120 BANNED BOOKS,

Second Edition

CENSORSHIP HISTORIES OF WORLD LITERATURE

Nicholas J. Karolides,
Margaret Bald and
Dawn B. Sova

Checkmark Books
An Infobase Learning Company

To the University of Wisconsin–River Falls Chalmer Davee Library staff
—N. J. K.
For Jonathan, André and Daniel
—M. B.
To my son, Robert Gregor
—D. B. S.

120 Banned Books, Second Edition

Copyright © 2011 by Nicholas J. Karolides, Margaret Bald and Dawn B. Sova

Checkmark Books
An imprint of Infobase Learning
132 West 31st Street
New York NY 10001

Library of Congress Cataloging-in-Publication Data
Karolides, Nicholas J.
120 banned books : censorship histories of world literature / Nicholas J. Karolides, Margaret Bald, and Dawn B. Sova. — 2nd ed.
p. cm.
Includes bibliographical references and index.
ISBN 978-0-8160-8232-2 (acid-free paper) 1. Censorship—United States—History—20th century. 2. Prohibited books—United States—History—20th century. 3. Challenged books—United States—History—20th century. 4. Censorship—History. 5. Prohibited books—United States—Bibliography. 6. Challenged books—United States—Bibliography. I. Bald, Margaret. II. Sova, Dawn B. III. Title. IV. Title: One hundred and twenty banned books. V. Title: One hundred twenty banned books.
Z658.U5K35 2011
363.6'1—dc22   2011013099

Checkmark Books are available at special discounts when purchased in bulk quantities for businesses, associations, institutions, or sales promotions. Please call our Special Sales Department in New York at (212) 967-8800 or (800) 322-8755.

You can find Facts On File on the World Wide Web at
http://www.infobaselearning.com

Text design by Cathy Rincon
Composition by Julie Adams
Cover printed by Sheridan Books, Ann Arbor, Mich.
Book printed and bound by Sheridan Books, Ann Arbor, Mich.
Date printed: August 2011

Printed in the United States of America

10 9 8 7 6 5 4 3 2

This book is printed on acid-free paper.

CONTENTS

LITERATURE SUPPRESSED ON
RELIGIOUS GROUNDS

LITERATURE SUPPRESSED ON
SEXUAL GROUNDS

LITERATURE SUPPRESSED ON SOCIAL GROUNDS

INTRODUCTION

For centuries, books have been banned, suppressed, and censored because of political, religious, sexual, and social reasons, according to the tastes and beliefs of a particular era or a locale. As times change, formerly banned books become acceptable or even "classic," while once-acceptable books are challenged, as the appearance of James Joyce's *Ulysses* and D. H. Lawrence's *Lady Chatterley's Lover* in college courses as required reading and the roller-coaster history of Mark Twain's *Adventures of Huckleberry Finn* attest. In many cases, the same book has been banned at different times for different reasons, as is the case with Erich Maria Remarque's *All Quiet on the Western Front*, Voltaire's *Candide*, and Aldous Huxley's *Brave New World*. The books do not change, but the social climate does.

This updated edition of *120 Banned Books* contains entries covering more than 2,000 years of censorship. Entries new to this edition range from best-selling works of popular fiction, such as the young-adult Twilight and Gossip Girl series, to highly acclaimed works of undeniable literary value, such as *Beloved* by Toni Morrison, *The Kite Runner* by Khaled Hosseini, and *The Appointment* by Herta Müller, winner of the 2009 Nobel Prize in literature. Entries from the past edition have been updated to reflect new challenges.

Each week brings new reports of challenges to books. In 2011, that may seem difficult to believe, but the reality remains. Parents and librarians are often shocked to hear that books in the Harry Potter series have been challenged in such diverse regions of the country as Massachusetts, California, and Georgia, yet some suggest that other books would be better banned, according to their own beliefs, biases, and prejudices. In some cases, readers who defend controversial works by academics, such as Stephen J. Dubner and Steven D. Levitt's *Freakonomics*, are quick to condemn Philip Pullman's trilogy His Dark Materials as unacceptably anti-religious.

As readers of the censorship histories in *120 Banned Books* will realize, the reasons for which these books have been banned, suppressed, and censored are often highly subjective, and the success or failure of efforts to ban, suppress, or censor books depends more upon how vocal the challengers are than upon the merits of the book. All books by an author who has offended in one book might be condemned, as was the case for Honoré de Balzac, or an author's lifestyle or politics may result in the banning of works, as occurred for Oscar Wilde and Dalton Trumbo. Threats to parental authority also drive challenges, as they have in regard to such diverse books as J. D. Salinger's *The Catcher in the Rye* and J. K. Rowling's Harry Potter series. Although the majority of challenges today in the United States occur in schools or public libraries, they are not limited to these venues.

120 Banned Books contains comprehensive information about books that have been banned, suppressed, or censored for political, religious, sexual, or social reasons across 20 centuries and in many nations. Each entry contains the author's name, original date and place of publication, and literary form, as well as a plot summary. A separate section of each entry provides details of the censorship history of the work, followed by a list of further readings for more in-depth examination of the challenges. The entries feature books in numerous genres, including fiction for children and adults, as well as nonfiction in the forms of biographies, autobiographies, political and religious tracts, philosophical treatises, histories, and books of science. In short, no one book or no one writer is protected from would-be censors.

—Dawn B. Sova, Ph.D.

LITERATURE SUPPRESSED ON POLITICAL GROUNDS

The phrase *suppressed on political grounds* casts a shadow of a heavy-handed government blocking its citizens from receiving information, ideas, and opinions that it perceives to be critical, embarrassing, or threatening. This image, unfortunately, is too often reality. It is not, however, limited to dictatorships such as those of Adolf Hitler's Nazi Germany, Joseph Stalin's Communist Soviet Union, Suharto's Indonesia, Augusto Pinochet's Chile, and Sani Abacha's Nigeria. The political turbulence of the 1990s dismantled several of these, establishing more open government in Indonesia, Chile, Nigeria, and Russia. The governments of democracies, however, also participate in attempts to censor such critical material in order to protect their own perceived state security. Indeed, repression of freedom of expression has been a significant operative factor in South Africa of the apartheid era, in pre-1990 South Korea, in Turkey, in postcommunist Ukraine, and recently in Russia. It is a factor, as well, in the United Kingdom and the United States today.

Further, the impression that censorship for political reasons emanates only from national governments is mistaken. Another common source of such activity, notably in the United States, is at the local community level, generated by school board members or citizens, individually or in groups, who attack textbooks and fiction used in schools or available in school libraries. In contrast to censorship challenges at the national level, challenges at the local level are aimed at the political values and images that children are receiving. In past decades, the chief targets were socialism, communism, and the portrayal of the Soviet Union. A companion concern was the portrayal of the United States. At the center of such objections was the fear that the Soviet Union would be viewed too positively or the United States too negatively. Continuing in the present, examining flaws in American society is deemed unpatriotic to critics, who become concerned when past and present policies of their government are questioned in school textbooks and library books.

Books conveying the dynamics of war situations are targets of censoring challenges as well.

The 30 censored titles discussed in this revised section vary considerably in subject and form. Some works have had comparably limited censorship exposure. Others have extensive and impressive censorship histories. *The Grapes of Wrath* was challenged and burned within a month of its publication in 1939 and has been subject to attacks ever since. The censorship of Aleksandr Solzhenitsyn's books by the Soviet government gained international notoriety. Four other novelists have had their entire oeuvre censored by their respective governments: Nobel Prize winner Miguel Angel Asturias of Guatemala (*El Señor Presidente*), Duong Thu Huong of Vietnam (*Novel Without a Name*), Pramoedya Ananta Toer of Indonesia (*The Fugitive*), and Herta Müller, also a Nobel Prize winner, by Romania (*The Appointment*). Harriet Beecher Stowe's antislavery novel *Uncle Tom's Cabin* was broadly censored in the South in the 19th century, and *My Brother Sam Is Dead*, the antiwar, nonromanticized Revolutionary War novel, by James Lincoln Collier and Christopher Collier, has drawn considerable fire since its publication in 1974. Other works have faced significant court cases, such as *I Am the Cheese*, by Robert Cormier; *Slaughter-House Five*, by Kurt Vonnegut, Jr.; and *Spycatcher*, by Peter Wright. Some censored writers discussed in this section are less well-known in the United States but still extremely important, such as Liao Yiwu of China (*The Corpse Walker*), Manuel Puig of Argentina (*Kiss of the Spider Woman*), Rajaa Alsanea of Saudi Arabia (*Girls of Riyadh*), and the anonymous German author of *A Woman in Berlin: Eight Weeks in the Conquered City*.

Not all objections are formalized or publicly announced; some are reported only in local newspapers. Self-censorship by teachers and librarians is common. I recall the comment of a librarian who accounted for the lack of challenges to her collection through her tactic of not ordering books that were censored elsewhere. Further, not all attacks are identified forthrightly; it is apparently more difficult to protest the politics of a text than it is to protest its offensive language. Lee Burress, who has conducted five state and national surveys of censorship of school library and classroom materials, referred to this mask as the "hidden agenda" of censorship.

The accounts of these attacks at local levels may seem to the glancing eye diversified and transient; those at the national and international levels may appear remote and arcane. These multiple streams of curtailed thought, however, combine to form a treacherous current. Its undertow can ensnare the mind in the tangled weeds of ignorance and irrationality. Denied both in individual incidents and en masse is the sine qua non of democracy, the right of fundamental inquiry, the ebb and flow of thought.

—Nicholas J. Karolides, Ph.D.
University of Wisconsin–River Falls

ALL QUIET ON THE WESTERN FRONT

Author: Erich Maria Remarque
Original dates and places of publication: 1928, Germany; 1929, United States
Publishers: Impropylaen-Verlag; Little, Brown and Company
Literary form: Novel

SUMMARY

> He fell in October 1918, on a day that was so quiet and still on the whole front, that the army report confined itself to the single sentence: All quiet on the Western Front.
> He had fallen forward and lay on the earth as though sleeping. Turning him over one saw that he could not have suffered long; his face had an expression of calm, as though almost glad the end had come.

This final passage of Remarque's renowned novel enunciates not only the irony of death of this unknown soldier, but also the irony of the wartime communiques that announced that there was nothing new to report while thousands were wounded and dying daily. (The German title of the novel, *Im Westen nichts neues*, translates as "nothing new in the West.") The final passage also signals the irony of the title, a bitterness that pervades the entire work.

There are many unknown soldiers in the novel on both sides of the trenches. They are the bodies piled three deep in the shell craters, the mutilated bodies thrown about in the fields, the "naked soldier squatting in the fork of a tree . . . his helmet on, otherwise he is entirely unclad. There is one half of him sitting there, the top half, the legs are missing." There is the young Frenchman in retreat who lags behind and then is overtaken, "a blow from a spade cleaves through his face."

The unknown soldiers are background. The novel focuses on Paul Baumer, the narrator, and his comrades of the Second Company, chiefly Albert Kropp, his close friend, and Stanislaus Katczinsky, the leader of the group. Katczinsky (Kat) is 40 years old; the others are 18 and 19. They are ordinary folk: Muller, who dreams of examinations; Tjaden, a locksmith; Haie Westhus, a peatdigger; and Detering, a peasant.

The novel opens five miles behind the front. The men are "at rest" after 14 days on the front line. Of the 150 men to go forward, only 80 have returned. A theme—and the tone of disillusionment—is introduced immediately, the catalyst being the receipt of a letter from Kantorek, their former schoolmaster. It was he who had urged them all to volunteer, causing the hesitant ones to feel like cowards.

> For us lads of eighteen [adults] ought to have been mediators and guides to the world of maturity. . . . in our hearts we trusted them. The idea of authority,

which they represented, was associated in our minds with greater insight and a manlier wisdom. But the first death we saw shattered this belief. . . . The first bombardment showed us our mistake, and under it the world as they had taught it to us broke in pieces.

This theme is repeated in Paul's conversation with adults at home during a leave. They evince deep ignorance of the nature of trench warfare and the living conditions and the dying. "Naturally it's worse here. Naturally. The best for our soldiers. . . ." They argue about what territories ought to be annexed and how the war should be fought. Paul is unable to speak the truth to them.

Vignettes of the solders' lives pile up in the first several chapters: inhumane treatment of the recruits at the hands of a militaristic, rank-conscious corporal; the painful death of a schoolmate after a leg amputation; the meager food often in limited supply; the primitive housing; and glimpses of the fear and horror, the cries and explosions of the front. The experienced men reveal their distance from their youth, not merely the trench warfare smarts in contrast to the innocent unready replacement recruits. Gone was the "ideal and almost romantic character" of the war. They recognized that the "classical conception of the Fatherland held by our teachers resolved itself here into a renunciation of personality." They have been cut off from their youth and from the opportunity of growing up naturally; they cannot conceive a future.

After a major battle, Paul narrates: "Today we would pass through the scenes of our youth like travellers. We are burnt up by hard facts; like tradesmen we understand distinctions, and like butchers, necessities. We are no longer untroubled—we are indifferent. We long to be there; but could we live there?"

Paul experiences the depths of this alienation during his leave. Beyond recognition and a vivid yearning, he knows he is an outsider. He cannot get close to his family; of course, he is unable to reveal the truth of his terror-filled experiences, so he cannot seek their comfort. Sitting in the armchair in his room, his books before him, he tries to recapture the past and imagine the future. His comrades at the front seem the only reality.

Rumors of an offensive turn out to be true. They are accompanied by a high double-wall stack of yellow, unpolished, brand-new coffins and extra issues of food. When the enemy bombardment comes, the earth booms and heavy fire falls on them. The shells tear down the parapet, root up the embankment and demolish the upper layers of concrete. The rear is hit as well. A recruit loses control and must be forcibly restrained. The attack is met by machine-gun fire and hand grenades. Anger replaces fear.

No longer do we lie helpless, waiting on the scaffold, we can destroy and kill, to save ourselves, to save ourselves and be revenged . . . crouching like cats we run on, overwhelmed by this wave that bears us along, that fills us with ferocity, turning us into thugs, into murderers, into God only knows what devils; this wave that multiplies our strength with fear and madness and greed of life, seeking and fighting for nothing but our deliverance. If your own father came over with them you would not hesitate to fling a bomb into him.

Attacks alternate with counterattacks and "slowly the dead pile up in the field of craters between the trenches." When it is over and the company is relieved, only 32 men answer the call.

In another situation the relative anonymity of trench warfare is erased. On patrol to scout out the enemy lines, Paul becomes separated from his own troops and finds himself in French territory. He hides in a shell hole, surrounded by exploding shells and sounds of activity. He is strained to the utmost, armed with fear and a knife. When a body crashes in upon him, he automatically slashes at and then shares the shell hole with the dying Frenchman who has become a person. He tries to dress the stab wounds. He is devoured by guilt:

> Comrade, I did not want to kill you. If you jumped in here again, I would not do it, if you would be sensible too. But you were only an idea to me before, an abstraction that lived in my mind and called forth its appropriate response. It was that abstraction I stabbed. But now, for the first time, I see you are a man like me. I thought of your hand grenades, of your bayonet, of your rifle; now I see your wife and your face and our fellowship. Forgive me, comrade. We always see it too late.

There is a respite for the company, and then it is sent out to evacuate a village. During the march, both Paul and Albert Kropp are wounded, Albert seriously. Hospitalized, they fear the amputation-prone doctors; Kropp loses his leg; he does not want to live a "cripple." Paul hobbles around the hospital during his recovery, visiting the wards, increasingly aware of shattered bodies:

> And this is only one hospital, one single station; there are hundreds of thousands in Germany, hundreds of thousands in France, hundreds of thousands in Russia. How senseless is everything that can be written, done, or thought, when such things are possible. It must all be lies and of no account when the culture of a thousand years could not prevent this stream of blood being poured out, these torture-chambers in their hundreds of thousands. A hospital alone shows what war is.

Back at the front the war continues, death continues. One by one the circle of comrades is killed. Detering, maddened for home by the sight of a cherry tree in bloom, attempts to desert but is captured. Only Paul, Kat, and Tjaden are alive. In the late summer of 1918 Kat sustains a leg injury; Paul attempts to carry him to a medical facility. Near collapse, he stumbles and falls as he reaches the dressing station. He rises only to discover that Kat is dead; en route he has sustained a splinter in the head.

In the autumn there is talk of peace and armistice. Paul meditates about the future:

And men will not understand us—for the generation that grew up before us, though it has passed these years with us here, already had a home and a calling; now it will return to its old occupations, and the war will be forgotten—and the generation that has grown up after us will be strange to us and push us aside. We will be superfluous even to ourselves, we will grow older, a few will adapt themselves, some others will merely submit, and most will be bewildered;—the years will pass by and in the end we shall fall into ruin.

CENSORSHIP HISTORY

When *All Quiet on the Western Front* was issued in Germany in 1928, National Socialism (Nazism) was already a powerful political force. In the social political context a decade after the war, the novel generated a strong popular response, selling 600,000 copies before it was issued in the United States, but it also generated significant resentment. It affronted the National Socialists, who read it as slanderous to their ideals of home and fatherland. This resentment led to political pamphleteering against it. It was banned in Germany in 1930. In 1933, all of Remarque's works were consigned to the infamous bonfires. On May 10, the first large-scale demonstration occurred in front of the University of Berlin: Students gathered 25,000 volumes of Jewish authors; 40,000 "unenthusiastic" people watched. Similar demonstrations took place at other universities; in Munich 5,000 children watched and participated in burning books labeled Marxist and un-German.

Remarque, who had not been silenced by the violent attacks against his book, published in 1930 a sequel, *The Road Back*. By 1932, however, he escaped Nazi harassment by moving to Switzerland and then to the United States.

Bannings occurred in other European countries. In 1929, Austrian soldiers were forbidden to read the book, and in Czechoslovakia it was barred from military libraries. In 1933 in Italy, the translation was banned because of its antiwar propaganda.

In the United States, in 1929, the publishers Little, Brown and Company acceded to suggestions of the Book-of-the-Month Club judges, who had chosen the novel as the club's June selection, to make some changes; they deleted three words, five phrases, and two entire episodes—one of makeshift latrine arrangements and the other a hospital scene during which a married couple, separated for two years, has intercourse. The publishers argued that "some words and sentences were too robust for our American edition" and that without the changes there might be conflict with federal law and certainly with Massachusetts law. A spokesperson for the publisher explained:

While it was still being considered by the [BOMC's] judges, the English edition was published, and while most of the reviews were favorable in the extreme, two or three reviewers condemned the book as coarse and vulgar. We believe that it is the greatest book about the war yet written, and that for the good of humanity it should have the widest possible circulation; we, therefore, concluded that it might be best not to offend the less sophisticated of its potential public and were, therefore, wholly satisfied to make the changes suggested by the Book-of-the-Month Club after the judges had unanimously voted for the book.

Another kind of publisher's censorship was revealed by Remarque himself. Putnam's had rejected the book in 1929, despite the evidence of its considerable success in Europe. According to the author, writing decades later, "some idiot said he would not publish a book by a 'Hun.' "

Nevertheless, despite its having been expurgated, *All Quiet on the Western Front* was banned in Boston in 1929 on grounds of obscenity. In the same year, in Chicago, U.S. Customs seized copies of the English translation, which had not been expurgated. Lee Burress, in *Battle of the Books: Literary Censorship in the Public Schools, 1950–1985*, reveals challenges on the grounds of its being "too violent" and for its depiction of war as "brutal and dehumanizing." A more recent example is identified in *Attacks on Freedom to Learn, 1987–1988*, the annual survey of school censorship of People For the American Way, in which the charge was "foul language" (California). The suggestion is, however, that censors have shifted their tactics, using these charges instead of such traditional accusations as "globalism" or "far-right scare words." It is identified in *The Encyclopedia of Censorship* as one of the "most often" censored books.

The 1930 U.S. film, *All Quiet on the Western Front*, acclaimed as one of the greatest antiwar films and the winner of Oscars for best film and best director, has been both banned and significantly expurgated. The leaders of the Reichswehr, the German army, protested its being filmed because of the negative portrayal of the army. On the opening night of its screening, December 5, 1930, brown-shirted Nazis demonstrated in the theater, causing the film not to be shown. This event and others on succeeding days, all orchestrated by Joseph Goebbels, effectively barred the screenings. While the German Left applauded the film, criticism by the political Right was "intense and uncompromising"; the Nazis identified the film as a "Jewish lie" and labeled it a "hate-film slandering the German soldier." A cabinet crisis ensued; within a week the film was banned for the reason that it "removed all dignity from the German soldier" and perpetuated a negative stereotype. According to historian Joel Simmons, nationalistic critics focused on "the film's anti-war theme and its characterization of German soldiers and the German army. In effect they condemned the film for being true to the novel. To them, its portrayal of German soldiers as frightened by their first exposure to gunfire and so disillusioned by the battlefield carnage as to question their superiors and the ultimate purpose of the war, denigrated the bravery and discipline of German fighting men and undermined the nation's confidence in its armed forces." Parallel reactions in Austria led to violent street confrontations after the film's preview on January 3, 1931; on January 10 it was banned. It was also denied exhibition in Hungary, Bulgaria, and Yugoslavia. However, in September 1931 as a result of a changed political situation, authorities in

Germany permitted a moderately edited *All Quiet on the Western Front* to be screened; there were no demonstrations or evident outrage.

Universal Studios began cutting the film as early as 1933, removing important scenes in the United States and abroad, these exclusions resulting from censorship, politics, time constraints (to shorten the film so that it would fit into a double bill), and film exhibitors' whims. When *All Quiet on the Western Front* was reissued in 1939 as an anti-Hitler film, it included narration about the Nazis. Another version added music at the film's conclusion, a segment that was originally silent.

FURTHER READING

Attacks on Freedom to Learn: 1987–1988. Washington, D.C.: People For the American Way, 1988.

Burress, Lee. *Battle of the Books: Literary Censorship in the Public Schools, 1950–1985.* Metuchen, N.J.: Scarecrow Press, 1989.

"Censorship Continues Unabated; Extremists Adapt Mainstream Tactics." *Newsletter on Intellectual Freedom* 37 (1988): 193.

Geller, Evelyn. *Forbidden Books in American Public Libraries, 1876–1939: A Study in Cultural Change.* Westport, Conn.: Greenwood Press, 1984.

Green, Jonathon, and Nicholas J. Karolides, reviser. *The Encyclopedia of Censorship, New Edition.* New York: Facts On File, 2005.

Haight, Anne L., and Chandler B. Grannis. *Banned Books: 387 B.C. to 1978 A.D.* 4th ed. New York: R. R. Bowker, 1978.

Hansen, Harry. "The Book That Shocked a Nation." In *All Quiet on the Western Front,* by Erich Maria Remarque. New York: Heritage Press, 1969.

Simmons, Joel. "Film and International Politics: The Banning of *All Quiet on the Western Front.*" *Historian* 52, no. 1 (1999): 40–60.

Tebbel, John. *A History of Book Publishing in the United States.* Vol. 3. New York: R. R. Bowker, 1978.

ANDERSONVILLE

Author: MacKinlay Kantor
Original date and place of publication: 1955, United States
Publisher: World Publishing Company
Literary form: Novel

SUMMARY

Andersonville is a novel of war—the Civil War; it does not, however, fit the stereotype of war novels, for it offers little action on the battlefield, strategies and troop movements, or individual responses to such situations in the manner of Stephen Crane's *The Red Badge of Courage* or Erich Maria Remarque's *All Quiet on the Western Front.* There are essentially two settings: Ira Claffey's Georgia plantation and Andersonville, a prison for captured Yankees.

Episodic in structure, the novel provides access to Ira's life and his emotional and intellectual reactions to the war and the prison. These episodes, interspersed among those that focus on Yankee prisoners and Confederate officers and guards, provide plot movement.

Managing his plantation from the outset of the war without the help of an overseer, Ira Claffey is perceived as capable and honest. In this last year of the war, he nurtures his family with compassion. Only two live on the plantation with him: Veronica, his wife, and Lucy, their daughter. They are joined during this year by surgeon Harry Elkins, formerly a comrade-in-arms of the Claffeys' eldest son. This son and another have already died in battle; their third son is reported dead early in the novel. This final bereavement casts a shroud over the mind of Veronica. She gradually distances herself from the living and fades into the past. Lucy bears these burdens and the death of her fiancé with pain and anger and courage.

Ira is not a secessionist; he does not favor the war. Initially angry and embittered, he grieves for his sons. His philosophy and nature help him to acknowledge the reality of war's destruction and that families in the North also grieve for their lost sons.

Deploring cruelty, Ira treats his slaves, now totaling 12 including children, with paternalistic kindness. He will not allow them to be mistreated by the Confederate soldiers; and when he must sell them, he assures himself that they will not be mistreated. At the end of the war he informs them of their freedom and their right to leave; however, out of concern for their safety and welfare, he urges them to remain on the plantation as salaried employees. When one couple decides to leave, he gives them a mule and cart so their young children won't have to walk.

Ira's sense of compassion is intensified with the advent of the stockade. At first he disbelieves the deliberate intent, as voiced by Captain Winder, to mistreat the prisoners by providing no shelter from the elements, to cause their deaths. He is increasingly horrified by the brutality and miserable conditions. He attempts to help—protesting to the officers, joining his neighbors to bring food and clothing for the prisoners (these are rejected), traveling to Richmond to gain the ear of President Jefferson Davis, a friend from his military days—but realizes his helplessness.

Others join him in these attitudes. Chief among them is Surgeon Elkins, who, having come to investigate the health conditions, returns out of a humane sense of obligation to tend the sick. The post commander, Lieutenant Colonel Persons, of like mind, puts his career on the line to protest the actions of Confederate brigadier general John H. Winder and his son, Captain Sid Winder. Other inspectors follow suit; Dr. Joseph Jones concludes his highly critical report with the following:

> This gigantic mass of human misery calls loudly for relief, not only for the sake of suffering humanity, but also on account of our own brave soldiers now captives in the hands of the Federal government. Strict justice to the gallant

men of the Confederate armies, who have been or who may be so unfortunate as to be compelled to surrender in battle, demands that the Confederate government should adopt that course which will best secure their health and comfort in captivity; or at least leave their enemies without a shadow of an excuse for any violation of the rules of civilized warfare in the treatment of prisoners.

In counterpoint to these beacons of humanity are Brigadier General Winder and Captain Winder, whose intentions are revealed in this statement by the captain in response to Surgeon Elkins's concern that there are no shelters built or trees left to shield the prisoners from the hot Georgia sun: "What the hell's the use of coddling a pen full of Yankees? I've got a pen here that ought to kill more God damn Yankees than you ever saw killed at the front." The general demonstrates a more rabid expression of these intentions.

General Winder assigns Captain Henry Wirz as superintendent of the prison. Wirz, a doctor by profession, made intensely irritable and vituperative by an arm wound, brutalizes the prisoners: they are tyrannized; their diet is insufficient in both quantity and nutrients; their living conditions are abominable. A failure as an administrator, his efforts are ineffectual. Wirz is in part victim of a situation he cannot control: the vindictiveness of the Winders; the overloading of the compound; lack or denial of food and medical supplies.

The stockade and the prisoners are, however, the core of the novel. The stockade's 27 acres, intended for some 10,000 men, held upward of 30,000 at one time. (Of the 50,000 prisoners received there, about 16,000 died.) With no sanitation facilities, the area soon becomes putrid, its limited water supply polluted, its stench befouling the surrounding neighborhood. The Yankees die from dysentery, scurvy, and polluted water; wounds, scratches, and stings festered into gangrene. Others die of starvation and violence, groups of "raiders" attacking and stealing from the weak, the innocent, the unprepared among them.

Against the background of ever-increasing privation and brutality, decay and death, individual prisoners are spotlighted. Their origins and childhoods, their initial responses to the war are counterpoints to their immediate situation. How they survive—whether they survive—reveals their natures. Edward Blamey, a New England fisherman, survives, though he initially resists, by selling his extraordinary eyesight to the raider, Willie Collins, in return for protection and creature comforts. Blamey spies goods among the other prisoners that can be stolen. Collins, surly and corrupt since childhood, uses his brute strength and amorality to build a power structure in which the "raiders" within the stockade terrorize fellow prisoners. He is finally tried, condemned, and hanged, along with others of his ilk, by a group of prisoners organized by Seneca MacBean and Nathan Dreyfoos, a semieducated midwesterner and an upper-class easterner. The Iowan Eben Dolliver's childhood is filled with a consciousness of birds, with birdsong; he is driven by starvation to attack a swallow for food. At age 13, Willie Mann of Missouri had rescued several immigrant German children from a bully;

subsequently he fell in love with one of them and now is sustained by dreams of returning to her. He survives because his doctor father had taught him the health value of pure water; he refuses to drink except when it rains.

A minor plot strand, the story of the poor white Tebbs family, particularly a vignette of the eldest son, brings the novel to fruition. Having enlisted at age 17, Coral returns home without a foot. Embittered, depressed, he flails at his family and at his life. While searching for a bird he has shot, he discovers an escaped prisoner lacking a hand, just about dead from starvation and weariness. Both have lost their limbs at Gettysburg. Coral on an impulse decides to help him with food and a hideout; the Yankee boy, Nazareth Strider from Pennsylvania, helps Coral in return by shaping a "peg-leg-foot" for him, with knowledge gleaned from his father's craft and using tools borrowed from Ira Claffey. When Ira discovers their secret, he shocks them both by helping. Again, Ira's humanity emerges; he muses as he works on the wooden foot, "It seemed odd to be performing a service for a wounded Yankee and a wounded Confederate in the same act and in the same breath." Acts of humanity unite the two boys.

The novel continues for another 40 pages beyond this episode to encompass the defeat of the Confederacy, the release of the prisoners, and the military arrest of Wirz. Two of Ira's adult slaves with their children take advantage of their freedom and leave; Coral Tebbs finds employment as their replacement. However, the crescendo of the novel is in the mutual salvation of Coral and Nazareth and in the symbolic healing and reunification it expresses.

CENSORSHIP HISTORY

Andersonville was challenged by Laurence Van Der Oord, the father of an Amherst (Ohio) High School student in 1967. Identifying the novel as "filth," he claimed his 16-year-old daughter could not read it because she did not understand the obscene words. He asserted that the book was 1 percent history and 99 percent filth and demanded that Donald Hicks, the history teacher who had assigned the novel as an optional choice, be dismissed.

Hicks countered that the relative worth of the novel outweighed the objectionable parts; about 30 of the 795 pages contain slightly obscene language. Defense of the novel was also offered by the school board president, Mrs. Clem Rice: ". . . maybe we should not shield high school students. . . . Perhaps they should know these facts exist even though they are bad and may not exist in our community." On August 24, the school superintendent announced that he would not order the removal of the book.

In 1973, a Buncombe County, North Carolina, school board member, Edna Roberts, removed several books, including *Andersonville*, from the high school library, claiming they were "unsuitable" for school libraries because they contained objectionable language. Subsequently, she introduced a resolution to the board that would have "expunged 'unsuitable' books from school libraries." The board rejected it, reaffirming its "Policies for Selection." Mrs.

Roberts's efforts were supported by the Christian Action League and Answer for America.

Buncombe County in 1981 was the scene of another controversy over classroom and library books, including, among others, *Andersonville*. The protest was initiated by a group of citizens meeting at Asheville's Owens High School in January; the meeting was led by several fundamentalist ministers, a chief spokesperson being Wendell Runion, who had organized the Concerned Citizens of Owens District group. The books on the list were labeled obscene. The group planned to file a grievance with the Buncombe County schools' administration to get the books removed. In February, an opposition group, calling itself "Books," was organized to provide an alternative perspective. On February 19, more than 1,000 residents attended a forum to air the two positions. Those opposed to the current book selection policy called for closing loopholes that "promote immorality." Pastor Randy Stone noted, "The use of God's name in vain, whether it be in a Pulitzer-prize winner or a book from an adult bookstore, is offensive to us and demands some sort of attention." Books's spokespersons included Loretta Martin, the president of the North Carolina Association of Educators, and Elsie Brumbeck, the director of educational media for the State Department of Public Instruction. Martin said, "Our schools are the only institution today that seeks to free the human mind." Brumbeck read a letter from the North Carolina Library Association in support of Buncombe County's current selection policy. Receiving the strongest accolade, however, was Pastor Fred Ohler, who, in support of the book selection policy, asked, "Why is immorality seen only as profanity and sexuality in Steinbeck, Salinger or Kantor and the larger issues of grinding poverty and social misjustice, of adult hypocrisy, of war camp atrocities never faced?" Referring to the list of quotations from the challenged books, he continued, "To read the Bible as some folks read *The Grapes of Wrath* would be like going through the Gospels and only seeing tax collectors, wine-bibers and Mary Magdalene." In March the Buncombe County Board of Education voted (5-2) to support the book selection policy.

Andersonville was withdrawn from the 11th-grade reading list at the Whitehall, Michigan, high school on December 12, 1963. An "unspecified number of unidentified complaints" were received by Superintendent of Schools Melvin Lubbers and County Prosecutor Harry J. Knudsen; the latter indicated he did not care if the book had won 20 Pulitzer Prizes; it was not fit reading for high school students. One parent, Jane Moog, angry about the dropping of the book, termed the act a "violation of civil liberties." Lubbers indicated that they did not quarrel with the author's message, but it was not of "sufficient benefit to justify putting it before the young mind." Despite a defense of the book by a school board member, Evelyn Robinson, and Circuit Judge John H. Piercy, the board of education voted 6-1 in support of Lubbers.

In 1961, under the leadership of J. Evetts Haley, Texans for America, a right-wing group, supported by the Daughters of the American Revolution (DAR) and the John Birch Society, attacked the language and concepts of a range of history books. They succeeded in causing the State Textbook Committee to reject 12 books opposed by the Texans for America and four opposed by the DAR. In addition, substantial changes in their texts were required of publishers for specific books.

These textbook battles spilled over to affect library books. *Andersonville* was banned from the four Amarillo high schools and at Amarillo College. The stated reasons were its political ideas and that its author was cited by the House Un-American Activities Committee. In 1962, a committee of inquiry, instigated by a Texas House of Representatives resolution, investigated the content of school books, searching for subversion of American principles and traditions. At an Austin hearing, excerpts from *Andersonville* were read as examples of obscenity and filth.

An attempt to ban *Andersonville* was also reported in Rock County, Wisconsin, in 1969.

FURTHER READING

Blake, Barbara. "Who Is the Rev. Wendell Runion and Why Does He Want Those Books Banned?" *Asheville Citizen*, January 31, 1981, [n.p.].

Burress, Lee. *The Battle of the Books: Literary Censorship in Public Schools, 1950–1985.* Metuchen, N.J.: Scarecrow Press, 1989.

Campbell, John, Jr. "Concern Expressed over Books in Schools." *Asheville Citizen*, January 23, 1981, [n.p.].

———. "Large Crowd Gathers for Sessions on Books." *Asheville Citizen*, February 20, 1981, p. 17.

Grisso, James L. "Amherst High Keeps *Andersonville*." *Cleveland Plain Dealer*, August 25, 1967, [n.p.].

Hoyle Bolick, Sandy. "Book Issue: Pros, Cons." *Asheville Times*, February 20, 1981, [n.p.].

Nelson, Jack, and Gene Roberts, Jr. *The Censors and the Schools.* Boston: Little, Brown, 1963.

Newsletter on Intellectual Freedom 13 (1964): 14; 22 (1973): 52; 30 (1981): 74.

"Official Removes 'Objectional' Books." *St. Louis Post Dispatch*, March 28, 1973, 22A.

"Pro Books Group Is Organized in County." *Asheville Citizen*, February 14, 1981, 7.

"Rock County Librarians United to Battle Would-Be Banners." *Beloit Daily News*, April 17, 1969, [n.p.].

THE APPOINTMENT

Author: Herta Müller
Original dates and places of publication: 1997, Germany; 2001, United States

Publisher: Rowohlt Verlag; Metropolitan Books/Henry Holt
Literary form: Novel

SUMMARY

> I've been summoned. Thursday at ten sharp. Lately I'm being summoned more and more often: ten sharp on Tuesday, ten sharp on Saturday, on Wednesday, Monday. As if years were a week, I'm amazed that winter comes so close on the heels of summer.

The subtle shuddering of this opening paragraph of *The Appointment* suggests, beyond mystery, something troubling and dark. (The German title translates to *Today I'd Rather Not See Myself.*) The unnamed female narrator is feeling threatened for good reason. Employed in a clothing factory, having separated from her first husband, anxious to find a way out of the country (Romania), she slipped a note into the pocket of ten suits bounds for Italy: "Marry me, *ti aspetto*" including her name and address. She is denounced. At the "meeting," which she is not allowed to attend, the notes, apparently ideologically offensive, were judged to be "prostitution in the workplace"; her supervisor, Nelu, whose advances she had rejected, had argued for "treason." Since this was her first offense and she was not a Party member, she was reprimanded. Following the discovery of three notes in trousers scheduled for Sweden: "Best wishes from the dictatorship," of which she is falsely accused, she becomes the object of the summonses from the secret police.

The novel in its entirety, in a stream-of-consciousness style, reveals the thoughts of the narrator during her walk from her apartment and ride on the tram to her meeting with her interrogator, Major Albu. She observes and considers the landscape and her fellow passengers; she reflects on family and her first and second husbands; she contemplates the nature of the world around her and herself. There is no sequential order or connectedness among her thoughts. The surface confusion it portrays represents her view of the world itself.

Two strong strands of thought and emotions, however, emerge: the representation of the dictatorial, malicious, and corrupt government and the demoralized repressed people who have been affected by the hollowness, constraints, and terror of their lives.

Bits and pieces of the brutality of the government are interspersed among the personal experiences and thoughts. Examples include: The narrator's good friend Lilli is shot while trying to escape to Hungary with her army officer lover. She is downed by one bullet but several more follow; five dogs shred her body. Only two factory coworkers—aside from Nelu and the narrator—attend the funeral. Others out of fear of association "refused to have anything to do with an escape attempt and the way it ended." Comparably, the narrator is fearful of missing her appointment with Alba: The summons is delivered orally. She worries that she may have misheard the date and will suffer consequences. During his session with her, Albu reveals that she is being shadowed; he knows of her activities with Paul, her second husband. Her shoemaker acquaintance whose wife was in a "mental home," apparently afflicted with senility, refers to two young women in the same institution "who lost their wits after what the police did to them. These women hadn't done anything either—one swiped a little candle wax from the factory, the other took a sack of corncobs that were lying in a field."

Paul also becomes a victim, first of clothing theft at his factory workplace and, subsequently, a political target. Stealing clothing while the owner is showering is apparently not unusual, but Paul is frequently a prey—indeed sometimes all of his clothes. This rationalization is expressed: Stealing isn't considered a bad thing in the factory. "The Factory belongs to the people, you belong to the people, and whatever you take is collectively owned, anyway—iron, tin, wood, screws, and wire, whatever you can get your hands on." However, in response to jokes about his "naked" situations, Paul remarked, "Socialism sends its workers forth into the world unclad. . . . Every week or so it's as if you were born anew. It keeps you young." This political statement is reported; Paul is required at the Party meeting (he is a Party member) to stand in front and "deliver public self-criticism for his quip." The narrator comments that if Paul had not made this blunder "some other pretext would have been discovered. False steps can always be found, unlike stolen clothes." This prediction presages Paul's clash with government inspectors.

A circumstantial family story reveals expropriation practices. The narrator's grandfather years before her first marriage was the victim of her father-in-law, a Party operative. He confiscated her grandfather's gold coins and jewelry; he had him and her grandmother deported to the harsh Baragon Steppe where her grandmother died under cruel, disheartening conditions. When her grandfather returned, his house having become state property, he had to go to court several times before he could reclaim his house. Her father-in-law, a danger to others, would ride a white horse from house to house, demanding that his horse be fed and watered, searching each house for grain and gold.

> First he rounded up the farmers with large holdings and turned them over to the security services, after that he went after medium-sized farmers, then he moved on to smallholders. He was a hard worker, after a while he was rounding up too many farmers, and ones who were too poor at that, so the gentlemen in the city sent whole groups of them back to the village on the next train.

This repressive persecution and brutal social-political environment are the backdrop to the chilling expression of the impoverished lives of the people and their inhumanity toward each other, mirroring, in effect, the government's behavior toward them. Given the prevailing threatening surveillance of the state, the constant awareness of needing to protect herself, given also the invasion of her privacy, the narrator trusts no one—even family and husbands. She begins to feel safe with Paul, but at the end of the novel a question is raised in her head. Personal relationships are fraught with betrayals: the narrator's father daily, seemingly, meets a young woman—a girl the narrator's age—from the market for sex—a great loss for the narrator who discovers them; her father-in-law, when his son reported for military duty, makes sexual overtures toward her to help her get over her husband's absence and when she resists him, he grumbled, "You rack your brains to come up with ways of helping your children, and this is what you get for your pains"; at a New Year's Eve party, the married couples by "mutual agreement had turned a blind eye to each other's whereabouts"; Lilly repeatedly urges her new stepfather to have sex with her when her mother/his wife is shopping, a plea to which he succumbs on a daily basis.

The overall impact upon the narrator of the political and social-personal environment is numbing, except in her careful scrutiny of everything about her. The events and images are dislocating and at times oppressive. She talks almost hopelessly about happiness and seems haunted by death. Her sanity may be at the brink. Suggestively, at the end of the novel when she accidentally sights Paul where she doesn't expect him to be, she thinks: "The trick is not to go mad."

CENSORSHIP HISTORY

Herta Müller's early career advocacy of freedom of speech and overt opposition to the Ceauşescu dictatorship in Romania started during the 1973–1976 period when she was a student at the university in Timişoara (Temeswar). She associated with Aktionsgruppe Banat, a circle of German-speaking authors who sought freedom of speech. (Müller's father served in the Waffen SS during World War II. After the war in 1945, her mother was deported to the Soviet Union to a work camp in present-day Ukraine for five years.)

Müller's first collection of short stories, *Niederungen (Lowlands)*, also titled *Nadirs*, was published, though heavily censored, in Romania in 1982; it was held by the publisher for four years. The Romanian press was very critical. An uncensored copy of *Niederungen* was smuggled into Germany and published in 1984. The German press gave it positive reviews; it was well received by the German public. In 1988 she published her first novel, *Drükender Tango*, in Romania where it experienced the same fate as her earlier work. (It was published in Germany in 1996.) These works spotlight life in a small German village in Romania, depicting the difficult life and harsh treatment of Romanian Germans under the repressive Ceauşescu regime. Major themes are corruption and intolerance. Indeed, because Müller had publicly criticized the dictatorship of Nicolae Ceauşescu, her works were banned from publication in Romania.

After her studies in Timis͵ oara, Müller worked as a translator in a tractor factory. However, when she refused to work for the Securitate (secret police), she was fired. Subsequently, she was harassed by the Securitate, subjected to threats, house searches, and bugging. She emigrated to Germany in 1987.

These practices are still active, the Securitate (CNSAS) only having been renamed—the Romanian Information Service (SRI)—40 percent of whose personnel are former secret police. On her visits back to Romania, as recently as spring 2009, Müller has experienced the bugging of her telephone, being shadowed, having an interview with a reporter interrupted, and the reporter also shadowed. Every year, she asked to see her file but was denied access. In 1999, as a result of the European Union's requirement, personnel files being held by CNSAS were released to the SRI, but her requests were denied; ostensibly the file was "still being worked on."

In 2004, "suddenly" her file was found under the name Cristina—three volumes totaling 914 pages. According to Müller, the reason given for opening the file was her "tendentious distortions of reality in the country particularly in the village environment," as depicted in her book *Nadirs*. The entry in the file for November 30, 1986, stated: "Every trip that Cristina takes to Bucharest and to other parts of the country, is to be reported in a timely fashion to the inland and counterespionage services, so that permanent control can be guaranteed" in order to "carry through with the appropriate control measures in connection with West German diplomats and West German citizens."

Müller also recounts a few incidents of physical abuse to herself and to other persons who planned to contact her, including a *Die Zeit* journalist who was "brutally" beaten, ending with broken toes on both feet. She notes, "My file also shows that a surreal punishment process was laid out because of spying for the BND (German police). I have the resonance of my books and the literary prizes to thank that the plan was not activated and I wasn't arrested."

Herta Müller was awarded the Nobel Prize in literature in 2009. Previously she won the German Kleist prize in 1994 and the International IMPAC Dublin Literary award in 1998 for her novel *The Land of Green Plums* (1993).

FURTHER READING

Baskin, Jason M. Review of *The Appointment*, by Herta Müller. *Chicago Review* 48, no. 4 (Winter 2002/2003): 136–138.

Eder, Richard. "Allegory of Oppression in Ceaucescu's [sic] Romania." *New York Times*, September 12, 2001, E8.

Filkins, Peter. "Betrayal as a Way of Life." *New York Times Book Review*, October 21, 2001, 18.

Müller, Herta. "The Secret Police Is Still in Service." *Die Zeit Online*. Available online. URL: http://www.zeit.de/2009/31Securitate. Accessed October 15, 2010.

Zaleski, Jeff. Review of *The Appointment*, by Herta Müller. *Publishers Weekly*, August 6, 2001, 61.

—German translations by Gretchen Toman,
Maple Grove Senior High School

AREOPAGITICA

Author: John Milton
Original dates and places of publication: 1644, England; 1888, United States
Publishers: [s.n.]; Cassell and Company
Literary form: Nonfiction essay

SUMMARY

Considered seminal in the defense of freedom of expression, *Areopagitica*, published in 1644, has been frequently cited by anticensors in promoting freedom of the press and of speech.

The title of John Milton's most famous prose work was derived from Areopagus, the hill of Ares in Athens named after Ares, one of the 12 major gods of ancient Greece. (In mythology, Ares, who had killed Poseidon's son for his having raped his daughter, was tried for murder by a council of the gods on this site; he was acquitted.) At this site the highest judicial court of ancient Athens met to debate political and religious matters. Its nearly 300 members were elected by a vote of all the free men of the city. Since the site Areopagus is identified with the glory of Athens's democratic institutions, Milton's title, *Areopagitica*, reveals his inclinations. The subtitle, *A Speech for the Liberty of Unlicensed Printing to the Parliament of England*, identifies his intent. In his "The Second Defense of the People of England," published in 1654, Milton noted:

> I wrote my Areopagitica in order to deliver the press from the restraints with which it was encumbered; that the power of determining what was true and what was false, what ought to be published and what to be suppressed, might no longer be entrusted to a few illiterate and illiberal individuals, who refused their sanction to any work which contained views or sentiments at all above the level of vulgar superstition.

It was specifically directed against the Order of Parliament of June 14, 1643, an ordinance requiring the licensing of all books and pamphlets in advance of publication. It also expresses significant ideas of religious liberty, interrelated with those of freedom of the press; however, these will not be discussed here.

Milton recognized the great concern the "Church and Commonwealth" had about the contents of books "for books are not absolutely dead things, but do contain a potency of life. . . . they do preserve as in a vial the purest efficacy and extraction of that living intellect that bred them." However, he argued that "Who kills a man kills a reasonable creature, God's image; but he who destroys a good book, kills reason itself, kills the image of God, as it were in the eye."

Milton decried censoring activities that represented what is now termed *prior restraint;* indeed, this becomes a basic tenet of his discussion. He likened the impulse to license to the prohibitory attitudes and actions of the papal court, which led to the Spanish Inquisition. He noted that their censoring acts spread from the heretical to any subject they found unsuitable, thus expressing a warning about the pattern of censorship. Before this "tyrannous inquisition," books were allowed to be born into the world, judgment about them reserved. Continuing this metaphor, rather than stand before a jury prior to birth to be judged in darkness without any public scrutiny, books should be examined more openly after publication.

Historical examples are used to support this position. He identifies practices in classical Athens and early Christianity, finding them free of control prior to publication and in all instances after publication except atheism, blasphemy, and libel. One example is the burning of the books of Protagoras and the banishing of the author himself upon command of the judges of Areopagus; Protagoras had written that he did not know "whether there were gods, or whether not."

The value of knowledge and learning forms a cornerstone of Milton's discussion. Books enhance our understanding of the known and introduce us to the new. The Order of Parliament would "suppress all this flowry crop of knowledge . . . to bring a famine upon our minds again" and allow the people to know only what the licensers permit. He likens this to the state of ignorance to which the decree of Julian the Apostate reduced the Christians, forbidding them to study the heathen texts. Thus, licensing would greatly discourage learning by reducing access to information and discussion. Restraining the freedom to write and the liberty of printing nullifies the privilege of the people and shackles the freedom to learn.

Knowledge thrives on the mind's exercise as does the discovery and affirmation of truth. His illustrations encompass the religious and scientific, attaining the truth by examining all opinions, even errors, so they may be known and evaluated. Individuals who base their beliefs solely on what they are told by their pastors or as determined by the assembly without knowing reasons cannot be said to understand. Even if the doctrine is true in an objective sense, it is not believed in the right way. It has not been questioned or examined, thus not really understood; the belief is superficial. An unlicensed press can propose challenges to cause thinking, thus enhancing the understanding of accepted beliefs or revealing new truths. Milton proposes these concepts for both the nation and individuals.

Extending this position, Milton promotes the reading of all texts, the good as well as those of "evil substance." The latter to a "discreet and judicious reader serve in many respects to discover, to confute, to forewarn, and to illustrate." Truth and virtue are attained by including all opinions, even errors, so they may be known and reasoned. Individuals are put in positions of having to make moral choices between the good and evil that surround them.

Since therefore the knowledge and survey of vice is in this world so necessary to the constituting of human virtue, and the scanning of error to the confirmation of truth, how can we more safely, and with less danger, scout into the regions of sin and falsity than by reading all manner of tractate, and hearing all manner of reason? And this is the benefit which may be had of books promiscuously read.

Milton drew a cause-and-effect connection between the actions of government and the nature of the populace. An "oppressive, arbitrary and tyrannous" government breeds a "brutish, formall, and slavish" people. A mild and free human government promotes liberty, the liberty of free writing, and free speaking. These in the past have enlightened the spirits, enfranchised and enlarged the apprehensions of the English people, making them more capable, more knowing, and more eager to pursue the truth. These attributes would be suppressed by the enforcement of this order.

The effectiveness of the order is also questioned. One aspect is the licensers themselves: They need to be above all other men to accomplish the task without bias, but are apt to be ignorant, corrupt, or overworked. Another is the assumption that books themselves are the sole source of ideas and behaviors that are perceived by the authorities to be censorable. Milton refutes both of these, arguing, as summarized above, the efficacy of books, thus the requirement of unlicensed printing.

CENSORSHIP HISTORY

Licensing of books, which should be understood as the suppression of undesired publications, was a frequent policy in England. As early as 1408, confirmed by Parliament in 1414, Archbishop Arundel's constitution forbade the reading of any book that had not been examined and approved by the University of Oxford or Cambridge. Henry VIII forbade the printing of any book concerning holy scripture unless it had been examined or approved. This was spread to the licensing of books of any kind. This policy was reasserted by the monarchs who succeeded him—Edward, Mary, Elizabeth, James, and Charles.

The practice and procedures of censorship had been developed in England over the 16th and 17th centuries, including the incorporation of a Stationers Company charged with the administration of the system. In 1637, in Charles's reign, the Star Chamber decree of July 11 established a broad range of censorship measures that forbade the printing, importing, or selling of seditious or offensive books; required the licensing of all books before being printed or reprinted; limited the number of master printers, specifying the number of presses and workers each might have; forbade the providing of space for unlicensed printers; and empowered the Stationers Company to search houses for such unlicensed printers.

In 1641, the Star Chamber had been abolished, an outcome of the defeat of Charles in the English Civil War. Though the Stationers Company was not abolished, its powers were diminished; for about 18 months there were no statutory restrictions on the press. Gradually, the openness was narrowed.

In 1643, the Puritans through a series of regulations, preceded by a 1642 regulation mandating that every publication bear the name of the printer, reinstated censorship practices until they were in full force. A significant factor underpinning these actions was the religious toleration controversy of the time.

In this context, John Milton published in 1643 *Doctrine and Discipline of Divorce* without benefit of authorization, registration, or signature, by then required. It was reprinted in February 1644, again without being authorized or registered, though it was signed. At this time the Royalists suffered a defeat, causing the Westminster Assembly (an advisory body to Parliament about reformation of the church, dominated by Presbyterians) to condemn tracts favoring toleration. A sermon on this subject, preached before Parliament, spoke against illegal books and identified *Doctrine and Discipline of Divorce* as immoral. Further, booksellers, united in a corporation, complained about illegal books to the House of Commons, denouncing Milton among others.

These were the direct catalysts of *Areopagitica*. Issued on November 23, 1644, it also was published without benefit of authorization or registration and in defiance of the restraining ordinance. (It was also delivered orally before Parliament.) On December 9, the booksellers complained to the House of Lords, but the lords took no action.

Milton's attack on licensing had no effect on Parliament's policy. Indeed, licensing was reasserted several times and continued to be practiced until 20 years after Milton's death, in 1694. Frederick Seaton Siebert notes that *Areopagitica* had "very little effect" on Milton's contemporaries; it "went unmentioned by most of the writers and public men of the times."

After the execution of Charles I and the abolition of the monarchy, Oliver Cromwell, named as lord protector in 1658, condemned *Areopagitica* as did the "Little Parliament" of Protestant England that had succeeded the expelled House of Commons.

Areopagitica appeared in only one edition and was not republished until 1738. At this time it aroused public support for the concept of freedom of the mind. According to Siebert, a significant factor in this change in public opinion was the Peter Zenger trial in a colonial courtroom in New York. Zenger's acquittal of libel of the royal governor was perceived as a freedom of the press issue; the publication of the trial transcript, four editions in London in 1728, notes Siebert, "undoubtedly set an example for English juries."

FURTHER READING

Green, Jonathon, and Nicholas J. Karolides, reviser. *Encyclopedia of Censorship, New Edition*. New York: Facts On File, 2005.

Haight, Anne Lyon, and Chandler B. Grannis. *Banned Books: 387 B.C. to 1978 A.D.* 4th ed. New York: R. R. Bowker, 1978.

Hunter, William B., ed. *A Milton Encyclopedia.* Lewisburg, Pa.: Bucknell University Press, 1978.

Saillens, Emile. *John Milton: Man, Poet, Polemist.* Oxford, England: Basil Blackwell, 1964.

Siebert, Fredrick Seaton. *Freedom of the Press in England, 1476–1776.* Urbana: University of Illinois Press, 1965.

Sirluck, Ernest. "Preface and Notes." In *Complete Prose Works of John Milton,* Vol. 2. New Haven, Conn.: Yale University Press, 1959.

BLACK BOY

Author: Richard Wright
Original date and place of publication: 1945, United States
Publisher: Harper and Row
Literary form: Autobiography

SUMMARY

"My days and nights were one long, quiet, continuously contained dream of terror, tension and anxiety. I wondered how long I could bear it." So concludes chapter 13 (there are 14) of Richard Wright's autobiography, expressing the crescendo of his feelings before finally in the last chapter achieving his secret dream of escaping the South to the North.

Subtitled "Record of Childhood and Youth," the memoir begins when he is four years old and takes him into his 19th year. His accounts of his experiences and relationships reveal how he has been shaped and conditioned, the person he has become.

Wright's childhood was one of trauma and indignity, narrowness and poverty. The family moved frequently, first from the plantation of his birth, where his father was a sharecropper, to Memphis. Other moves resulted from his father's abandoning his wife and two sons for another woman. These moves took the family to lower-rent accommodations, to new locations in search of jobs or to relatives where they lived on their sometimes grudging charity. Such dependence became virtually permanent after his mother at quite a young age suffered a stroke that caused paralysis of her legs.

Wright's dominant childhood memories are of hunger, deficiency, and fear. With his father's departure, there was no income until his mother was able to find work. Hunger, constant and gnawing, haunted the family; when food was available, it was insufficient in both quantity and nutrition. Often there was not enough money to heat their shack. Sometimes young Richard's mother brought the two boys to work with her; they stood in the corner of the kitchen where she was a cook, smelling the food but unable to eat. There was not enough money for clothes; ashamed of Richard's destitute appearance, his mother would not send him to school.

Beatings appear to have been "automatic" responses of adults toward children for misbehavior or stubborn resistance. Young Richard, an intractable, willful child, is often birched or strapped by his mother (before her illness) and relatives. Uncles and aunts attempt also to browbeat him into submitting to their wills. A parallel violence is evident in contacts with neighborhood gangs and in schoolyards. Richard, the new kid, the outsider, has to prove himself before he can gain entrance.

The sense of abandonment, exacerbated by being placed in an orphanage when his mother could not afford to take care of the two boys, and the feelings of loss—though perhaps not understood—were effective in forming Richard's personality. These dovetailed with his frequent outsider status; opportunities for deep and lasting relationships were thwarted by both the frequent moves and the suppressive attitudes of the significant adults. Warmth, tenderness and encouragement were lacking, except sporadically from his mother.

Religion was another source of agony and emotional browbeating, particularly during the period when he lived in his grandmother's house. Despite his young age, he resisted his grandmother's efforts to commit him to her fear-evoking religion, refusing to be bullied into submission. When his equally rigid and devout aunt, who is also his teacher, struck him across the knuckles with a ruler because she assumes he, rather than a devout classmate, is guilty of littering the floor, he vowed not to allow it a second time. When she came at him at home with a switch, he fought her off with a kitchen knife, fighting, in effect, for his sense of justice and independence.

A contrasting strand is woven through the autobiography: young Richard's curiosity, his eagerness to learn to read and the rapidity with which he learned. He began to pick out and recognize words in his playmates' schoolbooks at age six; in about an hour's time, the coalman taught him to count to 100. He questioned everything. His school attendance started late and was erratic; he was past 12 before he had a full year of formal schooling. But once fully enrolled, he excelled, graduating as the valedictorian of his class. Books became his salvation, both an escape from his tormenting environment and an avenue to a dreamed of future: "going north and writing books, novels." Books opened up the world of serious writing, opened up for him the life of the mind and encouraged his conviction to live beyond the constraints of the South.

Richard Wright acknowledges his limited contacts with whites during his early years. By age nine, a dread of whites had grown in him, fueled by frightening tales of repression, of the Ku Klux Klan, and of his family's experiences. His first jobs with whites when he is a young teenager corroborate his impressions of their meanness and mistreatment, projecting their view that blacks are children or idiots and less than human. A significant realization is his understanding that "the entire educational system of the South had been rigged to stifle" the aspirations of the black citizens.

As he gains experiences in the white world, Wright learns to keep secret his dream of going north and becoming a writer. It takes him considerably longer than his school and work acquaintances to learn appropriate obsequious mannerisms, language, and tone. His ignorance causes him to lose employment and to suffer harm. Part of his "problem," as a friend notes in his sixteenth year: "'You act around white people as if you didn't know that they were white.'" Wright silently acknowledges this truth:

> . . . it was simply impossible for me to calculate, to scheme, to act, to plot all the time. I would remember to dissemble for short periods, then I would forget and act straight and human again, not with the desire to harm anybody, but merely forgetting the artificial status of race and class.

His friend continues: "You know, Dick, you may think I'm an Uncle Tom, but I'm not. I hate these white people, hate 'em with all my heart. But I can't show it; if I did, they'd kill me."

Richard Wright did learn to control his public face and voice to a greater extent, but not without a sense of shame, tension, and mental strain. While the latter dissipated somewhat in the more urbane atmosphere of Memphis, he was frequently reminded of the need to be guarded. These experiences and responses reveal Wright's growth and cultural assimilation. They also reveal the survival training induced in blacks by the white threat: deception, dishonesty, lying, and irresponsibility.

When contemplating his present life and his future, Wright sees four choices: rebellion, organizing with other blacks to fight the southern whites; submitting and living the life of a genial slave, thus denying that his "life had shaped [him] to live by [his] own feelings and thoughts"; draining his restlessness by fighting other blacks, thus transferring his hatred of himself to others with a black skin; and forgetting what he's learned through books, forgetting whites and finding release in sex and alcohol. In this context, he continues:

> I had no hope whatever of being a professional man. Not only had I been so conditioned that I did not desire it, but the fulfillment of such an ambition was beyond my capabilities. Well-to-do Negroes lived in a world that was almost as alien to me as the world inhabited by whites.

Finally, however, "sheer wish and hope prevailed over common sense and facts." Planning with his mother, brother, and aunt, he takes the step; he boards the train bound for Chicago.

CENSORSHIP HISTORY

Richard Wright was not unfamiliar with the threat of censorship. A member of the Communist Party in 1940 when *Native Son* was published, he was threatened with expulsion because at least one party leader sensed a fundamental disagreement between the party's views and those expressed in the book. Wright had been saved by its popularity and acclaim, making Wright too important a member to lose. Wright had recognized other attempts by the party to constrain his thinking. In 1940 he renounced his affiliation with the party.

The Special Committee on Un-American Activities, the Dies Committee, had investigated him and called him subversive. Wright had also been the target of a top-priority investigation of the FBI regarding his affiliation with and activities for the Communist Party. Wright knew that his neighbors had been questioned. These events had preceded the publication of *Black Boy*. In the 1950s Richard Wright was identified unfavorably before the House Un-American Activities Committee and cited by the committee as belonging to one or more "fronts." According to existing directives, his work should have been withdrawn from U.S. libraries overseas.

Black Boy as originally submitted, titled *American Hunger*, included Wright's Chicago experience. Although it was initially accepted by Harper and Row, his editor later informed Wright that the book would be divided: The first two-thirds, the experiences in the South, would be published separately from the experiences in the North, Chicago, and New York. Initially, Wright accepted this suggestion without question; Constance Webb, Wright's biographer, notes, however, that subsequently he felt "in his whole being that his book was being censored in some way." He considered the possibility that Harper and Row did not want to offend the communists, since the United States and the Soviet Union were then allies, or that the Communist Party itself was exerting some influence over the publisher. He determined to find a way to publish the omitted final segment of his manuscript.

At the time of publication, despite its being a Book-of-the-Month Club selection and achieving both broad readership and significant acclaim in reviews, Mississippi banned it; Senator Theodore Bilbo of Mississippi condemned the book and its author in Congress:

> Black Boy should be taken off the shelves of stores; sales should be stopped; it was a damnable lie, from beginning to end; it built fabulous lies about the South. The purpose of the book was to plant seeds of hate and devilment in the minds of every American. It was the dirtiest, filthiest, most obscene, filthy and dirty, and came from a Negro from whom one could not expect better.

The autobiography has been met with controversy in school districts in all regions of the United States. Most of the challenges have been of mainly local interest, while one case received national attention and created precedent. In a 1963 school censorship survey of Wisconsin, *Black Boy* was reported removed because it was deemed unsuitable for high school students; a 1966 national survey reported the book challenged on the grounds of obscenity and that it teaches blacks to hate whites. In 1972, parents in Michigan objected to the book's sexual overtones and claimed it was unsuitable for impressionable sophomores, which resulted in its removal from the classroom. It was banned in Baltimore in 1974. In 1975, the book was removed from Tennessee schools for being obscene, instigating hatred between races, and encouraging immorality.

Complaints against five books, including *Black Boy*, were filed in November 1975 in East Baton Rouge, Louisiana, by Babs Minhinnette, chairperson of Concerned Citizens and Taxpayers for Decent School Books. This complaint emerged out of a controversy over the removal of two books, one by the school board and the other by the principal. This controversy had led to the adoption in May 1975 of a policy to handle objections. Subsequently, however, in September 1975, the school board had ordered a search for books and materials containing obscenity, filth, or pornography. Teachers and librarians criticized the search order, claiming it was a reversal of the policy adopted in May. The challenge to the five books by the Concerned Citizens chairperson was perceived as an attempt to test the new review procedure. The committee voted 6-1 to reject the request to remove the books after a review conducted in late November.

A comparable situation developed in Nashua, New Hampshire, in 1978. As a result of a complaint against the use of *Black Boy* in the ninth grade of the high school in Nashua, a review committee recommended that the book be removed from this grade level and that it be used only in elective courses in grades 11 and 12. The controversy over *Black Boy* gave rise to questions about the appropriateness of certain textbooks in schools across the state and gave impetus to the formation of a new organization, Concerned Citizens and Taxpayers for Better Education. This group's intention was to monitor books used in classes of several communities, from which its members were drawn, in order to safeguard "traditional Judeo-Christian values" in the schools.

The Anaheim (California) Secondary Teachers Association in September 1978 charged the Anaheim Union High School Board of Trustees with having "banned thousands of books from English classrooms of the Anaheim secondary schools." The trustees, acting on a recommendation of the district's administration, had removed more than half of the reading material available to English teachers. *Black Boy* was among the books banned from the classroom and from school libraries. The board's president, James P. Bonnell, claimed that the 270 books remaining on the grade 7 to 12 list were "adequate." Teachers were instructed to simply store the book, along with others, and cautioned that they were not permitted to provide the books for supplemental reading or to discuss the books with students. The local school board warned teachers that they risked dismissal if they taught any of the banned books. The result of the confrontation was the mounting of a recall campaign: Petitions were circulated to enforce a reelection ballot for Bonnell and another trustee, and "Notice of Intent to Recall" papers were served on these individuals. The recall election was successful in unseating these trustees.

In September 1987, Nebraska governor Kay Orr's "kitchen cabinet" met with leaders of a citizens' group, Taxpayers for Quality Education. The group made recommendations to the governor regarding curriculum, strategies for teaching reading, and school administration. It also indicated it would monitor books in school libraries and recommend reading lists. George Darlington, president of Taxpayers for Quality Education, identified *Black Boy* as one of the books that should be removed, asserting it had a "corruptive obscene nature" and citing the use of profanity throughout and the incidents of violence. He noted that such books "inflict a cancer on the body of education we want our children to develop." The book was removed from library shelves, then returned after the controversy abated.

Objectionable language was the basis for challenges in California (1977) and New York (1983); both failed. In Oxford, North Carolina (1994), objections focused on "filthy words," "lustful talk," and "immoral sex"; "the putting down of ALL kinds of people: the boy's family, the white people, the Jew, the church, the church school and even his friends." Also in 1994, a complaint in Fillmore, California, pointed to violence—the killing of a kitten—and profanity; the parent stated that the book is "not conducive to teaching what civilized people are supposed to behave like." The autobiography was also challenged in Round Rock, Texas, in 1996, for graphically describing three beating deaths and for having been "written while the author was a member of the Communist Party." The charges against the book in Jacksonville, Florida, in 1997, were made by a minister complainant, who alleged the book was profane, could stir up racial animosity, and was not appropriate for children; he urged the school board to ban the book and to fire the teacher who had assigned it.

In a landmark case, the autobiography was one of nine books that the school board of the Island Trees (New York) Union Free District removed from the junior and senior high school libraries in 1976; two books were removed from classrooms. The other books were *The Best Short Stories by Negro Writers, The Fixer, Go Ask Alice, Slaughterhouse-Five, Down These Mean Streets, A Hero Ain't Nothin' but a Sandwich, Laughing Boy, The Naked Ape, Soul on Ice,* and *A Reader for Writers.* Condemned with broad generalizations, the books were charged with being "anti-American, anti-Christian, anti-Semitic, or just plain filthy." As entered in the court record, the specific objections to *Black Boy* concerned the use of obscenity and the anti-Semitic remarks and other ethnic slurs, in such passages as the following: "We black children—seven or eight or nine years of age—used to run to the Jew's store and shout: . . . Bloody Christ Killers/Never trust a Jew/Bloody Christ Killers/What won't a Jew do/Red, white and blue/ Your pa was a Jew/Your ma a dirty dago/What the hell is you?"

The controversy began in March 1976 when the chair of a Long Island school board, Richard J. Ahrens, using a list of "objectionable" books and a collection of excerpts compiled by Parents of New York United (PONY-U), ordered 11 books removed from the Island Trees School District High School library. Teachers indicated that two of the books, Bernard Malamud's *The Fixer* and *The Best Short Stories of Negro Writers,* had been removed from classrooms, where they were being used in a literature course. The local teachers' union did file a formal grievance against the board, alleging a violation of the provisions of academic freedom in the union contract. A group of residents also objected to the censorship, stating they would protest to the state commissioner of education.

In defense against the protests of parents and students, the school board appointed a committee made up of parents and teachers to review the books and to determine which, if any, had merit. The committee recommended that seven of the books be returned to the library shelves, that two be placed on restricted shelves and that two be removed from the library, but the school board in July ignored these recommendations and voted to keep all but two of the books off the shelves. It authorized "restricted" circulation for *Black Boy* and circulation without restriction for *Laughing Boy.* The others would be "removed from . . . libraries and from use in the curriculum," that is, not to be assigned as required, optional, or even suggested reading, although the books might still be discussed in class. The vote was unanimous on most titles. Ahrens said, "It is not only our right but our duty to make the decision, and we would do it again in the face of the abuse heaped upon us by the media."

Five students—one junior high school student and four senior high school students—filed suit on January 4, 1977, against the school district, seeking an injunction to have the books returned to the library shelves. The students challenged the censorship, claiming that the school board had violated their constitutional rights under the guise of protecting their social and moral tastes.

A federal district court decision handed down in August 1979 (*Pico v. Board of Education*) favored the school board. U.S. District Court judge George C. Pratt rejected what he termed *tenure* for a book; in effect, he ruled that school boards have the right to examine the contents of library materials in order to determine their "suitability." At the center of the controversy was the constitutional role of the school board in public education, particularly in selection of content in relation to the perceived values of the community.

> In the absence of a sharp, focused issue of academic freedom, the court concludes that respect for the traditional values of the community and deference to the school board's substantial control over educational content preclude any finding of a First Amendment violation arising out of removal of any of the books from use in the curriculum.

After a U.S. Circuit Court of Appeals decision to remand the case for trial—in a 2-1 vote—the school board requested a review by the U.S. Supreme Court, which was granted. The appellate court had concluded that the First Amendment rights of the students had been violated and the criteria for the removal of the books were too general and overbroad.

The Supreme Court justices, sharply divided in a 5-4 decision (*Board of Education, Island Trees Union Free School District v. Pico*), upheld the appeals court. The Supreme Court mandated further trial proceedings to determine the underlying motivations of the school board. The majority relied on the concept that the "right to receive ideas" is a "necessary predicate" to the meaningful exercise of freedom of speech, press, and political freedom. Justice William Brennan, writing for the majority (which included Justices Thurgood Marshall, John Paul Stevens and Harry Blackmun; and Justice Byron White with qualifications), stated: "Local school boards have broad discretion in the management of school affairs but this discretion must be exercised in a manner that comports with the transcendent imperatives of the First Amendment."

> Our Constitution does not permit the official suppression of *ideas*. Thus whether [school board's] removal of books from their school libraries denied [students] their First Amendment rights upon the motivation. . . . If [school board] *intended* by their removal decision to deny [students] access to ideas with which [school board] disagreed, and if this intent was a decisive factor in [school board's] decision, then [school board] have exercised their discretion in violation of the Constitution. To permit such intentions to control official actions would be to encourage . . . officially prescribed orthodoxy. . . . [emphasis in original].
>
> [W]e hold that local school boards may not remove books from school library shelves simply because they dislike the ideas contained in those books and seek by their removal to "prescribe what shall be orthodox in politics, nationalism, religion, or other matters of opinion." . . . Such purposes stand inescapably condemned by our precedents.

In their dissenting opinion, Chief Justice Warren Burger and Justices Sandra Day O'Connor, Lewis Powell, and William Rehnquist issued a warning as to the role of the Supreme Court in making local censorship decisions: "If the plurality's view were to become the law, the court would come perilously close to becoming a 'super censor' of school board library decisions and the Constitution does not dictate that judges, rather than parents, teachers, and local school boards, must determine how the standards of morality and vulgarity are to be treated in the classroom." Thus, in their reluctance to place the Supreme Court in the position of local censor, the conservative justices recommended that the task of setting local community standards remain in local hands.

The controversy ended on August 12, 1982, when the Island Trees school board voted 6-1 to return the nine books to the school library shelves without restriction as to their circulation, but with a stipulation that the librarian must send a written notice to parents of students who borrow books containing material that the parents might find objectionable. The board also delayed action on whether *The Fixer* would be returned to the curriculum.

In February 2007, a citizens' group, the Livingston Organization for Values in Education (LOVE), complained to the Howell school board about the sexual content of four books in the Howell (Michigan) High School curriculum: *Black Boy*, by Richard Wright; *Slaughterhouse-Five*, by Kurt Vonnegut; *The*

Bluest Eye, by Toni Morrison; and *The Freedom Writers Diary*, by Erin Gruwell. Their challenge demanded that the books be removed from the curriculum; a LOVE spokesperson compared the books to *Penthouse* and *Playboy* magazines, asserting that they "contain similarly graphic materials in written form [and] are equally inappropriate." *The Bluest Eye* was described as a "graphic child rape book." Letters were also sent to the offices of the U.S attorney, state attorney general, and Livingston County prosecutor, requesting opinions about whether the books violate laws on obscenity and distribution of materials that are harmful to minors. The federal and state offices forwarded the request to the FBI which is a routine procedure with such complaints.

On February 12, the school board voted 5-2 to reject LOVE's complaint. They will continue to be used in AP classes. The district superintendent explained, "We should also be very careful about dismissing literary works because they test our own belief system or challenge our values." David Morse, the county prosecutor, concluded that the books are legal on two grounds: 1) Since the school board has approved use of these books, the teachers and administrators have complied with school codes and are exempted from criminal prosecution; 2) To qualify as obscene, a book must be found to appeal only to readers' prurient interest in sex and have no literary or educational merit.

". . . it is clear that the explicit passages [in the books] illustrated a larger literary, artistic or political message and were not included solely to appeal to the prurient interest of minors." Michigan attorney general Mike Cox and U.S. attorney Stephen Murphy concurred with Morse and indicated in mid-March that they would not prosecute.

FURTHER READING

"ASTA Release." *Anaheim Secondary Teachers Association* (September 27, 1978, and November 15, 1979).

Attacks on Freedom to Learn: 1980–1983, 1994–1995, and 1995–1996. New York: People For the American Way, New York Regional Offices, November 1983 and Washington, D.C.: People For the American Way, 1995 and 1996.

Gayle, Addison. *Richard Wright: Ordeal of a Native Son.* Garden City, N.Y.: Anchor Press/Doubleday, 1980.

Graham, Maryemma, and Jerry W. Ward, Jr. "*Black Boy (American Hunger)*: Freedom to Remember." In *Censored Books: Critical Viewpoints*, edited by Nicholas J. Karolides, Lee Burress, and Jack Kean, 109–116. Metuchen, N.J.: Scarecrow Press, 1993.

Hurwitz, Leon. *Historical Dictionary of Censorship in the United States.* Westport, Conn.: Greenwood Press, 1985.

Jenkinson, Edward B. *Censors in the Classroom: The Mind Benders.* Carbondale: Southern Illinois University Press, 1979.

Newsletter on Intellectual Freedom 24 (1975): 104, 120; 25 (1976): 34, 61–62, 85–86, 115; 26 (1977): 45; 27 (1978): 57; 28 (1979): 6, 141–145; 31 (1982): 12–13, 166, 197; and 36 (1987): 225.

North, William D. "Pico and the Challenge to Books in Schools." *Newsletter on Intellectual Freedom* 31 (1982): 195, 221–225.

Rich, R. Bruce. "The Supreme Court's Decision in Island Trees." *Newsletter on Intellectual Freedom* 31 (1982): 149, 173–186.

SIECUS. "FBI, State Deem Books Legal after Obscenity Complaints." March 2007. Available online. URL: http://www.familiesaretalking.org/index.cfm?fuseaction=feature.showFeature&featureID=1069. Accessed September 17, 2010.

Simoneau, Duke. "Book Controversy Flares in Nashua." *New Hampshire Sunday News*, March 5, 1978, pp. 1, 18.

Weathersby, Dorothy T. *Censorship of Literature Textbooks in Tennessee: A Study of the Commission, Publishers, Teachers, and Textbooks.* Ed.D. diss., University of Tennessee, 1975.

Webb, Constance. *Richard Wright: A Biography.* New York: Putnam, 1968.

BURGER'S DAUGHTER

Author: Nadine Gordimer
Original dates and places of publication: 1979, Great Britain; 1979, United States
Publishers: Jonathan Cape; Viking Press
Literary form: Novel

SUMMARY

Lionel Burger is not the center-stage character in *Burger's Daughter.* Yet the novel revolves around him as the life of his daughter, Rosa, emanates from and seems dominated by him. Lionel, a white Afrikaner from a wealthy family, is well reputed as a doctor, but has gained notoriety as a leader of the South African Communist Party and through his activities against the government's system of apartheid. He and his second wife, Cathy, have established a household that welcomes black Africans in an atmosphere of equality, a household in which social consciousness and responsibility are givens. Both parents constantly face the threat of arrest; indeed, Lionel dies of illness in prison during the third year of his life sentence, and Cathy dies of multiple sclerosis, her health damaged by imprisonment. The immediate sociopolitical context of these events is the South Africa of the March 1960 Sharpeville massacre in Rosa's childhood and the June 1976 Soweto school riots in her adulthood.

Despite the powerful presence of Lionel in the lives of this novel's characters, it is Rosa's story. Her early years are punctuated by activities that mark her parents' philosophy and expectations. Indeed, the story opens with Rosa, age 14, waiting outside a prison with a quilt and hot water bottle to deliver to her mother, who had been picked up by the police the night before and is being detained. But that act is not as revealing as the fact that she has secreted a note, seemingly innocuous in its message should it be discovered, inside the bottle cap to convey to her mother the status of her father. A few years later, at age 17, she takes on the pretense of being engaged to a political prisoner, a known associate of her father, to obtain permission to visit him in prison. At these monthly visits, she communicates information to him in the guise of a love letter and receives messages in return about the political prisoners through his vocal nuances and body language.

Rosa's early memories reveal her parents' activities and household. The evening of the Sharpeville massacre, African National Congress (ANC) leaders, Pan-African Congress people, lawyers, and others gather at their house, talking through the night about the changed political situation. At the opposite extreme, celebratory events—a successful boycott or march, a leader's release from prison, or Lionel found not guilty of a charge—also bring gatherings of the anti-apartheid faithful, white and black, to the house. Vivid in her memory is Boasie, a black child Rosa's age, the son of an ANC organizer, who is cared for by her family while his father travels on ANC business. She recurrently recalls their learning to swim together, fighting for "the anchorage of wet hair on Lionel Burger's warm breast in the cold swimming pool." They are separated once when both of Rosa's parents are arrested together; she does not see him again until many years later in London, a meeting that is emotionally traumatic for her.

In her recollections of her adolescent and young adult past, Rosa also reveals a note of resentment against the claim of familial relationship that enforces upon her certain situations—standing outside the prison, waiting for her mother and attending her father's trial for 217 days, both in the public eye. She expresses anger at her parents for their expectations of her playacting role as fiancée to the prisoner (for whom she really has tender feelings). After her mother's and then her father's death, the note of resentment swells at the expectations of the faithful that she will continue their activities, their social commitment. She muses:

> Even animals have the instinct to turn from suffering. The sense to run away. Perhaps it was an illness not to be able to live one's life . . . with justice defined in terms of respect for property, innocence defended in their children's privileges, love in their procreation, and care only for each other. A sickness not to be able to ignore that condition of a healthy, ordinary life: other people's suffering.

The suffering referred to is that of the black populace. This suffering is not actually visited, except in the connotations of shootings, protests and imprisonment, the oppression of pass laws and curfews. Instead, attention is given to raids that net one or another or both parents for periods of incarceration (the last leading to Lionel's trial and conviction to a life sentence) as well as others of the party. Cathy Burger and others are banned from certain occupations, from free movement around the country, even banned from house arrest, and banned from associations with particular people. There is a consciousness, too, of surveillance: The authorities' knowledge of Rosa's domiciles, her lovers, her movements, her contacts—her need to account for every visit and visitor just in case there is an interrogation.

The reader knows that the authorities are aware of her visits a year later to Pretoria; who she visits, the dates and frequency. Her purpose is to obtain a passport to leave the country (for she is forbidden access to a passport through normal channels), because, as she says, "I'd like to see Europe." After a year, Rosa is granted a passport (with understandings of where she is not to travel and with whom she is not to associate) and departs from South Africa, expecting to be stopped even as she is walking across the tarmac toward the plane. She isn't stopped, but "Surveillance watched her go in."

Book II chronicles Rosa's escape to France, first very briefly to Paris and then to the south of France to be with Lionel's first wife, whom she has never met. Katya (actually Colette), an aspiring ballerina, had been disciplined by the party for her "inactivity" and her "bourgeois tendencies to put [her] private life first." Rosa is overcome by the luminous landscape, its voluptuousness; the "pleasure of scents, sights and sounds exciting only in themselves, associated with nothing and nobody." She responds to a life lived for itself, without social mission and surveillance. Soon she has a lover; upon her impending departure for London he arranges for a rendezvous in London.

The sojourn in London does not evolve as anticipated. Her lover delayed by illness, Rosa spends relaxed hours wandering about London, chatting with people, taking a French class. She begins to think about meeting the people she had planned to avoid and does so. She goes to a gathering with other Africans in attendance, including South African revolutionaries. When she is recognized, she is introduced within the context of a speech about revolutionary heroes, particularly Lionel Burger.

Boasie is there. He seems guarded. Later that night, however, he telephones, but instead of reestablishing their childhood relationship, he rejects her, her memories, and her father. He is bitter that Lionel should be ennobled as heroic, while his own father, also a victim of the struggle, is forgotten, that whites should be credited and blacks neglected. Rosa is angered, her thoughts and emotions in turmoil.

Rosa returns to South Africa and to a job as a physiotherapist in a Johannesburg hospital. She is on duty in 1976 when the Soweto school riot victims fill the wards, after the police fire machine guns against the students' stones. A student rebellion ensues against the separate system of education; most never return to school after June 1976.

In October 1977 many people are detained, arrested, or banned; many organizations are banned as is the only black newspaper. Most of the banned people are black. Among the few whites is Rosa Burger, who is detained without charges. She is, however, subject to charges of collusion in a "conspiracy to further the aims of communism and/or the African National Congress. The charges would allege incitement and aiding and abetting of the students' and school children's revolt." One piece of evidence that will be identified in the indictment against her is her attendance at a leftist "rally" in London.

CENSORSHIP HISTORY

On July 5, 1979, *Burger's Daughter* was banned by the Republic of South Africa on the grounds that it "endangers the safety of the state" and that it depicts "whites as baddies, blacks as goodies." Further, it was deemed a "political novel" whose theme is black militancy and one that as a whole was harmful to relations between sections of population. The novel was also judged to be "indecent." The author was accused of using her central character "as a pad from which to launch a blistering and full-scale attack on the Republic of South Africa (and) its government's racial policies." The publications committee cited six categories of violation of the Publications Act of 1974.

In early October, however, the censoring committee was overruled by the Publications Appeal Board. The board's ruling was made on the advice of a committee of literary experts and an expert on security measures, and despite "crudities and profanity, derogatory references to whites and a distorted picture of the political situation in South Africa."

> The state security expert found there was no threat to the state from the novel. The literary experts concluded that the original censorship committee, in banning the book, stood "convicted of bias, prejudice, and literary incompetence. It has not read accurately, it has severely distorted by quoting extensively out of context, it has not considered the work as a literary work deserves to be considered, and it has directly, and by implication, smeared the authoress [sic]."

This turnabout resulted from a change of strategy by the Directorate of Publications, which administered the censorship system in South Africa. The 1974 Publications and Entertainments Act permitted appeals of censorship decisions made by committees appointed by the Directorate; the right to appeal was granted to the Directorate itself, to persons with financial interest and to the body that had originally submitted the text for censorship consideration. The change referred to above was that the Directorate itself appealed the decision of its own committee. *Burger's Daughter* was the first banned text so appealed and the first to be reinstated. However, as Gordimer herself stated, ". . . the censorship laws remain the same." Two previous novels, *World of Strangers* and *The Late Bourgeois World*, were banned for about a decade; the bans were lifted.

Ironically, in 1980, Gordimer was awarded the CNA Prize, one of South Africa's highest literary awards, for *Burger's Daughter.* She also was awarded the Nobel Prize in literature in 1991.

FURTHER READING

Gordimer, Nadine. *The Essential Gesture: Writing, Politics and Places.* New York: Alfred A. Knopf, 1988.
Index on Censorship 6 (November/December 1979): 69; 2 (April 1980): 73.
"Latest Gordimer Novel Banned in South Africa." *New York Times*, September 7, 1979, p. 8.

"South Africa Bans Two Novels." *Newsletter on Intellectual Freedom* 28 (1979): 147.
"South Africa Lifts Ban on Gordimer Novel." *New York Times*, October 7, 1979, p. 79.
"South Africans Cancel Ban on Gordimer Book." *New York Times*, October 5, 1979, p. 6.

BUS STOP (*CHEZHAN*)

Author: Gao Xingjian
Original dates and places of publication: 1983, People's Republic of China; 1998, United States
Publishers: *Shiyue* (literary quarterly); M. E. Sharpe (in anthology)
Literary form: Drama

SUMMARY

Subtitled *A Lyrical Comedy on Life in One Act, Bus Stop*, an experimental absurdist drama (referred to as Western modernism by Chinese critics), is set in the countryside. Six strangers assemble individually at a bus stop, apparently isolated from a community, joining the Silent Man who is already waiting, en route to a nearby city. They are identified but not named—Gramps, Young Woman, Hotheaded Youth, Spectacles, Mother, Master Worker. Director Ma, a party functionary, the section or division chief of a state-run store, also arrives to await the bus. Their missions seem urgent to themselves: Gramps, 60-some years old, has challenged a chess champion to a match; Young Woman, aged 28, has a blind-date rendezvous, perhaps her final opportunity to meet the right man; Spectacles, 30, plans to take the college entrance examination, later claiming this is his last opportunity; and Master Worker, 45, is relocating to the town to teach apprentices his craft so that the skills will not be squandered in the country. Mother, 40, will spend the weekend with her child and her husband, who lives in town because of his work assignment. The 19-year-old Hotheaded Youth wants to stroll in town and have a yogurt, and Director Ma, 50, has been invited by "someone with connections" to have a meal and drinks.

There is essentially little action in the drama: at the onset some jostling for position in the line, principally by the Youth; at midpoint, Silent Man abruptly and without comment leaves, heading for the city; and at the conclusion after a few false starts, steps are taken by the group to walk to the city. There is also the passage of time—10 years, if Spectacles's electric watch is to be believed, along with the evidence of two strands of white hair on Young Woman's head. Many buses have passed them by.

The real "movement" of the drama is in the relationships among the members of the group. Initially, quarrelsomeness and distance pervade. The angry complaints of Gramps aimed at the pushy, "obnoxious" Hotheaded Youth erupt into a near fistfight with Spectacles. The atmosphere of distance, however, gradually erodes—snatches of conversation about chess, about why parents with a child are, in effect, forced to live separately, and aspects in the operation of a "commercial unit." The realization of the passage of time—and that Silent Man has already left—begins to bring them together—emotionally and physically. At long last they decide to walk to town, helping one another, realizing at that moment that the bus stop had been abolished, thus explaining why none of the buses had stopped. They had waited for nothing.

Within the fragments of dialogue are embedded statements that express dissatisfaction with services and policies. Early on, when the bus does not arrive and when it passes by them, questions about "serving the customer" are raised, and Gramps responds, "On the contrary, the passengers have to serve them! If there's no one waiting at the bus stop how can they show off how vital they are?"

When Spectacles asks Mother why she does not get a job in town so that she can live with her husband and child, she responds, "Who doesn't want a work assignment in town, but you have to have a way to get to it," a reference to the 1980s system of government-assigned employment under which a desirable town work assignment, difficult to obtain, would frequently have the effect of separating a couple. She explains, "I have a child. . . . You know what the level of education is like in the schools on the outskirts of town. Hardly anybody from there can pass the college entrance exams!" Spectacles's concern about his last opportunity to take the college entrance exams, which require knowledge of a foreign language, and his not having studied a foreign language, echoes this concern.

Personal issues are also expressed. The Young Woman admits to being jealous of other, more privileged women and to her despair of her young man not waiting for her: "Never again. No one will ever wait for me again!" Mother mourns not being able to care for her husband and son, who need her. Hotheaded Youth, softened, also reveals parallel feelings: When Gramps suggests that he ought to apply himself to a craft, he admits, "There's no one to take me on. What's the use. . . ." After Master Worker agrees to take him on as an apprentice, his manner and attitude markedly change.

A ribbon of thought, of dismay, trails through the script. Spectacles says (furiously) to the Youth: "You don't understand what it is to suffer, so you're apathetic. Life has left us behind. The world has forgotten us. Your life is trickling away before your eyes." Gramps states: "I've waited a lifetime, waiting like this, and waiting. I've gotten old waiting." Young Woman observes: "Your whole life is wasted like this. To waste time like this, will we keep on wasting it forever?" Youth remarks: "Mister, we've been waiting for nothing. We've been cheated by the bus company." This implication that people should actively take charge of their lives rather than wasting their lives in passive waiting is solidified by character indecision about leaving the bus stop. At last, however, as a community, helping and caring for one another, they take to the road.

CENSORSHIP HISTORY

The play, titled *Chezhan* in Mandarin, was staged as a "rehearsal" by the Beijing People's Art Theatre, China's foremost theater company at the time, to which Gao Xingjian had been assigned. It was banned after 10 or 13 performances (reports differ). The play provoked controversy between two critical camps, those who found it creative and who approved its antipassivity message and those who argued that the "play contained a basic questioning if not a fundamental negation of the organization of contemporary Chinese society, a condescending attitude toward the deluded 'pitiable multitude,' and an elitist and individualistic impulse embodied in the 'silent man' walking alone to the city," as noted by University of Colorado professor Haiping Yan. A senior party member asserted that *Bus Stop* was "the most pernicious work since the establishment of the People's Republic." The "Anti-Spiritual Pollution Movement" under way at the time, targeted Gao, accusing him of being antisocialist. He was barred from publication for one year.

Earlier, Gao had attracted negative attention with his 1981 published booklet "A Preliminary Exploration into the Techniques of Modern Fiction," which, too radical for promoting decadent modernist ideas of the capitalist West, was condemned as a serious challenge to the party line. His experiential play known in English as "Signal Alarm" (1982) achieved positive audience response; it dramatized social issues of youth unemployment and juvenile delinquency. Nevertheless, its breakthrough aspects of staging aroused vehement sentiments about modernism and realism in theater. It was also banned in 1983.

Subsequently, facing rumors of further punishment—a labor camp in Quighai to "receive training"—Gao self-exiled himself to the mountains of southwestern China, walking over a 10-month period along the Yangtze River to get from its source to the coast. Returning to Beijing, he was permitted to publish, including the fictionalized memoir *Wild Man*, the play *The Other Shore*, and the novel *Soul Mountain*, but he left China in 1987, settling in France. The publication of the play *Fugitives (Taowang)*, which takes place against the background of the massacre on the Square of Heavenly Peace (Tiananmen Square) in 1989 led to his being declared persona non grata by China. All of his works were banned. Beijing also denounced the awarding of the Nobel Prize in literature (2000) to Gao, diminishing the merits of *Soul Mountain* and accusing the Nobel committee of being politically motivated. The Chinese press maintained a near blackout of the Nobel news. Gao's books are not available in bookstores in China.

Gao, now a citizen of France, has been awarded the Chevalier de l'Ordre des Artes et des Lettres, 1992; Prix Communauté francaise de Belgique, 1994, for *Le somnambule* (The sleepwalker); and Prix du Nouvel au Chinois, 1997, for *Soul Mountain.*

FURTHER READING

Gao Xingjian. *The Bus Stop: A Lyrical Comedy on Life in One Act.* Translaed by Kimberly Besio. In *Theater and Society: An Anthology of Contemporary Chinese Drama.* Edited by Haiping Yan. Armonk, N.Y.: M. E. Sharpe, 1998.

Yan Haiping, ed. *Theater and Society: An Anthology of Contemporary Chinese Drama.* Armonk, N.Y.: M. E. Sharpe, 1998.

THE CORPSE WALKER: REAL-LIFE STORIES, CHINA FROM THE BOTTOM UP

Author: Liao Yiwu
Original date and place of publication: 2008, United States
Publisher: Pantheon Books
Literary form: Oral History

SUMMARY

Real-Life Stories, China from the Bottom Up, the subtitle of *The Corpse Walker,* is more revealing of the subject of this collection of interviews. Liao Yiwu has interviewed 27 individuals, ranging in age from the 30s to the 100s and including a broad range of professions: a Professional Mourner, a Leper, an Abbot, a Retired Official, a Former Landowner, a Tiananmen Father, a Composer, a Yi District Chief's Wife, a Former Red Guard, and a Migrant Worker. They share a commonality: They all are from the bottom level of Chinese society, although some of them were well-to-do officials or business-men or working farmers-landowners prior to the defeat of the Nationalist government of Chang Kai-shek in 1949. Others were ordinary, often outcast, Chinese who reaped no benefits from the revolution.

Among the most compelling of those interviewed were those accused of being landowners, of having exploited the poor. Among these was the Buddhist Abbot (age 103 at the time of the interview). The monks abided by the vow of poverty, and none ever claimed ownership of the properties of the temple. Yet, during the land reform movement, a team of government officials and peasant activists set up a tribunal inside the temple to "dispense justice," calling him "a rich temple owner." He recalled the event:

> My captors dragged me onto the stage, stripped me of my kasaya, and forced me to stand in front of a large crowd of villagers, with my arms pulled up behind my back in the jet-plane position. One by one, peasant activists stood up to share with the crowd about my "crimes." I was accused of accumulating wealth without engaging in physical labor, and spreading feudalistic and religious ideas that poisoned people's minds.

Subsequently, public beating occurred during which the abbot was slapped, kicked, and hung from the ceiling. By the end of the land reform movement, the local government seized all the Buddhist treasures and confis-cated hundreds of hectares of pristine forest and farmland from the temple.

During the Great Leap Forward, launched by Chairman Mao in 1958, the temple was stripped of all its metal: incense burners, metal collection boxes, bells, the metal edges of wooden incense tables, the four bronze statues on the four corners of the temple roofs, and a pair of royal cast-iron cauldrons, a gift from Emperor Yongle in the Ming dynasty. These were melted. Hundreds of trees were chopped down to fuel the furnaces, stripping mountains bare.

The Former Landlord (age 89 when he was interviewed) suffered comparable treatment in 1950. His grandfather had purchased the property; his father had died of exhaustion from overwork. The land reform work team branded him an "evil landowner." His view of himself, being well versed in Confucianism, was that he was kind to others and had never harmed anyone or harbored any ill feelings.

> However, my fellow villagers, who used to be polite and respectful, had suddenly changed, as if they had all donned different facial masks. At the "speak bitterness meetings," two of my hired farmers accused me of exploiting them by forcing them to work in the cold winter days and randomly deducting their pay. I didn't agree with their accusations because I was working along with them in the field.

The Former Landlord's land titles, land leasing, and property rental agreements were annulled and everything he owned was confiscated. He remarked: "Of course, the world around me suddenly changed: rich people ended up suffering and the poor became masters. It was hard to accept at first."

The Former Landlord described the "speak bitterness" meetings:

> The militiamen beat me up pretty badly. I was in my forties then. Years of hard labor, such as carrying heavy sacks of salt on my back, made me pretty strong. . . . But as time went by, my back started to go because the militiamen forced me to bend down very deeply. I never complained or disobeyed. At the end of the Land Reform movement, the leader of the work team came to talk with me. He complimented me for being cooperative with the government. I was all smiles and bowed to him. In my heart, I felt as if someone had been stabbing me with a blunt knife.

Because some relations had been local officials during the Nationalist Chang Kai-shek government, the family of the former Yi District Chief suffered more torment. The district chief's wife was interviewed (age 84); she detailed the events in 1952, when she was 31 years old, after the land reform work team arrested her husband and brother. She was forced to witness their execution—rifles to their chests—and the cutting out of their tongues. When she screamed against this desecration, she was hit on her head with the butt of a rifle and knocked unconscious.

After the execution, the Yi District Chief's wife was locked up for more than 40 days. "Whenever there was a public speak bitterness meeting, the militiamen would drag me out in front of the podium, with hands tied behind my back and my head down. I had to carry a big cardboard sign on my neck. The cardboard sign said 'Wife of the Evil Landlord.' I would be asked to confess the crimes of my husband." All of her property was confiscated. While she was in detention, her youngest child, age two, died. Her two eldest sons, who had been caring for the children, were accused of crimes; the eldest hid in the mountains, the second, accused by a neighbor of writing anti-land reform slogans on a latrine wall, was sentenced to seven years in jail. The others begged for food or searched in the fields and trash cans.

The 1958–61 famine, "treated as a 'state secret'"— an estimated 30 millionpeople starved to death—is mentioned by many of those interviewed. The Illegal Border Crosser remarked, "You probably would say that people were desperate to leave China in 1962 because of the famine." Rejecting the official government explanation of "three years of natural disasters," the Retired Official identified the extreme policies of Chairman Mao as the cause of the disaster. In the 1950s, for example, Chairman Mao said that sparrows ate seeds and should be eliminated; a nationwide campaign essentially accomplished this goal in two years. "Little did we know that killing sparrows would disrupt the delicate balance of nature." Sparrows ate crops, but they also ate bugs, which flourished and brought disasters to many areas after the sparrows were gone.

The Great Leap Forward, the intention of which was to make China self-reliant and independent from the Soviet Union and to transform it into an industrialized country, was identified as a significant cause. The Retired Official, who headed a government work team at a rural region and who witnessed the devastating impact of the famine, reports that commune leaders followed Party instructions and ordered that peasants use the new "reasonable density" method: "Furrows were plowed very deep. Rice or wheat seedlings were planted very densely. The Party claimed that the method could increase the grain output ten times." This method didn't work. Many plants died and surviving ones did not pollinate. Nationwide displays of "agricultural miracles" were deceptions.

Then the Party switched focus from agriculture to steel production. Several results: All the peasants turned from farming to building and fueling brickyard furnaces—cutting down trees, neglecting harvesting; all metal objects—pots and pans, included—were collected for smelting; commune kitchens were set up. Early inspection of the communal dining rooms by the Retired Official suggests deception as to the quality and quantity of food to impress the inspectors, proven so by fall 1960 when the scarcity of food was evident. "In many places, commune leaders had turned over the grain that peasants saved over the years to meet [government grain] quotas. Peasants were left with little food for winter."

The Mortician (age 71 when interviewed) corroborates not only the number of famine-caused deaths—"in the second half of 1960, we were so overwhelmed here that I had to work overtime," but also the desperation of the people. In 1961:

> . . . food shortages got worse. As more bodies poured in, I didn't even have time to do any makeup. In that year, thousands of people roamed the mountain like locusts, desperately searching for things that were edible—tree

bark, grass roots, wild vegetables, even bugs. Unfortunately, all the mountain-tops had been deforested to feed the furnaces for iron and steel production. There wasn't much available for people to eat.

Both the Retired Official and the Mortician revealed the emergence of cannibalism: "As people became more and more desperate, they turned to their fellow human beings." A peasant was discovered secretly boiling the meat of his three-year old daughter; he explained that two children had died of starvation and they had no food for this daughter who was stunted; he sacrificed her for the rest of the family. After being lashed 50 times, the peasant was released.

[The villagers] took it as a sign of approval from the government and more families began to follow suit. Since boys were traditionally favored over girls, young girls were targeted. Some families ruthlessly murdered and ate their own daughters. Others would exchange their children with neighbors. Since a child could only last them for a couple of days, some, including Mo Erwa [the origi-nally discovered cannibal], began to kidnap children from other villages. Booby traps, which were used for wolves, were employed to capture kids.

The Mortician reported further that when the reclaimed bodies were brought back from the mountains, they "were mostly dismembered. The flesh around the thighs, the shoulders, the backs, and the buttocks was all gone."

The Great Proletarian Cultural Revolution, launched by Chairman Mao in 1966, deliberately engaged the support of college and high school students to, according to the Former Red Guard, give impetus to the Communist revolution rather than focusing on developing China's economy. Thus, stu-dents were mobilized and radicalized in defense of Chairman Mao. Their targets were government officials at several levels, hierarchal leaders, such as principals and teachers, former landlords. They were publicly discredited and beaten in the manner of the "speak bitterness" meetings. The Former Red Guard asserted: "Ordinary folks turned around en masse and began to target those in power"; "In those last days, it was very common to see students beat their teachers to death. So, if an accused capitalist was tortured to death, nobody cared"; "In those days, many of the Public Security Bureaus were paralyzed. Nobody was in charge. Nobody dared to question the case [of the six-month torture and ultimate death of a once honored high school princi-pal]. If they had they would have been accused of siding with the enemy. It was a lawless society. The words of Chairman Mao were the ultimate law of the land."

The Former Red Guard expressed his rationale for these activities:

I was born into a family of blue-collar workers. The Cultural Revolution offered me the opportunity to finally trample on those elite. It was glorious. I couldn't get enough of it. My youth, my dream, and my passion were all associated with the Cultural Revolution. The most exciting moment in those days was to see Chairman Mao in person, when he greeted millions of Red Guards in Beijing's Tiananmen Square.

His current responses parallel these: He does not have the same euphoric feelings, but cherishes the memories. "I will never forget them. We were so pure and innocent. . . . We were fighting for our beliefs. We were defending Chairman Mao and the Communist revolution. Anyone who obstructed the revolution deserved to be punished."

Among the more sensitive interviews was that of the Tiananmen Father who lost his elder son, Guofeng, at the massacre on June 4, 1989. This working class family was generationally quite poor, the father constantly hungry as a youngster and undereducated. Both parents worked. Guofeng excelled in school, the top of his high school class, and got the highest score of the township in the college entrance exams. He became the family's great hope for a change in their fortunes.

Guofeng became active politically, joining the students' pro-democracy movement. His parents became anxious:

My generation went through many political campaigns. We've seen them all. One minute, the Party seems to relax its political control. Once you let down your guard, they come out to get you. They've played this trick for years. The Communist leaders change their face like the April weather. I guess living with the fear of persecution made us jaded and overcautious.

Their fears were warranted: The student demonstrations initially identified as a patriotic movement were later called a riot—a counterrevolutionary riot. The troops were ordered to crack down on the student protestors. After warning the protesters to leave by 6:00 A.M. and permitting those who had negotiated safe passage to depart, the armed personnel carriers rolled up the road, firing on the crowds ahead and to the sides. Hundreds were killed, among them Guofeng. The devastated parents traveled to Beijing to bring their son's body home, but the Party Central Committee had ordered that all victims be cremated immediately. The parents, in response to their pleading, were allowed to take a picture of their son "on the condition that I keep those pictures confidential. [The Party secretary] made me promise not to use the pictures to tarnish the image of our government."

The family suffered further injuries: the death of the younger brother, a debilitating head concussion of the mother, and kidney cancer of the father. The family situation rolled downhill.

It's been sixteen years since the June 4 massacre happened. Sooner or later, justice will be done. We probably won't live long enough to see the day. Whatever happens, we can't let the Communist Party get away with the bloody debt owed to families like mine.

The above interviews were selected for their political orientation in keeping with this volume's focus. Other interviews relate traditions, rites, and roles, some of which are disappearing or have been declared illegal. Some of these are the Corpse Walker, the Professional Mourner, the Human Trafficker, and the Falon Gong Practitioner. Alas, the Migrant Worker is not disappearing.

CENSORSHIP HISTORY

In summer 2009, Liao Yiwu wrote: "I didn't witness the killings in Tiananmen Square. I was home in Fuling, a small mountain town well known for its pickled and shredded turnips. When I heard the news, I was outraged. I composed an epic poem, 'Massacre,' to commemorate the government's brutality against its people. With the help of a visiting Canadian friend, I made a tape, chanting my poem into an old toothless tape recorder."

Liao circulated the tape. (It was also smuggled out of China by sympathetic Western literary contacts.) He was arrested while making a movie about Tiananmen Square. Charged with organizing a large-scale counter-revolutionary group (later in 1992, changed to "engaging in individual counter-revolutionary activities"), he was sentenced to four years in prison. During his imprisonment, he was severely tortured; he twice tried to commit suicide. Liao's writings are officially banned in China, and he is frequently harassed. His works are circulated underground, however, and pirated versions can be found in some Chinese bookstores.

Liao has been denied travel opportunities outside of China, most recently in 2010 for a literary festival in Cologne; in 2009, he was prevented from attending a Berlin event affiliated with the Frankfurt Book Fair, at which China was designated the honored guest. All together, there have been 13 such travel denials.

Peter Gourevich's observation in the "Foreword" of *The Corpse Walker* is apt in the context of these censorial challenges:

> Liao is at once an unflinching observer and recorder, a shoe-leather reporter and an artful storyteller, an oral historian and deft mimic, a folklorist and satirist. Above all, he is a medium for whole muzzled swathes of Chinese society that the Party would like to pretend do not exist: hustlers and drifters, outlaws and street performers, the officially renegade and the physically handicapped, those who deal with human waste and with the wasting of humans, artists and shamans, crooks, even cannibals—and every one of them speaks more honestly than the official chronicles of Chinese life that are put out by the state in the name of "the people."

FURTHER READING

Kristof, Nicholas D. "Tiananmen Square." *New York Times*, June 11, 2010.
Liao Yiwu. "Nineteen Days." *Paris Review* 189 (Summer 2009). Available online. URL: www.theparisreview.org/letters-essays/5929/nineteen-days-liao-yiwu. Accessed January 24, 2011.

Wines, Michael. "For 13th Time, Critic of China Is Barred from Travel Abroad." *New York Times*, March 3, 2010, p. A4.

DOCTOR ZHIVAGO

Author: Boris Pasternak
Original dates and places of publication: 1957, Italy; 1958, United States
Publishers: Giangiacomo Feltrinelli Editore; Pantheon Books
Literary form: Novel

SUMMARY

Doctor Zhivago spans the life of its title character until his death before age 40. It spans also a vital period in Russia's history from just after the turn of the 20th century, through the 1917 revolution, the civil war, and up to the terror of the 1930s. An epilogue set during World War II (after Zhivago's death) affords a glimpse of the future as well as closure to the past.

Yurii Andreievich Zhivago is orphaned at a young age. His father, a rich industrialist who abandoned the family even before the early death of his mother, has squandered the family fortune. Yurii is brought up in the home of a cultured, intellectual family in Moscow. He studies to become a physician, earning esteem as a diagnostician, and marries Tonia, the daughter of his "adoptive" parents. A child is born, but their lives are sundered with Zhivago's induction into the military during World War I.

During this military service, Zhivago meets Lara—Larisa Feodorovna Antipova (née Guishar), the daughter of a Russianized, widowed Frenchwoman. He had encountered her twice during adolescence. Trained as a nurse, she is searching for her husband, Pasha—Pavel Pavlovich Antipov—who is rumored to have been injured or slain in battle. Lara carries with her the weight of a past bereavement—the loss of her innocence and purity, having been seduced during adolescence by the lecher Komarovsky, her mother's lover. Yurii and Lara gradually become friends before she departs for her home in Yuriatin in the Ural region and he to his family in Moscow.

> "Big news! Street fighting in Petersburg! The Petersburg garrison has joined the insurgents! The revolution!"

This announcement closes part one of the text and ushers in dramatic changes in the lives of the protagonists and of Russia.

Upon his return, Yurii finds Moscow disordered and depressed. Fuel and firewood are scarce. Maintaining subsistence is challenging and enervating. Yurii attempts to reestablish his medical practice and his social circle, but he finds himself feeling alienated from associates and friends. He begins to recognize the dangers to the family in the new political environment because of their past status.

After a brutal winter, Tonia and her father, with the help of Yurii's half brother, Evgraf, convince Yurii they must escape Moscow to Varykino, Tonia's grandfather's estate, a dangerous choice because it identifies them with its past. The long train ride in a freight car is itself dangerous; they must endure frequent searches. Along the way within sight of Yuriatin, Zhivago briefly meets the infamous Strelnikov, the fanatic officer of the Red Army. (He is in reality Lara's missing husband, who has taken the rumors of his death as an opportunity to change his identity.)

The Zhivagos' life at Varykino takes on an aura of peace and obscurity. Yurii's sense of peace, however, is broken by two events: his love affair with Lara, upon whom he chances in the Yuriatin library—he is tormented by this egregious betrayal of Tonia, whom he also loves; and his being conscripted at gunpoint by the Red partisans, the Forest Brotherhood, to replace their slain surgeon. This imprisonment lasts over a year before he is able to escape on his fourth attempt.

After a six-week walk, Yurii, black with grime, emaciated and weak, arrives in Yuriatin to find Lara. He learns his family has returned to Moscow and, later, that they have been exiled from Russia. However, because she is the wife of Strelnikov, he and Lara are not safe. They disappear to Varykino. Their paths separate when she escapes to a Pacific province, expecting him to follow. He stays behind, deceiving her for her safety, determined to go to Moscow. Before he leaves, Strelnikov arrives, seeking his wife and a hideout. The next day, anticipating capture, he shoots himself.

In Moscow again, Yurii seems unable to commit himself to either his work or his writing. Even his efforts to obtain an exit permit seem half-hearted. He deteriorates physically and intellectually. At last, with the help of his half brother, Evgraf, he takes initial steps toward revitalizing himself. He dies, however, of a heart attack, en route to a new hospital position.

Among those gathered for the wake is Lara. She has come to Moscow on an urgent mission—apparently to locate her and Yurii's lost child; for memory's sake she had come to visit her husband's student apartment, the very one in which Yurii had last lived. After the funeral, she stays to help Evgraf with Zhivago's papers—and then disappears.

> One day Larisa Feodorovna went out and did not come back. She must have been arrested in the street at that time. She vanished without a trace and probably died somewhere, forgotten as a nameless number on a list that afterwards got mislaid, in one of the innumerable mixed or women's concentration camps in the north.

Within this plot, Pasternak introduces an array of characters from all walks of life and portrays their life situations. He provides vignettes of personal and sociopolitical events to evoke the historical and human landscape. In the prewar, prerevolutionary period, the prosperity and charm of upper-class life is contrasted with that of the working class—musical evenings and a Christmas party of dancing, feasting, and card playing in opposition to an angry railroad strike and Cossack dragoons attacking and massacring a group of peaceful demonstrators.

In contrast to the Varykino interlude, a creative haven of happiness found in family, the rewards of work and the beauty of nature, there is the surrounding devastation—the shelled and burned villages viewed from the train, caught between the crossfire of the White and Red armies or destroyed because of uprisings. The peasants live in misery, their lives disrupted, their sons taken as soldiers.

Yurii's initial response to the revolution anticipates the "promises of a new order" as it had been expressed in the idealized revolutionary thought of 1905 and 1912–14; he had been cognizant of the oppression in czarist Russia. Subsequently, he is provoked by less familiar ideas growing out of the reality of a savage and ruthless war and the upheaval of the "soldiers revolution led by those professional revolutionaries, the Bolsheviks." While en route to Moscow, a train companion, a revolutionary, counters Zhivago's suggestion that the country must return to "relative peace and order" before embarking on "dangerous experiments":

> "That's naive. . . . What you call disorder is just as normal a state of things as the order you're so keen about. All this destruction—it's a natural and preliminary stage of a broad creative plan. Society has not yet disintegrated sufficiently. It must fall to pieces completely, then a genuinely revolutionary government will put the pieces together and build on completely new foundations."

Zhivago resists this siren song; as the train approaches Moscow, to him the war and the revolution seem empty and meaningless while his home, intact and dear, is meaningful.

Episodes of the revolution in progress provide glimpses beyond the surface devastation and deprivation and cast a shadow over the occasional political rhetoric of revolutionaries. A village is gratuitously shelled from an armored train because it is adjacent to another that had refused to adhere to the party line. Another is raided and burned to the ground for withholding food from the army, food supplies needed by the villagers. The second stage of the revolution is characterized as one of suspicion and intrigue—informers acting on hatred and envy, ready to destroy individuals in the "name of higher revolutionary justice."

Yurii, too often outspoken for his own safety, expresses his antagonism:

> "But, first, the idea of social betterment as it is understood since the October revolution doesn't fill me with enthusiasm. Second, it is so far from being put into practice, and the mere talk about it has cost such a sea of blood, that I'm not sure that the end justifies the means. And last—and this is the main thing—when I hear people speak of reshaping life it makes me lose my self-control and I fall into despair."

In another passage, he questions marxism and its leaders:

> "Marxism a science? . . . Marxism is too uncertain of its ground to be a science. Sciences are more balanced, more objective. I don't know a movement more self-centered and further removed from the facts than Marxism. Everyone is worried only about proving himself in practical matters, and as for the men in power, they are so anxious to establish the myth of their infallibility that they do their utmost to ignore the truth. Politics doesn't appeal to me. I don't like people who don't care about the truth."

At the height of his energy and power, Yurii dreams of living his life wholly and individually, "living by the sweat of [his] brow." He responds to "man's eternal longing to go back to the land." He embraces the beauty around him and loves to experience and express. He wants his freedom expanded, not diminished; he struggles to protect his privacy and the personal basis of his life. Zhivago maintains these values, although his lust for life and his life ebb away.

The epilogue, set during World War II in 1943, features two of Zhivago's childhood friends. They have been in Soviet penal camps but are now officers in the army. They mull over their past, the atrocities they have experienced. One of them comments on an important aspect of the Soviet system:

> "I think that collectivization was an erroneous and unsuccessful measure and it was impossible to admit the error. To conceal the failure people had to be cured, by every means of terrorism, of the habit of thinking and judging for themselves, and forced to see what didn't exist, to assert the very opposite of what their eyes told them. This accounts for the unexampled cruelty of the Yezhov period, the promulgation of a constitution that was never meant to be applied, and the introduction of elections that violated the very principle of free choice. And when the war broke out, its real horrors, its real dangers, its menace of real death were a blessing compared with the inhuman reign of the lie, and they brought relief because they broke the spell of the dead letter."

CENSORSHIP HISTORY

After the death of Stalin, during the Khrushchev period when the Kremlin eased its censorship policy in 1953, Boris Pasternak began writing *Doctor Zhivago*. He had been silent during the Stalinist period, which had "muted creative individualism and exacted conformity to party dictates from all writers." Upon submitting it to the State Publishing House and receiving a positive reaction, the author sent a copy to Giangiacomo Feltrinelli Editore, a publisher in Italy. Subsequently, the State Publishing House had second thoughts and condemned the book; its "cumulative effect casts doubt on the validity of the Bolshevik Revolution which it depicts as if it were the great crime in Russian history." Pasternak was required to request the book's return from the Italian publisher for "revisions." The publisher refused.

When Pasternak was awarded the Nobel Prize in literature in 1958, he was forced to refuse the award: "[I]n view of the meaning given to this honor in the community in which I belong, I should abstain from the undeserved prize that has been awarded me."

The Soviet Union denounced the award—and the Swedish judges—as a "purely political act hostile to our country and aimed at intensifying the cold war" and as a "hostile political act for recognizing a work withheld from Russian readers which was counter-revolutionary and slanderous." The award had "nothing in common with an impartial assessment of the literary merits of Pasternak's work." Further, Pasternak was expelled from the Soviet Union of Authors and deprived of the title "Soviet writer."

In 1986, reflecting more open policies under Mikhail Gorbachev, issues of censorship and bureaucratic interference in literature were debated at the Eighth Soviet Congress of Writers. A reform-oriented slate was elected to the leadership position of the Writers' Union. Its chief announced that the state publishing agency was considering the publication of *Doctor Zhivago*. It was published at last in 1988. In February 2004, publishers in Russia announced that the entire 11-volume set of Pasternak's writings would be published; two volumes were already available, including poems written between 1912 and 1959, the nine others being anticipated by February 2005. Nevertheless, *Doctor Zhivago* remains controversial with regard to its status as a school reading—whether it should be optional rather than required. The Education Ministry's recent ruling is that dissident writers be optional reading in schools.

In the United States in 1964, a Larchmont, New York, bookstore owner revealed that a man who identified himself as a member of the John Birch Society had telephoned to protest the great number of "subversive" books on the shelves. The titles identified were *Doctor Zhivago, Inside Russia Today* by John Gunther, and *Das Kapital* by Karl Marx; he also mentioned a book by Nabokov and a Russian-English dictionary. He threatened that if these and other "un-American" books were not removed from view, the society would organize a boycott of the bookstore. The editor of the *Newsletter on Intellectual Freedom* advised the bookseller, "Don't take any guff from a self-appointed censor." Presumably, the bookstore owner did not.

FURTHER READING

Chalidze, Valery. *To Defend These Rights: Human Rights and the Soviet Union.* New York: Random House, 1974.

Conquest, Robert. *The Pasternak Affair: Courage of Genius.* Philadelphia: J. B. Lippincott, 1962.

Haight, Anne Lyon, and Chandler B. Grannis. *Banned Books: 387 B.C. to 1978 A.D.* 4th ed. New York: R. R. Bowker, 1978.

Newsletter on Intellectual Freedom 13 (1964): 81; 35 (1986): 196–97; 36 (1987): 72.

Payne, Robert. *The Three Worlds of Boris Pasternak.* Bloomington: Indiana University Press, 1961.

Rowland, Mary F., and Paul Rowland. *Pasternak's Doctor Zhivago.* Carbondale: Southern Illinois University Press, 1967.

Salisbury, Harrison E. "Triumph of Boris Pasternak." *Saturday Review* 41 (November 8, 1958): 22.

Simmons, Ernest J. "Russia from Within." *Atlantic Monthly* 202 (September 1958): 67–68, 72.

THE FUGITIVE (*PERBURUAN*)

Author: Pramoedya Ananta Toer
Original dates and places of publication: 1950, Indonesia; 1990, United States
Publishers: Balai Pustaka Publishing; William Morrow and Company
Literary form: Novel

SUMMARY

Disguised as a beggar and living among beggars, Hardo is drawn out of his refuge to secretly visit Ningsih, his fiancée, at her home during the festivities celebrating her brother's circumcision. The celebratory scene is at odds with Hardo's condition and urgent self-denial as well as with the political condition of Java. The yoke of the Japanese occupation is heavy on the shoulders of the Javanese, their oppression and the concomitant loss of freedom insufferable to Hardo and his companion rebels.

Raden Hardo, we learn, had been a platoon leader in the Indonesian volunteer army. He and others had allied themselves with the Japanese military in order to force the Dutch colonialists out of Indonesia. Since his ultimate goal was independence for Indonesia, he became dissatisfied with the Japanese and, along with two other platoon leaders, Dipo and Karmin, conspired against them. The nationalist rebellion failed, however, when Karmin withdrew his support at the last moment for unspecified reasons. In the intervening six months, Hardo and Dipo have been fugitives, their capture and death by beheading seemingly imminent.

Now, on the eve of the Japanese surrender to the Allies, Hardo has been recognized, first by Ningsih's brother, Ramli, who idolizes him, and then by her mother, who came out to chase him away. Furthermore, he is followed by Ningsih's father, recently appointed village chief by the Japanese, who confirms the identification but is unable to convince Hardo to return with him to his home.

Hardo finds haven in a hut, seemingly isolated in a cornfield. Shortly, its owner, an old man, arrives, out of breath and fearful, for he is being chased by the police. It is Hardo's father. In the ensuing conversation, the old man reveals how he has come to this sorry state; he was fired from his position as district head of Karangjati, which includes the city of Blora. He has suffered the loss of his wife and his son—and then his selfhood and his job. Both he and his wife grieved upon hearing the news of their son's involvement in a rebellion against the Japanese, the failure of the rebellion and the search-to-kill order against him. The district head had been ordered to mobilize the search party; his wife, though ill, had been forced to accompany the search party. Devastated, weak, in pain, and filled with fear, she had died. This loss and the rumors of his son's death had taken away life's meaning; the father had escaped from his visions and empty life into gambling, losing his home and possessions. Now he is pursued by the police.

During this exchange, Hardo attempts to keep his identity secret, denying the old man's suspicions and pleas of acknowledgment. (Perhaps Hardo, in addition to protecting himself, is protecting his father in the event he is questioned and tortured.) The suspicions are not allayed and are indeed confirmed when Hardo talks in his sleep, providing evidence of his identity. Shortly thereafter, a patrol searching for Hardo arrives, but is finally put off by the father's denials of knowledge of his son's whereabouts. A Japanese officer, accompanied by the current district head and an Indonesian soldier, also fails to get information, though he strikes the old man down. It is revealed that Ningsih's father has betrayed Hardo.

That night Hardo rejoins the company of beggars, which includes his friend and coconspirator, Dipo. They debate their perilous situation: Dipo is critical of Hardo's "sentimentality" because he cannot control his feelings about his fiancée; he has forgotten his oath as a soldier and endangered himself and their cause. Dipo expresses a militaristic sense of behavior that rejects emotions and consideration of human frailty. These contrasting ideals are reflected in their argument about Karmin: Hardo would consider Karmin's reason for his actions and his human fallibility, and even defend him; Dipo would summarily decapitate him. During their discussion, another conspirator reports that Japan has surrendered to the Allies. But in Java, Japan is still in power and at that moment calling out the patrols. The conspirators disappear into the elephant grass.

The Japanese are determined to find Hardo and his companions. When they cannot find them among the beggars, they detain the village chief, Ningsih's father, and imprison Hardo's father. The village chief is brought before the Japanese officer, the district head, and the platoon commander, Karmin. He is questioned, threatened, and brutalized by the Japanese; he finally implicates his own daughter, Ningsih, to protect himself from further beatings.

Karmin's role is clarified in this and subsequent scenes. Aware that he has failed his friends for personal reasons, inaction rather than betrayal, he has been working for the past months to protect Hardo's personal and political interests. He has undermined the Japanese by making sure that the conspirators escape the raids, though this is becoming increasingly difficult. He goes to Ningsih's home to forewarn her. When the Japanese officer arrives, she, too, is threatened, but she is steadfast. At this moment of tension, almost simultaneously an uproar of voices broadcasts Japan's surrender and a patrol arrives with Hardo and Dipo in custody.

In the ensuing melee, among a riotous crowd of Indonesians, Karmin attacks the officer, who has taken out his gun and begun firing. During their fight, Dipo removes the officer's sword, presses its point into his back and attempts to decapitate him. At the crowd's urging that Karmin is a traitor, Dipo turns on him; Karmin bows his head, accepting the accusation and sentence. With a word, Hardo intervenes; he also dispels the crowd when Karmin places himself in its hands. "Hardo offered his scabby hand and Karmin took it in his own. They walked together toward the door, but there they were halted by the sight of the village chief bent over his daughter, Ningsih." A stray bullet from the Japanese officer's gun has found its victim.

The characters personify the political core of *The Fugitive.* The Japanese officer reveals the oppression and ruthlessness of that nation's occupation forces: threats, beatings and beheadings. The village chief and Ningsih are held hostage until Hardo is found and are subject to decapitation in his stead. These actions reflect an arrogance seen in the response to Ningsih's daring to ask why her father is being detained:

> "Silence!" the officer repeated. "Indonesians may not ask questions! You are Indonesian so you say nothing!" His fluency rapidly faded. "When Indonesians with Japanese . . . with Japanese, you understand? No telling stories. You remember that." The man's eyes bulged as he spoke. "Indonesians no good. Indonesians must learn to keep their mouths shut. You understand? Do you understand?"

Indonesian independence suffers from the words and behavior of Indonesians themselves. Ningsih's father's ready betrayal of Hardo expresses this demoralization. His act is dramatized by its evident self-serving nature. He admits to Karmin that he betrays Hardo for Ningsih's sake; he cannot see her marrying a beggar. Materialistic and status-oriented—he sells teak on the black market—he cannot countenance such a union. At critical moments, he thinks of himself, not merely his physical safety, but also of money dealings. When arrested, he complains about people who owe him money; during the concluding drama, when Japan's surrender is announced and Hardo has been captured, he reaches for his daughter and says: "It was for you . . . it was all for you that I did it." He loosens his hold to stand beside her. "I'm free, Ningsih! And you're free too. I saw him. And we're rich, Ningsih! We're rich."

Hardo is the heroic ideal, in contrast to Dipo, who lacks compassion, and Karmin, who is derailed from action at a crucial juncture. Hardo acts and argues for freedom from oppression. In response to his father's wearied comment that "there's no such thing as a free man" and that freedom from oppression is "rubbish," Hardo asserts:

> No, the fact is no one is completely sane. And there's no such thing as complete freedom. There's nothing that's one hundred percent in this world. That's just

a dream in a dreamer's mind. . . . All the same, we have to try to free ourselves from our present bonds and to climb upward, even if it means that we will be bound again. Freedom is upward, not downward!

In the responses of these characters to their situations and in their inter-relationships, Pramoedya exposes the variance and complexity of human values and aspirations. In the irony of his conclusion, he expresses the terror, injustice, and sorrow of the human condition. In expressing one day in the life of this fugitive, he spotlights the oppressive force of the occupying army and the energy and the persistence to gain independence.

Pramoedya's Buru tetralogy—*This Earth of Mankind, Child of All Nations, Footsteps,* and *House of Glass*—is also the object of censorship. Spanning 20 years, beginning in the 1890s, the novels are set in Java during the colonial rule of the Netherlands. "Colonial rule" signals a recognition of two factions: the rulers and the ruled. There is also the division of the Native peoples, those hierarchically operating in conjunction with the colonials, and the underclass outsiders. The cultures of these groups, their interactions, and the tensions among them, are revealed through the situations and difficulties that beset the two central characters, Minke and Nyai Ontosoroh, also identified as Sanikem, her birth name.

CENSORSHIP HISTORY

The works of Pramoedya Ananta Toer (1925–2006) have been banned in Indonesia, his native country. He was imprisoned for political reasons for 14 years and on house or city (Jakarta) arrest for an additional 20 years—from 1979 to 1999. Pramoedya wrote *The Fugitive* in 1949 while he was imprisoned by the Dutch from 1947 to 1950 for his role in Indonesia's anticolonial revolutions; he had been a member of the revolutionary underground and had printed and distributed revolutionary pamphlets. He wrote the book secretly when he was not doing forced labor and at night beneath his concrete bedstead. The text was smuggled out of the prison by a Dutch professor. With the success of the revolution in 1949, *The Fugitive*, published in 1950, was acclaimed and then banned; it contained elements of class conflict and was perceived as a potential threat to society.

FURTHER READING

Bald, Margaret. "For Indonesia's Rulers, the Fiction Hurts." *Toward Freedom* (August–September 1992): 17–18.

Charle, Suzanne. "Prisoner without a Cell." *The Nation,* February 3, 1992, 134–135.

Crosette, Barbara. "Banned in Jakarta." *New York Times Book Review,* January 19, 1992, p. 24.

Jones, Sidney. *Injustice, Persecution, Eviction: A Human Rights Update on Indonesia and East Timor.* New York: Asia Watch, 1990.

McDonald, Hamish. *Suharto's Indonesia.* Blackburn, Victoria, Australia: Dominion Press/Fontana Books, 1980.

Scott, Margaret. "Waging War with Words." *Far Eastern Economic Review* (August 9, 1962): 26–30.

Tickell, Paul. "Righting History." *Inside Indonesia* (May 1986): 29–30.

GIRLS OF RIYADH

Author: Rajaa Alsanea
Original dates and places of publication: 2005, Lebanon; 2007, United States
Publisher: Dar al Saqi (Arabic); Penguin (English)
Literary form: Novel

SUMMARY

Girls of Riyadh tells the story of a shillah, or clique, of four upper-class young women in Saudi Arabia: Gamrah, Sadeem, Lamees, Michelle. The story mostly focuses on their struggles to find true love and maintain romantic relationships within the rigid, oppressive, and repressive Saudi society. The novel also features the ups and downs of the intimate friendship shared by the four women, as they help each other understand and navigate their lives in Saudi Arabia. Sadeem's neighbor, Um Nuwayyir, provides her home for the women to meet with each other and occasionally with their love interests.

Girls of Riyadh is structured as a series of e-mails sent to a subscriber group. A first-person narrator, identifying herself as a friend to the four main characters, introduces each chapter (which is then narrated in the third person). In these introductions, she responds to readers and critics of her e-mails (both playfully and seriously) and addresses the growing popularity and scandal of her e-mails. She offers criticism of Saudi society and Saudi men but maintains optimism about love. She makes clear in these introductions that the desires, experiences, and perspectives of herself and the four women she writes about are not exceptional but typical of women in Saudi society.

Because of restrictive rules and social customs regarding interaction between the sexes, cell phones become the key means to maintain relationships. Single men frequently try to give their phone number to any single woman, and long-term romantic relationships are regularly maintained through late-night phone calls and frequent text messages:

> for so many [. . .] lovers in the country, the telephone was the only outlet, practically, for them to express the love that brought them together. The telephone lines in Saudi Arabia are surely thicker and more abundant than elsewhere, since they must bear the heavy weight of all the whispered croonings lovers have to

exchange and all their sighs and moans and kisses that they cannot, in the real world, enact—or that they do not want to enact due to the restrictions of custom and religion, that some of them truly respect and value.

It is difficult for a single man and single woman to be physically together in Riyadh; in some cases, it is a thrill for the women when their beloved men are able to drive in a car near them. Even acknowledging Valentine's Day is forbidden: "The Religious Police banned anything that might remotely suggest a celebration of the holiday of love [. . .] Love was treated like an unwelcome visitor in our region."

The story begins with Gamrah's wedding to Rashid, a man who treats Gamrah poorly and shows little personal or sexual interest in her. Gamrah lives with Rashid in America, where she feels increasingly isolated and miserable. She discovers that Rashid is having an affair with a woman named Kari, and later learns that Kari was Rashid's long-time girlfriend, but that his family disapproved and forced Rashid into marriage with Gamrah. Against Rashid's wishes, Gamrah does not take birth control and becomes pregnant; when Rashid learns about the pregnancy, he becomes enraged and sends her back to her family in Saudi Arabia, eventually divorcing her. Gamrah has a son, but Rashid never takes any part in his life. In Saudi Arabia, Gamrah struggles to find her place: as a divorced woman with a child, she feels restrained, rarely leaving her family home and despairing of ever finding another husband. She does find joy and fulfillment raising her son.

Sadeem meets a man named Waleed, and the two have a happy relationship that leads to an engagement. However, between the signing of the marriage contract and the actual wedding ceremony, Sadeem initiates a sexual encounter with Waleed. Afterward, Waleed avoids contact with Sadeem, eventually sending her divorce papers. Heartbroken, Sadeem goes to live temporarily in London, where she meets Firas, "a diplomat and a politician, widely connected and respected." Sadeem falls deeply in love with Firas, and while they maintain a long, passionate relationship (mostly through phone conversations), Firas avoids official commitment and hints that marriage will not be possible. Eventually, shortly after Sadeem's father dies, Firas becomes engaged to another woman, leaving Sadeem heartbroken once again, and she moves to Khobar to live with family. After the engagement, they again pick up their relationship, but five days later Sadeem, frustrated, breaks up with Firas, "finally cured of her love addiction' . . . los[ing] her respect for all men." In Khobar, Sadeem becomes a party planner, aspiring ultimately to plan weddings. She becomes a successful businesswoman, enlisting Um Nuwayyir and Gamrah to plan parties in Riyadh and planning for the possibility of Lamees running parties in Jeddah and Michelle in Dubai. Sadeem is pursued by her cousin Tariq, who offers love and security; Sadeem feels only fondness for Tariq. However, after Firas calls Sadeem offering to make her his second wife, Sadeem angrily hangs up and agrees to marry Tariq. The book is somewhat ambiguous: Sadeem has given up on passionate love, but she seems to have a happy relationship with Tariq.

Michelle is the most liberated of the four women; she spent her early life in America (her mother is American), and she "loathed Saudi society and its severe traditions." She often incisively and angrily criticizes the conservative Saudi society; for example, "She was well aware that genuine love had no outlet or avenue of expression in this country. Any fledgling love relationship, no matter how innocent or pure, was sure to be seen as suspect and therefore repressed." She falls in love with Faisal, but because Faisal's mother does not approve of their relationship, he breaks up with her rather than defy his family. Michelle becomes even more bitter about the rigid traditions and social customs of Saudi society. She attends school in America, but when she grows close to her American cousin, her parents force her to move back to Saudi Arabia. They eventually move to Dubai, where Michelle works her way up as a successful television producer. Michelle achieves "the best closure ever" when she appears at Faisal's wedding, forcing him to see her before she walks out laughing. But she knows "behind their smiles, many of those brides and grooms were concealing their own sad and yearning hearts because they had been kept from choosing their life's partner." While she ends the novel railing against Saudi society and the lack of courage in men, she holds hope for love: "I will never sell myself short and I can never be satisfied with crumbs."

Lamees attends college training to become a doctor. In college, Lamees develops a close friendship with a Shiite woman, Fatima, becoming interested in her religious beliefs and practices. Fatima introduces Lamees to her brother Ali. Lamees and Ali meet together at a café, where they are arrested by Al-Hai' ah, the religious police (a single man and woman together in public is enough cause for arrest), and though they are released after questioning, this ends her friendship with Fatima and relationship with Ali: "If Lamees had been allowed to continue seeing him, and more important if he hadn't been Shiite, she might actually have fallen in love with him." Eventually, Lamees goes to train at a hospital in Jeddah, where she meets Nizar, another medical student. In the end, she is the most romantically satisfied of the women: she marries Nizar, a man whom she loves and who treats her with caring, respect, and love. She is "the only one who had fulfilled the dream they all had, the dream of marrying the first love of their lives."

The novel ends with the narrator's bitter critique mingled with idealistic hope that characterizes most of the book:

> As for love, it still might always struggle to come out into the light of day in Saudi Arabia. You can sense that in the sighs of bored men sitting alone at cafes, in the shining eyes of veiled women walking down the streets, in the phone lines that spring to life after midnight, and in the heartbroken songs and poems, too numerous to count, written by the victims of love unsanctioned by family, by tradition, by the city: Riyadh.

CENSORSHIP HISTORY

According to James Adams,

> After completing her manuscript, Alsanea decided not to submit it to the Ministry of Information—a normal prepublication caution in Saudi society. Instead, she sought out a publisher in Beirut. "'In Saudi,' she explained, 'you're supposed to take your draft to the ministry and they kind of censor it for you or tell you it's horrible and unpublishable, or they take out some lines and then say it's okay for publication. Well, I didn't want to have to go through that stuff.'"

Indeed, the novel was banned in Saudi Arabia, according to Claudia Roth Pierpont, "apparently for suggesting that upper-class Saudi girls might wish to escape their luxurious designer cages." Harry De Quetteville notes, "In the kingdom where women are banned from driving and alcohol is forbidden, the behind-the-wheel exploits of her Dom Perignon-quaffing heroines have not been 'approved' for publication by the Ministry of Information." The initial banning only provoked interest: De Quetteville and Bruce Ward point out that copies of the book were selling in Saudi Arabia for hundreds of dollars. Fatema Ahmed writes that the book was "quickly withdrawn from bookshops and the ministry of information placed it for a while on its lengthy list of banned books," but that "Photocopies of *Girls of Riyadh* subsequently changed hands for up to $500." The BBC reports that Saudi customers often traveled to Bahrain, where they could purchase the book.

Eventually the book was approved for sale in Saudi Arabia, but that did not end problems. James Adams notes that the many e-mails Alsanea received included death threats, and that

> In February, 2006, her Lebanese publisher "brought in hundreds of copies to sell" at the Riyadh International Book Fair. Unfortunately, Sunni fundamentalists blasted the book as blasphemous and seditious and proceeded to buy up all available copies. Even now, [the novel is hard] to find in stores in Saudi Arabia.

According to Arabnews.com, in 2006 two Saudi men filed a lawsuit in the Court of Grievances against Rajaa Alsanea and "the Ministry of Information for giving the author permission to distribute the novel":

> The two Saudis had asked the court to withdraw the ministry's permission that allowed the author to distribute her book in the Kingdom through various bookstores. They also requested that all airports and seaports in the Kingdom ban the book's entry from abroad. They further said that the author be punished according to the laws of the land. In addition, they alleged that the Ministry of Information violated the laws of publication and distribution in Saudi Arabia by allowing the book to be sold at the International Book Exhibition held in Riyadh several months ago. According to the lawsuit, the book is "an outrage to the norms of Saudi society. It encourages vice and also portrays the Kingdom's

female community as women who do not cover their faces and who appear publicly in an immodest way."

The Court of Grievances rejected the lawsuit.

FURTHER READING

Adams, James. Review of *Sex and the City*. *Globe Review*, May 29, 2010.

Ahmed, Fatema. "Velvet Lives: Fatema Ahmed Goes Searching for Romance in Saudi Arabia." *Guardian Review*, July 14, 2007, p. 16.

De Quetteville, Harry. "Sex and the Saudi Kingdom a Hot Seller: Banned Novel Lifts the Veil on Conservative Society." *National Post*, February 8, 2006, p. A2.

McWatt, Jennifer. "Saudis Flock to Bahrain to Buy Book Banned by Riyadh." *BBC Worldwide Monitoring* (January 31, 2006).

Pierpont, Claudia Roth. "Found in Translation: The Contemporary Arabic Novel." *New Yorker*, January 18, 2010, pp. 74–80.

Qusti, Raid. "Court Rejects Case against Rajaa Al-Sanea." *Arab News* (October 9, 2006). Available online. URL: http://archive.arabnews.com/?page=1&section=0&article=87886&d=9&m=10&y=2006. Accessed January 24, 2011.

Ward, Bruce. "Carving out Their Own Way: Novel Has Ignited a Debate about Women in Saudi Arabia." *Montreal Gazette* (August 11, 2007): p. J4.

—Joseph K. M. Fischer
University of Wisconsin-River Falls

THE GRAPES OF WRATH

Author: John Steinbeck
Original date and place of publication: 1939, United States
Publisher: Viking Press
Literary form: Novel

SUMMARY

Set during the Great Depression in Oklahoma and California—the dust bowl and the verdant promised land—and the long road in between, *The Grapes of Wrath* expresses the travail of the Joad family in their journey to find a place for themselves. The dust claimed the land and destroyed their crops year after year; the people living on it are stranded. Hope, generated by handbills proclaiming job opportunities in California and emblazoned by images of verdant and fruited lands, lures the divested westward.

The Joad family is one of thousands of the dispossessed. They take to the road in a decrepit car turned into a truck, with a precariously low supply of money. They number 12, in addition to Casy, a former preacher, who joins them. Chief among them are Ma and Pa; Tom, just released on parole from prison, where he'd served time for murdering a man who had knifed him;

16-year-old Al, who is a capable driver and mechanic; and Rose of Sharon, who is pregnant.

The journey from Oklahoma is hazardous. Reminiscent of pioneer west-bound travelers, they face problems of supplies and water, transportation, and challenging landscape. Not unexpectedly, the car breaks down; tires give out. Al's alertness and skill, with help from Tom, salvage these exigent situations before disaster strikes. Their meager savings dwindle—gas, car repairs, food—so diet and health suffer. However, the Joads do make it.

Unfortunately, Grandpa Joad dies at the first encampment, and his wife, in a state of emotional collapse and physical exhaustion, dies while crossing the desert. The eldest son, Noah, decides to leave the family when they arrive in Needles, California; he is captivated by its river. Rose of Sharon's husband abandons her and the family when he realizes he will not have easy access to a job and personal advancement that he had expected. At the end of the novel, Rose of Sharon delivers a stillborn, apparently malnourished baby.

The promise of California proves to be barren. Before the journey, Ma Joad had said apprehensively, "I hope things is all right in California," and there are forewarnings along the way from returning emigrants that the handbill advertisements are a false lure, that the land is pretty but unavailable. There are two deceits: the jobs and the welcome. The handbills have lured thousands of workers for relatively few seasonal jobs. The Joads learn the script quickly. Out of food and money, they accept the first available work, picking peaches for five cents a box. They're ushered into the ranch area by police on motorcycles through throngs of striking men. They, too, had been offered five cents a box.

> "Lookie, Tom," [Casy] said at last. "We come to work, there. They says it's gonna be fi'cents. They was a hell of a lot of us. We got there an' they says they're payin' two an' a half cents. A fella can't even eat on that, an' if he got kids—So we says we won't take it. So they druv us off. An' all the cops in the worl' come down on us. Now they're payin' you five. When they bust this here strike—ya think they'll pay five? . . . We tried to camp together, an' they druv us like pigs. Scattered us. Beat the hell outa fellas . . . We can't las' much longer. Some people ain't et for two days. . . ."

The Joads and others hired with them are paid as promised, but as soon as the strike is broken, the wage is reduced to two and a half cents a box.

The living conditions add to the migrants' misery and dehumanization. Instead of the neat white house that Ma Joad and Rose of Sharon dream of, they find "Hooverville" (a reference to President Hoover's failed aid program) camps, a collection of some 40 tents and shacks: "The rag town lay close to water; and the houses were tents, and weed-thatched enclosures, paper houses, a great junk pile." These are scattered randomly, some neatly maintained, others surrounded by the debris of travel. Sanitary facilities do not exist, nor are there hot water and any other amenities.

The rare alternative is Weedpatch, the camp established by the government. Limited in the number of families it can house, it is a cooperative enterprise, operated and maintained by its residents, who establish its rules of order, conduct, and cleanliness through elected committees. The camp provides sanitary facilities—toilets, showers, and sinks, clothes-washing basins, and other amenities such as wood for fires. Equally meaningful to the Joads, who find space in the camp for a time, are the community relationships and support, the sense of being treated as human beings, the unity and mutual protectiveness.

The government camp is perceived by the landowners as a "red threat" (a reflection of the fear of socialism) to the status quo they wish to maintain. When Tom Joad asks about the availability of hot water at the peach ranch camp, he is treated contemptuously. A guard remarks,

> "Hot water, for Christ's sake. Be wantin' tubs next." He stared glumly after the four Joads.
> . . . "It's them gov'ment camps," he said. "I bet that fella been in a gov'ment camp. We ain't gonna have no peace till we wipe them camps out. They'll be wantin' clean sheets, first thing we know."

While the Joads are at the government camp, the local landowners and police indeed attempt to instigate a fight within the campgrounds to give them an excuse to send in a riot squad to destroy it.

The physical miseries are compounded by the attitude reflected in the hiring policies and the actions taken by police. The migrants are bullied and beaten, charged and jailed as vagrants for any resistance, even verbal. One "vagrant," who complains about the dishonest promises of pay rates, is labeled a "red": "He's talkin' red, agitating trouble." Other migrants are warned: "You fellas don't want to listen to these goddamn reds. Troublemakers. . . ." Hooverville communities are burned as well for such small infractions. The people themselves are judged by their surface condition: their poverty and hunger, their grime and tatters. They are condescendingly called "Okies": "Well, Okie use'ta mean you was from Oklahoma. Now it means you're a dirty son-of-a bitch. Okie means you're scum. Don't mean nother itself, it's the way they say it."

Two interlocking strands reveal aspects of the political-philosophic underpinnings of the novel. One strand signals the destruction of the family farm and the farmer; the second focuses on the tractor and other machinery that displace men and their animals, making them extraneous.

The family farm and farmer are victims of owners and banks, of companies with extensive acreage. In Oklahoma, when crops fail again and again, the owners, the Company, the Bank moved in. Eventually, the farmer is forced from the land. But the owners go one step further: "One man on a tractor can take the place of twelve or fourteen families." The tractor destroys the concept of the family farm and the farm itself: Keeping "the line straight," it drives through the dooryard, turns over buildings, tramples fences. The novel frequently refers to the farmers being "tractored off."

In California, the operation is essentially the same. The great owners and companies dominate: They control the land. The small landowner is pressured into line by the Farmers Association run by the Bank, which "owns most of this valley, and it's got paper on everything it don't own." They set the low wages and the cutthroat policies. Since this isn't enough to satiate their greed, a great owner buys a cannery, then sells the fruit to the cannery at a low price and the canned goods to consumers at a high price, ensuring a profit. The little farmer is squeezed out of business.

In direct contrast, the sharing ethic is evidenced among the migrants. From the outset when the Joads graciously welcome Casy as a travel companion despite the overcrowded vehicle, to the closing scene when Rose of Sharon readily nurses the starving man discovered in the barn, there is consistent expression of the need to help and to accept help without becoming a burden. Ma crystallizes the ethic and the contrast: "I'm learnin' one thing good. . . . Learnin' it all a time, ever' day. If you're in trouble or hurt or need—go to poor people. They're the only ones that'll help—the only ones."

Two opposing forces converge to climax the action and issues of the novel. The men, hungering for work until they are hired to pick peaches or cotton, wonder how they'll manage when all the picking seasons are over. "Fella had a team of horses, had to use 'em to plow an' cultivate an' mow, wouldn' think a turnin' 'em out to starve when they wasn't workin.'" The deprivation and desperation of the migrants brings them together; they begin to unite to create a solid front, culminating in a spontaneous strike. The owners, feeling the status quo threatened by the "reds" and needing to maintain control against a perceived insurrection, develop a counterforce of the police and citizens. The latter themselves feel threatened in their status and livelihood.

The clash of forces at the strike leads to Casy's death—he's the strike leader—and Tom's becoming a wanted man for battering Casy's murderer. While in hiding, Tom determines his future role: to take on Casy's mission, to unite his people, to help them to achieve their goal—"to live decent and bring up their kids decent."

> "I been thinkin' a hell of a lot, thinkin' about our people livin' like pigs, an' the good rich lan' layin' fallow, or maybe one fella with a million acres, while a hundred thousan' good farmers is starvin'. An' I been wonderin' if all our folks got together an' yelled, like them fellas yelled, only a few of 'em at the Hooper ranch—"

In the concluding chapters, the Joads, having helped Tom escape, are trapped by a flood, unable to leave their boxcar "home" because Rose of Sharon is delivering her stillborn child. When the birthing is over and the floodwaters have receded slightly, the three remaining adults carry Rose of Sharon and the two children through the chest-deep waters to higher ground where they find refuge in a barn. It is occupied, they discover, by a boy and his starving father; he had given all the food to his son. The Joads have found a temporary haven. Like their pioneer forebears, however, they have not found the promised land of opportunity.

CENSORSHIP HISTORY

The Grapes of Wrath faced censorship challenges just months after it was published (April 1939). National, regional, and state surveys attest to this, as well as to the novel's rating among the "most frequently" challenged books. Lee Burress in his five national surveys of librarians or schoolteachers/administrators reports multiple cases: 1966—five challenges (tied for fourth most frequently); 1973—four (tied for third); 1977—eight (second place); 1982—six (tied for sixth); 1988—two challenges. In Burress's master list of the 22 most frequently challenged books in American high schools 1965–81, *The Grapes of Wrath* placed second; on a comparable list for 1965–82, the novel was in fourth place. Surveys conducted by James Davis in Ohio (1982) and Kenneth Donelson in Arizona (1967) also identify challenges, as do those of Georgia (1982, 1984), North Carolina (1983), Minnesota (1991), and People For the American Way (1992). (Other titles reported by Burress among the top 25 most censored and included in this volume are 1984, *Slaughterhouse-Five*, and *Johnny Got His Gun*.)

Specifically documented attacks on the novel in its first year occurred in widely separated parts of the country: Kansas City, Kansas, where the board of education on August 18, 1939, voted 4-2 to order copies of the novel removed from the 20 public libraries for reasons of indecency, obscenity, abhorrence of the portrayal of women, and for "portray[ing] life in such a bestial way"; Buffalo, New York, where Alexander Galt, head librarian of the city libraries, barred it from being purchased because of its "vulgar words"; Kern County, California, where the county board of supervisors, voting 4-1 on August 21, 1939, "requested that the use, possession, and circulation of [the novel] be banned from the county's libraries and schools"; East St. Louis, Illinois, where five of nine library board members voted unanimously on November 15, 1939, to have three copies of the book burned on the courtyard steps (within a week, by a 6-2 vote, the board rescinded its burning order in response to the "national commotion it had aroused"; it placed the three copies on the "Adults Only" shelf); Greene County, Ohio, where in late November the library board members voted 4-3 to ban the novel as "unsuitable" for circulation among its patrons; and the USS *Tennessee*, where the chaplain removed it from the ship's library.

These challenges occurred as *The Grapes of Wrath* was becoming a best seller: 360,000 copies were in print, including a new printing of 50,000. The East St. Louis burning order occurred in 1939 during the week the novel had its largest sales order to date, 11,340 copies. A record 430,000 copies were sold by the end of the year. The East St. Louis librarian indicated that the waiting list for the novel was the largest of any book in recent years; a Greene County librarian noted that her library's five copies had been on reserve since it came out, the waiting list of 62 names in November stretching to March; there were 50 men on the waiting list of the USS *Tennessee*. In Kern County, with 60 copies in circulation at the time of the ban, 112 persons were on the several waiting lists.

Kern County, California

Of these challenges, the Kern County, California, event was the most organized in its opposition. Kern County is in the center of the agricultural region featured in *The Grapes of Wrath*. Though there had not been any registered complaints at the local libraries nor any articles or editorials debating the merits of the book, the board of supervisors—which also had not previously discussed the issue—passed the banning resolution proposed by Supervisor Stanley Abel on August 21, 1939. It read in part: "*The Grapes of Wrath* has offended our citizenry by falsely implying that many of our fine people are a low, ignorant, profane and blasphemous type living in a vicious, filthy manner." Another section objected to Steinbeck's choosing to ignore the education, recreation, hospitalization, welfare and relief services made available by Kern County. In addition to the banning of the book from the county libraries and schools, the resolution requested that Twentieth Century–Fox Film Corporation not complete its motion picture adaptation that was then in production. County librarian Gretchen Knief wrote immediately to Supervisor Abel. An excerpt follows:

> If that book is banned today, what book will be banned tomorrow? And what group will want a book banned the day after that? It's such a vicious and dangerous thing to begin and may in the end lead to exactly the same thing we see in Europe today.
>
> Besides, banning books is so utterly hopeless and futile. Ideas don't die because a book is forbidden reading. If Steinbeck has written truth, that truth will survive. If he is merely being sensational and lascivious, if all the "little words" are really no more than fly specks on a large painting, then the book will soon go the way of all other modern novels and be forgotten.

The offended citizens appear to have been the Associated Farmers of Kern County. Led by its president, Wofford B. Camp, a prominent rancher, it had sent a telegram of praise to Kansas City. Camp called Steinbeck's novel "propaganda of the vilest sort" and claimed, "We are defending our farm workers as well as ourselves when we take action against that book." Camp and two other men "ceremoniously burned" a copy of the book; a photograph of this act appeared in *Look* magazine.

The Associated Farmers group also organized a statewide action plan to suppress the book, to "remove the 'smear' to the good name of Kern, the state of California and agriculture." They urged all organizations in the San Joaquin Valley to approve a measure comparable to that of Kern County. Camp declared:

> We are angry, not because we were attacked but because we were attacked by a book obscene in the extreme sense of the word and because our workers with whom we have lived and worked for years are pictured as the lowest type of human life when we know that is not true.
>
> You can't argue with a book like that, it is too filthy for you to go over the various parts and point out the vile propaganda it contains. Americans have a right to say what they please but they do not have the right to attack a community in such words that any red-blooded American man would refuse to allow his daughter to read them.

Established in 1933 through the joint efforts of the California Farm Bureau Federation and the state Chamber of Commerce with the financial backing of the Canners League and large landholders, the Associated Farmers' original purpose was to organize local citizen committees to pass anti-picketing regulations so as to derail farm workers' strikes and unionizing activities; strike breaking efforts were a second phase of the organization's purposes.

During the ensuing week the battle lines were drawn. Supported, perhaps, by a series of articles and editorials that had appeared early in August in the *Bakersfield Californian*, which noted the irreconcilability between Steinbeck's fiction and the facts of assistance to migrants, adherents argued for even stronger action than a ban. Pro-America, a national women's organization, which was meeting in San Francisco, denounced the book as a "lie promoting class hatred" and indicated that the "farmworkers of California are better paid and better housed than agriculture workers anywhere else in the world."

Denunciations of the banning by the American Civil Liberties Union (ACLU) were joined by protests of several local unions—Oil Workers Union, Hod Carriers Union, Butchers Union, and the Brotherhood of Engineers—and the Workers Alliance, an organization of relief recipients, as well as library clients. The debate centered on the abridgement of constitutional rights; it also included discussion of the ethics of the supervisors' action and their "hidden motivation," that is, the influence of the Associated Farmers of Kern County.

Editorials and articles in newspapers throughout the Central Valley were highly critical of the censorship. In response to the endorsement of the banning by Pro-America, the *Selma Irrigator* editorialized about the politics of special interest groups:

> As for the meeting in San Francisco at which Mr. Steinbeck's book was denounced, wasn't it significant that the men and women who have read the book but don't want others to read it assembled in one of San Francisco's most luxurious hotels far from the San Joaquin cotton fields.

John Raymond Locke of the *Dinuba Sentinel* wrote:

It is absolutely foolish to try and deny the conditions pictured, whether of the Dust Bowl West or of our own California. Here in our own state most of the pioneers have been "run off" the land they brought into bearing. Look over files of the Sentinel for the past 20 years and see the hundreds that have been foreclosed.

The board of supervisors meeting on August 28 was crowded. Pickets carried banners urging the rescinding of the ban in front of the courthouse meeting room. The discussion was heated and lasted an entire day. R. W. Henderson of the ACLU argued that book censorship "could lead to partisan coloration of the library's contents"; Reverend Edgar J. Evans, in reaction to a supervisor's claim, after citing selected passages, that the "book was lewd," questioned whether it was language that was objected to, suggesting that instead it was "the exposure of a sociological condition." Supervisor Stanley Abel, the resolution's sponsor, admitted that the local Chamber of Commerce secretary had written the resolution. He pursued the morality issue for the most part, but at one point claimed that he was trying to bring national attention to the migrant workers in hopes of improving their lot. Despite the efforts of antiban partisans, the vote to rescind failed on a 2-2 vote, the chairperson being absent on vacation.

Some attempts to have the ban lifted were made at the following meetings of the board, but no action was taken until January 27, 1941, when such a vote did succeed. The books were returned to the Kern County library shelves. In the November 1940 election, Stanley Abel had been defeated. It was not until 1972, however, that the teaching of the book was permitted in Kern High School District at East Bakersfield High School. The official policy was at last overturned in July 2002; a resolution was adopted by the Kern County Supervisors officially rescinding the ban and praising Steinbeck for chronicling "the courage and humanity of common Americans during the Depression."

1970s

In April 1972, in Herman, New York, a petition from 100 residents, led by Rev. Barber, argued for the removal from the library and curriculum of books "containing profanity or descriptions of a sexual nature which arouse sexual desire" or those with "references and dialog that condone immorality or references that promote disrespect or defiance of parental or other constituted authority." Among the 10 books identified were three by Steinbeck—*The Grapes of Wrath*, *Of Mice and Men* and *In Dubious Battle*—as well as *The Catcher in the Rye* by J. D. Salinger and *To Kill a Mockingbird* by Harper Lee. Three committees were established, one to reevaluate the named books and one each to evaluate the high school and elementary school collections. In Richlands, Virginia, representatives of 17 churches complained in February 1973 about *The Grapes of Wrath* being in the Richland High School library; they characterized it as "pornographic, filthy, and dirty." In Buncombe, North Carolina, two challenges were issued, the first in the fall of 1973, the second in February 1981. The complaints: passages were objectionable to parents; the book was morally [in]decent to the community. The books in both cases were *The Grapes of Wrath*, *The Catcher in the Rye*, and *Andersonville* by MacKinlay Kantor; Steinbeck's *Of Mice and Men*, Eldridge Cleaver's *Soul on Ice*, and Gordon Parks's *The Learning Tree* were also included the first time. The board of education rejected the resolution, reaffirming its "Policies for Selection," in both instances. In Scituate, Rhode Island, in June 1975, after they had been denied their request to censor *The Grapes of Wrath* (and *Of Mice and Men*, *The Catcher in the Rye*, *Lord of the Flies* by William Golding, *The Art of Loving* by Erich Fromm, and *Listen to the Silence* by David Elliott) a group of ministers and other citizens protested by distributing leaflets with excerpts that would have "caused the devil to blush." Farmville, North Carolina, in 1977 established written guidelines for the classroom and library use of books like *The Grapes of Wrath*, *The Catcher in the Rye*, and *Of Mice and Men*. They were placed on restricted shelves, available only with written parental permission.

Kanawha, Iowa

The challenge to *The Grapes of Wrath* in Kanawha on February 11, 1980, emerged as a language issue. Marvin E. Stupka, the vice president of the bank and father of a 10th grader, read the first 11 pages of the novel assigned to his son's English class and "became incensed with the book's language." He concluded after reading "scattered portions" that the book is "profane, vulgar and obscene" because "it takes the Lord's name in vain dozens of times" and features a preacher who is an immoral hypocrite. He and others complained to superintendent Leroy Scharnhorst, who ordered the books collected and stored until the school board could decide the issue. At its February 11 meeting, the board voted 5-0 to permanently remove the books from two sophomore English classes. Teachers could not require it but might recommend it to their students; copies of the novel would remain in the school library.

While none of the parents told school officials they objected to the novel's message, school board president Wayne Rietema commented that the United States was "going pell mell downhill" morally and the Kanawha community had a chance to act and reverse that trend by banning the book from the classes. "This is the backbone of America—the small town." He added, "We do not intend to become a censoring committee," but he urged nevertheless that the board act to control the book. The attempt of one reporter to interview residents of Kanawha found them reluctant to be quoted, some out of fear of reprisals. However, letters and commentary in the Des Moines *Register* were entirely critical of the school board's action. One predictable result was that *The Grapes of Wrath* became a bestseller in surrounding communities' bookstores and libraries; the Kanawha Public Library borrowed a dozen copies to supplement its own single volume so as to meet reader demand.

In his discussion/analysis of the censoring of *The Grapes of Wrath*, Lee Burress points to the coincidence that in this instance a banker in Iowa should attack the novel for its language, ignoring the Jeffersonian agrarianism that permeates the book and Steinbeck's "charge that capital [of banks] is used to buy big tractors and drive the farmers off the land." He further notes:

> It is an interesting coincidence that approximately at the same time the book was removed from use in the English class at Kanawha, the Sioux City Diocese of the Roman Catholic Church issued a report concerning land ownership patterns in Iowa after two years of study. The report stated that in the 14 northwestern counties of Iowa, 77% of the land was owned by absentee owners.

Vernon, New York

Censorship of seven books from reading lists for junior and senior high students was demanded by Rev. Carl Hodley in February 1980. He labeled them "filthy, trashy sex novels." In addition to *The Grapes of Wrath*, his list included *Of Mice and Men* and *The Red Pony* by John Steinbeck, *A Separate Peace* by John Knowles, *It's Not the End of the World* by Judy Blume, *To Kill a Mockingbird* by Harper Lee, and *A Farewell to Arms* by Ernest Hemingway. The Vernon-Verona-Sherill school district refused to adhere to his request.

Buncombe County, North Carolina

The Grapes of Wrath was among the books challenged by a group led by several fundamentalist ministers. This censorship history is detailed in the discussion of *Andersonville*.

Richford, Vermont

In early fall 1981, five parents, led by Claire Doe, complaining *The Grapes of Wrath* contained immoral and offensive material, requested the book be banned from the high school library and dropped from the junior year American literature class. Objections centered on the image of the former minister, who describes how he used to "take advantage" of young women when he was a preacher, and on "the Lord's name being taken in vain." Doe, whose 16-year-old son was in the class, said that it was a good book for adults but not for children.

Following the school district's procedures, superintendent Forest Farnum appointed a nine-member committee, made up of teachers, parents, and church leaders, to study the book. Its chairperson, Edward Wilkins, an elementary school principal from a neighboring town, advised the members to consider historical value, literary merit, and religious symbolism. The committee heard the objections of Doe's group and reactions of some 25 parents who supported the book. The committee recommended to the school board that Steinbeck's novel be retained for classroom and library use without restrictions. The school board concurred. Carroll Hull, principal of Richford High School, said,

> "The decision reaffirms our right to require what we feel is necessary for a child's education. . . . In some cases, we allow students an alternative if the

parents object to the material. But some works, like The Grapes of Wrath, we consider essential."

Barry Steinhardt, executive director of the ACLU in Vermont, had indicated that legal action would be taken if the book was banned.

Anniston, Alabama

In fall 1982, a group of about 50 ministers together with church members, representing the Moral Majority, a fundamentalist conservative faction, targeted seven school library books, including *The Grapes of Wrath*, for removal. They labeled the books "ungodly" and "obscene" and circulated petitions to be presented to the Calhoun County Board of Education on October 18. They also planned to ask permission to form a church-assigned committee to review books on the library shelves as well as new selections. The other books were *Doris Day: Her Own Story*, Steinbeck's *East of Eden*, J. D. Salinger's *The Catcher in the Rye*, Anthony Burgess's *A Clockwork Orange*, Barbara Beasley Murphy's *No Place to Run*, and Frances Hanckel and John Cunningham's *The Way of Love*.

Before the school board met to hear the request, two principals ordered the removal of books. Principal Grover Whaley, of Alexandria High School, caused Steinbeck's books to be withdrawn because of some language in *Of Mice and Men* he found to be vulgar and profane; he had not been contacted by the ministers but had talked with one parent who disapproved of the book. He had received a few telephone calls protesting his action. Principal Wayne Wigley removed *Doris Day: Her Own Story* from the Pleasant Valley High School library upon a parent's complaint.

On a unanimous vote on November 16, the board of education returned all of the books to the library shelves but on a restricted basis. A 10-person committee consisting of Calhoun County superintendent Dan Henderson and school representatives so recommended after being advised by the board's counsel, H. R. Burnham, that comparable attempts to censor school library books around the country had failed in the courts. The ministers' request to screen library books was also rejected. Alternatively, a five-person committee to include a school administrator, teacher, librarian, and two parents was to be appointed at each county school to select and screen books, undertaking the function of the schools' librarians.

Burlington, North Carolina

"The book is full of filth. My son is being raised in a Christian home and this book takes the Lord's name in vain and has all kinds of profanity in it," complained Robert Wagner in March 1986. Though not formalized, his complaint about his son's 11th-grade literature class reading led to the assignment of an alternative text.

Carthage, North Carolina

A similar but formalized complaint about the use of the book in an 11th-grade class at Pinecrest High School by Marie Mofield on August 5, 1986, led the Moore County school system to appoint a study committee to evaluate whether *The Grapes of Wrath* should be required reading or banned per her request. The committee, led by Peggy Olney, the head librarian, met with Mofield, who subsequently withdrew her banning request, being satisfied that her 11th-grade child would not be required to read it.

Greenville, South Carolina

The purpose for the January 29, 1991, petition signed by 864 people and submitted to the Greenville County school board was the removal of five books from the approved reading list. The basis: They used the name of God and Jesus in a "vain and profane manner along with inappropriate sexual references." The school district's materials review committee had already approved the books' retention on the reading list; however, the instruction committee of the school board voted to conduct its own review. In addition to *The Grapes of Wrath*, the books objected to were *Second Heaven* by Judith Guest, *My Brother Sam Is Dead* by James L. Collier and Christopher Collier, *The Water Is Wide* by Pat Conroy, and *East of Eden* by John Steinbeck.

The argument was joined at a second board meeting with 13 speakers supporting the books, asserting, "It is vital that along with American pride, we have humility and show all aspects of American life"; and one speaker favoring the ban because "Under the definitions you have given tonight, we would have to approve *Playboy* and *Hustler,* too." At a third meeting on April 9, the school board affirmed by a 4-2 vote the district policy that allowed administration-appointed panels to review books about which parents raise concerns. The policy also authorized the parental option of refusing to have their children read a given book. A proposal from a school board trustee to provide reading lists with potentially offensive books identified was labeled as censorship by Pat Scales, a librarian:

> "[I]f the district does that, it might as well remove the books. Labeling books in any way is censorship. I do in my heart believe parents should be able to select reading material for their children. But our calling attention to [the fact the book may offend some] relieves them of that responsibility."

Union City, Tennessee

A somewhat more complex controversy emerged from Bobby Pegg's December 1993 objection to his daughter's 11th-grade advanced placement (AP) English class assignment of *The Grapes of Wrath*. His formal request of the Union City school board was for an alternative selection for his daughter without penalty to her grade. His claim: "Reading this book is against my daughter's religious beliefs." His request led to parental voices of support for the class and the book as well as parental opposition to the book; the latter individuals called for the book's being "outlawed and banned," citing "offensive and vulgar material" and language as being inappropriate for high school students. An eight-member ad hoc review committee denied Pegg's basic request for an alternative book assignment; the school board heard his appeal on January 10, 1994. The committee reviewed the book on specific criteria, including its appropriateness, content, and authenticity. Pegg had itemized the number of offensive passages: God's name taken in vain—129 times; vulgar language—264 times; and references to sex—31 times. After a two-hour debate the school board voted unanimously in support of the committee's recommendation of maintaining the reading list for the AP English class, which was not a required class. In opposition to the "moral consciousness of the student" and alternative-selection arguments, proponents of the book argued for the maintenance of standards of the AP national course requirements and resisting exceptions, reasoning that one would potentially lead to many. A selected spokesperson, Glenda Candle, said:

> There were books that could be deemed offensive by spokesmen for any number of religious, political, sexual and racial agenda. But does that capacity to offend mean these books should be ignored for their ultimate value and thus removed from the list of required reading? . . . I must respectfully suggest that if she wishes to continue as a student in the AP English program, she should be required to complete the work as assigned by her teacher.

Puyallup, Washington

After a series of racially charged incidents in 1999, a suit filed in U.S. District Court in 2000 by 36 students and 23 parents against the Puyallup School District accused the district of tolerating a racially hostile environment, citing assaults on minority students and racist graffiti and slurs. In addition, the group also complained of racial slurs in exams and in class discussion of several offending texts, identified as *The Grapes of Wrath*, *The Adventures Of Huckleberry Finn*, and *To Kill a Mockingbird*. Each text is similar in that it contains dialogue that refers to blacks with a particularly degrading slur, as alleged; however, each text also makes a powerful statement against racism, classism, and intolerance. The suit was settled in September 2002 before the scheduled trial: The school district agreed to pay $7.5 million and to make administrative and curricular changes, including the establishment of an office of diversity affairs, to encourage racial diversity.

International

By order of the Propaganda Administration, *The Grapes of Wrath* was banned in Germany in 1942–43. It was banned in Ireland in 1953. In Turkey, on February 21, 1973, 11 publishers and eight booksellers went on trial on charges of publishing, possessing, or selling books in violation of an order of the Istanbul martial law command. The charges: spreading propaganda unfavorable to the state.

The Film

The filming of *The Grapes of Wrath* was protested on the grounds that "it would be inflammatory and widely censored." Many conservatives, including most of Twentieth Century–Fox's board of directors, thought it was unsuitable for the screen—it was radical and subversive. The California Chamber of Commerce condemned the project, and the Agricultural Council of California, whose chairman, C. C. Teague, was also an official of the Associated Farmers of California, conducted a campaign in rural newspapers against the filming. Despite a clause in Steinbeck's contract with Twentieth Century–Fox that the film would "fairly and reasonably retain the main action and social intent," the final product, as Robert Morsberger points out, softens Steinbeck's "harsh criticism, generalizes the oppressors . . . leaves out the dialogue about reds, deletes the novel's tragic ending, reverses the sequences of the benevolent government camp and the vicious Hooper ranch, and ends with an upbeat note, leaving the impression that everything will be 'awright' and that nothing needs to be done."

Steinbeck was awarded the Nobel Prize in literature in 1962.

FURTHER READING

"Anniston Coalition Targets 'Obscenity.'" *Tuscaloosa News*, October 9, 1982, [n.p.].

Bixler, Paul. "Book Banned by Greene County Libraries, Is Offered to Public by Antioch College." *Steinbeck Newsletter* (Winter 1993): 10–11.

Bowden, Kevin. "Community Split on Steinbeck Novel." *Union City Daily Messenger*, December 13, 1993, pp. 1, 2.

———. "Request For Alternate Book Denied." *Union City Daily Messenger*, January 11, 1995, pp. 1, 2.

Burress, Lee. "*The Grapes of Wrath:* Preserving Its Place in the Curriculum." In *Censored Books: Critical Viewpoints*, edited by Nicholas J. Karolides, Lee Burress, and John M. Kean, 278–287. Metuchen, N.J.: Scarecrow Press, 1993.

Cowperthwait, Richard, and Alan Abbey. "Richford Parents Fermenting Over *Grapes of Wrath*." *Burlington Free Press*, November 11, 1981, pp. 1–2B.

"Fifty Years of Wrath." *Newsletter on Intellectual Freedom* 38 (1989): 121–123.

Gehrke, Donna. "Kanawha Bans Classic Book from Classes." *Des Moines Register*, February 12, 1980, p. 1A.

———. "School Board May Ban *Grapes of Wrath*." *Des Moines Register*, February 10, 1980, p. 1B.

Hollobaugh, Dix. "The Wrath of Kanawha." *Des Moines Sunday Register*, February 24, 1980, pp. 1A, 5A.

Jarvis, Richard. "Let Parents See Reading Lists, Trustee to Urge." *Greenville Piedmont*, April 10, 1991, p. 3.

Kappel, Tim. "Trampling Out the Vineyards—Kern County's Ban on *The Grapes of Wrath*." *California History* (Fall 1982): 210–221.

Karolides, Nicholas J., and Lee Burress, eds. *Celebrating Censored Books*. Racine: Wisconsin Council of Teachers of English, 1985.

"K. C. Libraries Ban *Grapes of Wrath*." *Bakersfield Californian*, August 18, 1939, [n.p.].

May, Lucy. "Group Wants Five Books Off Schools List." *Greenville News*, January 30, 1991, p. 1C.

———. "Proposal to Ban Some Books Draws Crowds to Board Meeting." *Greenville News*, March 13, 1991, p. 2.

———. "School Board Affirms Policy Allowing Panel to OK Books." *Greenville News*, April 10, 1991, p. 2.

McVicar, D. Morgan. "Disputed Books Go to Reserve Shelves." *Anniston Star*, November 17, 1982, pp. 1, 5A.

Morsberger, Robert E. "Steinbeck and Censorship." Available online. URL: http://www.csupomona.edu/~jis/2003/Morsberger.pdf. Downloaded August 23, 2004.

Mutter, John. "*Grapes of Wrath* Survives Banning Attempt in Vermont Town." *Publishers Weekly*, December 11, 1981, 9.

Newsletter on Intellectual Freedom 21 (1972): 103–04; 22 (1973): 88, 146; 24 (1975): 139; 30 (1981): 74; 31 (1982): 18, 58, 59–60; 32 (1983): 7, 37; 35 (1986): 210; and 36 (1987): 32–33.

Rintoul, William T. "The Banning of *The Grapes of Wrath*." *California Crossroads* (January 1963): 4–6.

———. "The Banning of *The Grapes of Wrath*." *California Crossroads* (February 1963): 26–28.

Roos, Jonathan. "Kanawha's Ban Turns Novel into Best-Seller." *Des Moines Register*, March 6, 1980, pp. 1A, 4A.

"Support of *Grapes* Ban Is Urged by Farmers Group." *Bakersfield Californian*, August 22, 1939, [n.p.].

Tebbel, John. *A History of Book Publishing in the United States.* Vol. 3. New York: R. R. Bowker, 1978.

Veon, R. J. Kern County Clerk and Clerk of the Board. Letter to Gretchen D. Knief, County Librarian. January 27, 1941.

THE GULAG ARCHIPELAGO 1918–1956

Author: Aleksandr Solzhenitsyn
Original dates and places of publication: 1973–1974, France; 1974 (Volume I), 1975 (Volume II), 1978 (Volume III), United States
Publishers: YMCA Press; Harper and Row
Literary form: Nonfiction

SUMMARY

Aleksandr Solzhenitsyn's purpose in his three volumes of *The Gulag Archipelago 1918–1956: An Experiment in Literary Investigation* is to document and reveal a great holocaust in the Soviet Union—exceeding that of Germany against the Jews and others during World War II. Tens of millions of Soviet citizens were imprisoned, savagely mistreated, and often murdered by their own government. The "archipelago" of the title refers to the forced-labor camps, "thousands of islands" scattered across the country geographically "from the Bering Strait almost to the Bosporus" but "in the psychological sense, fused into a continent—an almost invisible, almost imperceptible country inhabited by the zek people [prisoners]." "Gulag," an acronym, designates the Soviet penal system. Solzhenitsyn uses the background of his own prison experiences from 1945 to 1953; these are supplemented with reports by memoirs of and letters by 227 other eyewitnesses.

An early chapter in Volume I, "The History of Our Sewage Disposal System," establishes the origins and continuity of government repression from 1917 to 1956, in effect rejecting the Soviet government's acknowledged purges during Stalin's regime as being limited in time and scope. The text otherwise provides an internal structure from scenes of arrest to confinement and interrogation, then to first cell. Subsequently, the reader travels cross-country with the prisoner to the "ports," the prisons of the archipelago. The destinations are forced labor camps. Each chapter is illustrated with the experiences of individual prisoners, thus providing verifying detail. Another quartet of chapters expresses the shift in the Soviet government's laws and "justice"—attitudes and procedures, including the initial rejection of capital punishment to its massive, seemingly capricious utilization.

A significant assertion is that the arrests and imprisonments did not begin and end with the three biggest "waves" of repression. Of these the acknowledged purges in 1937 and 1938 of "people of position, people with a Party past, educated people" were not the main wave, nor were they accurately represented. Assurances that the arrests were chiefly of communist leaders are not supported by the fact that about 90 percent of the "millions arrested" were outside this circle. "The real law underlying the arrests of those years was *the assignment of quotas* . . . to every city, every district, every military unit. . . ." Before this, the wave of 1929 and 1930 "drove a mere fifteen million peasants, maybe more, out into the taiga and the tundra" and afterward the wave of 1944 to 1946 "dumped whole *nations* down the sewer pipes, not to mention millions and millions of others who . . . had been prisoners of war, or carried off to Germany and subsequently repatriated."

The chronology of purges begins with V. I. Lenin's edict in late 1917 and connects with those of Stalin, who refined and enlarged Lenin's tactics. Arrests encompassed a broad segment of the populace: tens of thousands of hostages; peasants revolting against the taking of their harvests without compensation; students for "criticism of the system"; religious practitioners and believers who were "arrested uninterruptedly"; workers who had not met quotas; and nationalist groups in Central Asia. Soviet soldiers who had been prisoners of war were also arrested and sent to labor camps, even those who had escaped and joined the resistance forces.

> It would appear that during the one thousand one hundred years of Russia's existence as a state there have been, ah, how many foul and terrible deeds! But among them was there ever so multimillioned foul a deed as this: to betray one's own soldiers and proclaim them traitors?

The presumption was that the soldiers had become traitors or had "acquired a very harmful spirit living freely among Europeans."

The Criminal Code of 1926, specifically Article 58, defined the crimes against the state. Operative for many years, the code's basic tenet was that any action—or any absence of action—directed toward the weakening of state power was considered to be counterrevolutionary. Along with armed rebellion, espionage and suspicion of espionage or unproven espionage, the list of criminal activities included subversion of industry, transport, and trade; propaganda or agitation containing an appeal, including face-to-face conversation between friends and spouses, private letters, and preparation of literary materials; failure to make a denunciation of any action and conscious failure to carry out defined duties or intentionally careless execution of them.

The charges against victims were unanswerable. Indeed, "interrogations under Article 58 were *almost never* undertaken to elicit the truth" but rather to induce a confession to an alleged crime or to draw the individual into statements that could be interpreted as self-incriminating. The burden of proof of innocence was upon the victims, who were given little opportunity to provide proof, nor were they apprised of their rights. Interrogation by torture was practiced:

> . . . that prisoners would have their skulls squeezed within iron rings; that a human being would be lowered into an acid bath; that they would be trussed up naked to be bitten by ants and bedbugs; that a ramrod heated over a primus stove would be thrust up their anal canal (the "secret brand"); that a man's genitals would be slowly crushed beneath the toe of a jackboot; and that, in the luckiest possible circumstances, prisoners would be tortured by being kept from sleeping for a week, by thirst, and by being beaten to a bloody pulp. . . .

Psychological torture was also employed, including interrogations at night, foul language, intimidation accompanied by false promises, threatening harm to loved ones, and being placed in a box without being informed of charges. "The more fantastic the charges were, the more ferocious the interrogation had to be in order to force the required confession."

Once condemned, the prisoners' miseries continued on the transport railroad cars, cattle cars, or barges. Subjected to severely overcrowded and underventilated conditions, at extreme temperatures and with insufficient food, they were brutalized by both the common criminals with whom they traveled and the guards.

A pervasive theme in *Gulag Archipelago I* is of corruption not merely of top officials but also of men and women at all levels of officialdom, who had been corrupted by power and, often, a justifiable fear that if they acted otherwise they would become victims. At base, Solzhenitsyn maintains that the destruction of millions of innocent people is derived from the Bolshevik revolution and the Soviet political system.

The author provides ironic counterpoints, such as the comparison of the Soviet and czarist practices. For example, during a 30-year period of revolutionary agitation and terrorism from 1876 to 1904, executions were rare—17 people a year for the whole country. In contrast, during the 1937–38 wave, a half-million political prisoners and almost a half-million thieves were executed in a year and a half; another source cited for the period identifies the execution figure as 1.7 million. Another counterpoint: The direct victims in the Soviet Union number between 15 and 25 million people; those of Nazi Germany number between 10 and 12 million.

The brutality of life and death in the "destructive-labor camps," or slave labor camps, is the focus of Volume II. During Stalin's reign, 10 to 15 million men, women, and children over age 12 were imprisoned in these "extermination factories" in any one year. Solzhenitsyn distinguishes between the prisons where a human being is able to confront "his grief face to face . . . to find space within himself for it" and the slave labor camps where survival, often at the expense of others, demanded every energy. The lives of the imprisoned consisted of "work, work, work; of starvation, cold, and cunning." Solzhenitsyn provides a brief capsule enumerating the range and types of work and expressing its exhausting, debilitating effects: back-breaking, hand-wearing labor with picks and shovels on the earth, in mines and quarries, in brickyards, tunnels, and on farms (favored for the food to be grabbed from the ground) and lumberjack work in the forests. The workday in the summer was "sometimes sixteen hours long." The hours were shortened during the winter, but workers were "chased out" to work in cold lower than 60 degrees below zero in order to "prove it was possible to fulfill" quotas.

> And how did they feed them in return? They poured water into a pot, and the best one might expect was that they would drop unscrubbed small potatoes into it, but otherwise black cabbage, beet tops, all kinds of trash. Or else vetch or bran, they didn't begrudge these.

In several chapters Solzhenitsyn scrutinizes the relationship between the penal system—the Gulag—and the Soviet economy "when the plan for superindustrialization was rejected in favor of the plan for supersupersuper-industrialization . . . with the massive public works of the First Five-Year Plan. . . ." Slave labor allowed Stalin to industrialize the nation cheaply. The laborers were expendable: The victims were sent to isolated regions and worked brutally without concern for their well-being and safety to construct railroads, canals, highways, hydroelectric stations, and nine cities. The laborers were not paid: "[F]orced labor should be set up in such a way that the prisoner should not earn anything from his work but that the state should derive economic profit from it." This system was termed "correction through labor."

The system did not work; corruption and thievery were rampant. Con-struction materials were stolen; machinery was damaged. The prisoners were not dutiful workers, nor did their weakened condition make for efficient and effective work.

As in Volume I, examples of individuals caught in the mesh provide details to reveal the extent of villainy. A particularly emotional chapter details the fate of children who are bereft as a result of the war or the imprisonment of their parents. They are swept up and sent away to be mistreated in colonies or workhouses. From the age of 12 they can be sentenced under the Criminal Code and end up in the Archipelago. "In 1927 prisoners aged sixteen (they didn't count the younger ones) to twenty-four represented 48 percent of all prisoners."

Solzhenitsyn enumerates and explains the "traits of *free* life," which were determined by the everpresent threat of the Archipelago: constant fear—of arrest, purges, inspections, dismissal from work, deprivation of residence permit, expulsion or exile; servitude; secrecy and mistrust; universal ignorance; squealing; betrayal as a form of existence; corruption; the lie as a form of existence; and cruelty.

Volume III turns away from the brutality and suffering of slave labor to focus on resistance within the camps. In Part V, *"Katorga"* (hard labor), Solzhenitsyn recounts the attempted escapes by individuals and small groups. An extended pair of chapters explores the reactions and behaviors of "a *committed* escaper," one who "never for a minute doubts that a man cannot live behind bars." The exploits of this individual, who does successfully escape but is recaptured because he refuses to kill innocent people, and the plans and procedures of others attest to the energy and determination of those who had not resigned themselves.

Particularly in the Special Camps, which had been established to separate the "socially irredeemable" political prisoners from the others, did the idea of rebellion begin to take shape and spread. Avengers emerged from the formed comradeships to murder informers. Though only a relatively few got the knife, the result was extensive: Informers stopped informing, and the air was "cleansed of suspicion." Insurrections occurred with varying degrees of success; military power was used to quell the major revolts. In May 1954, the prisoners of Kengir gained control of the camp for 40 days. Without any outside support, having been encircled by troops and deceived by an announcement that their demands had been accepted, the prisoners were crushed, literally (by tanks) and politically. More than 700 were killed.

Exile or banishment—the Soviet euphemism was "deportation"—was another instrument of power borrowed from the czars. The "export of undesirables" started shortly after the revolution; in 1929 a system of exile to remote localities in conjunction with forced labor was developed. The exile system grew steadily in capacity and importance in the World War II and postwar years, particularly from the "liberated" (occupied) territories and the western republics. The crimes for which a citizen was punished by exile or banishment included "belonging to a criminal nationality [including both whole nations and, as in the case of the Baltics, special categories of citizens]; a previous term of imprisonment in the camps [prisoners were 'released into exile' in perpetuity]; and residence in a criminal environment." All these deportations, "even without the exiled peasants, exceeded many times over the figure of 500,000 exiles which was all that Tsarist Russia, the prison house of nations, could muster in the whole course of the nineteenth century."

With Stalin's death there came a political thaw and some reprieve for the prisoners. Indeed, many were released. However, Solzhenitsyn points out that in the 40 pre-Khrushchev years, release meant "the space between two arrests." Even when the prisoner was rehabilitated, after being found to be falsely accused, the villains escaped judgment and punishment. Equally profound is the recognition that the camps, approved by the party, continued to exist; there are "still millions inside, and just as before, many of them are helpless victims of perverted justice: swept in simply to keep the system operating and well fed."

Solzhenitsyn specifically reveals his own error, the degree to which he had been deceived. He had let himself be persuaded by the state's authorization to publish *One Day in the Life of Ivan Denisovich* and by the "complacent mainland" that the relaxation was real. He writes, "But I (even I) succumbed and I do not deserve forgiveness."

CENSORSHIP HISTORY

Solzhenitsyn's works were barred from publication in the Soviet Union after Nikita Khrushchev lost power in 1964; previously under the Khrushchev regime, *One Day in the Life of Ivan Denisovich* had been approved for publication. J. M. Coetzee cites Dina Spechler's analysis of "permitted dissent" in the USSR from the death of Stalin in 1953 to 1970. Given the twists and turns of Soviet political life, Khrushchev, reacting to the "nagging resistance from the Party and bureaucracy, used *Novy Mir* [which first published *One Day in the Life of Ivan Denisovich* in 1962] as a vehicle to 'expose and dramatize problems and reveal facts that demonstrated . . . the necessity of the changes he proposed.'"

In February 1974, Aleksandr Solzhenitsyn was arrested and charged with treason; he lost his Soviet citizenship and was deported, that is, exiled from Russia. A Russian-language edition of *Gulag Archipelago I* had been published in Paris in September 1973. The American edition, which should have appeared immediately after the Russian, was delayed for six months, a delay to which the author attributes his arrest and exile, according to his memoir, *The Oak and the Calf*. He believes that "if all America had been reading *Gulag* by the New Year," the Soviets would have been hesitant to move against him.

The events leading to the publication significantly reflect the text. It had been completed in June 1968; a microfilm of the manuscript had been secretly and at great peril sent to the West, but the author had postponed its publication. The decision to publish was forced upon him in August 1973 when a Leningrad woman to whom Solzhenitsyn had entrusted the manuscript revealed the hiding place of a copy after having been terrorized through five sleepless days of interrogation by the KGB. (Released after the manuscript was located, she hanged herself.) The author understood that he had no alternative but to authorize publication immediately: The book contained the names of several hundred people who had provided him with information.

The underlying reason for the action against Solzhenitsyn with the publication of this volume was the rejection of the then-current Russian orthodoxy, that is, that "the abuses of justice under Stalinism were the direct consequence of the personality of the dictator." His data insist that the tyranny began with Lenin and continued under Nikita Khrushchev.

In contradiction of the United Nations (UN) Universal Declaration of Human Rights, which binds members to uphold the dissemination of ideas and information "through any media and regardless of frontiers," *Gulag Archipelago* was removed from two Swiss bookshops operating on United Nations premises. It was reported that the removal was instigated by the Soviet Union. Secretary-General Kurt Waldheim, at a July 1974 press conference, indicated a policy of giving "guidance" to the bookshops, that is, as indicated by Geneva director-general Vittorio Winspeare-Guicciardi, telling them it was their "duty" to avoid "publications *à caractère outrageant pour un Etat Membre*" (publications of an insulting character for a Member Nation). The press conference was held in response to the protest of the books' removal by more than 250 UN employees.

In addition to his works being barred from publication after 1964 (a collection of his short stories was published in 1963), Solzhenitsyn faced increasing criticism and overt harassment from authorities. In 1970, having been awarded the Nobel Prize in literature, he declined to go to Stockholm for fear that he would not be readmitted to the Soviet Union. During his exile, *Novy Mir* attempted to publish *The Gulag Archipelago*, but publishing was blocked by order from the Central Committee, particularly Vadim Medvedev, the Communist Party's chief of ideology. However, President Mikhail S. Gorbachev authorized the publication of extracts in 1989. On August 15, 1990, Gorbachev issued a decree restoring full citizenship to Solzhenitsyn and 22 other exiled dissident artists and intellectuals. In 1994, Solzhenitsyn returned to Russia.

An about-face was revealed on September 9, 2009, when Russia's Education Ministry announced that excerpts of the *Gulag Archipelago* have been added to the curriculum for high school students. The rationale behind the decision: the "vital historical and cultural heritage on the course of 20th century domestic history" contained in Solzhenitsyn's work.

Aleksandr Solzhenitsyn died in 2008.

FURTHER READING

Blake, Patricia. "*The Gulag Archipelago.*" *New York Times Book Review*, October 26, 1975, pp. 1, 18–21.

Burg, David, and George Feifer. *Solzhenitsyn*. New York: Stein and Day, 1972.

Chalidze, Valery. *To Defend These Rights: Human Rights and the Soviet Union.* New York: Random House, 1974.

Coetzee, J. M. "Censorship and Polemic: The Solzhenitsyn Affair." *Pretexts* 2 (Summer 1990): 3–26.

Conquest, Robert. "Evaluation of an Exile." *Saturday Review,* April 20, 1974, 22–24, 30.

"*Gulag* at the UN." *Newsletter on Intellectual Freedom* 23 (1974): 162.

Kramer, Hilton. "The Soviet Terror Continued." *New York Times Book Review,* June 18, 1978, pp. 1, 28–29.

Rubenstein, Joshua. "*The Gulag Archipelago.*" *The New Republic,* June 22, 1974, 21–22.

"Russia Makes Gulag History Required Reading." *Boston Globe* (September 10, 2009). Available online. URL: http://www.Boston.com/news/world9sep2009. Accessed June 14, 2010.

Solzhenitsyn, Aleksandr. *The Oak and the Calf.* New York: Harper and Row, 1980.

Steiner, George. "The Forests of the Night." *New Yorker,* June 16, 1974, 78–87.

I AM THE CHEESE

Author: Robert Cormier
Original date and place of publication: 1977, United States
Publisher: Pantheon Books
Literary form: Novel

SUMMARY

Two disparate alternating components—a narrative adventure and a series of transcripts of taped interviews—provide the structure and build the plot and ideas of *I Am the Cheese.* Adam Farmer, in the first, is journeying on his old-fashioned bicycle from Monument, Massachusetts, to Rutterberg, Vermont, to visit his father in the hospital. It is an adventure with a purpose, but Adam is afraid. The taped interviews between Adam and Brint, identified as a psychiatrist, an identity that is doubted by Adam and made suspect in the text, reveal an attempt to help Adam regain his memory; these tapes are supported by third-person narrative accounts of past events that fill in the memory blanks. These two components gradually intertwine, the tension mounting, the clues and bits of evidence fitting together to reveal what has happened and is happening to Adam Farmer.

Adam Farmer is really Paul Delmonte. He does not know this, however, until he is 14 when his father tells him the truth (the reader does not learn this until midway through the book). When Adam/Paul was young, his father, an energetic investigative reporter, had uncovered documents in the Albany, New York, state house that were damaging, indeed irrevocably ruinous, to both state and federal officials. The evident corruption involved links of government to criminal syndicates. After testifying in Washington in strict secrecy, under promises of protected identity, he returned home to resume his life. Two attempts on his life change that.

A "Mr. Grey" enters their lives. An agent of the U.S. Department of Re-Identification—a precursor of the Witness Re-Establishment Program—he provides the Delmontes with new identities and histories, new situations, even a newspaper article about their deaths by automobile accident. He causes them to be relocated to begin life anew. Mr. Grey remains in their lives, visiting their home once or twice a month for private conversations with David (Delmonte) Farmer in a sealed basement room.

But that is the past. In the present, Adam is on his bicycle pedaling toward Rutterberg, Vermont. He is fearful because it is his nature to be so, he says, but this is a striking foreshadowing. Remembering his father's singing, Adam tries to mimic his joyous rendering of "The Farmer in the Dell" to give himself courage. He is, however, terrified, first by a dog that tears after him and, subsequently, by three men in a lunchroom. Although they threaten him, he manages to escape from them temporarily. They follow him in a car, mockingly passing him, returning and passing him again and again, closer and closer until they knock him over the side into a gully. Adam is rescued and taken as far as Hookset, Vermont. There his bicycle is stolen by Junior Varney, but Adam is able to reclaim it after a tussle.

Two other incidents provide clues of wonder and suspense. Adam tries to telephone his best friend, Amy Hertz. But after calling the familiar number twice, he is told by a stranger who answers that he has had the number for three years. The information operator tells him there is no Hertz listing in Monument, Massachusetts. When Adam reaches Belton Falls, he goes to the Rest-A-While Motel, where he and his parents had happily stayed the year before, only to discover it is closed. The gas station attendant across the street tells him it has been closed for "two or three years . . . at least."

At last arriving at the hospital in Rutterberg, Adam is greeted by a doctor who walks with him. They pass Whipper, Dobbie, and Lewis, the three troublemakers from the lunchroom; he hears the growl of a ferocious dog and watches for the lurking Junior Varney. Adam is taken to his own room, where he sings "The Farmer in the Dell." He doesn't respond to the name Paul, nor does he recall his other name. But he knows who he is; "I am the cheese," he says. He stands alone.

The interviews are also in the present, conducted in a confinement facility. The interviews peel away the shrouds, sheet by sheet, from Adam's memory. These conversations help Adam remember the past, starting from an earliest memory of a stealthy trip when he was four, moving through the first clues to his first questions and suspicions, leading to the revelations about the changed identity and situation of his family. Adam also raises doubts about where he is—it does not seem like a hospital to him—and who Brint really is. Brint seems something more or other than a psychiatrist; his questions seem to reach beyond a search for Adam's personal life, but rather to a search for certain specifics, secrets. He seems at times "a predator, an enemy." Despite his constantly drugged condition, Adam suspects Brint and resists his inquiries, maintaining a slight degree of self-protective will.

Mr. Grey, always dressed in gray, is an important figure of the past. He does not merely protect the Delmontes by reestablishing them. He watches over them and maintains surveillance over them. He determines the options at every stage; he controls the family's movements and life. It is his "emergency" call that sets the stage for the demise of the family.

Mr. Grey had called, saying that their identities may have been discovered, that they had to leave town for a few days so that his men could check for any suspicious developments. The Farmers take this enforced holiday, staying the first night at the Rest-A-While Motel, enjoying each other and their escape. The next day, David Farmer notices a car following them. When they stop and get out of their car to admire a distant view and stretch their legs, a car hurtles toward them and crashes into them.

Adam remembers. In slow motion he remembers himself flying through the air, twisting and trembling. He remembers seeing his mother die instantly. He remembers a voice saying that his father, hurt, had run away but that "They'll get him—they never miss." He remembers the men coming toward him, looming over him: "Grey pants. Him. Hearing his voice again: 'Move fast. Remove her. The boy—check him. He may be useful. Fast now, fast.'"

The novel concludes with the annual report, filed presumably by Brint. It summarizes the third annual questioning of Subject A, Adam Farmer, establishing that he "discloses no awareness of data provided Department 1-R by Witness #599-6" (David Delmonte). It indicates that these results are consistent with the two previous interrogations and that "Inducement of medication . . . plus pre-knowledge interrogation failed to bring forth suspected knowledge. . . ."; also, it notes that "deep withdrawal" occurs when these topics are approached and "complete withdrawal accompanies recapitulation of termination of Witness #599-6 and affiliate (spouse)."

The report includes three advisories: 1) that the policy, which does not allow termination procedures by Department 1-R, be eliminated; 2) that the suspension of Personnel #2222 (Mr. Grey) be discontinued, granting him full reinstatement (the suspension had resulted from suspected complicity of Mr. Grey in the termination of Witness #599-6; the evidence of his contacting the Adversaries and revealing the location of the witness was only circumstantial); 3) that Subject A's confinement be continued, since he is "final linkage between Witness #599-6 and File Data 865-01," until "termination procedures are approved" pending revision of policy, or his "condition be sustained" until he "obliterates."

The closing paragraph of the novel is identical to the opening paragraph: Adam is on the bicycle, pedaling, pedaling.

CENSORSHIP HISTORY

The challenge in Panama City, Florida, against *I Am the Cheese* (winner of three awards—best young adult book by *Newsweek*, the *New York Times*, and the *School Library Journal*—and critical acclaim) was initiated by a formal complaint in April 1986 (which also included *About David* by Susan Beth Pfeffer). It eventually resulted in a federal court case (*Farrel v. Hall*) that was adjudicated on July 18, 1988; the situation was not finally resolved for another three years.

A preliminary pair of letters preceded the formal complaint. Marion Collins, grandmother of a student at Mowat Junior High School, complained by letter in fall 1985 to Leonard Hall, superintendent of the Bay County School District; she objected to vulgar language and advocacy of humanism and behaviorism. Hall immediately ordered Mowat's principal, Joel Creel, to ban the book. In follow-up letters to Hall and Creel, Collins further complained that the book was still in use.

The formal complainant was Claudia Shumaker, Collins's daughter and mother of a seventh grader in ReLeah Hawks's accelerated English class. Her complaint was filed upon the suggestion of Superintendent Hall after Hawks, anticipating the Shumaker complaint, had informed parents of her intent to teach *I Am the Cheese* and to offer an alternative text to students whose parents objected; she had received 88 favorable permission slips and only four declinations. Shumaker wanted the book banned altogether, noting her daughter would be ostracized.

Both *I Am the Cheese* and *About David* were withdrawn immediately from classroom use, pending consideration of the district review committee. That committee in a month's time recommended the reinstatement of *I Am the Cheese*. (It did not act on *About David* because it was not scheduled for classroom use.) However, Superintendent Hall did not act on the recommendation, thus effectively preventing Hawks and other teachers from using it in their classrooms.

Thereupon, the controversy heated up. Claudia Shumaker had protested that *I Am the Cheese*'s theme is "morbid and depressing," its language "crude and vulgar" and the "sexual descriptions and suggestions are extremely inappropriate." The offending words were *hell*, *shit*, *fart*, and *goddam*; the sexual descriptions included a scene of teens kissing, a description of breasts as "large" and "wonderful," and a reference to a supermarket display of Kotex. Her father, Charles E. Collins, who had served on the Bay County school board from 1954 to 1970, in a May 22, 1986, letter mailed to all the parents of Mowat students, protested in addition the novel's "subversive theme . . . which makes the 'government agents' out to be devious and 'hit teams' that killed the boy's parents, and now must kill the boy because he knows too much about the government's activities." In the letter and in an advertisement in the *Panama City News Herald*, he asked for telephone calls and mail-in coupons. M. Berry, M.D., in a letter to the editor, complained that the novel "slyly casts doubt on the U.S. government, parental authority and the medical profession."

The teachers called a public meeting on May 27, inviting students, teachers, and parents to discuss the issue. On that morning, Hall instructed the teachers not to discuss the First Amendment or the book controversy with their students; he also ordered them to tell the students not to attend the meeting and that their exclusion was the teachers' idea. About 300 parents attended the meeting; approximately two-thirds of them indicated support for the teachers and the English program.

Hall, on June 5, rejected the review committee's recommendation and ruled against use of *I Am the Cheese*. He argued that the book had never been officially adopted by the school board. In a later statement, however, he expressed a negative reaction to an idea he inferred from the novel: "You know what happens at the end? The mother and father are exterminated by the United States government. What does that tell you? I mean do you ever trust government again?" He said further that students should not be taught that a government agency might be corrupt and untrustworthy.

Beyond rejecting *I Am the Cheese* because the school board had not approved it, Hall added that any other materials that had not been approved, except state-approved textbooks, would also have to be approved by a five-step procedure: 1) the teachers would submit a detailed rationale for each book to be included in the curriculum and the classroom library; 2) the principal would either reject the rationale or send it to the county instructional staff; 3) the staff would either reject it or send it to the superintendent; 4) the superintendent would either reject it or send it to the school board; and 5) the board would make the final decision. Rejection at any stage would terminate the procedure; teachers would not be allowed to appeal. An additional procedure allowed citizens who objected to an approved book to appeal its inclusion; a procedure for a citizen to appeal a decision to reject a book was not included. This had the effect of eliminating classroom libraries and most classroom novels. Further, if a book was approved and then challenged, it would be withdrawn until judged by a series of review boards.

The proposed policy was debated at an extended school board meeting in August 1986. Parents and teachers who opposed Hall's proposed policy "protested that it was ham-fistedly authoritarian and heavily biased toward excluding, rather than including, material." Of the 25 citizens attending the meeting, 17 spoke against the proposal. Collins, however, submitted a stack of antiobscenity petitions, containing by his account 9,000 signatures. (An enterprising television journalist, Cindy Hill, discovered in the fall that there were actually only 3,549 signatures.) The school board voted to approve Hall's policy, changing it only to add a one-year grace period for books that had been taught in 1985–86. This still denied teachers and students access to *I Am the Cheese* and *About David*.

Gloria T. Pipkin, chair of the English department, filed a request to teach *I Am the Cheese* to her advanced eighth-grade English class. Creel, having consulted Hall, rejected her request. Pipkin revised the rationale and sent it to Hall, who responded that the principal's rejection terminated the procedure. Pipkin then asked to be placed on the school board agenda;

the chair at first attempted to prevent her from speaking, reminding her that "as a Mowat employee, she was subject to Creel's authority." Granted the right to speak, Pipkin asserted, "Make no mistake about it, *I Am the Cheese* has been banned in the Bay County school system because the ideas it contains are offensive to a few: no ruse can obscure that fact." Her request that the board go on record to restore the book to the classroom was ignored.

As the time arrived for the receipt of a rationale for teaching non-state-approved books, Hall added another step to the review process; he required senior high school teachers to categorize their books: Category I—no vulgar, obscene, or sexually explicit material; Category II—very limited vulgarity and no sexually explicit or obscene material; Category III—quite a bit of vulgarity or obscene and/or sexually explicit material.

When the review procedure was completed, Hall had eliminated 64 classics from Bay County classrooms. They included the following:

"Banned" from Bay High School: A Farewell to Arms by Ernest Hemingway; The Great Gatsby by F. Scott Fitzgerald; Intruder in the Dust by William Faulkner; Lost Horizon by James Hilton; Oedipus Rex by Sophocles; The Red Badge of Courage by Stephen Crane; A Separate Peace by John Knowles; Shane by Jack Schaefer; and Three Comedies of American Life by Joseph Mersand. "Banned" from Mosley High School: Adventures in English Literature; After the First Death by Robert Cormier; Alas, Babylon by Pat Frank; Animal Farm by George Orwell; Arrangement in Literature; The Autobiography of Benjamin Franklin by Benjamin Franklin; Best Short Stories; Brave New World by Aldous Huxley; The Call of the Wild by Jack London; The Canterbury Tales by Geoffrey Chaucer; The Crucible by Arthur Miller; Death Be Not Proud by John Gunther; Deathwatch by Robb White; Desire Under the Elms, The Emperors Jones, and Long Day's Journey Into Night by Eugene O'Neill; Exploring Life Through Literature; Fahrenheit 451 by Ray Bradbury; The Fixer by Bernard Malamud; Ghosts [sic] and Miss Julie by August Strindberg; The Glass Menagerie by Tennessee Williams; Great Expectations by Charles Dickens; The Great Gatsby by F. Scott Fitzgerald; Growing Up; Hamlet, King Lear, The Merchant of Venice, and Twelfth Night by William Shakespeare; Hippolytus by Euripides; In Cold Blood by Truman Capote; The Inferno by Dante (Ciardi translation); The Little Foxes by Lillian Hellman; Lord of the Flies by William Golding; Major British Writers (shorter edition); The Man Who Came to Dinner by George S. Kaufman and Moss Hart; The Mayor of Casterbridge by Thomas Hardy; McTeague by Frank Norris; Mister Roberts by Thomas Heggen; Oedipus the King: The Oedipus Plays of Sophocles; Of Mice and Men and The Pearl by John Steinbeck; The Old Man and the Sea by Ernest Hemingway; On Baile's Strand by W. B. Yeats; The Outsiders by S. E. Hinton; Player Piano by Kurt Vonnegut; The Prince and the Pauper by Mark Twain; Prometheus Unbound by Percy Bysshe Shelley; Tale Blazer Library: A Raisin in the Sun by Lorraine Hansberry; The Red Badge of Courage by Stephen Crane; A Separate Peace by John Knowles; To Kill a Mockingbird by Harper Lee; Watership Down by

Richard Adams; *Winterset* by Maxwell Anderson; and *Wuthering Heights* by Emily Brontë.

These exclusions engendered public protest and ridicule, including resolutions from the Chamber of Commerce. A letter of protest, signed by almost 2,000 county residents, was submitted to the school board on May 13. Hundreds of high school students wearing black armbands packed the boardroom in protest.

On May 12, 1987, a suit was filed by 44 Bay County parents, teachers, and students against Hall, Creel, and the school board. The suit, labeled *Farrell* (after a student, Jennifer Farrell, whose name headed the list of plaintiffs) *v. Hall*, went forward despite the school board's reactive effort to revise the review policy by permitting the inclusion of books used in 1986–87 that were recommended by the school principal. This "revision," while reinstating the 64 titles, maintained the Hall policy and the banning of *I Am the Cheese, About David*, and *Never Cry Wolf*, which had been barred in the interim. (The offense: one phrase shouted by a dogsled driver to his barking dogs— "FURCHRSAKE-STOPYOUGODAMNSONSABITCHES!")

The plaintiffs' case asked that *I Am the Cheese* and other young adult novels be restored to the curriculum; further, it asserted that the review policy denied students their First Amendment rights to receive information and be educated according to their parents' wishes and denied teachers their rights of free speech and academic freedom as well as placing an undue burden upon them in the preparation of rationales for every book taught and placed in their classroom libraries. At the core, the plaintiffs argued that Hall had acted counter to the First Amendment by using his position as superintendent of schools to reject books whose ideas violated his religious or political beliefs rather than because of their language. The defendants argued that the revised policy answered the plaintiffs' complaints and that the courts should not interfere in educational matters.

On July 18, 1988, Judge Roger Vinson of the U.S. District Court for the Northern District of Florida gave neither side a clear victory. He denied motions to dismiss the case. On behalf of the plaintiffs he noted in reference to Hall:

> [He] accepts as true . . . [that his] actions were motivated by his personal beliefs which form the basis for his conservative educational policy. Hall believes that his duty as superintendent is to restore Christian values to the Bay County school system. He thinks that one vulgarity in a work of literature is sufficient reason to keep the book from the Bay County school curriculum. Hall's opposition to I Am the Cheese arises solely from his personal opposition to the ideas expressed in the book. He believes that it is improper to question the trustworthiness of the government. Thus, students should not be presented with such ideas.

With regard to the accusation that books had been removed because of disagreement with the ideas they contained, he ruled:

Local school officials may establish and implement the curriculum to transmit community values, a task which requires decisions based on the social and ethical values of the school officials. . . . On the other hand, the discretion of state and local school authorities must be exercised in a manner that comports with the First Amendment. Local school officials may not suppress ideas simply because they disagree with those ideas so as to create a "pall of orthodoxy" in the classroom.

Thus, he supported the claims about the removal of *I Am the Cheese* and other works in order to suppress their ideas.

However, Judge Vinson did not support the plaintiffs' complaint relating to language; he asserted that rejecting books because of one vulgar word is within the school board's authority. So, too, the review policy was acceptable to the court because school boards have the right to approve books by whatever process they choose. The significant factor in this context is that board *decisions* may be challenged if deemed illegal or arbitrary. This applies also to books selected for school and classroom libraries.

Judge Vinson also ruled that federal courts, when First Amendment issues are involved, are obligated to intervene in educational matters.

The case was eventually settled out of court, after Hall decided not to run for reelection. Upon the request of his successor, Jack Simonon, to be given time to try to resolve the situation, a 60-day suspension of the trial was granted. The suspension lasted three years, during which time the People For the American Way organization negotiated on behalf of the teachers with the school board attorney to achieve a book review policy that was acceptable to all. Key features of this policy included time limits set for each stage of the review procedure; detailed procedures for handling challenges for existing materials; procedures established for the appeal of negative decisions; and provisions made to inform parents whose children would be affected by any complaint against a book so they could support or oppose the complaint.

Two additional challenges are recorded by the *Newsletter for Intellectual Freedom*, one in Cornwall, New York, in October 1984, and one in Evergreen, Colorado, in November 1993. In the former, Mrs. Oliver F. Schreiber objected to the contents of two of Robert Cormier's books: *I Am the Cheese* and *The Chocolate War*; her complaint described the books as humanistic and destructive of religious and moral beliefs and of national spirit. No action was taken on this complaint since, according to superintendent R. Lancaster Crowley, Schreiber's son was not required to read the novel and had been excused from class discussion.

The second incident was more complicated. Principal Larry Fayer removed 42 books from the Wilmot Elementary School Media Center after 10 parents objected to foul language and violence in six titles; *I Am the Cheese* was among them. The removal was appealed by librarian Theresa March. During the review procedure, Fayer agreed to display the books for parental inspection and to return to the shelves all those that were not challenged. Thirty-one of them met this criterion, including *I Am the Cheese*. When the challengers of the remaining 11 discovered that their complaints would become public information, the challenges were withdrawn, and those books, too, were reshelved.

FURTHER READING

Carlson, Peter. "A Chilling Case of Censorship." *Washington Post Magazine*, January 4, 1987, 10–17, 40–41.

Collins, Charles E. Letter to Parents, Mowat Middle School, Panama City, Florida. May 22, 1986.

Collins, Marion. Letter to Joel Creel, Principal, Mowat Middle School, Panama City, Florida. February 3, 1986.

DelFattore, Joan. *What Johnny Shouldn't Read: Textbook Censorship in America.* New Haven, Conn.: Yale University Press, 1992.

Foerstal, Herbert N. *Banned in the U.S.A.: A Reference Guide to Book Censorship in Schools and Public Libraries.* Westport, Conn.: Greenwood Press, 1994.

Gallo, Donald R. "Reality and Responsibility: The Continuing Controversy Over Robert Cormier's Books for Young Adults." In *The VOYA Reader,* edited by Dorothy M. Broderick, 153–160. Metuchen, N.J.: Scarecrow Press, 1990.

Linn, Jennifer. "Censorship Fight Has Just Begun." *Panama City News-Herald*, May 15, 1987, pp. 1A, 2A.

———. "Lawsuit Filed Against Hall, School Board." *Panama City News-Herald*, May 13, 1987, pp. 1A, 2A.

———. "Leonard Hall Bans 64 Books." *Panama City News-Herald*, May 8, 1987, pp. 1A, 2A.

May, Greg. "Hall Challenged: City Protests Categories." *Panama City News-Herald* (May 13, 1987): pp. 1B, 7B.

Newsletter on Intellectual Freedom 34 (1985): 45; 35 (1986): 209–10; 36 (1987): 52, 126–28, 168–69, 224; and 43 (1994): 97.

"One Arbitrary Policy Doesn't Justify Another." *Panama City News-Herald*, May 13, 1987, p. 6A.

Peyser, Andrea. "Battles over Book-Bans Getting Dirty." *Tampa Tribune*, May 17, 1987, pp. 1B, 10B.

Pipkin, Gloria. "Confessions of an Accused Pornographer." *Arizona English Bulletin* (1994): 14–18.

IN THE SPIRIT OF CRAZY HORSE

Author: Peter Matthiessen
Original date and place of publication: 1983, United States
Publisher: Viking Press
Literary form: Nonfiction

SUMMARY

Prefatory comment: As the censorship history will detail, two major libel suits against the author and publisher challenged *In the Spirit of Crazy*

Horse. The plaintiffs in these suits, William Janklow, then governor of South Dakota, and Special Agent David Price of the Federal Bureau of Investigation (FBI), will be given some prominence in this summary to provide a context for the cases.

While spotlighting the tensions and events of the 1970s on the Sioux reservations in South Dakota, *In the Spirit of Crazy Horse* provides in Book I a brief history of the Sioux nation from 1835 to 1965 as well as the origins (1968) and growth of the American Indian Movement (AIM). Four major issues emerge from the text: the loss and despoiling of Indian lands; the quest for sovereignty; FBI and BIA (Bureau of Indian Affairs) interference and brutality on the reservations; and the severe schism and distrust within the Sioux nation. These issues are represented through two major confrontations— Wounded Knee in 1973 and the Oglala shoot-out on June 26, 1975—as well as the subsequent manhunt for witnesses and fugitives, particularly Leonard Peltier, and their trials.

One of the major treaties of the Midwest region, the Fort Laramie Treaty of 1868, is at the heart of the claims of the Sioux (also designated Lakota) nation, which includes the Teton tribes from the western plains of North and South Dakota; and the Dakota, Santee, and Yankton tribes from the prairies of Minnesota and eastern North and South Dakota. This treaty guaranteed

> absolute and undisturbed use of the Great Sioux Reservation. . . . No persons . . . shall ever be permitted to pass over, settle upon, or reside in territory described in this article, or without consent of the Indians pass through the same. . . . No treaty for the cession of any portion or part of the reservation herein described . . . shall be of any validity or force . . . unless executed and signed by at least three-fourths of all the adult male Indians, occupying or interested in the same.

The lands so guaranteed, which included the sacred Black Hills area, were gradually taken away. As early as 1876, the Black Hills were invaded by miners seeking gold; they were supported by government troops. The forced sale of this sacred area along with 22.8 million acres of surrounding territory followed. The resident tribes were resettled elsewhere on the reservation lands, but were "forbidden to trespass on the 40 million acres of unceded land that was supposedly still a part of the Great Sioux Reservation." During President Benjamin Harrison's administration in 1889, the original reservation tract was dismantled, and the seven reservations that exist today were established.

In subsequent years, a series of "reforms," some of them well intentioned, further reduced the Indian lands: The General Allotment Act of 1887 broke down the Indians' communal attitude toward land by parceling it out; the Indian Claims Commission of 1946 in effect eliminated existing and potential land claims by monetary compensation; the termination legislation enacted in the 1930s, by relocating Indians off the reservations and giving them "independence" from tribal dependent status, made Indian reservation lands available to whites. Further, the BIA's land-tenure rules required that each family's allocation of land be equally divided among heirs, which created parcels too small to support a family.

A particular example illustrates the landmass lost:

> By 1942, nearly 1 million of the 2,722,000 acres assigned to Pine Ridge when the reservation was created in 1889 had passed into other hands, and by the 1970s, over 90 percent of reservation lands were owned or leased by white people or people with a low percentage of Indian blood, not because these people were more able but because the dispossessed traditionals had no money or means to work their land.

In recent years, the forests already having been stripped off and other minerals removed, the push to gain access to the uranium and coal fields on reservation lands had further threatened the reservations. However, resistance of the tribes had also mounted, accompanied by attempts to reclaim the lost lands.

The issue of sovereignty of Indian nations and the revalidation of Indian treaties are concomitant with the land claims. Two statements illustrate the opposing viewpoints. In the first, Judge Warren Urbom, a trial judge in some of the Wounded Knee cases, who dismissed 32 cases before trial, noted that, despite the "ugly history" and the "treaties pocked by duplicity," the Lakota claims to sovereignty were "squarely in opposition" to law and Supreme Court rulings, as developed in "an unbroken line." Judge Urbom pointed out that treaties were placed "by the Constitution of the United States on no higher plane than an Act of Congress, so if a self-executing treaty and an Act of Congress be in conflict, the more recent governs." In summary, he said, "the law is that native American tribes do not have complete sovereignty, have no external sovereignty, and have only as much internal sovereignty as has not been relinquished by them by treaty or explicitly taken by act of the U.S. Congress." The second statement is from Darrelle Dean (Dino) Butler's opening remarks at his trial for the murder of the two FBI agents at Oglala:

> We are members of a sovereign nation. We live under our own laws, tribal and natural. We recognize and respect our own traditional and elected leaders. The treaties that were made between Indian nations and the United States government state that we have the right to live according to our own laws on the land given to us in the treaties. That the laws of the United States government shall not interfere with the laws of our nations.

The conflict of these views of sovereignty is expressed in the behavior of United States official personnel, who presumed a proprietary status, and the reactions of the members of the Sioux nation. The overt conflict surfaces in the Wounded Knee episode, reported in Book I, and resurfaces in the Oglala shoot-out, detailed in Book II.

FBI and BIA agent intervention in reservation affairs is highlighted in the Wounded Knee and Oglala episodes, but it does not begin or end there. The agents of these bureaus are portrayed as vehemently antagonistic to AIM leaders and activities and, along with police, are frequently identified with injustice, harassment, and brutality. These range from intimidating and beating Indians, notably suspects or potential witnesses, to invasion of private property, presumably in search of suspects:

> Under cross-examination by the defense, [Wilford] "Wish" Draper [a young Navaho visitor] acknowledged without hesitation that he had lied to the grand jury in January and also as a prosecution witness in this trial; that when he had been apprehended in Arizona in January, he had been thrown against a car, then handcuffed and strapped for three hours in a chair while being threatened with a first-degree murder charge, until he finally agreed to supply useful testimony about the killings; that before the trial, he had told the defense attorneys that Peltier, Robideau, and Butler were all in camp when the shooting started; . . . and that most of his damning testimony on this subject was based on instruction from the FBI agents at the time of the grand-jury hearing, and also by Assistant U.S. Attorney Robert Sikma.
>
> That morning of September 5, an air-land-and-river operation had descended at daybreak on the Crow Dog and Running properties, in a massive racketing of helicopters that swept in over the dawn trees. More than fifty FBI agents in combat dress, with four large helicopters, military vehicles, trucks, vans, cars, and even rubber boats—presumably to prevent aquatic escapes down the narrow creek called the Little White River—surrounded the houses and tents, shouting, "This is the FBI! Come out with your hands up!" No one was given time to dress—Crow Dog himself was marched out naked—and even the small frightened children were lined up against walls as the agents ransacked and all but wrecked every house, tent, cabin, and car on both properties.

At the conclusion of the Dennis Banks–Russell Means conspiracy trial, federal judge Alfred Nichols severely criticized the FBI for its manipulation and unethical behavior. He had at first seemed sympathetic to the government's case and had indicated he had "revered" the FBI.

The FBI was also accused of fomenting discord among Indian factions on the reservations and promoting violence. Dino Butler, an AIM leader, is quoted as saying:

> The stories that go out from the reservations look like Indian versus Indian—you know, Dick Wilson and his goons versus the American Indian Movement. But we know different. The Federal Bureau of Investigation, the CIA, and the BIA, and all these different organizations working for the government—they are the ones causing all the trouble. They give Dick Wilson and his goons money. . . . When AIM gathers, the FBI buys ammunition and booze and stuff for these goons so that they will start drinking. That's how they get their courage.

Dick Wilson, the tribal chairman, and his "goon squad" (an acronym for Guardians of the Oglala Nation), identified in the book as Wilson's private police force, represent one faction. As accused by Butler, they are depicted as drunkenly brutal and repressive, holding the "traditionals" hostage, in effect. Outrageously corrupt, they milk the tribal coffers for their own benefit. The AIM organization is perceived as their enemy; thus, Wilson and his men are in league with the FBI, apparently to protect their privileges. The antagonism is decidedly bloody. These combined negative forces are evident in the Wounded Knee and Oglala incidents.

Judge Nichols was not the only judicial officer who started out with an anti-Indian bias, but not all changed their attitudes. Another legal officer, the attorney general of South Dakota during the Oglala episode, William Janklow, is quoted as having said, "The only way to deal with Indian problems in South Dakota is to put a gun to the AIM leaders' heads and pull the trigger." Janklow had taken his first job after law school as head of the legal services program on the reservation; he was serving effectively. In 1967, however, a 15-year-old girl accused Janklow of raping her. (He was her legal guardian.) "The hospital records included evidence, suggesting that an attack had occurred." Janklow was not prosecuted at the time after the FBI "smoothed over" the incident. In September 1974, during the Banks-Means trial, the charges resurfaced. "The would-be Attorney General refused to answer his summons, the BIA refused to deliver the subpoenaed file, and the FBI refused to cooperate in any way. Nevertheless, Janklow was charged by Judge Mario Gonzales with 'assault with intent to commit rape, and carnal knowledge of a female under 16.'" Janklow denied the charges and refused to appear in court; the charges were rejected repeatedly by the FBI, and the government did its best to thwart the investigation. In March 1975, the victim died as a result of a hit-and-run accident on a deserted road.

The siege at Wounded Knee began as a gesture of protest against injustices and the presence of federal officers on the reservation. The Oglala Sioux Civil Rights Organization (OSCRO) allied itself with AIM; on February 28, 1973, several hundred men, women, and children drove in caravan to Wounded Knee and took over the community. They issued a public statement demanding hearings on their treaty and an investigation of the BIA. Wounded Knee was surrounded the next day by an armed force consisting of the FBI, the U.S. Marshal Service, and the BIA police, supported by Dick Wilson's men. On May 9, after several attempts to negotiate and after exchanged gunfire that led to the death of a young Indian male, it was over. "The few Indians still left in the settlement submitted themselves to arrest by the U.S. government."

The Wounded Knee trials, particularly that of Dennis Banks and Russell Means, from January to September 1974, gained widespread notoriety. The prosecution, "dismissing past wrongs as irrelevant to this case, portrayed the two leaders as common criminals who had invaded, terrorized and looted a helpless community." At the end of this eight-and-a-half-week trial, the prosecution produced a surprise witness, former AIM member Louis Moves Camp, who "filled in every gap in the prosecution's case." Moves Camp had been assigned to FBI agent David Price, who, with his partner, had met daily with him from August 5 through August 10 and then had accompanied him from August 13 to 16, the day of his testimony. Moves Camp's testimony and the role played by Price were significantly questioned.

> More serious than Louis Moves Camp's lies was the all but inescapable conclusion that Agent Price and perhaps Agent Williams had knowingly prepared this man to give false testimony; or, at the very least, they had found his story so convenient that they had not bothered to find out if it was true.

There was a further assertion that Price was implicated in an "alleged cover-up of a disputed rape" committed by Moves Camp in River Falls, Wisconsin, on August 14. One of the Indians' legal aides is quoted as recalling: "Price can be friendly when he feels like it, and he can look you in the face and lie and know you know he's lying—and *still* not show a damned thing in his eyes."

Both Banks and Means were acquitted; others had charges dismissed, while a few received minor sentences for related charges. Of the leaders, only Crow Dog served any jail time—a few months—on charges directly related to Wounded Knee.

A little more than two years later, on June 26, 1975, the shoot-out at Oglala, specifically the Jumping Bull property, occurred. The firing erupted suddenly, catching the Indians off guard. Two special agents who had driven onto the property were wounded in the firefight, one seriously; subsequently, they were killed by shots at close range. One young Indian was also killed when a bullet struck him in the forehead. Federal reinforcements had arrived seemingly, to the Indians, almost immediately and set up roadblocks. Nevertheless, all but one—the dead Indian—had managed to escape.

What followed was a massive "reservation murders" investigation into the deaths of the two officers; the shooting death of the Indian was not considered. Public statements, printed in major newspapers, by FBI spokesmen and South Dakota attorney general William Janklow (who was subsequently reprimanded by Governor Richard Kniep for his inflammatory statements) that the agents' bodies had been "riddled with bullets" and that their cars had also been "riddled by machine-gun bullets" turned public opinion against AIM. (Each agent had actually been struck three times.) Outraged FBI officers "ransacked . . . house[s] without a warrant," harassed, coerced and bribed witnesses and, in the words of the U.S. Civil Rights Commission, overreacted so that the investigation took on "aspects of a vendetta . . . a full-scale military-type invasion." Special Agent David Price is identified as a member of some of these groups.

The activities of the fugitive Indians are also followed, from one camp or hideaway house to another. Some who had not been on the Jumping Bull property that fateful morning were pursued as AIM members. One of them, Anna Mae Aquash, died in a strange, questionable, hit-and-run accident. Eventually, four individuals were indicted on two counts of first-degree murder: James Theodore Eagle, Darrelle Dean Butler, Robert Eugene Robideau, and Leonard Peltier. Initially, Peltier was not in custody; he was later located in Canada, extradited to the United States with falsified documents, and tried separately.

The trial of Butler and Robideau was transferred from Rapid City, South Dakota, to Cedar Rapids, Iowa, based on the successful argument of anti-Indian prejudice. The trial opened on June 7, 1976, and concluded on July 16, 1976, with their acquittal on all counts. In addition to the significant testimony of a prosecution witness to defense cross-examination (quoted above relative to FBI manipulation of witnesses), the following argument to the court by a defense attorney regarding David Price's testimony was revealed:

> Mr. William Kunstler: We want to show this man fabricated testimony. That he has suborned perjury with witnesses in Indian trials involving A.I.M. people before. That he was the principal agent that produced witnesses they don't dare use now, produced witnesses that were to be used in this trial. John Stewart, Myrtle Poor Bear, Marvin Bragg, who was one they didn't produce on the stand, and that this man is notorious for producing fabricated evidence. They have put a witness like [James] Harper [a white man who had shared a cell with Dino Butler] on the stand and we are permitted to show, I think, under the rules of evidence that this is the way they prepare and work on witnesses, that they deliberately suborn perjury and use perjurious witnesses.

The case against James Theodore Eagle was abandoned as a result of the Cedar Rapids decision, but that of Leonard Peltier was pursued in Fargo, North Dakota. It ended on April 18, 1977, when the jury brought in a verdict of guilty on two counts of murder in the first degree. (The author comments that had Peltier been tried in Cedar Rapids, "it seems almost certain that he would have been acquitted" since there was "no good evidence that his actions had differed in a meaningful way. . . .")

Book III details Peltier's escape from prison, his recapture, and life in federal penitentiaries. Two chapters—one significantly titled "Forked Tongues"—investigate and analyze the evidence against Peltier. A third chapter, which includes a telephone interview with Special Agent David Price, investigates the situation of a potential prosecution witness, Myrtle Lulu Poor Bear, whom Price had been implicated in manipulating. There are also chapters on the "real enemy" of the Indians, that is, "the corporate state," that "coalition of industry and government that was seeking to exploit the last large Indian reservations in the West"; and on the attempt of the Indians in April 1981 to reassert their ownership of the Black Hills, the sacred Paha Sapa, by occupying sections of it.

CENSORSHIP HISTORY

The author and publisher of *In the Spirit of Crazy Horse* faced two libel suits two months after the book was published in 1983. The first plaintiff was William J. Janklow, then governor of South Dakota; the second was David Price, an FBI special agent. Peter Matthiessen, in his epilogue in the second edition, which came out after the trial, indicates that he assumed that the "FBI itself had sponsored [Price's] suit in order to lend some sort of credibility to the suit by Janklow" because Price himself "had assured me in our lengthy interview that he never made a move without the approval of his superiors, and since an FBI agent's salary could never pay for the very expensive attorneys he retained." There were altogether eight court decisions in eight years of litigation.

In April 1983, Governor Janklow called bookstores in Rapid City and Sioux Falls (he indicated he was attempting to call all bookstores in South Dakota) asking them to remove *In the Spirit of Crazy Horse* from their shelves because it was libelous and contained passages critical of him: "Nobody has the right to print lies and injure me or my family." While Janklow indicated he was acting as a private citizen, three of the booksellers reported that he had called from his office; one call was made by his secretary. Some stores removed the books; others did not. The disclosure of the governor's actions caused the sales of the book to increase.

Janklow filed a suit on May 19, 1983, asking $24 million in damages, against Viking Press, Peter Matthiessen and three bookstores. Janklow alleged that the book portrayed him as "morally decadent, a drunkard," "a racist and bigot," and "an antagonist of the environment." He claimed that Matthiessen's recounting of historical charges that he had raped a teenage Indian girl in 1967 and accusations against him by the American Indian Movement were "prepared either with a reckless disregard for truth or with actual malice for plaintiff." The defendants had edited all references to him and disregarded contrary evidence "in order to present a false and defamatory picture." His suit said that three federal investigations had determined that the rape charges were unfounded.

An attempt by the defendants for a change of venue from a state court in South Dakota to a federal court was denied on September 2, 1983, by U.S. District Court judge John B. Jones. The defendants had argued that Janklow had deliberately included the booksellers in his suit so that the case would be heard in the state courts. There was a presumption of bias in Janklow's favor at the state level.

On February 6, 1984, the booksellers' attorneys filed a joint memorandum asking Judge Gene Paul Kean of the Circuit Court of the Second Judicial Circuit in Sioux Falls to dismiss the case. The attorneys argued that courts had never required booksellers to investigate the accuracy of the books they sell. Further, a ruling to prove that the identified passages were

indeed libelous had not been made, nor had it been shown that the booksellers knew of the libel.

In support of the booksellers, the Freedom to Read Foundation on February 23 filed an amicus curiae brief in which they argued that if Janklow's

> contention were to be accepted, every bookseller, librarian, and other passive
> distributor of information would be confronted with a Hobson's choice: they
> would either have to review every potentially controversial book for factual ac-
> curacy and be prepared to defend such review in court, or accept at face value
> every claim made by a disgruntled reader who alleges that a particular work
> defames him and suppress all further distribution until such time, if ever, that
> the claim is resolved.
>
> It requires no prescience to recognize which choice must and will be made.
> Booksellers and librarians simply do not have the resources to undertake an in-
> depth review of every publication they are asked to distribute. . . . [therefore] the
> only way in which booksellers, librarians and other passive distributors of liter-
> ary materials could minimize their risk of litigation and liability under plaintiff's
> theory would be to categorically reject for distribution all works which address
> public controversy. . . .
>
> Plaintiff's theory of bookseller liability is not only insupportable under the
> First Amendment but also unconscionable in a society founded on the rule of
> law. . . . The hazard of self-censorship can be avoided only by equating "respon-
> sibility" with "authority." The remedy for libel must rest against the person
> responsible for it and by whose authority it was published. . . . To hold defendant
> booksellers proper defendants in this case would thus render their defense of
> First Amendment rights the very source of their liability for libel.
>
> A society which permits its legal process to become an instrument of co-
> ercion cannot long preserve the rule of law. And, as Justice Brandeis noted,
> silence coerced by law is the argument of force in its worst form. The defense
> of plaintiff's name does not require the "argument of force" he demands. The
> remedy for libel does not require the right to close the marketplace of ideas
> at will.

The booksellers were successful in their motion to have the suit against
them dismissed. On June 25, 1986, Judge Kean granted the defendants'
motion. Having noted the author's reputation as neither a sensationalist nor a
scandalous writer and the like reputation of the publisher, he stated:

> The calling up of booksellers and book distributors and expressing a view that
> something in the book may be false is not adequate. . . . If anyone who felt that
> he was libeled in written material could stop distribution in such fashion it would
> have a "chilling" effect on book distributors and book publishers.

Janklow did not appeal this decision.

Meanwhile, on July 13, 1984, Judge Kean issued an opinion granting
Viking and Matthiessen's motion to dismiss Janklow's entire case. He found
Matthiessen's reporting of the historical charges to be fair, balanced, and

protected as "neutral reportage." (This is an "evolving First Amendment doctrine that affords protection to reporting of charges.") Judge Kean stated further: "To force a writer to determine the responsibility of an organization or an original speaker at the risk of substantial liability would undoubtedly have a chilling effect on the dissemination of information." He also said that Matthiessen had the right to criticize Janklow in the book, which dealt with a longstanding public controversy.

Janklow's appeal of Judge Kean's decision was upheld on December 11, 1985, when the Supreme Court of South Dakota reversed the dismissal. It refused to adopt the principle of neutral reportage in South Dakota since the U.S. Supreme Court had not yet adopted the neutral reportage privilege. It remanded the case for summary judgment, requiring Judge Kean to rule on whether there was any evidence of wrongdoing by Viking and Matthiessen.

The Circuit Court of the Second Judicial Circuit in Sioux Falls again dismissed Janklow's case on June 2, 1989. Judge Kean ruled that "By no means are the statements concerning Janklow . . . a reckless publication about a public official. Defendants have provided evidence to support the statements in a lengthy affidavit by Matthiessen, accompanied by several exhibits totaling over 1,200 pages." Janklow's appeal to the South Dakota Supreme Court was rejected in a 4-1 decision, the majority citing First Amendment requirements.

This suit was formally ended in late October 1990 when Janklow allowed the 90-day deadline for appeal to the U.S. Supreme Court to lapse.

FBI special agent David Price filed his complaint of libel in January 1984 in state court in Rapid City, South Dakota, asking damages of $25 million. Price contended that he had been defamed by Matthiessen's charges that he and other FBI agents had engaged in illegal conduct in the events leading up to a gunfight between FBI agents and a few members of AIM living on the Pine Ridge Reservation. Specifically, he objected to allegations "that agents induced witnesses to commit perjury, and obstructed justice in the Peltier case . . . ; that they were racist and killers; and that they were 'corrupt and vicious' in their treatment of Indians on the reservation." He tried to impugn Matthiessen's sources by declaring that the AIM members among them had been convicted of criminal acts resulting from the Wounded Knee episode. Price also questioned the book's conclusion that Peltier's conviction had been a miscarriage of justice resulting from FBI misconduct.

In February 1985, South Dakota State Circuit Court judge Merton B. Tice, Jr., ruled that FBI agent Price's case against Viking Press and Matthiessen was not appropriate to South Dakota jurisdiction because Viking did not do enough business in South Dakota to establish the necessary "contact"; thus, if Price was harmed, it was not in South Dakota.

At the federal level, Judge Diana Murphy of the U.S. Federal District Court in Minneapolis in late January 1986 dismissed three of four counts in Price's suit. A significant rejection was Price's allegation of "group libel," that is, passages critical of the FBI had thereby defamed him personally. Judge Murphy's dismissal indicated that under these circumstances "the context of publication [must raise] a reasonable presumption of personal allusion." With regard to the remaining claims, Judge Murphy allowed Price two years of investigation. Thereafter, on January 13, 1988, she granted a motion for summary judgment and dismissal of the remaining claims. Judge Murphy upheld the right of an author "to publish an entirely one-sided view of people and events." Further, she noted that statements alleged by Price as defamatory were opinion and entitled to constitutional protection. With regard to factual statements about Price, the judge did not find that many were false; she also ruled that minor factual errors were not motivated by malice or negligence.

"The book deals with historical events, but does so from a very pointed perspective. The book's tone and style suggests the statements in question are opinion"; it seeks to persuade readers of the justice of a cause. She wrote, "The conduct of [FBI] agents in exerting their Federal authority is a matter of legitimate public interest" and noted that many statements of opinion were criticisms of government: "*In the Spirit of Crazy Horse* concerns speech about government officials, and it is this form of speech which the framers of the Bill of Rights were most anxious to protect. Criticism of government is entitled maximum protection of the First Amendment." She also pointed out that "Viking recognized that responsible publishing companies owe some duty to the public to undertake difficult but important works."

Price appealed the federal district court ruling. The unanimous decision of the U.S. Court of Appeals for the Eighth Circuit on August 7, 1989, granted summary judgment to Viking and Matthiessen, affirming all of Judge Murphy's rulings. The court, in effect, ruled that the challenged statements were constitutionally protected either as opinion or as "neutral reportage" in which the author transmits the views of others. Judge Gerald Heaney, writing for the three-judge panel, cited a 1964 precedent, *The New York Times v. Sullivan* decision of the Supreme Court. He wrote:

> The motivating factor in the Court's analysis was protection for criticism of public officials and speech regarding issues of political concern. The New York Times standard was constructed in light of three truths about public speech. First, false statements would necessarily occur in the course of a vigorous public debate. Second, absent protection for even false statements, destructive self-censorship would result. Third, the legal standards for defamation must protect defendants from the self-censorship imposed by threats of litigation. The Court felt that debate on matters of public concern "should be uninhibited, robust, and wide-open . . . [though] it may well include vehement, caustic, and sometimes unpleasantly sharp attacks on government and public officials. [Emphasis added by Martin Garbus, defense attorney for Viking Press and Matthiessen.]

While Price had relied on the previously accepted law that repeating a false accusation, even against a government official, could be libelous, Matthiessen had argued that some of the accusations he had printed were true and that reporting the historical fact that an accusation had been made was necessary to show the Indians' views. Further, the distinction between responsible critics and those whom Price labeled as leftists, that is, "good" and "bad" sources, was not accepted.

In conclusion, Judge Heaney reiterated Judge Murphy's sense that even if a government official could be injured by critical reports, to suppress them would unduly inhibit debate on issues of public significance:

> Sometimes it is difficult to write about controversial events without getting into some controversy along the way. In this setting, we have decided that the Constitution requires more speech rather than less. Our decision is an anomaly in a time when tort analysis increasingly focuses on whether there was an injury, for in debating this case we have searched diligently for fault and ignored certain injury. But there is a larger injury to be considered, the damage done to every American when a book is pulled from a shelf, as in this case, or when an idea is not circulated.
>
> In its entirety, *Crazy Horse* focuses more on public institutions and social forces than it does on any public official. The sentiments it expresses are debatable. We favor letting the debate continue.

Price made two separate applications to the U.S. Supreme Court to reverse the appellate court ruling. In his appeal for review, Price argued that the appeals court had created an "insurmountable hurdle" for plaintiffs in libel cases. "Any author with even a modicum of cleverness can publish purposely false allegations of criminal wrongdoing . . . or include clever and meaningless qualifiers to his defamatory allegations . . . he is absolutely protected by the opinion doctrine." In both instances, the Supreme Court refused to hear the appeal, thus leaving intact the appeals court ruling. The latter Supreme Court rejection occurred in January 1990.

Except for the initial printing of 35,000 copies, *In the Spirit of Crazy Horse* had been unavailable since the first lawsuit was filed in 1983. It was republished in 1991.

FURTHER READING

"Court Dismisses Janklow Suit against Viking and Matthiessen." *Publishers Weekly*, June 16, 1989, 14.

"Crazy Horse Suit Ends; Viking to Publish New Edition in 1991." *Publishers Weekly*, November 9, 1990, 12.

Fields, Howard. "High Court Rejects Libel Appeal against Viking." *Publishers Weekly*, January 26, 1990, 310, 312.

Garbus, Martin. Afterword to *In the Spirit of Crazy Horse*, by Peter Matthiessen. New York: Viking Press, 1991, 589–96.

Greenhouse, Linda. "Reviving Affirmative Action Issue, Court Will Decide." *New York Times*, January 9, 1990, pp. A1, 18.

"Libel Suit Against Viking Dismissed." *New York Times*, June 21, 1984, sec. 3, pp. 17.

Mitgang, Herbert. "Crazy Horse Author Is Upheld in Libel Case." *New York Times*, January 16, 1988, II 5.

Newsletter on Intellectual Freedom 32 (1983): 112; 33 (1984): 18, 75–76, 116, 148; 34 (1985) 34; 35 (1986): 52, 91; 37 (1988): 99; and 40 (1991): 55.

"South Dakota Governor Calls Stores to Ask Book's Removal." *New York Times*, May 1, 1983, p. I32.

"Viking and Matthiessen Prevail in Libel Suit." *Publishers Weekly*, January 29, 1988, 314.

"Viking, Matthiessen Win in Price Libel Suit." *Publishers Weekly*, September 1, 1989, 8.

JOHNNY GOT HIS GUN

Author: Dalton Trumbo
Original date and place of publication: 1939, United States
Publisher: J. B. Lippincott
Literary form: Novel

SUMMARY

Johnny Got His Gun is divided into Book I, "The Dead" and Book II, "The Living." "The Dead" is structured with chapters alternating from present to past as the protagonist, Joe Bonham, attempts to come to grips with what has happened to him. "The Living" concentrates on the present, though there are occasional reflections of the past. The novel is written in first person, an extended monologue—the mind, memories, and hallucinations of the protagonist.

> He was the nearest thing to a dead man on earth. He was a dead man with a mind that could still think. He knew all the answers that the dead knew and couldn't think about. He could speak for the dead because he was one of them.

These thoughts toward the close of Book I reflect Joe's realization and attitude. He has come far from the dull confusion and semiconsciousness of the first chapter. He begins to realize that he has been badly hurt and that he is deaf, but he is alive and in a hospital. In subsequent chapters, he realizes that he has lost one arm and then the other and then both legs. At last, he knows he has no mouth nor tongue nor nose and that he is blind.

The trauma and terror of these discoveries are like a bad dream; at times, Joe thinks he is dreaming or does not know when he is awake and when he is asleep. The nightmares shake him but being awake shakes him too.

The balancing chapters, Joe's recollections of the past, reveal Joe's *everyman* background—the normality of his life and love of his family; the buoyant adolescence and emerging manhood. His memories encompass the everyday: his mother's wordless singing while canning or making jelly; the smell and taste of freshly cooked hamburgers; camping-fishing holidays with his father; kissing and loving his sweetheart. By the close of Book I, Joe has established his sensibility and his stability of character. As his memories unravel and clarify, he establishes his sanity.

An antiwar element materializes in Book I. It is introduced in Chapter 2— "He lay and thought oh Joe Joe this is no place for you. This was no war for you. This thing wasn't any of your business. What do you care about making the world safe for democracy?" In Chapter 10 an extended stream-of-consciousness essay denounces fighting for empty words: freedom, liberty, honor, death before dishonor. The dead renounce these, for they died "yearning for the face of a friend . . . moaning and sighing for life." Joe knows for he is "the nearest thing to a dead man on earth."

In Book II, Joe tries to maintain control of his memory and gain cognizance and control of his environment. He works his mind, starting with recollections of numbers, quotations, and books; he tries to establish time, the passage of time. During a quite poignant moment, Joe solves this problem when he realizes he has identified the coming of dawn and opens up his memory bank of sunrise. He marks time, counting the days into years.

He works also on space and the message of vibrations until he can tell who is with him and what is being done. He is at first bewildered by a group of visitors in the fourth year of his hospitalization and then intensely angered when he realizes that he has been awarded a medal. His anger leads him to recall his use of a wireless set years before; he initiates efforts to communicate by tapping the Morse code "SOS" on his pillow.

Months later, a young substitute nurse recognizes the code, and Joe's attempt to communicate. His joy at being acknowledged a live man with a mind is a "new wild frantic happiness." When he answers her question, "What do you want?" the answer is, "What you ask is against regulations."

What did he want? He wants, of course, his life back—his senses, his limbs. He asks to be let out, to be released from the hospital "prison." He longs for air, sensations on his skin, to be among people. His mind runs ahead of his tapping, revealing his desire to make an exhibit of himself to show ordinary people— parents, schoolchildren—and legislators: "Here is war."

The text concludes in emotional antiwar rhetoric.

CENSORSHIP HISTORY

Dalton Trumbo's acclaimed World War I novel—it won the American Booksellers Award in 1940 as the "most original novel of the year"—is one of the finest by an American in the 1930s. *Johnny Got His Gun* was his statement against the war, against the United States getting involved in a European war. However, during World War II, Trumbo deferred his doubts, shifting from the antiwar attitudes to "militant support for the war effort."

In his 1959 introduction to *Johnny Got His Gun*, Trumbo recounts the book's "weird political history." "Written in 1938 when pacifism was anathema to the American left and most of the center, it went to the printers in the spring of 1939 and was published on September third—ten days after the Nazi-Soviet pact, two days after the start of World War II." Subsequently, serial rights were sold to *The Daily Worker* of New York City, becoming for months a rallying point for the left.

During World War II, after the book went out of print, Trumbo himself resisted requests to have it reprinted; his publishers agreed. These requests came from the extreme American right, which wanted a negotiated peace and which perceived the novel, according to Bruce Cook, to be "useful as propaganda . . . as the Axis fortunes began to fall" because of the antiwar message. "Anti-Semitic and native Fascist groups put on a big push for an early peace, demanding that Hitler be offered a conditional peace." Individuals of these persuasions claimed that Jews, communists, and international bankers had suppressed the novel. Trumbo was distressed that his book was being so used by these groups.

The army initiated a program, during World War II, of distributing books to soldiers overseas. From 1941 to 1943, 3 million books were shipped. Subsequently, the army invited the Council on Books in Wartime, an organization formed by the publishing industry to assist the war effort, to help in this program. In the next three years, 1,080 separate titles, more than 122 million books, were made available to servicemen.

There was an underlying censorship stance involved in the book selection. Prior to 1943, magazines and newspapers of Axis propaganda were rejected. In addition, three books were banned by the Special Services Division, two of them "by direction from higher authority." One of these was *Johnny Got His Gun*, presumably because of its pacifist message.

Johnny Got His Gun has been challenged and/or censored in schools: in the Midwest (1973) for vulgarity of incidents and language; in Michigan (1977) for too much profanity, too gruesome of details of a human being, expressing unpatriotic and anti-American ideas and sexual passages; in Wisconsin (1977) for too much profanity; in Texas (1977) as unpatriotic and anti-American; in Colorado (1977) for the description of the main character after he had been maimed in the war; in California (1977) for the language and for several passages describing sexual encounters; in Wisconsin (1982) as antiwar; in Vermont and Illinois (1982) as too violent.

Trumbo was also a successful screenwriter. Talented and prolific, he was nominated for and had won Academy Awards. In 1947, Trumbo was blacklisted as one of the Hollywood Ten. He had joined the Communist Party in 1943 (he left the party in 1948) when the United States and the Soviet Union were allies, and he had been active representing his views. As such, he was an obvious recipient of a subpoena to appear before the House Committee on Un-American Activities in Washington, D.C., on October 23, 1947. The hearings focused on the "Communist Infiltration of the Motion Picture

Industry": The presumption was that communist dogma and propaganda had been written into film scripts. The Hollywood Ten perceived the essential question to be one of freedom of speech.

Dubbed "unfriendly witnesses" because of their refusal to answer the committee's questions about membership in the Screenwriters Guild and the Communist Party, they, upon the committee's unanimous vote to seek indictments for contempt of Congress, were found guilty of contempt of the House of Representatives in a 346-17 vote. All 10 individuals served prison terms; Trumbo, sentenced to a year, served 10 months, starting on June 7, 1950.

Despite disclaimers that they would do anything so un-American, the motion picture industry prepared in November 1947 the notorious Waldorf Agreement which, in effect, declared the Hollywood Ten and others like them to be "no longer employable in the motion picture industry." The Hollywood Ten did bring suit on their contracts, but on November 14, 1949, the Supreme Court turned down their petition and refused to hear the case. Trumbo refers to this situation as a domestic manifestation of the cold war that was then developing: "We are against the Soviet Union in our foreign policy abroad, and we are against anything partaking of socialism or communism in our internal affairs. This quality of opposition has become the keystone of our national existence."

Before and after his imprisonment, Trumbo wrote for the movie black market under pseudonyms or under the cover of other screenwriters' names. In 1957, he won the Oscar for the Best Motion Picture Story for *The Brave One* under his pseudonym Robert Rich; this award "marked the beginning of the end of the black list," according to Cook, which by this time affected any writers implicated in the anticommunist witch-hunt. Cook quotes Trumbo as remarking that because there were so many screenwriters working in the movie black market under false or borrowed names, "no record of credits between 1947 and 1960 can be considered even remotely accurate." Cook also credits Trumbo with the dissolution of the blacklist in 1960: It was "a coordinated and deliberate personal campaign in the media . . . a crusade, a vendetta."

FURTHER READING

Cook, Bruce. *Dalton Trumbo*. New York: Charles Scribner's Sons, 1977.

DeMuth, James. "*Johnny Got His Gun:* A Depression Era Classic." In *Censored Books: Critical Viewpoints*, edited by Nicholas J. Karolides, Lee Burress, and John M. Kean, 331–337. Metuchen, N.J.: Scarecrow Press, 1993.

Jamieson, John. *Books for the Army: The Army Library Service in the Second World War.* New York: Columbia University Press, 1950.

Leary, William M., Jr. "Books, Soldiers and Censorship during the Second World War." *American Quarterly* 20 (1968): 237–245.

Trumbo, Dalton. "Introduction." In *Johnny Got His Gun*. New York: Bantam Books, 1983.

KISS OF THE SPIDER WOMAN (*EL BESO DE LA MUJER ARAÑA*)

Author: Manuel Puig
Original dates and places of publication: 1976, Spain; 1979, United
  States and Canada
Publisher: Seix Barral; Alfred A. Knopf
Literary form: Novel

SUMMARY

Molina and Valentín, sharing a cell in the penitentiary of the city of Buenos
Aires, are an unlikely pair. And not solely in temperament. Molina is
a homosexual accused of child molestation; he wants to be a woman.
Valentín is a political prisoner, "dedicated to political struggles, or, you
know, political action," the purpose of which is social revolution. He refers
to himself as a marxist. A further difference in that Molina is uneducated,
a window dresser, not intrested in books, and Valentín, college educated,
pursues knowledge, often commenting on texts he is studying.

Nevertheless, this unlikely pair gets along. Molina "entertains" Valentín
by recounting the plots of movies, six in total throughout the novel; some
are actual films and some are inventions. The movies give them something
to talk about, calming them down, diminishing their defensiveness, and
permitting escape from their confinement. Their conversations are self-
revealing.

The films are mainstream, rather than sophisticated art films, categorized perhaps as romantic adventures, with the exception of *Cat People*, a
classic horror film. They are melodramatic, using exotic landscapes. And
gimmicky—they feature voodoo and zombies for example. The women, with
whom Molina identifies, are often victims of their situation, the man in her
life, or herself; their suffering is horrific, as in the case of the cursed panther
woman, or noble, represented by the actress in the Nazi films, or the chan-
teuse, who having rejected her wealthy magnate for the reporter, stoops to
prostitution to support her lover. The heterosexual relationships are perceived as shallow or troubled, sometimes forced.

Midway through the novel we are privy to documents of the Ministry
of the Interior of the Argentine Republic, which identify the backgrounds
and prison behavior of the two inmates. Also, it is evident that both are
transferred to Pavilion D, cell 7, on the same date. We are also privy to an
interview of the warden of the penitentiary with Molina on the pretext of his
having a visitor. He is offered an early pardon if he can get Valentín to reveal
vital information about his political accomplices. (It is unclear whether this
offer was made at the time of the transfer to cell 7 or later.)

The warden also reveals that Valentín's food is "prepared" (read "poisoned") so that he becomes ill, the purpose being to weaken him. Molina eats

from this plate the first time and subsequently suffers from stomach cramps, pains, and extreme diarrhea. Valentín, who eats this prepared food again and again, is indeed sickened and weakened, losing control of his bowels. Out of need and compassion—and an emerging affection—Molina cares for Valentín during these crises, washing his body and both his clothes and the sheets. He advises—no, urges—Valentín not to eat the prison food, providing food, ostensibly gifted by his mother as in the past but provided this time by the warden. Gradually, Molina gains his cellmate's confidence. Further, while they are feasting, Molina reveals he's being nice to Valentín "because I want to win your friendship, and, why not say it? . . . your affection." Further, he differentiates himself from other "faggots," the "kind who fall in love with one another. But as for my friends and myself, we're a hundred percent female. We don't go in for those little games—that's strictly for homos. We're normal women; we sleep with men." The plan works so well that Valentín's resistance erodes, and he reveals features of his personal life and psyche. He seems to have regained a life force, revealing his memories of a woman he has loved.

Molina reveals that he is being considered for parole and, if so, that he will be removed from cell 7—part of the warden's enticement-for-information plan. Molina, however, having come to love Valentín, revises the objective to gain information about the political accomplices in order to insure parole. He cries and admits to being scared, not only of whether the release expectation will be fulfilled, but also of separation from his friend. This confession leads to a comforting massage which, in turn, leads to a sexual seduction.

Molina does get his early parole despite his having refused information from Valentín—probably another artifice of the warden—and has one last night in cell 7 and a final sexual experience. And a kiss. Valentín response to Molina's "I'm not the panther woman," is "It's true, you're not the panther woman. . . . You, you're the spider woman, that traps men in her web!"

The novel concludes with a transcript—a report on Luis Alberto Molina, prisoner 3.018, paroled on the 9th, placed under surveillance by CISL in conjunction with wiretap unit of TISL. It contains a meticulously detailed report of Molina's activity and phone calls. The conclusion: After a brief phone call, subsequent to dialing three times, Molina traveled by bus and subway; just after he was picked up by Central Bureau for interrogation, he was shot from a passing vehicle. He dies. Has he sacrificed his life consciously?

Meanwhile Valentín has been tortured. A medical intern, against regulations, gives him morphine, commenting on the "unbelievable" injuries and the burns on his groin. He is in a semiconscious state, dreaming of and talking to Marta, the woman he had loved before he got involved in subversive politics.

Homosexuality is expressed in two ways in *Kiss of the Spider Woman*. First, the plot itself in an honest and natural way portrays a love affair between two men without shame or apology. Second, a series of eight extended footnotes offers theories and clarifications to create understandings. Theorists and researchers are quoted to explore possible causes, to review controversies, to explain and deny misconceptions and stereotypes. Altogether, these footnotes are significant in educating the reader.

CENSORSHIP HISTORY

Between 1930 and 1983, Argentina experienced 31 military coups. Denial of civil liberties and censorship of newspapers and broadcasting media were the rule. Systematic repression became government policy under the military junta that overthrew the Perón government, ruling from 1976 to 1983. When released in July 1976, *Kiss of the Spider Woman* was immediately banned. The novel was responding in part to the brutality of this military regime: Citizens were tortured and killed; thousands who were suspected of subversion "disappeared," including educated young people. Valentín in this novel represents this last group. According to Jonathan Tittler, Puig wanted "to discredit the Argentine military in the eyes of the rest of Latin America." Also in 1977 at the International Book Fair in Buenos Aires, *Kiss of the Spider Woman* was included on a distinguished list of books that could not be imported, displayed, or sold. While political subversion is a significant theme in *Kiss of the Spider Woman*, so, too, is homosexuality, a taboo subject at the time. Its positive expression in this novel would have been a factor in the novel being suppressed.

The suppression was lifted upon the election of President Raúl Alfonsín (1983–89), who returned the Argentine government to more liberal principles.

Other novels written by Puig also faced censorship. Completed in 1965, *La traición de Rita Hayworth* (*Betrayed by Rita Hayworth*) was hampered by censorship problems but was eventually published in 1968. The first edition of *Fattaccio a Buenos Aires* (*The Buenos Aires Affair*) was confiscated by censorship agencies as soon as it was released in 1973. Shortly thereafter, Puig was threatened by Alinza Anticommunista Argentina (AAA) and forced to leave the country.

FURTHER READING

Balderston, Daniel, and Francine Masiello, eds. *Approaches to Teaching Puig's* Kiss of the Spider Woman. New York: Modern Language Association of America, 2007.

Green, Jonathon, and Nicholas J. Karolides, reviser. "Argentina." In *Encyclopedia of Censorship, New Edition*. New York: Facts On File, 2005.

Levine, Suzanne Jill. *Manuel Puig and the Spider Woman: His Life and Fictions*. New York: Farrar, Strauss and Giroux, 2000.

Tittler, Jonathan. *Manuel Puig*. New York: Twayne, 1993.

THE MANIFESTO OF THE COMMUNIST PARTY

Authors: Karl Marx and Friedrich Engels
Original dates and places of publication: 1848, Great Britain; 1872,
   United States (English translation)
Publishers: Communist League; Woodbull and Claflin's Weekly
Literary form: Nonfiction

SUMMARY

In the "Preface to the English Edition of 1888," Engels noted that "the history of the *Manifesto* reflects the history of the modern working-class movement" and identified it as the most international of all Socialist literature. Yet, he acknowledged significant differences between the Socialists of 1847, "adherents of the various Utopian systems," and Communists, "Whatever portion of the working class had become convinced of the insufficiency of mere political revolutions and had proclaimed the necessity of a total social change. . . ."

This definition lends itself to a central issue of section 1: class struggle. Such struggle between the oppressor, or the bourgeoisie, and the oppressed, or the proletariat, has existed throughout history and existed in the mid- and late 19th century. The bourgeoisie, equated with capital, developed in the same proportion as the proletariat developed. The latter is defined as "a class of laborers, who live only so long as they find work, and who find work only so long as their labor increases capital."

The bourgeois class developed from the feudal economic system, which was replaced by a manufacturing system to meet the demands of new markets that kept expanding, even establishing world markets. Politically oppressed by the feudal nobility in the preexisting system, the manufacturing middle class, itself revolutionized by the advance of industrialization, had achieved the position of power and control. "The executive of the modern state is but a committee for managing the common affairs of the whole bourgeoisie."

Beyond gaining political supremacy and massively altering the forms and extent of production, the bourgeoisie changed the face of society. By expanding the means of communication, all nations, even the most primitive, were drawn into civilization. The towns came to dominate the country, with significant increases in urban populations. The outcome of this was the creation of patterns of dependence: rural regions dependent on towns and cities; the primitive countries dependent on the developed ones. Also, the bourgeoisie destroyed the feudal patriarchal relations, "stripped of its halo every occupation, . . . and reduced the family relation to a mere money relation."

> It has resolved personal work into exchange value, and in place of the numberless indefeasible chartered freedoms, has set up that single, unconscionable freedom—Free Trade. In one word, for exploitation, veiled by religious and political illusions, it has substituted naked, shameless, direct, brutal exploitation.

Another outcome of centralized production was the concentration of property in a few hands and the creation of "more colossal productive forces than all preceding generations together." This means of production and its control are equated with social-political power. These movements of change are identified as constant, the "revolt of modern productive forces against modern conditions of production" leading to commercial crises during which existing products and previously created forces are destroyed. "The weapons with which the bourgeoisie felled feudalism to the ground are now turned against the bourgeoisie itself." The men who will wield the weapons of destruction are the modern working class, the proletarians.

Industrialization caused the work of proletarians to lose all its individual character. As a mere appendage of a machine, the worker's value is decreased, equal essentially to the cost of production, subsistence for his maintenance and for the propagation of his race.

> As privates of the industrial army they are placed under the command of a perfect hierarchy of officers and sergeants. Not only are they slaves of the bourgeois class, and of the bourgeois state; they are daily and hourly enslaved by the machine, by the over-looker, and, above all, by the individual bourgeois manufacturer himself. The more openly this despotism proclaims gain to be its end and aim, the more petty, the more hateful and the more embittering it is.

The worker is further exploited, beyond the factory, by other members of the bourgeoisie—the landlord, the shopkeeper—who take his wages from him.

In 1848, the proletariat was not yet organized in the worker's own behalf. Its struggle with the bourgeoisie was scattered and individualized or by factory, locale, or trade; it was misdirected against the instruments of production rather than the bourgeois conditions of production. However, the predicted change, given the development of industry—thus, the concentration of masses of workers and the equalization of life within the workers' rank and of wages at the same low level—was that the workers would unify.

The unifying force: communism. Defined as not forming a separate party in opposition to other working-class parties and as having no interests "separate and apart from those of the proletariat as a whole," the Communists' immediate aims are the formation of the proletariat into a class, the overthrow of bourgeois supremacy, and the conquest of political power by the proletariat. Marx and Engels saw the Communist Party as the only one that had as its purpose the advancing of the true interests of the proletariat as a class.

The "abolition of private property" was central in the theory of the Communists. This abolition focused on bourgeois property, "the final and most complete expression of the system of producing and appropriating products that is based on class antagonisms, on the exploitation of the many by the few." (The "hard-won, self-acquired, self-earned property . . . of the petty artisan and of the small peasant" was perhaps excluded from this abolition;

the issue was sidestepped by the view that such property had already been destroyed by the development of industry.)

Wage-labor does not create property for the laborer; it creates capital— "the kind of property which exploits wage-labor, and which cannot increase except upon condition of begetting a new supply of wage-labor for fresh exploitation." The solution to this antagonism between capital and wage-labor, given that capital is not a personal but a social power, was to convert capital into common property. The intention, further, was to change the "miserable character" of the "personal appropriation of the products of labor" so as "to widen, to enrich, to promote the existence of the laborer."

> The proletariat will use its political supremacy to wrest, by degrees, all capital from the bourgeoisie, to centralize all instruments of production in the hands of the state, i.e., of the proletariat organized as the ruling class; and to increase the total of productive forces as rapidly as possible.

The "Communist revolution is the most radical rupture with traditional property relations . . . [and] with traditional ideas." The *Manifesto of the Communist Party* is a call to arms, to revolutionary activity.

While recognizing the variation of this undertaking in different countries, the following goals were identified as generally applicable:

1. Abolition of property in land and application of all rents of land to public purposes.
2. A heavy progressive or graduated income tax.
3. Abolition of all right of inheritance.
4. Confiscation of the property of all emigrants and rebels.
5. Centralization of credit in the hands of the state, by means of a national bank with state capital and an exclusive monopoly.
6. Centralization of the means of communication and transport in the hands of the state.
7. Extension of factories and instruments of production owned by the state; the bringing into cultivation of waste lands, and the improvement of the soil generally in accordance with a common plan.
8. Equal obligation of all to work. Establishment of industrial armies, especially for agriculture.
9. Combination of agriculture with manufacturing industries; gradual abolition of the distinction between town and country, by a more equitable distribution of the population over the country.
10. Free education for all children in public schools. Abolition of child factory labor in its present form. Combination of education with industrial production.

The concluding pages of the text define and differentiate between communism and several socialism movements. Three broad categories of socialism are discussed: reactionary socialism, including feudal socialism, petty-bourgeois socialism, and German, or "true," socialism; conservative, or bourgeois socialism; and critical-utopian socialism. Each of these socialist movements is dismissed as inadequate, focusing on the dethroned aristocrat or the petty bourgeois; the preservation of the present state of society; the "redressing of social grievances, in order to secure the continued existence of bourgeois society"; and the rejection of political and revolutionary action, seeking to improve conditions through appeals to society at large, chiefly the ruling class.

CENSORSHIP HISTORY

Censorship of Karl Marx's works began before the publication of *Manifesto of the Communist Party*. The political and social journal, *Rheinische Zeitung*, was suppressed in 1843, one year after Marx became editor. He was exiled in Paris and Brussels. He was expelled from France about 1845 for contributing to the radical magazine, *Vorwarts*. In 1849, the *Neue Rheinische Zeitung*, edited by Marx, advocated nonpayment of taxes and armed resistance against Emperor Frederick William. The journal was suspended, and Marx was tried for treason; though acquitted by a middle-class jury, he was expelled from Germany.

Action to ban the *Manifesto* in Germany occurred in 1878. It grew out of two assassination attempts—on May 11 and June 2—on the life of Emperor William I, the second of which wounded him seriously. Chancellor Otto von Bismarck exploited the fact that the first assassin had once belonged to the Social Democratic Party and caused a bill to be drafted against the "socialists and their press." It failed because of opposition from the National Liberal Party. Though there was no evidence that the second assassin was a Socialist, Bismarck again "conjured up the red peril" and dissolved the Reichstag. The next election gave him a stronger conservative party base, which easily passed his antisocialism bill, the "Exceptional Law." In addition to limiting rights to form associations and organizations in support of social democratic, Socialist or Communist activities which "are designed to subvert the existing political order in ways that threaten the public order and particularly the harmony of the social classes," the law forbade the publication of newspapers or books, including the *Communist Manifesto*.

The Catholic Church undertook its anticommunist stance in the 19th century—"since *The Communist Manifesto* first appeared in 1848." Donald Crosby points out, "[T]he popes taught that communism was essentially atheistic and irreligious," representing the very Antichrist. They regarded the Communists as "anarchistic, violent and opposed to what was best for man," and their materialism as contrary to "the heart of the church, the world of God and of the spirit." The savage persecution of Russian Catholics after the Bolshevik Revolution intensified the church's hostility. The *Communist Manifesto* during this time was listed on the Index librorum prohibitorum, or Roman Index.

In the United States in the late 1930s, Catholics identified anticommunism as demonstrating compatibility with American patriotism and the greater American society. The anticommunism of the church's leaders did not waver and was indeed solidified by the "martyring" of Archbishop Aloysius Stepinac of Yugoslavia and Joseph Cardinal Mindszenty of Hungary. Two positions of anticommunism emerged, particularly evident in the post–World War II period: a militant, conservative effort that allied with Senator Joseph McCarthy in zealous pursuit of subversives and "fellow travelers" in government and other aspects of society; and a liberal effort that, while equally opposed to communism, believed the answer was not "an extension of Red hunts and repressive legislation but an expansion of social programs designed to end hunger, disease, deficient housing and other social and economic ills that drove men into the hands of the Marxists." This group vehemently opposed Senator McCarthy and his tactics.

Given this historic position and current attitudes, the revelations of a poll of libraries in 30 cities, reported in the *New York Times* in 1953, are understandable. While public institutions did not curb books by Communists—texts by Marx, Lenin, and Stalin could be borrowed without restriction—some private religious education institutions did limit their availability. Roman Catholic universities such as Loyola University in New Orleans, Creighton University in Omaha, and Marquette University in Milwaukee placed these texts under restricted access. Students could borrow them if related to assignments or if being used for reference under direction when studying the theories of communism for thesis work. At Marquette, the instructors submitted the names of students who borrowed these books; the list was subsequently turned over to the archbishop. The Marquette University spokesperson indicated as explanation for the restricted access of the *Manifesto* that it was listed on the Index.

The 1950–53 period in the United States was one of extensive criticism of Marx's works as well as other Communist writings. The period was dramatically punctuated by the activities and accusations of Senator Joseph McCarthy and of the House Committee on Un-American Activities. It included such disparate situations as a 1950s report before the Illinois legislature's Seditious Activities Investigation Committee in 1950 that urged limiting access of many books by Marx in the public library. "They develop the subject at length and by so doing put in the young mind a yearning for that." At another level in 1953, after students in Brooksfield, Florida, who were working on papers about Russia, reported finding materials favoring that country, Paul B. Parker, a retired colonel and a library board member, set himself up as a one-person censorship committee. He removed an unspecified number of books and magazines from the nearby Brooksville public library because they were "communist propaganda." These included the *Manifesto of the Communist Party*, *Mission to Moscow* by Joseph E. Davies, former United States ambassador to Russia, and both the *New Republic* and *Reporter* magazines. Mayor Howard B. Smith demanded their return despite Parker's threat to label him a "fellow traveler." With the library board also insisting on the return of the material and further rejecting Parker's motion that the books and magazines be stamped "Propaganda," some were returned. One exception: *Manifesto of the Communist Party.*

The Boston Public Library came under attack on September 23, 1952, when the *Boston Post*, recently purchased by John Fox, revealed that the library subscribed to the pro-Soviet monthly *New World Review* and to Russian newspapers *Pravda* and *Izvestia;* it also disclosed it had a lobby display of the *Manifesto* and "thousands" of Communist publications. The *Post* argued: "We believe that pro-Soviet literature should be suppressed in our public libraries. . . ." This position was counterargued by the director of the library, Milton E. Lord, who was supported by the *Boston Herald.* Lord was quoted: "It is essential that information in all aspects of the political, international and other questions be available for information purposes in order that citizens of Boston be informed about the friends and enemies of their country." Supporters of the *Post* included the American Legion and the Veterans of Foreign Wars; joining the *Herald* were the *Pilot*, a Catholic diocesan paper, and the *Christian Science Monitor.* On October 3, the Boston Public Library board voted 3-2 to maintain its collection of Communist materials.

The idea of "branding" books emerged in San Antonio, Texas, in 1953. Mayor Jack White suggested to the city council that it "consider branding all Communist-written volumes in the library," that is, books whose authors had been accused of affiliation with subversive organizations. The organizer of the San Antonio Minute Women, Myrtle Hance, provided a list of 600 titles by authors whose names had been gleaned from congressional investigation testimony. After the 15-member library board protested vehemently and the public's negative reaction to the proposal emerged, the branding idea was dropped.

During 1953, international repercussions resulted from the national debate. Senator McCarthy attacked the overseas libraries of the International Information Administration (IIA), claiming that there were some "30,000 volumes subversive of American interests" by 418 authors whose loyalty to the United States was suspect. The purpose of the libraries in the postwar period was to provide a balanced view of the opinion and thinking of the United States, to provide books that were nonpolitical in nature to accurately portray the American scene—without regard to the politics of the authors. The idea was to demonstrate the free marketplace of ideas to contrast and combat, in Germany, for example, the intellectual stagnation of the Nazi period. However, in practice during this period, according to David Oshinsky, "The rule of thumb, then, was to include 'controversial' books while excluding blatantly pro-communist or anti-American propaganda." The State Department, under its secretary, John Foster Dulles, reacted to McCarthy's attack by directing, with some confusion, the removal of all books by controversial authors— "communists, fellow-travelers, leftists, et cetera"—and books critical of U.S. policies. Even books without any political content were barred, including, for instance, the mysteries of Dashiell Hammett. In Australia and Singapore, the overseas library staffs actually burned books.

In his address to the graduating class of Dartmouth College on June 14, 1953, President Dwight D. Eisenhower spoke out against censorship: "Don't join the book-burners." He defended reading Marx and others as a way of maintaining awareness of the world crisis and the purposes of the Soviets; he defended the retention of "merely controversial" books in American libraries and overseas. However, at a subsequent press conference he objected to books advocating the overthrow of the United States and agreed to the elimination of books written by Communists, while recommending books written by anticommunists about communism.

Censorship on the international scene had been prevalent. In the 19th century, from 1882 to 1900, the Russian Federation banned the *Manifesto of the Communist Party* for political reasons. In 1878 in Prussia, Bismarck persuaded the Reichstag to prohibit the literature of the Social Democrats, including the *Manifesto*. Anne Haight identifies the attempts of the Nationalist Government of China in 1929 to stop the reading of the *Manifesto* and *Das Kapital*. Marx's works were among the 25,000 volumes publicly burned in Berlin, Germany, in 1933 in a large-scale "symbolic" bonfire demonstration. The destruction of books by the Nazis continued until World War II: In Austria, Vienna (1938) and Salzburg were notable sites; in Czechoslovakia, the education minister ordered all "unpatriotic" books, particularly by patriots, to be removed from public libraries and destroyed.

The entry "Marx, Karl" in *The Encyclopedia of Censorship* summarizes: "It is impossible to itemize every country in which Marxist works are prohibited, nor do such countries remain consistent in their bans, but it may be generally assumed that those governments pursuing right-wing totalitarianism or dictatorial policies are keen to ban the founder of communism." Germany suppressed the *Manifesto* in all occupied countries, as well as allied countries from 1940 to 1945: Denmark, Norway, France, Luxembourg, Belgium, the Netherlands, Lithuania, Latvia, Estonia, Belarus, Poland, Yugoslavia, and Greece. In this vein, a 1950 survey reported in the *New York Times* listed 16 countries as having outlawed the Communist Party, "legally or otherwise, and have taken steps in that direction." The list included Greece, Turkey, Lebanon, Syria, Korea, Burma, Indonesia, Indo-China, Malaya, Portugal, Spain, Peru, Bolivia, Chile, Brazil, and Venezuela. Other nations that then were considering such action included South Africa, Australia, Egypt, and Denmark.

In 1946, the coordinating council of the American military government in Germany ordered the destruction of Nazi memorials in order to eliminate the "spirit of German militarism and Nazism as far as possible." Darkly ironic, the "placement of books by Hitler, Goebbels, Mussolini and Karl Marx on restricted lists in libraries, or in some instances pulped," was ordered on the 11th anniversary of the Nazi book-burning demonstration.

On two occasions, October 18, 1988, and March 8, 1989, customs officials in Grenada confiscated boxes of books being shipped by Pathfinder Press, a publisher of political, historical, and academic books based in New York. The *Manifesto of the Communist Party* was one of the confiscated books. Other notable books then banned included *The State and Revolution* by V. I. Lenin, *The Struggle Is My Life* by Nelson Mandela, *Maurice Bishop Speaks: The Grenada Revolution 1979–83* by Maurice Bishop, *Malcolm X Speaks* by Malcolm X, and *Nothing Can Stop the Course of History: An Interview with Fidel Castro* by Congressman Mervyn Dymally and Jeffrey M. Elliott.

FURTHER READING

"Book Burning." *New Republic* 128 (June 29, 1953): 7–17.

"Branding of Books Stirs Texas Battle." *New York Times*, June 7, 1953, p. 61.

Cook, Fred J. *The Nightmare Decade: The Life and Times of Senator Joe McCarthy*. New York: Random House, 1971.

Crankshaw, Edward. *Bismarck*. New York: Viking Press, 1981.

Crosby, Donald F. *God, Church, and the Flag: Senator Joseph R. McCarthy and the Catholic Church, 1950–1957*. Chapel Hill: University of North Carolina Press, 1978.

"Firefighting." *New Republic* 129 (September 7, 1953): 5.

Green, Jonathon, and Nicholas J. Karolides, reviser. *The Encyclopedia of Censorship, New Edition*. New York: Facts On File, 2005.

Haight, Anne Lyon, and Chandler B. Grannis. *Banned Books 387 B.C. to 1978 A.D.* 4th ed. New York: R. R. Bowker, 1978.

Importation of Publications (Prohibition) Order. Grenada. Statutory Rules and Orders No. 6 of 1989. Gazetted April 14, 1989.

Inter-American Commission on Human Rights. Report No. 2/96, Case 10, 325 Grenada. Washington, D.C.: Organization of American States, March 1, 1996.

Kipp, Lawrence J. "Report from Boston." *Library Journal* 77 (1952): 1,843–1,846, 1,887.

Oshinsky, David M. *A Conspiracy So Immense: The World of Joe McCarthy*. New York: Free Press, 1983.

Pathfinder Press Releases. New York: October 19, 1988; March 10, April 5, and April 27, 1989.

"Poll of Libraries Shows Free Choice." *New York Times*, June 16, 1953, p. 22.

"St. George's, Grenada." *Newsletter on Intellectual Freedom* 38 (1989): 141–142.

"16 Countries Outlaw Reds, Survey Shows." *New York Times*, May 16, 1950, p. 20.

MEIN KAMPF

Author: Adolf Hitler
Original dates and places of publication: 1925, Germany; 1933, United States
Original publishers: Eher Verlag; Houghton Mifflin
Literary form: Biography

SUMMARY

Tormented and impoverished as a youth, optimistic yet often disappointed as an adolescent, determined and ultimately revered as a young man, Adolf Hitler's life echoes his work's title, which translates as *My Struggle*. In spite of the victories attained while rising to power and during his reign as führer, he met many failures; his success can be attributed to sheer determination and will to see a "dream" fulfilled, even though for most it was and will always be a nightmare.

Hitler was born in 1889 on Easter Sunday in Braunau, a small Austrian border town on the Inn River that was highly concentrated with people of German heritage. Depending on whose viewpoint one believes, Hitler's childhood was either an exercise in the development of discipline or pure hell. Charles B. Flood, author of *Hitler: The Path to Power*, paints a macabre beginning for the man who would one day rule the German empire. Alois Hitler, Adolf's father, was labeled "a small-town Henry VIII" for his exploits with women. Before Adolf he produced two children by two different women. The first was a widow who bore him a daughter. They would marry and be together for seven years until she filed for separation because Alois had moved on to a 19-year-old kitchen maid in the hotel where they were living. After his estranged first wife died, he and the kitchen maid had a son, Alois Jr. They married, but she too died, which allowed Alois to marry Klara Polzl, the children's nursemaid, 23 years younger than he. She was Adolf's mother. According to Alois Jr., Hitler's half brother, Alois Sr. would at times beat Junior unmercifully, and when Junior moved out at 14, the father's abusive behavior was shifted toward seven-year-old Adolf. Young Adolf bore many beatings by his father until one day he decided not to cry. After a total of 32 strikes with a stick, his father ceased, never to beat him again. This example of childhood misery, which some say worked to forge the mind of Hitler, goes unmentioned in the opening pages of *Mein Kampf*, due to the fact that, according to Otto D. Tolischus, reviewer for the *New York Times Magazine*, one of Hitler's primary goals was that the book be a tool of propaganda, not a solely biographical depiction highlighting, among other topics, his imperfect upbringing. This would explain Hitler's view of his father, which is very different from the account given by Flood. *Mein Kampf* has Hitler revering his father as "a gentleman . . . whose most ardent desire had been to help his son forge his career, thus preserving him from his own bitter experience (which had been growing up poor and without direction)." After his mother passed away, when Adolf was 18, his father having died when he was 13, Adolf said that "I honored my father, but my mother I had loved."

Mein Kampf is a work consisting of two volumes. The first, "A Reckoning," describes the period of Hitler's life when his thoughts on politics and the German Fatherland were combined to form his tenet of National Socialism; the second, "The National Socialist Movement," expands many of the ideas presented in the first volume. Those ideas stemmed from feelings and experiences of a young ambitious Hitler trying to forge a way of life for himself other than his father's suggestion of becoming a civil servant. Hitler's first love was art, which was squelched by his nonacceptance into the academy (few thought as highly of Hitler's work as he). As a result, he turned his attention to architecture, but because of his intolerance for study at the Realschule, this also became an unfulfilled dream.

As his misfortune grew, he began making connections with other Austrian Germans, noting many shortcomings that he and they shared. He sensed a lack of pride toward the German heritage, not only from other Germans, but also from all with whom he came into contact, as though somehow Germans were second-rate. He felt misplaced along with many other Austrian Germans, as if they were removed from a righteous existence. He saw the prevalence of Social Democrats in positions of power, positions that undermined the dignity of the working class, keeping the masses in line, obedient, and helplessly stuck in positions of servitude.

Hitler learned to despise Jews because, in his viewpoint, they were the Social Democrats who made life miserable for Hitler and other Austrian Germans in the working class. Slowly, he began to notice that the most prominent members of the Social Democratic movement, the authors of the press, those who protested against restraints upon business, and those against whom he argued about the policies of marxism, the tool he directly related to Social Democracy, were all Jews. His greatest revelation in all of this was that these people were not of the Austrian nation or the German nation, but were foreigners who had come to take total control. They had no nation really. Even if a Jew had been born in Austria or Germany and was a citizen of either country, it made no difference to Hitler. His goal and the goal of all Germans would be to fight against the people whose purpose, according to Hitler, was the defilement of all humanity and destruction of all established cultures and nations. He reasoned that if the German nation was preserved and advanced by self-propagation, then that was upholding the work of nature and performing the will of God: "By defending myself against the Jew, I am fighting for the work of the Lord."

Not only did his experience in Vienna further sour his feelings toward Jews and marxism, he also saw other inadequacies that shifted him into a career in politics where his involvement with the National Socialist movement blossomed. In Austria, Hitler viewed parliament as a self-serving system that totally neglected the working masses. If a problem or need arose that could not be remedied by the governing body, there seemed to be no blame placed upon anyone from within. Hitler could not recognize good government in a bureaucracy that did nothing but advance its own idleness and satisfaction of the status quo. Hitler was further infuriated with how the parliament continued to maintain power by lulling the people into a status-quo satisfaction which, especially before times of election, seemed to ice any chance of change or revolution, which he desperately desired.

Upon his arrival in Austria in 1904, Hitler became involved in the Pan-Germanic movement. He idolized Georg von Schonerer and Dr. Karl Lueger, who both worked to save the German people from ruin and to destroy the Austrian state. However, the movement ultimately failed. According to Hitler, the movement lost all momentum because 1) the social problem had an unclear conception, 2) the tactics of trying to win support from within parliament had failed, and 3) the public lacked the will to see the revolution take place. Each of these elements brought the movement to a standstill. However, these elements would not be forgotten by Hitler, who saw each as direct opposition to what must happen in order for all German people to one day be reunited and prosper over all of Europe and ultimately the world.

Hitler returned to Munich shortly before the outbreak of World War I, which he called the happiest time in his life. He immediately requested in writing to be enlisted, and was given permission via King Ludwig III to don the tunic of the Bavarian regiment, in which he served for six years. This experience led Hitler to another key discovery in terms of his personal philosophy. Throughout the war Hitler noticed that propaganda was a tool keenly utilized by the enemy, who portrayed the Germans as fierce, bloodthirsty fighting machines—but not by his own government. He claimed this as one of the factors that led to Germany's hard loss. He saw propaganda, when properly utilized, as one of the most effective tools of war, a means by which the masses are uniformly persuaded: simple, true in essence, and proven in methodology and message. He stored what he learned from this failure for certain future use.

Because the fall of the Reich happened so quickly, the defeat was recognized and immediately put aside, which according to Hitler provided more time for the rebuilding mentality to rapidly set in and grow. Building upon the earlier aims of the failed pan-Germanic movement from his time in Austria, Hitler's focus became the full development of National Socialism, rallying a lost nation around the concept of strength through a united Germany. Within this goal was the operating premise that only those of pure German heritage were worthy of citizenry; all others were deemed expendable for the good of the nation.

> Any crossing between two beings of not quite the same high standard produces a medium between the standards of the parents. That means: the young one will probably be on a higher level than the racially lower parent, but not as high as the higher one . . . if it were different, every further development towards higher levels would stop, and rather the contrary would happen . . . just as little as Nature desires a mating between weaker individuals and stronger ones, far less she desires the mixing of a higher race with a lower one, as in this case her entire work of higher breeding, which has perhaps taken hundreds of thousands of years, would tumble at one blow . . . The result of any crossing, in brief, is always the following: (a) Lowering of the standard of the higher race; (b) Physical and mental regression, and, with it, the beginning of a slowly but steadily progressive lingering illness. To bring about such a development means nothing less than sinning against the will of the Eternal Creator.

In Germany, *Mein Kampf* was responsible for the banishment of the Bible. In 1942, Dr. Alfred Rosenberg, a key supporter of the "new national church," released a 30-point doctrine of the National Reich Church, which outlined the plan for all churches to be transformed into instruments of the state and for Christianity to be systematically eliminated from all facets of religious existence. Seven of the 30 points specifically refer to the banishment of the Bible, which is to be subsequently replaced by *Mein Kampf:*

> 13) The National Reich Church demands the immediate cessation of the printing of the Bible, as well as its dissemination, throughout the Reich and colonies. All Sunday papers with any religious content also shall be suppressed.
>
> 14) The National Reich Church shall see that the importation of the Bible and other religious works into Reich territory is made impossible.
>
> 15) The National Reich Church decrees that the most important document of all time—therefore the guiding document of the German people—is the book of our Fuehrer [sic], *Mein Kampf.* It recognizes that this book contains the principles of the purist ethnic morals under which the German people must live.
>
> 16) The National Reich Church will see to it that this book spread its active forces among the entire population and that all Germans live by it.
>
> 17) The National Reich Church stipulates that the future editions of *Mein Kampf* shall contain its present number of pages and contents unmodified.
>
> 18) The National Reich Church will remove from the altars of all churches the Bible, the cross and religious objects.
>
> 19) In their place will be set that which must be venerated by the German people and therefore is by God, our most saintly book, *Mein Kampf,* and to the left of this a sword.

Hitler's observations in youth came to represent the foundations of Nazi Germany. To him the Aryan, Hitler's master race, was the strong, powerful, and culturally creative prototype of an ideal human being, the building block for humanity that reverberated the philosophy of the National Socialist Party. Diversity among races was a liability, not an asset; one race must rise above all others and claim absolute control. Only when Germans stood alone as the elite rulers of the world would his vision be complete. Until then, Hitler would use any tactic and force to attain that position.

The years leading up to World War II saw the most intense scrutiny of *Mein Kampf,* due to the fact that much of the world by now was certain that the text was a blueprint for Hitler's plan of world domination. Otto D. Tolischus, reporting for the *New York Times Magazine,* stated, "In content *Mein Kampf* is ten percent autobiography, ninety percent dogma, and one hundred percent propaganda. Every word in it . . . has been included . . . solely for the propagandist effect. Judged by its success, it is the propagandistic masterpiece of the age." The "masterpiece" also contains representations of Hitler's values: He recognized the futility of a government that was too large to uphold account-ability and solve problems effectively; he identified one downfall of education as information taught yet never utilized while he promoted the Greek ideal of a balance between the development of mind and body as one; and he identified merit and strength in a nation bound by patriotism and the will to succeed.

CENSORSHIP HISTORY

Mein Kampf had many challenges from the time of its publication to the height of World War II and, again, in the 1990s. In *The Encyclopedia of Censorship*, *Mein Kampf* is identified as one of the "most often" censored books. But perhaps the most documented history comes courtesy of James and Patience Barnes's text, *Hitler's Mein Kampf in Britain and America*, which highlights not only the publication wars in the United States, but also key censorship cases that both directly and indirectly were brought on by *Mein Kampf.*

The first U.S. publication in this country was in 1933 by Houghton Mifflin in Boston; that version was published in London the same year by Hurst and Blackett. The titles were, respectively, *My Battle* and *My Struggle.* The translator for the text was Edgar T. S. Dugdale. The translation had a complicated history: In 1928 Curtis Brown Limited was given the translation rights from Eher Verlag, the German publisher. However, Cherry Kearton, a former Curtis Brown employee who shifted over to work for rival Hurst and Blackett, had left the text when he transferred companies, figuring that noth-ing would ever come of Hitler. When Hitler's chancellorship was announced, Kearton tried to obtain the copy of the text in hopes of beating out his former firm with the publication. However, Curtis Brown now demanded a hefty sum for just the untranslated text, a move that made the decision to purchase it more difficult. That was when Dugdale stepped in and offered his translated abridged version to Kearton and Hurst and Blackett gratis. They accepted and went ahead with publication.

The Dugdale abridgment had been approved by Eher Verlag, but further expurgation of the text was accomplished by the Nazi government before the approval was granted. (According to Barnes and Barnes, "during the 1930s it was generally assumed, officially and unofficially, that Hitler would not authorize a full translation of his autobiography.") Some of the most blatant features, thus, were censored in the expurgated text by the Nazi government in addition to omissions at the hands of the translator. These included Hit-ler's tirades to details of German and Austrian politics and Hitler's reactions to them, much of Hitler's discussion of Austria-Hungary in chapters 1–4, Hitler's anti-Semitic theme of race pollution (though there remained many anti-Jew sentiments, including semi-obscene allegations), the Aryan race as the bearer or perpetuator of higher culture, Hitler's detailed pseudoscientific views about population growth, the impact of syphilis on modern society, and menacing passages about France. The complete translated text was issued in 1939, one published in London and two competing versions in the United

States. The latter competition was resolved in favor of Houghton Mifflin by the U.S. Circuit Court of Appeals for the Second Circuit in October 1939.

The reactions to *Mein Kampf* in Britain and the United States varied. The British populace, facing a significant potential threat, did not respond with censorial protests. In the United States, within a month of Houghton Mifflin's contracting with Hitler's German publisher, groups and individuals organized protests in an effort to suppress the book's publication. In August 1933, the *American Hebrew and Jewish Tribune* attacked the publisher: "We charge these publishers with an attempt to cash in on the misery and catastrophe of an important segment of the human family." The *New York Times* on August 18, 1933, included a quote from an *American Hebrew and Jewish Tribune* editorial: "that if Houghton Mifflin Company is bent on publishing Hitler's book 'they would do well to print the text in red, as symbolic of the blood that has dripped from Nazi bludgeons in the Third Reich. . . .' " David Brown, publisher of the Jewish periodical, stated, "we protest emphatically against the publication, sale and distribution of the English translation of Hitler's *Mein Kampf* in the United States."

Letters from Jews were written to Houghton Mifflin "by the hundreds," to President Roosevelt, urging his intervention, and to publishers such as the *Chicago Israelite*. One stated: "It is the utterance of venomous untruths about a large law-abiding peoples and I was wondering if there was not some way to stop publication of this book." A group of New York City residents petitioned the board of education to discontinue purchasing books from Houghton Mifflin: "an American firm that knowingly lends its assistance in spreading the lying propaganda of a common gangster—propaganda that strikes at the very foundations of American institutions—should have no right to participate in the distribution of taxpayers' money." In rebuttal, Edward Mandel, associate superintendent of education, asserted that the text must be placed so all "may see whether the book is worthy or is an exhibition of ignorance, stupidity, and dullness." The American Jewish Committee acted to counteract the effect of *Mein Kampf* by issuing a translation of a collection of excerpts from the original German text that had not been included in the abridged volume: "The diluted and bowdlerized version of the book as issued did not represent either the views or the temperament of its author."

In response to the public outcry, Roger L. Scaife, an officer with Houghton Mifflin, stated:

> In confidence I may add that we have had no end of trouble over the book—protest from the Jews by the hundreds, and not all of them from the common run of shad. Such prominent citizens as Louis Kirstein and Samuel Untermeyer and others have added their protest, although I am glad to say that a number of intellectual Jews have also written complimenting us upon the stand we have taken.

The prepublication challenges did not succeed.

As domestic complaints were high in number, so, too, did the banning of *Mein Kampf* begin to happen more frequently on a global level. Three incidents occurred in the latter part of 1933. The first occurred in Prague, Czechoslovakia, on September 18, when Hitler's book was banned from sale or circulation because of its fierce militaristic doctrine, along with two other Austrian monarchist books of propaganda. The government was targeting not only Hitler, but also a number of other National Socialist publications.

The second incident happened not a week later in Munich, Germany, where it was reported that the one millionth copy of the book had been put into circulation. Part of that article stated that Hitler's response to the apparent crushing of the National Socialist movement at the time he was thrown into Landsberg prison for his involvement in the famous "putsch" of 1923 was, "Give me five years after I am out of this and I shall have the party restored."

The third event occurred on October 1, 1933, when the court at Katowice in Warsaw, Poland, banned Hitler's book for being "insulting." German booksellers had previously protested a court-ordered confiscation of the work, but the court upheld its prior decision. Hitler's response to the ban was that the Poles had not been sufficiently Germanized before the world war.

Three years later, and on the eve of World War II, the Soviets began to increase their armaments significantly, fearing that an attack from Germany was imminent. Premier Vyacheslav M. Molotov, speaking before the Congress of the Central Executive Committee, stressed that "Hitler, in *Mein Kampf*, states it is necessary for Germany to acquire new territory, and he points to Russia and the Baltic Region"; therefore, he urged that it was essential to make marked increases in the military budget. Whether the book was ever banned by the Soviets is not identified.

The sale of *Mein Kampf* was also prohibited in Austria until July 12, 1937. On that date Austria and Germany signed a "press truce," which permitted the sale of the autobiography under the condition that it could not be used for propaganda purposes.

In the post–World War II period the most recent translation of *Mein Kampf*, by Ralph Manheim, was readily available in the United States. A new edition was not available in Great Britain until 1965, although the American edition could be imported. In Germany there was a total ban of the autobiography, which was initially suppressed by American de-Nazification efforts but then continued by the Federal Republic (West Germany) for reasons of national self-interest. Indeed, the Bavarian state government as executor of all surviving Nazi property, sought to prohibit the sale of the book throughout the world. In this regard, in the 1960s, when the Hutchinson Publishing Group, the British copyright holder, decided to reissue a British edition, its chairman encountered resistance from the West German government, the Board of Deputies of British Jews, and most Jewish organizations on the grounds that *Mein Kampf* would promote anti-Semitism and play into the hands of postwar fascist organizations. Opposition was surmounted on legal grounds; it was published in 1969.

In the decade of the 1990s, and the first years of the millennium, the European scene has evidenced considerable state-censored activity, driven in part by hate speech legislation and concerns for human rights; the rise of neo-Nazi activity appears to be an additional catalyst. Under German law, books promoting Nazi philosophy are banned from public display or sale, *Mein Kampf* having been barred for close to 60 years. The state of Bavaria, which still owns the copyright, in agreement with the federal government of Germany, does not allow any copying or printing in German. (It opposes copying or printing in other countries, as well, but with less success.) Owning and buying the book is legal, as is trading in old copies, unless such activity promotes hatred or war. Most libraries in Germany hold excerpted versions with numerous comments. Unexpurgated editions are available only to academic researchers, the original being too contentious for open sale. The book has been available for purchase on the Internet; however, German authorities have urged Internet booksellers to cease this activity. In late 1999, both Barnes&Noble.com and amazon.com had agreed to stop selling *Mein Kampf* in Germany. Pressure had also been exerted on these companies by the Simon Wiesenthal Center in Los Angeles. In 2001, a German court decided not to prosecute Yahoo! Deutschland for offering a copy of *Mein Kampf* in an online auction, recognizing it was only a supplier of Internet services and not responsible for their content.

In the Czech Republic action was taken against a publisher and an Internet distributor. The government ordered police raids on bookstores to confiscate copies of new nonexpurgated editions—without annotations or Nazi disclaimers—of *Mein Kampf*, the first in more than 50 years, part of the publisher's Books That Changed the World project. Of the more than 100,000 copies of the book that were printed, 90,000 were sold before the confiscation raids. Protests by Jewish and German groups led to the government's decision; Czech criminal code bars the dissemination of "national, racial, social or religious hatred or publicly expressing sympathy for fascism or other similar movement." Charged with disseminating Nazi propaganda—the book was alleged to promote hate groups and racism—the publisher, Michael Zitko, was found guilty of promoting a movement that suppresses human rights by three successive courts. Upon appeal, however, the Czech Supreme Court in 2002 overturned these convictions, asserting that Zitko could not be prosecuted for promoting fascism or Nazism because these movements are extinct. In 2004, Zitko was reconvicted, this time for repressing human rights. Zitko vowed to appeal this decision to the Supreme Court and perhaps the European Court of Human Rights. Subsequently, the Czech supreme court overturned the conviction, ruling he had not aimed to propagate the book's racist ideas. In a parallel case, Vitko Varak, who offered *Mein Kampf* for sale on the Internet, was fined in 2001, having been convicted of supporting and spreading a movement aimed at repressing the rights and freedoms of others. Vitko refused to pay the fine.

Several other European countries, as well as Canada, have had new editions of *Mein Kampf* translated into their native languages. The sales of the autobiography have been generally high, amid protest from Jewish groups that have led to actions by authorities. In Hungary, retail sales were suspended in December 1996, followed by a 1997 ban, on the grounds of incitement of hatred against minorities and a violation of human rights. The suspension initiated a debate over protecting free speech versus limiting viewpoints some persons considered offensive. In 1999 it was still being sold by street and subway vendors, despite complaints by the Jewish community. Sales in Portugal were blocked in 1998 after intervention by the German embassy. The copyright issue was cited, Bavaria not having granted the right to distribute the book to the Portuguese publisher; 4,000 books had already been sold, a large number in Portugal. A 1997 ban on publication in Sweden was upheld by Sweden's Supreme Court in 1998 on the grounds it would infringe copyright. A 2000 edition of *Mein Kampf* had been banned in Bulgaria; however, a 2001 edition (200,000 print run) circumvented the ban and was being sold, despite protests. The situation in Canada had a different orientation. The CEO and chair of Chapters and Indigo bookstore, Heather Rusman, withdrew the copies of *Mein Kampf* from the shelves. Considering the autobiography "hate literature," she said: "With freedom of expression, the line is drawn on hate literature. It's a corporate decision. It's what we stand for." The banning seems to have had the effect of increasing sales of the book.

The Netherlands, however, has maintained the banning of *Mein Kampf*. As recently as November 2007, Hitler's memoir was reported to be the only book not fully available since the end of World War II. As the former basis of Nazi ideology, it is regarded as "inciting hatred of, amongst others, the Jews." Thus, it remains on the blacklist. The Dutch Minister of Education, Ronald Plasterk, wants to maintain this status; yet he acknowledged that making it available in bookstores would educate readers about the "horrifying events of World War II"; however, this personal attitude is not reason enough to make *Mein Kampf* fully available.

In the context of these contradictory positions, Geert Wilders, a member of Parliament and leader of the Freedom Party, argued that the Quran is "also a hate inciting book that ought to be banned . . . as encouraging violence against disaffected Muslims and also endorsing violence by Islamic extremists." This action would parallel the blacklisting of *Mein Kampf*.

In contrast, authorities in Poland decided in 1992 to lift the ban on printing *Mein Kampf*, its publication having been determined to be legal and not in violation of Communist-era laws against fascism. Before it was re-banned in 1992 on the grounds of "eulogizing Fascism," 20,000 copies had been sold out in days, in part a response to the protests against its publication. Comparably, in 1993, Romania's chief state attorney acted against President Ion Iliescu's request to ban the book on the ground that it spreads fascism, which is forbidden by the constitution. Sales had been barred in the city of Sibiu until prosecutors released the prohibition. In 2001, *Mein Kampf* was published legally in Bulgaria for the first time.

Today only one version of *Mein Kampf* is easily attainable in the United States. Copyrighted in 1971, published by Houghton Mifflin, and translated by Ralph Manheim, it represents the work of, as the translator labels Hitler, "a half-educated writer, without clear ideas, [who] generally feels that to say a thing only once is rather slight." He also states that Hitler's style attempts to come off as highly educated and cultured but is at best redundant and without an edge.

Controversy over the republication has ensued as a result of the proposal in 2005 of the Institute for Contemporary History, based in Munich, to publish an academic edition—authoritative, annotated with comprehensive footnotes—of *Mein Kampf*. The Bavarian state government, which took over the rights of the main Nazi publisher, Eher-Verlag, after World War II as part of the Allies' de-Nazification program, has rejected this proposed project. The copyright, however, runs out in 2015; the German copyright law provides that an author's work enters the public domain 70 years after his or her death.

The basis for the rejection by the Bavarian Finance Ministry, which controls the copyright, is to prevent the distribution of Nazi ideology and the belief that publication might promote right-wing extremism. In contrast, Horst Möler, director of the Institute for Contemporary History, argues that "an academic edition could break the peculiar myth which surrounds *Mein Kampf*." Such a publication is perceived as the "best defense against those who might want to use the book to advance racist or anti-Semitic agendas." Although many German Jews still oppose the reissuing of Hitler's memoir, in 2009 the general secretary of Germany's Central Council of Jews backed the proposal as a method of informing future generations of the evils of Nazism. The Bavarian Finance Ministry hopes to prevent publication beyond 2015 under laws against incitement of hatred. An interesting paradox: Courts might rule that forbidding publication after 2015 constitutes a breach of freedom of expression.

Hitler's memoir has been under a de facto publishing ban in Germany, but it is not actually banned. While possession is not illegal, resale of old copies is tightly regulated, essentially limited to research purposes.

FURTHER READING

Baetz, Juergen. "Historians Hope to Publish *Mein Kampf* in Germany." *Washington Post*, February 5, 2010.

Barnes, James J., and Patience P. Barnes. *Hitler's Mein Kampf in Britain and America: A Publishing History 1930–1939*. Cambridge: Cambridge University Press, 1980.

Cohen, Carl, ed. *Communism, Fascism, and Democracy*. 2nd ed. New York: Random House, 1972.

"Czechs Ban Hitler's Book." *New York Times*, September 19, 1933, p. 12.

Flood, Charles Bracelen. *Hitler: The Path to Power*. Boston: Houghton Mifflin, 1989.

Green, Jonathon, and Nicholas J. Karolides, reviser. *The Encyclopedia of Censorship, New Edition*. New York: Facts On File, 2005.

Haight, Anne Lyon, and Chandler B. Grannis. *Banned Books: 387 B.C. to 1978 A.D.* 4th ed. New York: R. R. Bowker, 1978.

"Hitler Book Is Banned as 'Insulting' in Poland." *New York Times*, October 1, 1933, sec. 4, p. 2.

"Millionth Copy of Book by Hitler Off the Press." *New York Times*, September 28, 1933, p. 16.

"Nazi State Church Plan Proposes to Oust Other Faiths and Ban Bible." *New York Times*, January 3, 1942, p. 1.

Newsletter on Intellectual Freedom. "Amsterdam, Netherlands" 56 (2007): 271; "Munich, Germany" 58 (2009): 155–156.

Paterson, Tony. "German Jews Want *Mein Kampf* Reprinted." *Independent*, 10 August 2009.

"Publisher Scored for Hitler's Book." *New York Times*, August 18, 1933, p. 16.

"Reich and Austria Reach Peace Truce." *New York Times*, July 13, 1937, p. 15.

Sabine, George H., and Thomas L. Thorson. *A History of Political Theory.* 4th ed. Hinsdale, Ill.: Dryden Press, 1973.

"Soviets to Increase All Arms, Fearing Reich and Japan." *New York Times*, January 11, 1936, p. 1.

Tolischus, Otto D. "The German Book of Destiny." *New York Times Magazine*, October 28, 1936, pp. 1–2, 23.

—Eric P. Schmidt
Updated by Nicholas J. Karolides

MY BROTHER SAM IS DEAD

Authors: James Lincoln Collier and Christopher Collier
Original date and place of publication: 1974, United States
Publisher: Four Winds Press
Literary form: Novel

SUMMARY

The action of *My Brother Sam Is Dead* centers on the Meekers, a Connecticut village family during and after the American Revolution. The Meeker family's loyalties are divided—as are those of the community, the father being a Tory but promoting a neutral stance, anxious to protect his family and his livelihood. The elder son, Sam, drops out from college to join the rebel forces, leaving young Tim, the narrator, uncertain about whom and what to support. The emotional tensions and battlefield violence cause Tim to reconsider his values and political position over the span of the novel, from 1775 to 1778.

Disputes in the family—politics and relationships—upset its dynamics. Sam desires acknowledgment of his decision to fight with the Patriots; his father rejects this and demands that Sam remove his uniform and return to college or not come home. Sam requests the use of the family's Brown Bess during the war, the family's only gun, and is denied. He steals it. When Tim questions his father's decision in another instance, Mr. Meeker insists on Tim's obedience.

Disputes between the Tories, the colonists loyal to the king, and the Patriots, those loyal to the Continental Congress and the war effort, increase enmity between them. The war comes to the family and the community. A rebel group enters their tavern home and demands their weapon; when they are told the family no longer has it, an officer whips the flat side of his sword across Mr. Meeker's face. In 1776, en route to a Hudson River community to sell cattle, Tim and his father are surrounded and threatened by hostile men with rebel sympathies who are probably cowboys—cattle thieves; they are rescued by a Loyalist Committee of Safety. Attacked again on the way home during a blizzard, Mr. Meeker is captured, although Tim, using a ruse, escapes. (Later, the family learns that Mr. Meeker died of cholera on, unaccountably, a British prisoner ship.) Tim takes on the management of the household and business affairs with his mother, seeing himself suddenly to have achieved adult status. The British enter the community in 1777, taking several prisoners, including a nine-year-old boy, shooting down a messenger, and laying siege to a building. They attack, killing those inside and beheading a slave; these actions, witnessed by Tim, affect him physically as well as intellectually.

Later that year, the Continentals return and establish an encampment. The culminating event, the arrest and trial of Sam Meeker, occurs. The thieves, who Sam and Tim had chased, accuse Sam of stealing his family's cows. The court-martial goes against him; he is condemned to death by firing squad. General Putnam is steadfast in his decision to use Sam's case as an example for his troops to prevent such pillaging and theft. Putnam denies Mrs. Meeker's and Tim's requests for clemency. Sam's innocence may not be clear to the court or the general—evidence was lacking—but it is clear to the reader.

Against this backdrop of rite of passage, this novel focuses on questions of freedom—the sons' freedom from the authority of their father and the colonists' political freedom from the British Crown. Loyalties, competing at personal and political levels, are fraught with tension and hostility. While the novel opens with an eager-to-fight Sam, imbued with patriotic zeal, admired by an envious Tim, an antiwar stance evolves. This may be deduced by Tim's doubts and eventual rejection and from such comments as these from Mrs. Meeker, a sympathetic character: "War turns men into beasts. It's cheaper to shoot a boy than to feed him" and "Bah, patriotism. Your patriotism has got my husband in prison and one of my children out there in the rain and muck shooting at people and likely to be dead at any minute, and my business half ruined. Go sell your patriotism elsewhere. I've had enough of it." The violent events solidify this impression.

CENSORSHIP HISTORY

James Lincoln Collier and Christopher Collier, a professor of history at the University of Connecticut and the Connecticut state historian, collaborated in the writing of eight historical novels, most of them set during the Revolutionary War. *My Brother Sam Is Dead* is the most often challenged; it ranks 12th on the American Library Association's (ALA) "The 100 Most Frequently Challenged Books of 1990–2000." It also placed seventh in the ALA's annual rankings of the top 10 challenged books of 1996 and on the comparable lists of People For the American Way, which ranked it 11th in 1995–96 and 10th in 1994–95. Acclaimed for its literary quality and historical accuracy, it was named a Newbery Honor Book, a Jane Adams Honor Book, and a finalist for a National Book Award, all in 1975.

The two most frequent arguments presented by challengers and occasionally successful censors, often in relation to age appropriateness for elementary school readers, were foul and vulgar or profane and inappropriate language and too much violence. Specific words objected to include *dammit, Jesus, damn you, bastard, hell, Goddamn,* and *son of a bitch.* The diversity of these challenges in terms of time and place is widespread, reported from 1983 through 2004 in a range of states, among them California, Georgia, Pennsylvania, Ohio, Kansas, and Colorado. Some typical assertions are the "persistent usage of profanity" as well as references to "rape, drinking, and battlefield violence"; "In our house we do not allow God's name to be used in vain. Since God has been removed from our schools, how can we now speak about God in a derogatory way?" This complaint drew this response: "The literary, political, social, and historical significance outweighed the thirty occurrences of offensive language." Another explained: "We are obviously concerned about the decay in the way we speak to one another and the way we express ourselves. What we're trying to say is that it's not OK." A review committee in Maine countered the language complaint by explaining that the book had "a very strong moral theme, of benefit to students that outweighs the infrequent negative language. . . . It matters that the uses of bad language occur in emotional and difficult times and are not part of the normal speech." The graphic violence complaints refer to but do not often identify the decapitation and the execution scenes. A few complaints object to references to drinking, rape, and antireligious sentiments. A minister's request to ban the book asserted, in addition to obscene language, that it presented "a negative approach to God. . . . This is not about censorship, and it's not about First Amendment rights"; he indicated it was a matter of taste and whether the schools should "endorse the use of profanity." A member of a Florida school board, an air force veteran who was shot down in Vietnam, defended the language as realistic—"portrayal of war included profanity." In 2009, this novel was challenged—because of a parent's concern about profanity—in Muscoggee County, Georgia; it was retained in all elementary school libraries.

Direct confrontation with the unorthodox presentation of this war is mostly avoided by challengers. Two examples reflect this concern: In Connecticut, a challenger accused the book of "inflammatory propaganda" and as being "an inaccurate depiction of the Revolutionary War." Another challenger objected to the portrayal of "Americans as barbaric, unfeeling and almost inhumane."

FURTHER READING

Attacks on Freedom to Learn, 1992, 1993, 1995. Washington, D.C.: People For the American Way, 1991–92, 1992–93, 1994–95.

Collier, Christopher, ed. *Brother Sam and All That: Historical Context and Literary Analysis of the Novels of James and Christopher Collier.* Orange, Conn.: Clearwater Press, 1999.

Doyle, Robert P. *Banned Books: 2001 Resource Guide.* Chicago: American Library Association, 2001.

"Muscogee County, Georgia." *Newsletter on Intellectual Freedom* 58, no. 3 (May 2009): p. 93.

1984

Author: George Orwell
Original date and places of publication: 1949, London and United States
Publishers: Secker and Warburg; Harcourt Brace Jovanovich
Literary form: Novel

SUMMARY

The period after World War II was one of great turmoil. Although the immediate danger was over, many feared that the Communist ideologies that had taken over the USSR and parts of eastern Europe would spread throughout the world, meaning an end to the democracy and capitalism under which the United States and many other countries flourished. The novel *1984* took these fears to their furthest point, projecting a future world that is entirely totalitarian and describing in-depth the problems of humanity in such a world.

Winston Smith lives in London on the landmass known as Airstrip One in the country Oceania. The 39-year-old man is sickly and balding with a bleeding, open sore on his ankle that never heals. Every day he must climb the seven floors to his apartment, for the elevator never works. His main subsistence is the stale bread and pasty stew with unidentifiable meat that he can get for lunch at work. In order to keep sane, he drinks a lot of Victory Gin, which makes his eyes water as it painfully slides down his throat, and smokes many Victory Cigarettes, which he must always remember to hold carefully so the tobacco does not fall out. He is constantly surrounded by the lies his government tells, forced to listen to them at all hours from the telescreens blaring away in every room. He is one of the few aware that what is heard are lies, for he works as a fact-changer at the Ministry of Truth, which is responsible for all publications, propaganda, and entertainment for Oceania.

> What happened in the unseen labyrinth to which the pneumatic tubes led, he did not know in detail, but he did know in general terms. As soon as all the corrections which happened to be necessary in any particular number of the *Times* had been assembled and collated, that number would be reprinted, the original copy destroyed, and the corrected copy placed on the files in its stead. This process of continuous alteration was applied not only to newspapers, but to books, periodicals, pamphlets, posters, leaflets, films, sound tracks, cartoons, photographs—to every kind of literature of documentation which might conceivably hold any political or ideological significance. Day by day and almost minute by minute the past was brought up to date. . . . In no case would it have been possible, once the deed was done, to prove that any falsification had taken place.

At the same time as history is being revised, statistics are being faked so they are in accordance with the image the Party wishes to project:

But actually, he thought as he readjusted the Ministry of Plenty's figures, it was not even forgery. It was merely the substitution of one piece of nonsense for another. . . . For example, the Ministry of Plenty's forecast had estimated the output of boots for the quarter at a hundred and forty-five million pairs. The actual output was given as sixty-two millions. Winston, however, in rewriting the forecast, marked the figure down to fifty-seven millions, so as to allow for the usual claim that the quota had been overfilled. In any case, sixty-two millions was no nearer the truth than fifty-seven millions, or than a hundred and forty-five millions. Very likely no boots had been produced at all. Likelier still, nobody knew how many had been produced, much less cared. All one knew was that every quarter astronomical numbers of boots were produced on paper, while perhaps half the population of Oceania went barefoot.

In addition to the faking of statistics, historical facts are changed. Besides Oceania, the only other countries in the world are Eastasia and Eurasia. If Oceania is at war with one of these, it has always been at war with it. So, when the country changes allies and begins warring with a different nation, all of the past newspaper articles detailing the war must be changed to fit into this new world order. Then every individual must change the past in his or her mind, known as doublethink, and forget that anything other than this new truth was ever known.

It is this kind of deception that has Winston questioning his entire upbringing. He has always been told that Big Brother, the leader of the Party, saved the country from the terrible oppression of the capitalists. But he looks around him at the lack of many necessities and substandard quality of others and wonders if it has always been this way. If the Party lies about war, could it not also lie about saving society?

He has decided to begin consciously fighting the Party and attempting to discover the truth by keeping a diary of his thoughts, most of which are against Big Brother. He is careful to point out, though, that his first act of defiance began long ago. When one thinks about defying Big Brother, he or she has already committed a crime against him, known as thoughtcrime, which in and of itself is punishable by death. For this reason, Winston thinks he may as well go as far as possible in his defiance because he is essentially already dead.

Some day the Thought Police will catch him and he will die. Every room has a telescreen that simultaneously broadcasts Party news and monitors whatever is happening in the room for the Thought Police. People he knows could turn him in to save themselves. He has already reconciled himself to the fact that he will be caught someday and has given up any hope for his future. But he wants to find out the truth before he is discovered.

Winston's journey to discover this truth while rebelling against the Party encompasses many levels. The first is his fascination with the past. Winston frequents an antique shop where many relics of the age of capitalism are present—things that have no real purpose other than beauty, such as a blown glass paperweight filled with coral. He purchases the paperweight and takes the opportunity to talk with the proprietor about the time before Big Brother took over. The man does not know much, but he gives some credence to Winston's idea that the world was better before the reign of Big Brother.

A second level of rebellion is sexual. The Party does not like people to bond in that way, fearing that they may love one another more than they love the Party, and has set up many antisex leagues to promote its view. Winston is approached one day by a beautiful young woman named Julia, who also works at the Ministry of Truth. After many difficult encounters where they attempt to hide from the telescreens, they agree to meet in a clearing in the woods. Here they are able to be free with one another and have sex for the first time. They do it because they have been told not to, and the more rebellious they are, the better they like it. After a few more such meetings Winston gets the proprietor of the antique store to rent them the furnished room above his shop. There they have many encounters, which are more than just sex, but a sharing of feelings and desires.

The third level is a more active form of rebellion against Big Brother. Julia and Winston decide to attempt to join the underground organization called the Brotherhood. Winston has always felt a special comradeship with a member of the Inner Party who works in his building, O'Brien. In the hall one day, O'Brien tells him how much he admires his work and to stop by his house for a new edition of the dictionary of Newspeak, the official language of Oceania. Winston and Julia take the chance that this is a secret message and arrive at O'Brien's house together in order to proclaim their hatred of Big Brother and their alliance with the Brotherhood. O'Brien, after questioning them, agrees to let them join and gets a copy of the book that details the truth about Big Brother and the formation of Oceania.

The book, entitled *The Theory and Practice of Oligarchical Collectivism*, was written by the man on whom most of the anger and hatred of the Party members is focused, Emmanuel Goldstein. It appears that years before he was a highly influential charter member of the Party, but as its views changed, he was eliminated and has now become the scapegoat for all of the problems of Oceania. During the Two Minutes Hate, a daily ceremony in which all members are required to participate, his face is constantly shown so it can be insulted. The book discusses the truth behind the three Party slogans—"Ignorance is Strength," "War is Peace," and "Freedom is Slavery." For instance, war is peace because the constant preparation for war allows the economy to remain steady by using up surplus goods. Although battles rarely take place, war is a socially acceptable excuse for constant rationing. It also keeps the citizens in the state of fear, which makes them believe they need the protection of the government.

After receiving the book and reading it, Julia and Winston are caught in their room above the antique shop. A picture falls down to reveal the telescreen, which has been monitoring them the whole time. Then the proprietor, who has removed his disguise, is seen in his true form, a member of the Thought Police. They are brought to the Ministry of Love and put in separate jail cells. After much physical torture and starvation, which is standard procedure for all criminals, Winston begins his special sessions with O'Brien, who, along with the Thought Police, had been monitoring Winston for seven years. During these sessions O'Brien uses a type of shock therapy to get Winston to realize the power of the Party and the futility of opposing it. Winston holds firm to his belief that the Party cannot take the truth from him, believing there are certain truths that cannot be controlled. For instance, he thinks that 2 + 2 = 4, and there is no other way to think. O'Brien, though, gets him to believe that 2 + 2 = 5, which proves the end of his resistance and final acceptance of everything the Party tells him.

After he is released from the Ministry of Love, Winston is a pitiful shell of what he once was. He does not really work anymore, but spends his time drinking at a café and playing chess with himself. He sees Julia once, but their desire to be together has been taken from them, and both accept the Party's truth. He knows one day, when he is not paying attention, he will be shot in the back of the head. But he believes that he has discovered the ultimate truth of Big Brother and has been saved, so he is ready. The final lines of the novel show his ultimate acceptance of that which he vehemently denied his entire life.

> He gazed up at the enormous face. Forty years it had taken him to learn what kind of smile was hidden beneath the dark mustache. O cruel, needless misunderstanding! O stubborn, self-willed exile from the loving breast! Two ginger-scented tears trickled down the sides of his nose. But it was all right, everything was all right, the struggle was finished. He had won the victory over himself. He loved Big Brother.

CENSORSHIP HISTORY

Many attempts have been made to rid school libraries of *1984* in the nearly 50 years since its publication. In his introduction to *Celebrating Censored Books*, Lee Burress identified the 30 most frequently challenged books from a compilation of data from six national surveys of censorship pressures on American schools (1965–82); *1984* ranked fifth. This was especially true in the 1960s and 1970s when the nation was gripped by fear over the possibility of nuclear war with the Soviet Union, whose mere existence as a successful communist country threatened the United States and its democratic ideals. As such, the novel was frequently called into question.

More often than not, though, these claims surround the immorality and profanity of the novel. The sexual explicitness was often called inappropriate for adolescents or for any age group. Some did object to the study of the book because of its communistic ties. In the Lee Burress study of censorship in Wisconsin schools conducted in 1963, the John Birch Society is cited as objecting to the book for its "study of communism." A 1966 national survey completed by Burress, which does not cite specific names or places, identifies a principal who thought the novel "shows communism in a favorable light." A parent on the same survey complained that the "socialistic state shows utopia which is wrong." While in the latter case the request was denied, the principal's objection prevented the book from being purchased.

In a case cited in Jack Nelson and Gene Roberts's *The Censors and the Schools*, a teacher in Wrenshall, Minnesota, refused to remove *1984* from his reading list, leading to his dismissal. He was reinstated, though, after arguments "that the book 'illustrates what happens in a totalitarian society.'"

Nelson and Roberts also discuss the censoring of *1984* as a consequence of the "textbook battles" of the 1960s in Texas. Ten novels were removed from the libraries of the four Amarillo high schools and Amarillo College, including MacKinlay Kantor's *Andersonville*, Aldous Huxley's *Brave New World*, John Steinbeck's *The Grapes of Wrath*, and Oliver La Farge's *Laughing Boy*. According to Nelson and Roberts, most objections were raised because of obscenities in the novels, but some charges were due to the books' "political ideas or because the authors had once belonged to groups cited by the House Un-American Activities Committee."

As late as 1981, similar complaints were still being lodged. A Baptist minister in Sneads, Florida, Rev. Len Coley, attempted to have the book banned from school use on numerous occasions, often claiming the support of other church groups that later denied involvement. He said it was procommunist and contained explicit sexual material. As cited in the *Newsletter on Intellectual Freedom*, though, on January 13, 1981, the Jackson County school board voted unanimously to retain the novel as a "parallel reading text in a course on 'anti-communism' offered at Sneads High School."

However, many objections to the novel end with its removal from the classroom or the library or with it not being purchased. The continual objections to the novel are well evidenced by the fact that in a national survey completed by Burress in 1966, although the book was already considered a classic by many critics, it was present in only 43 percent of school libraries.

George Orwell's *Animal Farm*, subtitled *A Fairy Story*, has also endured many censorship challenges over the years, both national and international. Several studies reveal the frequency of these national objections. A Wisconsin survey in 1963 revealed that the John Birch Society requested its being withdrawn from classroom use, objecting to the phrase, "masses will revolt." A 1968 study of New York State English classrooms, conducted by the New York State English Council, based on 160 returns, identified *Animal Farm* as high on its list of "problem novels"; the reason cited was that Orwell was a communist. A comparable survey of censorship challenges in the schools, conducted in De Kalb County, Georgia, in 1982 for the period 1979 to 1982, revealed that *Animal Farm* had been objected to for its political theories. Also, *Animal Farm* was one of 64 literary books banned from classroom teaching at Bay and Mosely High Schools in Panama City, Florida, on May 7, 1987. (See the discussion of *I Am the Cheese*, by Robert Cormier, for details.) Internationally, the suppression of Animal Farm has occurred in disparate venues: the 1977 Moscow International Book Fair, the 1986 production of the Theatre of Nations Festival in the United States and a 1991 production in Kenya, and in the United Arab Emirates in 2002. All of these bans indicated political challenges, except the last, which was based on the book's supposed defiance of Islamic and Arab values—pictures and text depicting alcoholic drinks, pigs, and other "indecent images."

George Orwell's "fairy story" does have a conscious political orientation. Orwell, as quoted by C. M. Wodehouse in the preface (dated August 6, 1954) to the Signet Classics 29th edition, wrote, "Every line of serious work that I have written since 1936 has been written, directly or indirectly, against totalitarianism. . . . *Animal Farm* was the first book in which I tried, with full consciousness . . . , to fuse political purpose with artistic purposes into one whole."

FURTHER READING

Burress, Lee. *Battle of the Books: Literary Censorship in the Public Schools, 1950–1985.* Metuchen, N.J.: Scarecrow Press, 1989.
———. *Censorship Report.* Unpublished: 1966.
———. "The Pressure of Censorship on Wisconsin Public Schools." *Wisconsin English Journal* 6 (October 1963): 6–28.
Karolides, Nicholas J., and Lee Burress, eds. *Celebrating Censored Books.* Racine: Wisconsin Council of Teachers of English, 1985.
Nelson, Jack, and Gene Roberts, Jr. *The Censors and the Schools.* Boston: Little, Brown, 1963.
Newsletter on Intellectual Freedom 30 (1981): 73.

—Jane Graves

NOVEL WITHOUT A NAME

Author: Duong Thu Huong
Original date and place of publication: 1995, United States
Publisher: William Morrow and Company
Literary form: Novel

SUMMARY

Quan, a captain in the Vietcong who is fighting to evict the Americans from Vietnam and to defeat South Vietnamese forces, is the narrator-protagonist of *Novel Without a Name.* He was mobilized at age 18 from a northern village amid exuberant patriotic festivities. Now in 1975, 10 years later, Quan, despairing and increasingly cynical, recounts events and feelings of his present life against a backdrop of poignant recollections of his past and responses to the undesecrated environment amid the bombed ruins.

The war seems endless. One battle drags into another, some of them ending in victories, others in retreats. The battles themselves are not particularly represented; the after-effects tell the story.

> Every night, through a twilight swirling with ash, smoke, and dust, we dragged the corpses of our comrades away from the battlefield, from an earth soaked in blood, strewn with human flesh—that of the day's combat, the putrid shreds of the previous day, the rotting debris of a whole week shrouded in fog. No words will ever be able to describe the stench. . . . Cries dripping with blood and flesh. Caked in dried blood and sweat, we dragged our rifles and our dead on our backs. Some bodies were intact, some truncated, missing a head or a leg, others had their stomachs ripped open, their intestines dangling. The blood of our comrades mingled with our sweat and soaked into our clothes. We marched, stunned by

exhaustion and despair. We threw our last remaining energy into each retreat, not in the hope of saving our lives, but with the feverish desire to participate in the next day's butchery. We wanted to live so that in twenty-four or forty-eight or seventy-two hours we could spit fire on the enemy, watch the bodies tumble, the blood spurt forth, the brains shatter . . . to redress the balance.

At the end of the novel, the Vietcong momentum carries through to swift victory. Quan's company, however, has been decimated: Only 12 veterans are alive to participate in the celebration, 142 of the original group having been killed.

The effects of the war are visited upon individuals and groups, soldiers and the general populace. Aside from the deaths and wounds, there is rampant illness. Quan fights bouts of malaria. Once, when his company is ordered into battle, a third of them are stricken with malaria, but their order to march is maintained; that night "the company advanced single-file, a fierce, icy wind at our backs. Two able-bodied combatants carried each of the sick men and the weapons." While en route across the country, on a mission to rescue a childhood companion who is reported to have gone mad, Quan meets a soldier who has been suffering from dysentery for four years and seven months. Hunger and destruction are ubiquitous on his journey:

> At the front we had often been tortured by a hunger that blanched men's stares, that melted their bones. Sometimes the supply division would suddenly shower us with food. But here, behind the lines, people lived with a kind of hunger that raged without cease-fire, that went on and on: the hunger for protein.

Half-starved villagers eat manioc (cassava, source of tapioca) so the troops can have rice. Quan, on his mission, is insistently offered food despite meager rations and the hungry bellies of children. He is given refuge in makeshift bunkers during bombardments.

Behind the lines he begins to acknowledge another kind of brutality among the Vietcong forces and officials toward their own people. Quan finds his friend, Bien, not mad but pretending successfully to be so by throwing himself onto and rolling on barbed wire and banging his head against nails in a wall. Bien, a powerful yet gentle man, can no longer endure the carnage of war. He is kept locked up in a small shack with only a small peephole in his own excrement; he had not been allowed to bathe for two months. Bien is emotionally scarred by the war and its patriotic requisites as well; offered the opportunity by Quan to be discharged to return to the village's normal life, he cannot face the humiliation of returning without honor: "He dreamed of returning to the village, of decorating his obscure, colorless life with trophies of victory."

Another kind of brutality becomes evident. Quan, after his rescue mission, returns to his village on leave for the first time since he was mobilized. He discovers that his sweetheart, Hoa, to whom he had pledged himself, had been doubly violated: "Last year, the village Party committee drafted her. Poor girl. By the end of the year, she was pregnant. No one wanted to claim the child. She refused to denounce the father. Shamed, her parents threw her out." When Quan goes to her, their loneliness and anguish over lost years and lost love overwhelm them. However, Quan's bitterness and alienation seem to take over as he admits that the "beautiful dream that once bound us to each other had died."

These personal and global brutalities are experienced through the veil of patriotism and the rhetoric of marxism. Ten years later, Quan is haunted by his day of mobilization—the red flags in the courtyard, the beautiful girls singing, the slogans on the wall—"LONG LIVE THE NEW COMBATANTS FOR OUR COUNTRY!"—"THE YOUNG PEOPLE OF DONG TIEN VILLAGE UPHOLD ANCESTRAL TRADITION!"—"LONG LIVE INVINCIBLE MARXISM-LENINISM!"—and his own sense of "marching toward a glorious future." The war is perceived not merely as "against foreign aggression" but also as a "chance for a resurrection. . . . [O]ur country would become humanity's paradise. Our people would hold a rank apart. At last we would be respected, honored, revered." Armed with the "dialectical materialism of Marxist thought," the Vietcong victory would be more than success of a tiny country against the imperialists. It would be a victory for marxism—to build communism on earth, to realize the dream of a paradise for humankind.

These memories are tainted with irony, recalled as they are in moments of despair, jarred as they are by the reality of mud and carnage: "The blood and filth had filed words down, gnawed through them just as they had rotted through the soles of our soldier's shoes. I had my dose of glory and adulation."

Quan's doubts may have been initiated by coincidence when he had read an old issue of the Communist Party daily; it was celebrating the glorious victories during the Tet Offensive:

> We had been there. I had buried with my own hands countless numbers of my companions, had dragged away from the line of fire little Hoang's corpse, one of the many angels lost in the war. All he had left was one arm, one leg, and a diary filled with gilded dreams.

Quan frequently mentions the deaths of gentle and intellectual youths, including his younger brother, and the agony of mothers over their lost sons.

The questioning deepens as the Communist Party officials are implicated. Bien's father is derisive about the local village secretary:

> Before, out of every ten of them you could find at least seven who were honest, civilized. Even during the worst intrigues, at least they feared public disgrace. Now the ones who hold the reins are all ignoramuses who never even learned the most basic morals. They study their Marxism-Leninism, and then come and pillage our vegetable gardens and rice fields with Marx's blessing. In the name of class struggle, they seduce other men's women.

He continues his diatribe in the safety of an isolated field.

And no one dares say it. Even I don't, and I'm the most rebellious person in the village. I brought you out here to speak freely. For so long, it's just been misery, suffering, and more suffering. How many have died since the great De Tham, Phan, and Nguyen Thai Hoc—how many lives were sacrificed to gain independence? The colonialists had only just left Vietnamese soil and these little yellow despots already had a foothold!

An overheard conversation in a train compartment further unsettles Quan. A pair of elitist, middle-aged Party functionaries, having usurped seats from sleeping soldiers, reveal hypocritical cynicism and corruption about the ideals and doctrines of the revolution. One of them is arrogant about the use of power to subdue the people to Party purposes.

All you need to do is mount a podium perched above a sea of rippling banners. Bayonets sparkling around you. Cannons booming. Now that's the ultimate pleasure: the gratification of power. Money. Love. Why, next to it, they're nothing. So we need a religion. . . . We demolished the temples and emptied the pagodas so we could hang up portraits of Marx, enthrone a new divinity for the masses. Remember the army's ideological rectification campaigns? With the cadres from 1952 to 1953? Were those really any different from confessions in church? We invented sins. We tortured ourselves. We repented in exchange for a pure soul, hoping it would bring us one step closer to the Supreme Being. Today, it's the same story.

Karl Marx is slandered:

Obviously, a great man can't be judged on the basis of his private life. But just for a laugh, do you know what kind of a man Karl Marx was in real life? Well, he was a debauched little dwarf. As a student, he hung out in brothels. He particularly liked gypsy girls. As for his mature years, everybody knows that he got his own maid pregnant. It was only when he died that his wife Jenny forgave him and adopted the bastard kid. Ha ha ha ha!

The final "truth" is revealed to Quan by one of his soldiers who points out after he is reprimanded for destroying medicine containers and television sets—the people's property—in a South Vietnam warehouse that "the people, that's my mother, my father, your parents, the soldiers . . . will [never] get a crumb." He illustrates from a personal experience that money collected for charity was confiscated by officials for personal use.

Weary in body and spirit as the war draws to a close, old before his time, Quan realizes he has lost everything. He feels "barren, emptied, beaten." His dreams are shadowed by Hoa's youthful image, the memory of his brother's birth and his bright talent and a warrior ancestor. This ancestor, a wraith, speaks to Quan of "triumphal arches"; Quan curses him in response. The dream closes with Quan remarking, "My poor ancestors. Wretched architects of glory."

In discussing the future with his deputy, who is worried about what they will do, he tells him, "You think too much! Try to concentrate on your nerves and muscles instead so you can get out of this war alive. After that, we'll see about the rest." At the victory celebration, having noted that "glory only lasts so long," he responds to the question "What happens afterward" by saying, "How do I know? We're all in the same herd of sheep." He hears nothing more of their conversation, only the sounds of: a mournful chant, "rising from the fields, from the solitude of the countryside."

CENSORSHIP HISTORY

For 10 years, starting at age 21, Duong Thu Huong led a Communist Youth Brigade unit at the front during the Vietnam War, living in tunnels and underground shelters alongside regular North Vietnamese troops. She was part of a theatrical troupe, responsible for arranging performances to entertain soldiers and people in bombed-out areas. Their purpose: to enhance morale. She was one of three survivors of a unit of 40 men and women.

After decades of activism with the Vietnamese Communist Party, Duong became disillusioned; in the 1980s she wrote and spoke about the political and spiritual chaos of Vietnam, for the most part at official Party and Writers' Union Congress functions or in interviews with official Party literary magazines. The first censorship and banning of Duong's books occurred in the early 1980s. In 1982 she publicly protested, at the Third Congress of the Writers' Union, the censorship of a screenplay. Between 1982 and 1985, a party banning order ensured that none of her work was published. A documentary she had independently produced during 1985–87, *A Sanctuary for the Despairing*, about the inhumane conditions in a camp for 600–700 "mentally ill" war veterans, was destroyed by security police under orders of party secretary Nguyen Van Linh. In 1988, *Paradise of the Blind*, Duong's third novel, was denounced by Nguyen, who issued a second banning order. In 1990 *Novel Without a Name* was sent to France and the United States since publication was forbidden in Vietnam; the third banning order identified this novel. None of her recent novels or screenplays, including *Memories of a Pure Spring* (1996) and *No Man's Land* (1999), has been published in Vietnam.

An advocate of democratic reform, specifically supporting multiparty politics, Duong in July 1989 was expelled from the Communist Party (party officials say she resigned), accused of espousing heresies about democracy and human rights. On April 13, 1991, she was arrested and imprisoned without trial. She was charged with having contacts with "reactionary" foreign organizations and with having smuggled "secret documents" out of the country. Duong responded to these charges by asserting that she was expelled from the Party because of her dissident views; the "secret documents" were her writings, including the manuscript of *Novel Without a Name*. She was held in prison for seven months, first in a compound outside Hanoi and then in a prison. She described her cell as having "no windows—only a door with a hole for me to look out of." She was not done any physical harm, but she lost nearly 35 pounds because of inedible prison food. She commented: "They wanted to know if I had communications with anybody who was dangerous—foreigners or overseas Vietnamese. It was all a pretext to harass me, to frighten me." She was released in November 1991.

In 2002, having published one of her controversial articles in a Vietnamese newspaper in Australia and another, "The Flap of Raven Flock" (*"Tung Vo Canh Cua Bay Qua Den"*) in the *Saigon Times*, she was identified as a "national traitor," a "woman ungrateful for what Vietnamese martyrs have done for the country's liberty." In the cited articles, she expresses Vietnam's past as "the ill-fated history of a humble nation in which any brave soldier can become a dim-witted and cowardly citizen . . . and authority in Vietnam lies in the barrel of a gun held by right-wing extremists and village bullies."

An alternative interpretation of the banning of Duong's works indicates that they are not formally banned except in effect: "Government-controlled publishing houses will not reprint the popular old works, nor will they publish her new works." Her books, among the most beloved works in modern Vietnamese literature, are difficult to obtain. A bookseller in Hanoi said, "We all love her novels, but we cannot have them on our shelves."

During a 2005 visit to France—only the second time that she has been allowed to travel to Europe—Duong asserted that her priority is to denounce the Hanoi government as irremediably corrupt and abusive. "It is my mission to do so on behalf of those who have died under this shameful regime. . . . I have to empty what is inside me to keep my conscience clear. The people have lost the power to react, to reflect, to think. Perhaps I will give people courage." Duong has been living in exile in France since 2006, but she has not chosen—nor sought—political asylum.

Duong Thu Huong was nominated for the 1991 Prix Femina Étranger. On December 13, 1994, she was awarded the French chevalier order of arts and letters. The Vietnamese government in Hanoi expressed unhappiness over this "deplorable action"; the incident caused a rift—*un coup de froid*—between the two countries. France was accused of "a new form of colonialism" for giving an award to a dissident Vietnamese writer.

FURTHER READING

Klepp, Lawrence. "In Dubious Battle." *Far East* (April 4, 1994): 37.

McPherson, Nina. "A Note about the Author." In *Paradise of the Blind*, by Duong Thu Huong. New York: William Morrow, 1993, pp. 268–70.

Proffitt, Nicholas. "The Mission of Comrade Quan." *New York Times Book Review*, February 12, 1995, pp. 13–14.

Riding, Alan. "Vietnamese Writer Won't Be Silenced!" *New York Times*, Jully 11, 2005.

Shenon, Philip. "In This Author's Book, Villains Are Vietnamese." *New York Times International*, April 12, 1994, p. A43.

THE PRINCE *(IL PRINCIPE)*

Author: Niccolò Machiavelli
Original dates and places of publication: 1532, Italy; 1640, England
Publishers: Antonio Blado; R. Bishop
Literary form: Nonfiction

SUMMARY

Dedicated to Lorenzo de' Medici (though initially to Giuliano de' Medici, his uncle, who died in 1516), *The Prince*, or *Il Principe*, was written in 1513–14, against a backdrop of 16th-century Italian intrigue, strife, and political upheaval. Machiavelli had been a casualty of this upheaval when the republican government of Florence in which he had been a civil servant, chiefly in the diplomatic corps, fell and the Medici family returned to power. (Three generations of Medicis had ruled prior to the formation of the republican government in 1494.)

Machiavelli's purpose in this treatise on politics, at least on the surface, is to offer advice on successful governance, including gaining and maintaining control of territories. Ultimately, he wanted a "strong state, capable of imposing its authority on a hopelessly divided Italy" and the expulsion of foreign powers. Underlying his analysis is a basic tenet: "the real truth of things rather than an imaginary view of them," favoring political realism and rejecting idealist views of human behavior, including rulers and the ruled, with regard to political practice and response. In this context of politics, Machiavelli subordinated morals to political expediency.

Having minimized the problems of princes of hereditary states in maintaining control of their territory—"it is simply a matter of not upsetting ancient customs, and of adjusting them instead to meet new circumstances," for the people have grown accustomed to their prince's family—Machiavelli turns his attention to the greater difficulties of "mixed principalities," that is, a new territory grafted onto the old states, and of new states. These difficulties increase when the language, customs, and laws of the new possession differ from those of the conquering prince.

One of the chief difficulties is the conquered, some of whom may have welcomed the opportunity to change masters but are fickle in their friendship when they discover that their expectations of bettering their lives have not been borne out. Additionally, those who have been harmed in the power seizure become enemies. Machiavelli recommends extinguishing the family line of the previous prince but maintaining the old way of life and customs, laws and taxes, thus earning the good will of the people, so as to incorporate the new territory into the old in the shortest possible time.

For new possessions, Machiavelli recommends that the new prince go to the new territory to live; troubles may be spotted and dealt with before they expand. Another tactic is to establish colonies rather than maintain any army because fewer are hurt and they are poor and scattered.

> All the others remain untouched, which is a persuasion to keep quiet; yet they also become fearful of making a mistake and suffering like those who have already been despoiled. . . . And in this connection it should be re-marked that men ought either to be caressed or destroyed, since they will seek revenge for minor hurts but will not be able to revenge major ones. Any harm you do to a man should be done in such a way that you need not fear his revenge.

Further, the conqueror should become the protector of his weak neigh-bors, should act to weaken his strong neighbors, and should fight an invad-ing force of a powerful foreigner. In this vein, Machiavelli asserts, using the Romans as his example, that war should not be avoided: ". . . wars don't just go away, they are only postponed to another's advantage." A critical error in this regard is to allow or assist another state to become powerful. "From this we can draw a general rule, which never fails or only rarely: the man who makes another powerful ruins himself."

Machiavelli distinguishes between those princes who acquire territories through chance or good fortune and those who acquire territories through their own arms and energy. While the latter may endure more problems in gaining and securing power, they will more easily hold power because of the strength of character they exhibited. "Such men meet with great difficulties in their rise to power; all their dangers are on the way up, and must be over-come by their talents (*virtù*) but once they are on top, once they are held in veneration, and have destroyed all their envious rivals, they remain powerful, secure, honored, and happy." In contrast, men who achieve new states with other people's arms and by good luck are at a loss because they are dependent on the goodwill and good fortune of those who elevated them. They cannot command because they lack capability and do not have their own loyal troops unless they corrupt them.

Cesare Borgia exemplifies one who became established through the power of his natural father, Pope Alexander VI, and his troops. However, Cesare, a man of shrewdness and ambition, solidified his position by attacking neigh-boring cities. Having taken control of the Romagna and realizing the people had been plundered by their former masters and had become lawless, he cre-ated peace and obedience by establishing good government based on absolute authority and cruelty. When his ends were achieved, he caused his agent, the man held responsible for the excessive harshness, to be publicly and savagely murdered, thus removing the onus of blame from himself. Machiavelli does not condemn Cesare but offers him as a model for those who rise to power through the fortune and arms of others.

While he credits their courage and their ability to overcome adversity, Machiavelli does not acknowledge as excellent those who come to power by crime. It is a factor neither of fortune nor of virtue to "murder his fellow citizens, betray his friends, to be devoid of truth, pity, or religion."

In discussing empowerment to rule in a civil princedom, Machiavelli identifies two forces: the nobles, who desire to command and oppress the people, and the people, who desire not to be dominated and oppressed. Becoming a prince with the help of the nobles is more difficult than with the help of the people. The nobles claim equality, so he cannot command or manage them; also, the nobles are apt to be self-interested and independent and, thus, not dependable in times of adversity. If the people have selected him, the prince needs only take them under his protection and provide benefits for them; he should do this even if they did not select him in order to gain their support and obligation. This is all the more important when it is recognized that a prince cannot make himself safe against a hostile people; there are too many of them. He can, however, safeguard against hostile nobles who are few. "And because men, when they receive benefits from a prince whom they expected to harm them, are especially obligated to him, such a prince's subjects may feel more warmly toward him than if he had risen to power with their help."

Several chapters focus on character and behavior attributes of princes that lead to praise or blame. In introducing these, Machiavelli identifies basic generalizations: "I know everyone will agree that among these many qualities a prince certainly ought to have all those that are considered good. But since it is impossible to have and exercise them all, because the conditions of human life simply do not allow it, a prince must be shrewd enough to avoid the public disgrace of those vices that would lose him his state." These also reveal a practical imperative: success of the enterprise.

Machiavelli compares several key virtues and vices. Among these are generosity and stinginess; he opts for the latter because by being stingy a prince can save his resources to support the defense of his state and to engage in wars and ventures without taxing his people. Generosity is not recognized unless it is so ostentatious as to deplete his funds, causing him to raise money through taxes. Princes can afford to be generous with what belongs to strangers.

While being thought merciful is preferable, princes will find cruelty advantageous. Cesare Borgia used cruelty to unify, to restore order and obedience. Cruelty can also compel loyalty and respect, particularly among soldiers. However, such behavior should be tempered with humanity to avoid being hated. For a prince to be feared is more advantageous than to be loved. Men—"ungrateful, fickle, liars and deceivers, fearful of danger and greedy for gain"—don't worry about offending a man who makes himself loved when it is to their advantage; fear, however, involves dread of punishment from which there is no escape. To avoid being hated, though feared, a prince should refrain from taking the property of his subjects and citizens and from taking their women. "Cruelty is badly used when it is infrequent at first, but increases with time instead of diminishing."

Comparably, Machiavelli argues that a crafty, cunning, manipulative prince is more successful than one who keeps his word. A prince needs to be flexible in this regard to suit his interests. He cites Pope Alexander VI as a master at such deception; while appearing virtuous, convincing in his assertions and solemn in his oaths and using these characteristics, when possible, he was ready for the contrary when the situation warranted. Men judge by appearances. The prince's task is to "win victories and uphold his state."

By avoiding contempt and hatred, by demonstrating in his actions that he isn't fickle or frivolous, that he is courageous, sober and strong, the prince will be highly esteemed. This respect and the goodwill of his people whom he keeps satisfied will avert internal subversion against which the prince must be on guard. Conspirators will not act against him if they know the people will be outraged and will not support them. The prince must also be on guard against foreign powers. This defense is secured by good weapons and good friends; "if he has good weapons, he will never lack for good friends."

The Prince concludes with an impassioned "exhortation to restore Italy to liberty and free her from barbarians," a plea seemingly connected to his dedication. The times are propitious; the country is ready to be released from "cruel insolence of the barbarians." He calls particularly on the House of the Medici to raise a citizen army to disperse and defeat the invaders.

Machiavelli's name has become synonymous with unscrupulous political behavior. He has been identified as an agent of Satan and charged with "deliberately advocating evil." Segments quoted out of context, as exemplified by the Gentillet publication (see Censorship History), effectively illustrate Machiavelli's iniquity. Such interpretations still obtain, as exemplified by the opinion of Leo Strauss: "If it is true that only an evil man will stoop to teach maxims of public and private gangsterism, we are forced to say that Machiavelli was an evil man."

A more modern interpretation focuses on Machiavelli's intent to express the reality of political action based on analysis of history in contrast to the ideal behavior. J. R. Hale infers that Machiavelli "was concerned only with *il vero*, the true picture of what actually happened, and that he only talked about politics in terms directly deduced from the way in which men had behaved and did behave." An extension of this position, as identified by numerous critics, is Machiavelli's low esteem of men, evident in *The Prince* in his derisive language and attitude describing the populace, the nobles, and the rulers themselves.

Robert M. Adams relates a 180-degree variation in the 20th century, which is, "tradition [which] has emphasized the idealistic, enthusiastic, patriotic, and democratically minded Machiavelli." In this context he acclaims Machiavelli as "a great moral conscience"; "he resurrects . . . the undying worm of man's bad conscience at pretending to rule his fellow men."

CENSORSHIP HISTORY

Despite Antonio Blado having received permission from Pope Clement VII (Giulio de' Medici) to publish Machiavelli's writing, in 1559 all of Machiavelli's works were placed on the Index librorum prohibitorum, the Roman

Index of Paul IV, in the "banned absolutely" category. Compiled by the Holy Inquisition in Rome at the urging of Pope Paul IV (described as "implacably anti-heretical"), the Index forbade Catholics to read the works, including *The Prince*, or even own copies. The prohibition resulted from the Council of Trent, meeting from 1545 to 1563 in order to strengthen the discipline of the Roman Catholic Church against Protestantism. Pope Paul IV, a lifelong inquisitor and mortal enemy of heresy, widened the scope of the Index to include, beyond heresy, morality and manners in general. This was the first appearance of Machiavelli on an Index list.

This censorship system was finally abandoned in 1966; the last Index, that of Leo XIII, had been published in 1881 with supplements in 1884, 1896, and 1900. Books previously banned but published prior to 1600 were removed from the Index, "although," as noted in the *Encyclopedia of Censorship*, "they are to be considered as much condemned today as they ever were."

The 1572 massacre of some 50,000 French Huguenots by Catholic leaders, known as the Saint Bartholomew's Day Massacre becasue it began on Saint Bartholomew's night and extended for several weeks, was blamed on Machiavelli by the Protestants. This was because Catherine de' Medici, the queen mother and power behind the throne of her 22-year-old son, was a reader of Machiavelli; she was hated as an Italian and a Medici and as a secret and treacherous person. The irony of the accusation against Machiavelli is that the Catholics were at this time forbidden to read him.

In 1576, a French Huguenot, Innocent Gentillet, published (in French) *A discourse on the meanes of evel governing and maintaining in good peace, a kingdome, or other principalitie: Divided into three parts, namely, the counsele, the religion, and the policie, which a prince ought to hold and follow. Against Nicholas Machiavelli, the Florentine*. It was translated and published in English in 1602. Gentillet, who held Machiavelli directly responsible for the Saint Bartholomew massacre, used selected maxims to attack *The Prince*. His text was considerably influential since translation of *The Prince* itself into the languages of Protestant countries was delayed for many years. The English translation was published in 1640 when the episcopal censorship broke down. See the Censorship History discussion of *Areopagitica* by John Milton. The Elizabethans' understanding of and hostility to *The Prince* derived from Gentillet's book.

Most recently, in 1935, Benito Mussolini, Fascist dictator of Italy, encouraged the distribution of *Il Principe*, thereby demonstrating Italy's need for an all-powerful dictator supported by a national army. And shortly after Fidel Castro overthrew the government of Fulgencio Batista y Zaldívar in Cuba in 1959, a newspaper reported that *The Prince* was on Castro's revolutionary reading list.

FURTHER READING

Adams, Robert M. "The Interior Prince, or Machiavelli Mythologized" and "The Rise, Proliferation, and Degradation of Machiavellism: An Outline." In *The Prince*, edited by Robert M. Adams, 238–250. New York. W. W. Norton, 1977.

Bull, George. "Introduction." In *The Prince*. Trans. George Bull. Baltimore: Penguin Books, 1961, pp. 9–26.

Green, Jonathan, and Nicholas J. Karolides, reviser. *The Encyclopedia of Censorship, New Edition*. Facts On File, 2005.

Haight, Anne Lyon, and Chandler B. Grannis. *Banned Books 387 B.C. to 1978 A.D.* 4th ed. New York: R. R. Bowker, 1978.

Hale, J. R. "The Setting of *The Prince*." In *The Prince*, edited by Robert M. Adams, 141–152. New York: W. W. Norton, 1977.

Magill, Frank N., ed. *Masterplots*. Rev. ed. Englewood Cliffs, N.J.: Salem Press, 1976.

Strauss, Leo. "Machiavelli the Immoralist." In *The Prince*, edited by Robert M. Adams, 180–185. New York: W. W. Norton, 1977.

EL SEÑOR PRESIDENTE (THE PRESIDENT)

Author: Miguel Angel Asturias
Original dates and places of publication: 1946, Mexico; 1963, United States
Publishers: Costa-Amic; Murray Printing Company
Literary form: Novel

SUMMARY

The events of *El señor presidente*, or *The President*, are immediately precipitated by the "murder" of Colonel José Parrales Soriente, a favorite officer of the president of an unnamed country believed to be Guatemala. However, the machinations behind the events reveal that the president and his regime are the chief catalyst for the terrors and tyranny that emanate from the death of the colonel.

There are other victims, including the "murderer," a "halfwit beggar" called "the Zany," who is traumatized by the word *mother*. Terrorized by hearing the word jeered at him, he reacts violently when Parrales Soriente creeps up to him while he is asleep and shouts it in his ear. The witnesses, other beggars, are captured, imprisoned, interrogated, and tortured—all at the orders of the judge advocate general—until at last they change their story of the Zany's guilt to betray two men, General Eusebio Canales and Abel Carvajal, the lawyer, whose names are provided by the judge advocate. Thus, Canales and Carvajal, though innocent, become political victims, as do a host of others.

The president, who is portrayed as a self-centered, suspicious, and vindictive man, orders his favorite confidential adviser, Miguel Angel Face (Don Miguel Cara de Angel), to secretly warn Canales of his anticipated arrest so that he will "take to flight at once" because "it doesn't suit the government for him to go to prison." Angel Face orchestrates the escape with help from Lucio Vasquez, a member of the secret police whom he chances to meet in a bar, under the guise of kidnapping Camila Canales, the general's daughter, so they might elope. Angel Face succeeds in capturing Camila while accompanied by a collection of rough men who are to loot the house so as to create a diversion. The police join in the looting.

General Canales does escape. The failed attempt to kill him during his escape brings down the wrath of the judge advocate. Arrests are made, the first being that of Fedina Rodas, who has innocently come to warn Camila, after hearing the plan from her husband, who was told about it by Vasquez. She is incarcerated in a tomblike cell and interrogated. She tells her story, but the judge advocate prefers to disbelieve her. She is mistreated and beaten; her captors bring her infant son, crying for nourishment, to the next room to force her to reveal the "truth" of the general's whereabouts. Since she cannot, the child is allowed to die within earshot; she goes mad. Subsequently, the judge advocate sells her for 10,000 pesos to a madam of a brothel to be enslaved in prostitution.

The judge advocate causes the arrests of Carvajal and Vasquez. Astounded (and innocent), Carvajal is charged with sedition, rebellion, and treason. After days in the dungeon, he is brought to trial before the Council of War. Actually, there is no trial, only ritual; he is sentenced to death by the tribunal, whose members are drunk. No indulgences are granted to political prisoners.

> A few steps further on they entombed him in an underground dungeon three yards long by two and a half wide, in which twelve prisoners condemned to death were already standing packed together like sardines, motionless for lack of space, satisfying their physical needs where they stood and trampling on their own excrement. Carvajal was Number 13. When the soldiers left them, the painful breathing of the mass of doomed men filled the silence of the cell, already disturbed by the distant cries of a walled-up prisoner.

Vasquez is also sentenced to death for shooting the Zany, though he claims that he was an agent of the secret police and had orders to do so.

Meanwhile, Angel Face has had a change of mind and of heart, both before and after the abduction of Camila.

> And the more he thought about his project the blacker it seemed; the idea of kidnapping the daughter of a man doomed to die seemed to him as horrible and repugnant as it would have been congenial and pleasant to help him to escape. It was not good nature which made such a naturally unfeeling man dislike the thought of ambushing a trusting and defenceless citizen. . . . No. Very different were the sentiments which made Angel Face bite his lips with silent disapproval of this desperate and diabolical plan. He had believed in all good faith that as the general's protector he possessed certain rights over his daughter, but he now saw them sacrificed to his accustomed role of unreasoning tool, myrmidon and executioner.

Afterward, upon looking into her pale face and anguished eyes, he abandons the prospect of forcing his attentions on her, becoming first fatherly, then protective. He attempts to place her in the homes of her uncles and aunts; one after the other, they reject her. Out of fear for their own lives, reputations, and fortunes, they repudiate their brother and, thus, his daughter.

During this interlude, Camila becomes seriously ill with pneumonia. At the point of death, having received final absolution, she is married to Angel Face. This step is predicted to bring about the miracle of saving her life: "[T]he only thing that can fight death is love." He has come to love her and, after she recovers, she also loves him. Briefly, they share a life of dangerous bliss. The danger, of course, is that the president's confidential adviser has married the daughter of the president's presumed enemy—without his permission. Beneath the surface, the terror cauldron bubbles. The judge advocate submits a letter denouncing Angel Face, whom he feels has insulted him. The president acts as if he still trusts Angel Face and sends him to Washington as his special envoy to mend international relations. It turns out to be a trap. (Though it is not stated, the president is implicitly the activator.) At the border, Angel Face is arrested, given no opportunity to defend himself and beaten. Another man who resembles him takes on his identity and his papers. Angel Face is cast into solitary confinement in the most foul and dire conditions. He wastes away and dies.

General Canales becomes a changed man. His journey across his country opens his eyes to the deceptions and injustices perpetrated on his countrymen by the government he had been defending. He hears stories of his benefactors—a farmer who rescues him in the mountains and three elderly sisters who take him in to hide him and arrange for him to be smuggled across the border. They have been defrauded by local government officials in league with greedy, dishonest lawyers. They lose their lands, property and, in the farmer's case, the lives of his wife and sons.

> A storm of feelings was raging in old Canales' breast, such feelings as are always aroused in the heart of a good man when confronted with injustice. He suffered on behalf of his country. . . . It is a more despicable and therefore a sadder thing to be a soldier simply in order to keep a gang of ruffians, exploiters and self-important betrayers of their country in power, than it is to die of hunger in exile.

Canales leads a revolutionary army to reassert justice but dies just when he is about to lead his troops of defrauded men into action. Empowering these activities is the president. He hates his countrymen, as he reveals:

> "Ungrateful beasts!. . . . I loved and shall always love Parrales Soriente; I was going to have made him a general, because he trampled on my countrymen and humiliated them, and if it hadn't been for my mother he would have finished them off altogether and avenged me for all the grudges I bear against them, things I alone know about. Ungrateful beasts!"

Indeed, the best way to get on his right side is "to commit a public outrage on defenceless people," "to demonstrate the superiority of force to public opinion," or "to get rich at the expense of the nation."

The text is steeped in treachery and riddled with ironies. The police called to rescue Camila loot her home, allowing her to be abducted. Vasquez bludgeons Camila's nurse with a massive iron bar and groans when her inhuman cries pierce the air. The bordello madam's private apartment is crowded with engravings, sculptures, and religious images and relics. The major whom Angel Face warns against informers and advises to get on the good side of the president is the very officer who is in charge of his entrapment and who mercilessly has him brutalized. The overpowering irony is the honoring of the president—"Long live the President! Long live the Constitutional President of the Republic!"—a celebration at its height during those events.

The focus of another work by Asturias, his so-called Banana Plantation trilogy—with its implicit political orientation—also invited censorial attention. Composed of *Viento fuerte* (*Strong Wind*), 1950, *El papa verde* (*The Green Pope*), 1954, and *Los ojos de los enterralos* (*The Eyes of the Interred*), 1960 (respectively issued in the United States in 1967, 1971, and 1973), the novels describe the exploitation of plantation workers and the influence exercised by U.S. companies in Guatemala until the second half of the 20th century.

CENSORSHIP HISTORY

The political life of Miguel Angel Asturias is significantly interwoven with his literary career. His participation as a student in opposing the dictatorship of Manuel Estrada Cabrera in Guatemala and subsequent activity as a political journalist led to 10 years of voluntary exile, beginning in 1923. The Cabrera regime had been overthrown in 1920, but Cabrerista forces soon regained power. *El señor presidente* was written in 1932. Its situations and events are identified as being based on the author's experiences with the totalitarian Cabrera regime.

Asturias returned to Guatemala in 1933. Elected to the National Assembly in 1942, he again actively participated in an overthrow, this time in 1944 of the dictatorial regime of General Jorge Ubico. Diplomatic assignments for Asturias followed during the brief period of democracy in the succeeding years until the 1954 counterrevolution.

Once empowered, the right-wing forces of Carlos Castillo Armas ("the Liberator") banished Asturias in 1954, stripping him of his Guatemalan citizenship. (He never returned, but his passport was returned in 1959 at the insistence of the University of Guatemala.) Among the actions taken by Armas subordinates was the burning of "subversive" books. These included Asturias's novels *El señor presidente*, *Strong Wind*, and *The Green Pope*. (Also burned were Victor Hugo's *Les Misérables*, Dostoyevsky's novels, and the writings of Juan José Arvalo Bermejo and other revolutionaries.) The first two books of the trilogy were banned because of their evidently strong criticism of a U.S. corporation (the United Fruit Company). It is reported that United Fruit actively promoted the intervention of the United States to overthrow the government of Jacobo Arbenz. The action was supported by the Central Intelligence Agency (CIA).

Journalists Stephen Schlesinger and Stephen Kinzer make a detailed case, based on U.S. State Department documents released to them through the Freedom of Information Act, of U.S. complicity in the overthrow of the democratic government of Arbenz in 1954. CIA director Allen Dulles is identified as the "godfather of Operation Success, the plot to overthrow Arbenz," while Secretary of State John Foster Dulles is represented as planning the Guatemalan coup; he is depicted as building justification for his planned coup at the 10th Inter-American Conference at Caracas, Venezuela, where he lobbied for two weeks for passage of a resolution condemning communism in the Americas and, subsequent to the coup, insisting that Arbenz's followers in asylum in foreign embassies be seized and prosecuted as communists.

When Miguel Angel Asturias was awarded the Nobel Prize in literature in 1967, *El señor presidente* was one of the works specifically identified in the award statement.

FURTHER READING

Callan, Richard J. *Miguel Angel Asturias.* New York: Twayne, 1970.
Flynn, Gerard, Kenneth Grieb, and Richard J. Callen. *Essays on Miguel Angel Asturias.* Milwaukee: University of Wisconsin Press, 1973.
Grieb, Kenneth. "Miguel Angel Asturias as a Political Propagandist." In *Essays on Miguel Angel Asturias,* edited by Gerard Flynn et al., 10–22. Milwaukee: University of Wisconsin Press, 1973.
Schlesinger, Stephen, and Stephen Kinzer. *Bitter Fruit: The Untold Story of the American Coup in Guatemala.* Garden City, N.Y.: Doubleday, 1982.
Wiskari, Werner. "Guatemalan Author of Anti-U.S. Works Wins Nobel Prize." *New York Times,* October 20, 1967, pp. 1, 44.

SLAUGHTERHOUSE-FIVE, OR THE CHILDREN'S CRUSADE

Author: Kurt Vonnegut, Jr.
Original date and place of publication: 1969, United States
Publisher: Delacorte Press
Literary form: Fiction

SUMMARY

Many years after World War II, Kurt Vonnegut visited Bernard V. O'Hare, a friend from the war, to discuss the destruction of Dresden. The Allied forces annihilated Dresden with so much firepower that it resembled the ruins one might imagine seeing after an atomic bomb had been dropped. Vonnegut and other American prisoners of war (POWs) survived the ordeal in

"Schlachthof-fünf," Slaughterhouse-Five, a cement fortress originally used as a stockyard killing shed. The two men later returned to Dresden, which, along with personal experience, provided Vonnegut with material to write his "famous book about Dresden."

Billy Pilgrim, the protagonist, was born in Ilium, New York, in 1922. He served in the army as a chaplain's assistant. After his father is accidentally killed in a hunting accident, Billy returns from furlough and is assigned as an aide to a regimental chaplain whose assistant has been killed. However, the chaplain is killed in the Battle of the Bulge, leaving Billy and three other Americans lost and wandering deep in German territory. One of the other Americans, Roland Weary, is an antitank gunner who has been plagued throughout his life by being the unpopular person everyone likes to ditch. More than once Weary pushes Billy out of the line of enemy gunfire, but Billy is so exhausted and in such poor condition that he does not realize his life has been spared. This attitude infuriates Weary, who "had been saving Billy's life for days, cursing him, kicking him, slapping him, making him move." Weary and the other two in the quartet, both scouts, have become "The Three Musketeers" in Weary's mind. However, as Weary's obsession to keep the hallucinating Billy alive grows, the scouts' contempt of Billy and Weary also grows, and they ditch Billy and Weary. Weary is set on destroying Billy, but just as he is about to send his heel crashing through Billy's exposed spine, the two are discovered by a band of German soldiers and taken as prisoners of war.

Billy and Weary are searched, deprived of their weapons and valuables, and paraded away to a cottage that has been transformed into a holding place for POWs. The men are placed with about 20 other Americans. For a propagandist technique, Billy is singled out and photographed as an example of how the American army prepares its men for the war. The Germans and the POWs travel on and meet with more POWs until they form a human river. They arrive at a railyard and are separated by rank, privates with privates, colonels with colonels, and so on. Billy and Weary are separated, but Weary's continuous testimony of how Billy was responsible for the breakup of "The Three Musketeers" eventually spreads to the car where Billy is being held, causing a general feeling of hatred from the occupants of the car toward Billy. On the ninth day of their journey, Weary dies of gangrene. On the 10th day the train finally stops and the occupants are released into a prison camp. Billy is the next to last to leave his car. A corpse stays behind.

The men are stripped, they shower, and their clothes are sanitized. Among them is Edgar Derby, a middle-aged man whose son is fighting in the Pacific theater, and Paul Lazzaro, a tiny shriveled-up man who is covered with boils. Both men were with Weary when he died; Derby cradled his head, and Lazzaro promised to enact revenge upon Billy. The men are given their clothes and dogtags, which they must wear at all times. They are led to a shed that houses a number of middle-aged Englishmen who have been POWs since the beginning of the war. Unlike their American counterparts, however, the Englishmen have made the most of their imprisonment by keeping themselves in shape and properly groomed. They have also cleverly hoarded enough rations that they can afford to trade with the Germans for supplies like lumber and other building materials that they use to maintain their shed.

In poor condition and in a hallucinatory state, Billy is billeted in the hospital portion of the British compound, which is in reality six beds in another room of the shed. Here he is injected with morphine and watched by Derby, who reads *The Red Badge of Courage* to pass the time. Billy awakens from his morphine-induced sleep, not knowing where he is or what year it is. Derby and Lazzaro are sleeping in adjacent beds. Apparently Lazzaro's arm has been broken for stealing cigarettes from an Englishman, and he is now lecturing Billy and Derby on how he will someday enact revenge for that and for Weary's death, for which he holds Billy responsible.

The Americans are informed by the head Englishman that they will be "leaving this afternoon for Dresden—a beautiful city. . . . [they] needn't worry about bombs. . . . Dresden is an open city. It is undefended, and contains no war industries or troop concentrations of any importance." The Americans arrive to find that what they have been told is true. They are led to a cement fortress that had been a slaughterhouse of livestock and is now their dwelling place—"Schlachthof-fünf." The Americans are assigned to work in a factory that produces malt syrup enriched with vitamins and minerals, to be used by pregnant German women.

Four days later, Dresden is destroyed. Billy, some Americans, and four German guards are safe in the underground slaughterhouse while the entire city is firebombed. As they emerge the next afternoon, "the sky was black with smoke. The sun was an angry little pinhead. Dresden was like the moon now, nothing but minerals. The stones were hot. Everybody else in the neighborhood was dead." The soldiers order the Americans to line up in fours, and they all march away until they come to a country inn that is far enough removed from Dresden to not have been affected.

Two days after the war ends, Billy and five other Americans ride back to Dresden, looting through abandoned homes and taking as many souvenirs as they please. The Russians come along soon afterward and arrest the Americans, who are sent home on the *Lucretia A. Mott* two days later.

Throughout his war experience, Billy Pilgrim is a time traveler. His trips stem from a few incidents, namely, when he is near death or when he is on drugs. As he is being pushed along by Weary, he travels in time forward and backward. For example, he goes back to when he was a boy, when he and his father were at the YMCA. His father wanted to teach Billy how to swim by using the "sink-or-swim" technique. Having been pushed into the deep end, Billy ended up "on the bottom of the pool, and there was beautiful music everywhere. He lost consciousness, but the music went on. He dimly sensed that somebody was rescuing him. [He] resented that." From the pool he goes forward in time to 1965 to visit his mother in Pine Knoll, a rest home; then he returns to 1958 to his son's little league banquet; from there he goes ahead to a New Year's Eve party in 1961, where he is caught cheating with another woman; finally he is back in the German outland, being shaken against a tree by Weary.

While under the morphine-induced sleep in the British-run prison camp, Billy travels through time to 1948, to the veterans' hospital near Lake Placid. He is being introduced by Eliot Rosewater, a former infantry captain, to the works of Kilgore Trout, a little-known science fiction writer who will become Billy's favorite author and whom Billy will meet some years later. Billy also goes ahead to a time when he is 44 years old and a captive in the zoo on Tralfamadore. The Tralfamadorians, telepathic beings who live in four dimensions and have a firm understanding of the concept of death, have captured Billy and put him into a "human exhibit," where he is naked in a setting consisting of furniture and appliances from the Sears & Roebuck warehouse in Iowa City, Iowa. Not long after Billy is captured, the Tralfamadorians capture a female earthling, Montana Wildhack, a 20-year-old motion picture star whom they hope will mate with Billy. In time she gains Billy's trust and they mate, much to the awe and delight of the Tralfamadorians.

Not long after their sexual experience, however, Billy wakes up. It is 1968, and he is sweating profusely because his electric blanket is on the highest setting. His daughter had laid him in bed upon his return from the hospital, where he had been placed after being the lone survivor in a plane crash in Vermont, en route to an optometrists' convention in Canada. His wife, the former Valencia Merble, is the daughter of a well-to-do optometrist, who had placed Billy in charge of his business in Ilium, thus making Billy a wealthy man. She died while rushing to visit Billy in the hospital after the plane crash, apparently from carbon monoxide poisoning.

Billy Pilgrim drives to New York City the next day, hoping to be on a television show so he can tell the world about the Tralfamadorians. Instead, he ends up on a radio talk show where the topic is "Is the novel dead or not?" Billy speaks of his travels, Montana, the Tralfamadorians, multiple dimensions and so on, until "He was gently expelled from the studio during a commercial. He went back to his hotel room, put a quarter into the Magic Fingers machine connected to his bed, and he went to sleep. He traveled back in time to Tralfamadore." Billy Pilgrim dies on February 13, 1976.

CENSORSHIP HISTORY

As one of the most censored books in recent years—ranked 15th, according to Lee Burress on his national surveys–based list of the 30 most challenged books from 1965 to 1985 and ranked 69 on the American Library Association's list of "The 100 Most Frequently Challenged Books of 1900–2000"—*Slaughterhouse-Five, or the Children's Crusade: A Duty-Dance with Death* can boast dozens of cases when students, parents, teachers, administrators, librarians, and members of the clergy have called for the removal or destruction of the Vonnegut novel for one or many of the following reasons: obscenity, vulgar language, violence, inappropriateness, "bathroom language," "R-rated" language, ungodliness, immoral subject matter, cruelty, language that is "too modern," and an "unpatriotic" portrayal of war.

In an early suit in Michigan—*Todd v. Rochester Community Schools* (1971)—circuit judge Arthur E. Moore told an area high school to ban the book for violating the Constitution's separation of church and state; the novel "contains and makes references to religious matters," was a "degradation of the person of Christ," and was full of "repetitious obscenity and immorality." Thus, it fell within the ban of the establishment clause. The Michigan Appellate court reversed the circuit court's decision; the court had overstepped its bounds in venturing into the area of censorship. According to the appellate court, judgments about books resided with "students, the teacher, and the duly constituted school authority. Such action [by the circuit court] is resolutely forbidden by the Constitution."

June Edwards focuses on the charge of parents and the religious right: "The book is an indictment of war, criticizes government actions, is anti-American, and is unpatriotic." This charge defies the reason why Vonnegut wrote the novel, which was to show that "there is nothing intelligent to say about a massacre." Edwards supports this position by also countering the final two arguments: "Young people may refuse to serve in future combats after reading about the horrors of war in novels like *Slaughterhouse Five* . . ., but this does not make them un-American. They do not want their country to engage in violence, to exterminate whole populations, but to find other ways to resolve conflicts."

Nat Hentoff reports that Bruce Severy, the only English teacher in North Dakota's Drake High School in 1973, used *Slaughterhouse-Five* in his classroom as an example of a "lively contemporary book." Severy submitted the text to the superintendent for review and, after receiving no response, went ahead and taught it. A student's objection citing "unnecessary language" led to a school board meeting where the text was denounced and labeled "a tool of the devil" by a local minister. The school board decided that the novel would be burned, even though no board member had read the entire book. Severy, after discovering his contract would not be renewed, stated, "A few four-letter words in a book is no big deal. Those students have all heard these words before; none learned any new words. I've always thought the purpose of school was to prepare these people for living in the 'big, bad world,' but it evidently isn't so." Severy, with help from the American Civil Liberties Union, sued the school district; the following verdict was reached in an out-of-court settlement: 1) *Slaughterhouse-Five* could be used by teachers in Drake High School in connection with the teaching of English in grades 11 and 12; 2) Severy's performance could not be in written or oral terms deemed unsatisfactory; and 3) Severy was awarded $5,000.

The Librarians Guide to Handling Censorship Conflicts gives a detailed account of the suits and countersuit of the *Pico v. Board of Education*, Island Trees Union Free School District cases of 1979, 1980, and 1982. It is noted for being the first case of school library censorship to have reached the Supreme Court. The case stemmed from the actions of school board members attending a meeting in 1975 of Parents of New York United (PONY-U), where one of the issues concerned "the control of textbooks and library books in the schools." Using a list that contained books considered objectionable in other high school libraries, Richard Ahrens, then president of the school board, along with board member Frank Martin, descended upon the school library one evening to see which listed books were shelved there. They discovered nine, including *Slaughterhouse-Five*. At a subsequent meeting in February 1976 with two high school principals, the board decided to remove the nine books, along with two others from the junior high school. Two of the books were removed from classrooms as well. That decision prompted a memo from Superintendent Richard Morrow, who stated, "I don't believe we should accept and act on someone else's list. . . . we already have a policy . . . designed expressly to handle such problems." At the March 30 meeting, President Ahrens disregarded the memo and ordered the books removed from the district's libraries. After the media got word of the brewing controversy, the board wrote a rebuttal that stated:

> This Board of Education wants to make it clear that we in no way are BOOK BANNERS or BOOK BURNERS. While most of us agree that these books have a place on the shelves of the public library, we all agree that these books simply DO NOT belong in school libraries where they are so easily accessible to children whose minds are still in the formulative [sic] stage, and where their presence actually entices children to read and savor them. . . .

Superintendent Morrow responded that it was "wrong for the Board—or any other single group—to act to remove books without prolonged prior consideration of the views of both the parents whose children read these books, and the teachers who use these books to instruct . . . and to by-pass the established procedure for reviewing the challenged books." On April 6 the board and Morrow voted to appoint a review committee of four parents and four teachers to review the books and make recommendations concerning their future status. In the meantime, Morrow requested that the books be returned to the shelves until the review process was completed. They were not. In subsequent meetings, the review committee determined that six of the 11 books, including *Slaughterhouse-Five*, should be returned to the school shelves. Three were not recommended, and two others could not be decided upon. However, on July 28, the board in an open meeting voted to return only one book, *Laughing Boy*, to the shelves without restrictions and one, *Black Boy*, with restrictions despite the committee's stance. Ahrens stated that the other nine books could not be assigned as required, optional, or suggested reading, but could be discussed in class.

A lawsuit was filed on January 4, 1977, by Stephen Pico and other junior and senior high school students, who were represented by the New York Civil Liberties Union. Pico claimed that First Amendment rights had been violated via the board's removal of the books.

As entered in the court record, the school board condemned the books as "anti-American, anti-Christian, anti-Semitic, and just plain filthy"; it cited passages referring to male genitalia, to sexuality, to lewd and profane language, and to sacrilegious interpretations of the Gospels and of Jesus Christ. According to Leon Hurwitz, "A federal district court gave summary judgment for the board, but an appellate court remanded the case for a trial on the students' allegations." The Supreme Court to which the school board appealed this decision, in a 5-4 decision, upheld the appellate court, rejected the idea that "there are no potential constitutional constraints on school board actions in this area." The case came full circle on August 12, 1982, when the school board voted 6-1 to return the books to the school library shelves, with the stipulation that the librarian send a notice to the parents of any student who might check out a book containing objectionable material. (For further discussion of this case, refer to the censorship history of *Black Boy*.)

Many other incidents have occurred throughout the seventies, eighties, and nineties concerning *Slaughterhouse-Five*. According to *Banned Books: 387 B.C. to 1987 A.D.*, an unidentified Iowa town's school board in 1973, the same year as the Drake burning, ordered 32 copies burned because of objectionable language. The teacher who assigned the text had his job threatened. In McBee, South Carolina, a teacher using the text was arrested and charged with using obscene materials.

Newsletter on Intellectual Freedom reports that a review committee in Lakeland, Florida, in 1982 voted 3-2 to ban *Slaughterhouse-Five* from the Lake Gibson High School library, citing explicit sexual scenes, violence, and obscene language. The complaint originated from a board member and was backed by then Polk County deputy school superintendent Cliff Mains, who stated that the book review policy maintained the decision's legal validity.

On May 27, 1984, in Racine, Wisconsin, William Grindeland, the district administrative assistant for instructional services, barred the purchase of *Slaughterhouse-Five*, stating, "I don't believe it belongs in a school library." Unified school board member Eugene Dunk countered, "Denial of quality reading materials for our youngsters is criminal." This stirred up a heated controversy, which was compounded by the board's banning of five textbooks, three in social studies and two in home economics, on June 12. Board member Barbara Scott proposed that a "reserved list" be developed that contained books for which written parental permission would be required for students to check them out. Meanwhile, the Racine Education Association (REA) threatened to take legal action and file a lawsuit in federal court against the United school board if the book was banned. REA executive director Jim Ennis said the suit's goal would be to "prevent the school board from excluding 'contemporary and relevant literature' from Unified libraries and courses." On June 14, a committee of administrators did recommend that the school district purchase a new copy of *Slaughterhouse-Five* and also recommended a new library book selection policy, which called for the formation of a committee consisting of parents, librarians, and directors of instruction, who together would be responsible for the selection of new library materials. This news prompted the REA to hold off on any legal action against the school district.

On May 15, 1986, Jane Robbins-Carter, president of the Wisconsin Library Association, wrote to inform the Racine Unified School District that a resolution of censure had been developed "due to the conflict between the policies and practices of the District as they relate to library materials selection and purchase and the principles of intellectual freedom as supported by the Library Bill of Rights of the American Library Association." The charges stemmed from the actions undertaken by William Grindeland, which allowed him "the authority to delete orders for library materials 'not in keeping with the standards of the selection policy,'" to use "vague and subjective criteria" in choosing what materials could be used, and to refer "requests for materials of a highly controversial nature . . . to the public library, local bookstores or newsstands." Robbins-Carter added that "the censure will remain in effect until such time as the Board of Education adopts a revised Library Materials Selection and Purchase Policy." The Racine Unified School District adopted a policy in June 1985; on December 9, the Racine Unified School District's Library Materials Review Committee voted 6-2 to place *Slaughterhouse-Five* under limited access to students with parental permission. Grindeland, a member of the committee that reviewed the book, said, "I objected to the book being in a school library, and I still do. But restricting it is a good compromise."

In October 1985, in Owensboro, Kentucky, parent Carol Roberts filed a complaint stating that *Slaughterhouse-Five* was "just plain despicable," referring to the passages about bestiality, Magic Fingers, and the sentence, "The gun made a ripping sound like the opening of the zipper on the fly of God Almighty." She had also prepared a petition with the signatures of over 100 parents. In November, a meeting consisting of administrators, teachers, and parents voted unanimously that the text remain on the school library shelves. Judith Edwards, director of the city schools' department of instruction, commented that the committee "felt the book was meritorious." In April 1987, in LaRue, Kentucky, the LaRue County Board of Education refused to remove *Slaughterhouse-Five* from the school library shelves despite numerous complaints citing foul language and deviant sexual behavior. Principal Phil Eason defended the book, stating that it "show[s] the obscenity of war," and "We don't make them [the people opposing the text] read them [books in the library]."

In August 1987, in Fitzgerald, Georgia, school officials decided that a policy used to ban *Slaughterhouse-Five* from all city schools would also offer the same protection against other "objectional" materials. The book was permanently banned by a 6-5 vote after Farise and Maxine Taylor, whose daughter had brought the book home, filed a formal complaint in June, citing that "[I]f we don't do anything about it, they're putting that garbage in the classroom and we're putting our stamp of approval on it."

In February 1988, in Baton Rouge, Louisiana, school board member Gordon Hutchinson stated that he wanted to ban *Slaughterhouse-Five* and all books like it, which he described as being "a book of dirty language." The complaint was brought to his attention by parent Brenda Forrest, whose daughter had selected the book from a suggested reading list at Central High School. Baton Rouge District PTA president Beverly Trahan commented, "You can get into some very serious problems with book bans." Dick Eiche, executive director of the East Baton Rouge Association of Educators, echoed Trahan's view supporting the book. School board president Robert Crawford, a Vietnam veteran, agreed with Eiche and Trahan's views when he stated, "I think it's dangerous to start banning books. We could clean out the libraries if we wanted to." In March, Superintendent of Schools Bernard Weiss said a committee would be formed to evaluate the book. The 12-member committee voted 11-0 with one abstention to retain the book. Community member Bill Huey stated, "I can hardly believe this community . . . is even discussing removing a book from library shelves. I don't want to live in a community that sanctions bingo and bans books."

Slaughterhouse-Five was challenged, but retained, in Monroe, Michigan, in 1989, as required reading in a modern novels course for juniors and seniors because of its language and the portrayal of women: "Many similes or metaphors are used to describe things or events, but they are generally stated in sexual terms. . . . Or the language is just plain offensive. Any claim to be using this language for emphasizing is invalidated by its frequent use. I feel this book is degrading to life, sex, women and men, and above all, God." Another attack occurred in 1991, in Phemmer, Idaho, where parents objected to the book's use in an 11th-grade English class, citing profanity. Because the school had no policy in effect to deal with the challenge, an official ordered that the book be removed from the school and that the teacher using the book throw away all copies. In Round Rock, Texas, in 1996, 12 novels used in honors or advanced placement classes were charged with portraying excessive violence and sexual situations. The challenger, a school board member, claimed the request for removal was not censorship: "It's deciding what is consistent with society's standards and appropriate for everyone to use in the classroom." A student remarked, "The whole thing is motivated by fear. They're afraid we're actually going to have to think for ourselves." The novel was retained.

Complaints in Prince William County, Virginia, in 1998 centered on profanity and explicit sex scenes. A school board member, responding to excerpts from three challenged novels, indicated he was "completely appalled. I feel that this is a degradation to the human race." In Coventry, Rhode Island, in 2000, the novel was removed as required reading in the summer reading program although retained as an option; the challenger complained of vulgar language, violent imagery, and sexual content. After the novel was challenged in 2001 as being too graphic for high school students in Moreno Valley, California, the school board voted unanimously against a request to withdraw it from the Advanced Placement English curriculum.

A controversy over books deemed inappropriate for students ensued in May 2006 in a suburban Chicago school district, Arlington Heights–based

Township High School District 214. The district includes six high schools of about 13,000 students. School board member Leslie Pinney identified nine books, including *Slaughterhouse-Five*, as containing explicit sexual images, graphic violence, and vulgar language; their educational value was questioned. The school board voted 6-1 to retain the nine books after a school board meeting attended by some 500 persons. Other books on the list included *Beloved*, by Toni Morrison; *The Things They Carried*, by Tim O'Brien; *The Awakening*, by Kate Chopin; *Freakonomics*, by Steven D. Levitt and Stephen J. Dubner; *The Botany of Desire: A Plant's-Eye View of the World*, by Michael Pollan; *The Perks of Being a Wallflower*, by Stephen Chbosky; *Fallen Angels*, by Walter Dean Myers; and *How the García Girls Lost Their Accents*, by Julia Alvarez.

In February 2007, a citizens' group, the Livingston Organization for Values in Education (LOVE), complained to the Howell school board about the sexual content of four books in the Howell (Michigan) High School curriculum: *Slaughterhouse-Five*, by Kurt Vonnegut; *Black Boy*, by Richard Wright; *The Bluest Eye*, by Toni Morrison; and *The Freedom Writers Diary*, by Erin Gruwell. Their challenge demanded that the books be removed from the curriculum; a LOVE spokesperson compared the books to *Penthouse* and *Playboy* magazines, asserting that they "contain similarly graphic materials in written form [and] are equally inappropriate." *The Bluest Eye* was described as a "graphic child rape book." Letters were also sent to the offices of the U.S attorney, state attorney general, and Livingston County prosecutor, requesting opinions about whether the books violate laws on obscenity and distribution of materials that are harmful to minors. The federal and state offices forwarded the request to the FBI, a routine procedure with such complaints.

On February 12, the school board voted 5-2 to reject LOVE's complaint. The books will continue to be used in AP classes. The district superintendent explained, "We should also be very careful about dismissing literary works because they test our own belief system or challenge our values." David Morse, the county prosecutor, concluded that the books are legal on two grounds: 1) Since the school board has approved use of these books, the teachers and administrators have complied with school codes and are exempted from criminal prosecution; 2) To qualify as obscene, a book must be found to appeal only to readers' prurient interest in sex and have no literary or educational merit. ". . . it is clear that the explicit passages [in the books] illustrated a larger literary, artistic or political message and were not included solely to appeal to the prurient interest of minors." Michigan attorney general Mike Cox and U.S. Attorney Stephen Murphy concurred with Morse and indicated in mid-March that they would not prosecute.

FURTHER READING

"Board Reverses Censorship Stand." *Racine Journal Times*, June 22, 1984, n.p.
"Book Banning." *Racine Journal Times*, June 13, 1984, n.p.
Burress, Lee. "Introduction." In *Celebrating Censored Books!*, edited by Nicholas J. Karolides and Lee Burress. Racine: Wisconsin Council of Teachers of English, 1985.

Edwards, June. *Opposing Censorship in the Public Schools: Religion, Morality, and Literature.* Mahwah, N.J.: Lawrence Erlbaum Associates, 1998.
"FBI, State Deem Books Legal after Obscenity Complaints." Available online. URL: www.familiesaretalking.org/index.cfm?useaction=feature.show feature & feature ID= 1069. Accessed June 14, 2010
Foerstel, Herbert N. *Banned in the U.S.A.: A Reference Guide to Book Censorship in Schools and Public Libraries.* Westport, Conn.: Greenwood Press, 1994.
Francisco, Jamie. "School Board Averts Ban." *Chicago Tribune* (May 26, 2006). Available online. URL: http://www.alliancelibrarysystem.com/pdf/2006Schoolboard avertsbookban.pdf. Accessed February 18, 2011.
Haight, Anne Lyon, and Chandler B. Grannis, *Banned Books: 387 B.C. to 1978 A.D.* 4th ed. New York: R. R. Bowker, 1978.
Hentoff, Nat. *The First Freedom: The Tumultuous History of Free Speech in America.* New York: Delacorte Press, 1980.
Hurwitz, Leon. *Historical Dictionary of Censorship in the United States.* Westport, Conn.: Greenwood Press, 1985.
Jenkinson, Edward B. *Censors in the Classroom: The Mind Benders.* Carbondale: Southern Illinois University Press, 1979.
Jones, Frances M. *Defusing Censorship: The Librarian's Guide to Handling Censorship Conflicts.* Phoenix, Ariz.: Oryx Press, 1983.
Newsletter on Intellectual Freedom 23 (1974): 4; 29 (1980): 51; 31 (1982): 155, 197; 33 (1984): 158; 35 (1986): 9–10, 57, 114; 36 (1987): 51, 224; 37 (1988): 86–87, 139–40.
"OK for *Slaughterhouse Five.*" *Racine Journal Times,* June 14, 1984, n.p.
"Unified Bans 5 Books." *Racine Journal Times,* June 12, 1984, n.p.
"Unified Lifts Book Ban." *Racine Journal Times,* June 19, 1984, n.p.
"Unstocking the Shelves." *Racine Journal Times,* May 27, 1984, n.p.

—Eric P. Schmidt
Revised by Nicholas J. Karolides

SNOW

Author: Orhan Pamuk
Original dates and places of publication: 2002, Turkey; 2004, England and United States
Publishers: İletişm; Faber & Faber; Alfred A. Knopf
Literary form: Novel

SUMMARY

An exile living in Germany for 12 years for having been part of a Marxist-Leninist movement as a student, Ka (an appellation he prefers to Kerin Alakuşeğlu) returns to Istanbul to attend his mother's funeral, then travels by bus to Kars (*kar* is the Turkish word for snow), an isolated community on the Turkey-Armenia border. When asked why he's there, he claims to be a journalist, covering the upcoming municipal elections and the spate of suicides by young women. In fact, Ka is a poet; he is traveling to Kars to connect again with a university classmate, İpek, who is extraordinarily beautiful. He imagines himself to be in love with her.

As the bus exits from Erzurum, it begins to snow, heavy and thick, continuing throughout the trip and the four days he stays in Kars. The blizzard blankets the city, at once masking the streets, covering the grime and the evidence of poverty, creating an aura of silence and wonder. It spoke to Ka of purity, a sense of innocence that is soon lost. The roads leading into Kars are blocked to all traffic, Kars becoming in effect totally isolated.

Kars's turbulent history—"endless wars, rebellions, massacres, and atrocities . . . , occupied alternately by Armenian and Russian armies" in the past, the Turkish army arriving in 1920—predicts the ethnic diversity and divisiveness of the present. There are animosities among political, religious, and ethnic factions: democratic republicans, secularists, Muslims, atheists, separatist Kurds, revolutionaries, old-style socialists, and the military. There is also hostility toward the Westerner attitude of the central government and distrust of those, like Ka, who reflect Western behaviors—or, on the contrary, envy of these individuals. Tension seems a constant, propelled by corruption: poverty and joblessness, a sense of constant surveillance, police (brutal) invasion of homes, bugged rooms, double agents, informers, an oppressive military presence, and the MIT—National Intelligence Agency.

The suicide phenomenon (Ka was given details of six incidents) was fraught with rumors and religious-political accusations. With one exception, the young women's stories revealed that marital abuse, paternal repression, poverty, and a besmirched reputation were critical causal factors. Yet, the exception, the "head scarf girl," became the cause célèbre. Many women and girls refused to obey the edict of national authorities that outlawed the wearing of head scarves in educational institutions. This led to these girls being barred from the classroom—in effect, from an education. The head scarf was perceived as a symbol of political Islam: "When a girl has accepted the head scarf as the Word of God and the symbol of faith, it's very difficult for her to take it off." Despite the Islamic condemnation of suicide as a major sin and the urging of her parents to remove her head scarf, this girl "began to tell her father that life had no meaning and that she no longer wanted to live," and she committed suicide.

Ka becomes embroiled in the Kars political and religious maelstrom on his first day. He and İpek witnessed the murder of the director of the Education Institute, who had ordered the head scarf removal; then he is taken to meet Blue, identified in Turkish papers as a terrorist, a militant political Islamist, rumored to be a murderer, who is hiding out in Kars for reasons unknown. Later, Ka is confronted by three boys, who assert Ka is an atheist and question his motives for being in Kars.

There are two strands to the plot: Ka's relationship with İpek, which becomes intense, and her family, including her sister, Kadife; Ka's becoming involved in a plan to bring a proclamation to a German reporter (actually a person of Ka's invention), professing a statement of values, signaling a kind of unanimity among oppositional forces in Kars. Ka agrees to Blue's insistence that he convince İpek's father to attend a secret meeting to write and sign the "announcement."

Readers witness or are informed of inhumane practices and degrading conditions. We visit the district of shanties; some residents who "opened their doors fearfully, assuming, after so many years of police intimidation, that this was yet another search." We are told of Muhtar's (İpek's former husband who is a mayoral candidate) "look of miserable resignation . . . he knew he would get a beating,"—and he did, apparently simply by being with Ka. We are part of the audience with Ka at the National Theatre when a "revolution" occurs on stage; seemingly part of the play's plot, a violent secular/antipolitical group mounts a coup, taking over the city government; soldiers on the stage fire at the audience, five volleys, killing 17. At a second performance at the National Theatre, a character, played by Kadife (a head scarf wearer), is required to remove her head scarf and shoot the hero; she does, but the gun is unexpectedly loaded. Taken to the police headquarters to identify the suspects in the murder of the Education Institute's director, we look with Ka's eyes into one cell "about the size of a double bed . . . five people inside, one of them a youth with a bloody face." Ka did not as a matter of principle identify anyone in any of the cells, though he recognized two of them from the theatre episode.

Almost two-thirds through the novel, leaving Ka and İpek in a passionate embrace, the text shifts to Frankfurt four years later; the narrator (the author) enters the novel. He has come to Germany to reclaim Ka's possessions—especially his green notebook in which he had written his Kars poems—and to uncover the details of his death. Ka had been shot at about midnight outside a shop, three bullets in his body. The green notebook was not found. But he did find a packet of love letters, written to İpek but never sent.

Conversations and debates among the characters reveal significant concerns. Faith is a primary one, as evident in the head scarf controversy: the "'covered girls' who have put everything at risk for the sake of their faith. But it is the secular press that calls them 'covered girls.' For us, they are simply Muslim girls, and what they do to defend their faith is what all Muslim girls must do." When an actress on stage attempted to burn a head scarf, a boy from the religious high school in the audience shouted, "Down with the enemies of religion! Down with the atheists! Down with the infidels." The head scarf agitation pits the secular government's suppression against Islamic militants. The women speak of pride in honoring the "Word of God and the symbol of faith."

The "disease" of atheism is a parallel concern. It is not uncommon for Ka to be asked if he is an atheist as is the case with his exchange with three students from the religious school. They lecture him about believing in God, and they assume as an atheist he has an urge to commit suicide.

State-sponsored oppression is frequently represented in the novel. Blue's proposed proclamation to the West is a critical feature of the novel: "Will the West, which takes its great invention, democracy, more seriously than the Word of God, come out against this coup that has brought an end to democracy in Kars?" The "Announcement" that is created at the secret meeting, beyond calling attention to the interruption of the democratic election process, includes also "A brief reference . . . to the Kurds who'd been shot or taken from their homes and killed, and to the torture and intimidation suffered by the boys from the religious high school. . . . An assault on the people, the spirit and religion." It called for the "whole world to unite in protest against the Turkish Republic."

The overarching theme of *Snow* is the conflicting nature of life in Turkey, the challenge to the secular government and attitudes by the Islamic militants. This is expressed in the rejection of the Westernization attitudes of the state, the rejection of Ka's European attitudes and character. This friction is evident also in the Turks' defensive inferiority complex, at once resentful and self-protective about their situation. Conscious of the people's poverty and the stereotypical reaction of contempt by Westerners, a passionate Kurd asserts, "We're not stupid, we're just poor!"

The plot, intrigue-filled and convoluted, draws Ka into the center of the action as a conspirator and mediator. Yet, his personal goal—to gain happiness with İpek—which he seems to have achieved when she agrees to join him in Germany, is affected by his actions on behalf of the political-social life of the city. At the conclusion of the "present" of the novel, Blue has been located in his hiding place and killed, and Ka sends a note to İpek stating that he is under military "protection" and "they are forcing me to leave on the first train." He asks İpek to join him at the train station, as they have planned, with their luggage. She did not.

CENSORSHIP HISTORY

Orhan Pamuk's statement, quoted in the Swiss newspaper *Tages Anzeiger* in February 2005 that "a million Armenian and 30,000 Kurds were killed in these lands, and nobody but me dares to talk about it" was the catalyst for the onslaught leveled against him and his books. He was charged under Turkey's Article 301 in the then new penal code, which states: "A person who being a Turk, explicitly insults the Republic Turkish Grand National Assembly, shall be punishable by imprisonment of between six months to three years." Pamuk was retroactively charged in June; the newspaper interview occurred four months earlier. Such accusations of genocide are rejected by Turkey in both the deaths of ethnic Armenians in the early 20th century and, more recently, the deaths of Kurdish separatists.

The trial began on December 16, but it was suspended; another law requires that ex post facto charges be approved by the Ministry of Justice. On January 22, 2006, the Justice Ministry asserted it had no authority to open a case against Pamuk under the new penal code, thus refusing to issue an approval of the prosecution. Nevertheless, there was an outcry in the international press against this "repressiveness," and members of the European Parliament reacted against the case as "unfortunate" and "unacceptable."

The reactions in Turkey by conservative nationalist groups were much less benign. A hate campaign forced Pamuk to flee the country; during the trial nationalists shouted traitor and threw eggs at his car. Censoring attacks also occurred. A local government authority in Isparta ordered the "seizure and destruction" of Pamuk's books in libraries within his jurisdiction in protest of the author's remarks. The Turkish press reported that in Bilecik, a community about 93 miles (150 km) south of Istanbul, Pamuk's books were burned at a "Respect the Flag" rally. These were "calls from fellow journalists for Pamuk to be forever 'silenced.'"

In a BBC News interview, Pamuk asserted that his purpose was to defend freedom of speech in Turkey: "What happened to the Ottoman Armenians in 1915 was a major thing that was hidden from the Turkish nation; it was a taboo. But we have to be able to talk about the past."

This was not the first instance of Pamuk's legal trials. A supporter of Kurdish political rights, in 1995 he was among a group of authors tried for essays that criticized Turkey's treatment of the Kurds, a minority group within its borders.

The so-called Ergenekon scandal was the outcome of the arrest in January 2008 of 13 ultranationalists, including retired military officers and Kemal Kerinçsiz (who had led the attempt to bring Pamuk to trial in 2005). These participants in a Turkish nationalist underground organization named Ergenekon were suspected of conspiring to assassinate political figures, such as the Turkish-Armenian newspaper editor and intellectual Hrant Dink, who was murdered in 2007; Orhan Pamuk was among the figures targeted by the group. The author himself acknowledged that the police informed him of the assassination plan.

Orhan Pamuk was awarded the 2006 Nobel Prize in literature.

FURTHER READING

"The Curious Case of Orhan Pamuk." *Harvard Political Review* (April 1, 2009).
Hacaoglu, Selcan. "Turkish Court Drops Charges against Novelist." *Independent,* January 23, 2006.
Hitchens, Christopher. "Mind the Gap." *Atlantic Monthly* (October 2004): 188–93.
"International PEN Calls for Government Condemnation of Attacks on Author Orhan Pamuk." *International Freedom of Expression Exchange* (IFEX) (April 6, 2005).
Lea, Richard. "Plot to Kill Nobel Laureate." *Guardian* (London), January 28, 2008.
Tonkin, Boyd. "From Public Enemy to National Hero." *Independent,* October 16, 2008.
Updike, John. "Anatolian Arabesques." *New Yorker,* August 30, 2004, 98–99.

SPYCATCHER

Author: Peter Wright
Original dates and places of publication: 1987, Australia; 1987, United States

Publishers: William Heinemann; Viking Penguin
Literary form: Autobiography

SUMMARY

Subtitled *The Candid Autobiography of a Senior Intelligence Officer, Spycatcher* reveals the activities of MI5, the "Security Service" of Great Britain, while focusing on the role of Peter Wright. MI5's central function is domestic counterintelligence in contrast to the foreign intelligence mission of MI6, alias the "Secret Service." The MI stands for "Military Intelligence," but MI5 is operated entirely by civilians.

Wright entered the service initially prior to 1955 as a research scientist and worked as an agent for MI5 from 1955 to 1976. Wright's first appraisal was that the services were woefully out of date technologically, needing new techniques of eavesdropping that did not require entry to premises. His first project, a sensitive microphone, established the underpinnings of his reputation. This success was followed by the development of other devices. He describes the early 1950s as "years of fun," detailing a series of spysearching and eavesdropping incidents that illustrate technological inventiveness.

The saga continues through the 1960s, but the tone begins to change with the appointment of Roger Hollis as director-general of MI5 in 1956. Clearly, Wright doubts Hollis's ability to lead the Security Service and questions his negation of or hesitation to pursue active measures. Nevertheless, targets were pursued, among them the Egyptian government. Wright was able to develop a method of determining the settings of the cipher machines in the Egyptian embassies, thus enabling the British to decode the cipher. This ability was significantly helpful during the Suez Crisis.

In the context of the Suez conflict, Wright also mentions that MI6 developed a plan to assassinate Gamel Abdel Nasser, the president of Egypt. Two alternative plans, he claims, had been approved by Prime Minister Anthony Eden. Another revelation is that MI5 had gone beyond attempting to bug the avowed cold war enemy, Russia, but had also bugged the embassies of Britain's ally, France. This intelligence eavesdropping occurred during the 1960–63 interval when Great Britain was attempting to enter the Common Market.

A persistent, sometimes overriding concern relates to the infiltration of the British intelligence operations at the hands of an elaborate "Ring of Five" spy group. A Russian defector had so identified a conspiracy group. Double agents Guy Burgess, former executive officer of the British Foreign Service, and Donald Maclean, British diplomat, had defected to Russia in 1951. Harold "Kim" Philby, a high-level British diplomat and senior intelligence officer, was cleared after interrogation by MI6; however, Philby's reinterrogation by MI5 in 1962 led to his confession that he, too, was a double agent. He defected to Russia in 1963. In 1964, Sir Anthony Blunt, about whom there had been suspicions for years, also confessed to being a Russian spy. Wright, at the heart of these investigations, provides extended details of them along with his efforts to track down the fifth man. He reveals evidence that MI5's plans and procedures had often been leaked; he is sure that the culprit is in a high-level position. He and a colleague narrow down the choices to the director himself, Roger Hollis. Wright time and again asserts his belief in this finding even after Hollis is cleared after he has retired in 1965.

With regard to these revelations Wright reports considerable dismay and embarrassment within the intelligence community and the government. The revelations cast doubt on the effectiveness of the services, in particular their ability to maintain secrecy.

Another major operation, which may have grown out of fervor to track down subversives in government, is directed against Prime Minister Harold Wilson. Wilson came under suspicion, a suspicion, according to Wright, fed by James Angleton, chief of counterintelligence of the CIA, who would not reveal his source. Wilson's office was bugged while he was prime minister. Wright claims that MI5 had enough information to cause "a political scandal of incalculable consequences" that would have led to Wilson's resignation. He further states that he was approached by a group of MI5 officers to participate in a plot to leak information to "contacts in the press and among union officials . . . that Wilson was considered a security risk." The purpose was to bring down the government.

The book closes with Wright's retirement. He reiterates in the last chapter his conviction that Hollis was the "fifth man" and that "fear of scandal" became the most important consideration affecting everyone for the "turmoil of the 1960s." Throughout the book he asserts his own devotion to the cause represented by MI5 and acknowledges his many efforts on behalf of that cause.

CENSORSHIP HISTORY

The censorship challenge of *Spycatcher* emerged on two fronts: the publication of the book and the publication of excerpts and reports of its contents in newspapers. The government of Prime Minister Margaret Thatcher argued that publication would cause loss of confidence in MI5's ability to protect classified information, would damage national security, and would violate secrecy oaths taken by intelligence officers.

The Book
In September 1985, having learned of the planned publication of *Spycatcher* in Australia, thus avoiding litigation in Britain (the publisher had sent an advance copy to the attorney general, suggesting he could remove offensive passages, but a review of the text had determined that the book should be totally suppressed), the British government began legal action to suppress release of the book. It sought and was granted a temporary injunction by an Australian court, blocking publication until a trial had settled the legal issues.

The civil suit was tried in the New South Wales Supreme Court, Sydney, in November 1986, having been preceded by pretrial hearings. Essentially two major arguments emerged, those of national security and those of Wright's violation of his lifetime agreement to maintain secrecy about his MI5 activities. The defense argued that a previous publication, *Their Trade Is Treachery* by Chapman Pincher, published in 1981, had already revealed the information in *Spycatcher* (Wright had been an unnamed consultant to Pincher) and that the government had not taken action to prevent its publication. Thus Wright was not violating the secrecy code. The government claimed that Pincher the journalist was different from Wright the public official. The five-week trial ended on December 20, 1986, with Justice Philip Powell questioning the veracity of British cabinet secretary Sir Robert Armstrong, the chief witness for the Thatcher government.

Justice Powell announced his ruling on March 13, 1987. In a 286-page document, he rejected the claim of the government that *Spycatcher* would be harmful to British security and denied the request for a permanent injunction. He reasoned that the material in Wright's book was either harmless or already disclosed. He agreed that the government had the right to expect intelligence agents to keep secrets. However, two general reasons were offered why the British government could not claim that right in this instance: Earlier books and other publications had not been banned; disclosure to the public should be permitted when intelligence officers conducting secret operations break the law.

Within days, the British attorney general announced that the ruling would be appealed. The appeal hearing began on July 27, 1987, and the verdict on that appeal was announced on September 24, 1987. The New South Wales Court of Appeals rejected the government's request on a 2-1 vote. The court allowed the injunction against publication for three days. The government then appealed this decision that would have allowed publication to the High Court, Australia's highest judicial body. It was denied on September 27, 1987, allowing publication of the book in Australia. (About 240,000 copies of *Spycatcher* were sold in Australia after the lower court had ruled in favor of publication.)

The appeal to the High Court went forward, scheduled for March 8, 1988. The High Court's seven judges announced their unanimous decision on June 2, 1988, rejecting the government's attempt to ban further publication. These judges also accepted Britain's reasoning that Wright was bound by his lifetime oath to remain silent. They indicated, however, that the Australian court had no jurisdiction to enforce a British security regulation.

The Newspapers

In June 1986, the British government obtained legal rulings barring two newspapers, the *Guardian* and the *Observer*, from publishing leaks of Wright's allegations. The two newspapers had already each published an article in relation to the Australia trial. The newspapers appealed on the grounds that the information was already in the public domain and in the public interest since serious wrongdoing of the secret service was alleged. The appeal was denied: If the original publication was unauthorized, then republication would also be unauthorized.

Three different newspapers published articles on April 17, 1987. The *Independent* first included a full front-page summary of Wright's allegations with verbatim quotes from his book; the *Evening Standard* and the *Daily News* followed suit. The attorney general charged them with criminal contempt of court, citing the existing ban on the first two newspapers. The initial verdict supported the newspapers on the grounds that one newspaper was not bound by an injunction on another. However, on July 15, the appellate court overturned this verdict, in effect setting wide-ranging restrictions on any newspaper that published any material that another had been prevented from publishing.

Meanwhile, the *Sunday Times* on July 12, 1987, had begun a serialization of *Spycatcher*. This series, however, was stalled by a temporary injunction by the government on July 16.

In the succeeding week, the *Sunday Times*, the *Guardian*, and the *Observer* appealed the injunction. Days later, a High Court judge sided with the newspapers by dismissing the injunction. However, the government's appeal to the court of appeals resulted in a decision favorable to the government, but modified: Extracts were disallowed, but publication of Wright's allegations was legitimate news. Both parties appealed to the law committee of the House of Lords, the "Law Lords," Britain's highest appellate body. Its decision, a 3-2 ruling, on July 30, 1987, not only favored the government, but also extended the original ruling to include any evidence or arguments from the Australian court hearings. The Law Lords stated in their written opinions, issued in mid-August, that their ruling was temporary, pending a full trial. Further publication would destroy the government's case in advance of a trial. The minority opinion, calling attention to the release of *Spycatcher* in the United States and its availability in Britain, indicated that the claim of confidentiality was an empty one since it had already been lost; another point noted that the attempts to insulate the British public were "a significant step down the very dangerous road of censorship."

In the interim between ruling and opinions, the newspapers had violated the ban: The *Guardian* had reported the Australian court's hearings; the *News on Sunday* printed excerpts from *Spycatcher*. The attorney general announced it would prosecute the *News on Sunday* for contempt of court. Prime Minister Margaret Thatcher indicated the fight was a matter of principle because of the violation of a lifelong vow. Editor Brian Whitaker's reaction: "It is unacceptable that in a democracy like ours the British press should not be allowed to print stories concerning this country which are appearing in other newspapers throughout the world."

The trial to determine whether the injunctions should be permanent began in late November 1987; it concluded on December 21, 1987, when the

High Court judge found in favor of the newspapers, rejecting a permanent injunction. Justice Richard R. F. Scott was critical of the government: The duty of the press to inform the public had "overwhelming weight" against potential government embarrassment because of scandal. "The ability of the press freely to report allegations of scandal in government is one of the bulwarks of our democratic society. . . . If the price that has to be paid is the exposure of the Government of the day to pressure or embarrassment when mischievous or false allegations are made, then . . . that price must be paid."

The court of appeals, to which the government had immediately appealed, ruled unanimously in favor of the newspapers in February 1988. The ban on press publication remained in effect while the government appealed to the House of Lords. In October, that body unanimously upheld the court of appeals, lifting the temporary injunctions barring the newspapers from printing news about and excerpts from Wright's book and the trial. The government lost a two-and-a-half-year struggle.

The language of the ruling did not express a legal right to publish. Rather, the finding in favor of the newspapers was based on the reality of the information no longer being secret. In the majority opinion, Lord Keith declared, "[G]eneral publication in this country would not bring about any significant damage to the public interest beyond what has already been done."

The *Guardian*, the *Observer*, and the *Sunday Times* filed a suit against the British government with the European Court of Human Rights, which issued its final judgment on November 16, 1991. The first ruling, unanimous, determined that the British government had violated the European Convention on Human Rights in its attempt to prevent the three newspapers from disclosing the evidence of serious wrongdoing by MI5 contained in *Spycatcher*. Specifically, Article 10, which guarantees "the right of freedom of expression" to everyone, was violated. The second ruling, however, on a 14-10 vote, upheld the principle of prior restraint, supporting the government's injunctions on the *Guardian* and the *Observer* after they published the first articles about Wright's allegations. In confirming the legality in banning the publication of potentially sensitive material, the majority of the European Court acknowledged an "interests of national security exception." The dissenting judges were critical of a government being able to suppress disclosures before they are published. Once published—as was the case in the United States in July 1987—the contents could no longer be described as secret. In this context, the government's continuing the gag after July 1987 prevented newspapers from exercising their right and duty to provide information on a matter of legitimate concern.

U.S. Publication

With regard to the publication of *Spycatcher* in the United States, letters dated between March 6 and July 5, 1987, and published in London's *Independent* revealed that Assistant Treasury Solicitor David Hogg suggested to Viscount Blankenham, chair of Pearson—owner of Pearson, Inc., in the

United States whose subsidiary, Viking Penguin, was considering publishing *Spycatcher*—that Blankenham could "remove the directors of the American subsidiaries" if they persisted in their plans. Blankenham, while admitting his sympathy for the government's position, nevertheless stated:

> "[P]redisposition to sympathy [cannot] lead—in an international publishing group—to any insistence by Pearson . . . that overseas publishing houses in the group acknowledge and act on that sympathy." It is not open to an English court, he said, to control the exercise of power arising in the internal management of a foreign company.

Spycatcher was published in the United States in July 1987.

FURTHER READING

"British Official Suggests Ousting Viking Board to Stop *Spycatcher.*" *Publishers Weekly*, August 7, 1987, 311.

Clines, Francis X. "*Spycatcher* Judge Rules Against Thatcher." *New York Times*, December 22, 1987, p. 16.

Fysh, Michael, ed. *The Spycatcher Cases*. London: European Law Centre, 1989.

Kirtley, Jane E. "The Law Lords Take a Detour: Chapter Two of the *Spycatcher* Saga." *Government Information Quarterly* 7 (1990): 53–58.

———. "A Walk Down a Dangerous Road: British Press Censorship and the *Spycatcher* Debacle." *Government Information Quarterly* 5 (1988): 117–135.

Newsletter on Intellectual Freedom 36 (1987): 229.

Pincher, Chapman. *The Spycatcher Affair*. New York: St. Martin's Press, 1988.

———. *Their Trade Is Treachery*. London: Sidgwick and Jackson, 1981.

Turnbull, Malcolm. *The Spycatcher Trial*. Topsfield, Mass.: Salem House Publishers, 1989.

THE THINGS THEY CARRIED

Author: Tim O'Brien
Original date and place of publication: 1990, United States
Publisher: Houghton Mifflin/Seymour Lawrence
Literary form: Fiction

SUMMARY

A true war story, according to Tim O'Brien, is never moral, never able to separate fact from fiction, never ending, never diminutive, never uninquisitive, and never about war. Instead, a true war story is about the things that war is not: "sunlight . . . the way dawn spreads out on a river . . . love and memory." A true war story serves as a healing tool to anesthetize the sting of war. In *The Things They Carried*, O'Brien has a true war story for every path that he, Lieutenant Jimmy Cross, and Alpha Company travel. The purpose of O'Brien's story, which is made up of many smaller stories, is to make the reader think about not just the Vietnam War, but also the aspects and experiences that take place before and after the war within the hearts of those directly and indirectly involved. For those who were in the war, the book raises many questions and provides some answers. For those who were not involved with combat, the book sheds light on aspects least thought of when Vietnam is mentioned, including the feelings, thoughts, and challenges raised by the experience.

At first Tim O'Brien is strongly against U.S. involvement in Vietnam, perhaps more so than a typical 21-year-old, but he, like the rest of a nation divided, is mostly confused and unsure as to how the whole experience will develop. "Certain blood was being shed for uncertain reasons," and he wants no part of the turmoil. In fact, he did work for various antiwar factions toward the end of his college days, nothing to be jailed for, but his activism still served to solidify his liberal views. When his draft notice arrives, it is as though his entire life has been shrouded with a cape of hopelessness and desperation. Feeling already defeated, as though this can only be the passage to an early death, O'Brien one day sets out for a haven from his future.

Fear drives O'Brien to a derelict old resort in northern Minnesota run by one Elroy Berdahl, an old man who has seen nothing too surprising lately and can pretty easily surmise O'Brien's peril. For six days O'Brien fantasizes about the many ways he can escape his predicament. However, the reality of what others will think of him clamps down his motivations, keeping them well in check. During the last day of his stay, the two take to the river for a fishing excursion. Wise in his years, Berdahl pilots his old watercraft to a quiet inlet, which O'Brien immediately recognizes as his opportunity to escape. Twenty yards astern and up a rocky and jagged shoreline lays the thick brush of the undisturbed Canadian border. His body, tense yet eager, will not budge, not because he does not want to jump, but because he fears what others will say. He cannot face his family or friends as one labeled an abandoner. He can only sob and resign himself to the war, and the many stories in which he will partake.

O'Brien's time on Rainy River with Elroy Berdahl shows another side to the peril of Vietnam: the battle within. The actual battle in the field is well enough documented; what of the battles that occur away from that venue? What becomes of the young man with a prosperous future when faced with the gripping apprehension of a bleak situation: Kill or be killed? What happens to the weary yet ever thankful patriot who finds less than a sliver of a hero's welcome upon returning home after a hellish ordeal? The most intense battles may be those that take place internally, like his time on Rainy River, not in a wet, sticky, smoldering trench.

One particular mind battle occurs when O'Brien is injured and nearly dies of shock, due largely to the inexperience of the new medic, Bobby Jorgenson, who replaces Rat Kiley as the medic of Alpha Company well into the war. O'Brien is more than bitter about Jorgenson and wants to take revenge.

He strikes one night while Jorgenson has night watch: Carefully rigging trip lines, sheets and devices designed to emit strange sounds, O'Brien carefully plays hell with Jorgenson's nerves, leading the medic to believe that he not only is being watched, but also stalked and possibly a sitting-duck target. O'Brien is near giddiness as he pulls on a line that makes a sharp rustling sound, and Jorgenson pivots toward it, furiously clutching his rifle and peering into the blackness. However, as this goes on, O'Brien wonders if it has been too much. He thinks about how it must have been for Jorgenson to be thrust into a difficult situation, and if he could have performed any better, considering the circumstances. O'Brien decides to end the game but cannot because the friend he enlisted to help him is now more wrapped up in the prank than O'Brien ever was and refuses to back down. O'Brien is now a powerless spectator as the prank continues throughout the night, tormenting Jorgenson while inflicting guilt on O'Brien as well. The next day, O'Brien confesses to Jorgenson and offers an apology, which is accepted. Both become friends, but O'Brien still feels as though his retaliation went too far.

The Things They Carried is told by an older, more critical, yet more inquisitive O'Brien. Storytelling is combined with fierce antiwar sentiment and the belief that, right or wrong, the soldiers were justified because they had to do their patriotic duty. O'Brien fictionalizes events that actually occurred on the line along with those that happened just before the war, directly after the war, when he was a boy growing up, and in the present. O'Brien invents names and places to make the action seem more real to those who actually were there and to those who can only read about it. The author Tim O'Brien was in Vietnam for about one year and saw the enemy in human form only once. The character Tim O'Brien is a 21-year-old kid going off to war. The only link between the two is the feelings such as fear, doubt, excitement, and anger they both experienced.

CENSORSHIP HISTORY

Attacks on the Freedom to Learn: 1992–1993 Report cites an attempt to ban *The Things They Carried.* The incident occurred in Waukesha, Wisconsin. The school board was presented with a teacher's request to order 120 copies of the text for classroom use in a modern literature class. Objections raised at the school board meeting on September 9, 1992, cited the text "for profanity and for discussion of the Vietnam War." The motion to vote on the adoption of the text was brought up by L. Brecka and seconded by J. Cuevas. The discussion that ensued was highlighted with concerns including "anti-American attitudes, offensive language, political bias, and disturbing fiction. . . ." A vote of 8-1 against adoption was the end result, with the request that the book remain suitable for library reference but not for required classroom reading. Also noteworthy is the fact that the teacher who originally requested the book for classroom use was not mentioned in the meeting minutes, perhaps disabling the defense of the book even further. Since that decision was made, none of the members serving on the 1990 Waukesha school board remain and were thus unavailable for comment.

Two challenges, one in Pennridge, Pennsylvania (2001), the second in George County, Mississippi (2003), both for the book's language, had opposite results. The novel was retained in Pennridge, despite the protest of its "strong language"; the novel was removed in George County for profanity and violence, along with *Fallen Angels*, by Walter Dean Myers, and *Of Mice and Men*, by John Steinbeck. The negative vote resulted despite the explanation by Principal Paul Wallace of the school's policy of parental approval of readings, based on information about the works' contents and the provision of alternate reading materials.

A controversy over books deemed inappropriate for students ensued in May 2006 in a suburban Chicago school district, Arlington Heights–based Township High School District 214. The district includes six high schools of about 13,000 students. School board member Leslie Pinney identified nine books, including *The Things They Carried*, as containing explicit sexual images, graphic violence, and vulgar language; their educational value was questioned. The school board voted 6-1 to retain the nine books after a school board meeting attended by some 500 persons. Other books on the list included *Beloved*, by Toni Morrison; *Slaughterhouse-Five* by Kurt Vonnegut, *The Awakening*, by Kate Chopin, *Freakonomics*, by Steven D. Levitt and Stephen J. Dubner; *The Botany of Desire*: *A Plant's-Eye View of the World*, by Michael Pollan; *The Perks of Being a Wallflower*, by Stephen Chbosky; *Fallen Angels*, by Walter Dean Myers; and *How the García Girls Lost Their Accents*, by Julia Alvarez.

FURTHER READING

Attacks on the Freedom to Learn 1992–1993 Report. Washington, D.C.: People For the American Way, 1993, p. 189.

Francisco, Jamie. "School Board Averts Book Ban." Available online. URL: alliancelibrarysystem.com/PDF/2006. Accessed October 25, 2010.

Harris, Robert R. "Too Embarrassed Not to Kill." *New York Times Book Review*, March 11, 1990, p. 8.

Prescott, Peter S. "The Things They Carried." *Newsweek*, April 2, 1990, p. 57.

—Eric P. Schmidt
Updated by Nicholas J. Karolides

UNCLE TOM'S CABIN

Author: Harriet Beecher Stowe
Original date and place of publication: 1852, United States
Publisher: John P. Jewett
Literary form: Novel

SUMMARY

When Harriet Beecher Stowe wrote *Uncle Tom's Cabin,* her main goal was to paint a picture of slavery so heartrending as to cause white people to rise up against it. Her goal was not one of political change, however, for she believed that change that did not include a change of heart would not last. She thought the only way to effect a proper change was through conversion of the entire nation to Christianity. If everyone believed not only in but also practiced an equality ordained by God, the slaves would necessarily be set free and everyone would be able to go to Heaven. As such, every plot line focuses on a character who is a model of acceptance of Christianity, or a character whose faith is tested. Whether characters are good or evil depends upon their religious nature more than their deeds.

One plot line tells of the slave Eliza, her husband, George, who lives on another plantation, and their son, Harry. When Eliza discovers that her owner, Mr. Shelby, has sold her son to pay off a debt, she decides her only option is to run away. Her husband has already done so, as he is afraid his master will not allow his marriage to Eliza to continue, but will instead force him to live with another woman on his plantation. George feels his only hope is to run away to Canada and earn enough money to buy his wife and child. Once Eliza decides to escape, she realizes that her only hope, too, lies in Canada. She runs with her child toward the river that separates her home state of Kentucky from the free state of Ohio. With the slave trader Haley about to capture her, she has few choices; she crosses the ice-covered Ohio River, baby in her arms and no shoes on her feet, and arrives on the free side, tired and full of gashes. Unfortunately, due to the Fugitive Slave Law of 1850, being in a free state means relatively little. The new law forbids the people of the free states from helping runaway slaves and requires the slaves to be captured and returned to their proper owners. Quakers, notorious for their hatred of slavery, reject this law, becoming her main assistants, offering her food and shelter and reuniting her with her husband. The family is still in danger, however, as the slave trader has hired two men to find and capture Eliza and Harry, and they have set up a posse toward that end. The family attempts its escape to Canada, then is cornered by the posse, but George is unwilling to give up easily and begins shooting, wounding one of the group and scaring the others away.

Eliza and George are virtuous Christians, while Haley and the men he has hired are not. Eliza has faith that God will do what is best, as shown by her belief that He will help her across the river. George's faith, however, is tested. He feels that he and all blacks have been deserted by God. According to the beliefs of the narrator, George must accept Christianity as a necessary part of becoming a good man. This acceptance comes when, at the home of a Quaker with his wife and son, George is treated as an equal for the first time. The narrator says that "a belief in God, and trust in His providence, began to encircle his heart, as, with a golden cloud of protection and confidence, dark, misanthropic, pining, atheistic doubts, and fierce despair, melted away before the light of a living Gospel. . . ." George has converted in his soul, and thus is saved; Haley and the two slave trackers, however, are seen as evil, not because they sin daily by treating humans as property, but because they are not Christians. The narrative makes clear that their lack of Christian virtue will most certainly be dealt with harshly on Judgment Day.

The second major plot line follows the journeys of a virtuous man, Uncle Tom. He was also sold to Haley, but unlike Eliza, he is not willing to run away. He believes that he must do what his master says in this life and in the next. The plantation owner has put his trust in Tom, and Tom feels he cannot disobey. More important, Tom believes that whatever is to happen is ordained by God, and he will not risk becoming wicked by breaking His laws. While Tom has a wife and several children, he passively allows himself to be taken away and is soon found on a ship going down the Mississippi River. Also aboard is a young girl, little Eva. Tom is drawn to befriend her because she is angelic and pure. When he saves her life after she falls into the river, her father, Augustine St. Clare, agrees to purchase him.

Tom is brought to his new home in New Orleans, where the reader is introduced to a variety of characters. Eva's mother, Marie, is an extremely selfish hypochondriac who cares more for her own fabricated illnesses than the real illness of her child. St. Clare, on the other hand, cares deeply for his child and for his slaves. He believes slavery is wrong but does not see any way he can stop it. He believes it is his own fault if his slaves misbehave because being slaves has made them immoral. St. Clare also does not care much for religion because, as he says, religious slave owners are hypocritical, and he does not want to attend a church where the ministers tell the owners what they want to hear instead of the truth. Miss Ophelia is St. Clare's cousin from Vermont, whom he has engaged to run his household while his wife is "sick." She is hypocritical in a different way because she is religious and believes slavery is wrong, but she cannot stand to think of black people as her moral or intellectual equals.

St. Clare, while himself against slavery, details why his brother, Alfred, is in favor of it. Alfred, an "aristocrat," gives several arguments in defense of slavery by comparing it to other political systems.

> ". . . . 'the American planter is only doing, in another form, what the English aristocracy and capitalists are doing by the lower classes;' that is I take it, *appropriating* them, body and bone, soul and spirit, to their use and convenience. . . . there can be no high civilization without enslavement of the masses, either nominal or real. There must, [Alfred] says, be a lower class, given up to physical toil and confined to an animal nature; and a higher one thereby acquires leisure and wealth for a more expanded intelligence and improvement, and becomes the directing soul of the lower."

Eva is the ideal type of person Stowe wanted everyone to become—purely Christian and not hypocritical. Even in death, Eva remains pure, for she welcomes the opportunity to see her savior and converts others to the path of righteousness. Unlike her mother, she does not use the Bible to prove that God made slavery for a reason. Unlike Ophelia, she practices love and kindness. Unlike her father, she believes ending slavery is possible and that it is her mission to change the feelings of those around her so they feel compelled to free their slaves. She accomplishes this goal through her death. Her father is so moved that he becomes more religious and begins the paperwork necessary to free Tom, while Topsy, a mischievous and self-proclaimed "wicked" young slave girl, becomes good, and Ophelia begins to think of Topsy as a human, capable of loving and being loved.

Unfortunately, the papers that would give Tom his freedom have not been completed by the time St. Clare is stabbed trying to break up a fight—the ultimate act of Christian selflessness—so Tom is sold by Marie. He is bought at an auction by Simon Legree, a man who uses constant beatings to keep his slaves in line and drives them until they die, then buys new ones. More than his lack of respect for human life, his desire to make Tom give up his religion makes him a villain; when he finds Tom's hymnbook while rooting through his belongings, he says, "'Well, I'll soon have *that* out of you. I have none o' yer bawling, praying, singing niggers on my place; so remember. Now, mind yourself . . . *I'm* your church now! You understand,—you've got to be as I say.'" When Tom refuses Legree's order that he beat another slave, Legree becomes incensed. He tells Tom that he owns him, body and soul, but Tom responds:

> "Mas'r Legree, as ye bought me, I'll be a true and faithful servant to ye. I'll give ye all the work of my hand, all my time, all my strength; but my soul I won't give up to mortal man. I will hold on to the Lord, and put his commands before all,—die or live; you may be sure on't. Mas'r Legree, I an't a grain afeard to die. I'd as soon die as not. Ye may whip me, starve me, burn me,—it'll only send me sooner where I want to go."

This attitude forces Legree into a state of fear because he knows himself to be wicked and that, in the end, he will go to Hell. This fear manifests itself in a hatred of Tom so strong that he eventually beats him to death. Tom is another exemplary Christian who would rather accept his own death than inflict pain on another. His death causes the conversion of Cassy, an older slave woman who has turned away from God because she believes He has turned away from her. He also converts Sambo and Quimbo, Legree's slaves, who run the plantation and willingly beat their fellow slaves; when he dies, they realize the wrongs they have done to him and others and repent. Finally, Tom's death causes a different kind of conversion, when George Shelby, son of Tom's old owner, frees all of his slaves.

CENSORSHIP HISTORY

Uncle Tom's Cabin, from the moment it was published, was extremely controversial. The topic of slavery lay at the ideological heart of America and caused a great split, for how could a nation founded on principles of equality support a system in which 5 million of its populace were degraded and forced into submission? For this reason, the novel spurred many debates. Many in the North wanted to know if the stories were true; not living in slavery and seeing it firsthand, they could not believe that it was so cruel. That is why at the end Stowe included a chapter entitled "Concluding Remarks," in which she vouches for the truth of each incident she details, including the flight of Eliza across the icy Ohio River and the sad tales of familial separation on the auction block. Despite the controversy surrounding the novel and the fact that, as Joseph Conlin says in his book *Our Land, Our Time*, it "was banned in the South," the novel quickly became a best seller, with 3 million copies in print before the Civil War. In addition to responding to censorship, a dialogue was created between the proslavery and antislavery activists of both the North and the South. Those who disagreed with Stowe's conclusions countered them with criticism of her novel and with what John Tebbel calls "'anti–Uncle Tom' books," such as *Aunt Phillis's Cabin; or, Southern Life as It Is*.

Uncle Tom's Cabin was not only potentially dangerous to the American system of slavery, however. The idea of equality offended many others. Anne Haight notes that in 1852 it was "banned under the 'censorship terror' of Nicholas I." Censorship was a large part of Russian history, not just of books, but also of periodicals, plays, music, and other forms of expression. This trend was started long before Nicholas became czar, but his reign reinforced and extended the prohibitions. According to the statute on censorship of 1828:

> Works of literature, science, and art are to be banned by the censorship: (a) if they contain anything that tends to undermine the teachings of the Orthodox Greco-Russian church, its traditions and rituals, or in general the truths and dogmas of the Christian faith; (b) if they contain anything infringing upon the inviolability of the supreme autocratic power or upon the respect for the imperial house, or anything contradicting basic government legislation.

Uncle Tom's Cabin was seen as a threat to both of these conditions and was, therefore, censored. The system of aristocracy that Stowe criticizes as inhumane existed in Russia as well. The czar and other nobles prospered, while the lower classes worked very hard for relatively little. The free circulation of such ideas was understood as dangerous to the czar, so the novel was censored. Similar censorship took place for many other authors.

Also based on the statute of 1828, the novel was censored for undermining religious ideals. While the novel is extremely pro-Christian, it often takes sides against the church and the clergy. Both St. Clare and Stowe herself discuss the hypocrisy of the Christian church, which twists scripture to the advantage of slaveholders. When Marie tells how a sermon discussed scripture that showed how slavery was properly ordained by God, St. Clare scoffs at the idea: "'This religious talk on such matters,—why don't they carry it a little further, and show the beauty, in its season, of a fellow's taking a glass too much, and sitting a little too late over his cards, and various providential arrangements of that sort, which are pretty frequent among us young men; we'd like to hear that those are right and godly, too.'" Stowe, in her final paragraph, says, "Both North and South have been guilty before God; and the *Christian Church* has a heavy account to answer. . . ." She believed that it was the church's responsibility to teach the Christian virtues of kindness and equality, not to help support the unkind and unequal system of slavery.

The belief that the church allows so unjust a system to continue was also the reason behind papal censorship of this novel. Haight notes that in the Italian states and in the papal state in 1855 "the sale of the volume was prohibited, though not listed on the index." The Index librorum prohibitorum, or Roman Index, listed the works Catholics were forbidden to read, due to their blasphemous nature.

In addition to censorship in other countries, the novel was often protested and censored in the United States in later years by people who felt it was racist. Haight writes that in Bridgeport, Connecticut, in 1955, "a dramatized version . . . was protested by blacks as a caricature of reality." Stowe's novel, in fact, presents a stereotypical view of blacks and whites. For example, while Aunt Chloe is delightedly describing a dinner she made, she compares herself to her mistress, and several implicitly racist statements are made:

> "I and Missis, we come pretty near quarreling about dat are crust. . . . and, finally, I got kinder sarcy, and, says I, 'Now Missis, do look at dem beautiful white hands o' yourn, with long fingers . . . and look at my great black stumpin' hands. Now, don't ye think dat de Lord must have meant *me* to make de pie-crust, and you to stay in de parlor?'"

Remarks like these, found throughout the narrative, upset readers. Elsewhere in the story, Stowe paints a picture of blacks who are so happy as slaves that when George Shelby gives them their freedom, they refuse it. She also ends the plot of George and Eliza by sending them to Liberia, a colony in Africa set aside for freed slaves, making it obvious that educated, free blacks are not welcome in America. Also, many felt the character of Tom to be overly passive and unwilling to fight for his own life and freedom or that of his family. As Haight points out, during the 1950s, "'Uncle Tom' was becoming a derogatory phrase implying submissiveness."

In 1984, in Waukegan, Illinois, the book was protested by Alderman Robert B. Evans, Sr., along with Mark Twain's *Adventures of Huckleberry Finn*, Harper Lee's *To Kill a Mockingbird*, and Margaret Mitchell's *Gone with the Wind*. As Lee Burress points out, students and parents joined the protest in objection of "'racism' and 'language.'" Specifically, as the *Newsletter on Intellectual Freedom* says, Evans objected to the books' use of the word *nigger* and requested that they be removed from the curriculum: "There are no books in the district that talk about 'honkies,' 'dagos,' 'spics,' 'polacks,' or 'Hymies.' Just like people of those nationalities are offended by use of those words, black folks are offended by use of the word 'nigger.'" Since only *Huckleberry Finn* was required reading, the result was removal of this novel from the required reading list.

FURTHER READING

Burress, Lee. *Battle of the Books: Literary Censorship in Public Schools, 1950–1985.* Metuchen, N.J.: Scarecrow Press, 1989.

Conlin, Joseph R. *Our Land, Our Time: A History of the United States.* San Diego, Calif.: Coronado Publishers, 1985.

Haight, Anne Lyon, and Chandler B. Grannis. *Banned Books: 387 B.C. to 1978 A.D.* 4th ed. New York: R. R. Bowker, 1978.

Monas, Sidney. *The Third Section: Police and Society in Russia under Nicholas I.* Cambridge, Mass.: Harvard University Press, 1961.

Newsletter on Intellectual Freedom 33 (July 1984): 105.

Tebbell, John. *A History of Book Publishing in the United States.* Vol. 3: *The Creation of an Industry: 1630–1865.* New York: R. R. Bowker, 1972.

Vernadsky, George, ed. *A Source Book for Russian History from Early Times to 1971.* Vol. 2. New Haven, Conn.: Yale University Press, 1972.

—Jane Graves

A WOMAN IN BERLIN: EIGHT WEEKS IN THE CONQUERED CITY

Author: Anonymous
Original dates and places of publication: 1954, United States; 1959 (German edition), Switzerland
Publishers: Harcourt Brace; Kossodo
Literary form: Diary

SUMMARY

Friday, April 20, 1945, 4:00 P.M. The anonymous diarist (hereafter "She") begins her memoir with sounds of war in the background, yesterday's "distant rumble," today "a constant roar." The Russian invasion is thus forewarned, an outcome never anticipated when the war started. There is little news. She has been bombed out of her apartment and is living in a borrowed one out of her suitcase. Food is scarce; hunger is a constant. Electricity and running water are erratic—soon to disappear altogether. At night, the building's residents huddle in the basement shelter, protection from air raids, and later, briefly, from the Russians.

The atmosphere is fraught with despair and fear. "My sole concern as I write these lines is my stomach. All thinking and feeling, all wishes and hopes begin with food." Three early contrasting scenes illuminate the situation, the first of soldiers: "I stood in the doorway and watched some soldiers pass by our building, listlessly dragging their feet. Some were limping. Mute, each man to himself, they trudged along, out of step, toward the city. Stubbly chins and sunken cheeks, their backs weighted down with gear. . . . They all seem so miserable, so little like men anymore. The only thing they inspire is pity, no hope or expectation." Another scene: the discovery of food in the former police barracks, recently used by the Luftwaffe; a frantic mass in the pitch-black basement shoving, shouting, grabbing what they could find. Plunder—and anger. The author's apartment destroyed by a bomb, She moves in with the widow.

April 27 is the "day of catastrophe." The Russians have arrived, have taken over the street—troops, horses, vehicles—initially seeming friendly. Soon, since She knows a rudimentary Russian, having traveled to Russia, She is called upon to intercede in behalf of two women being molested. Though She manages to save them, She becomes a victim. Caught in a dark corridor, She is raped by two soldiers, twice each. Then, shortly thereafter back in her apartment, hemmed in by four soldiers, She is raped by one of them, who, asserting ownership, briefly becomes her protector against the others. But the next day another rapes her, an older man who spits in her mouth. She determines to find a protector, an officer who would, by rank, shield her from others. In effect, She gives herself to him, becoming his property. Anatole, a lieutenant, the chosen one, dispels other "suitors" and brings food and drinks. So begins a way of life. When his unit is repositioned, he is replaced by the major.

Few women escape these assaults—even grandmothers. Young girls, virgins, were concealed in false ceilings. Others used the same tactic as the author. One detailed event reveals the abuse of Elvira, a redhead who was hiding in a liquor distillery. She and the widow climb up to the fifth floor apartment to which Elvira had escaped

> "They lined up," [the distiller's] wife whispers to us, while the redhead stays silent. "Each took his turn. She says there were at least twenty, but she doesn't know exactly. . . ." I stare at Elvira. Her swollen mouth is sticking out of her pale face like a plum. "Show them," says the distiller's wife. Without a word the redhead opens her blouse and shows us her breasts, all bruised and bitten. I can barely write this; just thinking about it makes me gag all over again.

Berlin is covered with a blanket of fear among the women and an accompanying deep sense of despondency.

In contrast, the Russian soldiers, speak of German atrocities on the eastern front. On April 27, when the German women ask an officer to protect them, he cites a Stalin decree, but one of the men being reprimanded "voices his objection, his face twisted in anger: 'What do you mean? What did the Germans do to our women?' He was screaming. 'They took my sister and . . .' and so on." Another brutality is revealed in a May 5 conversation between two German women protected it seems by the presence of two young children, an infant and a four-year old, and two young soldiers, clearly enchanted by the children. One of them, a 17-year old "looks at [the author], brow deeply furrowed, and asks me to translate that in his village German soldiers stabbed some children to death and took others by the feet and bashed their heads against a wall. Before I translate, I ask, 'Did you hear that? Or see it yourself?' He gazes off and says in a stern voice, 'I saw it twice myself.' I translate."

Distinctions among the Russians are identified. As contrasts to the brutal, lewd men who force themselves on the women and even Lieutenant Anatole, a peasant and somewhat refined, we are introduced to an intellectual sergeant, a schoolteacher by profession and an orthodox marxist; his conversations are political and economic. Another, Anatole's orderly, solicitous and linguistically sophisticated, discusses Pushkin. Having been rejected by the author, his advances were made during Anatole's absence. Another lieutenant is "distant and formal and flawlessly polite."

Aiming to replace Anatole in the author's bed, the major is discreet, politely cautious. "He speaks a sophisticated Russian: as always I can tell by the fact that whole sentences go by without my understanding a word. He seems to be well read and quite musical, and he's clearly taking pains to behave like a gentleman even now." During their first intercourse, when She complains of being miserable and sore, he is gentle and silently tender. He wants her to join him in Russia.

Early in the diary, an April 26 entry, She notes how her attitudes—and those of other women—and interpretation of men are changing.

> These days I keep noticing how my feelings toward men—and the feeling of all the other women—are changing. We feel sorry for them; they seem so miserable and powerless. The weaker sex. Deep down we women are experiencing a kind of collective disappointment. The Nazi world—ruled by men, glorifying the strong man—is beginning to crumble, and with it the myth of "Man." In earlier wars men could claim the privilege of killing and being killed for the fatherland was theirs and theirs alone. Today we women, too, have a share. That has transformed us, emboldened us. Among the many defeats at the end of this war is the defeat of the male sex.

She notes her prewar instinct with German men to "play down my intelligence for them" because a German man wants to be smarter.

The reactions of German men to the abuse of their wives was "reasonable—they react with their heads, they're worried about saving their own skins, and their wives support them in this. No man loses face for relinquishing a woman to the victors. . . . On the contrary, they would be censured if they provoked the Russians by resisting. The husband of the author's friend so acted but "torment[ed] himself with reproach" for not interceding when "the Ivans took their pleasure with his wife." He was "within hearing range."

Two exceptions to this reasonable code are represented. When a Russian attacked the bookseller's wife, her husband yelled at him, running toward him with "red-eyed wrath," thus causing the Russian to back off. Another husband, whose wife had drunk and slept with the same Russian several times, shot her in the back and then shot himself in the mouth.

While not a constant commentary, the flaws of the Nazi regime are frequently enough expressed to assert a position. Early in the diary, on April 23, She reflects on the government's abandonment of the civilians:

> There were rolls at the baker's, the last ones. My last ration cards for bread, too. No new cards in sight. No decrees and no news, either. Nothing. Not a soul cares about us anymore. We're suddenly mere individuals, no longer members of the tribe, the German Nation. Old ties are broken; friendships don't extend farther than three buildings away. There's only the group of us, huddled in the cave, a clan, just like in prehistoric times. The horizon has shrunk to three hundred paces.

On May 8, Herr Pauli, the widow's tenant, curses the government about the *Volksturm* [People's militia] "senselessly" sending old, tired men "to die at the last moment . . . just left to bleed to death, helpless with not even a rag to dress their wounds." A reference to Göering, reported as crying like a child upon his arrest, identifies him as "a colossus with feet of clay." In reacting on May 17 to a former Nazi party boss having been denounced and picked up, She reflects, "We have mixed feelings, talking about this. A bit of *schadenfreude* [taking joy in other's suffering] cannot be denied. The Nazis were too pompous and subjected the *volk* to too many harassments, especially in the last few years, so it's right that they should atone for the general defeat."

The shortage of food—hunger—is introduced on April 20 and persists throughout the eight weeks, excepting the two weeks when her Russian protectors are also providers and when She, as a drafted laborer along with other women, is fed a hearty barley soup. There are days when She and the widow lived solely on bread or nettles or a thin flour soup. Throughout the post-Army period, women are described as gaunt and hollow-eyed; on June 11, She notes, "I was very low on energy; my diet has no fat. There's always this wavy mist in front of my eyes, and I feel a floating sensation, as if I were getting lighter and lighter."

Throughout her diary, She contemplates her situation and herself: "I'm constantly repulsed by my own skin. I don't want to touch myself, can barely look at my body . . . and all for the filth I am now" (April 29). After the departure of the lieutenant and the appearance of the major, she writes, "I cannot force myself into this role, to feel at ease so quickly. I have this repulsive sense of being passed from hand to hand; I feel humiliated and insulted, degraded into a sexual thing" (May 2). When both the lieutenant and the major are on the scene, She is apprehensive: "What am I supposed to do? I'm nothing but booty-prey that has to stand back and let the hunters decide what to do with their game and how to parcel out" (May 4). "Sleeping for food is another new concept. . . ." (May 16). She also recognizes her growing resilience and strength: "On the other hand, things are looking pretty good for me. I'm healthy and refreshed. Nothing has harmed me physically. I feel extremely well armed for life. . . . I'm well equipped for the world" (May 13).

On June 16, Gerd, the author's fiancé, returns from the front in civilian dress and suntanned and bearing food; he had simply left the army. She was "feverish with joy." The relationship sours: He does not understand her unwillingness to share food with his guests. He responds negatively to her stories of her experiences, becoming angry. "You've all turned into a bunch of shameless bitches, everyone of you in the building. Don't you realize?" He grimaced in disgust. "It's horrible being around you. You've lost all sense of measure." He read her diary; when she translated her shorthand "*schdg*" as *schändung*" (rape), he "looked at me as if I were out of my mind but said nothing more." The next day he left to visit a buddy's parents and would return with food. The diary ends a page later.

By the conclusion of the diary in mid-June, some semblance of order and normality had been achieved. Running water and electricity had been restored to the apartment on May 19 and May 27 respectively. Germany had surrendered; peace had been declared. Germany had been divided into sectors, and on June 10, 1945, it was announced that Berlin, too, would be divided among the three allies. On June 15, the radio broadcasts another concentration camp report. Some rations were being distributed. Walking through the streets seemed safe. Yet, "everywhere you turn you can sense the fear. People are worrying about their bread, their work, their pay, about the coming day. Bitter, bitter defeat."

CENSORSHIP HISTORY

The republication in 2003 after 50 years of A *Woman in Berlin: Eight Weeks in the Conquered City* was received with critical acclaim, becoming a best seller in Germany for at least 19 weeks. It was praised for its unsentimental honesty, its "determination to see beyond the acts themselves" and the author's "fierce, uncompromising voice." Its style is acclaimed for its precise detail and keen observation. In contrast, the first publication in Germany in 1959 was controversial and the author felt humiliated. Thus, she had refused to allow it to be reprinted until after her death. She died in 2001.

The first publication—an incomplete translation—was in the United States in 1954 in the cold war years, presumably when western audiences might have been more receptive. In addition to English, it was translated into seven other languages. The 1959 German-language edition, published in Switzerland, perhaps because it was banned in Germany, faced a hostile or silent response. Germans, during a period of great forgetting, were not ready for "uncomfortable truths"; sexual collaboration for survival was a taboo subject. Germans were outraged, accusing the author of "besmirching the honor of German women." Further, German men were affronted by their images in the diary: standing aside or acquiescing to their women being violated. The author, in fact, does refer to the myth of the strong man as being eradicated.

Thus, the diary was "virtually banned," quickly going out of print; "the book sank without trace in a country that had *decided* to deal with the horrors of its immediate past through collective silence."

Hans Magus Enzensberger, the literary executor of the author, in keeping with his perception of her wishes, maintained the "anonymous" authorship for the 2003 edition. However, Jens Bisky, a German journalist with *Süddeutsche Zeitung* revealed his discovery that the author was Marta Hillers, a not altogether confirmed fact. In response to this revelation, Enzensberger accused Bisky of "shamelessness."

FURTHER READING

Bourke, Joanna. "Living with a Brutal Bear." *Independent*, June 17, 2005.
Connolly, Cressida. "She Screamed for Help but Her Neighbors Barricaded the Door." *Daily Telegraph*, April 17, 2005.
Enzensberger, Hans. "Enzensberger and Anonyma." *Der Spiegel*, September 29, 2003.
Esch, Christian. "An Unimportant Person?" *Süddeutsche Zeitung*, September 25, 2003.
Gottesmann, Christoph. "A Woman in Berlin." *New York Times Book Review*, September 11, 2005, 6.
Grant, Linda. "The Rubble Woman." *Observer*, July 2, 2005.
Harding, Luke. "Row Over Naming of Rape Author." *Observer*, October 5, 2003.
Kanon, Joseph. "*A Woman in Berlin*: My City of Ruins," *New York Times*, August 14, 2005.

—German translations by Gretchen Toman,
Maple Grove Senior High School

LITERATURE SUPPRESSED ON
RELIGIOUS GROUNDS

In 1989, an edict from Tehran brought a shocking reminder of religious censorship, regarded by many as a specter from the distant past of the Inquisition and the burning of heretics. The Ayatollah Khomeini's fatwa (death decree) against author Salman Rushdie and the widespread banning of Rushdie's novel *The Satanic Verses* for blasphemy against Islam was a startling example of a phenomenon that is as old as history and, with the current wave of religious fundamentalism, as recent as today's headlines.

Censorship has existed in every society to protect the prevailing moral and social order. Book censorship in Western culture can be traced to the earliest years of Christianity, when the church began to suppress competing views as heretical. In the second century, the Council of Ephesus burned superstitious works and prohibited the *Acta Pauli*, a history of St. Paul, and in the fifth century, the pope issued the first list of forbidden books.

The flood of unauthorized Bible translations and religious tracts that followed the invention of the printing press in 1450 and the rise of religious dissent during the Protestant Reformation motivated the church to expand its censorial functions. In 1559, Pope Paul IV published the first Index librorum prohibitorum (Index of Forbidden Books). The Index, often referred to as the Roman Index, was administered by the Roman Inquisition. It was binding on all Roman Catholics, who represented most of the population of continental Europe, and was enforced by government authorities. At the same time, similar indexes were also prepared by theological faculties in Paris and Louvain and by the Spanish Inquisition.

As church and state in Europe began to separate in the 16th century, national monarchies instituted their own mechanisms of religious and political censorship to supplement or substitute for that of the church. In the areas where they had political control, the new Protestant faiths began to ban the writings of Catholics or dissenters.

From the earliest times, religious orthodoxy and politics have been intimately connected. To be a heretic was often to be considered a traitor, subject to punishment by secular authorities. And manipulation of religious sensibilities for political purposes has a long and sordid history, with recorded examples dating to the trial of Socrates in 399 B.C.

As Europe became more politically fragmented and means of communication more sophisticated, state censorship was rarely thorough enough to prevent forbidden books from circulating. By the 18th century, the proliferation of underground publishing, as France's book censor Chrétien-Guillaume de Lamoignon de Malesherbes said, meant that "a man who had read only books that originally appeared with the formal approval of the government would be behind his contemporaries by nearly a century."

It is impossible to discuss religious censorship of books without referring to the Roman Index, one of the most successful and enduring censorial devices in history. When it was finally abolished by the Vatican in 1966 after four centuries, it had outlived its effectiveness. The church had long before lost the authority to enforce it, and this list was widely viewed as anachronistic.

In the 42nd and final Index issued in 1948 and in print until 1966, a total of 4,126 books were still prohibited to Catholics: 1,331 from the 17th century or earlier, 1,186 from the 18th century, 1,354 from the 19th century, and 255 from the 20th century. Though many were obscure theological titles or works that were controversial in their day but had been forgotten for centuries, literary and philosophical classics by dozens of authors representing a Who's Who of Western thought also were included: among them, Bentham, Bergson, Comte, Defoe, Descartes, Diderot, Flaubert, Gibbon, Hobbes, Hume, Kant, Locke, Mill, Montaigne, Montesquieu, Pascal, Rousseau, Sand, Spinoza, Stendhal, Voltaire, and Zola. Rather than banning books, the church's post-Index book censorship has focused primarily on sanctioning dissident Catholic theologians for their writing or pressuring the occasional Catholic author to hew to orthodoxy.

Though the First Amendment bars government authorities from practicing religious censorship in the United States, individuals and organized religious fundamentalists have successfully pressed to remove books viewed as anti-Christian from public and school libraries and curricula. The majority of these instances have focused on perceived immorality, profane language, or treatment of sexuality rather than religious content per se. Their targets, however, have included textbooks that teach evolution without presenting the alternative theories of "creationism," or "intelligent design," books said to promote the religion of "secular humanism," and material with references to Eastern religions, "New Age" thought, and witchcraft or the occult, such as J. K. Rowling's Harry Potter books and Roald Dahl's *The Witches.*

Although Rushdie's *Satanic Verses* is the most notorious international case of book censorship in the 20th century, it is not unique. The freedom of expression and safety of authors, editors, and publishers continues to be threatened by governments that censor or prosecute those whose writing offends Islamic religious authorities and by militant Islamic groups and terrorists.

Since the Islamic revolution of 1979 in Iran, thousands of writers, journalists, and other intellectuals have been jailed, and unknown numbers executed or assassinated. Iranian novelist Shahrnush Parsipur, for example, was repeatedly imprisoned because of her writing and had to leave the country. During the 1990s, fundamentalist terrorists murdered Egyptian writer Farag Fouda and Algerian novelist and journalist Tahar Djaout, among many others. In 1994, the Egyptian Nobel laureate Naguib Mahfouz was stabbed and seriously wounded. Other writers, such as Taslima Nasrin of Bangladesh, have been driven into exile by death threats or, like Egyptian novelist Alaa Hamed, sentenced to prison for blasphemy. The writing of feminists such as Nasrin, Nawal El Saadawi of Egypt, and Fatima Mernissi of Morocco, who challenge interpretations of Islamic dogma that restrict women, has particularly angered both governments and Islamists.

The books discussed in this section represent a sampling of the thousands that have been targets of religious censorship over the centuries. They include texts of the world's major religions, novels, and classic works of philosophy, science, and history representing the intellectual heritage of Western civilization. They also include contemporary works that offended church authorities, governments, or Christian, Hindu, or Muslim fundamentalists. A few entries, such as Charles Dickens's *Oliver Twist*, chronicle censorship attempts in the United States that were ultimately unsuccessful but that merit attention because they involved legal challenges.

Many of these books were branded with the charge of heresy. Heresy is defined as opinion or doctrine that is at variance with orthodox religious teaching, or, as religious historian David Christie-Murray observed, "the opinion held by a minority of men which the majority declares is unacceptable and is strong enough to punish." Others were charged with blasphemy, speaking in a profane or irreverent manner of the sacred. All were censored because they were seen as dangerous—to orthodoxy, to faith and morals, or to the social and political order.

Yet to review the censorship of the books discussed in this section is to be struck by its futility. As historian Leonard W. Levy observed, the verdicts of time mock judgments and alter sensibilities. Insurgent faiths become established and revolutionary ideas lose their power to shock. For centuries censorship has created best sellers because, as Michel de Montaigne said, "To forbid us anything is to make us have a mind for it." Like water leaking slowly through a dike to become a steady trickle or a flood, words and ideas inexorably elude the censor's grasp.

"A book cannot be killed," commented Moroccan writer Nadia Tazi on Rushdie's censorship. "It lives and dies on its own. Once the 'vases' are 'broken,' the fragments of life spread throughout the world; voices escape, going their adventurous ways; and there are always encounters, mutations, and festivals of the spirit."

NOTES ON THE SECOND EDITION

Since the first edition of this book was published in 2005, would-be censors have found new targets, but their motives and methods remain the same. In the United States, public schools and public libraries are still the primary arenas for battles over book banning. During the period 1990 to 2008, the American Library Association (ALA) logged more than 9,600 attempts to limit access to books or remove them entirely from schools or libraries. Many of the people who would restrict the freedom to read are parents and organized Christian conservatives who wish to shield young people from sexual content, offensive language, portrayals of violence, or political, social, or religious viewpoints with which they disagree. During the years 2000 to 2009, J. K. Rowling's Harry Potter novels were at the top of the ALA's list of "challenged" books because their depiction of wizards and witches offended Christian fundamentalists. In 2007 and 2008, Philip Pullman's award-winning His Dark Materials trilogy of fantasy novels, *The Glass Compass*, *The Subtle Knife*, and *The Amber Spyglass*, were among the most frequently targeted books because they were seen as anti-Catholic and antireligious. And more than 85 years after the Scopes "monkey trial," the teaching of evolution and its discussion in textbooks is still hotly contested around the country on religious grounds.

Writers around the world continue to face bans, persecution, and violence for offending religious authorities or religious sensibilities or for diverging from political ideology masquerading as religion. This edition discusses the stepped-up suppression of writers in Iran and the increase in book banning since 2005 by the hard-line Islamic regime of Mahmoud Ahmadinejad—including international best sellers such as *The Da Vinci Code* (also banned in Lebanon, Pakistan, Egypt, and some Indian states). It also sheds light on an ominous development, an example of the stranglehold that extremism can have on freedom of expression—preemptive censorship by publishers motivated by fear of violence. In 2008, Random House, the world's largest trade book publisher, canceled the publication of *The Jewel of Medina*, a novel by Sherry Jones about Muhammad's wife A'isha, because the company feared terrorist attacks by radical Muslims. After Random House's decision, the London home of the book's British publisher was firebombed. In 2009, also fearing violence, Yale University Press decided to remove all the images of the prophet Muhammad from *The Cartoons That Shook the World*, a scholarly study by Jytte Klausen of the international furor that erupted after a Danish newspaper published 12 cartoons of Muhammad in 2005.

After September 11, 2001, we realized that the fatwa against writer Salman Rushdie was the harbinger of a greater tragedy: wholesale murder by terrorists in the name of religion. "When people first started to make a connection between me and 9/11, I resisted because of the disparity of the scale," Rushdie told the *Times* of London in 2005. "But I have come to feel that what happened with *The Satanic Verses* was a kind of prologue and that now we are in the main event."

—Margaret Bald

THE AGE OF REASON

Author: Thomas Paine
Original dates and place of publication: 1794–95, France
Literary form: Philosophical treatise

SUMMARY

The Anglo-American political theorist, writer, and revolutionary Thomas Paine was one of the greatest pamphleteers in the English language. *The Age of Reason*, an uncompromising attack on Christianity based on the principles of rationalism, became the most popular deist work ever written.

The son of an English Quaker, Paine immigrated to America in 1774 and became active in the independence movement. His pamphlet, *Common Sense*, published in January 1776, called for the founding of an American republic and galvanized the public toward independence.

In 1787, Paine returned to England, where he published in 1791–92 *The Rights of Man*, a work defending the French Revolution and attacking social and political inequities in Britain. It was to sell an estimated half-million copies in the next decade and become one of the most widely read books in England. Indicted for seditious libel by the British government for *The Rights of Man*, Paine fled to Paris, where he participated in the French Revolution as a member of the National Convention. For 10 months in 1794, during the Reign of Terror, he was imprisoned by Maximilien Robespierre and the Jacobins before being rescued by the American ambassador to France, James Monroe.

On his way to prison Paine delivered to a friend the manuscript of part one of *The Age of Reason*, which was published in Paris in 1794. After his release from prison, he completed part two, which appeared in 1795. During his stay in France, Paine became convinced that popular revulsion against the reactionary activities of the French clergy, who plotted against the Revolution in alliance with the forces of aristocracy and monarchy, was leading the French people to turn to atheism. In *The Age of Reason*, Paine resolved to rescue true religion from the Christian system of faith, which he regarded as a "pious fraud" and "repugnant to reason."

Paine, in common with many prominent American and European intellectuals, such as Benjamin Franklin, Thomas Jefferson, Voltaire, and Jean-Jacques Rousseau, was a deist. Deism, a religious expression of scientific rationalism, proposed that the existence of God could be inferred from the order and harmony of creation. Deists saw formal religion as superfluous and scorned claims of supernatural revelation as a basis for belief. God's creation, deists believed, was the only bible.

In *The Age of Reason*, Paine popularized deism, removed it from the sphere of the intellectual elite, and made the philosophy accessible to a mass audience. Though critics described the book as "the atheist's bible," Paine repudiated atheism. He opened the book with a profession of faith: "I believe in one God, and no more; and I hope for happiness beyond this life."

Paine's declared objective in all his political writings, beginning with *Common Sense*, was to rescue people from tyranny and false principles of government. *The Age of Reason* was written in the same vein. "Of all the tyrannies that affect mankind," Paine wrote, "tyranny in religion is the worst; every other species of tyranny is limited to the world we live in; but this attempts to stride beyond the grave, and seeks to pursue us into eternity." Organized religion was set up to "terrify and enslave mankind, and monopolize power and profit." The only true theology was "natural philosophy, embracing the whole circle of science."

Paine criticized insincere claims of belief as "mental lying." Every national church or religion claims some special mission from God, communicated to certain individuals, and every church proclaims certain books to be revelation or the word of God. "It is a contradiction to call anything a revelation that comes to us second-hand, either verbally or in writing," Paine wrote.

Paine believed that mystery, miracle, and prophesy were three frauds and that the Old and the New Testaments could not be attributed to revelation. "I totally disbelieve that the Almighty ever did communicate anythingto man . . . other than by the universal display of Himself in the works of the creation, and by that repugnance we feel in ourselves to bad actions, and the disposition to do good ones." It was the "Bible of Creation," not the "stupid Bible of the Church," to which men should turn for knowledge. "My own mind is my own church," he proclaimed.

While in part one of *The Age of Reason* Paine disputed in general terms the tenets of Christianity, in part two he attacked both the Old and the New Testaments in tones of ridicule and sarcasm. Challenging the authenticity of the five books of Moses, Paine asserted that they had not been written in the time of Moses; rather, they represented an "anonymous book of stories, fables and traditionary or invented absurdities, or of downright lies." He described the Old Testament as being full of "obscene stories, the voluptuous debaucheries, the cruel and tortuous executions . . . a history of wickedness that has served to corrupt and brutalize mankind; and for my part, I sincerely detest it as I detest everything that is cruel."

Criticizing the New Testament, Paine wrote that the Gospels, having appeared centuries after the death of Christ, were not written by the apostles. He admitted that Jesus was a virtuous and honorable man but denied that he was God. He took offense at the Christianity of the church, "a religion of pomp and revenue" contradictory to the character of Jesus, whose life was characterized by humility and poverty. He described the story of the Immaculate Conception as "blasphemously obscene." He deplored the depiction of miracles for "degrading the Almighty into the character of a showman."

Of all the systems of religion, none is "more derogatory to the Almighty, more unedifying to man, more repugnant to reason, and more contradictory in itself, than this thing called Christianity," Paine wrote. "As an engine of power, it serves the purpose of despotism; and as a means of wealth, the avarice of priests; but so far as respects the good of man in general, it leads to nothing here or hereafter."

As Christianity worships a man rather than God, it is itself a species of atheism, a religious denial of God, Paine contended. "The creation is the Bible of the Deist. He there reads, in the handwriting of the Creator himself, the certainty of his existence and the immutability of His power, and all other Bibles and Testaments are to him forgeries."

CENSORSHIP HISTORY

Paine wrote *The Age of Reason* in an accessible, easy-to-read style. Deistic organizations distributed it free of charge or at low cost in America and Europe. In America, in the mid-1790s, Paine's book went through 17 editions, selling tens of thousands of copies. *The Age of Reason* became the bible of American deists, Paine their hero, and deism a mass movement allied with republicanism.

However, the book also aroused the hostility of clergy and believers on both sides of the Atlantic—a hostility that endured even long after Paine's death. A century later, for example, Theodore Roosevelt referred to Paine as "a filthy little atheist." *The Age of Reason* outraged the leaders of the religious establishment. But it also angered religious reformers who shared Paine's critique of religious conservatism but who parted company with him when he rejected the Bible and all forms of Christianity.

Like its seditious predecessor, *The Rights of Man*, *The Age of Reason* was regarded by the British government as genuinely dangerous because it appeared in the context of mass unrest stirred by the French Revolution. Though Paine was out of reach of British law in France and America, his publishers and booksellers in Britain were not. They were relentlessly prosecuted and imprisoned by the British government over a period of more than 25 years.

In 1797, Thomas Williams of London was tried by a special jury before the Court of King's Bench and found guilty of the crime of blasphemy for having published *The Age of Reason*. The prosecution contended that Paine's book, by subverting the truths of Christianity, undermined the government and the constitution, both of which rested on Christianity. Further, *The Age of Reason* robbed the poor by depriving them of a belief in a happier afterlife. Williams was sentenced to a year at hard labor and a £1,000 fine.

In 1812, the British Crown prosecuted publisher Daniel Isaac Eaton for blasphemy for publishing and selling a new edition of *The Age of Reason*. Eaton had earlier been imprisoned for publishing *The Rights of Man*. "Our civil and religious institutions are so closely interwoven together," the prosecutor told the jury, "that they cannot be separated—the attempt to destroy either is fraught with ruin to the state." Eaton was sentenced to stand in the pillory and to serve 18 months in Newgate Prison. Upon his release from prison, he again defied authorities by publishing *The Age of Reason;* once again, he was prosecuted and convicted of blasphemy. However, because of his age and poor health, he was not sentenced.

The highest price for the defense of Paine's right to publish his ideas was paid by publisher Richard Carlile, a radical exponent of freedom of the press, who between 1817 and 1835 served more than nine years in prison for publishing *The Age of Reason* and other deist tracts. In 1818, he read *The Age of Reason* for the first time and became a deist. He decided to republish the book knowing that its previous publishers had been imprisoned for blasphemy. Indicted for blasphemy, Carlile defiantly kept selling the book. He was brought to trial in October 1819 and in his own defense read the entire book to the jury, taking 12 hours the first day of the trial. By reading it into the court proceedings, he ensured that the work would be republished as part of the public record. It sold 10,000 copies in this form thanks to publicity surrounding the trial.

Carlile was found guilty of blasphemy and sentenced to two years in prison and a £1,000 fine for publishing *The Age of Reason,* as well as another year in prison and a £500 fine for publishing Elihu Palmer's deist book, *The Principles of Nature.* Within an hour of his conviction, government officers seized the contents of his shop and closed it down. Carlile was bankrupted and spent six years in prison, as he could not pay his fines. His wife, his sister, and more than 20 of his workers were also prosecuted and jailed in the years that followed for continuing to publish *The Age of Reason* and other material judged blasphemous.

Rather than succeeding in suppressing Paine's work, Carlile's prosecution aroused interest in it. Four years later more than 20,000 copies were in circulation in England. According to the philosopher John Stuart Mill, writing in 1824, "as among the poorer classes it is notorious that there are several readers to one purchaser, it may be estimated that at least one hundred thousand persons have been led to the perusal of that work under circumstances highly favourable to its making an impression on their minds."

FURTHER READING

Foner, Eric. *Tom Paine and Revolutionary America.* London: Oxford University Press, 1976.

Levy, Leonard W. *Blasphemy: Verbal Offense against the Sacred, from Moses to Salman Rushdie.* New York: Alfred A. Knopf, 1993.

Paine, Thomas. *The Age of Reason.* Introduction by Philip S. Foner. Secaucus, N.J.: Citadel Press, 1974.

THE BIBLE

Literary form: Religious text

SUMMARY

The Bible is a collection of books containing the sacred writings of the Jewish and Christian religions. Both religions regard the Bible as inspired by God. The Christian Bible has two parts: the Old Testament, which includes the Hebrew Bible that is sacred to Jews, and the New Testament, which includes specifically Christian writings. The Hebrew Bible is divided into three sections: the Law, or Torah (also known as the Pentateuch), consisting of the first five books—Genesis, Exodus, Leviticus, Numbers, and Deuteronomy—the Prophets, books of history and prophecy; and the Writings, containing prayers, poems, and maxims.

The books of the Bible were written over centuries by many different authors. The authorship of the Old Testament was traditionally attributed to great Jewish leaders, among them Moses, Samuel, David, Solomon, and various prophets. Modern scholars, however, have concluded that many of the books are later compilations of early traditions and writings. Scholars believe that the earliest books of the Bible began as oral literature and were first written down following the reign of King David, after 1000 B.C. The Book of Genesis, for example, contains passages that may date to the 10th century B.C., but the entire book was probably not written down in its present form until the fifth century B.C. The whole Torah, or first five books of the Bible, was in use by about 400 B.C.

The Old Testament—written in Hebrew, with some sections in Aramaic—tells the story of Creation and provides information on pre-Israelite times and the history and religious life of ancient Israel from about 1300 B.C. to the second century B.C. Christians and Jews regard the Old Testament as the record of a covenant or testament made by God with man and revealed to Moses on Mount Sinai.

The canonical books of the Old Testament and their order vary within the Jewish, Catholic, and Protestant religions. The Hebrew Bible revered by Jews consists of 24 books. The Christian Old Testament divides some of the books, increasing their number to 39. The Catholic Bible also includes as authentic seven books of the Old Testament that Protestants consider to be of doubtful authority and refer to as the Apocrypha.

The 27 books of the New Testament, sacred only to Christians, chronicle the years from the birth of Jesus Christ to about A.D. 100 and consist of the earliest documents extant on the life and teaching of Jesus and the establishment of the Christian church. Christians believe that Jesus Christ proclaimed a new covenant, or new testament, that both fulfilled and superseded the covenant revealed to Moses.

The New Testament is divided into four sections: the Gospels, or biographies of Jesus; the Acts of the Apostles; the Letters, or Epistles, of the apostles; and Revelation, a book of prophecy. Written in Greek between A.D. 70 and 100, the New Testament was compiled in the second century. Although the New Testament is traditionally considered to have been written by the apostles and disciples of Jesus, modern scholars have questioned the apostolic authorship of some of the books.

Both the Old and New Testaments were translated into Latin by Saint Jerome in about A.D. 400 and compiled as the standard and definitive text in the sixth century. The Roman Catholic Church designated his translation, known as the Vulgate, as the authorized Bible. It remained so for 1,000 years, up to the time of the 16th-century Reformation. The first book printed in Europe, the famous Gutenberg Bible of 1456, was an edition of the Vulgate.

CENSORSHIP HISTORY

"Both read the Bible day and night, But thou read'st black where I read white." These words of the poet William Blake aptly describe the origins of censorship of the Bible. Battles over the correct version of the Bible began in the early years of Christianity, when many of the church's first decrees established certain books as acceptable parts of the Bible and disclaimed others. Throughout the later Middle Ages, the Catholic Church discouraged translation of its official Latin Vulgate edition for fear that the text might be corrupted or misinterpreted. In the late 14th century, in defiance of the church's restrictions, the first complete translation of the Vulgate into English appeared, the work of the scholar and reformer John Wycliffe and his followers.

Wycliffe, whose treatise *On Civil Lordship* was condemned for heresy, maintained that all people had the right to read the Gospel "in that tongue in which they know best Christ's teaching." Reading the Wycliffe Bible was forbidden in England except by ecclesiastical permission. In 1409, the Synod of Canterbury at Saint Paul's in London issued a decree forbidding translation of the Scriptures or the reading of any new translations without a special license, under penalty of excommunication. Although Bible translations were undertaken in other European countries, no others appeared in England until the Protestant Reformation. Despite the ban, the Wycliffe Bible was frequently copied, and some portions of it were later adopted by William Tyndale, the first of the Reformation translators.

The 16th-century Protestant reformers held that because God speaks directly to human beings through the medium of the Bible, it is the right and duty of every Christian to study it. They either sponsored or undertook themselves translations of the Bible into their own languages. By 1522, when Martin Luther's German translation was published, or shortly thereafter, there were already 14 printed German Bibles, and vernacular versions had appeared in France, Italy, Spain, Portugal, Bohemia, the Netherlands, and Scandinavia.

Protestant reformers believed that the Bible should be understood literally and historically by readers without interpretation by church authorities. This doctrine, *sola scriptura* (Scripture alone), was seen as threatening by the Catholic Church, faced with a widespread loss of its authority as the Protestant revolt spread throughout Europe. Catholic censorship focused on the burgeoning number of Protestant vernacular versions of the Bible, notably Luther's in Germany, Tyndale's in England and Robert Estienne's in France. Protestants also censored biblical material, banning titles by dissenting Protestants as well as by Catholics. But Protestants could censor only within their own political boundaries. Because of the fragmentation of Protestant Europe, Protestant censorship was not as comprehensive as that of the Catholic Church.

The most violently suppressed Bible translation was Tyndale's. He was the first person to translate the Bible into English from its original Hebrew and Greek and the first to print it in English. His translation of the New Testament, printed in Cologne and Worms, Germany, in 1524–26, was smuggled into England, where the church banned and publicly burned it. His translations of the Pentateuch in 1530, the Book of Jonah in 1531, and a revised New Testament in 1534 were also prohibited and burned. Despite the bans, many reprints of Tyndale's translations were smuggled into the country and circulated.

In a plot masterminded by English authorities, Tyndale was arrested by authorities in Antwerp, Belgium, tried for heresy, and strangled and burned at the stake near Brussels in 1536 with copies of his Bible translation. Despite its repression, Tyndale's translation survived to form a considerable portion of later Bibles, including the Authorized or King James Version published in 1611.

Miles Coverdale, Tyndale's colleague, produced a complete English Bible in 1535. Because it could not be licensed to be printed in England, it was published in Germany. The popular demand for the Bible in English and the growing difficulty of suppressing its publication led King Henry VIII to name an authorized version, Matthew's Bible, based on Tyndale's and Coverdale's work. It appeared in 1537 with prefaces and annotations by John Rogers, who used the pseudonym John Matthew. Rogers was a Catholic priest who converted to Protestantism and a friend of Tyndale's. Matthew's Bible was the first in English to be licensed by the government. But on the accession of the loyal Catholic queen Mary I, Rogers was among the first of 300 martyrs to be imprisoned and burned as heretics in 1554.

Bans on new Bible versions were not confined to England. In 1539, Henry VIII issued his own Great Bible, a revision by Coverdale of his earlier work, which was to be the official version in the newly reformed Church of England. When he decided to print it in Paris, authorities moved to stop it. François Regnault, the famous Parisian printer of English books, was seized by the Inquisition and imprisoned. Sheets of the Great Bible were smuggled out of France in hats and taken to every church in England with the king's directive that each man should interpret Scripture for himself.

In 1546, the doctors of theology at the Sorbonne secured the condemnation in the Louvain Index of Forbidden Books of a Bible edition printed by the renowned humanist Robert Estienne, the official printer of King Francis I. The king responded by prohibiting the printing or circulation in France of the Louvain Index and ordering the withdrawal of strictures on the Estienne Bible. With the death of the king in 1547, however, the prohibition was renewed and Estienne had to move his press to Geneva. But Protestant Geneva, under the authority of the Protestant reformer John Calvin, was not a bastion of religious toleration. The Calvinists also condemned the Estienne Bible.

Spain under the Inquisition moved to suppress Bible editions influenced by Protestantism. In 1551, the Index of Valladolid listed 103 editions condemned because of errors and heresies to suppression, correction, or cancellation.

The restoration of papal authority, ecclesiastical courts, and the laws against heresy in England under the Catholic regime of Mary I reconfirmed the ban on Protestant Bibles. In 1555, a royal proclamation commanded "that no manner of persons presume to bring into this realm any manuscripts, books, papers . . . in the name of Martin Luther, John Calvin, Miles Cover-dale, Erasmus, Tyndale . . . or any like books containing false doctrines against the Catholic faith." Protestants from England who took refuge in Frankfurt and Geneva published the Calvinist "Breeches Bible" in 1560. Although its use was forbidden in churches in England, it went into 140 editions between 1560 and 1644.

In 1546, the Catholic Church's Council of Trent declared the Latin Vulgate of Saint Jerome to be the sole canonical text of the Bible. In opposition to the Protestant reformers, the council decreed that dogma is transmitted through the church's teaching, whose authority is equal to that of the Bible, and forbade the reading of any unapproved translation. The first English version approved for Catholics was a translation of the New Testament from the Vulgate by church scholars published in Rheims in 1582 and printed in 1610 with an approved Old Testament as the Rheims-Douay version.

In 1631, the word *not* was inadvertently omitted from the seventh commandment (Thou shalt not commit adultery) in an edition of 1,000 copies of the Bible printed in England by R. Barker. The printers were heavily fined, and the edition, known as the "wicked Bible," was so vigorously suppressed that few copies have survived.

Because the copyright of the Authorized (King James) Version was held by the British Crown, the right to print in England in the 17th century was held by the royal printers. Only the universities of Oxford and Cambridge were exempt from the restriction. This meant that no authorized Bible could be printed in the American colonies until after their independence. The first Bible printed in America was not the King James Version, but the *Up-Biblum God*, John Eliot's Bible translation for the Algonquian Indians, published in 1661–63. The Bible in English was probably not published in the United States until 1782 in Philadelphia, though historians have found evidence that a Bible may have been secretly printed in Boston about 1752.

The prudish sensibilities of the 19th century in England and the United States led to a new kind of censorship of the Bible—the publication of expurgated editions. *The Holy Bible, Newly Translated*, by John Bellamy, a Swedenborgian, was published in 1818. Declaring that no major biblical figure could have committed actions he found unacceptable, Bellamy decided that the translation from Hebrew must be at fault, and he revised passages he considered indecent. *The New Family Bible and Improved Version*, by Dr. Benjamin Boothroyd, a Congregationalist who wanted to circumvent "many offensive and indelicate expressions" in the Bible, was published in several editions beginning in 1824. That year, in *The Holy Bible Arranged and Adapted for Family Reading*, John Watson, a Church of England layman, replaced offensive sections with his own writing and dropped the numbering of traditional chapters and verses so that it was difficult for readers to notice what had been cut. In 1828, William Alexander, a Quaker printer, published *The Holy Bible, Principally Designed to Facilitate the Audible or Social Reading of the Sacred Scriptures.* He changed words and passages "not congenial to the views and genius of the present age of refinement."

The first expurgated Bible in America was published in 1833 by the lexicographer Noah Webster, who made thousands of alterations in material he considered indecent. Although his Bible was adopted by the state of Connecticut in 1835, endorsed by Yale, and widely used in Congregational pulpits for about 20 years, Webster's desire to make changes even in "decent" parts of the Bible met with criticism. The third edition, published in 1841, was the last.

Twentieth-century government censorship of the Bible has been most widespread in socialist countries. In 1926, the Soviet government instructed libraries throughout the USSR to remove all religious books such as the Bible. It was allowed to remain only in the country's largest libraries. Its importation was forbidden, and it was not printed again in the Soviet Union until 1956. In China, during the Cultural Revolution of the 1960s and 1970s—a campaign to destroy "the four olds" of culture, thinking, habits, and customs—Bibles were burned, and all places of Christian worship were closed.

A 1986 government-authorized printing of a Bible used by the Baptist Church in Romania marked the first time since 1951 that the Bible had been published there. The socialist military government of Ethiopia in 1986 banned several books of the Bible as "contrary to the ongoing revolution." A shipment of more than 45,000 Bibles destined for a church in Ethiopia was held indefinitely in customs.

Many attempts to censor the Bible have been recorded in the United States. Parents or religious groups who denounced the teaching of the Bible as comparative literature or believed it should be taught only as the sacred word of God from their own perspective and interpretation have tried to remove it from school libraries or curricula. Challenges to the Bible have also often been based in misunderstanding of Supreme Court decisions prohibiting prayer in the public schools. In 1963, in *District of Abington Township v. Schempp*, the U.S. Supreme Court prohibited devotional exercises in public schools. The Court, however, did not forbid the study of the Bible as literature, or of religion in historical or social studies. In its decision the Court declared, "In addition, it might well be said that one's education is not complete without a study of comparative religion or the history of religion and its relationship to the advancement of civilization. Nothing we have said here indicates that such study of the Bible or of religion, when presented objectively as part of a secular program of education, may not be effected consistently. . . ."

In an early challenge to the Supreme Court decision, a conservative religious organization sued the University of Washington for having offered an elective course on the Bible as literature. It argued that such a course could not be offered in a public institution and that the approach taken conflicted with its religious views. The Washington state courts upheld the inclusion of the course in a broad curriculum.

A 1982 study of 17 surveys conducted of school libraries during the previous two decades found that the presence or use of the Bible in schools had been challenged by students, parents, or teachers who thought it was illegal or who objected to the interpretation used. Similar challenges were reported during the 1980s and 1990s. For example, in 1989 an elementary school in Omaha, Nebraska, banned the reading or possession of the Bible on school premises. In a settlement of a suit in federal district court that never came to trial, it was agreed that students could read the religious literature of their choice at school during their free time. In 1991, a library patron who believed that public funds could not be spent on religious books challenged the presence of the *Evangelical Commentary on the Bible* and the *Official Catholic Directory* in the Multnomah, Oregon, public library. The books were retained by the library. In May 1981, Christian fundamentalists burned copies of *The Living Bible* in Gastonia, North Carolina.

A spate of attempts during the 1990s to restrict access to the Bible, reminiscent of Victorian-era attempts to bowdlerize it, were motivated by the view that it contains indecent material. In 1992 in the Brooklyn Center, Minnesota, independent school district, an atheist "seeking to turn the tables on the religious right" challenged use of the Bible, declaring that "the lewd, indecent, and violent contents of that book are hardly suitable for young children." In 1993, the Bible was challenged as "obscene and pornographic," but was retained at the Noel Wien Library in Fairbanks, Alaska. Near Harrisburg, Pennsylvania, protesters attempting to remove it from the West Shore schools cited "more than 300 examples of obscenities in the book" and objected that it "contains language and stories that are inappropriate for children of any age, including tales of incest and murder."

Though the Bible is among the most censored books in history, it has been translated more times and into more languages than any other and has outsold every book in the history of publishing. In the English language alone, some 450 different editions are in print. The long history of Bible censorship has had little impact on its availability and influence today.

FURTHER READING

Burress, Lee. *Battle of The Books: Library Censorship in the Public Schools, 1950–1985.* Metuchen, N.J.: Scarecrow Press, 1989.

Daniell, David. *Let There Be Light: William Tyndale and the Making of the English Bible.* London: British Library, 1994.

———. *William Tyndale: A Biography.* New Haven, Conn.: Yale University Press, 1994.

Doyle, Robert P. *Banned Books: 2004 Resource Guide.* Chicago: American Library Association, 2004.

Haight, Anne Lyon. *Banned Books: 387 B.C. to 1978 A.D.* Updated and enlarged by Chandler B. Grannis. New York: R. R. Bowker, 1978.

Hentoff, Nat. *Free Speech for Me, but Not for Thee.* New York: HarperCollins, 1992.

Jenkinson, Edward B. "The Bible: A Source of Great Literature and Controversy." In *Censored Books: Critical Viewpoints*, edited by Nicholas J. Karolides, Lee Burress, and John M. Kean, 98–102. Metuchen, N.J.: Scarecrow Press, 1993.

Lofmark, Carl. *What Is the Bible?* Buffalo, N.Y.: Prometheus Books, 1992.

Manguel, Alberto. *A History of Reading.* New York: Viking Press, 1996.

New York Public Library. *Censorship: 500 Years of Conflict.* New York: Oxford University Press, 1984.

O'Neil, Robert M. "The Bible and the Constitution." In *Censored Books: Critical Viewpoints*, edited by Nicholas J. Karolides, Lee Burress, and John M. Kean, 103–108. Metuchen, N.J.: Scarecrow Press, 1993.

Perrin, Noel. *Dr. Bowdler's Legacy: A History of Expurgated Books in England and America.* Garden City, N.Y.: Anchor Books, 1971.

Putnam, George Haven. *The Censorship of the Church of Rome.* Vol. 1. New York: G. P. Putnam's Sons, 1906–07.

Tinguet, Margaret. "Ethiopia: Destroy the Muslims." *Index on Censorship* 16, no. 4 (April 1987): 33–35.

THE CARTOONS THAT SHOOK THE WORLD

Author: Jytte Klausen
Original date and place of publication: 2009, United States
Original publisher: Yale University Press
Literary form: Scholarly political science analysis

SUMMARY

On September 30, 2005, the Danish newspaper *Jyllands-Posten* published 12 cartoons depicting the prophet Muhammad. The cartoons, drawn by different artists, were accompanied by statements explaining that they were being published as a blow against intimidation and self-censorship because various artists "were afraid—or should be afraid—to treat Muslims as they would members of any other religious group." The publication of the cartoons touched off violent protests during which 200 or more people died and sparked an international debate on free speech, blasphemy laws, and modern Islam.

The Cartoons That Shook the World examines the events following the publication of the cartoons in *Jyllands-Posten*. The book's author, Jytte Klausen, is a native of Denmark who lives in the United States and teaches comparative politics at Brandeis University. She deconstructs the arguments and motives that drove the escalation of the conflict and concludes that the reaction was primarily "an orchestrated," though uncoordinated, "political action" by those who wished to influence elections in Denmark and Egypt. Later, the issue was taken up by Islamic extremists whose aim was to destabilize governments in Pakistan, Lebanon, Libya, and Nigeria, rather than a spontaneous emotional outburst and "a colossal cultural misunderstanding," which is how it was widely perceived.

Klausen describes the 12 drawings at the center of the conflict, as well as the cartoonists' bewildered and angry responses to the developing crisis. Some of the cartoons were, in fact, caricatures, or wordless line drawings that satirize, mock, or ridicule; others could be properly described as political cartoons, which tell a story or comment on current events. One cartoon in particular, by Kurt Westergaard, which depicted Muhammad with a bomb in his turban, inspired the most rage—although Westergaard, says Klausen, intended only "to show that radical Muslims use the Prophet's name to justify violence."

Klausen explains that the early reaction to the cartoons was nonviolent, though Muslims and others saw them as derogatory and evidence of an Islamophobic environment in Denmark. It was to call attention to an ongoing "smear campaign" against Muslims that, following the cartoons' publication, a group of Muslim ambassadors in Copenhagen wrote to the Danish prime minister Anders Fogh Rasmussen and requested a meeting. Among their concerns were demeaning statements made by the Danish culture minister Brian Mikkelsen and representatives of the far-right Danish Peoples' Party (DPP), an ally of the governing party. When Fogh Rasmussen responded, as he did similarly to two other letters from the Organization of the Islamic Conference (OIC) and the Arab League (who would become key players in the controversy), he defended Denmark's tradition of free speech, said that the government had no influence over the press, and ignored the request for a meeting. He maintained this stance in the ensuing weeks and months as the crisis simmered. This response (or lack of it), Klausen asserts, all but guaranteed the subsequent controversy, of which, she says, Fogh Rasmussen and his government should have been well aware.

Klausen examines Fogh Rasmussen's possible motives, which include his political ambitions and his ties to the DPP, a party that wielded considerable political clout. Moreover, says Klausen, the issue was not just free speech; it was the perception that *Jyllands-Posten* had exploited the issue of free speech specifically to deride Muslims. Many decried what they saw as a double standard that favored Christians and Jews—the most common complaint that Muslims expressed during the crisis. (Denmark, like other countries in Europe, has laws against blasphemy and racial hate speech.)

Klausen traces the events as they unfolded, beginning with diplomatic efforts in fall 2005 to quell a growing crisis that included death threats against the cartoonists and the *Jyllands-Posten* editors. Egypt, in particular, became a major player in the events that followed. Toward the end of October, the Egyptian foreign ministry voiced its expectation that the Danish government should condemn "the mockery of the Prophet" and complained to the United Nations, the Organization for Security and Co-operation in Europe, and the European Union that the Danes had violated nondiscrimination resolutions. Klausen discusses the possible reasons for Egypt's involvement, including the government's wish to compare favorably with the opposition party, the Muslim Brotherhood; an attempt to discourage Western pressure to democratize; and an effort to help establish Islamophobia as a human rights offense. At around the same time, the Arab League and the OIC accused Denmark of violating UN resolutions on human rights.

In December 2005, a group of Danish imams assembled a dossier containing, among other documents, copies of the cartoons and more incendiary drawings (which were incorrectly attributed to *Jyllands-Posten*, though they had never appeared in the paper). Copies of these materials, which were distributed at an OIC summit meeting, became "the primary source of information for Middle Eastern religious authorities, and it shaped their view about the treatment of Muslims in Denmark," despite the fact that, as Klausen notes, the "impression conveyed by the dossier was . . . misleading and on some points plainly false." Following the OIC summit and the release of a communiqué condemning the cartoons, the world's Muslims—who by and large knew little about the controversy until that time—were put on alert. The OIC meeting "encouraged the religious establishments to become involved and various governments and parliaments in Islamic countries to publicly condemn the cartoons."

In January 2006, expressing disappointment at the Danish government's continuing refusal to apologize, the Muslim Brotherhood clerics who belonged to the International Union of Muslim Scholars condemned the cartoons, encouraged Arab and Muslim governments to apply political and diplomatic pressure on Denmark, and recommended a trade boycott. In February 2006, Islamic scholar and preacher Yusuf al-Qaradawi, who had ties to the Muslim Brotherhood, urged Muslims to stage a "day of rage" against the cartoons, though not all Muslims—including his supposed allies—agreed with him. At that time, "clerics and political leaders from the radical opposition in Muslim countries . . . joined the campaign," and violence erupted around the world.

The protests, says Klausen, ultimately "had less to do with outrage at the cartoons than with a broader strategy of collective mobilization and agitation," as radical groups across the Muslim world co-opted the cartoons "to mobilize popular anger against local governments for purposes that had nothing to do with the feelings of observant Muslims or the human rights of Danish Muslims." She notes that only a small fraction of Western Europe's small population of Muslims support Islamist extremism, and she highlights the mixed reactions of Muslims to the cartoons, observing that "the protests against the cartoons revealed deep fissures in the Muslim countries between secularists, electoral Islamists, and extremists," with "political arguments . . . as common as religious opinions."

The violent protests that erupted in February and March 2006 were brought on, Klausen writes, by a combination of motives that, while appearing to be part of a "coordinated global protest," were actually part of a fragmented movement with varying goals and players. "The governments of Muslim countries aimed to make symbolic statements and influence international debates about human rights, democracy, and Muslims. . . . The radical extremists aimed to destabilize Islamic governments and turned the cartoons against them. The Danish mosque activists wanted to change things in Denmark and shake up Danish Muslims, and . . . European Muslim associations and the Muslim Brotherhood pursued legal avenues of redress in order to obtain recognition and promote the rights of Muslims in the context of national politics."

Klausen emphasizes that it was not until other European newspapers began to reprint the cartoons, months after their initial publication, that the crisis became full blown. While a number of European newspapers reprinted them as a way to demonstrate their solidarity in refusing to cave in to "political correctness," many Muslims saw the reprinted cartoons "as a coordinated campaign of denigration." (In fact, during two weeks in February, the cartoons were also reprinted in Russian, African, Latin American, Asian, and Australian papers. By the end of February, one or more of the cartoons had been reprinted in at least 143 newspapers in 56 countries. Among the news outlets that reproduced the cartoons were 12 or more papers, magazines, or news stations in Arab and Muslim countries.)

"A domestic chain-reaction of protests and counterprotests" followed each reprint, Klausen explains. Except in the British and American media, which by and large did not reprint the cartoons, this chain reaction occurred worldwide. Finally, says Klausen, "The cartoons were made into a chapter in the undeclared war between the West and Islam only as a result of the political processes that took place before the eruption of violent demonstrations." In the end, the "cartoons and the protests against them confirmed existing prejudices on both sides."

CENSORSHIP HISTORY

In August 2009, Jytte Klausen noted, in an address to members of a Washington think tank, "It is obviously a strange situation for an author to end up becoming another chapter in her own book." In July, a few months before the scheduled fall publication of *The Cartoons That Shook the World*, Klausen learned that Yale University Press, the book's publisher, had decided to remove the illustrations of the 12 cartoons from the book. They also excised all representations of Muhammad, including renderings of the scene of "Muhammad in Hell" in Dante's *Inferno*, drawn by such masters as Doré, Rodin, and Blake, and an image from a children's book.

In a publisher's statement printed at the front of the book, Yale University Press said that it had considered the civil unrest occasioned by the publication of the cartoons and, in consulting with "experts in the intelligence, national security, law enforcement . . . fields, as well as with leading scholars in Islamic studies," was persuaded that reprinting the images risked inciting violence.

In an author's statement, printed on the same page, Klausen "reluctantly" consented to the removal of the illustrations, saying that Muslim scholars and political activists and leaders with whom she had spoken "urged me to include the cartoons . . . with the purpose of encouraging reasoned analysis and debate" on the entire episode.

Debates over Yale's action began to rage, in a more intellectual way, with as much passion as Muslim demonstrators displayed in their condemnation of the cartoons. James Bone, writing in the *Times* of London, and Christopher Hitchens, posting on *Slate*, berated Yale for its cowardice in censoring itself. PEN American Center, the National Coalition Against Censorship, the American Booksellers Foundation for Free Expression, the American Civil Liberties Union, the American Library Association, and the American Association of University Professors (AAUP) were among the groups that protested. "What is to stop publishers from suppressing an author's words if it appears they may offend religious fundamentalists or groups threatening violence," wrote Cary Nelson, president of the AAUP in an open letter. The university's action "compromises the principle and practice of academic freedom, undermines the independence of the press, damages the university's credibility, and diminishes its reputation for scholarship," wrote Joan Bertin, executive director of the National Coalition Against Censorship on behalf of 11 other organizations.

John Donatich, director of Yale University Press, defended the removal of the images. He cited the arrest in 2008 by Danish police of Muslims who attempted to murder Kurt Westergaard, the artist who depicted Muhammad with a bomb in his turban, as a continued reaction to the publishing of the cartoons. Donatich also quoted one of the experts consulted by Yale—Ibrahim Gambari, United Nations special adviser to the secretary-general—as saying, "You can count on violence if any illustration of the prophet is published. It will cause riots, I predict, from Indonesia to Nigeria."

However, Reza Aslan, a scholar of religion and author of *No god but God: The Origins, Evolution and Future of Islam,* disagreed and withdrew the blurb he had written in praise of the book. The book is "a definitive account of the controversy," he said, "but not to include the actual cartoons is to me, frankly, idiotic. . . . This is an academic book for an academic audience by an academic press. . . . There is no chance of this book having a global audience, let alone causing a global outcry."

Klausen, also, found Gambari's assertions "laughable," but was more disturbed by Yale's insistence that as a condition of being able to read the summary of recommendations made by the consultants, she sign a confidentiality agreement forbidding her to discuss their findings. She refused. One of the consultants, Fareed Zakaria, then editor of *Newsweek International*, who serves on Yale's governing board, came forward and said that he told Yale he believed reprinting the images would have provoked violence.

As Brendan O'Neill wrote in London's *Independent* (and as others have observed), publishing the cartoons in an academic work is very different from reprinting them in various newspapers, which was the action that gave rise to the riots. The real problem, he wrote, "is the cultural cowardice in the West itself, over-caution amongst the supposed guardians of ideas and arguments, that leads to the removal of offending material." Citing other cases in which material was suppressed before it reached the public—including Random House's reneging on its contract to publish Sherry Jones's *The Jewel of Medina* (about Muhammad's wife A'isha and which was later released by another publisher)—O'Neill notes that, "In each case, it wasn't threats or actions by agitated Muslims that gave rise to censorship; rather, elite fear of agitated Muslims generated self-censorship."

The *Washington Post*'s editorial of August 23, 2009, said: "Yale's self-censorship establishes a dangerous precedent. If one of the world's most respected scholarly publishers cannot print these images in context in an academic work, who can? . . . In effect, Yale University Press is allowing violent extremists to set the terms of free speech. As an academic press that embraces the university's motto of *Lux et Veritas*, it should be ashamed."

Jytte Klausen herself has observed that, as her book shows, the violence had "little connection to the original protests in Denmark or the international diplomatic protests." She notes that most of the deaths occurred in Nigeria, where a "virtual civil war" is ongoing. And al-Qaeda's bombing of the Danish embassy in Islamabad in 2008 had more to do with "a string of attacks on diplomatic foreign missions" than with the cartoons. "The deaths," she wrote, "resulted from violence in long-running conflicts where the cartoons became a new symbol in an old terrorist campaign or a rallying point in a protracted standoff between extremists and local governments."

So while Klausen reluctantly agreed to go ahead with the book's publication on Yale's terms, she has written subsequently that "nothing could substitute for looking at the cartoons and parsing their multiple and contradictory meanings and interpretations." In addition, she observed, "The removal of the other illustrations poses problems for the text, which was written to the illustrations . . . these illustrations were intended to awake the reader to the history of depiction of Muhammad in Ottoman, Persian, and Western art—and to show also how we live with images and do not examine them. Well, they will not be examined this time."

In December 2009, the self-censorship controversy took a startling new turn when *Index on Censorship*, a respected British organization and publication that documents and campaigns against censorship, declined to publish images of the cartoons alongside an interview with Klausen about Yale's censorship. Jonathan Dimbleby, chair of *Index*, cited the firebombing of the home and offices in London of the publisher of Gibson Square Books, who had proposed publishing the novel *The Jewel of Medina*, and wrote: "Re-publication of the cartoons would put at risk the security of our staff and others, which on balance, could not be justified on 'freedom of expression' grounds alone."

Critics of *Index's* decision could not resist pointing out the obvious. "They at least know the value of free expression, and would not let purely notional imaginary projected risks cause them to censor themselves," wrote Ophelia Benson in London's *Guardian*. "Surely. But Index on Censorship did just that, thus seeing and raising Yale's bet in the irony stakes."

Dissenting *Index* board member Kenan Malik wrote, "[W]e cannot in good conscience criticize others for taking decisions that we ourselves have taken and for the same reasons. . . . Almost every case of pre-emptive censorship, including that of Yale University, has been rationalised on the grounds that the censored material was not necessary anyway. Once we accept that it is legitimate to censor that which is 'unnecessary' or 'gratuitious', then we have effectively lost the argument for free speech. . . . what I fear is that in refusing to publish the cartoons, *Index* is not only helping strengthen the culture of censorship, it is also weakening its authority to challenge that culture."

—Alice Tufel and Philip Milito

FURTHER READING

Applebaum, Anne. "Chipping Away at Free Speech." *Washington Post* (September 15, 2009). Available online. URL: http://www.washingtonpost.com. Accesssed June 6, 2010.

Benson, Ophelia. "Fear and Censorship." *Guardian* (January 5, 2010). Available online. URL: http://www.guardian.co.uk/commentisfree/belief/2010/jan/04/religion-islam. Accessed June 6, 2010.

Bone, James. "Yale University Press Accused of Cowardice over Muhammad Cartoons." *Times* (London) (August 18, 2009). Available online. URL: http://www.timesonline.co.uk/tol/news/world/us_and_americas/article679968. Accessed June 6, 2010.

Broder, Henryk M. "After Attack on Danish Cartoonist, the West Is Choked by Fear." *Spiegel Online International* (January 4, 2010). Available online. URL: http://www.spiegel.de/international/Europe/0,1518,669888,00.html. Accessed June 6, 2010.

Christoffersen, John. "Yale Criticized for Nixing Muslim Cartoons in Book." Associated Press (September 8, 2009). Available online. URL: http://abcnews.go.com/US/wireStory?id=8512341. Accessed June 6, 2010.

Cohen, Patricia. "PEN Urges Yale to Publish Images of Muhammad." *New York Times* (September 11, 2009). Available online. URL: http://www.campus-watch.org/article/id/8289. Accessed June 6, 2010.

————. "Yale Press Bans Images of Muhammad in New Book." *New York Times* (August 13, 2009). Available online. URL: http://www.nytimes.com/2009/08/13/books/13book.html. Accessed June 6, 2010.

Devi, Sharmilia. "Book on Danish Cartoons Sparks Ruckus." *National* (September 9, 2009). Available online. URL: http://www.campus-watch.org/article/id/8273. Accessed June 6, 2010.

Dimbleby, Jonathan. *Index on Censorship* (December 18, 2009). Available online. URL: http://www.indexoncensorship.org/2009/12/jonathan-dimbleby/. Accessed June 6, 2010.

Dworkin, Ronald. "The Right to Ridicule." *New York Review of Books* (March 23, 2006). Available online. URL: http://www.nybooks.com/articles/18111. Accessed June 6, 2010.

Eltahawy, Mona. "Yale's Misguided Retreat." *Washington Post* (August 29, 2009). Available online. URL: http://www.washingtonpost.com. Accessed June 6, 2010.

Flood, Alison. "Publisher Bans Images of Muhammad in New Book." *Guardian* (August 14, 2009). Available online. URL: http:/www.guardian.co.uk/books/2009/aug/14/publisher-bans-images-muhammad/print. Accessed June 6, 2010.

Goldstein, Evan R. "The Book That Shook Yale." *Chronicle of Higher Education* (September 29, 2009). Available online. URL: http://chronicle.com/article/The-Book-Shook-Yale/48634. Accessed June 6, 2010.

Hitchens, Christopher. "Yale Surrenders." Slate (August 17, 2009). Available online. URL: http://www.slate.com/toolbar/aspx?action=print&id=2225504. Accessed June 6, 2010.

Howard, Jennifer. "Academic and Free-Speech Groups Join Criticism of Yale U. Press Over Cartoons in Book." *Chronicle of Higher Education* (September 16, 2009). Available online. URL: http://chronicle.com/article/AcademicFree-Speech/48441/. Accessed June 6, 2010.

Klausen, Jytte. "'Not Everything Can Be Explained by Words Alone.'" *Yale Alumni Magazine* (September 9, 2009). Available online. URL: http:/www.yalealumnimagazine.com/extras/yup/klausen149.html. Accessed June 6, 2010.

Malik, Kenan. "Why We Should Not Censor Ourselves." *Index on Censorship* (December 18, 2009). Available online. URL: http://www.kenanmalik.com/debates/index_cartoons.html. Accessed June 6, 2010.

O'Neill, Brendan. "Censorship Is Being Justified by Imaginary Muslim Outrage." *Independent* (October 22, 2009). Available online. URL: http://license.icopyright.net/user/viewFreeUse.act?fuid=NTQ3MTY3NA%3D%3D. Accessed June 6, 2010.

Pasha, Kamran. "Yale and the Danish Cartoons." Huffington Post (September 8, 2009). Available online. URL: http://www.huffingtonpost.com/kamran-pasha/yale-and-the-danish-carto_b_279463.html. Accessed June 6, 2010.

Ritter, Karl. "Muhammad Cartoonist Defiant After Attack." Associated Press (May 13, 2010). Available online. URL: http://www.google.com/hostednews/ap/article/ALeqM5gfyTngzJoXl5VLnRYFKryLwR. Accessed June 6, 2010.

"Self-Muzzled at Yale." *Washington Post*. Editorial (August 23, 2009). Available online. URL: http://www.washingtonpost.com. Accessed June 6, 2010.

"Somali Charged over Attack on Cartoonist." BBC News (January 2, 2010). Available online. URL: http://news.bbc.co.uk/2/hi/Europe/8437652.stm. Accessed June 6, 2010.

Sjolie, Marie Louise. "The Danish Cartoonist Who Survived an Axe Attack." *Guardian* (January 4, 2010). Available online. URL: http://www.guardian.co.uk/world/2010/jan/04/danish-cartoonist-axe-attack. Accessed June 6, 2010.

"Writers Issue Cartoon Row Warning." BBC News. (March 1, 2006). Available online. URL: http://news.bbc.co.uk/2/hi/Europe/4663520.stm. Accessed June 6, 2010.

CHILDREN OF THE ALLEY

Author: Naguib Mahfouz
Original dates and places of publication: 1959, Egypt; 1988, United States
Original publishers: *Al-Ahram* newspaper; Three Continents Press
Literary form: Novel

SUMMARY

The Egyptian author Naguib Mahfouz (1911–2006), awarded the Nobel Prize in literature in 1988, was the most celebrated contemporary Arab writer of his time, with 33 novels, 13 anthologies of stories, and 30 screenplays to his credit over a half-century. Many of Mahfouz's richly detailed novels portray life in Cairo's teeming working-class neighborhoods. Among them are the three novels of his masterpiece *The Cairo Trilogy*, written between 1945 and 1957, chronicling the fortunes of three generations of a Cairo family.

Children of the Alley (also known by the title *Children of Gebelawi*) is the history of an imaginary Cairo alley and a retelling in allegorical form of the lives of Adam and Eve, Cain and Abel, and Moses, Jesus, and Muhammad. The novel can be read on many levels. It is an evocative account of the vanished world of Mahfouz's childhood in the alleys of Gemalia, in Cairo, and an engrossing fictional narrative. It is also a fable that echoes the history of Judaism, Christianity, and Islam, as well as a critique of religious intolerance and political and economic repression.

Narrated by an unnamed resident of the alley who is a professional writer, the story begins in the shadow of the mansion of Gabalawi, master of the estate at the foot of Muqattam Mountain. Gabalawi, whose despotic presence looms over generations of his descendants, represents God, or as Mahfouz has said, a certain idea of God that people have created.

Gabalawi's son, Adham, and Adham's wife, Umaima, tempted and tricked by Adham's dissolute brother, Idris, are permanently expelled by Gabalawi from the mansion and its fragrant gardens for seeking a look at his forbidden book. One of their two sons, Qadri, kills the other, Humam, in a fight. Qadri marries Hind, the daughter of Idris. They have several children, and from these ancestors all the people of the alley descend.

Gabalawi shuts himself away in his mansion and is not seen again. The management of his estate subsequently becomes a source of conflict. Though the estate's overseer at first follows the good example of Gabalawi, sharing its benefits with all the descendants, greed eventually gets the better of him and he exploits the poor. The neighborhood is run by young gangsters in the overseer's employ, who extort protection money from its hard-working inhabitants.

The first to rise up and rebel against injustice in the alley is the snake charmer Gabal, who defeats the gangsters and takes over leadership of the quarter. Gabal, who applies eye-for-an-eye justice, is honest and upright and shares the estate revenues equally, but he is also feared. He is a symbol of justice and order, but after his death, the era of the dishonest overseers and their threatening gangsters returns.

In another generation, a new leader—Rifaa, the carpenter's son—comes forth to preach against violence and materialism. He calls on Gabal's followers to trust him so that he can deliver them from evil spirits. Rifaa is murdered by the overseer and his gangsters, who see him as a threat to their social order.

A third leader, Qassem, eventually emerges from among the Desert Rats, the poorest and most wretched people of the neighborhood. He says that the people of the alley are all Gabalawi's children and the rule of gangsters must end. Following Rifaa's example, he ushers in an era of brotherhood and peace among the followers of Gabal, Rifaa, and his own disciples. He proclaims that no neighborhood is more closely related to Gabalawi than any other and that the estate belongs to everyone.

But those who succeed Qassem as overseer return to the old system of violence and exploitation. The alley is again divided against itself, with separate quarters for the followers of Gabal, Rifaa, and Qassem. "Gabalawi," the old man Shakrun cries out facing the mansion, "how long will you be silent and hidden? Your commandments are ignored and your money is being wasted. . . . Don't you know what has happened to us?"

Arafa, a magician, resolves to liberate the alley from the overseer's tyranny. He wants to find Gabalawi's book, the cause of Adham's exile, believing that it holds the magic secret of Gabalawi's power. When he breaks into the mansion to search for the book, he kills a servant. Having come in a quest for power to use against evil, he has turned into an evildoer.

In murdering a servant, Arafa indirectly kills Gabalawi, who dies from the shock of the murder in his house. The followers of Gabal, Rifaa, and Qassem squabble over where Gabalawi should be buried, each group believing they have a closer relationship with their ancestor. The overseer instructs the storytellers to sing the story of Gabalawi, emphasizing how he died at the hands of Arafa. But the people favor Arafa and his magic, exalting his name above those of Gabal, Rifaa, and Qassem. Gabalawi is dead, the people of the alley say: "We have nothing to do with the past. Our only hope lies in Arafa's magic, and if we had to choose between Gabalawi and magic, we'd choose magic." The final line of the book looks to the future with hope: "Injustice must have an end, as day must follow night. We will see the death of tyranny, and the dawn of light and miracles."

CENSORSHIP HISTORY

Children of the Alley was serialized in 1959 in the semiofficial Cairo newspaper *Al-Ahram*. Devout Muslims took to the streets in protest, demanding a ban because Mahfouz had suggested in allegorical fashion that the God of Adam, Moses, Jesus, and Muhammad might be dead. It was only upon the intervention of Egypt's president, Gamal Abdel Nasser, a friend of *Al-Ahram*'s editor, Mohammed Heikal, that the serialization was published uncut to the end. However, the scholars of Cairo's powerful government-recognized religious authority, Al-Azhar University, banned *Children of the Alley*, condemning it as "blasphemous," and calling its author a heretic for causing offense to the prophets of Islam and for misrepresenting the character of Muhammad.

Since that time, militant Islamic groups have sustained a relentless campaign against the book and its author, which successfully ensured its banning for more than three decades. *Children of the Alley* was passed from hand to hand in its newspaper version until 1967, when a pirated edition of the novel was published in Beirut, Lebanon, in slightly expurgated form. Smuggled into Egypt, it was sold under the counter at some Cairo bookstores.

In 1979, Mahfouz again incurred the wrath of Islamic fundamentalists in Egypt and elsewhere in the Arab world when he was among the first to support the peace treaty between Egypt and Israel. His novels were banned for several years in many Arab countries.

In 1988, Mahfouz won the Nobel Prize. Fundamentalists, who had never forgiven him for writing *Children of the Alley*, renewed their attacks, fearing that the prize would be used as a pretext to remove the book from the proscribed list. "The novel had basically been forgotten for a period of 30 years," Mahfouz said in a 1989 interview, "but following the prize it was subjected to very heavy attack in all the Islamicist-oriented newspapers and magazines. So the idea of publishing it here isn't even a topic for discussion."

In view of Egyptian president Hosni Mubarak's statement that the novel should be published and its availability in much of the rest of the Arab world, renewed attempts were made to lift the ban on the book. But when the Egyptian monthly *Al-Yasar* began to serialize it in 1989, the Islamic press campaigned so virulently against it that Mahfouz himself asked the magazine to stop the serialization.

Mahfouz again ran afoul of militants that same year when he spoke out against Iran's Ayatollah Ruhollah Khomeini's edict calling for the death of British author Salman Rushdie for having written *The Satanic Verses*. Sheikh Omar Abdel Rahman, the Egyptian fundamentalist leader of the militant Gamaat Islamia sect (who was later convicted in a plot to blow up New York City landmarks and assassinate U.S. political leaders), issued a statement calling on both Mahfouz and Rushdie to repent. "If they do not, they will be killed," he said. "If this sentence had been passed on Naguib Mahfouz when he wrote *Children of the Alley*, Salman Rushdie would have realized that he had to stay within certain bounds."

In June 1992, Islamist terrorists in Cairo shot and killed Farag Fouda, a prominent Egyptian secular writer, who, like Mahfouz, had spoken out against violent censorship. Shortly after Fouda's slaying, the Egyptian government uncovered a death list including Mahfouz and several other leading writers and intellectuals. Mahfouz was offered but declined police protection.

In early 1994, the weekly magazine *Rose el-Youssef* published extracts from several banned works, including *The Satanic Verses* and *Children of the Alley*, accompanied by a statement in defense of freedom of expression. Most Arab countries, with the exception of Egypt and Kuwait, banned the magazine's distribution. In October 1994, Mahfouz was stabbed several times in the neck as he sat in a car outside his Cairo home. (Two Islamic militants were convicted of attempted murder and executed, and others received lesser sentences.) Mahfouz never regained full use of his right arm and hand after the assault and had to dictate his writings.

Shortly thereafter, the government's minister of information, speaking from Mahfouz's hospital bed, said the government did not support a ban on any of his works. His statement was interpreted as ending the official prohibition of *Children of the Alley*. As Egyptian newspapers rushed to serialize the novel, Mahfouz asked that publication come at a later time. "The issue is diverting attention from a crime against my life to whether this novel is, or is not, against religion," he said. But his request was ignored. A few weeks after the attack, the novel was published in the Egyptian press for the first time in 35 years, but its publication in book form in Egypt remained officially prohibited. Despite the ban, the Lebanese edition of the book had continued to be sold on the black market, and an English translation was available from American University in Cairo Press. Mahfouz died in August 2006 at the age of 94. Four months later, the book was officially published in Arabic in Egypt and became a best seller in Egypt.

FURTHER READING

Abou El-Magd, Nadia. "Book That Nearly Cost Naguib Mahfouz His Life Resurfaces in Egypt." Associated Press (January 12, 2007). Available online. URL: http://thedailynewsegypt.com/article.aspx?ArticleID=4933. Accessed June 6, 2010.

Appignanesi, Lisa, and Sara Maitland, eds. *The Rushdie File*. Syracuse, N.Y.: Syracuse University Press, 1990.

El-Hennawy, Noha. "Publish and Perish." *Egypt Today* (February 2006). Available online.URL: http//www.egypttoday.com/article.aspx?ArticleID=6361. Accessed June 6, 2010.

Pipes, Daniel. *The Rushdie Affair*. New York: Carol Publishing Group, 1990.

Weaver, Mary Anne. "The Novelist and the Sheikh." *New Yorker*, January 30, 1995, 52–59.

CHRISTIANITY RESTORED

Author: Michael Servetus
Original date and place of publication: 1552, France
Literary form: Theological treatise

SUMMARY

The Spanish theologian and physician Michael Servetus earned his reputation for religious deviationism at the age of 20. During his law studies at Toulouse, France, he had discovered in the Scriptures the historical person of Jesus of Nazareth, leading him to reject traditional formulations of the nature of Christ and the relationship of the three persons of the Trinity.

Servetus believed that Protestant reformers Martin Luther, John Calvin, and Huldrych Zwingli were not revolutionary enough, because they accepted the doctrine of the Trinity, which he viewed as incomprehensible. Failing to convince the reformers in Basel and Strasbourg of his ideas, Servetus decided to write a book that would persuade all Christians of the truth of his discoveries.

In 1531, he published *On the Errors of the Trinity*, a treatise asserting that traditional Scholastic theology introduced Greek philosophical terms and nonbiblical concepts into the definitions of the Trinity that were abstract, speculative, and unrelated to the living God. "Not one word is found in the whole Bible about the Trinity, nor about its Persons, nor about an Essence, nor about a unity of the Substance, nor about one Nature of the several beings," he wrote. Orthodox Catholics and many Protestants viewed Servetus's theology as having revived the fourth-century heresy of Arianism, which denied the doctrine of the Trinity by teaching that Jesus as the Son of God was neither equal to nor eternal with God the Father.

In 1552, Servetus recast his earlier tracts in a new book, *Christianity Restored*. It contained a revised edition of *On the Errors of the Trinity* and new material, including 30 letters on theology that he had sent to Calvin. In *Christianity Restored*, Servetus challenged the established churches, both Catholic and Protestant, to return Christendom to the purity of its origins: "A calling of the whole apostolic church to make a fresh start, restored completely in the knowledge of God, the faith of Christ, our justification, regeneration, baptism, and the Lord's Supper. Our restoration finally in the kingdom of heaven, with the loosing of the captivity of ungodly Babylon and Antichrist and his own destroyed."

In the new work, he claimed that Christianity had failed because it had become corrupted in the early fourth century by pagan doctrines and by the church's acquisition of temporal power. He attacked the definition of the Trinity established by the church's Council of Nicaea in the fourth century, as well as the practice of infant baptism, which he termed as unchristian. He accepted the heretical Anabaptist tenet that baptism should be deferred until maturity, when a sinner has experienced Christ and repented. Christ himself was not baptized until he was an adult, Servetus wrote, and becoming a Christian meant sharing a spiritual communion that an infant could not understand.

CENSORSHIP HISTORY

The publication in 1531 of *On the Errors of the Trinity* made Servetus notorious and a hunted man, threatened by both the French and Spanish Inquisitions and the Protestants, who banned his book and closed cities to him. In 1532, the Inquisition in Toulouse issued a decree ordering his arrest. He went underground in Paris and assumed a new identity, adopting the name of Michel de Villeneuve, from the family home of Villanueva, Spain. Fear of persecution in Paris drove him to Lyon, where he worked as a printer's editor, eventually settling in 1540 in the suburb of Vienne.

Using his own name, Servetus began to correspond with Protestant reformer John Calvin in Geneva, instructing him on theology. In all he sent 30 epistolary discourses to Calvin. Calvin sent him a copy of his *Institutes of The Christian Religion*, which Servetus boldly returned annotated with criticisms. Servetus also presented Calvin with a manuscript copy of part of *Christianity Restored*, apparently hoping that Calvin would view it favorably.

A thousand copies of *Christianity Restored* were printed anonymously and in secret in Vienne by the publishers Balthasar Arnoullet and Guillaume Guéroult in 1552 after publishers in Basel refused to have anything to do with the book. Some copies were sent to the Frankfurt book fair and others to a bookseller in Geneva. There a copy came into the hands of Calvin's colleague, Guillaume Trie, who forwarded the first four leaves of the book to a Catholic cousin in Lyon, revealing Villeneuve's identity and location in Vienne. The cousin placed the material in the hands of the Inquisition, which began an investigation.

Servetus and his publisher Arnoullet denied any knowledge of the book. But at the request of the Inquisition, Trie provided the investigators the manuscript copy of the book sent by Servetus to Calvin, implicating Servetus. Servetus was arrested and held for trial but escaped. In June 1553, the civil tribunal of Lyon condemned him in absentia for heresy, sedition, rebellion, and evasion of prison, fining him 2,000 livres and sentencing him to be burned. In his absence, bales of copies of his books were incinerated with his effigy. His publisher was imprisoned.

In August, on his way to seek refuge in Italy, Servetus passed through Geneva, Calvin's stronghold. There he was recognized and, on Calvin's orders, arrested. Charged with 39 counts of heresy and blasphemy, for more than two months he stood trial before the judges of the Geneva city council. The verdict of the council was that the book Servetus had secretly printed in Vienne had spread "heresies and horrible, execrable blasphemies against the Holy Trinity, against the Son of God, against the baptism of infants and foundations of the Christian religion." The Geneva authorities consulted the magistrates of all the Swiss cantons, who unanimously agreed on the verdict.

Servetus was sentenced to be burned to ashes with his book for trying "to infect the world with [his] stinking heretical poison." The verdict stated further, "And so you shall finish your days and give an example to others who would commit the like." Servetus's last request was to see Calvin. "I told him to beg the pardon of the son of God, whom he had disfigured with his dreams . . .," Calvin reported. "But when I saw that all this did no good I did not wish to be wiser than my Master allows. So following the rule of St. Paul, I withdrew from the heretic who was self-condemned."

Servetus asked to die by the sword rather than by burning. Although Calvin supported this request for mercy, it was denied by the magistrates. "He asked forgiveness for his errors, ignorance and sins, but never made a full confession," wrote Calvin's colleague, Guillaume Farel. "But we could never get him openly to admit his errors and confess that Christ is the eternal son of God." On October 27, 1553, Servetus was burned at the stake.

Calvin urged the destruction of *Christianity Restored* in Protestant countries, as it contained "prodigious blasphemies against God." Only three copies survived. In part the tragic result of a power struggle between Calvin and his opponents, Servetus's execution damaged Calvin's reputation. As Church historian Roland H. Bainton wrote, Servetus had "the singular distinction of having been burned by the Catholics in effigy and by the Protestants in actuality." Servetus was the first person to be executed as a heretic on the authority of a reformed church. His martyrdom came to have a significance greater than any other in his century, as it marked the first important controversy over the issue of toleration within Protestantism.

The movement on behalf of toleration, reflected in Sebastian Castellio's 1554 defense of toleration, *Concerning Heretics*, was galvanized by widespread revulsion at Servetus's punishment. Yet the systematic repression of *Christianity Restored* minimized Servetus's posthumous influence on religious thought. Almost two centuries later, Richard Mead, the physician to the king of England, tried to publish Servetus's work. In 1723, the government seized and burned the whole printing and imprisoned Mead and his printer.

FURTHER READING

Bainton, Roland H. *Hunted Heretic: The Life and Death of Michael Servetus.* Gloucester, Mass.: Peter Smith, 1978.
Christie-Murray, David. *A History of Heresy.* Oxford: Oxford University Press, 1989.
Haight, Anne Lyon. *Banned Books: 387 B.C. to 1978 A.D.* Updated and enlarged by Chandler B. Grannis. New York: R. R. Bowker, 1978.
Levy, Leonard W. *Blasphemy: Verbal Offense Against the Sacred, from Moses to Salman Rushdie.* New York: Alfred A. Knopf, 1993.
Parker, T. H. L. *John Calvin.* Batavia, Ill.: Lion Publishing Corporation, 1975.
Smith, George H. *Atheism, Ayn Rand, and Other Heresies.* Buffalo, N.Y.: Prometheus Books, 1991.

Spitz, Lewis W., ed. *The Protestant Reformation*. Englewood Cliffs, N.J.: Prentice Hall, 1966.

Zagorin, Perez. *How the Idea of Religious Toleration Came to the West*. Princeton, N.J.: Princeton University Press, 2003.

CHURCH: CHARISM AND POWER: LIBERATION THEOLOGY AND THE INSTITUTIONAL CHURCH

Author: Leonardo Boff
Original dates and places of publication: 1981, Brazil; 1985, United States
Publishers: Editora Vôzes; Crossroad
Literary form: Theological essays

SUMMARY

The Brazilian Catholic theologian Leonardo Boff is a leading exponent of liberation theology, an interpretation of Christian faith drawn from the experience of the poor. *Church: Charism and Power*, a collection of essays, speeches, and lecture notes, contains some of the sharpest criticisms of the Roman Catholic Church to come from Latin America. Boff argues from his experience with the poor in Brazilian base communities—grassroots, Catholic communities led by laity. He urges institutional reform of Catholicism and its transformation into a "liberation Church," not simply *for* the poor, but *of* the poor. Criticizing abuse of hierarchical power, he calls for a return to the collegial structure of early church communities, in which both clergy and laity exercised power.

Boff's central thesis is that the struggle for justice and human rights cannot be separated from a similar struggle within the church itself. The preferential option for the poor demands shifts within Catholicism. The institutional church must move away from its reliance on power and coercion and toward a democratic model of openness and tolerance, the original model upon which Christ founded the church. Boff contends that the church hierarchy took its form only after Jesus' death. When Christianity became the official religion of the Roman Empire, the church began to reflect the empire's feudal structure of authority, including its institutions, laws, and bureaucratic centralization.

Boff distinguishes between two kinds of power: *exousia*, the power of love employed by Jesus, and *potestas*, the power to dominate and rule that characterized Roman officialdom. He describes the exercise of *potestas* by the clergy and the division between the clergy and the laity as a cancer within the church. The charismatic essence of the church, in which everyone has a charism, or gift, to offer, has been extinguished. "Christianity is not against power in itself," Boff writes, "but its diabolical forms which show themselves as dominion and control." Using marxist terminology, Boff refers to the "gradual expropriation of the spiritual means of production from the Christian people by the clergy."

The church must contain charisms, such as teaching, serving, preaching, and administering, as well as power. The papacy does have a special position within the church in maintaining doctrinal unity based on the emerging consensus of the community. Power can be a charism, Boff believes, as long as it serves everyone and is an instrument for building justice in the community.

CENSORSHIP HISTORY

Boff's orthodoxy already had been investigated by the Vatican in 1976 and again in 1980 on suspicion of doctrinal deviation. The 1980 investigation centered on his book *Jesus Christ, the Liberator.* But the Vatican had been generally willing to leave the question of orthodoxy of individual Latin American theologians to their own bishops.

When *Church: Charism and Power* was published in Brazil, Spain, and Italy in 1981, it was not expected to spark widespread debate. It was a further development of ideas expressed in Boff's doctoral thesis and in a previous book on ecclesiology, or the study of the structure of the church. Boff was not optimistic that the book, a loosely connected collection of disparate writings and talks rather than a comprehensive analysis, would find an audience.

Almost immediately, however, it provoked an unusual amount of discussion. Boff had applied the insights of liberation theology, previously directed at the reform of secular society, to the church itself. His choice of the words "symbolic violence" to refer to the Vatican's methods for discouraging dissent and his use of quasi-marxist terminology to analyze the church's structure angered critics.

In the book, he quotes at length a Brazilian Catholic who makes a point-by-point parallel between Kremlin and Vatican styles of governance. In another highly controversial passage, he writes: "It is strange to see that the Church institution has developed into exactly that which Christ did not want it to be."

Boff had earlier described the Vatican's Congregation for the Doctrine of the Faith (CDF) as relying on procedures that are unacceptable in civil society, a "Kafkaesque process wherein the accuser, defender, the lawyer and judge are one and the same." In 1982, a similar process was initiated to investigate Boff's views.

In February 1982, Boff, who knew that his critics had already complained to the Vatican, mailed to Rome as a courtesy a copy of some negative reviews of his book and a response by Rev. Urbano Zilles of Brazil. Three months later, he received a letter from Joseph Cardinal Ratzinger, prefect of the CDF (who became Pope Benedict XVI in April 2005), asking him to respond to criticisms. He wrote a response and published it.

In May 1984, Boff received a six-page letter from Ratzinger criticizing Boff's views as expressed in the book and saying they "did not merit acceptance." The letter referred to Boff's theological method, his analysis of church structure, his concepts of dogma and revelation, and his description of the exercise of power in the church. It criticized his "ecclesiastical relativism" and his "sociological" analysis. Ratzinger accused Boff of using language that was "polemic, defamatory and pamphleteering, absolutely inappropriate for a theologian," drawing on "ideological principles of a certain neo-Marxist inspiration," proposing "a certain revolutionary utopia which is foreign to the church," and holding a "relativizing conception" of church structure and doctrine.

Boff replied with a 50-page document, insisting that he wrote "only to right the balance in the direction of the experience of the laity, the poor, and the contributions of the social sciences." He concluded, "Of one thing I am sure: I prefer to walk in the church than go it alone with my theology. The church is a reality of Faith that I assume. Theology is a product of reason that I discuss."

Rather than going through the Brazilian bishops, who would have supported Boff, Ratzinger summoned him to Rome for a "colloquy" in September 1984. Boff took with him to Rome petitions signed by 50,000 Brazilians and was accompanied by two Brazilian cardinals, who came to show their support. Although Boff would not have selected *Church: Charism and Power* to fully represent his ideas, the colloquy turned out to be a full-scale interrogation on his views as expressed in the book.

In March 1985, the CDF published a Notification, making public the letter Ratzinger had sent the previous year and labeling it an official public document approved by the pope. The CDF stated that its reservations about his book "had not been substantially overcome" and that Boff was guilty of three errors: his statement that the church borrowed societal characteristics from contemporary Roman and later feudal society, his relativistic interpretation of dogma as good for specific circumstances and times, and his statements that clergy had expropriated spiritual means of production from the laity. "The options of Leonardo Boff analyzed herein endanger the sound doctrine of the Faith which this congregation has the task of promoting and safeguarding," the Notification concluded.

In May 1985, Boff received an official notice from the CDF ordering him to begin immediately to observe an "obedient silence" for an unspecified period of time. The notice stated that the period of silence "would permit Friar Boff a time for serious reflection." It required him to abstain completely from writing and publishing, from his duties as editor of the *Revista Ecclesiastica Brasileira*, the most influential theological journal in Brazil, from his work as editor of books on theology at the publishing house Editora Vôzes, and from teaching or lecturing. Boff submitted to the silencing, saying, "As a Christian, Franciscan friar and theologian, it is for me to listen and adhere."

Ten Brazilian bishops, who viewed the Vatican's attack on one of liberation theology's most prominent figures as an unwelcome intrusion of Rome into Latin American matters and a threat to the right of Catholics to think and write freely, took the highly unusual step of publicly criticizing the Vatican's treatment of Boff. Senior Brazilian bishops met with Pope John Paul II in Rome during March 1986. That month, after 10 months of the silencing, Boff's punishment was lifted. Boff said he received the news "as an Easter present" and was sure that it was a gesture of goodwill on the part of the Vatican toward the bishops of Brazil.

In 1991, Boff published a series of articles calling for change in the church's prohibition against marriage for priests. When church officials denied approval for publication of his next manuscript, he resigned from the priesthood. In an open letter to his followers he wrote, "I am leaving the priestly ministry, but not the church. . . . I continue to be and will always be a theologian in the Catholic and ecumenical mold, fighting with the poor against their poverty and in favor of their liberation."

FURTHER READING

Boff, Leonardo. Leonardo Boff's official Web site. Available online. URL: http://fly.to/boff.
"Leonardo Boff." Inter Press Service (December 30, 1999).
Cox, Harvey. *The Silencing of Leonardo Boff: The Vatican and the Future of World Christianity.* Oak Park, Ill.: Meyer Stone Books, 1988.
Sigmund, Paul E. *Liberation Theology at the Crossroads: Democracy or Revolution?* New York: Oxford University Press, 1990.

CONCERNING HERETICS

Author: Sebastian Castellio
Original date and place of publication: 1554, Switzerland
Literary form: Theological treatise

SUMMARY

French Protestant theologian Sebastian Castellio was Europe's first great defender of religious tolerance, and his book *Concerning Heretics, Whether They Are to Be Persecuted and How They Are to Be Treated (De haereticis)* was a landmark in the struggle against religious persecution.

In 1553, at the instigation of the Protestant leader John Calvin, the Spanish theologian Michael Servetus was burned at the stake in Geneva for his unorthodox views on the Trinity and the efficacy of infant baptism as expressed in his treatise *Christianity Restored.* The execution of Servetus prompted Castellio to write the most important work of the century in support of religious toleration. Published in Latin and in French and German translations in 1554 under three different pseudonyms and with a false printer's name, *Concerning Heretics* courageously protested cruelty and persecution carried out by Christians in the name of religious doctrine.

The book consisted of two parts: a preface by Martin Bellius (a pseudonym for Castellio), addressed to a German prince, Christoph, duke of Württemburg, and an anthology of selections from the writing of the early church fathers and Protestant writers on the subject of toleration. The selections included writings by Erasmus, Martin Luther, Calvin, and Castellio himself, under his own name and the pseudonyms Basil Montfort and Georg Kleinberg.

In the book's preface, Castellio presented a parable illustrating that tolerance and mutual love are imperative to Christians. He asked the prince to imagine that he had instructed his subjects to prepare to meet him clad in white garments at some time in the future. When he returned, he found that instead of preparing their robes, they were disputing among themselves about his whereabouts and how he would reappear. What if then, Castellio asked the prince, the controversy degenerated into violence and one group killed those who disagreed with them? And what if those who killed others claimed to have done it in his name and in accord with his commands, even though he had previously expressly forbidden it?

"Although opinions are almost as numerous as men, nevertheless there is hardly any sect which does not condemn all others and desire to reign alone," Castellio continued. "I ask you, then, most Illustrious Prince, what do you think Christ will do when He comes? Will He commend such things? Will He approve of them?"

Castellio declared that he wrote to "stanch the blood" shed by those who are called heretics. After investigating the meaning of heresy, he concluded that heretics are those with whom one disagrees. Each sect views the others as heretical, "so that if you are orthodox in one city or region, you must be held for a heretic in the next." If one travels, one must change one's religion like one's money.

The points of religion on which Christians disagree and persecute one another are uncertain. "Were these matters obvious, that there is one God, all would agree." The wisest course is to condemn no one who believes in God, whatever their religion. Because people will never agree on religious matters, conduct alone should be punishable, never religious belief or worship. On such matters as the doctrine of the Trinity, "each may be left to his own opinion and revelation of the Savior." Religion resides "in the heart, which cannot be reached by the sword of kings and princes." Since faith cannot be compelled, coercion is futile.

In the book's concluding statement by Basil Montfort, Castellio stressed that neither Christ nor the apostles did violence to their enemies and that when religion is not left free, spiritual tyranny and error can flourish.

CENSORSHIP HISTORY

By the time Castellio wrote *Concerning Heretics* in 1554, Calvin already regarded him as an enemy. As a colleague of Calvin, in Geneva, Castellio became head teacher of the Collège de Rive and preached at nearby villages. When he split with Calvin over doctrinal differences, the Geneva magistrates censured him for misconduct. In 1545, he moved to the more tolerant city of Basel, where he worked as a corrector for the noted printer and publisher Johannes Oporinus and became a professor of Greek at the university. Castellio wrote epic poems in Greek and Latin and translated the Bible. The preface to his Latin Bible translation published in 1551 contained his first notable defense of religious toleration and an indictment of religious persecution by Christians. It was Castellio's first salvo in a long battle against Calvinist intolerance, which was galvanized by the execution of Servetus in 1553.

The Calvinists stepped up their harassment of Castellio after the publication of *Concerning Heretics*. Despite Castellio's use of pseudonyms, the Calvinists suspected that he was the author. Calvin and his followers condemned the work as an evil influence and Castellio as a blasphemer who deserved Servetus's fate. Calvin urged the Swiss synods to prohibit the book's circulation.

Later that year, Castellio wrote another tract in defense of his views, an anonymous satirical polemic attacking Calvin's ideas, titled *Against Calvin's Book*. Calvin was able to ensure, however, that no publisher would print it. It circulated only in manuscript form until 1612, when it was published for the first time in the Netherlands. "If Servetus had attacked you by arms, you had rightly been defended by the magistrate," Castellio wrote. "But since he opposed you in writings, why did you oppose them with sword and the fire?. . . Does your piety consist only in hurrying to the fire strangers passing peacefully through your city?"

Christ and his disciples died as heretics and seditious blasphemers, Castellio reminded his readers. "This ought to fill us with fear and trembling when it comes to persecuting a man for his faith and his religion." Servetus had fought with "reasons and writings" and should have been answered the same way, Castellio declared. Now that Servetus has been burned, everybody desires to read his books. "To kill a doctrine is not to protect a doctrine, but it is to kill a man. When the Genevans killed Servetus, they did not defend a doctrine, but they killed a man."

Calvin's disciple, Theodore Beza, wrote a refutation of *Concerning Heretics* in which he described toleration as a diabolical doctrine and its defenders as "emissaries of Satan." In 1555, Castellio responded to Beza with his third major treatise on toleration, *Concerning the Nonpunishment of Heretics*, written again under the pseudonym Basil Montfort. It offered a critique of the theoretical underpinnings of religious persecution, asserting that the killing of heretics was antithetical to Christianity and that heresy was a vice rather than a crime. The work circulated in manuscript copies but remained unprinted during the author's lifetime. It was not published in book form until 1971.

For the next decade, the Calvinists hounded Castellio as he continued to defend the principles of religious freedom. In 1557, Calvin and Beza had

Castellio brought before the Basel City Council, but he was cleared of any wrongdoing. In 1563, they finally were able to bring Castellio to trial for religious unorthodoxy. However, he died in December of that year at age 48, while the proceedings were pending, At the time of his death, he had been considering immigrating to Poland, which offered a haven to victims of religious persecution.

In spite of Calvin's efforts to suppress *Concerning Heretics*, it was widely influential in Western Europe. It sparked the first great controversy within Protestantism over the issue of religious freedom and inspired other writers during the 16th and 17th centuries to argue in favor of freedom of conscience.

FURTHER READING

Castellio, Sebastian. *Concerning Heretics, Whether They Are to Be Persecuted and How They Are to Be Treated.* Translated and with an introduction by Roland H. Bainton. New York: Columbia University Press, 1935.

Christie-Murray, David. *A History of Heresy.* Oxford: Oxford University Press, 1989.

Levy, Leonard W. *Blasphemy: Verbal Offenses Against the Sacred, from Moses to Salman Rushdie.* New York: Alfred A. Knopf, 1993.

Smith, George H. *Atheism, Ayn Rand, and Other Heresies.* Buffalo, N.Y.: Prometheus Books, 1991.

Spitz, Lewis W., ed. *The Protestant Reformation.* Englewood Cliffs, N.J.: Prentice Hall, 1966.

Zagorin, Perez. *How the Idea of Religious Toleration Came to the West.* Princeton, N.J.: Princeton University Press, 2003.

THE DA VINCI CODE

Author: Dan Brown
Original date and place of publication: 2003, United States
Original publisher: Doubleday
Literary form: Novel

SUMMARY

Few works of popular fiction have captured the imagination of the reading public and stirred as much controversy as the historical thriller *The Da Vinci Code* and its revelation of the secret of the Holy Grail—that Jesus Christ was a mortal man who married Mary Magdalene and sired a bloodline that has endured to this day.

The story begins at the Louvre, where an albino monk named Silas has assassinated Louvre curator Jacques Saunière, who is a Grand Master for the Priory of Sion. The Priory of Sion was founded in 1099 to conceal the Holy Grail relics and protect them from those who would destroy them, most notably the Roman Catholic Church, which views the Grail and its story as a threat to its power. Silas is the ward of Bishop Aringarosa, head of Opus

Dei, a conservative Catholic Church organization. Before killing Saunière, Silas forces him to reveal the location of the keystone to the Grail. Aringarosa covets those remains, to ensure and augment Opus Dei's own power. Before Saunière's murder, a figure known only as "the Teacher" had approached Aringarosa about having the Vatican finance his efforts to attain the Grail, and Aringarosa agreed, putting Silas at the service of the Teacher.

The book's hero enters the narrative here. Robert Langdon, Harvard professor of religious symbology, is in Paris to deliver a lecture and to meet with Saunière at a reception afterward, but Saunière does not show up. Langdon is summoned by the Judicial Police (the French equivalent of the FBI) for questioning and for help in deciphering the bizarre clues Saunière left in his remaining minutes alive. Langdon and Captain Bezu Fache, head investigator of the crime, enter the Louvre's Grand Gallery, where the corpse lies. Saunière is naked on the floor, arms and legs spread-eagle, with a pentacle (a five-pointed star) drawn on his abdomen with the blood of his fatal wound. Fache calls Langdon's attention to a marker in Saunière's hand and uses black-light illumination on the area around the corpse to reveal a series of numbers, two odd phrases, and a circle in which Saunière positioned his dying body, which Langdon at once recognizes as a replica of Leonardo da Vinci's "Vitruvian Man," a symbol of male and female harmony.

At this moment, police cryptographer Sophie Neveu, Jacques Saunière's estranged granddaughter, arrives at the murder scene. She quickly gains Langdon's trust and, together, while Fache absents himself for a moment, they solve these three lines of riddles, which lead them to a key with the Priory's fleur-de-lis symbol and the letters "PS" written on it, along with an address on note paper. Sophie then reveals to Langdon that a tracking device was planted in his coat pocket and that Fache had erased a fourth line of the clue before Langdon arrived on the scene: "PS: Find Robert Langdon." Langdon removes the device, tossing it out a window onto a truck waiting below at a traffic light.

Fache, led to believe Langdon has escaped, has his agents give chase to the truck, orders arrest warrants for Langdon and Sophie, and releases their names and pictures to the media. Langdon and Sophie, meanwhile, flee the museum and locate the address given with the key, which turns out to be that of the Paris branch of the Depository Bank of Zurich. A watchman admits Langdon and Sophie to the bank, where they are confronted by bank president André Vernet, a friend of Jacques Saunière. He is suspicious, but allows them to access Saunière's deposit box, gained by a code composed of the numbers found near Saunière's body. The deposit box contains a rosewood box with a rose inlay on the lid; inside the box is a large cryptex, a cylinder invented by Leonardo himself, which works like a combination lock, for transporting messages securely. Inside the cryptex is a message written on papyrus. If the cryptex is opened incorrectly, a vial of vinegar breaks and dissolves the message. Under the lid inlay is a paper bearing a riddle giving clues to the cryptex's combination.

Vernet returns, having heard the news bulletin of Saunière's murder and the fugitive status of Langdon and Sophie, but he is coerced into helping them escape. Langdon and Sophie hide in a bank transfer truck while Vernet drives through the waiting line of police outside the bank's garage. The truck is let past, but a suspicious agent informs Fache, and the chase resumes. Meanwhile, Silas goes to the Church of Saint-Sulpice, where Saunière has told him to look for the keystone to the Grail, and is admitted by a nun. But Saunière had lied in order to defend the Grail's secret, and Silas realizes he has been tricked. The nun reveals herself to be in league with the Priory, and Silas kills her. Confused, he calls the Teacher to relate what has transpired and awaits further instructions.

Langdon and Sophie ditch Vernet, who calls bank security to activate the truck's homing device, as Langdon and Sophie head for the chateau of Sir Leigh Teabing, Langdon's friend and fellow Grail expert. Grudgingly admitted by Rémy, Teabing's surly manservant, Langdon and Sophie meet with Teabing, who enlightens Sophie on the true nature of the Grail. It is the womb of Mary Magdalene herself, who was of royal descent (the House of Benjamin) and married to Jesus (the House of David). At the time of the Crucifixion, Mary Magdalene was pregnant and fled to Gaul, where she gave birth to a daughter, Sarah, thus establishing the sacred bloodline that was to become the Merovingian dynasty of France. The Priory and the Knights Templar were established to protect the secret and to hide the Grail relics, including the bones of Mary Magdalene.

Silas now breaks into the house, looking for the keystone. He is subdued and taken with Langdon, Sophie, Teabing, and Rémy, as they flee from the police, who have tracked the bank transport truck to Teabing's chateau. They go to a nearby airfield, where they are able to flee for England on Teabing's private jet. In the interim, Bishop Aringarosa has learned of Silas's murderous rampage. Aringarosa realizes that his plan to obtain the Grail has collapsed and suspects that the Teacher may be double-crossing him. Filled with remorse for his arrogance, Aringarosa contacts Fache to confess.

Police at Teabing's villa discover an enormous surveillance setup with bugs in Saunière's office and at the homes of other Priory members. When it is determined that Teabing's jet is bound for England, Fache contacts the English authorities to hold the escapees until he can arrive there himself. He also establishes contact with Aringarosa, hears his confession, and has him travel to England, where he is to wait for Fache at the London headquarters of Opus Dei.

Sophie's estrangement from her grandfather is alluded to throughout the narrative, and now she reveals her story to Langdon: Paying a surprise visit to her grandfather at his country home, Sophie had let herself in and followed strange chanting sounds to a lower-level room. There she found a group of men wearing black tunics and shoes and women wearing white gossamer gowns and golden shoes, holding golden orbs, and all wearing androgynous masks. In their midst, engaged in the sex act, was her grandfather and a large woman with long gray hair. Horrified, Sophie fled and broke contact with her grandfather. Langdon explains to her that what she had witnessed was a pagan sex ritual known as Hieros Gamos, or "sacred marriage," which constituted a spiritual act of worship.

As Langdon and the others are en route to England, he solves the riddle that allows the large cryptex to be safely opened. Inside is a smaller cryptex with another riddle, which speaks of ". . . a knight a Pope interred." On landing in England, the group evades the waiting police and, on a hunch, goes to Temple Church, built by the Knights Templar themselves. They do not find the tomb they are looking for. At the church, Rémy pretends to kidnap Teabing, leaving Langdon and Sophie shaken but able to continue searching for the knight's tomb. Once they have gone, Rémy and Teabing remove Silas's binds, telling him to wait at Opus Dei's London office, while Teabing informs the police anonymously that Silas is hiding there. He then kills Rémy. Teabing is himself the Teacher, who, with information gained by his surveillance, had dispatched Silas on his murderous errands. Teabing had played on Opus Dei's desire to obtain the Grail, never intending to let them have it, and Rémy had been his collaborator. Teabing felt that the Priory had broken its own vow to reveal the secret of the Grail at the so-called End of Days and had vaingloriously taken it upon himself to do so.

Once the riddle is solved, revealing Isaac Newton as the "knight" eulogized by Alexander Pope ("a pope"), Langdon, Sophie, and Teabing meet at Westminster Abbey before Newton's tomb, where Teabing fully reveals his plan. Langdon secretly opens the second cryptex and removes the contents, before smashing it in front of Teabing. Teabing is arrested. He begs to know the answer to the final riddle, but Langdon lets him be led away.

Meanwhile, Silas tries to flee the police and, in the confusion, accidentally shoots Aringarosa. Wounded in the confrontation, Silas escapes but is later found dead in Kensington Gardens. With Silas dead, Teabing in custody, and Aringarosa in the hospital, all that remains is the solving of the final riddle:

The Holy Grail 'neath ancient Roslin waits.
The blade and the chalice guarding o'er her gates.
Adorned in masters' loving art, She lies.
She rests at last beneath starry skies.

Langdon and Sophie go to Rosslyn Chapel and see a Star of David on the chapel floor (the interlocking blade and chalice triangles). However, Sophie discovers that a young docent at the chapel is her long-lost brother, and the guardian of the chapel is none other than Marie Chauvel Saint-Clair, of the Merovingian line, wife of Jacques Saunière, Sophie's grandmother, and the unrecognized participant in the sex rite that Sophie had witnessed. Sophie is a descendant of Jesus Christ and Mary Magdalene, and the Priory hid her identity to protect her life after suspected Opus Dei operatives had killed her parents. Marie assures Langdon that the Grail is no longer at the chapel, and he and Sophie part company.

Back in Paris, Langdon remembers the final riddle and, on a hunch, heads for the Louvre, following the ancient "Rose Line" (the original prime meridian) to the museum's inverted pyramid (the Chalice) and the small upright pyramid (the blade) below it. Looking up at the starlit night, he realizes that the Grail is buried under these pyramids. Langdon sinks to his knees, as much in amazement as in adoration.

CENSORSHIP HISTORY

The Da Vinci Code quickly became an international blockbuster. By 2009, it had sold some 80 million copies and been translated into 44 languages. It soon also became a target of protest. While some authors and critics disparaged the book for its dubious literary value and inaccurate historical information, and Catholic sources denounced it as a dishonest attack on the church, others objected to what they referred to as the blasphemous nature of the book's subject matter. Both evangelical Protestants and Catholics circulated rebuttals, ranging from church-issued pamphlets and study guides to books such as Rev. Erwin W. Lutzer's *The Da Vinci Deception* and Rev. James L. Garlow's and Peter Jones's *Cracking the Da Vinci Code*. These writings sought to refute the book for fostering, in Garlow's words, "an incorrect and historically inaccurate view . . . people are buying into the notion that Jesus is not divine . . . is not the son of God."

Even though Christians were in the forefront of protests against the book, it was banned primarily in predominantly Muslim countries. The first country to ban it was Lebanon, for fear of reviving the sectarian tensions between Christians and Muslims that lay at the heart of Lebanon's 15-year war (1975–90). The government's national security agency issued the ban after protests by the Catholic Information Center. Lebanese who wanted to read the book, however, were able to download it on the Internet or buy black-market copies. In 2006, Iran, after allowing the publication of eight previous editions of the book, banned any further editions at the request of Christian clergy.

Further bans came in the wake of the new international attention brought to the book by the release of a film adaptation in 2006. The predominantly Christian, northeastern Indian state of Nagaland banned both the film and the book in May 2006, declaring them blasphemous, offensive, and a direct assault on the Christian faith. Following Nagaland's lead in June 2006 and after protests by local Christian leaders, the Indian states of Goa, Punjab, Tamil Nadu, and Andhra Pradesh also banned both the film and the book. India's national government did not ban either. (Indian censors cleared the film after its makers agreed to insert a legal disclaimer saying "it was of a fictitious nature.")

Later that month, after protests by members of Pakistan's small Christian community, Pakistan banned the film as blasphemous and also announced intentions to ban the book, which had been available there for some time. The country's cultural affairs minister, Ghazi Gulab Jamal, said that the decision had been made because the *Code* contravenes Islamic teachings. "Islam teaches us to respect all the prophets of Allah Almighty, and degradation of any prophet is tantamount to defamation of the rest," he said.

Also in 2006, Egypt's Ministry of Culture banned both the film and the Arabic- and English-language editions of the novel, which had been sold in the country since 2003. The police also confiscated 2,000 copies of a pirated DVD of the film and arrested the owner of a local production company.

—Philip Milito

FURTHER READING

Bhaumik, Subir. "India State in Total *Da Vinci* Ban." BBC News (May 23, 2006). Available online. URL: http://news.bbc.co.uk/go/pr/fr/2/hi/south___asia/5009778.stm. Accessed July 8, 2009.

"Da Vinci Code Ban in India State." BBC News (June 1, 2006). Available online. URL: http://news.bbc.co.uk/go/pr/fr/-/2/hi/south___asia/5036094.stm. Accessed July 8, 2009.

"Da Vinci Code Book Banned in Iran" BBC News (July 26, 2006). Available online. URL: http://news.bbc.co.uk/go/pr/fr/-/2/hi/entertainment/5216490.stm. Accessed July 27, 2009.

Faroaq, Umer. "Pakistan Bans *Da Vinci Code*, Christians Happy." Islam Online (June 5, 2006). Available online. URL: http://www.islamonline.net/servlet/Satellite?c=Article__C&cid=1162385911282&pagename. Accessed July 8, 2009.

Garlow, James L., and Peter Jones. *Cracking Da Vinci's Code*. Wheaton, Ill.: Victor Books, 2004.

Goodstein, Laurie. "Defenders of Christianity Rebut *The Da Vinci Code*." *New York Times*, April 27, 2004, A22.

Hiel, Betsy. " 'Da Vinci' Unlikely to Pass Egypt Censors." *Pittsburgh Tribune-Review* (May 14, 2006). Available online. URL: http://www.pittsburghlive.com/x/pittsburghtrib/mostread/s_453828.html. Accessed August 25, 2009.

"Iran Bans *Da Vinci Code* Book after 8 Editions." Christians of Iraq (July 26, 2006). Available online. URL: http://www.christiansofiraq.com/irandavinci.html. Accessed July 8, 2009.

Lutzer, Erwin W. *The Da Vinci Conspiracy*. Carol Stream, Ill.: Tyndale House, 2004.

"Pakistan Bans *Da Vinci Code* Film." BBC News (June 4, 2006). Available online. URL: http://news.bbc.co.uk/go/pr/fr/-/2/hi/south___asia/5045672.stm. Accessed July 8, 2009.

"Punjab Ban for *Da Vinci Code* Film." BBC News (May 25, 2006). Available online. URL: http://news.bbc.co.uk/go/pr/fr/-/2/hi/south___asia/5017498.stm. Accessed July 8, 2009.

Wilson, Scott. "Fearing Repeat of the Past, Lebanon Bans a Book." *Washington Post* (October 17, 2004). Available online. URL: http://www.washingtonpost.com/wp-dyn/articles/A38753-2004Oct16.html. Accessed June 4, 2009.

DIALOGUE CONCERNING THE TWO CHIEF WORLD SYSTEMS

Author: Galileo Galilei
Original date and place of publication: 1632, Italy
Literary form: Scientific monograph

SUMMARY

The work of the great Italian astronomer, mathematician, and physicist Galileo Galilei had a profound effect on the development of science and philosophy, laying the foundations for modern experimental science and enlarging human understanding of the nature of the universe. Although the Polish astronomer Nicolaus Copernicus had argued in *On the Revolution of Heavenly Spheres*, published in 1543, that the Sun was the center of the universe and the Earth a planet that moved, belief in the geocentric Ptolemaic system (named for the second-century astronomer Ptolemy) remained prevalent in the early 17th century. The Ptolemaic theory placed the Earth motionless at the center of the universe, with the Sun, the Moon, and the five planets moving around it in complex circular motions.

When Galileo, a professor of mathematics at the University of Pisa, first gazed at the sky through the refracting telescope he had designed, it had been a half-century since Copernicus introduced his theory of a heliocentric, or Sun-centered, universe. For the first time, however, actual observations of the heavens through a telescope seemed to confirm Copernicus's hypothesis. In 1610, Galileo published *The Starry Messenger*, a 24-page pamphlet reporting his astronomical observations of the Moon and the planets. Galileo recounted his discovery of four previously unknown heavenly bodies moving around the planet Jupiter, proof that Copernicus's theory was correct. He also noted that the Moon was not a self-luminous body, but was lit by the Sun.

The Venetian senate granted Galileo a salary for his discoveries, and he was appointed mathematician to the duke of Tuscany. In 1613, he published *Letters on the Solar Spots*, in which he declared his belief in the Copernican theory. Galileo was convinced that "the Book of Nature is written in mathematical symbols," and that in observation and quantification lay the science of the future. In 1632, Galileo published the work that was to mark a turning point in the history of science, *Dialogue Concerning the Two Chief World Systems, Ptolemaic and Copernican*.

In this dialogue in the Platonic tradition, Galileo allowed arguments for and against the Copernican system to emerge from a conversation among three friends: a Florentine who believes in the Copernican system, an Aristotelian supporter of the geocentric theory, and a Venetian aristocrat for whose benefit they propose their arguments. Galileo wrote in Italian for the nonspecialist, rather than in Latin, the language of scholars and intellectuals.

In structuring the *Dialogue*, Galileo complied with the church's orders that the heliocentric theory be discussed as a useful mathematical hypothesis, rather than as a representation of physical reality. But the views he expressed in the *Dialogue* were clearly supportive of the Copernican system. Galileo found that the Earth, like the other planets, rotated on its axis and that the planets revolved around the Sun in elliptical paths determined by gravity. He rejected the idea of a finite universe bounded by an outer sphere of unchanging perfection. By showing that the Earth was not the center of creation but, rather, an insignificant part of it, Galileo overturned the medieval system of cosmology based on Aristotelian theories of the motion of bodies.

Galileo expressed two principles in the *Dialogue* that have become the guiding principles of modern science. First, statements and hypotheses about nature must always be based on observation, rather than on received authority; and second, natural processes can best be understood if represented in mathematical terms.

CENSORSHIP HISTORY

In 1616, the system of Copernicus was denounced as dangerous to the faith and Galileo, summoned to Rome, was warned by Pope Paul V not to "hold, teach or defend" Copernican theories. Galileo promised to obey the papal injunction and returned to Florence. In 1619, the pope banned similar theories, published by the German astronomer Johannes Kepler in *The New Astronomy*. According to the papal bull accompanying these bans, teaching or even reading the works of Copernicus and Kepler was forbidden.

In 1624, Galileo went to Rome again to pay his respects to the newly anointed Pope Urban VIII. Despite the prohibition of 1616, he requested papal permission to publish a book comparing Ptolemaic and Copernican doctrines. The pope refused his request.

Despite warnings by the Vatican, which had cited numerous corrections required before any of Copernicus's theories might be promulgated, in 1632 Galileo published *Dialogue Concerning the Two Chief World Systems*. He attempted to satisfy the authorities by including a preface by a leading Vatican theologian describing Copernican theory as merely an interesting intellectual exercise. But the pope was unconvinced. The book had attracted the attention of all of Europe. The rising threat of Protestantism spurred the pope to respond aggressively to preserve the integrity of the church's dogmas.

Further, Galileo's enemies at the Vatican implied that by publishing the book under the colophon of three fishes—the usual imprint of the Florentine press of Landini—Galileo had made a libelous reference to Pope Urban VIII's three incompetent nephews, whom he had promoted to the church hierarchy. They further suggested that one of the characters in the dialogue, Simplicio, the conservative defender of the geocentric view of the universe, was meant to be a caricature of the pope himself.

In February 1633, the pope summoned Galileo to Rome. Although he was gravely ill in Florence and his doctors warned that a journey in the dead of winter might prove fatal, the pope threatened to forcibly remove him in chains if he did not appear. The grand duke of Florence provided a litter to carry Galileo to Rome, where he was imprisoned. In June he was put on trial for heresy.

The trial focused on technicalities regarding what church authorities had told him during his visit to Rome in 1616 and on how clearly he had understood the papal disapproval of Copernican doctrines. The Inquisition's verdict was that Galileo was "vehemently suspected of heresy, namely of having believed and held the doctrine which is false and contrary to the sacred and divine scriptures that the sun is the center of the world and does not move from East to West and that the earth moves and is not the center of the world and that an opinion may be held and defended as probable after it has been declared and defined to be contrary to Holy Scripture. . . ."

Galileo was sentenced to prison for an indefinite period and required to make a public and formal abjuration. On the morning of June 22, 1633, at the age of 70, Galileo knelt before the court and declared, "With sincere heart and unpretended faith I abjure, curse, and detest the aforesaid errors and heresies and also every other error and sect whatever, contrary to the Holy Church, and I swear that in the future I will never again say or assert verbally or in writing, anything that might cause a similar suspicion toward me. . . ." "And yet it [the Earth] moves," he is said by legend to have muttered after his recantation.

In 1634, the *Dialogue* was formally condemned and banned along with all of Galileo's works. Galileo was confined to a secluded house in Arcetri, outside Florence, where he was allowed no visitors except with the permission of the pope's delegate. During his confinement Galileo was able to complete a new work, *Dialogue Concerning Two New Sciences*, which was smuggled out of Italy and published by the Protestants in Leiden in 1638, four years before his death. During the last four years of his life, Galileo was blind. Eventually the pope allowed him the companionship of a young scholar, Vicenzo Viviani. Still in seclusion, Galileo died on January 8, 1642, a month before his 78th birthday.

The Index of Forbidden Books of 1664 confirmed the condemnation of the works of Copernicus and Galileo and of all other writings affirming the movement of the Earth and the stability of the Sun. In 1753, the Index of Benedict XIV omitted the general prohibition covering books that teach the heliocentric theory.

However, it was not until 1824, when Canon Settele, a Roman astronomy professor, published a work on modern scientific theories, that the church finally announced its acceptance of "the general opinion of modern astronomers." In the next papal Index of 1835, the names of Galileo, Copernicus, and Kepler were removed. On October 31, 1992, Pope John Paul II formally rehabilitated Galileo—359 years, four months, and nine days after Galileo had been forced to recant his heresy that the Earth moved around the Sun.

FURTHER READING

Boorstein, Daniel J. *The Discoverers: A History of Man's Search to Know His World and Himself.* New York: Random House, 1983.
Collinson, Diané. *Fifty Major Philosophers: A Reference Guide.* London: Routledge, 1988.
Garraty, John A., and Peter Gay. *The Columbia History of the World.* New York: Harper & Row, 1972.
Green, Jonathon. *Encyclopedia of Censorship.* New York: Facts On File, 1990.

ESSAYS

Author: Michel de Montaigne
Original date and place of publication: 1580, France
Literary form: Essays

SUMMARY

Michel de Montaigne was the originator of the personal essay as a literary form and the inventor of a new form of autobiography. In his *essais*, or "trials," he set out to test his judgment on a wide range of subjects of interest to him, revealing his inner life and personality. Written over a period of 20 years, beginning in 1571 when Montaigne was 38 until his death in 1592, the 94 essays trace the evolution of Montaigne's thinking as he added to and changed his earlier writings. Books one and two were published in 1580. Revised and enlarged editions of the first two books appeared with book three in 1588; a final complete edition was published posthumously in 1595.

The earliest essays, which began as notes on Montaigne's reading, are mainly compilations of anecdotes with brief commentary. Over the years the essays became longer and more personal. His most influential philosophical essay was the book-length "Apology for Raymond Sebond," composed in 1576. Montaigne's skepticism, summed up in his famous motto *"Que Sçay-je?"* (What do I know?), is revealed in this essay, a sustained argument on the impotence and vanity of presumptuous human reason. In the later essays his self-portrait emerges as the central theme.

Essays opens with Montaigne's preface, "To the Reader," in which he sets the conversational, personal and modest tone that is characteristic of his writing: "This book was written in good faith, reader. It warns you from the outset that in it I have set myself no goal but a domestic and private one. I have had no thought of serving either you or my own glory. . . . If I had written to seek the world's favor, I should have bedecked myself better, and should have presented myself in a studied posture. I want to be seen here in my simple, natural, ordinary fashion, without straining or artifice; for it is myself that I portray."

Drawing on his own recollections, conversations with neighbors and friends, readings in classical literature, and the narratives of historians and ethnographers, the essays range over a vast array of subjects, from cannibalism to education, politics, friendship, nature, and death. Montaigne reveals himself as intellectually curious, tolerant, skeptical, and unafraid to contradict himself. His aim is to provide an unvarnished picture of his experience and attitudes, for if a man does not know himself, what does he know?

"My sole aim is to reveal myself," he writes, "and I may be different tomorrow if some new lesson changes me. . . . Contradictions of opinion, therefore, neither offend nor estrange me; they only arouse and exercise my mind."

Through his quest for self-knowledge, Montaigne is led to recognize common human traits and values. In his last essay, "On Experience," he concludes, "It is an absolute perfection and virtually divine to know how to enjoy our being rightfully. We seek other conditions because we do not understand the use of our own, and go outside of ourselves because we do not know what it is like inside. . . . The most beautiful lives, to my mind, are those that conform to the common human pattern, with order, but without miracle and without eccentricity."

CENSORSHIP HISTORY

The first attempt to censor the *Essays* took place in 1580–81, shortly after the first publication of books one and two, when Montaigne traveled to Germany, Switzerland, and Italy. Upon his entry into Rome, as Montaigne recounted in his *Travel Journal*, his baggage was thoroughly examined by customs. Although he had passed through Germany and "was of an inquiring nature," he carried no forbidden books. Nevertheless, all the books he had, including a copy of the *Essays*, were confiscated for examination. They included a prayer book (suspect only because it was published in Paris, rather than Rome) and "also the books of certain German doctors of theology against the heretics, because in combatting them, they made mention of their errors."

Though Montaigne had been cordially received by Pope Gregory XIII, he was later summoned to the Vatican's Holy Office and advised that some passages in his *Essays* should be changed or deleted in future editions. The papal censor, theology professor Sisto Fabri, who did not read French, discussed with Montaigne various errors that had been identified upon the report of a French friar. The censor objected to the overuse of the word *fortune;* the defense of the fourth-century Roman emperor Julian, who abandoned Christianity; the praise of heretical poets; the idea that one who prays should be free from evil impulses; the critical comments on torture ("All that is beyond plain death seems to me pure cruelty"); and the recommendation that children should be fit to do either good or evil so that they may do good through free choice. Though Fabri was "content with the excuses I offered," Montaigne commented, "on each objection that his Frenchman had left him he referred it to my conscience to redress what I thought was in bad taste."

Montaigne responded that these were his opinions, which he did not feel were erroneous, and suggested that perhaps the censor had improperly understood his thoughts. He did promise, however, to consider some revisions. Ultimately, he made none of the recommended revisions in the essays.

In 1595, an unauthorized, expurgated edition was published in Lyon by Simon Goulart. As it was produced for Calvinist consumption, the publisher suppressed a number of chapters and omitted passages critical of Protestants. In its complete edition, as edited by Montaigne's literary executor Marie de Gournay and published in 1595, *Essays* remained a best seller in France into the mid-17th century and was reprinted every two or three years. The book was considered a classic and Montaigne a standard author.

Though the Spanish Inquisition prohibited Montaigne's writing in 1640, it was not until 84 years after Montaigne's death, when the *Essays* had been circulating for close to a century, that the Vatican condemned it. In 1676, it was placed on the Index of Forbidden Books and remained there for almost 300 years.

Montaigne was a faithful Catholic, but he felt that the spheres of faith and reason should be separate. He believed that when faith and reason are contradictory, faith must prevail in religious matters. Not even the most important church dogmas, such as the existence of God and the immortality of the soul, can be proved. They must, rather, be accepted on faith. Theology and philosophy were thus separated, and modern scientific discoveries, such as the new astronomy combatted by the church, could be accepted as a matter of reason without challenging religious doctrine.

"No proposition astounds me, no belief offends me," Montaigne wrote, "however much opposed it may be to my own." Montaigne's skepticism, tolerance, and mistrust of dogmatic systems of belief reflected an open-minded humanistic spirit. This attitude was still possible in Montaigne's day while the liberal philosophy of Renaissance humanism prevailed. But as the Counter Reformation gained strength and church traditions were secured against the innovations of Protestant theology, Montaigne's views on the separation of faith and reason were attacked as the heresy of "fideism." The placement of the *Essays* on the Index in 1676 is thought to be the result of criticisms by theologians influenced by the rationalism of Descartes, which declared that faith could appeal to reason.

FURTHER READING

Boase, Alan M. *The Fortunes of Montaigne: A History of the Essays in France, 1580–1669.* New York: Octagon Books, 1970.

Frame, Donald M., trans. and intro. *The Complete Works of Montaigne.* Stanford, Calif.: Stanford University Press, 1967.

————, trans. and intro. *The Complete Essays of Montaigne.* Stanford, Calif.: Stanford University Press, 1958.

Montaigne, Michel de. *Essays.* Ed. and introduction by J. M. Cohen. Middlesex, England: Penguin Books, 1958.

Tetel, Marcel. *Montaigne: Updated Edition.* Boston: Twayne Publishers, 1990.

Toulmin, Stephen. *Cosmopolis: The Hidden Agenda of Modernity.* Chicago: University of Chicago Press, 1990.

HARRY POTTER AND THE SORCERER'S STONE

Author: J. K. Rowling
Original dates and places of publication: 1997, United Kingdom; 1998, United States
Original publishers: Bloomsbury Publishing; Scholastic Press
Literary form: Novel

SUMMARY

Harry Potter and the Sorcerer's Stone (published in the United Kingdom as *Harry Potter and the Philosopher's Stone*) is the first volume of J. K. Rowling's seven-part series chronicling the adventures of young Harry Potter in wizardry school. The story begins on a dull, gray Tuesday outside the home of Vernon and Petunia Dursley and their son, Dudley, at No. 4 Privet Drive. That night a half-giant on a flying motorcycle leaves a baby boy on the Dursleys' doorstep. It is their nephew Harry Potter.

We learn that the evil wizard Lord Voldemort murdered Harry's parents, the renowned wizards Lily and James Potter, and then mysteriously disappeared. Harry survived Voldemort's attack with a lightning bolt–shaped scar on his forehead and is famous in the wizard world as "the boy who lived." Headmaster Albus Dumbledore and Professor McGonagall of the Hogwarts School of Witchcraft and Wizardry have left Harry with his Muggle (nonwizard) relatives until he is old enough to attend Hogwarts.

Ten years later, Harry is living a miserable life with the odious Dursleys and has been told nothing about his wizardly heritage. One day, a letter arrives addressed to him. Uncle Vernon confiscates it, yet the letters continue to arrive by the dozens. He flees with his family to a shack on an island in the middle of the sea, but the letters follow them there. Finally, Rubeus Hagrid, the half-giant who is keeper of keys and grounds at Hogwarts, appears at the door. He explains to Harry that Voldemort had killed his parents, that Harry, too, has magical powers, and that he has been accepted at Hogwarts.

On September 1, Harry's new life begins, as he takes the Hogwarts Express from Platform Nine and Three-Quarters at King's Cross Station, a platform accessible only to wizards. On the train, Harry meets the students who will become his best friends: Ron Weasley, Hermione Granger, and Neville Longbottom, as well as the school bully, Draco Malfoy. When the students are divided into houses, Harry, Ron, Hermione, and Neville are assigned to the noble house of Gryffindor, and Malfoy to the sinister Slytherin, run by malicious Severus Snape, the teacher of potions.

During Harry's first flying lesson, it is evident that he is a natural talent on the broomstick. He is recruited to be the Seeker, a pivotal position on Gryffindor's Quidditch team, a kind of soccer played in the air on broomsticks.

When Malfoy challenges Harry to a midnight wizard's duel, Harry, while evading the ever-vigilant custodian, Argus Filch, and his cat, Mrs. Norris, discovers an enormous three-headed dog guarding a trap door in a forbidden third-floor corridor. During his first Quidditch game, Harry escapes an attempt on his life by someone using sorcery. He suspects Snape. Hagrid inadvertently reveals that the dog, Fluffy, is guarding a secret and that a certain Nicholas Flamel is involved.

Harry remains at school for the Christmas holidays. Among his Christmas presents is the Invisibility Cloak that had belonged to his father. Hidden beneath his cloak, he explores the deserted school and discovers a magnificent mirror, in which he sees his parents and grandparents for the first time. Though his family appears to be alive, Dumbledore explains that the Mirror of Erised reflects neither knowledge nor truth but rather only the deepest desires of those who look upon it.

After Christmas, Harry and his friends learn that Nicholas Flamel is the only known maker of the Sorcerer's Stone. This stone transforms metal into gold and produces the Elixir of Life, which grants immortality to those who drink it. They realize that Flamel had asked Dumbledore to keep the stone safe and that Fluffy now guards it.

Professor McGonagall catches Harry and his friends at midnight at the top of the tallest astronomy tower, off limits for students, while they are doing a favor for Hagrid. As punishment they are sent into the Forbidden Forest for the night. They come upon a hooded figure drinking the blood of a dead unicorn. A centaur rescues Harry and explains that the hooded man was Voldemort, who seeks the Sorcerer's Stone to achieve immortality.

Harry finds out that Fluffy goes to sleep to the sound of music and that Hagrid has revealed this information to a hooded stranger in a bar. The night after exams end, Harry, Ron, and Hermione, in an attempt to protect the stone, go to the third floor, put the dog to sleep, and pass a series of tests and obstacles to reach the chamber where the stone is kept. Harry is shocked to encounter Quirrell, the timid professor of Defense Against the Dark Arts, who admits that he was the one who had tried to kill him.

Quirrell orders Harry to look into the Mirror of Erised, the final seal protecting the Sorcerer's Stone, and reveal its location. When Harry lies about what he sees, Quirrell's turban falls away. At the back of his head, Harry sees a terrible, snakelike face. It is Voldemort, who is sharing Quirrell's body. Quirrell tries to strangle Harry, but his hands burn when he touches Harry's skin. Harry loses consciousness and then awakens in the school infirmary to find out that Dumbledore had arrived just in time to save him. Dumbledore destroyed the stone, but Voldemort is still out there somewhere, perhaps looking for another body to share.

Quirrell could not touch Harry without burning, Dumbledore explains, because "if there is one thing Voldemort cannot understand, it is love. He didn't realize that love as powerful as your mother's for you leaves its own mark. . . . It is in your very skin."

At the Hogwarts' year-end banquet, the bravery of Harry and his friends wins the House Cup for Gryffindor. Now Harry must return to the Muggle world and face another summer with the Dursleys, but this time, he has magic tools at hand.

In volumes two through seven—*Harry Potter and the Chamber of Secrets* (1998), *Harry Potter and the Prisoner of Azkaban* (1999), *Harry Potter and the Goblet of Fire* (2000), *Harry Potter and the Order of the Phoenix* (2003), *Harry Potter and the Half-Blood Prince* (2005), and *Harry Potter and the Deathly Hallows* (2007)—J. K. Rowling chronicles Harry's second through sixth year at Hogwarts and beyond, as he grows from a bright-eyed 10-year-old into an angst-filled teenager and continues his battle against evil, learning about his past and his own dark connections to Voldemort.

CENSORSHIP HISTORY

The seven books in the Harry Potter series have been an international publishing sensation, translated into at least 60 languages and sold in more than 200 countries. In June 2008, the number of books sold worldwide had reached 400 million.

But Rowling's series has also achieved a more dubious distinction: According to the American Library Association (ALA), every year from 1999 to 2002, Harry Potter topped the list of titles "challenged," or targeted for censorship, in libraries and schools in the United States because it portrays wizardry and magic. In 2003, it ranked second. The ALA defines a challenge as a formal written complaint filed with a library or a school requesting that materials be removed because of content or appropriateness. The ALA documented 125 attempts during 1999–2003 to restrict access or remove the Potter books from classrooms, curricula, or school or public libraries.

In most cases, the efforts were unsuccessful. However, in Zeeland, Michigan, in November 1999, school superintendent Gary L. Feenstra ordered that *Harry Potter and the Sorcerer's Stone* could not be used in classrooms or displayed on library shelves, that students could check it out or write reports about it only with parental permission, and that no new copies could be purchased for school libraries. Zeeland students, parents, and teachers joined with groups representing booksellers, librarians, publishers, and writers to form an organization to fight the restrictions, Muggles for Harry Potter. The Zeeland Board of Education set up a committee composed of parents and educators from each school in the district to evaluate the superintendent's restrictions. On May 11, 2000, Feenstra accepted the committee's recommendations to rescind the ban, retaining only the restriction on classroom readings in kindergarten to grade 5.

The first legal challenge to a ban on Potter books came in July 2002, when a student and her parents sued the Cedarville, Arkansas, school board. It had restricted access to the books in school libraries by placing them in a section that was off limits to students unless they had their parents' permission, overruling a unanimous decision by the district's library committee to allow unrestricted access. The board acted in response to a parent's complaint that the books show "that there are 'good witches' and 'good magic' and that they teach 'parents/teachers/rules are stupid and something to be ignored.' " The complaining parent said in court depositions that she became concerned about children's exposure to Harry Potter after hearing anti-Potter sermons by the pastor of the Uniontown Assembly of God church, who was also a member of the Cedarville school board.

In April 2003, U.S. District Court judge Jimm L. Hendren in Fort Smith, Arkansas, ordered the Cedarville school district to return the books to the open shelves of its libraries "where they can be accessed without any restrictions other than those. . . that apply to all works of fiction in the libraries of the district." Hendren said there was no evidence to support the school board's claim that the books threatened the orderly operation of the schools and concluded that the majority of the board members voted to "restrict access to the books because of their shared belief that the books promote a particular religion." This violated the First Amendment rights of the students. "Regardless of the personal distaste with which these individuals regard 'witchcraft,' " the judge said, "it is not properly within their power and authority as members of defendants' school board to prevent the students at Cedarville from reading about it."

Conservative groups and Christian fundamentalist organizations such as Focus on the Family, Family Friendly Libraries, Freedom Village USA, and activist Phyllis Schafly's Eagle Forum organized efforts to remove Harry Potter from schools or libraries. They believe that the books are dangerous to children because they promote the occult, Satanism, and antifamily themes and encourage witchcraft and drug use.

On its Web site in 2002, Family Friendly Libraries explained that it promotes book policies it believes "are necessary to protect children, preserve parental rights, re-establish decency as a standard for the classroom, encourage higher educational standards, and uphold Constitutional law as today's courts seem to interpret it."

The group singled out categories of books and other materials that "constitute family sensitive materials that deserve special handling in the public school library setting on special shelves that do not allow general student access." They include "those with religious symbolism and language (Harry Potter and C. S. Lewis' Narnia series falls in this category)."

Family Friendly Libraries also recommended that "a family-friendly attorney send a letter on his/her official stationary [sic] to school officials reminding them that although teacher-led objective discussions about religious history, holidays etc are not forbidden within relevant educational planning, nevertheless . . . the teacher also cannot present Harry Potter or other materials celebrating a pagan religious system."

Other organizations that have targeted Harry Potter cite the Hatch Amendment (the Protection of Pupil Rights Amendment to the General Education Provisions Act), which prohibits federally funded schools from conducting psychological testing or surveys of students on certain subjects and restricts the types of physical exams children can receive without parental consent.

According to form letters made available by Christian fundamentalists on the Internet, the Hatch Amendment gives parents the right to excuse children from classroom activities involving discussion of alcohol and drug education; nuclear issues; education on human sexuality; "globalism"; "one-world government" or "anti-nationalistic curricula"; evolution, including Darwin's theory; and witchcraft, occultism, the supernatural, and mysticism.

Jim Bradshaw, a spokesman for the U.S. Department of Education, told the *South Bend* (Indiana) *Tribune* in April 2004 that the Hatch Amendment is often misinterpreted by the public. "There are many form letters out there created and distributed by parental rights groups that misapply the Protection of Pupil Rights Amendment (PPRA) to certain situations," he said. "PPRA has to do with surveying students, not with what is taught to students. Thus, whether a particular book can be taught is a local issue. The Department of Education is specifically prohibited by law from telling a school what they can or cannot teach." Nevertheless, parents have presented form letters citing the Hatch Amendment to school officials as justification for restricting access to the Harry Potter series and other books in schools.

In an interview with the *Baltimore Sun* in 2000, Rowling commented on the attempts to keep Harry Potter out of the hands of schoolchildren: "I think it's shortsighted in the sense that it is very hard to portray goodness without showing what the reverse is and showing how brave it is to resist that. You find magic, witchcraft, and wizardry in all sorts of classic children's books. Where do you stop? Are you going to stop at *The Wizard of Oz?* Are you going to stop at C. S. Lewis? The talking animals in *Wind in the Willows?*"

During 2001–03, the Potter books were publicly burned or shredded by fundamentalist church groups in the United States in Butler County, Pennsylvania; Lewiston, Maine; Alamogordo, New Mexico; and Greenville, Michigan. Harry Potter books have also been banished from some Christian religious schools in the United States, as well as in Australia, Britain, and Sweden.

Although a few U.S. Catholic schools banned the books, the Vatican informally approved them. In February 2003, Rev. Peter Fleetwood, former official of the Pontifical Council for Culture, introducing a Vatican document on New Age religious beliefs to the press, commented that the books helped children "to see the difference between good and evil." "I don't think there's anyone in this room who grew up without fairies, magic, and angels in their imaginary world," he told reporters. "They aren't bad. They aren't serving as a banner for an anti-Christian ideology."

In July 2005, however, it was revealed that when Pope Benedict XVI was a cardinal (Joseph Cardinal Ratzinger) and head of the Vatican's Congregation for the Doctrine of the Faith, he had criticized the Potter books. In 2003, Ratzinger had written two letters replying to Gabrielle Kuby, a Catholic sociologist from Germany and author of *Harry Potter: Gut oder Böse* (Harry Potter: Good or evil). Kuby's book alleges that the books prevent the young from developing a proper sense of good and evil and harm their relationship with God.

In the first letter, written in German, dated March 7, 2003, Ratzinger thanked Kuby for her "instructive book" and suggested she send a copy to Monsignor Fleetwood. "It is good that you enlighten us in matters relating to Harry Potter," Ratzinger wrote, "for these are subtle temptations, which act imperceptibly and, for that reason, deeply, and subvert Christianity in the soul, before it can really grow properly." Despite the pope's negative assessment of the books in the past, the Vatican has not attempted to bar them from Catholic schools or recommend that Catholics refrain from reading them.

As *Harry Potter and the Half-Blood Prince* hit U.S. bookstores in July 2005, it appeared that some of the steam had gone out of the anti–Harry Potter movement. The ALA announced that in 2004, for the first time in five years, the series did not appear on its list of "most challenged" books. A number of observers noted that the frequency of protests against the books had diminished markedly in 2004 and 2005.

Only a few incidents of attempted censorship of the Harry Potter books were reported to the ALA during 2004–2009. In 2006, trustees of the Wilsona School District in California removed Harry Potter and 23 other books from a reading list recommended by a parent-teacher committee for the Vista San Gabriel elementary school library. Also in 2006, in Gwinnett County, Georgia, a parent asked that the books be removed from school libraries because they promote witchcraft. The county school board rejected the request. The parent appealed, and in December 2006 the Georgia Board of Education supported the school board's decision and ruled that the parent had failed to prove her contention that the books "promote the Wicca religion." In May 2007, a state superior court judge upheld the state board of education's decision. In October 2007, the pastor of St. Joseph's School in Wakefield, Massachusetts, removed the books from the school library, declaring that the themes of the witchcraft and sorcery were inappropriate for a Catholic school.

Though the epicenter of the anti-Harry Potter movement is in the United States, the book has also been targeted abroad. In February 2002, board of education officials in the United Arab Emirates banned 26 books from schools, including the Harry Potter series and George Orwell's *Animal Farm*, because "they have written or illustrated material that contradicts Islamic and Arab values." They nonetheless remained available in bookstores.

In December 2002, a representative of the International Foundation for Slavic Writing and Culture filed criminal hate-crime charges against Rosman Publishing in Moscow for publishing a Russian translation of *Harry Potter and the Chamber of Secrets,* claiming that it "instilled religious extremism and prompted students to join religious organizations of Satanist followers." After an investigation, the Moscow City Prosecutor's Office decided that there were no grounds for a criminal case.

FURTHER READING

American Library Association. *Newsletter on Intellectual Freedom* 54, no. 3 (May 2005).

Blakely, Rhys. "Pope Criticises Harry Potter." *Times* (London) (July 13, 2005). Available online. URL: http://www.timesonline.co.uk/article/0,,1=1692541,00.html.

Chansanchai, Athima. "Darkness and Delight of Potter's Creator." *Baltimore Sun* (October 20, 2000). Available online. URL: http://www.baltimoresun.com. Accessed November 2, 2000.

Churnin, Nancy. "Bible Belt Beware: Harry Potter Isn't So Controversial Anymore." *Dallas Morning News* (July 13, 2005). Available online. URL: http://www.free republic.com/focus/f-news/1443583/posts. Accessed November 15, 2005.

deLuzuriaga, Tania. "Man from Ministry Bans Potter." *Boston Globe* (October 25, 2007). Available online. URL: http://www.boston.com/news/local/articles/2007/10/25/man_from_ministry_bans_potter/. Accessed June 6, 2010.

Doyle, Robert P. *Books Challenged or Banned in 2008–2009.* Chicago: American Library Association, 2009.

———. *Books Challenged or Banned in 2006–2007.* Chicago: American Library Association, 2007.

———. *Books Challenged or Banned in 2005–2006.* Chicago: American Library Association, 2006.

———. *Banned Books: 2004 Resource Book.* Chicago: American Library Association, 2004.

———. "Books Challenged or Banned in 2002–2003." Chicago: American Library Association, 2003.

———. "Books Challenged or Banned in 2001–2002." Chicago: American Library Association, 2002.

———. "2000–2001: Books Challenged or Banned." Chicago: American Library Association, 2001.

Family Friendly Libraries. "Family-Friendly Public School Book Policies." 2002. Available online. URL: http//www.fflibraries.org/Book_Reports/PSBookPolicies.htm.

Kern, Edmund. "Pope Should Spell Out Views on Potter." *The Scotsman* (July 29, 2005). Available online. URL: http://www.scotsman.com/opinion.cfm?id=1700982005.

Meenan, Jim. "Mom: Parental Rights Central to Book Issue." *South Bend Tribune* (April 16, 2004). Available online. URL: http://www.southbendtribune.com. Accessed April 27, 2004.

Rowling, J. K. J. K. Rowling Official Site. Available online. URL: http://www.jk
rowling.com.
Scholastic Press. "Harry Potter." Available online. URL: http://scholastic.com/harry
potter.

THE HIDDEN FACE OF EVE: WOMEN IN THE ARAB WORLD

Author: Nawal El Saadawi
Original dates and places of publication: 1977, Lebanon; 1980, United
States
Publishers: al-Mu'assassat; Zed Books
Literary form: Sociological text

SUMMARY

A physician, sociologist, novelist, and author of nonfiction essays and books
on Arab women's issues, Nawal El Saadawi is one of the most widely translated Egyptian writers and an outspoken feminist. In this personal and disturbing account, the author exposes the hidden abuses of girls and women
in the Muslim world and the ideologies she holds responsible for their
oppressed condition.

Covering a wide range of topics, from female genital mutilation and
sexual abuse of girls, to prostitution, sexual relationships, marriage, and
divorce, El Saadawi advances the thesis that the problems of Arab women
stem not from the substance and values of Islam, but rather from an economic and political system based on male domination. One of the primary
weapons used to suppress the revolt of women against patriarchy and its
values is the misuse of the doctrines of Islam, the exploitation of religion for
social and political ends.

The oppression of women in any society is an expression of an economic
structure built on landownership, systems of inheritance and parenthood,
and the patriarchal family as a social unit, El Saadawi contends. Arab cultures
are not exceptional in having transformed women into commodities. In the
very essence of Islam, the status of women is no worse than it is in Judaism or
Christianity.

El Saadawi recounts her own genital mutilation at the age of six, a
prevalent custom for Egyptian girls when she was growing up. "Society
had made me feel, since the day that I opened my eyes on life, that I was
a girl, and that the word *bint* (girl) when pronounced by anyone is almost
always accompanied by a frown." Recalling her experiences as a doctor
working in rural areas of Egypt, she analyzes the psychological and physical damage of genital mutilation, which is aimed at denying sexual pleasure
to women in order to ensure their virginity before marriage and chastity
throughout.

Society, as represented by its dominant classes and male structure, El Saadawi contends, realized at an early stage the power of female sexual desire. Unless women were controlled and subjugated, they would not submit to moral, legal, and religious constraints, in particular those related to monogamy. An illicit intimacy with another man could lead to confusion in succession and inheritance, since there was no guarantee that another man's child would not step into the line of descendants.

El Saadawi also discusses another taboo subject, sexual molestation of girls by male family members. She cites a study she conducted in 1973, involving 160 Egyptian girls and women from different social classes, from both educated and uneducated families. One of her findings showed that sexual molestation of female children by men was a common occurrence. The increasing number of men unable to marry for economic reasons, the segregation of the sexes, the lack of sexual outlets for men, the convenient proximity of female family members or young domestic servants, and the low status of women are all contributing factors to the problem.

El Saadawi systematically analyzes other abuses against women, including marriage customs and laws that transform women into merchandise to be bought in exchange for dowry and sold for the price of alimony; laws that punish a woman for committing adultery; prohibitions on abortion that result in maternal deaths from illegal abortions; and marriage regulations giving the husband the right to refuse his wife permission to leave the house to work or travel.

Looking back into Egyptian history, she finds in the predominance of the female goddesses of pharaonic Egypt a reflection of the high status of women before the advent of the systems characterized by the patriarchal family, land ownership, and division into social classes. In Islamic history, she points to one of Muhammad's wives, Aisha, as an example of a liberated woman known for her strong will, eloquence, and intelligence. Aisha did not hesitate to oppose or contradict the Prophet; she fought in several wars and battles and was actively involved in politics and cultural and literary activities. The complete emancipation of women, whether in the Arab countries or elsewhere, El Saadawi says, can occur only when humanity does away with class society and exploitation and when the structures and values of the patriarchal system have been erased.

CENSORSHIP HISTORY

El Saadawi has long been a thorn in the side of Egyptian religious and political authorities, whom she has angered by her unyielding demands for women's rights, daring writings on gender and sexuality in 35 books, and questioning of religious and secular foundations of patriarchal authority.

She was the first feminist in the Arab world to publicly confront issues such as female genital mutilation, prostitution, incest, and sexual abuse of Arab girls and women. Her first study of Arab women's problems and their struggle for liberation, *Women and Sex*, published in Egypt in 1972, was a best seller, but it offended religious and government leaders. As a direct result of the book's publication, she was dismissed from her post as director general of health education in the Ministry of Health. She also lost her job as editor of the journal *Health* and was removed as assistant general secretary of the Medical Association. Her publisher was ordered to recall all copies of *Women and Sex* and put them in storage.

The 1977 publication of *The Hidden Face of Eve: Women in the Arab World* in Arabic and its subsequent translation into several languages brought her international attention but also more harassment in Egypt. During the presidency of Anwar Sadat, from 1970 until 1981, despite the absence of official censorship, emergency laws allowed the prime minister to withhold printing permits for publications. When a permit was denied for *The Hidden Face of Eve*, El Saadawi had it published in Beirut, Lebanon. The book was prohibited from entry to many Arab countries, including Egypt, where Egyptian customs and excise authorities barred it under the Importing of Foreign Goods Act. "Islamicists considered its critical examination of the links between the Middle East's three social taboos—religion, sex and the ruling establishment—blasphemous," El Saadawi wrote. "A disobedient woman writer is doubly punished," she contended, "since she has violated the norm of her fundamental obligation to home, husband and children."

When the Center for New Ideas in Tehran, Iran, translated the book into Farsi in 1980, Islamic extremists among followers of the Ayatollah Ruhollah Khomeini burned the book and its publishing house. Despite the bannings, the book, smuggled from Lebanon and sold surreptitiously, has been widely read in Egypt and in many of the other Arab countries where it is prohibited.

El Saadawi's writings and her left-wing political views—she opposed the 1979 Camp David peace treaty between Egypt and Israel—led to her arrest and imprisonment in 1981 under the Sadat regime. Along with many other Egyptian intellectuals, she was jailed for three months for alleged "crimes against the state" and released after Sadat's assassination.

Only in the early 1980s was she able to publish a book in Egypt, though she remained blacklisted from Egyptian television and radio. After her release from prison she founded the Arab Women's Solidarity Association, an international Arab women's network to support women's rights and secularism. In July 1991, the Egyptian government under President Hosni Mubarak banned the Egyptian branch of the association and also closed down its feminist magazine.

El Saadawi has been the target of numerous death threats by Muslim fundamentalists. Sheikh Mohammed al-Ghazzali, a well-known faculty member at Al-Azhar University, Egypt's state-funded religious establishment, called her "an animal." In June 1992, the government posted armed guards outside her home to protect her. "I never trusted them," says El Saadawi. "I did not believe that those in power were so concerned about my life." In 1993, she left Egypt, fearing for her life, and moved to the United States, where she was a visiting professor for four years at Duke University. She returned to Egypt in 1999.

In 2001, El Saadawi faced charges of apostasy in Cairo's Civil Affairs Court brought by an Islamist lawyer who sought to divorce her forcibly from her Muslim husband of 37 years, Dr. Sherif Hetata. The lawyer, Nabih El-Wahsh, claimed that El Saadawi's views, as quoted in a local weekly newspaper, on the veil, Muslim inheritance laws and the pagan aspects of the pilgrimage to Mecca "ousted her from the Muslim community."

El Saadawi said that her statements were taken out of context as "part of a campaign by the political religious trend against me." The lawyer based his case on the claim that Islamic law, or sharia, prohibits Muslims from marrying those who have abandoned their Islamic faith and that the Muslim community is empowered by sharia to defend its tenets against such transgressions through the exercise of *hisba*. *Hisba* allows any Muslim to file a case on behalf of society when the plaintiff feels that great harm has been done to Islam.

In July 2001, the court rejected the lawyer's claim on grounds that under Egyptian law, only a state prosecutor can bring *hisba* cases. A number of Islamist lawyers had brought Egyptian intellectuals and writers to court using *hisba* during the 1990s. A notorious suit in 1995 against university professor Nasr Hamed Abu Zeid, alleging that his writings denied some of the basic teachings of Islam, resulted in a court order for Abu Zeid's separation from his wife, Ibtihal Younes. The couple went into exile in the Netherlands to avoid the forcible divorce and escape death threats by militant Islamists. In the wake of international criticism and embarrassment over the Abu Zeid case, the government asked Parliament in 1998 to amend the law to allow only the state's prosecutor-general to file *hisba* cases.

During the 33rd International Cairo Book Fair in 2001, government censors confiscated four books written by El Saadawi, including her memoirs. In May 2004, the Islamic Research Academy of Al-Azhar, Egypt's leading Muslim religious institution, called on the government to ban El Saadawi's 1987 novel, *The Fall of the Imam*, on the grounds that it offends Islam. "Almost every year," El Saadawi said, "they launch a campaign against me in order to draw people's attention away from crucial issues and to frighten creative writers."

In January 2007, five of her books were again barred from display at the Cairo International Book Fair, including her 2006 play, *God Submits His Resignation from the Summit Meeting*. Later that year, Al-Azhar filed suit against El Saadawi for blasphemy for publishing the play. In January 2008, the owner of Egypt's Madbouli bookstore and publishing company, who had published dozens of El Saadawi's books in the past, destroyed the entire inventory of the play, as well as *The Fall of the Imam*, in the presence of the government's book controller, "once we learnt it offends religion." After Islamists called for revocation of her Egyptian citizenship, El Saadawi fled Egypt for Brussels.

FURTHER READING

Anis, Mona, and Amira Howeidy. " 'I Dream of a Better Future.' " *Al-Ahram Weekly* (June 22–29, 1995). In *World Press Review* (October 1995): 19–21.

Dawoud, Khaled. "Did *Hisba* Ever Go Away?" *Al-Ahram Weekly On-line* 539 (June 21–27, 2001). Available online. URL: http://weekly.ahram.org.eg/2001/539/eg7.htm.

Ehab, John. "Publish and Be Damned." *Daily News Egypt* (April 11, 2008). Available online. URL: http://www.dailystaregypt.com/article.aspx?ArticleID=13056. Accessed June 6, 2010.

Howeidy, Amira. "The Persecution of Abu Zeid." *Al-Ahram Weekly* (June 22–28, 1995). In *World Press Review* (October 1995): 18–19.

Malti-Douglas, Fedwa, and Allen Douglas. "Reflections of a Feminist." In *Opening the Gates: A Century of Arab Feminist Writing*, edited by Margot Badran and Miriam Cooke, 394–404. Bloomington: Indiana University Press, 1990.

El Saadawi, Nawal. "Defying Submission." *Index on Censorship* 19, no. 9 (October 1980): 16.

———. *The Hidden Face of Eve: Women in the Arab World*. Preface by Nawal El Saadawi. Trans. Sherif Hetata. London: Zed Books, 1980.

———. *The Hidden Face of Eve: Women in the Arab World*. Foreword by Irene L. Gendzier. Boston: Beacon Press, 1982.

———. Nawal El Saadawi's official Web site. Available online. URL: http://www.nawalsaadawi.net.

Al-Tahhawi, Amira. "Egypt's 'Woman Rebel' Back in the Line of Fire." *Menassat* (July 2, 2008). Available online. URL: http://www.menassat.com/?q=en/news-articles/4034-egypts-woman-rebel-back-line-fire. Accessed June 6, 2010.

HIS DARK MATERIALS TRILOGY, BOOK I: *THE GOLDEN COMPASS*

Author: Philip Pullman
Original date and places of publication: 1995, United Kingdom; United States
Original publishers: Scholastic Children's Books; Alfred A. Knopf
Literary form: Novel

SUMMARY

The Golden Compass (originally published under the title *Northern Lights* in the United Kingdom) is Book I of Philip Pullman's His Dark Materials trilogy, which follows the adventures of young Lyra Belacqua and her daemon, Pantalaimon (Pan), on a fated quest.

Pullman has, in convincing fashion, created an alternate version of Earth as Lyra's birth-world, where all humans have daemons (animalistic manifestations of the soul's qualities), and the Church has almost absolute control of society. With the abolition of the papacy, the Holy Church has become a hierarchy of courts and councils known as the Magisterium, chief among them being the

General Oblation Board. The traditional Church teachings of heaven and hell are threatened by the notion of the existence of other universes in different dimensions and by the alleged presence of mysterious particles known as Dust.

It is in this atmosphere of theological and political intrigue that the tale begins. Lyra, brought up at Jordan College, learns that her uncle, the powerful Lord Asriel, has come to the school with photographic evidence of Dust and of an alternative universe, revealed in the light of an aurora. Lord Asriel persuades the Master and the Scholars of the College to grant his request for further funding and returns to the North to continue his experiments regarding Dust.

Shortly thereafter, children and their daemons from the surrounding area are being kidnapped by what have come to be called Gobblers by the locals. On the day Lyra's friend, Roger, is kidnapped, she is summoned by the Master to meet Mrs. Coulter, a one-time Scholar mounting her own expedition north. Lyra is made Mrs. Coulter's assistant. Before she goes with Mrs. Coulter, the Master gives her an alethiometer, a device for revealing the truth of a situation, telling her she must keep it hidden from Mrs. Coulter. Lyra assumes that the Master wants her to bring the device to Lord Asriel.

Lyra slowly becomes suspicious of Mrs. Coulter and her golden monkey daemon. At a social function, Lyra overhears several startling conversations: She learns that Lord Asriel is being held prisoner by order of the Magisterium in an arctic kingdom called Svalbald, ruled by sapient armored bears; she also learns that the Gobblers are from the General Oblation Board and that Mrs. Coulter herself is the head of the board. When Pan discovers the golden monkey daemon leaving Lyra's quarters, Lyra realizes that Mrs. Coulter must now know about the alethiometer; Lyra gathers her possessions and flees with Pan.

While escaping, Lyra is accosted by two slave traders but is rescued by a group of gyptian men, who know Lyra from Jordan College. The gyptians are a gypsy-like boat people who value loyalty above all else and whose children have been targeted by the Gobblers; when Lyra learns of the gyptian's plan to go North and rescue all the children, she offers to accompany them so that she may use the alethiometer to help find Roger and free her uncle. However, she learns from the gyptians' leaders, John Faa and Farder Coram, that, in actuality, she is the offspring of Lord Asriel and Mrs. Coulter; after the adulterous scandal, both of them shunned the child, and the courts placed her at Jordan College. Despite this emotional shock, Lyra manages to master the alethiometer.

Before the gyptians begin their expedition, they build their supplies and try to gain support from their allies, the witches. Like the gyptians, the witches honor obligations, and Farder Coram, who once saved the life of witch queen Serafina Pekkala, asks for and receives her pledge of aid. John Faa engages itinerant aeronaut Lee Scoresby and his hot-air balloon for the trip, while Lyra enlists Iorek Byrnison, a renegade armored bear who was deposed as king of his clan and exiled from Svalbald. Soon after the expedition sets out, they are attacked by Tartars who are in league with Mrs. Coulter. They kidnap Lyra and Pan and take them to Bolvangar, where the Oblation Board conducts its own experiments, which, Lyra learns, entail cutting daemons away from their children. Lyra stumbles into one of the operating rooms, where three technicians about to subject her to the procedure are interrupted by the timely arrival of Mrs. Coulter, who has been relentlessly following Lyra.

Mrs. Coulter tells Lyra that Dust is first attracted to people at the time of puberty, when their daemons begin to trouble them with the normal awakenings of sexuality, which is why the Magisterium holds Dust to be the source of Original Sin. The board's attempt to eradicate what they feel is sin results in the depersonalization of the child, incurring a servile attitude. But now that Lord Asriel has given proof of Dust and of alternative universes, the Magisterium can no longer dismiss them as heresies and is now trying to gain control of access to Dust, since Lord Asriel's findings have shown a link between Dust and the ability to cross over into those alternative worlds.

Lyra escapes from Mrs. Coulter and sets a fire in the kitchen, which consumes the whole compound. The Tartars begin to stalk the children, but the gyptian expedition arrives in time to rescue them. Lyra means to continue on with Roger and Iorek Byrnison to find Lord Asriel. Lee Scoresby, accompanied by Serafina Pekkala, takes them farther north by balloon. While en route, they are attacked by bat-like creatures called cliff-ghasts. As the balloon nears the ground, Lyra is thrown from the basket and taken prisoner by the armored bears. Iorek Byrnison and Roger also manage to get off the balloon and arrive in time for Iorek to fight the bear-king to the death and reclaim his throne. The bears now turn and fight Mrs. Coulter and the Tartars, who have come by airship, while Lyra, Roger, and Iorek Byrnison go on to the cabin where Lord Asriel is being held.

They find Lord Asriel, and he affirms to Lyra that there is a connection between Dust and sex and, more important, that there is an energy released when a child is separated from his daemon that, properly conducted, can create a portal into one or more of the alternative universes. This would mean the end of the Magisterium's power. Lord Asriel thinks that Dust comes from these other worlds and is determined to destroy its source. Lyra realizes it was not the alethiometer he wanted but Roger, a child to complete his experiment.

As an aurora reveals a city in the sky, Lord Asriel separates Roger from his daemon, killing them both. The released energy creates an opening in the sky, through which Lord Asriel passes. Lyra and Pan follow him over, determined to locate the source of Dust before he does.

In Book II of the His Dark Materials trilogy, *The Subtle Knife*, the adventures of Lyra Balacqua continue as Lyra meets Will Parry, a fugitive boy from our own universe, who journeys with Lyra from world to world in search of the answers behind Dust. In Book III, *The Amber Spyglass*, Lyra and Will find themselves at the center of a brutal battle whose outcome will reveal the secret of Dust.

CENSORSHIP HISTORY

Since its publication in 1995, *The Golden Compass* has enjoyed considerable critical acclaim and popular success, as have Books II and III of Pullman's His Dark Materials trilogy, *The Subtle Knife* (1997) and *The Amber Spyglass* (2000). Protest against the books began only in 2007, after a film adaptation of *The Golden Compass* was announced. As the December release date approached, Pullman helped promote the film with provocative interviews, in which he proclaimed his atheism and affirmed that the books of his trilogy were an inverted retelling of John Milton's epic poem *Paradise Lost*, this time with God as the vanquished instead of Satan.

Even though the film of *The Golden Compass* watered down Pullman's references in the novel to abuses of power by a religious institution very much like the Catholic Church, the Vatican condemned the movie. An editorial in the Vatican newspaper, *L'Osservatore Romano*, stated that the film and Pullman's writings showed that "when man tries to eliminate God from his horizon, everything is reduced, made sad, cold and inhumane."

In the United States, William Donohue, president of the ultraconservative Catholic League, called for a boycott of the film and the books of the trilogy. The league felt that if children could not see the film, they would not be enticed to read the trilogy, which a league spokesperson described as "a candy-coated message of atheism." The league sent out pamphlets to hundreds of groups, ranging from Roman Catholic bishops to Protestant and Muslim organizations, as well as to Catholic schools around the country, urging them to pull *The Golden Compass* and its companion volumes from their shelves.

This campaign met with success. In 2007, according to the American Library Association (ALA), *The Golden Compass* was the fourth most-challenged book in the United States, with reports of 420 formally submitted complaints to libraries or schools asking for the book's removal, and in 2008, the His Dark Materials trilogy was listed second on the ALA's list. In some cases, the volumes remained on the shelves; in others, the books were removed but later returned; and in yet other cases, such as at a Christian school library in Montrose, Texas, use of *The Golden Compass* was permanently discontinued, even though it had been on the school's eighth-grade recommended reading list for 10 years.

The Golden Compass was also targeted in Canada. The Catholic School Board of Ontario's Halton district removed it from circulation on the strength of one anonymous complaint that the book was "written by an atheist where the characters and text are anti-God, anti-Catholic, and anti-religion." The Catholic School Board of Calgary followed suit. Board officials said that its decision came in response to concern voiced by parents as well as publicity about the film. In Ontario, the decision was reversed in a matter of days; however, the book was removed from public display and made available only upon request. In Calgary, the book was returned to library shelves two months later.

In 2008, the school board of the publicly funded Dufferin-Peel Catholic School District in Mississauga, Ontario, asked principals to remove the books of the trilogy from school library shelves pending review. They were eventually returned to libraries with a sticker on the inside cover telling readers that "representations of the church in this novel are purely fictional and are not reflective of the real Roman Catholic Church or the Gospel of Jesus Christ."

Commenting on the censorship of *The Golden Compass* in Canada, Lorne Gunter, writing in *The Edmonton Journal*, suggested that Christian parents use the book as a teaching opportunity, rather than demand that it be pulled from library shelves. In the *Boston Globe*, Donna Freitas, a Catholic theologian at Boston University, wrote a vigorous defense of the trilogy. She said that it is a thoroughly Christian work, albeit one that reflects the influence of heterodoxy—the notion of the feminized God of love and mercy, represented by Dust, versus the patriarchal God of judgment and unyielding authority, the false God who dies at the end of the trilogy.

As it happened, the film received mixed reviews and did poorly at the box office. But it did draw attention to the books after all, which saw an enormous spike in sales (15 million copies worldwide as of December 2007).

Writing almost a year later in *The Guardian*, Pullman explained his views about religion and expressed his delight at being listed on the ALA's list of most challenged books. "Religion, uncontaminated by power, can be the source of a great deal of private solace, artistic expression, and moral wisdom," he wrote. "But when it gets its hands on the levers of political or social authority, it goes rotten very quickly indeed. The rank stench of oppression wafts from every authoritarian church, chapel, temple, mosque, or synagogue—from every place of worship where the priests have the power to meddle in the social and intellectual lives of their flocks, from every presidential palace or prime ministerial office where civil leaders have to pander to religious ones." Pullman also said that the controversy about *The Golden Compass* moved interested readers from the library, "where they couldn't get hold of my novel" to the bookstores, "where they could. . . . The inevitable result of trying to ban something—book, film, play, pop song, whatever—is that far more people want to get a hold of it than would ever have done if it were left alone. Why don't the censors realise this?"

—Philip Milito

FURTHER READING

Associated Press. "Ontario Catholic School Board Pulls Fantasy Book following Complaint about Atheist Author." *International Herald Tribune* (November 22, 2007). Available online. URL: http://www.iht.com/bin/printfriendly.php?id=8443713. Accessed June 12, 2009.

Borst, John, et al. "Golden Compass 'Review' Causes Media Firestorm." Tomorrow's Trust, A Review of Catholic Education, blog archive (November 26, 2007). Available online. URL: http://tomorrowtrust.ca/?9=1129. Accessed June 12, 2009.

"Calgary Catholic School Board Dumps Golden Compass." Globe and Mail (December 5, 2007). Available online. URL: http://www.theglobeandmail.com/servlet/story/RTGAM.20071205.wgoldcompass1205/B. Accessed December 6, 2007.

Freitas, Donna. "God in the Dust." Boston Globe (November 25, 2007). Available online. URL: http://www.boston.com/bostonglobe/ideas/articles/2007/11/25/god_in_the_dust

Gunter, Lorne. "Faith Strengthened by a Good Test." Edmonton Journal (November 25, 2007). Available online. URL: http://lgunter@shaw.ca. Accessed June 12, 2009.

Pullella, Philip. "Vatican Blasts 'Golden Compass' as Godless and Hopeless." Reuters (December 19, 2007). Available online. URL: www.reuters.com/article/entertainmentNews/idUSL1958884920071219. Accessed November 18, 2009.

Pullman, Philip. "The Censor's Dark Materials." Guardian (September 28, 2008). Available online. URL: http://www.guardian.co.uk/books/2008/sep/29/philip.pullman.amber.spyglass.golden.compass. Accessed June 12, 2009.

Viren, Sarah. "Does Film 'Compass' Steer Kids in Wrong Direction?" Houston Chronicle, December 7, 2007, A1.

IMPRESSIONS READING SERIES

General editor: Jack Booth
Original date and place of publication: 1984, Canada
Original publisher: Holt, Rinehart and Winston of Canada
Literary form: Textbook series

SUMMARY

Impressions was a literature-based language arts reading series for kindergarten through sixth grade used in schools in the United States and Canada during the 1980s and 1990s. The 59 books of the series contained 822 literary selections followed by suggested learning activities and included excerpts from the works of authors such as C. S. Lewis, Laura Ingalls Wilder, A. A. Milne, Rudyard Kipling, Lewis Carroll, Martin Luther King, Jr., Dr. Seuss, Ray Bradbury, L. Frank Baum, Maurice Sendak, and the Brothers Grimm.

Impressions implemented a "whole language" rather than a phonics-based approach to the teaching of reading and writing through exposure to fiction, poetry, myths, folk tales, and songs. During the early 1990s, the textbook series was at the top of the list of challenged or banned books in the United States. Christian fundamentalists claimed the schoolbooks promoted paganism, satanism, and New Age religion and organized campaigns to remove them from schools.

Among the titles in the series, which consisted of student texts, workbooks, and teacher resource books, were: *Catch a Rainbow, Good Morning*

Sunshine, Fly Away Home, Ready or Not, How I Wonder, Cross the Golden River, Thread the Needle, Under the Sea, Wherever You Are, East of the Sun, and *Run Forever.*

Catch a Rainbow, a beginning reader, for example, included 12 illustrated selections by such noted children's book authors as John Burningham, Elizabeth Bridgman, Pat Hutchins, and Meguido Zola. The book's cover displayed a colorful picture of a unicorn flying over a rainbow. The first selection was "What Will I Wear" by David Booth: "Here is my hat. It is orange. Here is my T-shirt. It is red. Here is my belt. It is yellow. Here are my jeans. They are blue. Here are my socks. They are green. Here are my shoes. They are purple. Here is a rainbow. (Sometimes it hides in my closet.)" Margaret Wise Brown's "Little Black Bug" also appeared: "Little black bug, / Little black bug, / Where have you been? / I've been under the rug, / Said the little black bug. / Bug-ug-ug-ug." One of the poem's illustrations is a green fly buzzing over a rainbow.

The student workbook for *Good Morning Sunshine* contained 63 fill-in-the-blank worksheets, including, for example, "The Chicken and the Princess": "One day the ch_cken was g_ing to town. The chicken g_t l_st, b_t a princ_ess found h_m." Another entry is titled "A Goblin in Our House" and is illustrated by a drawing of a comical ghost: "He knocks and he __ and he rattles at the __."

A small number of the selections in the series—22 of 822 stories—mentioned ghosts, goblins, or witches or included fantasy from fairy tales such as The Gingerbread Man or Beauty and the Beast.

CENSORSHIP HISTORY

"Nightmarish Textbooks Await Your Kids—Concerned Parents Say *Impressions'* Violent and Occultic Content Torments Even Happy, Well-Adjusted Children" read the cover headline of *Citizen Magazine,* published by the Colorado-based conservative Christian group Focus on the Family in 1991. The Impressions reading series had been well reviewed by educators. At the time, it was in use in 1,500 schools in 34 states and was the leading elementary school text in Canada. Some attempts to ban the series occurred during 1987–89 in Washington, Oregon, California, and Idaho after its publisher first began to market the book in the western states. By 1990 the Religious Right had begun a national campaign against Impressions, charging that it taught lessons in the occult, New Age religion, and witchcraft.

Protests against the textbooks sprang up in 400 school districts. More than 30 districts in California alone banned it, and it was challenged in Alaska, Georgia, Illinois, New Mexico, Maine, Maryland, Mississippi, New York, North Carolina, South Dakota, and Tennessee. According to a report by the civil liberties organization People For the American Way (PFAW) in Washington, D.C., it topped the list of books most frequently targeted for banning in the United States between 1990 and 1992.

The source for many complaints appeared to be a packet of materials circulated by several conservative religious groups, including Educational Research Analysts, the Texas-based textbook review organization founded by conservative activists Mel and Norma Gabler, and Citizens for Excellence in Education (CEE), based in Costa Mesa, California. In a letter to its members in 1990, CEE's head, Robert Simonds, called the fantasy tales of supernatural characters and monsters in the books "an affront to all decent people."

The CEE published a manual titled "How to Elect Christians to Public Office" and encouraged Christian conservatives to run for local school board offices. According to PFAW, 31 percent of the Religious Right's candidates were elected in California school board elections in 1992. Focus on the Family, the Rutherford Institute, Concerned Women for America (CWA), and Phyllis Schlafly's Eagle Forum also spearheaded attempts to remove the Impressions series from schools.

While most of the objections focused on witchcraft and the occult, some of the groups opposing the reading series distributed a book called *N.E.A.: Trojan Horse in American Education* (1984) by Samuel L. Blumenfeld, which contends that there is a conspiracy by the National Education Association to create a socialist government and that teachers "have been deliberately trained to produce functional illiterates" by using the whole-language method of teaching reading skills, rather than phonics.

In 1990, parents in Coeur d'Alene, Idaho, and Stockton, California, pressed for the removal of Impressions because the third-grade reader included "A Wart Snake in a Fig Tree" by George Mendoza, a parody of "The Twelve Days of Christmas." In Yucaipa, California, some parents contended that the face of the devil could be seen in the series' illustrations by photocopying them and holding them upside down and up to a mirror.

In Winters, California, parents complained to the school board in 1990 that Impressions emphasized witchcraft and the occult, promoted disrespect for parents and other authorities, and had a Canadian bias. A list of objections presented to the school superintendent and board of trustees said that Impressions promoted drug and alcohol abuse, as the troll princess in Beauty and the Beast puts a sleeping tablet in the prince's wine; cannibalism in The Gingerbread Man; satanic ritual, because it encouraged children to chant rhymes; rainbows as a symbol of New Age religion; and witchcraft and the Wicca religion, because witches appeared in some stories, including in excerpts from C. S. Lewis's *The Lion, the Witch and the Wardrobe*. Despite the protests, the school board unanimously voted to retain the textbooks.

In November 1990, in Wheaton, Illinois, 300 parents attended a school board meeting to urge the removal of Impressions. When the board refused to abandon the series, used in the district since 1988, a group of parents sued, alleging that assignment of the books to their children violated their religious freedom under the First Amendment. The parents claimed that the series "fosters a religious belief in the existence of superior beings exercising power over human beings by imposing rules of conduct with the promise and threat of future rewards and punishments" and focuses on supernatural beings, including "wizards, sorcerers, giants and unspecified creatures with supernatural powers." They also said that it "indoctrinates children in values directly opposed to their Christian beliefs by teaching tricks, despair, deceit, parental disrespect and by denigrating Christian symbols and holidays," and requires students "to prepare and cast chants and spells and to practice being witches."

In October 1992, district judge James B. Moran dismissed the action: "It is not the province of this court . . . to sit as some sort of reviewer of the decisions of local school boards. Plaintiffs must be able to establish that the series fosters a partial religious belief, and a review of the series establishes that it cannot be reasonably concluded that it does so."

The parents appealed to the Court of Appeals of the Seventh Circuit, which on February 2, 1994, in *Fleischfresser v. Directors of School District 200* ruled in favor of the school board. The court declared: "While the parents and their children may be sincerely offended by some passages in the reading series, they raise a constitutional claim only if the use of the series establishes *a religion*. The parents insist that the reading series presents religious concepts, found in paganism and branches of witchcraft and Satanism; this hardly sounds like the establishment of a coherent religion."

In reaching its decision, the appeals court applied the three-pronged *Lemon* test, formulated by U.S. Supreme Court justice Warren Burger in the majority opinion in a 1971 case, *Lemon v. Kurtzman*, to determine whether a law had the effect of establishing religion. Under that test, the school district's choice of texts would violate the Constitution if it did not have a secular purpose, if its principal or primary effect advanced or inhibited religion, or if it fostered an excessive government entanglement with religion.

In *Fleischfresser*, the appeals court determined that fantasy and make-believe did not establish a religion: "The parents would have us believe that the inclusion of these works in an elementary school curriculum represents the impermissible establishment of pagan religion. We do not agree. After all, what would become of elementary education, public or private, without works such as these and scores and scores of others that serve to expand the minds of young children and develop their sense of creativity?"

A few months after the *Fleischfresser* decision, the Court of Appeals of the Ninth Circuit heard a similar challenge to Impressions. In Woodland, California, during the 1989–90 school year, several parents of children in the Woodland Joint Unified School District filed a written complaint asking the school board to remove the reading series. The school board offered to give their children alternate reading assignments but declined to remove the books. In 1991, two parents sued the school district. The Mississippi-based American Family Association, headed by Rev. Donald E. Wildmon, and the American Center for Law and Justice in Virginia, affiliated with Rev. Pat Robertson, supported the parents in their suit. Those who backed the school board's position included PFAW, the American Association of School Administrators, the American Association of University Women, the Association of American Publishers, the National Congress of Parents and Teachers, the Association for Supervision and Curriculum Development, the California Teachers Association, and the American Library Association's Freedom to Read Foundation.

In *Brown v. Woodland Unified Joint School District*, the parents alleged that the district's use of portions of Impressions endorsed and sponsored the religions of "witchcraft" and "neo-paganism" and thereby had violated federal and state constitutional requirements regarding the separation of church and state. U.S. District Court judge William B. Schubb rejected their claims and ruled that he found no evidence that school officials were seeking to promote any religion: "A school district may incorporate folk traditions into learning exercises. . . . [F]ar from preferring one religion over another, *Impressions* materials were chosen in part to reflect the cultural diversity of North American society." The Woodland parents appealed the ruling to the U.S. Court of Appeals for the Ninth Circuit. The court applied the *Lemon* test and upheld Schubb's decision.

In September 1990, Georgia's state textbook commission decided against adopting the texts in the state's schools by a 13-8 vote. The decision came after parents allied with the local conservative Christian group Family Concerns lobbied the committee, armed with guidelines on how to fight the series published by Focus on the Family's *Citizen Magazine*. Robert Hess, *Citizen*'s editor, acknowledged that the objectionable material in the readers might amount to only 5 percent of their content. But "you find a pattern of darker themes that include witchcraft and fear," he added.

The *Atlanta Journal and Constitution* responded in an editorial: "This is, of course, utter gibberish, just the latest of those occasional damn fool notions that, for obscure reasons, strike a spark that spreads like wildfire through the state's considerable forests of ignorance. . . . Charged with the solemn and, you would think, inspiring task of getting Georgia's children up to educational speed for the 21st century, the state textbook committee has instead brought back the book-burning and witch-hunting of the 16th."

In North Carolina, state representative Connie Wilson (R) led a campaign against the series, and the North Carolina Textbook Commission and the state Board of Education voted against its adoption. It also was rejected by the textbook adoption committee in Mississippi but was adopted in New Mexico after a heated debate.

In 1991, opponents of the series in Coeur d'Alene, Idaho, asserted that the books taught children to disrespect parents, teachers, and authority figures and brought religion into the public schools. They claimed that 52 percent of the series' contents dealt with the occult, as they identified certain words and symbols as occult, including six-pointed stars and rainbows. A local minister of the Nazarene church told the state's textbook committee that illustrations of the Aztec calendar, which contained eight points, subliminally inculcated children into the occult, as each of the points represented a day on which a child was sacrificed.

In November 1990, a group of parents in Willard, Ohio, filed a $1.6 million civil lawsuit in federal court against their school district, charging that Impressions taught their children about witchcraft. PFAW joined the school district's defense team, and the American Family Association backed the parents. In January 1991, U.S. District Court judge Nicholas Walinski rejected a motion that would have halted the use of Impressions in the schools until the lawsuit was settled. That month, the plaintiffs decided to drop their suit.

Impressions was also the subject of protests organized by conservative religious groups in Canada, where the series had been part of the curriculum since 1984. In Manning, Alberta, in September 1991, a group of parents at Rosary Catholic School claimed that an illustration contained a subliminal image of the devil and that the line "In Napanee I'll eat your knee," from a nonsense poem by Dennis Lee, promoted cannibalism. A group of parents entered the school, threatened the staff and the principal, and warned that they would burn the Impressions texts if they were not immediately removed. Within a few days, the Catholic school board instructed the school superintendent to cease using the books. In 1982, the Manning Elementary School also decided to remove them from its first-through third-grade curriculum.

In 1993, a parent group in Burns Lake, Vancouver, petitioned for removal of the books, used since 1985, because the stories were frightening and taught the occult, promoted violence, undermined parental authority, and discredited "basic human morals." The school board voted to remove them from six elementary schools. In 1995, some trustees of the Metropolitan Toronto Separate School Board asked that the series be dropped. As more than three-quarters of the district's schools used Impressions, this would have cost the school system $1 million in replacement texts. The board ultimately decided against replacing the series.

As Diane Ravitch pointed out in her study of textbook censorship, *The Language Police: How Pressure Groups Restrict What Children Learn*, although the Religious Right consistently lost court battles to ban Impressions, its campaign had an impact on educational publishers. "The *Impressions* series, for all its literary excellence, was not republished and quietly vanished," she wrote, and the furor that sank Impressions has made textbook publishers cautious about including material that might anger Christian conservatives.

FURTHER READING

Brown, Ron. "Children's Book Challenges: The New Wave." *Canadian Children's Literature* 68 (1992): 27–32.

Carver, Peter. "Good Impressions—and Bad." *Canadian Children's Literature* 68 (1992). Available online. URL: http://libnt_lib.uoguelph.ca. Accessed September 29, 2004.

Clark, Charles S. "Why Are Complaints about American Schoolbooks on the Rise?" *CQ Researcher* (February 19, 1993). Available online. URL: http://www.college ofsanmateo.edu/library/cqresrre1993021900.htm.

DelFattore, Joan. *What Johnny Shouldn't Read: Textbook Censorship in America*. New Haven, Conn.: Yale University Press, 1992.

Foerstel, Herbert N. *Banned in the U.S.A.: A Reference Guide to Book Censorship in Schools and Public Libraries*. Westport, Conn.: Greenwood Press, 2002.

Institute for First Amendment Studies. "Groups Unite to Ban Textbooks." *Freedom Writer* (March/April 1991). Available online. URL:http://www.publiceye.org/ifas/fw/9103/textbooks.html.

Junas, Dan. *Report on the Religious Right in Washington State*. Seattle: American Civil Liberties Union of Washington, 1995. Available online. URL: http://www.aclu-wa.org/Issues/religious/3.html.

Newsletter on Intellectual Freedom 39, no. 3 (March 1990): 46; 39, no. 6 (November 1990): 201; 40, no. 1 (January 1991): 16; 40, no. 2 (March 1991): 47; 42, no. 1 (January 1993): 11.

"Parents' Pressure Leads Trustees to Vote to Scrap Reading Series." *Vancouver Sun*, May 10, 1993, p. A-3.

Ravitch, Diane. *The Language Police: How Pressure Groups Restrict What Children Learn*. New York: Alfred A. Knopf, 2003.

"Textbook Panel Goes Witch-Hunting." *Atlanta Journal and Constitution* (September 29, 1990). Available online. URL: http://www.holysmoke.org/wicca/textbook.htm. Accessed November 15, 2005.

INFALLIBLE? AN INQUIRY

Author: Hans Küng
Original dates and places of publication: 1970, Germany; 1971, United States
Original publishers: Benzinger Verlag; Doubleday and Company
Literary form: Theological analysis

SUMMARY

To err is human. To err is also papal, contends Catholic theologian Hans Küng. Küng's rejection of the doctrine of papal infallibility, as expressed in *Infallible? An Inquiry*, embroiled him in conflict with Vatican authorities.

Infallibility is defined by the Roman Catholic Church as exemption from the possibility of error, bestowed on the church by the Holy Spirit. Infallibility is vested in the pope when he speaks as the head of the church on matters of faith and morals. Definitive pronouncements resulting from an ecumenical council, when ratified by the pope, are also held to be infallible. In *Infallible? An Inquiry*, Küng examines papal encyclicals and statements, conciliar pronouncements, Scripture, and church history and concludes that there is no such thing as an infallible proposition. No church teaching is automatically free from error, because the church is composed of human beings. God alone is a priori free from error in detail and in every case.

Küng believes the dogma of papal infallibility should be discarded, as it has been disproved by historical and biblical research. He suggests that it be replaced by the notion of "indefectibility"—the perpetuity of the whole church in the truth of God's word despite the possible errors of any of its parts. In the long run, he believes, in spite of errors by the teaching authority of the church, the truth of the message of God in Jesus Christ will prevail.

Küng contends that the Second Vatican Council (1962–65), for which he served as a theological consultant, despite its efforts to renew the church by broadening ecumenical understanding and opening out toward the modern world, did not go far enough in reforming church structures. The ecclesiastical teaching office is still conceived by the pope and the hierarchy in a preconciliar, authoritarian way.

"The conception of continuity, authority, infallibility of the Church and the Church's teaching has led the Catholic Church into a dangerous tight corner," Küng writes in *Infallible*. He lists numerous and indisputable past errors of the ecclesiastical teaching office, now largely recognized by the church, including the condemnation of Galileo Galilei and the excommunication of the Greek church. "A close scrutiny of the Index of Forbidden Books would be particularly revealing in this respect," he adds, "yet the teaching office found it difficult to admit these errors frankly and honestly."

Küng raises doubts about the authority of Pope Paul VI's 1968 encyclical on birth control, "Humanae Vitae," which reaffirmed the church's traditional prohibition of contraception. In this encyclical, Küng contends, the ecclesiastical teaching office counts for more than the gospel of Christ, and papal tradition is placed above Scripture. Jesus himself did not found a church, Küng says, but rather his life and death set in motion a movement that over the course of time took on increasingly institutional forms.

Küng calls for a new age of leadership, one in which "the pope exists for the Church and not the Church for the pope," in which the pope's primacy is not one of ruling, but of service. Küng writes that he remains for all his criticism a convinced Catholic theologian. But because he is deeply bound to his church, he claims the right and the duty in full awareness of his own human inadequacy and fallibility to raise a protest.

CENSORSHIP HISTORY

When *Infallible? An Inquiry* first appeared in 1970, on the centennial of the First Vatican Council's enunciation of the doctrine of papal infallibility, it sparked an international debate that was unprecedented in recent theology. The assertion of infallibility of the teaching office in the Catholic Church has long been unacceptable to non-Catholic theologians. But Küng was the first major Catholic theologian to question dramatically and forcefully the most basic concept of church authority. The divergence on this issue by a theologian as distinguished as Küng represented the extent to which the doctrine had become questionable.

In his preface to *Infallible? An Inquiry*, Küng wrote: "It is true that the Index has been abolished and another name given to the Roman Inquisition. But

there are still inquisitional processes against troublesome theologians. . . ."
Küng himself became subject to such processes for his dissident views. In
obvious reaction to Küng's ideas, the Vatican's Congregation for the Doctrine of the Faith (CDF) issued on June 24, 1973, a "Declaration Against
Certain Errors of the Present Day," which reiterated Catholic teaching
on the infallibility of the church and the pope and declared that the pope
and bishops are indeed guaranteed immunity from error when they define
doctrine.

Küng's best-selling 1974 book, *On Being a Christian,* an effort to make
the traditional articles of faith intelligible to modern believers, raised further doubts within the hierarchy about his orthodoxy. In 1975, the Vatican
admonished Küng not to advocate two theses drawn from his 1967 book
The Church and from *Infallible? An Inquiry:* that in case of necessity, the
Eucharist might be consecrated by an unordained person and that propo-
sitions defined by the church might be erroneous. In addition, church
authorities instituted an official process to examine the orthodoxy of his
views. They requested repeatedly that he come to Rome for discussions.
Küng called for due process, demanded the right to see the full dossier
on his case before submitting to any inquiry, and asked to choose his own
defense counsel. In 1968, 1,360 theologians had signed a statement calling
for such due process for theologians in cases where authorities in Rome
objected to their teachings. Claiming he would not receive a fair trial, Küng
refused to come to Rome.

When Pope John Paul II succeeded Paul VI in 1978, he moved to confront dissident theologians. On December 18, 1979, the CDF withdrew
Küng's *missio canonica,* thereby barring him from teaching "in the name of the
Church." The CDF accused him of "causing confusion" among the faithful
by casting doubt in his writing and teachings on the dogma of papal infallibility and questioning the doctrine of Christ's divinity. Küng was informed that
he could no longer be considered a Catholic theologian. He was forbidden
to teach Catholic doctrine, and Catholic institutions were prohibited from
employing him.

Küng remained a Catholic priest, however, as well as a tenured professor at the University of Tübingen until his retirement in 1996, a position
protected by German law. He founded the Global Ethics Foundation in 1991
and has continued to write and publish.

FURTHER READING

Bokenkotter, Thomas S. *A Concise History of the Catholic Church.* Garden City, N.Y.:
    Doubleday, 1977.
Collins, Paul. *The Modern Inquisition: Seven Prominent Catholics and Their Struggles with
    the Vatican.* Woodstock, N.Y.: Overlook Press, 2002.
Küng, Hans. *Infallible? An Unresolved Inquiry.* Preface by Herbert Haag. New York:
    Continuum, 1994.

THE JEWEL OF MEDINA

Author: Sherry Jones
Original date and place of publication: 2008, United States
Original publisher: Beaufort Books
Literary form: Novel

SUMMARY

The Jewel of Medina is a work of historical fiction based on the story of Muhammad's rise to power, narrated by his child bride and purported favorite wife, A'isha bint Abi Bakr. The story begins in Mecca in A.D. 619, when six-year-old A'isha is beginning purdah, the Islamic custom of secluding women. Sick at heart, the spirited A'isha dreams of marrying her friend Safwan and living as a Bedouin.

A'isha's father, Abu Bakr—Muhammad's friend and one of the first converts to Islam—builds a mosque where he and other "Believers" (Muslims) can pray. At this time, Muhammad has not yet gained full acceptance as God's prophet, nor has his belief in "the one true God," al-Lah (Allah). Muhammad's *qur'an* ("recitations"), proclaiming that the other gods in Mecca's holy shrine are false, angers his kinsmen, the Quraysh, a merchant tribe who depend on the idols to attract worshippers and their money into the city. Among Muhammad's fiercest enemies is his cousin, Abu Sufyan. Abu Sufyan and his men routinely slit the throats of Believers in Mecca, and hundreds—including Muhammad, Abu Bakr, and their families—flee to the Jewish city of Yathrib (called al-Medina, "The City," by Muhammad), where they have been promised asylum.

Shortly after arriving in Medina, nine-year-old A'isha is married to Muhammad. Though she knows and cares for him, she is distraught; he is 43 years her senior, and she loves Safwan. But she does not live with Muhammad until age 12, and even then, he delays consummation of the marriage, teaching her instead how to wield a sword. The novel relates A'isha's maturation from a spoiled, willful girl to become Muhammad's respected adviser and *hatun* (first wife), as well as someone whom his other wives come to love and respect. Alongside her own personal story—of her troubled attraction to Safwan; her impetuousness and her desire to be a warrior; her growing love for Muhammad and her jealousy over each new wife he takes; and, most of all, her wish to control her own destiny—she describes Muhammad's increasing power as more and more people convert to Islam, and the ongoing clashes between the Muslims and the Quraysh.

In 625, the Believers defeat Abu Sufyan and his army in battle at Badr. Their continuing raids on the Qurayshi caravans, along with Muhammad's claim that he is the prophet that the Jewish book foretold, also exacerbate tensions with their Jewish Kaynuqah and Nadr neighbors, who trade with the Quraysh and do not believe that God would send an Arab to minister to Jews.

When the Muslims ride into battle at Uhud, A'isha is thrilled to be permitted to join them, if only to carry water and tend the wounded. But the Believers are outnumbered, outsmarted, and nearly massacred, and Muhammad is seriously wounded.

Meanwhile, Muhammad's marriage to the beautiful young widow Hafsa bint Umar, whose father, a former enemy, has become an important member of his circle, inspires the first of A'isha's many jealous rages. After taking two more wives—Zainab bint Khusainah, known as Umm al-Masakin (Mother of the Poor) for her charitable works, and the beautiful widow Umm Salama—Muhammad reminds a jealous A'isha that these "alliances" are important for extending Muslim influence and increasing their chance of survival, for as they grow in power, they acquire more enemies. But Muhammad soon becomes smitten with Zaynab bint Jahsh, the wife of his cousin and adopted son, Zayd. Zaynab leaves Zayd for Muhammad, though she is forbidden to marry him because it would be considered an act of incest—whereupon Muhammad says that Allah has told him in a "revelation" that he may marry her to protect her from the shame of divorce. He defends his decision by observing that since Zayd is not a blood relation, the charge of incest does not hold. At the same time, A'isha fumes at the thought that Muhammad is ignoring his own rule forbidding Muslim men to marry more than four wives. Tongues wag at the wedding reception, and the Prophet is advised to sequester his wives to prevent more gossip. While he stops short of this move, he claims that Allah has said his wives may be addressed only from behind a curtain and that they must be covered "from head to toe, every inch, except for a single eye." Upon his death, his widows will be forbidden to remarry.

A'isha is stung by this seeming change in Muhammad, who had always been gentle and fair to women and had even extended some of their rights. Suffocated by the new restrictions and humiliated because her marriage remains unconsummated, A'isha runs off with Safwan. She soon has misgivings, however, and returns, scandalized, to Medina. She understands that, as a woman, she will always be chained and that resisting those chains will only make things worse for her—yet she knows that women often "found ways to slip those bonds . . . and then return to their so-called captivity before anyone noticed." To be free, she must learn to become politically useful to Muhammad by advising him well. Eventually, Muhammad declares that Allah has revealed that A'isha is innocent of adultery, and the marriage is finally consummated. Now A'isha assumes the role of adviser: Faced with an onslaught from Abu Sufyan's approaching army, which strongly outnumbers the Muslim army, A'isha suggests building a trench around Medina. Muhammad likes her plan. Protected by the trench for nearly a month while Abu Sufyan tries to gain entry to the city via an alternative route, the Believers are spared at the last minute when a sandstorm destroys the enemy camp, and Abu Sufyan flees with his army. In the wake of this news, many people convert to Islam, increasing Muhammad's power. He soon signs a treaty with the Quraysh, which Abu Sufyan later breaks.

A'isha, meanwhile, hatches a plan to help her neglected sister-wives earn some sorely needed cash, for they often go hungry and thinly clothed: They hire themselves out to prepare brides for their wedding ceremonies. Meanwhile, Muhammad takes two more wives—Saffiya bint Huyayy, a traitor's daughter, and Umm Habiba bint Abu Sufyan, Abu Sufyan's daughter—and takes the Christian courtesan Maryam, a gift from Egypt, as his concubine. When another bride-to-be—the exotic Alia—arrives as a gift from Yemen, A'isha learns that Alia is part of a Yemenite plot to assassinate Muhammad on his wedding night, and she tries to stop it by tricking Alia into antagonizing Muhammad in bed. Muhammad, enraged, does not believe A'isha when she explains that she was trying to save his life. Meanwhile, A'isha sees Abu Sufyan slip into his daughter's hut and suspects Umm Habiba of spying, but it turns out that Abu Sufyan has only come to plead mercy, terrified at rumors of a Muslim invasion. Muhammad is merciful and reinstates the treaty with the Quraysh.

Learning that his wives have started a business without consulting him, Muhammad stalks away angrily to pray for one month and decide their fate. At the end of the month, Muhammad tells A'isha that he loves her spirit but that a wife cannot constantly defy her husband. He gives her the choice of following the rules of the *harim* or claiming her freedom. Recognizing his generosity and their love for each other, she chooses to stay. She also defends her sister-wives, quelling Muhammad's anger and securing her permanent position as *hatun*.

A'isha is now 17 years old, and new converts to Islam arrive in Medina every day. Muhammad decides that he must prove his strength by ruling the Quraysh once and for all, which means invading Mecca. He emerges victorious and is proclaimed the Prophet of the One God, becoming the most powerful man in the kingdom.

Maryam, meanwhile, bears a long-awaited son, Ibrahim, to Muhammad, but at the age of two, Ibrahim contracts a fever and dies. With no heir, Muhammad is inconsolable and, within months, he is dying. Infighting begins in Medina, as the people wonder who will take Muhammad's place. But Muhammad refuses to name anyone, saying that Allah must decide. In his final days, Muhammad chooses Abu Bakr to lead the weekly prayers, though he does not name him as his formal successor.

On the day he dies, in June 632, Muhammad gives his sword to A'isha, his "warrior bride." Abu Bakr is poised to become Medina's next leader, though he faces challengers from within. A'isha understands that the jihad of which Muhammad spoke on his deathbed has already begun and that she must fight to preserve what he has built. The book ends with an affirmation that A'isha—a name that has been associated with scandal—means "life."

CENSORSHIP HISTORY

Described by its author, Sherry Jones, as "a book about women's empowerment and the origins of Islam," *The Jewel of Medina* was suppressed before it was ever published. Recalling the events surrounding the publication of Salman Rushdie's *The Satanic Verses* some 20 years earlier, the story of the suppression and subsequent publication of *The Jewel of Medina* stands as a sobering example of the stranglehold that extremism can have on free expression. Unlike Rushdie, however, this book's author was not threatened or harmed. Neither were any employees of Random House or its imprint, Ballantine Books, the publisher that bought the rights to the book in 2007 in a $100,000, two-book deal. But in spring 2008, shortly before the book's scheduled release, Random House executives told Jones, a veteran, award-winning journalist and first-time novelist, that they wanted to "indefinitely postpone" its publication because they feared terrorist attacks by radical Muslims.

It seems that one Denise Spellberg, associate professor of history and Middle Eastern studies at the University of Texas at Austin, had read the book's galleys at Random House's request and the author's suggestion. Spellberg, the author of *Politics, Gender, and the Islamic Past: The Legacy of A'isha Bint Abi Bakr*—which Jones says she used in her research and originally listed in her novel's bibliography—concluded that it was a "very ugly, stupid piece of work" that "deliberately misinterpret[ed] history" and would offend Muslims. Spellberg contacted Shahed Amanullah, editor in chief of the online newsmagazine altmuslim.com, and asked him to warn Muslims about the book, which, she said, "made fun of Muslims and their history." Amanullah, who had not read the book, sent an e-mail to a listserv of Middle East and Islamic studies graduate students, which appeared out of context the next day on a Web site for Shiite Muslims under the headline, "Upcoming Book, 'Jewel of Medina': A New Attempt to Slander the Prophet of Islam." Things escalated from there, with demands from Muslims that the book be withdrawn and that the author apologize to "all the Muslims across the world."

Meanwhile, Spellberg warned Random House that the book's publication presented a "national security issue" that could cause a backlash of violence from some Muslims. Spellberg and her attorney also sent a letter to Random House stating that she would sue the publisher if her name was associated with the book. Random House, in turn, after consulting with other "credible and unrelated sources," concluded that the book's publication "could incite acts of violence by a small, radical segment," and pulled it from publication, "for the safety of the author, employees of Random House, booksellers and anyone else who would be involved in distribution and sale of the novel." No threats of any attacks had been made at the time, just "threats of terrorist threats," as Jones put it.

Salman Rushdie, reacting to the Random House decision, said, "I am very disappointed to hear that my publishers, Random House, have cancelled another author's novel, apparently because of their concerns about possible Islamic reprisals. This is censorship by fear and it sets a very bad precedent indeed."

Jones reported that she was stunned by the news. In many interviews following Random House's decision, Jones said that she emphasized her "respect for Islam; about what a gentle, wise, and compassionate leader Muhammad really was; Muhammad's respect for women, especially his wives; and women's crucial roles in the formation of the early Islamic community"—themes that she hoped her book would make plain, if anyone ever got the chance to read it.

Determined to see the book published elsewhere, she terminated her contract with Random House. In August 2008, the *Wall Street Journal* published an opinion piece about the incident ("You Still Can't Write about Muhammad") by Asra Nomani, a Muslim-American who had read *Jewel* in galleys. "The series of events that torpedoed this novel are a window into how quickly fear stunts intelligent discourse about the Muslim world," Nomani wrote, giving a detailed account of the events that had occurred and placing Spellberg at the center of the maelstrom. "I don't have a problem with historical fiction," Spellberg told Nomani in an interview. "I do have a problem with the deliberate misinterpretation of history. You can't play with a sacred history and turn it into soft core pornography."

With regard to that characterization, two brief sections in particular were quoted most often in the press accounts of the controversy. In one, A'isha expresses her anxiety about the impending consummation of her marriage to Muhammad: "Soon I would be lying on my bed beneath him, squashed like a scarab beetle, flailing and sobbing while he slammed himself against me." In another, A'isha describes the actual consummation: "Desire burned like a fire in Muhammad's loins, unquenchable in one night, or two, or three. As for me, the pain of consummation soon melted away—Muhammad was so gentle, I hardly felt the scorpion's sting. To be in his arms, skin to skin, was the bliss I had longed for all my life."

Responding to both Nomani's piece and the uproar caused by Random House's decision, Spellberg sent a letter to the *Wall Street Journal*, denying that she was the "instigator" of Random House's decision and refuting the book jacket's claim that the novel was "extensively researched." She also wrote, "As an expert on A'isha's life, I felt it was my professional responsibility to counter this novel's fallacious representation of a very real woman's life . . . . I felt it my duty to warn the press of the novel's potential to provoke anger among some Muslims. . . . I do not espouse censorship of any kind, but I do value my right to critique those who abuse the past without regard for its richness or resonance in the present. . . ." In her letter, Spellberg also charged that *Jewel* "follows in the oft-trodden path" of "anti-Islam polemic that uses sex and violence to attack the Prophet," a bewildering statement given the mildness of this book's contents by almost any standards.

The Jewel of Medina was soon sold to independent publisher Beaufort Books in the United States and Gibson Square Books in Britain. In August 2008, the book was published in translation in Serbia. When the Muslim community there protested, the novel's Serbian publisher withdrew it from bookstores but quickly restored it upon learning that pirated copies were being sold, and it soon became a best seller in that country. Shortly before the book's scheduled October 2008 release, the North London home of Jones's British publisher, Martin Rynja—which doubles as the office of Gibson Square—was fire-bombed. Three Islamic extremists—Ali Beheshti, 40; Abrar Mirza, 22; and Abbas Taj, 30—were arrested, later found guilty of conspiracy to recklessly damage property and endanger life (Beheshti and Mirza pleaded guilty to conspiracy to commit arson), and sentenced to four and a half years in jail. Beheshti's attorney said that "it was an act of protest born of the publication of a book felt by him and other Muslims to be disrespectful, provocative and offensive."

Following the incident, Jones postponed a planned publicity tour, and Gibson Square Books announced that she had decided to delay publication. Jones denied this and said that the decision was the publisher's alone. As of mid-2010, the book had not been published in the United Kingdom. Soon after the firebombing, radical Muslim clerics warned of further attacks, and on October 6, 2008, a Muslim organization run by Anjem Choudhary and Omar Bakri released an article that called the book "blasphemous" and Jones "an enemy of Islam." Beaufort Books, however, proceeded with its plans and released the book in the United States in October 2008. No new incidents of violence relating to its publication have been reported.

Many of those who had opposed the book's release consistently sidestepped the fact that *Jewel* is a work of fiction or echoed Spellberg's comment that "even historical fiction should take some responsibility for the past." But others, such as writer and poet Marwa El-Naggar of IslamOnline.net, who criticized the book for its "inaccuracies, its faults, and its biases," nonetheless supported its publication. So did Shahed Amanullah, the journalist whom Spellberg had first contacted about the book: "The best response to free speech is simply more speech in return," he wrote. "Anyone should have the right to publish whatever they want about Islam or Muslims—even if their views are offensive—without fear of censorship or retribution. Muslims, however, shouldn't be expected to be passive consumers of these views. An offended Muslim has the right—indeed, the responsibility—to vigorously critique anything written about them or their religion, provided they do not cross the line into intimidation and coercion. In an ideal world, both parties would open their minds enough to understand the other point of view."

Still other critics were concerned mostly with what they say was Jones's poor scholarship and the quality of her prose ("lamentable" and "purple"), and the *Los Angeles Times* went so far as to describe the book as "a second-rate bodice ripper," though that characterization seems overstated. In her *New York Times* review, Lorraine Adams referred to Jones as "an inexperienced, untalented author" who had written a book that does not "qualify as art."

Ethar El-Katatney, writing in *Egypt Today*, called Jones to task for using mostly English books and Arabic books translated by Western authors to do her research, adding, "Jones has taken great literary license in depicting history in a manner that fits best with how she wanted her novel to develop." But Katatney also observed, "While there is plenty of sexuality, there are no sex scenes," and concluded, "Rather than alienating her [Jones], Muslims should aim to win her over as an ally and use her novel to teach non-Muslims about the true history of Islam."

Literary theorist Stanley Fish wrote in his blog for the *New York Times* that Random House's decision did not constitute censorship, and that, rather, it was "a minor business decision," arguing that the term *censorship* should only be used in relation to a government's interference with free expression. Linguist Bill Poser, writing in the linguistics blog Language Log, disagreed and observed that "A free society cannot permit anyone, government, corporation, church, or individual, to decide what may and what may not be published. That a publisher should cancel publication of a novel out of fear of violence by religious fanatics has everything to do with the Western tradition of free speech." And in a widely circulated editorial that appeared in the *New Republic*, Álvaro Vargas Llosa wrote, "Any time, any place in which the threat of violence inhibits the exercise of free expression, the imperfect freedoms of Western civilization that so many people around the world struggle to imitate are in danger. . . . The problem is not whether Random House was entitled to its decision, but what the decision to go against its own desire to publish the book tells us about the fear that fanaticism has instilled in Western countries through systematic acts of intolerance."

Readers who objected to the book's portrayal of Muhammad were most likely, as suggested by Lorraine Adams in the *New York Times*, put off by Jones's portrayal of his sexuality, the potentially self-serving nature of his revelations, his decision that Muslim women must speak from behind a curtain (which, Adams says, is "the basis for the veiling of Muslim women"), and his marriage to 12 women, despite his decree that Muslim men be forbidden to take more than four wives—the latter two being "among the most contested criticisms of Muhammad," according to Adams.

As far as its historical accuracy is concerned, Jones notes openly, in a Q&A at the back of the book, that she took literary license with the facts—in particular, A'isha wielding a sword, her near-adulterous encounter with her childhood sweetheart Safwan, her obsessive struggle to become *hatun* (first wife), and, mostly, details about Muhammad's other wives. She attempted, she explained, to use fiction to symbolize an individual trait or suggest a characteristic of the times: The sword both represents A'isha's strength and demonstrates that some women fought in early Islamic battles under Muhammad, for instance, and the stories about the other wives were invented to explore the reasons for their behavior. A'isha's struggle to become *hatun* (which is rooted in Turkish, but not Islamic, tradition) is emblematic of harem behavior at that time, Jones has said. "I had to invent motives, which, as a fiction writer, I appreciated being able to do," she noted.

By late 2009, *The Jewel of Medina* had been published in translation in some 20 countries. A sequel to the book, *The Sword of Medina*, was published in the United States by Beaufort Books in October 2009.

—Alice Tufel

FURTHER READING

Adams, Lorraine. *"Thinly Veiled." New York Times Sunday Book Review* (December 12, 2008). Available online. URL: http://www.nytimes.com/2008/12/14/books/review/Adams-t.html?_r=1&scp=1&sq=publisher%20of%20O.J.%20book%20to%20handle%20Muhammad%20novel&st=cse. Accessed November 16, 2009.

Allen, Nick, and Aislinn Simpson. "Mohammed Novel: Academic Faces Calls to Apologise Over 'Pornographic' Remarks." *Daily Telegraph* (September 29, 2008). Available online. URL: http://www.telegraph.co.uk/news/3102416/Mohammed-novel-Academic-faces-calls-to-apologise-over-pornographic-remarks.html. Accessed October 12, 2009.

Bingham, John. "Radical Islamic Clerics Warn of Further Attacks after Publisher Is Firebombed." *Daily Telegraph* (September 28, 2008). Available online. URL: http://www.telegraph.co.uk/news/uknews/3097350/Radical-Islamic-clerics-warn-of-further-attacks-after-publisher-is-firebombed.html. Accessed November 14, 2009.

Bone, James. "Salman Rushdie Attacks 'Censorship by Fear' over The Jewel of Medina." *Times* (London) (August 16, 2008). Available online. URL: http://entertainment.timesonline.co.uk/tol/arts_and_entertainment/books/article4543243.ece. Accessed June 2, 2009.

El-Katatney, Ethar. "Flawed Jewel." *Egypt Today* (October 2008). Available online. URL: http://www.egypttoday.com/article.aspx?ArticleID=8171. Accessed October 12, 2009.

Fish, Stanley. "Crying Censorship." Think Again blog *New York Times.* (August 24, 2008). Available online. URL: http://fish.blogs.nytimes.com/2008/08/24/crying-censorship/index.html. Accessed August 27, 2008.

Flood, Alison. "Publication of Controversial Muhammad Novel Delayed." *Guardian* (October 10, 2008). Available online. URL: http://www.guardian.co.uk/books/2008/oct/10/jewel-of-medina-sherry-jones-aisha/print. Accessed July 9, 2009.

Fresno, Adam. "Radical Muslims Guilty of Firebomb Plot on Publisher of Prophet Mohammed Book." *Times* (London) (May 15, 2009). Available online. URL: http://www.timesonline.co.uk/tol/news/uk/crime/article/article6295795.ece. Accessed November 14, 2009.

Goldenberg, Suzanne. "Novel on Prophet's Wife Pulled for Fear of Backlash." *Guardian* (August 9, 2008). Available online. URL: http://www.guardian.co.uk/books/2008/aug/09/fiction.terrorism/print. Accessed July 9, 2009.

Hogan, Ron. "Judge for Yourself: *Jewel of Medina* in U.S. Bookstores." GalleyCat (October 6, 2008). Available online. URL: http://www.mediabistro.com/galleycat/authors/judge_for_yourself_jewel_of_medina_in_us_bookstores_96577.asp. Accessed October 12, 2009.

Hume, Mick. "A Festival of Grovelling to Terrorists." *Times* (London) (August 12, 2008). Available online. URL: http://www.timesonline.co.uk/tol/comment/columnists/article4509698.ece?print=yes&rand... Accessed July 23, 2009.

Jones, Sherry. Afterword to *The Jewel of Medina.* New York: Beaufort Books, 2008.

———. "Censoring 'The Jewel of Medina.'" PostGlobal: Islam's Advance. Posted by Jack Fairweather (August 11, 2008). Available online. URL: http://newsweek.washingtonpost.com/postglobal/islamadvance/2008/08/censoring_islam.htm. Accessed October 12, 2009.

———. "Our Own Worst Enemy." *New Humanist* 124, no. 6 (November/December 2009). Available online. URL: http://newhumanist.org.uk/2163/our-own-worst-enemy. Accessed June 6, 2010.

———. "Q&A with 'The Jewel of Medina' Author Sherry Jones." In *The Jewel of Medina*, 355–358. New York: Beaufort Books, 2008.

Llosa, Álvaro Vargas. "The Freedom to Publish." *New Republic* (September 10, 2008). Available online. URL: http://www.tnr.com/story_print.html?id=6c96c81a-63d0-4bcd-8d06-fcfb9b84fccd. Accessed June 6, 2010.

Nomani, Asra Q. "You Still Can't Write about Muhammad." Op-Ed. *Wall Street Journal* (August 6, 2008). Available online. URL: http://online.wsj.com/public/article_print/SB121797979078815073.html. Accessed October 12, 2009.

Poser, Bill. "Rushdie 1, Fish 0." Language Log (August 25, 2008). Available online. URL: http://languagelog.ldc.upenn/edu/nll/?p=525. Accessed August 27, 2008.

Spellberg, Denise. "I Didn't Kill 'The Jewel of Medina'." Letters. *Wall Street Journal* (August 9, 2008). Available online. URL: http://online.wsj.com/article/SB121824366910026293.html#printMode. Accessed October 12, 2009.

Trachtenberg, Jeffrey A. "Bride of the Prophet." *Wall Street Journal* (October 4, 2008). Available online. URL: http://online.wsj.com/article/SB122306918228703347.html#. Accessed October 12, 2009.

Walker, Peter. "Three Jailed for Arson Attack over Muhammad Bride Novel." *Guardian* (July 7, 2009). Available online. URL: http://www.guardian.co.uk/2009/jul/07/muslims-jailed-arson-book-protest. Accessed July 9, 2009.

Washington Post. "Random Error." Editorial. (August 22, 2008). Available online. URL: http://www.washingtonpost.com/wp-dyn/content/article/2008/08/21/AR2008082103104.html. Accessed October 12, 2009.

Willis, Simon. "The Jewel of Medina." *Granta* (September 20, 2008). Available online. URL: http://www.granta.com/Online-Only/The-Jewel-of-Medina. Accessed November 14, 2009.

Wilson, G. Willow. "Sherry Jones Has the Right to Offend Me." Red Room (August 13, 2008). Available online. URL: http://www.redroom.com/blog/g-willow-wilson/sherry-jones-has-the-right-to-offend-me. Accessed November 14, 2009.

THE KORAN (QUR'AN)

Original date and place of composition: Seventh century A.D., Arabia
Literary form: Religious text

SUMMARY

The Koran, or Qur'an (Recitation), is the earliest and the finest work of classical Arabic prose and the sacred book of Islam. Muslims believe that it was revealed by God to the prophet Muhammad, transmitted over time by the angel Gabriel, beginning in A.D. 619 until the Prophet's death in 632. To Muslims, the Koran is an unalterable reproduction of original scriptures that are preserved in heaven. Originally committed to memory and recited by Muhammad's followers, the Koranic revelations were written down during the Prophet's lifetime on palm leaves, stones, bones, and bark. The verses of the

Koran were collected by the caliph Umar, and the canonical text was established in 651–652 under the caliph Uthman by Arabic editors following the instructions of the Prophet's secretary.

The Koranic revelations are divided into 114 suras, or chapters, each beginning with the phrase, "In the Name of Allah, the Compassionate, the Merciful." Excepting the brief first chapter that is included in Muslim daily prayers, the suras are arranged generally by length, with the longest first and the shortest last. The longest suras relate to the period of Muhammad's role as head of the community in Medina. The shorter ones, embodying mostly his ethical teachings, were revealed earlier during his prophethood in Mecca.

The Koran preaches the oneness of God; God's omnipotence and omniscience are infinite. He is the creator of heaven and earth, of life and death. The Koran also emphasizes God's divine mercy and compassion. As his omnipotence is tempered with justice, he is forgiving to the sinner who repents. In the Koran, God speaks directly in the first person and makes known his laws. The Koran provides the basic rules of conduct fundamental to the Muslim way of life. Believers must acknowledge and apply both beliefs and acts in order to establish their faith as Muslims. The religion took on the title of Islam because Allah decreed in the Koran: "Lo the religion with Allah is *al-Islam* (the Surrender) to His will and guidance."

Duties in Islam are incumbent on all the faithful, regardless of status in society. "Verily there is no preference for any of you except by what ye enjoy in good health and your deeds of righteousness," says the Koran. The most important duties for the believer, known as the Five Pillars of Islam, are the profession of faith in Allah and his apostle, daily prayer at appointed hours, almsgiving, fasting in the month of Ramadan and, if possible, the pilgrimage to Mecca. "Lo! Those who believe and do good works and establish worship and pay the poor-due, their reward is with their Lord and there shall no fear come upon them, neither shall they grieve," the Koran says.

For Muslims, the Koran is the living word of God, "the Scripture whereof there is no doubt," and, as such, contains not only eternal Truth but also the most perfect representation of literary style.

CENSORSHIP HISTORY

Around 1141, Peter the Venerable, the abbot of Cluny, translated the Koran into Latin. During the period of the medieval Crusades, Christian hostility toward Arabs and their religion mounted. The church fathers regarded Islam as a heresy, Muslims as infidels, and Muhammad as a "renegade bishop, an imposter" who rebelled against the central mission of Christ. By 1215, the church had introduced legislation severely restricting Muslims in Christendom.

The Arabic text of the Koran was not published in Europe until 1530, in Venice. The pope ordered the burning of this edition. Latin translations of the Koran were prohibited by the Spanish Inquisition, a ban that remained in effect until 1790.

In 1541, Johannes Oporinus, a printer in Basel, Switzerland, began printing Robert of Ketton's 12th-century Latin translation of the Koran. City authorities confiscated the entire edition. Protestant reformer Martin Luther argued that the edition should be released because knowledge of the Koran would work to "the glory of Christ, the best of Christianity, the disadvantages of the Moslems, and the vexation of the Devil." The edition was allowed to appear in 1542 with prefaces by both Luther and Protestant reformer Philipp Melanchthon.

The first English edition of the Koran and a new Latin translation were produced in the 17th century. The Koran had still not been printed in the Islamic world; it could be reproduced only in the original handwritten format used by the Prophet's disciples. In the late 17th century, a Turkish printer in Istanbul, Ibrahim Müteferrika, secured the sultan's permission to set up the first printing press in a Muslim country. In 1727, despite protests by calligraphers, he was granted an imperial edict to print books. But the printing of the Koran itself was still expressly forbidden. It was not until 1874 that the Turkish government gave permission to print the Koran, but only in Arabic. In modern times an English translation was tolerated. In the rest of the Muslim world, printing of the Koran was still prohibited.

The first printed edition of the Koran in Egypt appeared in 1833 under Muhammad Ali Pasha, credited with having laid the foundations of modern Egypt. His Bulaq Press became the first and most distinguished publisher in the Arab world. But on his deathbed, religious leaders persuaded his successor, Abbas Pasha, to lock up all printed copies and ban their circulation. Only under Said Pasha, who ruled from 1854 to 1863, were they released.

The Egyptian government published the first official printed version of the Koran in 1925. But this version and other late 20th-century editions of the Koran published in other Muslim countries were reproduced in block printing or lithography, considered closer to handwritten script, rather than movable type. Although Islamic law prohibits only the liturgical use of the Koran in a language other than Arabic, some Muslim theologians today believe that it is a sacrilege to translate the Koran because Allah declared to Muhammad, "We have revealed unto thee an Arabic Koran." Yet, despite such objections, unauthorized translations have been made into 43 different languages.

In 1995, the government of Malaysia banned *Bacaan*, a Malay translation of the Koran by Othman Ali, published in Singapore. The banning was part of an official policy aimed at outlawing "deviant" Islamic sects. *Bacaan* was labeled as "deviational" because it offered an interpretation that differed from the official government-approved version and did not include the original text in Arabic.

Modern government censorship of the Koran has been recorded in socialist countries. In 1926 in the Soviet Union, government directives to libraries stated that religiously dogmatic books such as the Gospels, the Koran, and the Talmud could remain only in large libraries, accessible to students of history, but had to be removed from the smaller ones. Such restrictions were lifted after a modus vivendi was worked out between Muslims and the state during World War II.

In China during the Cultural Revolution of the 1960s and 1970s, study of the Koran and its reading in mosques were prohibited. The Koran had been printed in China since the 19th century and translated into Chinese since the 1920s. The Communist government had published an authorized Chinese translation in 1952.

In 1986 in Ethiopia, under the socialist military government, it was reported that copies of the Koran were destroyed or confiscated by the army, Koranic schools and mosques were closed or razed, Muslims were prohibited from praying, and some were ordered to convert to Christianity and burn the Koran. Ethiopia's ruling military council, the Derg, feared that a resurgence of Islamic fundamentalism would provide moral and financial aid to Muslims who opposed the Marxist-Leninist revolution.

In March 2001, a group of right-wing Hindus in New Delhi, India, burned copies of the Koran to protest the destruction of ancient Buddhist statues in Afghanistan by the Taliban.

The Koran is today the most influential book in the world after the Bible and, with the Bible, is the most widely read of sacred texts. More portions of it are committed to memory than those of any other similar body of sacred writings.

FURTHER READING

Boorstein, Daniel J. *The Discoverers: A History of Man's Search to Know His World and Himself.* New York: Random House, 1983.
Dawood, N. J., trans. and intro. *The Koran.* Baltimore: Penguin Books, 1968.
Farah, Caesar E. *Islam: Belief and Observances.* New York: Barron's Educational Services, 1987.
Lippman, Thomas W. *Understanding Islam: An Introduction to the Muslim World.* New York: Penguin Books, 1990.
Nugent, Philippa. "Of Such Is Reputation Made." *Index on Censorship* 25, no. 2 (March/April 1996): 160.

LAJJA (SHAME)

Author: Taslima Nasrin
Original dates and places of publication: 1993, Bangladesh; 1994, India
Publishers: Ananda Publishers; Penguin Books
Literary form: Novel

SUMMARY

Taslima Nasrin, a former physician from Bangladesh, is a poet, novelist, and journalist and an outspoken feminist. *Lajja* (*Shame*) is a documentary novel about the plight of a Hindu family in Bangladesh persecuted by Muslim fundamentalists during an outbreak of anti-Hindu violence in 1992. On December 6, 1992, Hindu extremists demolished the Babri Masjid, a 16th-century mosque in Ayodha, India. The incident set off weeks of mob violence in India during which more than 1,200 people were killed. In Bangladesh, Muslims terrorized Hindus and ransacked and burned Hindu temples, shops, and homes in retaliation. Hindus are a minority in Bangladesh, which has an Islamic constitution.

The novel traces the events of 13 days in the life of a fictional family, the Duttas—Sudhamoy Dutta, a physician, his wife Kironmoyee and their grown children Suranjan and Maya—in the aftermath of the razing of the Babri mosque. It also reflects Hindu complaints of persistent violation of their rights.

Many Hindu friends of the Dutta family crossed the border into India to settle with relatives, particularly after a 1990 wave of anti-Hindu violence. But Sudhamoy, now an invalid, had long ago moved from the countryside to the capital, Dhaka, after being forced from his house and land. He chooses to stay, though his wife wants to flee to India.

Sudhamoy, an atheist who fought for the independence of Bangladesh from Pakistan, believes with a naive mix of optimism and idealism that his country will not let him down. His son, Suranjan, rebels against the prospect of having to flee his home as they had in 1990, when the family took shelter in the home of Muslim friends.

"After independence the reactionaries who had been against the very spirit of independence had gained power," Suranjan thinks, "changed the face of the constitution and revived the evils of communalism and unbending fundamentalism that had been rejected during the war of independence." Unlawfully and unconstitutionally, Suranjan recalls, Islam became the national religion of Bangladesh.

Suranjan catalogs the hundreds of violent incidents representing the heavy toll that communalism—chauvinism and prejudice based on religious identity—and religious fundamentalism have taken in Bangladesh over the years. He remembers the looting and burning by Muslims in Hindu communities in October 1990. Women were abducted and raped, people were beaten and thrown out of their houses, and property was confiscated. Suranjan is critical of the failure of the government to protect Hindus.

"Why don't we work to free all State policies, social norms and education policies from the infiltration of religion?" he asks. "If we want the introduction of secularism, it does not necessarily mean that the Gita must be recited as often as the Quran is on radio and TV. What we must insist on is the banning of religion from all State activities. In schools, colleges and universities all religious functions, prayers, the teachings of religious texts and the glorifying of lives of religious personae, should be banned."

The terror finally reaches the Dutta family when a group of seven young men invade the house and abduct 21-year-old Maya. Suranjan and his Muslim friend, Haider, search the streets of Dhaka for Maya but can find no sign of her. Maya is never found and is presumed dead. In the end Suranjan and his family decide to flee to India, their lives and their hopes for their country in ruins. "There was absolutely no one to depend upon," Nasrin writes. "He was an alien in his own country."

CENSORSHIP HISTORY

Nasrin is an uncompromising critic of patriarchal religious traditions that she sees as oppressive to women and an outspoken advocate of women's social, political, and sexual liberation. In her crusading syndicated newspaper columns, collected and published in two books, she protested religious intolerance and increasing incidents of violence against women by local *salish*, or Islamic village councils in Bangladesh, as well as the failure of the government to take adequate measures to stop them. According to Amnesty International, *salish* have sentenced women to death by stoning, burning, or flogging for violating the councils' interpretation of Islamic law.

Nasrin's newspaper columns, her bold use of sexual imagery in her poetry, her self-declared atheism, and her iconoclastic lifestyle aroused the fury of fundamentalist clerics. By early 1992, angry mobs began attacking bookstores that sold her works. They also assaulted Nasrin at a book fair and destroyed a stall displaying her books. That year, en route to a literary conference in India, her passport was confiscated by the Bangladeshi government, ostensibly because she listed her employment as a journalist rather than a doctor. (Nasrin is a gynecologist and at the time was employed by the Ministry of Health.)

Lajja (*Shame*) was published in Bangladesh in the Bengali language in February 1993, three months after the razing of the Babri mosque in India that touched off a wave of violence against Hindus in Bangladesh. Nasrin states in a preface to the English-language edition of the novel that she wrote the book in seven days soon after the demolition of the mosque because "I detest fundamentalism and communalism. . . . The riots that took place in 1992 in Bangladesh are the responsibility of us all, and we are to blame. *Lajja* is a document of our collective defeat."

During the first six months after its publication, the novel sold 60,000 copies in Bangladesh. Though panned by some critics as a didactic political tract, it was a commercial success in both Bangladesh and neighboring Bengali-speaking Calcutta, India. Pirated copies of the novel were widely circulated in India by militant Hindus. In 1994, the novel was published in English in New Delhi. (It was published in the United States in October 1997.)

After protests by Muslim fundamentalists in Bangladesh, in July 1993 the Bangladeshi government banned *Lajja* on the grounds that it had "created misunderstanding among communities." On September 24, 1993, Nasrin opened the daily newspaper and saw a prominently displayed notice calling for her death. A fatwa, or death decree, had been issued by a mullah, or Muslim cleric, of the Council of Soldiers of Islam, a militant group based in Sylhet, Bangladesh. It called for her execution for blasphemy and conspiracy against Islam.

The group offered a $1,250 bounty for her death. In the following weeks, additional bounties were promised. Thousands of Muslim fundamentalists attended mass rallies and marched through the streets of Dhaka, hanging and burning Nasrin in effigy. Nasrin was able to obtain police protection only after suing the government, which, in response to international pressure, posted two police officers outside her home.

The International PEN Women Writers' Committee organized a campaign on Nasrin's behalf, enlisting the support of human rights and women's organizations around the world. It called on Bangladesh's government to protect Nasrin, prosecute those who sought her death, lift the ban on her book, and restore her passport. The governments of Sweden, Norway, the United States, France, and Germany lodged official protests. Sweden and Norway ultimately threatened to cut off all economic assistance.

Almost overnight, Nasrin, who was unknown outside Bangladesh and India, became a symbol in the Western world of freedom of expression and women's rights. The government of Bangladesh returned Nasrin's passport, but no arrests were made, even though making a death threat and offering a reward for it is a crime in Bangladesh.

At the time, Bangladesh was governed by the Bangladesh Nationalist Party under Prime Minister Khaleda Zia, the widow of President Ziaur Rahman, an army general assassinated in 1981. Prime Minister Zia was elected with the support of the Muslim party, Jamaat-e-Islami, which held 20 seats in Parliament. Critics of the government contended that she capitulated to fundamentalist demands in the Nasrin case to preserve her electoral coalition.

In April 1994, after the return of her passport, Nasrin traveled to France, where she spoke at a meeting marking International Press Freedom Day. Returning to Bangladesh through India, she gave an interview to the English-language daily the *Calcutta Statesman*, which quoted her as saying, "The Koran should be revised thoroughly." In an open letter to the Bangladeshi and Indian press, Nasrin denied making the reported remarks, but in her denial she wrote that "the Koran, the Vedas, the Bible and all such religious texts" were "out of place and out of time."

In Bangladesh, fundamentalists took to the streets by the tens of thousands in daily demonstrations calling for her death. Mobs attacked the offices of newspapers that showed sympathy for her and ransacked bookstores carrying her books. Religious groups pressed the government for her arrest. On June 4, 1994, the Bangladeshi government brought charges against her under a rarely used 19th-century statute dating from the era of British colonialism that proscribes statements or writings "intended to outrage the religious feeling of any class by insulting its religion or religious believers." The crime carries a maximum penalty of two years in prison.

When a warrant was issued for her arrest, Nasrin left her apartment and went underground. In an interview given just before going into hiding, Nasrin explained, "So many injustices are carried out here in the name of Allah. I cannot stop writing against all these simply to save my own skin. . . . The Koran can no longer serve as the basis of our law. . . . It stands in the way of progress and in the way of women's emancipation. . . . The problem is the intolerance of the fundamentalists. I fight with my pen, and they want to fight with a sword. I say what I think and they want to kill me. I will never let them intimidate me."

On August 3, after protracted negotiations among her legal advisers, Western ambassadors, and the government of Bangladesh, Nasrin was granted bail and ordered to appear for trial at a later, unspecified date. She fled to Stockholm, Sweden, and remained in exile in Europe and the United States. (In 1998, she returned to Bangladesh to care for her critically ill mother and was again forced to go into hiding because of threats and demonstrations against her.) In 2005, Nasrin moved to Kolkata, India, where she hoped to obtain permanent residency. The Indian government, instead, granted her a series of temporary visas. After violent protests by Muslim groups in Kolkata in 2007, the government moved her to Jaipur, then to a safe house in Delhi, and restricted her movements. In March 2008, Nasrin, protesting her confinement in Delhi, left India for Europe and the United States.

"The mullahs who would murder me will kill everything progressive in Bangladesh if they are allowed to prevail," Nasrin wrote in her preface to *Lajja*. "It is my duty to try to protect my beautiful country from them, and I call on all those who share my values to help me defend my rights. I am convinced that the only way the fundamentalist forces can be stopped is if all of us who are secular and humanistic join together and fight their malignant influence. I, for one, will not be silenced."

More than a 16 years after the first efforts to censor Nasrin, she still faced bans of her writing and threats against her life. All four volumes of her autobiography published in 1999–2004, including *Meyebela: My Bengali Girlhood* (1999), were banned in Bangladesh.

FURTHER READING

Crossette, Barbara. "A Cry for Tolerance Brings New Hatred Down on a Writer." *New York Times,* July 3, 1994, p. 7.

Dhar, Sujoy. "Bangladeshi Author's New Book Upsets Prurient Fans." Inter Press Service (November 27, 2003).

Irvine, Lindesay. "Taslima Nasrin to Leave India." *Guardian* (March 17, 2008). Available online.URL: http://www.guardian.co.uk. Accessed June 6, 2010.

Nasrin, Taslima. Taslima Nasrin's official Web site. Available online. URL: http://taslimanasrin.com

Riaz, Ali. "Taslima Nasrin: Breaking the Structured Silence." *Bulletin of Concerned Asian Scholars* 27, no. 1 (January–March 1995): 21–27.

Tax, Meredith. "Taslima Nasrin: A Background Paper." *Bulletin of Concerned Asian Scholars* 25, no. 4 (October–December 1993): 72–74.

Weaver, Mary Anne. "A Fugitive from Justice." *New Yorker*, September 12, 1994, 47–60.

Whyatt, Sara. "Taslima Nasrin." *Index on Censorship* 23, nos. 4–5 (September/October 1994): 202–207.

THE LAST TEMPTATION OF CHRIST

Author: Nikos Kazantzakis
Original dates and places of publication: 1953, Greece; 1960, United States
Publishers: Athenai; Simon & Schuster
Literary form: Novel

SUMMARY

The Last Temptation of Christ by the Greek novelist, poet, dramatist, and translator Nikos Kazantzakis, best known for his novel *Zorba the Greek*, retells the life story of Jesus of Nazareth, imagining the human events of the gospel accounts in a vivid mosaic colored by extravagant imagery. Kazantzakis's Jesus is not the self-assured son of God following a preordained path but a Christ of weakness, whose struggles mirror those of human beings who face fear, pain, temptation, and death. Though Jesus is often confused about the path he should choose, as the story proceeds his sense of mission becomes clear. When he dies, it is as a hero who has willed his own destiny.

Though the story follows the gospel narrative, its setting and atmosphere derive from the peasant life of Kazantzakis's native Crete. The novel was written in the rich, metaphor-laden vocabulary of demotic Greek, the everyday language of modern Greece.

In the 33 chapters of *The Last Temptation of Christ*, corresponding to the number of years in Jesus' life, Kazantzakis portrays what he describes as "the incessant, merciless battle between the spirit and the flesh," a central concern explored in his novels and philosophical writings. Jesus is tempted by evil, feels its attractiveness, and even succumbs to it, for only in this way can his ultimate rejection of temptation have meaning.

The novel opens with the scene of a young man in the throes of a nightmare, dreaming that hordes are searching for him as their savior. Jesus of Nazareth, the village carpenter, has been gripped since childhood by strange portents and has felt the hand of God clawing at his scalp. He shrinks from these signs and visions, hoping that, if he sins, God will leave him alone.

Jesus has loved Mary Magdalene, the daughter of the village rabbi, since childhood. He had wished to marry her but had been mercilessly forced by God to reject her. She has become a prostitute in order to forget Jesus. Overwhelmed by remorse, Jesus seeks refuge in a desert monastery. A reluctant

Messiah, he cries out to God, "I love good food, wine, laughter. I want to marry, to have children. . . . Leave me alone. . . . I want Magdalene, even if she's a prostitute. I want you to detest me, to go and find someone else; I want to be rid of you. . . . I shall make crosses all my life, so that the Messiah you choose can be crucified."

During his stay in the desert, Jesus finds the courage and determination to embark on his public ministry. The central chapters of the novel trace the familiar episodes of the Gospel, leading to the moment of the Crucifixion, where the last temptation comes to Jesus in his delirium on the cross in the form of a dream of erotic bliss and a worldly life: His guardian angel snatches him away from the Crucifixion, and Jesus takes the smooth, easy road of men. He has at last married Magdalene. Upon Magdalene's death, he marries Martha and Mary, the sisters of Lazarus, and fathers children. Now, as an old man, he sits on the threshold of his house and recalls the longings of his youth and his joy to have escaped the privations and tortures of the cross.

He comes face to face with his former disciples, led by Judas, who accuses him of being a traitor, a deserter, and a coward. "Your place was on the cross," Judas says. "That's where the God of Israel put you to fight. But you got cold feet and the moment death lifted its head, you couldn't get away fast enough." Jesus suddenly remembers where he is and why he feels pain. Though temptation captured him for a split second and led him astray, he has stood his ground honorably to the end. The joys of marriage and children were lies, illusions sent by the devil. He has not betrayed his disciples, who are alive and thriving, proclaiming his gospel. "Everything had turned out as it should, glory be to God."

CENSORSHIP HISTORY

Critics recommended Kazantzakis's unorthodox portrait of Jesus as a powerful and important novel, an extraordinary and original work of art, which in the deepest sense celebrates the spiritual struggles of humankind. It was widely acknowledged, however, that from an orthodox point of view, his interpretation might be considered as heretical or blasphemous.

Kazantzakis's primary motive in writing *The Last Temptation of Christ* was not, however, to disagree with the church. He wanted, rather, to lift Christ out of the church altogether, to portray Jesus as a figure for a new age, in terms that could be understood in the 20th century. In a 1951 letter, Kazantzakis explained his intentions: "It's a laborious, sacred creative endeavour to reincarnate the essence of Christ, setting aside the dross—falsehoods and pettiness which all the churches and all the cassocked representatives of Christianity have heaped up on His figure, thereby distorting it."

"That part of Christ's nature which was profoundly human helps us to understand him and love Him and pursue his passion as if it were our own," Kazantzakis wrote in the prologue of the novel. "If he had not within him this warm human element, he would never be able to touch our hearts with such assurance and tenderness; he would not be able to become a model for our lives. . . . This book was written because I wanted to offer a supreme model to the man who struggles; I wanted to show him that he must not fear pain, temptation or death—because all three can be conquered, all three have already been conquered."

The Eastern Orthodox Church excommunicated Kazantzakis in 1954 as a result of publication in Greece of *The Last Temptation of Christ.* Kazantzakis wrote, "The Orthodox Church of America convened and damned *The Last Temptation* as extremely indecent, atheistic and treasonable, after admitting they hadn't read it. . . ." Kazantzakis wrote to Orthodox church leaders, quoting the third-century Christian thinker Tertullian: "At Thy Tribunal, Lord, I make my appeal," adding, "You have execrated me, Holy Fathers; I bless you. I pray that your conscience may be as clear as mine and that you may be as moral and as religious as I am."

The same year, the Catholic Church placed the novel on its Index of Forbidden Books. Kazantzakis commented, "I've always been amazed at the narrow-mindedness and narrow-heartedness of human beings. Here is a book that I wrote in a state of deep religious exaltation, with a fervent love of Christ; and now the Pope has no understanding of it at all. . . ."

The furor over the novel, however, had the result of increasing its sales. "I have ended up by becoming famous in Greece," Kazantzakis wrote in 1955. "All the newspapers, except two, have declared themselves on my side, and from all over Greece telegrams are being sent in protest over the priests' wanting to seize my books. . . . And the books are sold out the moment they are printed and certain booksellers buy up a number of copies and sell them at very high black market rates. What a disgrace! How medieval!"

Ultimately the Greek Orthodox Church was pressured to halt its anti-Kazantzakis campaign. Princess Marie Bonaparte read the book and recommended it to the queen of Greece. The queen "kept the Greek Orthodox church from making itself ridiculous," wrote Helen Kazantzakis in her biography of her husband.

In 1962–65 in Long Beach, California, the novel, in the company of Jessica Mitford's *The American Way of Death* and poetry by Langston Hughes, was the target of a three-year campaign by a right-wing group aimed at removing it from the public library. The campaign was unsuccessful.

A 1988 film of the novel directed by Martin Scorsese caused worldwide controversy and was banned in several countries mainly because of the sequence drawn from the novel in which a delirious Jesus on the cross imagines that he has loved, married, and fathered children. Scorsese and the director of the Venice Film Festival were prosecuted for blasphemy in Rome but were acquitted. In the U.S., Roman Catholic authorities criticized the film as blasphemous. Three Republican congressmen introduced a resolution to force the withdrawal of the film. The Dallas, Texas, city council passed a resolution condemning it. Blockbuster Video announced that it would not carry the film. In Escambia County, Florida, the board of county commissioners passed an ordinance to prohibit the showing of the movie in the county at risk of 60 days in jail and $500 fine, or both. U.S. District Court judge Roger Vinson issued a restraining order against the ban as an unconstitutional violation of the First Amendment.

Director Scorsese's response to the film's censorship echoed that of Kazantzakis 34 years earlier. "My film was made with deep religious feeling. . . . It is more than just another film project for me. I believe it is a religious film about suffering and the struggle to find God." In December 1988, the novel was banned in Singapore as a result of pressure from fundamental-ist Christians related to the controversy over the film.

In 2005, another story of the life of Jesus, the satirical *Das Leben des Jesus* (*The Life of Jesus*) by Austrian cartoonist Gerhard Haderer, fell afoul of Greek censors. It was the first book to be banned there in more than 20 years. The best-selling illustrated book, which was published in Germany and Austria in 2002, depicts Jesus as a binge-drinking friend of Jimi Hendrix and a naked surfer high on marijuana.

Haderer did not realize that his book had been translated and published in Greece until he received a summons in late 2003 to appear before an Athens court. The Greek Orthodox Church had filed a complaint against the author. The book was confiscated and Haderer, his Greek publisher, and four booksellers were tried for blasphemy. The publisher and book-sellers were acquitted, but Haderer was convicted and given a six-month suspended sentence in absentia. Artists and writers in the European Union rallied around Haderer and raised concerns that the European arrest warrant system instituted in 2002 as an antiterrorist measure was being used to curtail freedom of expression. Haderer appealed his conviction and ultimately the court of appeals in Athens overturned the lower-court ruling, describing the case as "daft," and ordered that the book could be sold openly again.

In 2006, Iran's Ministry of Culture banned *The Last Temptation of Christ*, which had been published in Iran four times previously.

FURTHER READING

"Court Laughs at Cartoonist's Trial." *Kathimerini* (April 4, 2005). Available online. URL: http://www.ekathimerini.com/4dcgi/_w_articles_politics_100014_14/04/2005_55187.

Diver, Krysia. "Cartoonist Faces Greek Jail for Blasphemy." *The Guardian* (March 23, 2005). Available online. URL: http://www.guardian.co.uk/arts/news/story/0,11711,1443908,00.html.

Heins, Marjorie. *Sex, Sin, and Blasphemy: A Guide to America's Culture Wars.* New York: New Press, 1993.

Kazantzakis, Helen. *Kazantzakis: A Biography Based on His Letters.* Translated by Amy Mims. New York: Simon and Schuster, 1968.

Kazantzakis, Nikos. *The Last Temptation of Christ.* Translation and afterword by P. A. Bien. New York: Simon and Schuster, 1960.

Levy, Leonard. *Blasphemy: Verbal Offense against the Sacred, from Moses to Salman Rushdie.* New York: Alfred A. Knopf, 1993.

Sarkouhi, Faraj. "Iran: Book Censorship the Rule Not the Exception." Radio Free Europe / Radio Liberty (November 26, 2007). Available online.URL: http://www.vferl.org/articleprintview/1079193.html. Accessed July 8, 2009.

Thompson, David, and Ian Christie, eds. *Scorsese on Scorsese.* London: Faber and Faber, 1989.

THE NEW TESTAMENT

Translator:　William Tyndale
Original date and place of publication:　1526, Germany
Literary form:　Religious text

SUMMARY

The English Protestant reformer and linguist William Tyndale was the first person to translate The Bible into English from the original Greek and Hebrew and the first to print it in English. Many scholars consider his influence on English literature comparable to William Shakespeare's.

In 1524, when Tyndale, an Oxford graduate and Catholic priest, resolved to translate the Bible, England was the only European country without a printed vernacular version. The 1408 synod of Canterbury had forbidden translation into English of any portion of the Scriptures by an unauthorized individual. Only the fifth-century Latin Vulgate edition of the Bible translated by Saint Jerome was considered acceptable.

Translation of the Bible into the vernacular remained illegal in England for fear that anarchy and schism would be brought about by the spread of Lutheranism. Lutheran books had been publicly burned in Cambridge and London in 1520. Martin Luther's doctrine of *sola scriptura*, Scripture alone, which emphasized the ability of believers to read and understand the Bible themselves without church intervention, was considered to defy church authority. Scripture could be interpreted only by the infallible pope and the hierarchy.

Tyndale could find no religious authority in London who would support his work. "And so in London I abode for almost a year, and marked the course of the world . . . ," he later wrote, "and saw things whereof I defer to speak at this time and understood at the last not only that there was no room in my lord of London's palace to translate the New Testament, but also that there was no place to do it in all England, as experience doth now openly declare."

In 1524, Tyndale left England for Germany. The following year in Cologne, he began printing his translation of the New Testament from the Greek. The printing had reached Matthew 22 when it had to be suspended. His translation was violently opposed by the clergy, who, fearing Lutheranism, saw it as "pernicious merchandise." When the Cologne authorities moved to arrest him and his assistant and impound their work, they fled to Worms, where publication of the 700 pages of the New Testament was completed clandestinely and anonymously at the press of Peter Schoeffer in 1526. Six thousand copies of Tyndale's New Testament were smuggled into England the following year and widely distributed. For the first time, all 27 books of the New Testament were available in clearly printed portable form in a language that every reader could understand.

The primary source for Tyndale's New Testament was the original Greek, although he drew from both the Latin Vulgate and Martin Luther's German translation. Because he believed that the word of God should speak directly to the reader in an understandable way, his first aim was clarity, to write in everyday spoken English. "If God spare my life, ere many years, I will cause a boy that driveth a plough shall know more of the Scripture than thou dost," he told a learned man before leaving England.

His ability to write in simple, direct, and rhythmic prose and, as his biographer David Daniell says, "to create unforgettable words, phrases, paragraphs and chapters, and to do so in a way that . . . is still, even today, direct and living" had an indelible impact on both the language of the Bible and English prose.

"Am I my brother's keeper?" "Blessed are the pure of heart; for they shall see God." "No man can serve two masters." "Ask and it shall be given to you." "There were shepherds abiding in the fields." These and hundreds of proverbial phrases such as "the signs of the times," "the spirit is willing," and "fight the good fight" come from Tyndale's New Testament.

Tyndale's 1534 revision of the New Testament, published in Antwerp under his own name, was carried forward into later Renaissance Bibles and formed the basis of the Authorized, or King James, Version of the Bible published in 1611.

Living in concealment in the Low Countries, Tyndale also translated the first half of the Old Testament from the original Hebrew. His masterly translation of the Pentateuch appeared in 1530, beginning with Genesis: "In the beginning God created heaven and earth. . . . Then God said: let there be light and there was light." The Book of Jonah was completed in 1536. Tyndale's Old Testament books were published in pocket volumes and smuggled into England. His Old Testament was also adopted in large part into the King James Version of the Bible.

CENSORSHIP HISTORY

Church dignitaries in England immediately denounced Tyndale's 1526 edition of the New Testament. In the summer of 1526, the English bishops met and agreed that "untrue translations" should be burned, "with further sharp corrections and punishment against the keepers and readers of the same." The Catholic cardinal Thomas Wolsey, who controlled domestic and foreign policy for Henry VIII, instructed the English ambassador to the Low Countries to act against printers or booksellers involved in the production and distribution of the English New Testament. Tyndale's New Testament was the first printed book to be banned in England. Wolsey ordered Tyndale to be seized at Worms, but Tyndale found refuge with Philip of Hesse at Marburg.

Although Henry VIII was to break with Rome in the early 1530s, he had no sympathy with Protestant views and saw Tyndale's New Testament as Lutheran in its influence. Tyndale had translated the Greek word *ekklesia*, for example, as "the congregation," which is the body of Christ, rather than "the church." The English bishops saw this as heretical in that the word *congregation* implied equality of the gathering of believers. They believed that this idea was Lutheran and denied the church's authority. Copies of the book were publicly burned at Saint Paul's Cathedral in 1526. In May 1527, church authorities ordered all copies to be bought up and destroyed. But despite the ban, reprints continued to be distributed, many imported clandestinely from the Low Countries.

Tyndale, in hiding in Antwerp, continued to publish polemics from abroad in defense of the principles of the English reformation, including *The Obedience of a Christian Man* and *The Parable of the Wicked Mammon* in 1528, an exposition of the New Testament teaching that faith is more important than works. When *Wicked Mammon* began to circulate in England, the church, viewing it as containing Lutheran heresies, moved to suppress it. Those who were found with it were arrested and severely punished. *Wicked Mammon*, like the New Testament translation, was widely read, nevertheless, and continued to be influential, even years later when it was still prohibited.

The English ambassador to the Low Countries was instructed to demand that the regent extradite Tyndale and his assistant, William Roye, to England, but they could not be found. In 1530, Tyndale further enraged King Henry VIII by publishing *The Practice of Prelates*, which condemned the king's divorce. In May 1535, Tyndale, working in Antwerp on his translation of the Old Testament, was arrested as the result of a plot masterminded by English authorities. He was imprisoned in Vilvoorde Castle near Brussels, charged with Lutheran heresy and disagreeing with the Holy Roman Emperor. Tyndale was put on trial, formally condemned as a heretic, degraded from the priesthood, and handed over to the secular authorities for punishment. In early October 1536, he was strangled at the stake, and his body was burned with copies of his Bible translation. His last words were "Lord, open the king of England's eyes."

At the time of Tyndale's death, about 50,000 copies of his Bible translations in seven editions were in circulation in England. A small portion of Tyndale's translation was included in a complete English Bible published illegally in Germany by his colleague Miles Coverdale. In 1537, Matthew's Bible appeared in England under the pseudonym John Matthew. Its editor, John Rogers, was a Catholic priest who converted to Protestantism and Tyndale's friend. Two-thirds of Matthew's Bible contained Tyndale's translations.

Matthew's Bible was the first Bible in English to be licensed by the government. Despite its inclusion of Tyndale's translations, it was approved by Henry

VIII. His break with the Catholic Church had been completed by the Act of Supremacy in 1534, which established the Church of England. Tyndale's and Coverdale's translations were also included in Henry VIII's Great Bible of 1539, which was declared the official Bible of the Church of England.

In 1546, the Catholic Church's Council of Trent said that the Latin Vulgate of Saint Jerome was the sole canonical text of the Bible. Catholics were forbidden to read any translation, such as Tyndale's, without special permission of the pope or the Inquisition. This restriction remained in effect until the late 18th century.

During the reign of the Catholic queen Mary I in England from 1553 to 1558, the ban on Protestant Bibles was reinstated. In 1555, a royal proclamation commanded "that no manner of persons presume to bring into this realm any manuscripts, books, papers . . . in the name of Martin Luther, John Calvin, Miles Coverdale, Erasmus, Tyndale . . . or any like books containing false doctrines against the Catholic faith."

The committee assembled in 1604 by King James I to prepare the Authorized Version of the Bible—often acclaimed as the greatest work ever produced by a committee and ranked in English literature with the work of Shakespeare—used as its basis Tyndale's work. Nine-tenths of the Authorized Version's New Testament is Tyndale's. Many of its finest passages were taken unchanged, though unacknowledged, from Tyndale's translations.

The tragedy of Tyndale's execution at the age of 42 is compounded by the knowledge that he was cut down before having completed his life's work. Tyndale was unable to go on to translate the poetic books and prophecies of the Old Testament or revise again his New Testament translation. As his biographer Daniell laments, it is as though Shakespeare had died halfway through his life, before his greatest tragedies had been written.

In 2000, Tyndale's New Testament was given its first complete reprint after more than 400 years by the British Library in a pocket-sized edition that mirrors the original.

FURTHER READING

Daniell, David. *Let There Be Light: William Tyndale and the Making of the English Bible.* London: British Library, 1994.
———. *William Tyndale. A Biography.* New Haven, Conn.: Yale University Press, 1994.
Haight, Anne Lyon. *Banned Books: 387 B.C. to 1978 A.D.* Updated and enlarged by Chandler B. Grannis. New York: R. R. Bowker, 1978.

NINETY-FIVE THESES

Author: Martin Luther
Original date and place of publication: 1517, Switzerland
Literary form: Theological tract

SUMMARY

Martin Luther, a German monk of the Augustinian order, was the founder of the Protestant Reformation in Europe. He was a doctor of divinity and town preacher of Wittenberg, where he taught theology at the university. A visit to Rome had convinced him of the decadence and corruption of the Catholic pope and clergy. In 1516, he began to question the efficacy of indulgences in a series of sermons.

In 16th-century Roman Catholic doctrine, the pope could transfer superfluous merit accumulated by Christ, the Virgin Mary, or the saints to an individual sinner in order to remit temporal penalties for sin later to be suffered in purgatory. Such transfers of indulgences could benefit both the living and the dead. Luther's evangelical emphasis on the complete forgiveness of sins and reconciliation with God through God's grace alone led him to question the doctrine of indulgences and the pervasive ecclesiastical practice of selling them.

The following year, Johann Tetzel, a Dominican monk, hawked indulgences to pay a debt that Albert of Brandenburg had incurred to purchase the Bishopric of Mainz and to help pay for the new basilica of Saint Peter in Rome. Luther resolved to voice his pastoral concern about the spiritual dangers of indulgences as an obstacle to the preaching of true repentance and interior conversion.

On October 15, 1517, Luther challenged his academic colleagues to debate the subject. Luther issued his challenge in the traditional manner—by posting a placard written in Latin on the door of the castle church in Wittenberg. Luther's notice contained his 95 theses on indulgences. To his surprise, the theses were circulated in Latin and German throughout Germany and within a few weeks to much of Europe, unleashing a storm of controversy that was to lead to the Protestant Reformation.

In his Ninety-five Theses or *Disputation on the Power and Efficacy of Indulgences,* Luther argued that the pope could remit only those penalties he had imposed himself and denied the pope's authority to remit sin. Luther rejected the idea that the saints had superfluous merits or that merit could be stored up for later use by others.

The pope has no control over the souls in purgatory, Luther asserted. "They preach only human doctrines who say that as soon as the money clinks into the money chest, the soul flies out of purgatory." If the pope does have such power, Luther asked, "why does not the pope empty purgatory for the sake of the holy love and the dire need of all the souls that are there if he redeems an infinite number of souls for the sake of miserable money with which to build a church?"

He branded indulgences as harmful because they gave believers a false sense of security. By implying that the payment of money could appease the wrath of God, the sale of indulgences impeded salvation by diverting charity and inducing complacency. "Christians should be taught that he who gives to the poor is better than he who receives a pardon. He who spends his money for indulgences instead of relieving want receives not the indulgence of the pope but the indignation of God." Those who believe that their salvation is assured because they have indulgence letters will face eternal damnation, "together with their teachers," who preach unchristian doctrine.

Luther objected to the church's intent to raise money for a basilica by sale of indulgences. "Why does not the pope, whose wealth is today greater than the wealth of the richest Crassus, build this one basilica of St. Peter with his own money rather than with the money of poor believers?" Luther asked. Luther believed that to repress by force the objections of the laity to the sale of indulgences, rather than resolving them reasonably, "is to expose the church and the pope to the ridicule of their enemies and to make Christians unhappy."

Luther's theses were directed toward church reform. He did not see them as an attack on the pope's authority or as the beginnings of a schism. But the church's response to Luther's proposals pushed him toward a more radical stance that led ultimately to a break with Rome and the founding of a new church.

CENSORSHIP HISTORY

At first Pope Leo X did not take serious notice of Luther's theses, viewing them instead as a reflection of the rivalry between Luther's Augustinian order and the Dominicans, who were Luther's most vociferous critics. But the theses, rapidly distributed in Germany, found active support among the peasantry and civil authorities, who objected to Rome's siphoning of local funds. The hierarchy became convinced that the abuses of indulgences should be corrected and Luther silenced.

In 1518, the pope asked Hieronymus, bishop of Ascoli, to investigate Luther's case. Luther was summoned to Rome to answer charges of heresy and contumacy, or insubordination. Frederick III, elector of Saxony, stepped in to demand that Luther's hearing be held on German soil. When the hearing before the papal legate was transferred to Augsburg, where the imperial diet (the legislative assembly) was unsympathetic to papal claims, Luther refused to retract any of his theses. In a debate in Leipzig in 1519 with the German professor Johannes Eck, Luther argued that because the authority of the pope was of human origin, rather than rooted in divine right, he could be resisted when his edicts contravened the Scriptures.

Johannes Froben of Basel had published the Ninety-five Theses in an edition with Luther's sermons. In February 1519, Froben reported that only 10 copies were left and that no book from his presses had ever sold out so quickly. Taking full advantage of the new potential of the printing press, the book had been distributed not only in Germany, but in France, Spain, Switzerland, Belgium, England, and even in Rome. The same year, the theological faculties of the Universities of Louvain and Cologne ordered copies of the theses to be burned for heresy.

The pope appointed commissions to study Luther's writings. On June 15, 1520, the pope proclaimed in the papal bull "Exsurge Domine," "Rise up O Lord and judge thy cause. A wild boar has invaded thy vineyard." The bull pronounced 41 errors of Luther as "heretical, or scandalous, or false, or offensive to pious ears, or seductive of simple minds, or repugnant to Catholic truth, respectively." In his preface the pope wrote, "Our pastoral office can no longer tolerate the pestiferous virus of the following forty-one errors. . . . The books of Martin Luther which contain these errors are to be examined and burned. . . . Now therefore we give Martin sixty days in which to submit." It was forbidden to print, distribute, read, possess, or quote any of Luther's books, tracts, or sermons.

Then in August, October, and November of 1520, Luther published three revolutionary tracts that dramatically raised the stakes of his disagreement with the church: *Address to the Christian Nobility of the German Nation*, which attacked the claim of papal authority over secular rulers; *The Babylonian Captivity of the Church*, which rejected the priesthood and the sacraments; *The Freedom of Christian Man*, which reiterated his doctrine of justification by faith alone. The first edition of 4,000 copies of the *Address* sold out within a week. Riding the crest of a wave of public support, Luther in his sermons, debates, and writings proposed a radical alternative to the Catholic Church.

On October 10, the papal bull reached Luther in Germany. Luther wrote a stinging reply to the bull: *Against the Execrable Bull of Antichrist*. "They say that some articles are heretical, some erroneous, some scandalous, some offensive," Luther wrote. "The implication is that those which are heretical are not erroneous, those which are erroneous are not scandalous, and those which are scandalous are not offensive." Calling on the pope to "renounce your diabolical blasphemy and audacious impiety," he concluded, "It is better that I should die a thousand times than that I should retract one syllable of the condemned articles."

Luther's books were burned in Louvain and Liège during October and the following month in Cologne and Mainz. On December 10, 1520, Luther and his followers publicly burned the papal bull at Wittenberg, along with copies of canon law and the papal constitutions. "Since they have burned my books, I burn theirs," Luther said. In January 1521, the pope issued a new bull, "Decet Romanum Pontificum," which affirmed the excommunication of Luther and his followers and the burning of his works.

Luther's enormous popularity, bolstered by his appeal to German nationalist objections to Roman intervention in their affairs, saved him from the fate of other heretics. Elector Frederick III of Saxony, Luther's temporal ruler, refused to give him over for trial to Rome. The only power in Europe capable of suppressing Luther was the Holy Roman Emperor Charles V, a devout Catholic determined to root out the heresy.

On April 18, 1521, Luther was called before the Diet of Worms. Before the emperor and the assembled princes of the empire he refused to recant or disown his writings. "Should I recant at this point," he said, "I would open the door to more tyranny and impiety, and it will be all the worse should it appear that I had done so at the instance of the Holy Roman Empire." He continued, "Unless I am convicted by Scripture and plain reason—I do not accept the authority of popes and councils, for they have contradicted each other—my conscience is captive to the Word of God."

On May 26, 1521, Charles V decreed in the Edict of Worms that Luther was "a limb cut off from the Church of God, an obstinate schismatic and manifest heretic. . . . [N]o one is to harbor him. His followers are also to be condemned. His books are to be eradicated from the memory of man." The edict included a Law of Printing, which prohibited printing, sale, possession, reading, or copying Luther's work or any future works he might produce.

Though the emperor had persuaded most of the princes of Germany to sign the condemnation, few strongly supported it. Though the edict called for Luther's arrest, his friends were able to harbor him at the castle in Wartburg of Elector Frederick III of Saxony. There he translated the New Testament into German and began a 10-year project to translate the entire Bible. He returned to Wittenberg in March 1522 at considerable risk and spent the rest of his life spreading his new gospel.

Censorship of Luther's writing was pervasive throughout Europe. His works and those of his disciples were destroyed and banned in England, France, Spain, and the Netherlands. In 1524, the Diet of Nürnberg declared that "each prince in his own territory should enforce the Edict of Worms in so far as he might be able." As the edict implied, it could not be enforced in most of northern Germany. Cities in southern Germany and elsewhere in northern Europe joined the Lutheran reform. "Lutheran books are for sale in the marketplace immediately beneath the edicts of the Emperor and the Pope who declare them to be prohibited." a contemporary commented.

In 1555, Charles V signed the Peace of Augsburg, giving up further attempts to impose Catholicism on the Protestant princes. The peace allowed each prince to choose the religion of his state and declared that people could not be prevented from migrating to another region to practice their own religion. Lutheranism had taken hold.

Luther's works remained on the Vatican's Index of Forbidden Books until 1930. They were still prohibited, however, according to the church's canon law barring Catholics under penalty of mortal sin from reading books "which propound or defend heresy or schism."

FURTHER READING

Bainton, Roland H. *Here I Stand: The Life of Martin Luther.* New York: Penguin, 1995.

Bokenkotter, Thomas S. *A Concise History of the Catholic Church.* Garden City, N.Y.: Doubleday, 1977.

Christie-Murray, David. *A History of Heresy.* Oxford: Oxford University Press, 1989.

Haight, Anne Lyon. *Banned Books: 387 B.C. to 1978 A.D.* Updated and enlarged by Chandler B. Grannis. New York: R. R. Bowker, 1978.

Putnam, George Haven. *The Censorship of the Church of Rome.* Vol. 1. New York: G. P. Putnam's Sons, 1906–07.

Spitz, Lewis W., ed. *The Protestant Reformation.* Englewood Cliffs, N.J.: Prentice Hall, 1966.

Wilcox, Donald J. *In Search of God and Self: Renaissance and Reformation Thought.* Boston: Houghton Mifflin, 1975.

Zagorin, Perez. *How the Idea of Religious Toleration Came to the West.* Princeton, N.J.: Princeton University Press, 2003.

OLIVER TWIST

Author: Charles Dickens
Original date and place of publication: 1838, United Kingdom
Literary form: Novel

SUMMARY

The publication of *Oliver Twist,* Dickens's second novel, the story of an orphan who falls into the hands of a group of thieves in the slums of London, firmly established the literary eminence of its 25-year-old author. Within a few years, Dickens was the most popular and widely read writer of his time. Beginning in 1837, *Oliver Twist* appeared in monthly installments in a London magazine. The following year it was published in three volumes in book form. *Oliver Twist* offers the first glimpse of the genius of Dickens that would reach full flower in his later novels. It is among the most powerful works of fiction portraying the misery of daily life for the urban poor and the uncaring bureaucracies that sustain an oppressive system.

When Dickens was 12, his father was taken to debtors' prison. While the rest of the family accompanied his father to the workhouse, Dickens was sent to paste labels on bottles in a blacking factory. This experience left him with a bitter and passionate opposition to child labor and inhumane treatment of the poor and is reflected in the biting sarcasm that animates the early chapters of *Oliver Twist.*

When Oliver's destitute mother, found lying in the street, dies giving birth to him in a nearby workhouse, the infant becomes the ward of the local parish overseers. He is dispatched to a parish institution where he and other orphans are brought up under cruel conditions, "without the inconvenience of too much food or too much clothing."

At age nine, Oliver is returned to the workhouse by Mr. Bumble, the unctuous parish beadle. The workhouse boys are fed three meals of thin gruel a day, with an onion twice a week and half a roll on Sunday. "Please, sir, I want some more," Oliver says. In punishment for the "impious and profane offence of asking for more," Oliver is ordered into instant solitary confinement.

He is then apprenticed by Mr. Bumble to the undertaker, Mr. Sowerberry, where he lives and works in mean circumstances. After fighting with his bullying coworker, Noah, Oliver is beaten and runs away to London. There he unwittingly falls into the hands of Fagin, the nefarious leader of a gang of thieves, whose other chief members are the burglar Bill Sikes, Sikes's companion, Nancy and the pickpocket known as the Artful Dodger. When the

Dodger picks the pocket of an elderly gentleman, Oliver is caught and brought to the police magistrate. Injured and ill, Oliver is rescued by the benevolent Mr. Brownlow, who takes him into his household. But Nancy finds Oliver and brings him back to the gang. When Oliver is made to accompany Sikes on a burgling expedition and is shot and wounded, he comes into the hands of Mrs. Maylie and her protégée, Rose, who treat him kindly.

A sinister person named Monks, who is known to Fagin, appears to have a special interest in Oliver. Nancy, who overhears a conversation between Fagin and Monks, goes to Rose and reveals to her that Monks is Oliver's older half brother, knows the secret of Oliver's parentage, and wishes all proof of it destroyed. When Nancy's betrayal is discovered by the gang, she is brutally murdered by Sikes.

While trying to escape capture by a mob, Sikes accidentally hangs himself. Fagin is arrested and sentenced to execution. Monks confesses that he pursued Oliver's ruin so that he could retain the whole of his late father's property. Upon the death of his mother, Oliver was to have inherited the estate, as long as he had in his minority never stained the good name of his family. Fagin had received a reward from Monks for turning Oliver into a thief. It turns out that Rose is the sister of Oliver's late mother. In the end Oliver is adopted by Mr. Brownlow. Mr. Bumble ends his career as a pauper in the very same workhouse over which he formerly ruled.

In Dickens's preface to the third edition of the novel, he wrote, "I wished to show, in little Oliver, the principle of Good surviving through every adverse circumstance and triumphing at last." All ends happily in *Oliver Twist*, yet the haunting memory of the evils that beset Oliver in the poorhouses and streets of London remains.

CENSORSHIP HISTORY

"The walls and ceiling of the room were perfectly black with age and dirt. . . . Some sausages were cooking; and standing over them, with a toasting fork in this hand, was a very old shriveled Jew, whose villainous-looking and repulsive face was obscured by a quantity of matted red hair." The sinister and evil Fagin is introduced to readers of *Oliver Twist* with an archetypal anti-Semitic image dating back many centuries in Western culture, that of the Satanic and fiendish Jew. Dickens's caricature of Fagin has been the subject of protest and debate since the time of the novel's publication.

Dickens shaped the character of Fagin, referred to as "the Jew" hundreds of times throughout the novel, according to a traditional pattern commonly employed to portray Jews in literature and on the stage in the 19th century. Fagin's red hair and beard were commonly associated with ancient images of the devil. He has a hooked nose, shuffling gait, a long gabardine coat, and broad-brimmed hat and is a dishonest dealer in secondhand clothes and trinkets. Fagin is portrayed, like Satan, as serpentlike, gliding stealthily along, "creeping beneath the shelter of the walls and doorways . . . like some loathsome reptile, engendered in the slime and darkness through which he moved. . . ."

Though literary critics believe that Dickens did not intend to defame or injure Jews in his creation of the character of Fagin, Dickens was a product of the anti-Semitic culture of his time. Reflected in laws, public discourse, literature, and popular entertainment, prejudice against Jews was a part of the early Victorian heritage. In the 1830s, Jews were barred from owning stores within the city of London, could not work as attorneys, receive a university degree, or sit in Parliament. Because they were confined to certain occupations, the majority of England's 20,000 to 30,000 Jews made their living by buying and selling old clothes, peddling, and moneylending.

In a letter to a Jewish woman who had protested the stereotypical treatment of Fagin, Dickens wrote, "Fagin is a Jew because it unfortunately was true, of the time to which the story refers, that class of criminal almost invariably was a Jew." The 1830 trial of Ikey Solomons, a Jewish fence, who, like Fagin, dealt in stolen jewelry, clothing, and fabrics, had been extensively publicized and was one of the influences on Dickens's portrayal of Fagin.

The years 1830 to 1860 saw a rise in the status of Jews in England. Legal barriers and commercial restrictions were removed, Jews were elected to posts in local and national government, and many became socially prominent. Social attitudes also changed, reflected in Dickens's increased awareness of and sensitivity to anti-Semitism in the years that followed the initial publication of *Oliver Twist*. "I know of no reason the Jews can have for regarding me as inimical to them," Dickens wrote in 1854.

In 1867–68, a new edition of Dickens's works was published. Dickens revised the text of *Oliver Twist*, making hundreds of changes, most in relation to Fagin. He eliminated the majority of the references to Fagin as "the Jew," either cutting them or replacing them with "Fagin" or "he." Nevertheless, "Fagin remains 'the Jew,'" literary critic Irving Howe commented, "and whoever wants to confront this novel honestly must confront the substratum of feeling that becomes visible through Dickens's obsessive repetition of 'the Jew.'" A critical reading of the novel can lead to a better understanding of the anti-Semitic stereotypes that were part of the popular culture of early 19th-century England. "There is nothing to 'do' [about Fagin]," wrote Howe, "but confront the historical realities of our culture, and all that it has thrown up from its unsavory depths."

In 1949, a group of Jewish parents in Brooklyn, New York, protested that the assignment of *Oliver Twist* in senior high school literature classes violated the rights of their children to receive an education free of religious bias. Citing the characterization of Fagin in *Oliver Twist* and Shylock in William Shakespeare's play *The Merchant of Venice*, they sued the New York City Board of Education. They asked that both texts be banned from New York City public schools "because they tend to engender hatred of the Jew as a person and as a race."

In *Rosenberg v. Board of Education of City of New York*, the Kings County Supreme Court decided that the two works should not be banned from New York City schools, libraries, or classrooms, declaring that the Board of Education "acted in good faith without malice or prejudice and in the best interests of the school system entrusted to their care and control, and, therefore, that no substantial reason exists which compels the suppression of the two books under consideration."

In denying the plaintiffs' bid to ban the books, the presiding judge stated, "Except where a book has been maliciously written for the apparent purpose of fomenting a bigoted and intolerant hatred against a particular racial or religious group, public interest in a free and democratic society does not warrant or encourage the suppression of any book at the whim of any unduly sensitive person or group of person, merely because a character described in such book as belonging to a particular race or religion is portrayed in a derogatory or offensive manner." Removal of the books "will contribute nothing toward the diminution of anti-religious feeling," the court said.

FURTHER READING

Dickens, Charles. *Oliver Twist*. Introduction by Irving Howe. New York: Bantam Books, 1982.

Doyle, Robert P. *Banned Books: 2004 Resource Guide*. Chicago: American Library Association, 2004.

Kaplan, Fred, ed. *Oliver Twist: A Norton Critical Edition*. New York: W. W. Norton, 1993.

Veidmanis, Gladys. "Reflections on 'the Shylock Problem.' " In *Censored Books: Critical Viewpoints*, edited by Nicholas J. Karolides, Lee Burress, and John M. Kean, 370–378. Metuchen, N.J.: Scarecrow Press, 1993.

ON THE INFINITE UNIVERSE AND WORLDS

Author: Giordano Bruno
Original date and place of publication: 1584, France
Literary form: Philosophical treatise

SUMMARY

The Italian philosopher Giordano Bruno entered the Dominican order at a young age and was expelled in 1576 at the age of 28 when he was charged with heresy. He traveled throughout Europe for 15 years, one step ahead of the censors, teaching at Toulouse, Paris, Oxford, Wittenberg, and Frankfurt. In *On the Infinite Universe and Worlds*, his major metaphysical work, published in 1584, he refuted the traditional cosmology of Aristotle and its limited conceptions of the universe. Instead, Bruno asserted that the physical universe is infinite and includes an indefinite number of worlds, each with its own sun and planets. He pictured the world as composed of individual, irreducible elements of being, called monads, governed by fixed laws of relationship.

Bruno's philosophy prefigured modern cosmic theory. He accepted Nicolaus Copernicus's hypothesis that the Sun, rather than the Earth, is the center of our world. But he went further than Copernicus in arguing that the Sun is simply one star among others. All judgments about position are relative, since there are as many possible modes of viewing the world as there are possible positions. Therefore, no one star or planet can be called the center of the universe. Human beings cannot conclude that they are unique, because the presence of life, even that of rational beings, may not be confined to Earth. There is no absolute truth, and there are no limits to the progress of knowledge.

The infinite universe is the product of a pantheistic infinite divine power or cause whose work is manifest in human beings and in all of nature. "The Divine one extols his own glory and sets forth the greatness of his sway, not in one sun, but in uncountable suns; not in one earth, but in worlds without end."

Because God's power is infinite, his creation must also be infinite. The agent would be imperfect if his works did not fulfill his power. Bruno believed that understanding of the universe as the manifestation of God would free the human spirit. "[It] opens the senses, contents the soul, enlarges the mind and brings true blessed news to man. . . . For deeply considering the Being and substance in which we are fixed, we find that there is no such thing as death, not for us alone, but for the true substance."

CENSORSHIP HISTORY

"I wish the world to possess the glorious fruits of my labor," Bruno wrote in *On the Infinite Universe and Worlds*, "to awaken the soul and open the understanding of those who are deprived of that light, which, most assuredly, is not mine own invention. Should I be in error, I do not believe I willfully go wrong."

In the view of his contemporaries, Bruno had indeed gone wrong. His assault on Aristotelian views of the universe and his construction of a "new philosophy" challenged the Scholasticism that dominated the universities. It ran counter to the beliefs held by all the ecclesiastical institutions, whether Catholic, Lutheran or Calvinist. His speculation about an endless number of celestial worlds was viewed as heretical pantheism.

In 1577, the Inquisition in Naples initiated proceedings against him, and Bruno fled Italy. In 1592, he rashly returned and, denounced by a Venetian nobleman, was delivered to the Inquisition in Venice. He was imprisoned and tried on charges of blasphemy, immoral conduct, and heresy. On May 26, 1592, the Holy Tribunal met to consider his case. Bruno told the judges: "I have ever expounded philosophically and according to the principles of Nature and by its light . . . although I may have set forth much suspicious matter occasioned by my own natural light . . . never have I taught anything directly contrary to the Catholic religion. . . ." When asked whether he believed that the Father, Son, and Holy Spirit were one in essence but distinct persons, he admitted "I have never been able to grasp the three being really Persons and have doubted it. . . ." Bruno offered to submit to all church doctrines, but he refused to abjure his philosophy.

Bruno remained in prison for months awaiting the decision of the Venetian Inquisition. Because he was regarded as a "heresiarch," an originator and leader of heresy, the chief inquisitor at the Holy Office in Rome demanded that he be delivered there for trial. He was extradicted to Rome and on February 27, 1593, was imprisoned for seven years. He was allowed neither books nor writing material, and his only visitors were officials of the Inquisition and priests sent to urge him to repent. In 1559, several cardinals interrogated him regarding heresies extracted from his books. At a final interrogation he declared he would recant nothing. In January 1660, at a meeting presided over by the pope, it was decreed that he would be burned at the stake for "many various heretical and unsound opinions." He was executed in Rome on February 17, 1600.

On August 7, 1603, all of Bruno's writings were placed on the Index of Forbidden Books, where they remained through the last edition of the Index, in effect until 1966. Robert Cardinal Bellarmino, who had overseen Bruno's trial and punishment, was declared a saint by the Catholic Church in 1930. Bruno's works had never been popular in England or on the Continent and were scarce in Catholic countries because of their suppression. John Toland, the 17th-century English deist and author of *Christianity Not Mysterious*, recognized Bruno as a forerunner of the freethinkers of his own era; Toland translated part of *On the Infinite Universe and Worlds* and wrote an account of the book. Bruno's philosophy also had an important influence on the philosophers Baruch Spinoza and Gottfried Wilhelm Leibniz.

In 2000, on the 400th anniversary of the execution of Bruno, the Vatican's secretary of state, Angelo Cardinal Sodano, said that his death was "a sad episode of modern Christian history" but that his writing was "incompatible" with Christian thinking and that he therefore remains a heretic.

FURTHER READING

Boulting, William. *Giordano Bruno: His Life, Thought and Martyrdom.* New York: Books for Libraries Press, 1972.

Copleston, Frederick. *A History of Philosophy.* Vol. 3: *Late Medieval and Renaissance Philosophy.* New York: Doubleday, 1993.

George, Leonard. *Crimes of Perception: An Encyclopedia of Heresies and Heretics.* New York: Paragon House, 1995.

Green, Jonathon, and Nicholas J. Karolides, reviser. *The Encyclopedia of Censorship, New Edition.* New York: Facts On File, 2005.

Jaspers, Karl. *The Great Philosophers.* Vol. 3. New York: Harcourt Brace, 1993.

Levy, Leonard W. *Blasphemy: Verbal Offense Against the Sacred, from Moses to Salman Rushdie.* New York: Alfred A. Knopf, 1993.

ON THE ORIGIN OF SPECIES

Author: Charles Darwin
Original date and place of publication: 1859, United Kingdom
Literary form: Scientific text

SUMMARY

The British naturalist Charles Darwin published his groundbreaking work, *On the Origin of Species*, 22 years after he initially wrote it, in response to competition from other scientists who were preparing to publish similar ideas. In this book, Darwin outlines the observations he made while sailing around South America on the HMS *Beagle* from 1831 to 1836.

Darwin believed in "descent with modification," that generations of organisms changed over time, and those that best withstood climatic and other changes were most likely to survive and multiply. Darwin stated that these changes occurred through natural selection, controlled by the organisms themselves, over millions of years. *On the Origin of Species* discussed these broad concepts through specific examples of evolution in pigeons and ants, as well as in discussion of embryology and morphology. Though his theory was based on careful measurements and observations, Darwin understood that it would be seen as radically at odds with prevailing ideas about the design of nature. Attempting to head off criticism, Darwin acknowledged that "nothing at first may be more difficult to believe than that the more complex organs and instincts should have been perfected . . . by the accumulation of innumerable slight variations, each good for the individual possessor."

Most readers of Darwin's book had been taught that God created the world according to an orderly plan, placing humans on Earth with dominion over nature. Darwin's ideas provided much less certainty than traditional, biblical-based explanations of nature. Popular impressions of Darwinism, however, differed from Darwin's actual writings. Social scientists summed up his concept of descent with modification through natural selection as "survival of the fittest" and used this term to explain relations between social classes. To so-called Social Darwinists, wealthier, more powerful people deserved to hold on to their advantages because they were the "fittest" human beings. Under Social Darwinism, any aid to the disadvantaged became an unnatural act, needlessly prolonging the lives and traits of the "unfit." Social Darwinists shortened Darwin's ideas by using the term *evolution* and added a belief that evolution always resulted in progress.

Darwin never intended this linear approach to the study of nature. He was most interested in the mutations that occurred over generations of organisms, whether the mutations resulted in progress or not. Further, Darwin never wished to explore his theories in the realm of human behavior and social organization. When he discussed his ideas in relation to humans, he focused on the development of organs and systems in the body, not in society.

Darwin was part of a movement in science toward reliance on empirical data. He was a contemporary of scientists such as John William Draper, author of *History of the Conflict between Religion and Science*, who questioned religious-based models for scientific observation. While Darwin was careful not to attack religion directly, as Draper did, his quiet, measured arguments did not include any mention of a divine power ordering the universe.

CENSORSHIP HISTORY

Historians of science believe that one of the reasons Darwin delayed publishing his work for so long was his fear that his ideas were too radical for the time and would be greeted with hostility. In 1844, he wrote to a friend that to publish his thoughts on evolution woud be akin to "confessing a murder." Seeing himself as a scientist, he refused to comment on the wider importance of his ideas. Near the end of his life, after publishing several other works in which he affirmed his belief in natural selection, he continued to think only in terms of advancing science and hoped that his quiet example would win people to his ideas.

On the Origin of Species by means of Natural Selection, or the Preservation of Favoured Races in the Struggle for Life was published on November 24, 1859, in an edition of only 1,250 copies by the reluctant John Murray, who did not anticipate much interest in the book. The first edition was sold out on the day of publication and a second edition of 3,000 copies soon after. The book appeared in six editions through 1872. An American edition appeared in May 1860 and was greeted with widespread controversy.

"Sixteen thousand copies have now (1876) been sold in England," Darwin wrote in his autobiography, "and considering how stiff a book it is, it is a large sale. It has been translated into almost every European tongue." He counted more than 265 reviews and numerous essays. Darwin's ideas gained wide currency in academic scientific circles almost immediately and became the foundations of modern evolution theory.

However, the publication of *On the Origin of Species* also unleashed one of the most dramatic controversies of the Victorian era. Darwin was accused of "dethroning God," as one critic put it, by challenging the literal interpretation of the Book of Genesis. Clergy railed against him from pulpits all over Britain. His book was barred from Trinity College at Cambridge, even though Darwin was a graduate. Darwin, referring to occasions when he was "contemptuously criticised," declared that "I could not employ my life better than in adding a little to natural science. This I have done to the best of my abilities, and critics may say what they like, but they cannot destroy this conviction."

Unlike *Zoonomia*, a scientific treatise written by Darwin's grandfather, Erasmus Darwin, in the late 18th century, which was banned by the Catholic Church because it expressed a theory of evolution, *On the Origin of Species* was never placed on the Roman Index of Forbidden Books.

A resurgence of opposition to Darwinism began in the 1920s in the United States. By the early 20th century, American high school science textbooks had begun to incorporate Darwinian evolution in discussing human origins and biology. In 1919, the World Christian Fundamentals Association (WCFA) was founded to oppose teaching of evolution in American public schools. Local school boards and state boards of education in areas with large fundamentalist Christian populations were pressured to reject the new textbooks and legislatures around the country were lobbied to pass antievolution resolutions. More than 20 state legislatures considered such measures.

In 1925, in the most famous example of antievolutionary sentiment, Tennessee passed a law prohibiting teachers from teaching the theory of evolution in state-supported schools. A combination of factors compelled the Tennessee state legislature to pass such a sweeping measure. The 1920s were an era of pleasure-seeking in popular culture, especially among teenagers; at the same time, fundamentalist religion and nativism were on the increase as a reaction to these "modern" ideas. Fundamentalist Christians feared that a materialistic philosophy such as natural selection would send a damaging, nihilistic message to schoolchildren. They believed that schools would produce more orderly students if they taught the biblical account of Creation, with a God designing nature according to a set plan. Local leaders in the small town of Dayton, Tennessee, welcomed the chance to put their town on the map in the context of this battle.

John T. Scopes, a science teacher in Dayton, volunteered to be the test case for Tennessee's antievolution law. Representing the state was William Jennings Bryan, a populist leader and three-time Democratic presidential candidate who had served as Woodrow Wilson's secretary of state and was popular among fundamentalists for his biblically inspired rhetoric and his devotion to maintaining traditional, rural ways of life. Clarence Darrow, a noted defense lawyer and avowed agnostic, defended Scopes, arguing that academic freedom was being violated and that the legislation violated the separation of church and state. Members of the American Civil Liberties Union (ACLU), at that time a new organization devoted to defending free speech, also contributed to Scopes's side.

The Scopes "monkey trial," as it became known, was an event of national importance during the summer of 1925. Newspapers from around the country sent correspondents to Dayton to cover the proceedings, and Dayton merchants sold souvenirs of the trial, including stuffed monkeys to represent the idea that Darwin claimed humans were descended from apes. Reporters from big-city newspapers reported on the trial with amusement, while fundamentalist observers saw the proceedings as a crucial battle against the forces of modernism.

Both sides claimed victory. Scopes was found guilty of violating Tennessee's statute prohibiting the teaching of evolution. As a state employee, the judge ruled, Scopes could not disobey state laws. His backers were also pleased, as the decision gave them the chance to appeal the matter to a higher court, where the case for evolution and freedom of expression could get even more publicity. The Scopes case, however, was thrown out on a technicality. In the original case the judge, rather than the jury, had fined Scopes $100. This procedural error reversed the verdict that found Scopes guilty.

Antievolution efforts did not end with the conclusion of the Scopes trial. The Tennessee antievolution law remained on the books until 1967, and grass-roots fundamentalists in the United States launched efforts to remove Darwin's ideas from public school textbooks. In 1968, the U.S. Supreme Court considered a case similar to Scopes's. Susan Epperson, a high school biology teacher, challenged the constitutionality of the Arkansas Anti-Evolution Statute of 1928, which provided that teachers who used a textbook that included Darwin's theory of evolution could lose their jobs. The Supreme Court ruled that the law was unconstitutional and conflicted with the First and Fourteenth Amendments. Government power could not be used to advance religious beliefs.

Having been defeated in the courts, antievolutionists shifted their focus to requiring instruction in "creationism" as an alternative to evolutionary theories. They defined creationism as the theory that all life forms came into existence instantaneously through the action of a single intelligent creator. In the early 1980s, Arkansas and Louisiana state boards of education required the teaching of both creationism and evolution in public schools. These laws were ruled unconstitutional in 1987 by the U.S. Supreme Court in *Edwards v. Aguillard* as advocating a religious doctrine and violating the establishment clause of the First Amendment. However, battles about the teaching of evolution still rage on, especially at the local school board level.

In 2002, the Cobb County, Georgia, school system decided to place stickers in science textbooks that said "evolution is a theory not a fact" and should be "approached with an open mind, studied carefully and critically considered." The stickers were added after more than 2,000 parents complained that the textbooks presented evolution as fact, without mentioning rival ideas about the beginnings of life, such as the biblical story of the Creation.

Five parents sued the school district, claiming that the stickers were unconstitutional. In January 2005, a federal judge in Atlanta ordered the schools to remove them, as they send "a message that the school board agrees with the beliefs of Christian fundamentalists and creationists," "convey a message of endorsement of religion," and violate the First Amendment's separation of church and state, as well as the Georgia Constitution's prohibition against using public money to aid religion.

The case was only one of many battles waged around the country since 2000 over the teaching of evolution in science classes. In 2004, Georgia's education chief proposed a science curriculum that substituted "changes over time" for the word "evolution." The idea was dropped after teachers protested. The same year, a school district in Dover, Pennsylvania, became the first in the nation to mandate that science students be told about "intelligent design," the concept that the universe is so complex that it must have been created by a higher power. Teachers were to read students a brief statement introducing intelligent design in ninth-grade biology class and referred students for more information to an intelligent design textbook, *Of Pandas and People.* The ACLU of Pennsylvania and 11 parents filed suits in federal court, saying that teaching intelligent design in public school classrooms violated their religious liberty by promoting particular religious beliefs.

In December 2005, after a six-week trial in federal district court in Harrisburg, Pennsylvania, U.S. District Judge John E. Jones III ruled that it was unconstitutional for the school district to present intelligent design as an alternative to evolution in high school biology courses. He declared that intelligent design is "a religious alternative masquerading as a scientific theory" and that evidence at the trial proved that it was "creationism relabeled." "We find that the secular purposes claimed by the Board amount to a pretext for the Board's real purpose, which was to promote religion in the public school classroom in violation of the establishment clause," Jones wrote in his ruling. The ruling was unlikely to be appealed by the school board, because the board members who supported intelligent design were unseated in elections in November 2005 and replaced by a slate that opposed intelligent design.

In the first seven months of 2005 alone, 17 pieces of antievolution legislation were introduced in 12 states, according to the National Center for Science Education in Oakland, California, a group that advocates teaching evolution in public schools. Most of the bills were efforts to limit teaching of evolution and include alternate theories in science classes.

In November 2005, a creationist majority on the Kansas Board of Education voted to include criticism of evolution in the school science standards used to develop statewide tests in the fourth, seventh, and 10th grades. The most significant change was in the definition of science. Instead of "seeking natural explanations for what we observe around us," the new standards describe it as a "continuing investigation that uses observation, hypothesis testing, measurement, experimentation, logical argument, and theory building to lead to more adequate explanations of natural phenomena."

Board member Kathy Martin, who supported the new standards, told the *Kansas City Star* that she hoped the changes would encourage teachers and students to look at "all the scientific research and data and evidence and whether it supports or refutes evolution because evolution is not a sacred cow." The majority of the 26-member committee that had originally drafted the standards objected to the changes made by the Board of Education. The changes include "intelligent design–inspired language," the committee wrote in a reply to the board, and "intelligent design has no scientific basis."

In 2006, the makeup of the Kansas Board of Education shifted to a pro-science majority, and new standards were approved that ended the requirement to include antievolution concepts.

In August 2009, the National Center for Science Education reported that there was currently no explicit requirement in any of the states' science standards that creationism be taught or evolution not be taught. However, creationists and proponents of intelligent design have reduced their advocacy of state-level legislation and policies that explicitly endorse creationist claims or attack evolution. Having been struck down by the courts, "blanket bans of evolution and policies requiring 'balanced treatment' of evolution and creationism have given way to more innocuous language," the center reported, "such as 'teaching the controversy,' 'critical analysis,' 'strength and weaknesses,' 'academic freedom,' and 'discussing the full range of scientific views.' " Creationists are using such language to justify the use of teaching material that casts doubt on the theory of evolution.

In 2009, the Texas Board of Education approved a science curriculum that opened the door for teachers and textbooks to present creationists' claims. Although the board voted to remove a long-standing requirement that students analyze the "strengths and weaknesses" of evolutionary theory, it approved standards requiring students to analyze and evaluate the completeness of the fossil record and the complexity of the cell. Social conservatives on the board, the *Wall Street Journal* reported, "have made clear that they expect books to address those topics by raising questions about the validity of evolutionary theory." As Texas represents the largest single publishing market for high school textbooks, scientists and educators said that they feared the decision in Texas would have deleterious effects on the teaching of science in other states.

Living Waters, an antievolution evangelical group, announced plans in October 2009 to distribute on American university campuses 175,000 copies of a special edition of *On the Origin of Species* with an introduction promoting creationism. The group's fund-raising materials said that the introduction "gives a timeline of Darwin's life, and his thoughts on the existence of God. It lists the theories of many hoaxes, exposes the unscientific belief that nothing created everything, points to the incredible structure of DNA, and notes the absence of any undisputed transitional forms. To show the dangerous fruit of evolution, it also mentions Hitler's undeniable connections to the theory, Darwin's racism, and his disdain for women. In addition, it counters the claim that creationists are 'anti-science' by citing numerous scientists who believed that God created the universe."

It was reported in March 2005 that the controversy over evolution had gone beyond the schools to affect Imax theaters. Some dozen theaters, particularly in the South, including some in science museums, had refused to show movies that mention evolution, the big bang, or the geology of Earth, as they feared protests from people who believe that evolution contradicts the Bible. Because only a few dozen Imax theaters routinely show science documentaries, barring such films from even a few cinemas could affect a film's bottom line and ultimately a producer's decision in the future to make similar documentaries.

Opponents of evolution have made significant inroads among the American public. In 2004, a national Gallup poll found that only 35 percent of those asked were confident that Darwin's theory was "supported by evidence," and 37 percent of those polled by CBS News said creationism should be taught in schools instead of evolution.

On the 200th anniversary of Darwin's birth in 2009, a Gallup poll found that only 39 percent of Americans said they "believe in the theory of evolution." A quarter said that they did not believe in the theory, and 36 percent had no opinion.

There have been some reports from abroad of censorship of *On the Origin of Species* in the 20th century. In 1935, it was prohibited in Yugoslavia, and in 1937 it was banned under the right-wing Metaxas regime in Greece. In Malaysia, in 2006, an Indonesian translation of *On the Origin of Species* was among 56 books banned by the Internal Security Ministry. But unlike other cases of book censorship, the book was generally not removed from bookstore or library shelves in the United States. It was, rather, the ideas expressed in the book that were censored.

—with Jonathan Pollack

FURTHER READING

Alter, Alexandra. "Decades after the 'Monkey Trial,' Creationists Turn to Science." *Miami Herald* (August 15, 2005). Available online. URL: http://www.centredaily.com/mid/centredaily/news/12424164.htm.

"Anti-Evolution Teachings Gain in U.S. Schools." *Newsletter on Intellectual Freedom* 54, no. 1 (January 2005).

Boorstein, Daniel J. *The Discoverers: A History of Man's Search to Know His World and Himself.* New York: Random House, 1983.

Carroll, Diane. "Evolution Issue Again Gets Look from Board." *Kansas City Star* (August 9, 2005). Available online. URL: http://www.kansascity.com/mld/kansas city/news/local/12336247.htm.

DelFattore, Joan. *What Johnny Shouldn't Read: Textbook Censors in America.* New Haven, Conn.: Yale University Press, 1992.

Demac, Donna A. *Liberty Denied: The Current Rise of Censorship in America.* New York: PEN American Center, 1988.

Goodstein, Laurie. "Judge Rejects Teaching Intelligent Design." *New York Times* (December 21, 2005). Available online. URL: http://www.nytimes.com. Accessed December 27, 2005.

Gould, Stephen Jay. *Ever Since Darwin: Reflections on Natural History.* New York: W. W. Norton, 1977.

Hart, Ariel. "Judge in Georgia Orders Anti-Evolution Stickers Removed from Textbooks." *New York Times* (January 14, 2005). Available online. URL: http://www. nytimes.com. Accessed January 14, 2005.

Jaschik, Scott. "Darwin, From the Creationists." *Inside Higher Ed* (October 7, 2009). Available online. URL: http://www.insidehighered.com/news/2009/10/07/darwin. Accessed June 6, 2010.

Larson, Edward J. *Trial and Error: The American Controversy over Creation and Evolution.* New York: Oxford University Press, 1985.

Mead, Louise S., and Anton Mates. "Why Science Standards Are Important to a Strong Science Curriculum and How States Measure Up." National Center for Science Education (August 7, 2009). Available online. URL: http://springerlink. com/content/9u0610162rn51432/fulltext.html. Accessed June 6, 2010.

Newport, Frank. "On Darwin's Birthday, Only 4 in 10 Believe in Evolution." *Gallup Daily News* (February 11, 2009). Available online. URL: http://www.gallup.com/ poll/114544/darwin-birthday-believe-evolution.aspx. Accessed June 6, 2010.

Numbers, Ronald L., ed. *Creation-Evolution Debates.* New York: Garland, 1955.

Raffaele, Martha. "Controversial Step Taken in Rural Pennsylvania District." Associated Press (November 12, 2004).

Rogers, Donald J. *Banned! Book Censorship in the Schools.* New York: Julian Messner, 1988.

Simon, Stephanie. "Texas Opens Door for Evolution Doubts." *Wall Street Journal* (March 28, 2009). Available online. URL: http://www.wsj.com/article/ SB123819751472561761.html. Accessed June 6, 2010.

Southeast Asian Press Alliance/International Freedom of Expression eXchange. "Authorities Ban Films, Books, Television Talk Show; Film Director Appeals Ban" (March 1, 2007). URL: Available online: http://www.ifex.org/malaysia/2007/03/01/ authorities_ban_films_books_television/. Accessed June 6, 2010.

THE SATANIC VERSES

Author: Salman Rushdie
Original dates and places of publication: 1988, United Kingdom; 1989, United States
Original publishers: Penguin Books; Viking Penguin
Literary form: Fiction

SUMMARY

The Satanic Verses, by the Indian-born British author Salman Rushdie, holds a unique place in the history of literary censorship. In 1989, Iran's leader, Ayatollah Ruhollah Khomeini, condemned the book for blasphemy against Islam and issued an edict calling for its author's execution. The death threat drove Rushdie into hiding, and the furor over the novel escalated to become an unprecedented event of global dimensions.

Rushdie's complex and challenging novel is a surreal and riotously inventive mixture of realism and fantasy. In a cycle of three interconnected tales set in present-day London and Bombay, an Indian village, and seventh-century Arabia, it explores themes of migration and dislocation, the nature of good and evil, doubt and loss of religious faith. "It is a migrant's-eye view of the world," Rushdie explained, commenting on the intentions of his novel. "It is written from the experience of uprooting, disjuncture and metamorphosis (slow or rapid, painful or pleasurable) that is the migrant condition, and from which, I believe, can be derived a metaphor for all humanity."

The novel opens at 29,000 feet in the air as two men fall toward the sea from a hijacked jumbo jet that has blown up over the English Channel. The two—both Indian actors—mysteriously survive the explosion and wash up on an English beach. Gibreel Farishta, formerly Ismail Najmuddin, is a legendary star of Indian movies; Saladin Chamcha, formerly Salahuddin Chamchawala, is an urbane Anglophile who makes a successful living in London doing voiceovers for television commercials.

As Rushdie describes his protagonists, "*The Satanic Verses* is the story of two painfully divided selves. In the case of one, Saladin Chamcha, the division is secular and societal; he is torn, to put it plainly, between Bombay and London, between East and West. For the other, Gibreel Farishta, the division is spiritual, a rift in the soul. He has lost his faith and is strung out between his immense need to believe and his new inability to do so. The novel is 'about' their quest for wholeness."

To their surprise and puzzlement, Gibreel and Saladin find after their fall from the sky that they have undergone a metamorphosis, acquiring characteristics alien to their own personalities. Gibreel, the womanizer, develops a halo, assuming the appearance of the archangel Gibreel (Gabriel), while the mild and proper Saladin grows horns, hooves, and a tail in the image of Satan. The fantastic adventures in England and India of these two walking symbols of good and evil form the central thread of the narrative.

The second tale, told in alternating chapters, evokes the historical origins of Islam in narratives dealing with the nature and consequences of revelation and belief. It takes place in the dreams of Gibreel Farishta, in which he becomes the archangel Gibreel, and in a film based on his imaginings in which he plays the role of the archangel. The dream-film sequences, which parallel the story of the prophet Muhammad in Mecca, tell the story of Mahound. He is a businessman turned prophet of Jahilia, the city of sand, who receives divine revelation through the intercession of the angel Gibreel and founds a religion called Submission (the literal English translation of the Arabic word *Islam*).

In the third tale, also dreamed up by Farishta, a charismatic holy woman cloaked in butterflies leads the faithful of a Muslim village in India on a pilgrimage to Mecca. As they walk toward Mecca, they perish when the waters of the Arabian Sea do not part for them as expected.

The parts of the novel recounting Gibreel's painful visions, set in Mahound's city of Jahilia, are the primary focus of the controversy about the book. They allude to a legendary episode in the Prophet's life in which Muhammad added verses to the Koran that elevated to angelic status three goddesses worshipped by the polytheistic citizens of Mecca. Later, Muhammad revoked these verses, realizing that they had been transmitted to him not by Allah but by Satan posing as the angel Gabriel.

In contrast to the version of the incident recounted in Islamic history, Gibreel in his dream says that he was forced to speak the verses by "the overwhelming need of the Prophet Mahound," implying that Mahound, rather than Satan, put the false verses into Gibreel's mouth for opportunistic reasons. "From my mouth," Gibreel says, "both the statement and the repudiation, verses and converses, universes and reverses, the whole thing, and we all know how my mouth got worked."

In another dream passage alluding to an incident drawn from Islamic historical accounts, a scribe called Salman alters the text of the book dictated to him by Mahound. "Mahound did not notice the alterations," the scribe says, "so there I was, actually writing the Book, or re-writing anyway, polluting the word of God with my own profane language. But, good heavens, if my poor words could not be distinguished from the Revelation by God's own Messenger, then what did that mean?" Salman notices that the angel Gibreel's revelations to Mahound are particularly well timed, "so that when the faithful were disputing Mahound's views on any subject, from the possibility of space travel to the permanence of Hell, the angel would turn up with an answer, and he always supported Mahound."

Another provocative episode from Gibreel's dreams is a cinematic fantasy about a brothel in Jahilia called The Curtain (a translation of the Arabic word *hijab*, the Muslim women's veil), where business booms after 12 prostitutes assume the names and personalities of Mahound's 12 wives. A line of men awaiting their turns circles the innermost courtyard of the brothel, "rotating around its centrally positioned Fountain of Love much as pilgrims rotated for other reasons around the ancient Black Stone."

Hearing the news of the prostitutes' assumed identities, "the clandestine excitement of the city's males was intense; yet so afraid were they of discovery, both because they would surely lose their lives if Mahound or his lieutenants ever found out that they had been involved in such irreverences, and because of their sheer desire that the new service at The Curtain be maintained, that the secret was kept from the authorities."

Rushdie prefaces the story of the brothel with a statement that proved to be prescient in view of the events that engulfed his novel: "Where there is no belief, there is no blasphemy." Only because the men of Jahilia had accepted the tenets of their new faith could they find illicit pleasure in patronizing a brothel serviced by prostitutes impersonating the wives of the Prophet.

As the novel ends, Saladin Chamcha has become reintegrated into Indian society. He has completed a process of renewal and regeneration in his embrace of love and death and his return to his roots in India. Gibreel Farishta, tormented by his epic dreams and visions of doubt and skepticism, has lost his faith and failed to replace it by earthly love. Unable to escape his inner demons, he is driven mad and commits suicide.

CENSORSHIP HISTORY

The Satanic Verses was published in the United Kingdom on September 26, 1988. Rushdie's eagerly awaited fourth novel received laudatory reviews in the British press. It was hailed as "a masterpiece," "truly original" and "an exhilarating . . . extraordinary contemporary novel . . . a roller coaster ride over a vast landscape of the imagination."

Even before its publication, however, the controversy about the novel had already begun. Syed Shahabuddin and Khurshid Alam Khan, two Muslim opposition members of India's Parliament, alerted to the book's content by articles in Indian publications, launched a campaign to have it banned.

"Civilization is nothing but voluntary acceptance of restraints," Shahabuddin wrote in defense of censorship. "You may hold whatever private opinions you like but you do not enjoy an absolute right to express them in public." Expressing a view that was echoed by many opponents of the book as the controversy continued, Shahabuddin admitted that he had not read *The Satanic Verses* and did not intend to. "I do not have to wade through a filthy drain to know what filth is," he declared.

India's government, fearing civil disorder among the country's Muslim population, was the first to censor the book. On October 5, 1988, only nine days after its publication in Britain, the importation of the British edition was prohibited under a ruling of the Indian Customs Act. Muslims in India contacted Islamic organizations in Britain, urging them to take up the protest campaign. Two London publications sponsored by the Saudi Arabian government prominently featured stories denouncing the novel. At his home in London, Rushdie began to receive death threats.

The U.K. Action Committee on Islamic Affairs released a statement demanding withdrawal and destruction of the book, an apology, and payment of damages to an Islamic charity. "The work, thinly disguised as a piece of literature," the statement read, "not only greatly distorts Islamic history in general, but also portrays in the worst possible colours the very characters of the Prophet Ibrahim and the Prophet Mohamed (peace upon them). It also disfigures the characters of the Prophet's companions . . . and the Prophet's holy wives and describes the Islamic creed and rituals in the most foul language."

The British-based Union of Muslim Organisations called for Rushdie's prosecution under rarely enforced British laws prohibiting blasphemy against the doctrines of the Church of England. The British government declined to consider expansion of the laws to include transgressions against the Islamic faith. On November 11, Prime Minister Margaret Thatcher announced that "there are no grounds on which the government could consider banning the book." On November 21, the grand sheik of Egypt's Al-Azhar, the mosque and university that is considered the seat of Islamic authority, called on all Islamic organizations in Britain to join in taking legal steps to prevent the book's distribution.

In the United States, where the novel had not yet appeared, its publisher, Viking Penguin, received bomb threats and thousands of menacing letters. On November 24, 1988, *The Satanic Verses* was banned in South Africa, even though it had not yet been published there. A planned visit by Rushdie was canceled when its sponsors feared that his safety could not be guaranteed. Within weeks, the book was also banned in several countries with predominantly Muslim populations: Pakistan, Saudi Arabia, Egypt, Somalia, Bangladesh, Sudan, Malaysia, Indonesia, and Qatar.

In November 1988 in England, *The Satanic Verses* received the Whitbread literary prize for best novel. In December and again in January 1989, Muslims in Bolton, near Manchester, and in Bradford, Yorkshire, held public book burnings. A large group of demonstrators marched in London to protest the book. The Islamic Defence Council in Britain presented a petition to Penguin Books, demanding that the publisher apologize to the world Muslim community, withdraw the book, pulp the remaining copies, and refrain from printing future editions.

The petition listed as insulting to Muslims the fact that Abraham was referred to in the books as "the bastard"; that the prophet Muhammad was given the archaic medieval name of Mahound, meaning "devil" or "false prophet"; that the text states that revelations the Prophet received were well timed to suit him when "the faithful were disputing"; that the Prophet's companions were described in derogatory terms and the namesakes of his wives were depicted as prostitutes; and that the Islamic holy city of Mecca was portrayed as Jahilia, meaning "ignorance" or "darkness."

Penguin Books refused to comply with the petitioners' demands. On January 22, 1989, Rushdie published a statement in defense of his novel. *The Satanic Verses* is not an antireligious novel, he said. "It is, however, an attempt to write about migration, its stresses and transformations, from the point of view of migrants from the Indian subcontinent to Britain. This is for me, the saddest irony of all; that after working for five years to give voice and fictional flesh to the immigrant culture of which I am myself a member, I should see my book burned, largely unread, by the people it's about, people who might find some pleasure and much recognition in its pages."

Rushdie's repeated efforts throughout the controversy to clarify the intentions and meaning of his book had little impact on the fervent opposition to it. Few of those who protested against the book had read it, and for many, the very title of the novel, which seemed to imply that the Koranic verses were written by the devil, was sacrilegious and sufficient to condemn it.

It is never stated within Gibreel Farishta's dreams that Satan wrote the sacred book. However, the passages in which Gibreel claims to have received the verses directly from Mahound, rather than from God, imply that the book was written without divine intervention. Attributing the *koran* (Qur'an) to human composition is considered blasphemous in Muslim belief.

Rushdie explained that Gibreel's blasphemous visions were intended to dramatize the struggle between faith and doubt, rather than to insult the Muslim religion. "Gibreel's most painful dreams, the ones at the center of the controversy," Rushdie wrote, "depict the birth and growth of a religion something like Islam, in a magical city of sand named Jahilia (that is 'ignorance,' the name given by Arabs to the period before Islam). Almost all of the alleged 'insults and abuse' are taken from these dream sequences. The first thing to be said about these dreams is that they are *agonizingly painful to the dreamer.* They are a 'nocturnal retribution, a punishment' for his loss of faith. . . . The first purpose of these sequences is not to vilify or 'disprove' Islam, but to portray a soul in crisis, to show how the loss of God can destroy a man's life."

The novel's would-be censors frequently cited the tale of the brothel as particularly offensive to Muslims. Rushdie pointed to a distinction often ignored by his critics, that the prostitutes only take the names of the Prophet's wives. The real wives are "living chastely in their harem." "The purpose of the 'brothel sequence,' then," Rushdie explained, "was not to 'insult and abuse' the Prophet's wives, but to dramatize certain ideas about morality; and sexuality, too, because what happens in the brothel . . . is that the men of 'Jahilia' are enabled to act out an ancient dream of power and possession. . . . That men should be so aroused by the great ladies' whorish counterfeits says something about *them*, not the great ladies, and about the extent to which sexual relations have to do with possession."

Critics also noted Rushdie's use of the name "Mahound," the Satanic figure of medieval Christian mystery plays, for the Muhammad-like character in the novel, as evidence of his invidious intentions. Rushdie described his choice of the name as an example of how his novel "tries in all sorts of ways to reoccupy negative images, to repossess pejorative language." "Even leaving aside the obvious fact that my Mahound is a dream-prophet and not the historical Muhammad," Rushdie wrote, "it may be noted that on page 93 of the novel there is this passage: 'Here he is neither Mahomet nor Moehammered; has adopted, instead, the demon tag the farangis hung around his neck. To turn insults into strengths, whigs, tories, blacks all chose to wear with pride the names that were given in scorn. . . .'"

Rushdie's view that "there are no subjects that are off limits and that includes God, includes prophets" was clearly not shared by those who urged banning of the novel. "The use of fiction was a way of creating the sort of distance from actuality that I felt would prevent offence from being taken," Rushdie declared. "I was wrong."

On February 12, 1989, during violent demonstrations against the book in Islamabad, Pakistan, six people died and 100 were injured. The next day in Srinigar, India, rioting led to the death of another person and the injury of 60. On February 14, Iran's leader, Ayatollah Ruhollah Khomeini, issued a fatwa, or religious edict, against the book.

Khomeini's edict stated: "I inform all zealous Muslims of the world that the author of the book entitled *The Satanic Verses*—which has been compiled, printed, and published in opposition to Islam, the Prophet, and the Qur'an— and all those involved in its publication who were aware of its contents, are sentenced to death. I call on all zealous Muslims to execute them quickly, wherever they find them, so that no one else will dare to insult the Islamic sanctities. God willing, whoever is killed on this path is a martyr. In addition, anyone who has access to the author of this book, but does not possess the power to execute him, should report him to the people so that he may be punished for his actions."

The 15 Khordad Foundation, an Iranian charity, offered a reward for Rushdie's murder: $1 million if the assassin were non-Iranian and 200 million rials (approximately $750,000) for an Iranian. The reward was later raised by the foundation to $2.5 million. During the days following Khomeini's edict, several Middle East terrorist organizations sponsored by the Iranian government publicly declared their determination to execute Rushdie. Demonstrations were held outside the British embassy in Tehran, and all books published by Viking Penguin were banned from Iran.

On February 16, Rushdie went into hiding under protection of the British government. Two days later, he issued a public statement regretting that some Muslims might have been offended by his book. "As author of *The Satanic Verses*," he said, "I recognize that Muslims in many parts of the world are genuinely distressed by the publication of my novel. I profoundly regret the distress that the publication has occasioned to sincere followers of Islam. Living as we do in a world of many faiths, this experience has served to remind us that we must all be conscious of the sensibilities of others." Khomeini responded with a statement refusing the apology and confirming the death sentence. "Even if Salman Rushdie repents and becomes the most pious man of [our] time," he declared, "it is incumbent on every Muslim to employ everything he has, his life and his wealth, to send him to hell."

On February 22, *The Satanic Verses* was published in the United States. Hundreds of threats against booksellers prompted two major bookstore chains temporarily to remove the book from a third of the nation's bookstores. On February 28, two independently owned bookstores in Berkeley, California, were firebombed.

Violent demonstrations continued to occur in India, Pakistan, and Bangladesh during the month after Khomeini's edict. On February 24, 12 people died during rioting in Bombay. Nonviolent protests against the book also took place in Sudan, Turkey, Malaysia, the Philippines, Hong Kong, and Japan. On March 7, Britain broke off diplomatic relations with Iran. Later that month, two moderate Muslim religious leaders in Belgium who had publicly expressed opposition to the death sentence against Rushdie were shot dead in Brussels.

In mid-March, the Organization of the Islamic Conference, while it refused to endorse the death threat, voted to call on its 46 member governments to prohibit the book. Most countries with large Muslim populations banned the sale or importation of *The Satanic Verses*. The Revolutionary Government of Zanzibar, for example, threatened a sentence of three years in prison and a fine of $2,500 for possession of the book. In Malaysia, the penalty was set at three years in prison and a fine of $7,400. In Indonesia, possession of the book was punishable by a month in prison or a fine. Turkey was the only country with a predominantly Muslim population where it remained legal. Several countries with Muslim minorities, including Bulgaria, Papua New Guinea, Thailand, Sri Lanka, Kenya, Tanzania, and Liberia, also imposed bans.

In some cases, countries with negligible Muslim populations took steps to suppress the book. In Venezuela, owning or reading it was declared a crime under penalty of 15 months' imprisonment. In Japan, the sale of the English-language edition was banned under threat of fines. The government of Poland also restricted its distribution. Many countries banned the circulation of issues of magazines, such as *Time*, *Newsweek*, *Asiaweek*, and *Far Eastern Economic Review*, that had published articles about the controversy.

Despite the bannings, the book was imported and circulated clandestinely in countries where it was forbidden, such as Kuwait, Senegal, Egypt, India, and even Iran, where a few copies were smuggled in and passed from hand to hand. As a result of its notoriety, *The Satanic Verses* became a best seller in Europe and the United States. By the end of 1989, more than 1.1 million copies of hardcover English-language editions had been sold.

On June 3, 1989, the Ayatollah Khomeini died. The edict against Rushdie, however, remained in force, reaffirmed by Iranian government officials. Acts of terrorism related to protests against the book continued to occur. During 1990, five bombings targeted booksellers in England. In July 1991, in separate incidents, Hitoshi Igarashi, the Japanese translator of *The Satanic Verses*, was stabbed to death, and its Italian translator, Ettore Capriolo, was seriously wounded. In July 1993, Turkish publisher Aziz Nesin, who had printed translated excerpts from the novel in a newspaper, was attacked by Islamist rioters in the city of Sivas. They cornered him in a hotel and set it on fire, killing 37 people, but Nesin escaped. In October 1993, William Nygaard, its Norwegian publisher, was shot and seriously injured.

For a total of nine years, Rushdie was in hiding in 30 safe houses in Britain under Scotland Yard's protection. In 1998, the Iranian government, headed by President Mohammad Khatami, publicly disassociated itself from the fatwa against Rushdie and assured the British government that Iran would do nothing to implement it. Though Rushdie remained under partial protection, he began to travel and appear in public again.

Possession or distribution of *The Satanic Verses* remained illegal in Iran. In 2000, a U.S. federal appeals court halted the deportation to Tehran of Abbas Zahedi, an Iranian businessman, after he provided documentary evidence that he faced torture or death for distributing copies of *The Satanic Verses*. Zahedi had fled Tehran for the United States in 1996, when a warrant was issued for his arrest because he had asked a colleague to translate the book, which he had obtained in Turkey, into Farsi. The translator, Moshen, was tortured to death in the custody of Iranian security forces.

Although Rushdie has been able to resume the normal life of a literary celebrity, dividing his time between New York and London, he remains shadowed by the fatwa. In January 2004, he was threatened on a visit to his native city of Bombay by demonstrators outside his hotel calling for his death. Islamic groups in India offered to pay 10,000 rupees to anyone who succeeded in shaming Rushdie by blackening his face with boot polish or soot.

Despite the Iranian government's renewed disavowal of the fatwa, in January 2005, just before its 16th anniversary, Iran's supreme spiritual leader, Ayatollah Ali Khameini, reiterated that Rushdie was an apostate and that killing him remained an act authorized by Islam. Religious authorities in Iran maintain that the only person who can lift the death sentence against Rushdie is the man who imposed it, Ayatollah Khomenei, and as he is dead, the fatwa is permanent. In February 2005, Iran's Revolutionary Guards renewed calls for Rushdie's death, stating, "The day will come when they [Muslims] will punish the apostate Rushdie for his scandalous acts and insults against the Koran and the Prophet." The head of the Khordad Foundation was quoted in 2003 as saying that the reward for killing Rushdie had risen to $3 million. In February 2004, the foundation declared that a new "committee for the glorification of the martyrs of the Muslim world" was offering an additional bounty of $100,000 for Rushdie's assassination.

In June 2005, a reporter for the *Times* (London) uncovered evidence of how serious the threat against Rushdie had been. In the Behesht Zahra cemetery in Tehran, in an area dedicated to foreign terrorists or "martyrs," stands a shrine bearing the words: "Mustafa Mahmoud Mazeh, born Conakry, Guinea. Martyred in London, August 3, 1989. The first martyr to die on a mission to kill Salman Rushdie." According to Scotland Yard, on that date in the Beverley House Hotel, Paddington, in London, an explosion that leveled two floors of the building killed Mazeh in his room. Antiterrorist squad detectives said he had died while trying to prime a bomb hidden in a book. At the time, British authorities said that there was a "hint" that he had belonged to a terrorist group but had not publicly linked the bombing to Rushdie.

When the British government announced in 2007 that Rushdie would be awarded a knighthood, protests and demonstrations erupted in Pakistan and Malaysia. A hard-line Pakistani cleric called for the author's death, and Pakistan's religious affairs minister, Mohammed Ejaz ul-Haq, said it would now be justified for suicide bombers to kill Rushdie. After the British government protested, ul-Haq explained that his comments were a statement of fact and not intended to incite violence. Rushdie received his knighthood in June 2008.

On the 20th anniversary of the publication of *The Satanic Verses* in October 2008, Sir Salman Rushdie told the *Times* (London) that he did not regret writing his book. "The question I'm always asking myself is: are we masters or victims? Do we make history or does history make us? Do we shape the world or are we just shaped by it? The question of do we have agency in our lives or whether we are just passive victims of events is, I think, a great question and one that I have always tried to ask. In that sense I wouldn't not have wanted to be the writer that asked it."

FURTHER READING

Appignanesi, Lisa, and Sara Maitland, eds. *The Rushdie File.* Syracuse, N.Y.: Syracuse University Press, 1990.

Barnes, Julian. "Staying Alive." *New Yorker* (February 21, 1994): 99–105.

Campbell, Duncan, and Julian Borger. "Rushdie Furore Stuns Honours Committee." *Guardian* (June 20, 2007). Available online. URL: http://www.guardian.co.uk/uk/2007/jun/20/books.pakistan. Accessed June 6, 2010.

For Rushdie: Essays by Arab and Muslim Writers in Defense of Free Speech. New York: George Braziller, 1994.

Harrison, James. *Salman Rushdie.* New York: Twayne, 1992.

Hoyle, Ben. "Salman Rushdie Unrepentant About Satanic Verses." *Times* (London) (October 1, 2008). Available online. URL: http://entertainment.timesonline.co.uk/tol/arts_and_entertainment/books/clive_james/article4856150.ece. Accessed June 6, 2010.

"Iran Adamant over Rushdie Fatwa." BBC News (February 17, 2005). Available online. URL: http://news.bbc.co.uk/2/hi/middle_east/4260599.stm.

Levy, Leonard W. *Blasphemy: Verbal Offense Against the Sacred, from Moses to Salman Rushdie.* New York: Alfred A. Knopf, 1993.

Lloyd, Anthony. "Tomb of the Unknown Assassin Reveals Mission to Kill Rushdie." *Times* (London) (June 8, 2005). Available online. URL: http://www.timesonline.co.uk/article/0,,3-1645223,00.html.

Pipes, Daniel. *The Rushdie Affair: The Novel, the Ayatollah, and the West.* New York: Carol Publishing Group, 1990.

Rushdie, Salman. *Imaginary Homelands: Essays and Criticism 1981–1991.* New York: Penguin Books, 1991.

Ruthven, Malise. *A Satanic Affair: Salman Rushdie and the Wrath of Islam.* London: Hogarth Press, 1991.

Weatherby, W. J. *Salman Rushdie: Sentenced to Death.* New York: Carroll and Graf Publishers, 1990.

SHIVAJI: HINDU KING IN ISLAMIC INDIA

Author: James W. Laine
Original date and place of publication: 2003, United States
Publisher: Oxford University Press
Literary form: History

SUMMARY

Shivaji: Hindu King in Islamic India by James W. Laine, a professor of religious studies at Macalester College in St. Paul, Minnesota, is a scholarly work about the 17th-century Hindu warrior and king Shivaji (1627–80). In 1674, Shivaji established an independent Hindu kingdom in western India, in what is now Maharashtra state, in defiance of the Muslim Mughal Empire, which controlled much of what is now India. The stories of Shivaji's life are legendary among the Marathi-speaking Hindu population of western India, who revere him as a hero of nearly divine status. He is also an icon for Hindu nationalists, who see him as the standard-bearer of opposition to Muslim domination.

Laine's book explores the Shivaji legend, analyzing the way various texts and stories have been woven into a commonly known narrative. He traces its development from the 17th century to the present, noting the different ways the story has been told. His primary interest is to examine critically the growth of Shivaji's legend as it relates to narratives of Maharashtrian Hindu identity.

"Good history is rarely about good guys and bad guys," Laine writes. A simplistic reading of Shivaji's story "leaves Maharashtrians with history in which Muslims (12 percent of the current population of Maharashtra) can only play the role of aggressors, usurpers and oppressors. The modern descendants of those Muslims are thus vilified as outsiders to a society which, though founded on secular principles, is easily swayed by the rhetoric of Hindu chauvinism." His aim is to be "a disturber of the tranquility with which synthetic accounts of Shivaji's life are accepted" and to rescue Shivaji's biography "from the grasp of those who see India as a Hindu nation at war with its Muslim neighbors."

Laine begins his study with early accounts of Shivaji's life at the end of the 17th century, composed by balladeers, court poets, and chroniclers patronized by Shivaji and his immediate descendants. The best-known tales of Shivaji from this period are intimately familiar to Maharashtrians today: his first great act of heroism, the killing of the general Afzal Kahn who had been dispatched by the Muslim sultan Adil Shah to conquer Shivaji; the raid against the Muslim noble Shaista Khan; Shivaji's escape from house arrest at the imperial court in Agra; and the conquest of Simhagad, a fort that had been ceded to the Mughals. The stories also tell of Shivaji's crowning in 1674 as *chatrapati* of an independent Hindu kingdom in an orthodox ceremony that had fallen out of favor in Islamicate (meaning the culture and society associated with Islam) India.

In these heroic texts, Laine sees a complex articulation of ideas and values that construct a Hindu identity. But it would be a misrepresentation to picture Shivaji in 17th-century Maharashtra as leading a band of united Hindu liberationists against a united Muslim oppressor, Laine writes. Elite Hindus were able to participate in the Islamicate world of 17th-century Deccan politics, Laine explains, and elite Muslims often accommodated themselves to Hindu social structures. Though Muslims were different in their beliefs and practices, they were not alien, nor were they a uniform group.

Some Maratha nobles supported Shivaji; others served Adil Shah or the Mughals. Shivaji himself began as a nominal servant of Adil Shah. He later made an alliance with the general Jai Singh and fought as a Mughal general. At that time, it was clear that religious identity was not a major factor for Maratha nobles in determining how they forged military and political alliances. Yet Shivaji stood apart. He attempted to rule as an independent Hindu monarch, to be faithful to his religious traditions, and to challenge the hegemony of the Islamicate world.

In the 17th century, Shivaji's legend was as an epic and martial hero. But in the 18th century, when the complexities of Hindu and Muslim interaction had receded in memory, Shivaji's story became wedded to that of the prominent 17th-century saints of Maharashtra—Tukaram and Ramdas—and he was transformed into a religious figure.

A primary preoccupation of 18th-century chroniclers was the warrior Shivaji's desire to renounce the world of wealth, power, and violence. He became a character who embodied the core values of an "essentialized, universalist Hinduism" in opposition to a single monolithic Islam. The complex picture of cross-religious alliances and internal differences within the Hindu and Muslim communities was replaced by "a picture of mythic clarity." "[S]uch universalism is the necessary precursor to the ideology of nationalism," Laine writes, "for nationalism presumes that all the members of the 'imagined community' participate equally in the common cultural tradition."

From the mid-19th century to the present, the retelling of the Shivaji story has reflected awareness of European culture and power. In 1900, Shivaji was portrayed not only as the father of a Maharashtrian nation but also as the leader of an independence movement with significance for all of India.

By the end of the 20th century, Shivaji's legend had become standardized as the patriotic tale of a great man whose kingdom represented a golden age, who lifted up the oppressed common man and gave him freedom. He is brave, fair-minded, compassionate, and pious and a devoted son who is without vice. Shivaji's life story is currently governed by the dictates of neo-Hindu nationalism, Laine says, "and the story has become so naturalized that it is difficult to imagine the story in any other way."

Laine concludes his study with a chapter examining what he describes as the "cracks" in the Shivaji narrative, "the places where we see efforts to construct a meaningful tale against corrosive forces of disharmony, contradiction and hypocritical compromise," where the writers of Shivaji's story seem to have avoided saying something. "Such a pursuit will allow us not to see the 'real' Shivaji but to better appreciate the ideological concerns of the many authors who have shaped the narrative tradition of Shivaji's legendary life. The real issue is what the authors are saying about themselves, about the dreams they hold, the dreams they see expressed in the tales of their hero."

Laine considers some "unthinkable thoughts, carefully held at bay by the narrators who have shaped the Shivaji legend": that Shivaji might have had an unhappy family life, that he had a harem, that he was uninterested in the religion of bhakti saints, that his personal ambition was to build a kingdom rather than liberate a nation, and that he lived in a cosmopolitan Islamicate world and did little to change that fact. It was Laine's expression of the "unthinkable thought" about Shivaji's family life that led to the controversy about his book.

The traditional accounts describe Shivaji's family life in positive terms, Laine writes, but Shivaji's parents lived apart for most if not all of his life. "Perhaps he was born at a time when his parents were already estranged? How would the narrative look in light of such a supposition?" Laine asks. "The repressed awareness that Shivaji had an absentee father is also revealed by the fact that Maharshtrians tell jokes naughtily suggesting that his guardian Dadaji Konddev was his biological father. In a sense, because Shivaji's father had little influence on his son, for many narrators it was important to supply him with father replacements, Dadaji and later Ramdas."

In an epilogue, Laine sums up the trajectory of the Shivaji story. "The narrative of Shivaji's life, already reshaped by *bhakti* writers by 1800, was thoroughly overtaken by the nationalist narrative in 1900 and has been sustained as a grand narrative of Hindu nationalist identity, despite all the inner inconsistencies, anachronisms, and communalism that imaginative enterprise has entailed."

CENSORSHIP HISTORY

An Indian edition of *Shivaji: Hindu King in Islamic India* was published in June 2003 by Oxford University Press India. The book was an English-language best seller in Pune, Maharashtra's second-largest city after Mumbai (Bombay) and the traditional center of Maharashtrian culture, and there were some positive reviews in national newspapers. But later that year, Laine began to receive e-mails, phone calls, and letters referring to the section of his book where he discusses Shivaji's parentage, demanding that he apologize for defaming a national hero.

Shivaji is a highly symbolic figure and a rallying point for Hindu nationalist groups, which include the Bharatiya Janata Party (BJP), the ruling party in India when Laine's book was published, and the Maharashtra-based right-wing Shiv Sena party. Hindu fundamentalists have been particularly vocal in their opposition to any criticism of Shivaji, his father, Shahji, and his mother, Jijabai, all of whom are highly revered.

On November 10, 2003, a group of Indian historians sent a letter to Oxford University Press India, calling for the book's withdrawal. "Though we do believe in freedom of expression," the scholars wrote, "we cannot subscribe to the practice of maligning the life and character of any person, especially of one who commands the love, respect and admiration of crores [tens of millions] of people and is a source of inspiration to them, by casting baseless aspersions." Ten days later, the publisher withdrew the book from the Indian market.

Laine had conducted some of his research at the venerable Bhandarkar Oriental Research Institute (BORI) in Pune. On December 22, activists from Shiv Sena confronted scholars attached to the institute. Sanskrit scholar Shrikant Bahulkar, whom Laine thanked in his preface, was assaulted and his face tarred. Bahulkar had helped Laine to translate Sanskrit and Marathi texts. On December 28, Shiv Sena leader Raj Thackeray apologized to Bahulkar and promised that Sena activists would have to get clearance from their leaders before embarking on "such aggressive campaigns" in the future.

In late December, Laine faxed a statement to Indian newspapers, apologizing for causing offense. "It was never my intention to defame the great Maharashtrian hero," he wrote. "I had no desire to upset those for whom he is an emblem of regional and national pride and I apologize for inadvertently doing so. I foolishly misread the situation in India and figured the book would receive scholarly criticism, not censorship and condemnation."

On January 5, 2004, a mob of some 150 people led by a little-known group called the Sambhaji Brigade stormed and ransacked BORI, destroying books, valuable manuscripts, and artifacts. Four days later, Maharashtra's state government filed charges against Laine and his publishers under Section 153 and 153A of the Indian penal code ("wantonly giving provocation with intent to cause riot;" "promoting enmity between different groups on grounds of religion, race, place of birth, residence, language, etc., and doing acts prejudicial to maintenance of harmony"). Even though the book was no longer being sold in India, the Maharashtra state government proceeded to ban it. The Oxford University Press showroom in Pune was forced to close by Maratha organizations supporting the Sambhaji Brigade.

On January 16, India's prime minister, Atal Bihari Vajpayee, regarded as a moderate within the BJP, spoke out against the book ban while unveiling a statue of Shivaji in Mumbai. "If you do not like anything in a particular book, then sit and discuss it. Banning a book is not a solution. We have to tackle it ideologically," he said. Hindu nationalist groups allied to his party swiftly denounced his comments. By March 20, when Vajpayee was launching the BJP general election campaign in Maharashtra, he had changed his position. "We are prepared to take action against the foreign author," he said. "This was a warning to all foreign authors that they do not play with our national pride." It was clear that the book had become fodder for politicians jockeying for the support of Maharashtra voters during a high-stakes national election campaign.

On March 22, Maharashtra home minister R. R. Patil confirmed that the state was pursuing criminal charges against Laine and his publisher and said that he wished to bring Laine in for interrogation. "If he does not show up on his own, then we will seek the assistance of Interpol to bring him, as a criminal offense has been registered against him for the book, which contains alleged slanderous remarks against Shivaji and his mother Jijamata." The next day Pune police commissioner D. N. Jadhav told reporters that he would write to Laine to summon him to India for questioning. If Laine ignored the summons, he said, the police would go to India's Central Bureau of Investigation and Interpol for help in extraditing him to India.

In fact, it was highly unlikely that Laine could be extradited, as the charges he faced are not crimes under U.S. law and the extradition would have to be ordered by a U.S. court. Days later, the police commissioner said that the police would not be sending a letter to Laine after all, as a petition had been filed by Laine and his publishers in the Bombay High Court challenging the charges.

In April, Laine submitted a formal apology to the high court. "It was never my intention to denigrate Shivaji or outrage sentiments," he wrote. "It is obvious that there can be no historical basis for jokes. Historical evidence suggests that Shahji was Shivaji's biological father and that is also my view. In writing the book, I had hoped to contribute in some way to a rich understanding of this great man. I forthwith direct my publishers to henceforth delete the offending paragraph on page 93 from all future publications of the book worldwide."

Nevertheless, on May 6 the Bombay High Court decided to allow Maharashtra police to proceed with their criminal investigation. On May 20, Laine and his publishers were granted relief when India's Supreme Court overruled the high court. It stayed further investigation or arrests pending the Supreme Court's consideration at a later date of the petition filed by the publishers and author to quash the case against them. At the end of 2005, no further legal action had been taken against Laine and his publishers, but the book remained banned in Maharashtra.

In 2007, India's Supreme Court quashed the criminal proceedings against Laine, declaring that he had no "intention to cause disorder or incite the people to violence," which is an essential element to prove offense under the law. In the meantime, yet another book by Laine, *The Epic of Shivaji*, was banned in Maharashtra. *The Epic of Shivaji*, Laine's first book on the subject, had been published by Orient Longman in 2001 without protest. It is a translation of the Sanskrit poem *Shivbharat*, written in 1674 by Kavindra Paramananda and commissioned by Shivaji himself to celebrate his life. In July 2006, a descendant of Shivaji and former BJP legislator filed a case against Laine for the use of the term *Oedipal rebel* in his introduction to the translation to refer to Shivaji's relationship with his father. The state government banned the book and seized 24 copies from its publisher on the grounds that it may hurt "public sentiments" and threaten law and order.

In an interview in 2004 with the Macalester College student newspaper, Laine, who has received death threats, expressed concern for the chilling effect on scholarship in India. "Storytellers have gone to great lengths to preserve the popular image of their hero," Laine said. "The purpose of academics is not to support the heroes of the state. There is no way scholarship can function under the restriction [of upholding] an ideal portrait as some kind of moral standard."

The events surrounding Laine's books are consonant with a pattern of violence, threats, and censorship against authors, artists, and filmmakers in India who offend the sensibilities of Hindu militants. "Today's new intimidating social censorship knows no limits," wrote Rajeev Dhavan in the Indian daily *The Hindu*, echoing the comments of the Indian journalists and scholars who decried the attacks on Laine and those connected to his book. "Direct threats are handed out by lumpen elements. Powerful informal censorship systems have crippled performance, films, shows and publications. Faced with this barrage, state censorship has retreated or capitulated. Governance has been abandoned to mob intimidation at the price of free speech."

Laine is not the only American scholar to be targeted. Paul Courtright, a professor of religion at Emory University in Atlanta, was threatened with death in 2004 by Hindu militants who were offended by a book he wrote in

1985, *Ganesa: Lord of Obstacles, Lord of Beginnings.* Courtright's Indian publishers recalled the book, which draws on psychoanalytical theories to study the stories of the Hindu god, Ganesha, after U.S.-based Hindus mounted a campaign on the Internet against it.

FURTHER READING

Baldauf, Scott. "How a U.S. Historian Sparked Calls for His Arrest—in India." *Christian Science Monitor* (March 29, 2004). Available online. URL: http://www. csmonitor.com/2004/0329/p01s04-wosc.html.

Barnes, Michael "Warrant for Professor's Arrest Issued in India." *The MAC Weekly*, (April 2, 2004). Available online. URL: http://www.macalester.edu/weekly. Accessed October 2, 2004.

Courtright, Paul. "Studying Religion in an Age of Terror: Internet Death Threats and Scholarship as a Moral Practice." The Academic Exchange, Emory University (April 15, 2004). Available online. URL: http://www.emory.edu/ACAD_EXCHANGE/2004/aprmay/courtright.html.

Dhavan, Rajeev. "Ban, Burn, Destroy." *The Hindu* (January 23, 2004). Available online. URL: http://www.hindu.com/2004/01/27/stories/2004012701571004.htm.

Engineer, Asghar Ali. "The Politics of Attack on Bhandarkar Institute." Centre for Study of Society and Secularism (February 1–5, 2004). Available online. URL: http://www.csss-isla.com/archive/archive.php?article=http://www.css-isla.com/archive/2004/feb 1_15.htm.

"James Laine's *Shivaji: Hindu King in Islamic India* and the Attack on the Bhandarkar Oriental Research Institute." *The Complete Review* (February 2004). Available online. URL: http://www.complete-review.com/quarterly/vol5/issue1/laine0. htm.

Katakam, Anupama. "The Politics of Vandalism." *Frontline* (January 17–30, 2004). Available online. URL: http://www.flonet.com/fl2102/stories/20040130003802800. htm.

Katakam, Anupama, and Nandagopal R. Menon. "Politics of a Ban." *Frontline* (February 11–24, 2006). Available online. URL: http://www.hinduonnet.com/fline/fl2303/stories/20060224002609300.htm. Accessed June 6, 2010.

Laine, James W. "In India, 'the Unthinkable' Is Printed at One's Peril." *Los Angeles Times*, January 12, 2004, p. B-13.

"Laine to Be Summoned to India, Says Police Chief." Express News Service, Mumbai, India (March 23, 2004). Available online. URL: http://cities.expressindia.com/fullstory.php?newsid=79728.

Nandgaonkar, Satish. "Author Explains Oedipus Parallel—Not Derogatory, Says Laine." *Telegraph* (January 12, 2006). Available online. URL: http://www.telegraphindia. com/1060112/asp/nation/story_5711098.asp. Accessed June 6, 2010.

"Pune Institute's Desecration Shocks Author." *Mid Day* (January 6, 2004). Available online. URL: http://ww1.mid-day.com/news/nation/2004/january/73060.htm.

Singh, Vijay. "Bringing Laine Back: Easier Said Than Done." Rediff.com (March 27, 2004). Available online. URL: http://us.rediff.com/news/2004/mar/27laine. htm.

Vedantam, Shankar. "U.S. Scholars' Writings Inspire Hatred in India." *Washington Post*, April 10, 2004, p. A-1.

THE TALMUD

Original date and place of publication: Ca. A.D. 200–500, Palestine and
   Mesopotamia
Literary form: Religious text

SUMMARY

The Talmud, a collection of teachings set down by the Jewish scholars of
antiquity, is the compendium of the oral law and tradition of Judaism. The
word *Talmud* comes from the Hebrew word meaning "instruction." The collection has two main components: the Mishnah, the book of law written in
Hebrew, and the commentaries on the Mishnah, known as the Talmud or
Gemarah, written in Aramaic. Talmudic sages believed that God revealed
two Torahs to Moses. One was the Scriptures, or written books. The other,
the Mishnah, was preserved in oral traditions handed down through many
centuries and compiled toward the end of the second century A.D. The material of the Mishnah is arranged in six groups, called orders, that deal with
agriculture, the sabbath and festivals, marriage, civil and criminal law, ritual
sacrifices, and cleanliness. The orders are subdivided into 63 tracts or books.

   Oral explanations and commentaries that developed around the Mishnah
over the centuries were later put into written form and called the Gemarah.
The Mishnah serves as text and the Gemarah as a series of comments and notes.
Two versions of the Gemarah exist: one compiled in the fourth century by the
scholars of Palestine, and the other in the fifth century by the scholars of Baby-
lonia, which became the authoritative work. The Talmud is considered, with the
Hebrew Bible, as the central pillar of Judaism and the most important book in
Jewish culture. It is the accepted religious authority among all Orthodox Jews.

CENSORSHIP HISTORY

The history of suppression of the Talmud is many centuries long. Early
attempts to ban it date at least to the seventh and eighth centuries. During
the Middle Ages, with the revival of learning and the appearance of books of
theological speculation, the Catholic Church began to adopt a more severe
attitude toward suspect books. It began to examine Jewish literature and the
Talmud more intensively.

   In 1144 in Paris, the Catholic Church ordered the burning of the Talmud on charges of blasphemy and immorality. Other incidents of censorship
were recorded during the next hundred years. The anti-Talmudic campaign
reached its height in 1239, when Pope Gregory IX ordered all Jewish books
to be burned. He acted on allegations of heresy in the Talmud brought by
Jewish converts to Christianity. Gregory sent letters to the kings and prelates of England, France, Navarre, Aragon, Castile, and Portugal, ordering
that on a sabbath during the following Lent, while Jews worshiped in their
synagogues, the books should be seized and delivered to the mendicant friars

for examination, and that these books, deemed heretical, should be destroyed. The order was carried out fully only in France.

In 1244, Pope Innocent IV ordered Louis IX of France to burn all copies of the Talmud. This order was repeated in 1248, when 20 wagonloads of books were burned in Paris, and again in 1254. In 1264 in Rome, Pope Clement IV appointed a committee of censors to expunge all passages from the Talmud that appeared derogatory to Christianity, allowing Jews to keep only expurgated versions. Three years later, Clement IV instructed the king of Aragon to force Jews to deliver Talmuds to inquisitors.

Numerous instances of official burnings of the Talmud were recorded in France in the 14th century, as the anti-Jewish polemic continued. In 1415, Pope Benedict XII ordered all copies of Talmudic books delivered to bishops for preservation subject to papal instructions. Jews themselves were forbidden to possess copies of any material considered antagonistic to Christianity and could not read or study the Talmud. A church synod in Basel in 1431 reaffirmed the stringent ban.

Because so many copies of the Talmud had been lost over the centuries, there was great interest among Jews in the new 15th-century technology of the printing press. The first printed edition of the Talmud appeared in Guadalajara, Spain, in 1482. But the Talmud soon became a target of the Spanish Inquisition. In 1490 in Spain, the grand inquisitor, Tomás de Torquemada, burned Hebrew books by order of Ferdinand and Isabella; he later conducted at Salamanca an auto-da-fé, or burning, of more than 6,000 volumes described as books of magic or infected with Jewish errors. When the Jews were expelled from Spain and Portugal, in 1492, all Jewish books were confiscated.

In 1509, Johannes Pfefferkorn, a priest and Jewish convert to Christianity, advocated destruction of Hebrew books in all countries under the rule of the Holy Roman Emperor. Emperor Maximillian requested the opinion of another priest, Johann Reuchlin. Reuchlin, who had published the first Hebrew grammar for Christians, argued that to understand the Old Testament it was necessary to collect and study Hebrew manuscripts rather than destroy them. He suggested that Jews be required to furnish books for the universities and that chairs of Hebrew learning be instituted in every university in Germany. His recommendation was met by intense opposition, to which he responded with *Augenspiegel* (Mirror of the eye) in 1511. He distinguished anti-Christian polemics from classical works in Hebrew, which he believed should be preserved. A sustained controversy developed between the humanists who supported Reuchlin and the clerics and leaders of the Inquisition who supported Pfefferkorn. In 1521, the Roman curia suppressed Reuchlin's writings against Pfefferkorn.

In 1520, Pope Leo X gave permission for the publication and printing of the Talmud in Venice, and several editions appeared in the next few decades. In the 1530s, Martin Luther, convinced that Christians in Moravia were being induced to convert to Judaism, urged that Jews be deported to Palestine and forbidden to practice usury, and that their synagogues be burned and their books destroyed. German principalities expelled Jews from certain localities and suppressed their books. In other German cities, such as Frankfurt and Worms, Jews were tolerated.

As the Counter-Reformation and the church's battle against heresy and the power of the printing press intensified, Pope Julius III in 1553 halted the printings of the Talmud allowed by Pope Leo X. In 1555, the houses of Jews were searched, and Jews were ordered under pain of death to surrender all books blaspheming Christ. Princes, bishops, and inquisitors were instructed to confiscate the Talmud. The books were collected and burned on the first day of Rosh Hashanah, the Jewish New Year. Christians were forbidden under threat of excommunication to possess or read Jewish books or to aid Jews by producing copies in script or by printing. Jewish books, including rare rabbinic manuscripts, were burned by the thousands in Italian cities. Some 12,000 volumes of Hebrew texts were burned after the inquisitor Sixtus of Siena destroyed the library of the Hebrew school at Cremona. The Talmud was not published again in Renaissance Italy.

The harshness of Julius III's decree was somewhat alleviated by Pope Pius IV in 1559, who allowed distribution of the Talmud only if those sections that offended Christianity were erased. As a result of this decision, a truncated and expurgated edition was printed in Basel under the supervision of Catholic monks. Subsequent editions were often similarly expurgated. In many European countries, where the Talmud could be printed only with official permission, licensing was confined to Christian printers.

The church's first Index of Forbidden Books, in 1559, included the Talmud. Under the revised Index prepared by the Council of Trent in 1564, all works of Jewish doctrine were banned, except those permitted by the pope after the Jewish community offered a substantial financial "gift."

In 1592, Pope Clement VIII issued a bull forbidding either Christians or Jews from owning, reading, buying, or circulating "impious talmudic books or manuscripts" or writings in Hebrew or other languages that "tacitly or expressly contain heretical or erroneous statements against the Holy Scriptures of the Old Law and Testament." Any such work, whether expurgated or not, was to be destroyed. In 1596, this ruling was modified when the publication of the Machsor, the basic Hebrew prayer book, was permitted, but only in Hebrew.

Active suppression of the Talmud by the Catholic Church lasted through the 18th century. In 1629, an Italian cardinal boasted of having collected 10,000 outlawed Jewish books for destruction. As late as 1775, Pope Clement XIV confirmed the prohibitions of previous papal bulls. No Hebrew books could be bought or sold until examined and approved by the church.

In the 20th century, the most extensive censorship of the Talmud was reported in Europe under the Communist Party in the Soviet Union and under the Nazis during the Holocaust. In 1926, the government of the Soviet Union ordered that religiously dogmatic books such as the Talmud could be left in the large libraries but must be removed from the small ones. Virtually no printing of the work was allowed after that time. A Russian translation, the first in any language to be permitted since the 1917 revolution, was undertaken during the 1990s under the sponsorship of the Russian Academy of Sciences.

In 1939, most of the schools of Jewish learning in Europe were totally destroyed by the Nazis. Innumerable copies of Jewish religious texts were lost during the Holocaust.

The Second Vatican Council in 1965 brought about a change in attitude toward the Talmud. It deplored anti-Semitism and the persecution of Jews, emphasizing the church's biblical connection to Judaism and the common religious heritage of Christians and Jews.

FURTHER READING

Bainton, Roland. *Here I Stand: A Life of Martin Luther.* New York: Penguin, 1995.

Burman, Edward. *The Inquisition: Hammer of Heresy.* New York: Dorset Press, 1992.

Green, Jonathon. *Encyclopedia of Censorship.* New York: Facts On File, 1990.

Haight, Anne Lyon. *Banned Books: 387 B.C. to 1978 A.D.* Updated and enlarged by Chandler B. Grannis. New York: R. R. Bowker, 1978.

Hertzberg, Arthur. "Swimming without Drowning: New Approaches to the Ocean of the Talmud." *New York Times Book Review*, March 27, 1994, pp. 12–14.

Lea, Henry Charles. *History of the Inquisition of the Middle Ages.* Vol. 1. New York: Russell and Russell, 1955.

Levy, Leonard W. *Blasphemy: Verbal Offense Against the Sacred, from Moses to Salman Rushdie.* New York: Alfred A. Knopf, 1993.

Peters, Edward. *Inquisition.* New York: Free Press, 1988.

Putnam, George Haven. *The Censorship of the Church of Rome.* Vol. 1. New York: G. P. Putnam's Sons, 1906–07.

Steinsaltz, Adin. *The Essential Talmud.* New York: Basic Books, 1976.

THE WITCHES

Author: Roald Dahl
Original date and places of publication: 1983, United Kingdom and United States
Original publishers: Jonathan Cape; Farrar, Straus and Giroux
Literary form: Novel

SUMMARY

The Witches by Roald Dahl, the award-winning British author of 19 children's books, is the story of a seven-year-old boy and his Norwegian grandmother who together battle a plot by witches to exterminate the world's children.

In fairy tales, witches wear black hats and cloaks and ride on broomsticks. "But this is not a fairy tale," the author warns his readers in "A Note about Witches." "This is about REAL WITCHES. . . . *REAL WITCHES dress in ordinary clothes and look very much like ordinary women. They live in ordinary houses and they work in ORDINARY JOBS.* That is why they are so hard to catch." Real witches hate children. They are particularly dangerous because they don't look dangerous. "She might even be your lovely school-teacher who is reading these words to you at this very moment."

Twice a year, a boy goes to Norway from England with his family to visit his grandmother. Shortly after his seventh birthday, during a Christmas visit, his parents are killed in a car accident. The day after the accident, the grandmother, an expert on witches, begins telling stories about children who were kidnapped by witches and vanished off the face of the Earth.

How do you recognize a witch? Grandmother explains that a real witch always wears gloves, because witches have thin curvy claws instead of fingernails. Witches never have toes, and their feet have square ends. They are always bald and wear a wig. The wigs make their scalp itch and cause nasty sores on the head. They also have slightly larger nose holes than ordinary people and keen powers of smell. But the dirtier a child is, the less he smells to a witch. A clean child smells to a witch like dog droppings.

One of their favorite tricks is to mix up a powder that will turn a child into a creature that all grown-ups hate. Once a year in each country, the witches meet secretly to hear a lecture by the Grand High Witch of All the World. Grandmother says that when she was younger, she traveled the world trying to track down the Grand High Witch.

The boy and his grandmother move back to his family house in England. One day, he is in his tree house when a peculiar woman appears below, wearing a small black hat and long black gloves. She says that if he comes down she will give him a present, a small green snake. He refuses, and the woman leaves. When his grandmother arrives, he realizes that he has seen a witch for the first time. "It is hardly surprising," he says, "that after that I became a very witch-conscious boy."

Grandmother gets pneumonia, and when she recovers, the doctors recommend that she go to a nice hotel on the south coast of England. She books rooms at the Hotel Magnificent in the seaside town of Bournemouth. Looking for a place to play with his two pet mice, the boy finds an empty ballroom, reserved for the annual meeting of the Royal Society for the Prevention of Cruelty to Children, and settles behind a large folding screen. The ladies from the Royal Society stream in. The boy notices that many of the women are scratching their heads and are wearing wigs and gloves.

A pretty young woman in a long black dress appears on the platform. Her gloved fingers unhook something behind her ears, and the whole of her face comes away in her hands, revealing her real face, a fearsome and ghastly sight. The boy knows immediately that she is none other than the Grand High Witch. As the women remove their wigs, he sees a sea of red and itchy-looking naked scalps. The Grand High Witch gives her orders: Every child in the country "shall be rrrubbed out, sqvashed, sqvirted, sqvittered and frr-rittered before I come here again in vun year's time. . . . Vee vill vipe them all avay! Vee vill scrub them off the face of the earth. Vee vill flush them down the drain!"

The Grand High Witch instructs the other witches to return to their hometowns and buy the best sweet shops in England. They are to announce a gala grand opening with free sweets and chocolates for every child. The sweets will be filled with the latest magic formula: Formula 86 Delayed Action Mouse-Maker. When the children arrive at school the next day, they will turn into mice. "Down with children! Do them in! Boil their bones and fry their skin!" sings the Grand High Witch.

The boy realizes that he is in danger and that his only hope of avoiding discovery is that he has not washed for days. The Grand High Witch announces that she has already given a dose of Formula 86 in a chocolate bar to a smelly boy in the hotel lobby and has promised to give him more chocolate if he will meet her in the ballroom at 3:25 P.M. Bruno Jenkins, who is staying in the hotel with his parents, arrives to collect the chocolate bars. As the witches and the boy watch, Bruno is changed into a mouse.

Then the witches smell dog droppings and begin to sniff the air. The boy is discovered. The Grand High Witch pours the entire contents of a little bottle down his throat and he, too, turns into a mouse. While the witches are getting a mousetrap, he runs away. "I was feeling remarkably well," the boy thinks. Perhaps it isn't so bad being a mouse. "Little boys have to go to school. Mice don't. Mice don't have to pass exams. Mice don't have to worry about money. . . . My grandmother is a human, but I know that she will always love me whoever I am."

The boy finds Bruno, and the two mouse-boys make their way to his grandmother's room. There the boy vows to stop the witches. He will go to the Grand High Witch's room, steal a bottle of her Delayed Action Mouse-Maker, give the witches a dose, and turn them into mice. Grandmother lowers the boy over the balcony in a sock into the Grand Witch's bedroom, and he escapes with 500 doses of the mouse-maker.

Grandmother hides the mice-boys in her purse and goes to the dining room. She gives Bruno's parents the bad news that Bruno has been altered. Meanwhile, the boy sneaks into the kitchen and pours the mouse-maker dose into the soup. But before he can escape to the dining room, a cook chops off the tip of his tail with a carving knife.

In the dining room, the Grand High Witch screams and goes shooting up into the air. Suddenly all the other witches begin to scream and jump up out of their seats. Then, all at once, they become still, stiff, and silent. They shrink and turn into mice. Waiters smash the mice with chairs, wine bottles, and frying pans, and behind them comes the cook with his carving knife. Grandmother exits the hotel with her grandson safe in her purse and returns to Norway.

Back in grandmother's fine old house, the boy asks how long he can expect to live as a mouse-person. Grandmother estimates that he will survive about nine years. "Good," the boy says. "It's the best news I ever had. . . . Because I would never want to live longer than you." "Are you sure you don't mind being a mouse for the rest of your life?" Grandmother asks. "I don't mind at all," he says. "It doesn't matter who you are or what you look like so long as somebody loves you."

Grandmother calls the chief of police in Bournemouth and gets the name and address of the lady who disappeared from room 454 in the hotel (the Grand High Witch). Her home is a castle in the mountains above a small village. There the grandmother expects to find the names and addresses of all the rest of the witches in the world. The boy and his grandmother plot to use the doses to destroy the new Grand High Witch and the other witches in the castle. They will turn them into mice and send in cats to destroy them. Then the boy and his grandmother will travel the world, leaving deadly drops of Mouse-Maker in the food of witches. "It will be a triumph, my darling!" says the grandmother. "A colossal unbeatable triumph. We shall do it entirely by ourselves, just you and me! That will be our work for the rest of our lives."

CENSORSHIP HISTORY

Dahl's books for children are among the most frequently targeted for removal from school classrooms and libraries in the United States. His most popular books, including *The BFG, Charlie and the Chocolate Factory, James and the Giant Peach,* and *Matilda,* have all been challenged or banned. Their detractors say the books do not teach moral values or a good philosophy of life, contain rude or offensive language, or encourage children to disrespect adults. Because of its theme of witchcraft, *The Witches* is at the top of the list of censored Dahl books. It ranked number nine among the books most frequently challenged or removed from school curricula and libraries during 1990–92, according to a study by Herbert N. Foerstel. It was number 27 on the American Library Association's (ALA) list of most frequently challenged books during 1990–2000.

A witch's potion in a children's book is a recipe for censorship. Christian fundamentalists who believe that portrayal of magic and witchcraft is dangerous or incompatible with their beliefs have objected to the presence in schools of fantasy fiction with references to sorcery, wizardry, incantation, spells, or witchcraft, such as J. K. Rowling's Harry Potter books, or even fairy tales.

Educators and critics who have evaluated *The Witches* agree that, although the book is macabre and grotesque, it is more than just a scary story. It is a tale of heroism, in which good triumphs over evil, and the unmistakable message of the book is one of love and acceptance. As novelist Erica Jong commented in her review of the book in the *New York Times,* "Children love the macabre, the terrifying, the mythic," and stories that allow them to confront their own fears. *The Witches* is "a parable about the fear of death and separation and a child's mourning for the loss of his parents. . . . It is a curious sort of tale but an honest one, which deals with matters of crucial importance to children: smallness, the existence of evil in the world, mourning, separation and death."

Since 1990, *The Witches* has been challenged in at least 10 school districts in the United States, according to reports collected by the ALA. The ALA estimates that for every challenge about which it receives information, four or five go unreported.

In 1990, parents attempted to remove *The Witches* from the Amana, Iowa, first-grade curriculum because the book was "too sophisticated and did not teach moral values," and from the Goose Lake (Iowa) Elementary School because it had violent content and used the word *slut* and because the boy was turned into a mouse. In 1991, it was challenged at the Dallas (Oregon) Elementary School library because it might entice impressionable or emotionally disturbed children into becoming involved in witchcraft or the occult.

In 1992, Escondido Union Elementary School in Escondido, California, placed the book on the library's restricted list after four parents filed a complaint contending that it would cause "desensitization to violence" and "increased interest in the practice of witchcraft." The restriction requiring a parent's written permission before a child under 12 could check out the book was the first ever imposed in the district. In 1993, the Escondido school district board voted to lift the restriction and return the book to open library shelves. The district still retained bans on four other books that parents charged were promoting the occult, including poet Eve Merriam's *Halloween ABC*, which has frequently been targeted for "satanic" content.

In 1992, in La Mesa, California, a group of parents argued that *The Witches* should be banned from school libraries because it included horrifying depictions of witches as ordinary-looking women and promoted the religion of Wicca or witchcraft. The school board declined to remove the book from libraries. In Spencer, Wisconsin, in 1993, parents objected to the book's presence in a fourth-grade classroom, as they believed it could desensitize children to crimes related to witchcraft. The Spencer school board voted 3-2 to concur with a citizen-teacher committee that recommended its continued use and decided to leave the decision on what books to read in the classroom to faculty and school administrators.

In May 1994, the Lakeview Board of Education in Battle Creek, Michigan, voted to keep *The Witches* on elementary library school shelves despite protests from parents who said it was "satanic." The school board's president said it was inappropriate to debate the book's religious connotations. In Stafford, Virginia, in 1995, the book was removed from classrooms and restricted to school libraries because protesting parents said it contained crude language and encouraged children to disobey their parents and other adults.

In 1997, the librarian at Kirby Junior High School in Wichita Falls, Texas, announced that *The Witches* and three other books had been removed from the library and were in the possession of a parent who was a member of the First Assembly of God Church. The parent asked trustees to ban books with "satanic" themes and said the books would not be returned to library shelves until the school board approved them. A school board member said it was unlikely that *The Witches* and other books would be returned unless there was more academic value to them than he could see from the excerpts he had read.

In February 1998, a parent presented a complaint signed by eight people demanding that *The Witches* be removed from classrooms and libraries in the Dublin, Ohio, school district because it was derogatory toward children, harmful to their self-esteem, and conflicted with the family's religious and moral beliefs. "I find this type of material extremely objectionable and cannot understand why an educator, librarian or parent would knowingly choose this type of reading material for their students or children," the parent said. The complainant objected particularly to passages on how to recognize witches when they are "demons in human shape" and that would encourage children to avoid baths so witches couldn't smell them.

In response to the complaint, the school superintendent recommended discontinuing classroom use but leaving the book in school libraries. In June 1998, the Dublin Board of Education overruled the superintendent and voted 3-2 to allow the book to be read aloud in classrooms and to remain in libraries.

Dahl, who died in 1990, commented in 1989 on an attempt by parents to remove *The Witches* from a school library in Billings, Montana. "This book is a fantasy and an enormous joke," he told the Associated Press. "We all know that witches don't exist, not the way I've written about them. They are parents without any sense of humor at all." Dahl suggested that the school district let the children help decide the book's fate in the school library. "The banning of any book, you know, especially a children's book, is unforgivable."

The Associated Press saw the protest against Dahl's book in the context of a campaign by religious fundamentalists against Halloween. The incident in Montana came a week after parents in Maryland and Texas urged school officials to limit observance of Halloween because they said the holiday is linked to devil worship. Several Maryland school officials canceled traditional Halloween costume parties, opting to hold fall and harvest celebrations instead, while officials in that state and in Texas said they would take a look at the role of Halloween in the schools.

FURTHER READING

Associated Press. "Ban on 'The Witches' Sought." (October 19, 1989).

Doyle, Robert P. *Banned Books: 2004 Resource Book.* Chicago: American Library Association, 2004.

Foerstel, Herbert N. *Banned in the U.S.A.: A Reference Guide to Book Censorship in Schools and Public Libraries,* Revised and expanded edition. Westport, Conn.: Greenwood Press, 2002.

Jong, Erica. "The Boy Who Became a Mouse." *New York Times Book Review* (November 13, 1983). Available online. URL: http://roalddahlfans.com/books/witcrev1.php.

Newsletter on Intellectual Freedom 41, no. 3 (May 1992): 78; 41, no. 6 (November 1992): 196; 42, no. 4 (July 1993): 127; 42, no. 5 (September 1993): 157; 43, no. 3 (May 1994): 200; 47, no. 5 (September 1998): 156.

WOMEN WITHOUT MEN: A NOVEL OF MODERN IRAN

Author: Shahrnush Parsipur
Original dates and places of publication: 1989, Iran; 1998, United States
Original publishers: Noghreh Publishing; Syracuse University Press
Literary form: Novel

SUMMARY

Shahrnush Parsipur's *Women Without Men: A Novel of Modern Iran* (*Zanan-e-Bedoon-e-Mardan*), drawing on Persian and Islamic mythology and the fantastic elements of tales such as *The Thousand and One Nights*, weaves together stories of five women in contemporary Iran whose lives intersect in a mystical garden in the city of Karaj.

Mahdokht, a teacher, sits in the garden of her brother's house in Karaj, a city 25 miles west of Tehran known for its gardens, river, and cool climate, where she is spending the summer. She knits sweaters for children and, in her interest in performing charitable acts for children, compares herself to Julie Andrews's character in the film *The Sound of Music*. She witnesses a sexual encounter in the gardener's greenhouse between the gardener and a 15-year-old girl. Both the gardener and the girl disgust her. When the girl begs her not to tell anyone, Mahdokht secretly hopes the girl's brothers will find out and beat her to death.

"My virginity is like a tree," Mahkokht thinks. "I'm a tree. I must plant myself." She decides to stay in the garden and plant herself at the beginning of winter. She wants to grow on the riverbank, sprout new leaves, and give them to the wind. She will become thousands of branches and cover the entire world.

Faizeh's story begins on August 25, 1953 (when Mohammad Mosaddeq, the prime minister of Iran, was overthrown in a U.S.-backed coup). That evening, Faizeh puts on her chador and leaves the house in a taxi. There is rioting in the streets. Faizeh arrives at her friend Munis's house. Faizeh's brother's wife, Parvin, has separated from him, and Faizeh recounts a comment that Parvin once made to her: "A woman who spends half her time making out with Farid [Parvin's brother] in the hall should do something about the curtain of virginity, not waste all her time cooking."

"First I thought of slapping her so hard upside the head that her eardrum would break," Faizeh tells Munis. "Besides, virginity is not a curtain, it's a hole." Munis replies, "Virginity is a curtain, my mother says. If a girl jumps down from a height she'll damage her virginity. It's a curtain, it can be torn."

Faizeh insists that it is a hole. "It's narrow, and then it becomes wide." Munis's brother, Amir, arrives and agrees to take Faizeh home before nightfall.

On August 27, Munis is standing on the roof looking down at the street. Amir has said she must not go out, as there is fighting in the streets. It has been three days and two nights since she found out that virginity is a hole, not a curtain. She is filled with rage, recalling her childhood fear of climbing a tree lest she tear the curtain of her virginity. As she watches a man staggering in the alley below, Munis bends forward, then falls to the pavement. The man in the alley says he is dead and that she must go away.

Munis leaves and spends a month walking the streets. One day she sees a book in a stall, *The Secrets of Sexual Satisfaction or How to Know Our Bodies*, and after the 13th day of passing the bookstall, she buys the book. After reading it for three days, she looks up. The trees and sunshine and streets have new meaning for her. "She had grown up."

Munis returns home. Amir says that she has destroyed the family's reputation. He takes the fruit knife from the lunch table and stabs her to death. When Faizeh arrives in search of news about Munis and sees that Amir has killed his sister, she feels that the hand of fate has finally showed her the way. "You're a brother, you upheld your family's honor," she says. "You killed her? You did the right thing. Why not? A girl who disappears for a month is as good as dead."

Faizeh helps Amir bury Munis in the garden. Faizeh tells Amir, "Now after this incident, you must get married as soon as possible so that people will forget about Munis. Anyway you need a partner in life who can take care of you." A few days later Amir announces his intention to get married, not to Faizeh, but to the 18-year-old daughter of Haj Mohammad Sorkhchehreh. She is "very beautiful, soft and quiet, modest, shy, kind, diligent, hardworking, dignified, chaste, elegant, and neat. She wears a chador, always looks down when she's in the street, and blushes constantly." When Faizeh hears the news, she bangs her head against the wall and hits the window with her fist, breaking the glass.

On the night of Amir's wedding, Faizeh appears at his house. The servant, Alia, who suspects that Amir has killed Munis, lets her in. Faizeh goes straight to the garden to bury a talisman at the foot of Munis's corpse to bring bad luck for Amir. Suddenly, she hears Munis's voice saying, "Faizeh dear! I can't breathe." Faizeh digs in the dirt until Munis's face appears. She brings water to Munis, who comes to life, gets dressed, and sits down in her usual place by the radio.

Now that Munis has risen from the dead, she can read minds. Munis accuses Faizeh of conspiring with her brother to kill her. After the members of the household arrive, Munis goes to the bridal chamber and tells Amir that his new wife had become pregnant by a cousin and had an abortion. But Amir will have to get along with his bride anyway, or she will punish him. Then Munis announces that she will live with Faizeh, and the two women walk out the door and disappear into the night.

Mrs. Farrokhlaqa Sadraldivan Golchehreh, age 51, is sitting in a rocking chair on the terrace. Her domineering husband of 30 years, Golchehreh, is in the living room tying his tie. Farrokhlaqa is patiently waiting for him to go out. Since he has retired, Golchehreh is home more often, and his presence is suffocating. Fakhredin, a young man Farrokhlaqa had loved, who left for America when she was 13, appears in her memory. He always told her that she looked like Vivien Leigh in *Gone With the Wind.*

Farrokhlaqa tells her husband that she wishes they had a garden in Karaj. "Do you think that after menopause you can still enjoy a garden?" her husband asks. Farrokhlaqa becomes frightened by the strange way her husband is looking at her. She punches him in the stomach. He trips and dies falling down the terrace stairs. Three months later, Farrokhlaqa sells the Tehran house, buys a house and garden in Karaj, and moves there.

Zarrinkolah is a 26-year-old prostitute, working at Golden Akram's house. She has 20 to 30 customers a day and is tired of working but sees no way out of her life of prostitution. One day a customer comes in. It is a man without a head. From that day on, all Zarrinkolah's customers are headless. Zarrinkolah goes to the bathhouse, performs ablutions 50 times, and prays at a shrine. She asks the owner of a diner where to go to drink cool water. He suggests Karaj, and she sets off for the city.

Two girls are on the road to Karaj. One is Faizeh, age 28, and the other is Munis, 38. They are both virgins. They meet a truck driver and his assistant, who rape them. The truck driver leaves the scene, but further down the road he loses control of the truck and crashes. The rapists are killed. A passenger in the truck, a gardener, survives and heads for Karaj.

Farrokhlaqa arrives at the house and garden she has bought in Karaj. She is planning a busy social life and envisions turning her house into a literary salon. She sees a tree on the riverbank. It is Mahdokht, the sister of the garden's former owner, who had lost her mind and planted herself in the earth. A man arrives who offers to work as a gardener. Zarrinkolah is with him. They had met on the road to Karaj. She said he was the first person she had seen in six months who had a head.

Then two tired women in dusty chadors, Munis and Faizeh, knock on the door. They tell of their rape by the truck drivers. Faizeh cries that she was a virgin and that the disgrace has ruined her reputation. Munis says, "Well, Faizeh dear, I was a virgin too. To hell with it. We were virgins, now we're not. It's nothing to cry over." Farrokhlaqa invites them to stay, and they tell one another about their lives.

The women help the gardener repair the main house, and Zarrinkolah and the gardener feed the tree with morning dew. When the house is finished Farrokhlaqa prepares a party room and invites journalists, poets, painters, writers, and photographers, who come every Friday and stay until late at night. Zarrinkolah and the gardener marry, and she becomes pregnant. As she grows fatter, she changes color and becomes transparent. She and the gardener feed her breast milk to the tree. Farrokhlaqa leaves the women in the house and returns to Tehran.

In midwinter, as Mahdokht is nourished by human milk, she has an explosive feeling. In midspring, her body explodes. The tree turns into seeds that blow into the water. Mahdokht travels with the water all over the world.

Faizeh has been traveling to Tehran to meet Amir. Amir and Faizeh marry secretly, and Amir finds a better job and is able to buy a new house. "Their life is neither good nor bad. It just goes on." Munis decides to become light. She flies off into the sky and spends seven years passing through seven deserts. After seven years, she arrives at the city, puts on a clean dress, and becomes a simple schoolteacher.

Farrokhlaqa stays in Tehran, where a young painter paints her portrait day after day. Eventually she gives him money to go to Paris to paint. She meets Mr. Marikhi, an old friend of her childhood love, Fakhredin. They marry, and when Marikhi is stationed in Europe, Farrokhlaqa goes with him. "Their relationship is satisfactory, neither warm or cold."

Zarrinkolah gives birth to a lily, which grows up in a small hole on the riverbank in Karaj. She and her husband sit on the lily together, become smoke, and rise into the sky.

CENSORSHIP HISTORY

Parsipur published her first novel, *The Dog and the Long Winter*, in 1974. While attending college in Tehran, she worked as a producer for Iranian National Radio and Television. After she resigned her position in 1974 to protest the execution of two poets by the shah's regime, she was arrested by the shah's notorious intelligence agency, SAVAK, and imprisoned for a short period.

In 1976, she traveled to France to attend the Sorbonne. During her four-year stay there, she completed her second novel, *The Simple and Small Adventures of the Tree Spirit*. Shortly after her return from Paris to Iran, she was arrested, along with her mother and two brothers, and imprisoned without formal charges by the revolutionary regime as a result of one of her brother's attempt to create an archive of political publications.

Parsipur spent a total of four years, seven months, and seven days in prison. Under the Ayatollah Ruhollah Khomeini's regime, hundreds of writers and journalists were arrested. According to the London-based human rights organization Article 19, by early 1983 at least 39 writers, translators, and journalists had been executed after summary trials.

Parsipur was released from prison in 1986 and, in 1989, her novel, *Touba and the Meaning of Night*, the story of a young girl's coming of age in 19th-century Iran, was published and became a national best seller. The same year, she found a publisher for *Women Without Men*. The novel received a great deal of attention in Iran and was widely discussed by literary critics.

Soon after its publication, the government banned it as un-Islamic and subsequently banned all of her other writings. Censorship laws prohibit the publication of material contrary to the principles of Islam and the authorities reserve the right to ban any work postpublication and take legal action against the author and publisher.

The censors took issue with Parsipur's treatment in the novel of the topics of virginity, rape, prostitution, and failed marriages, as well as references to Western culture, such as the films *The Sound of Music* and *Gone with the Wind.*

Parsipur was arrested twice in connection with the banning of *Women Without Men* and jailed each time for more than a month. Mohammad Reza Aslani, the book's publisher, was also arrested, and his publishing house, Noghreh Publishing, was closed.

As Parsipur was unable to make a living in Iran as a writer, she sought political refugee status and moved to the United States in 1994. All eight of her novels and a prison memoir continue to be banned in Iran. Yet her books continue to circulate underground and are widely read there.

FURTHER READING

Article 19. "Iran: Press Freedom Under the 'Moderates.' " *Censorship News* no. 15 (August 17, 1992).

Parsipur, Shahrnush. *Women Without Men: A Novel of Modern Iran.* Afterword by Persis M. Karim. Translator's note by Kamran Talattof. New York: The Feminist Press at the City University of New York, 2004.

ZHUAN FALUN: THE COMPLETE TEACHINGS OF FALUN GONG

Author: Li Hongzhi
Original dates and places of publication: China, 1994; United States, 2001
Publisher: Fair Winds Press (United States)
Literary form: Spiritual text

SUMMARY

Zhuan Falun (Revolving of the law wheel) is the main book of teachings of a philosophy of spiritual cultivation introduced by Li Hongzhi in China in 1992. Falun Gong, or Falun Dafa, stresses the integration of high ethical standards and physical well-being and the cultivation of one's inner nature by upholding the three principles of truth, compassion, and forbearance.

Falun Dafa reflects the Buddhist and Taoist traditions of Chinese culture and is based in *qigong:* a form of traditional Chinese exercise that cultivates qi (chi), or vital energy. It prescribes a set of five exercises involving routines of physical movements and meditation. Its adherents regard it as a powerful mechanism for healing and health and believe that it is different from other *qigong* techniques in having a higher objective of spiritual enlightenment.

Zhuan Falun: The Complete Teachings of Falun Gong is composed of nine lectures originally given by Li during the period 1992–94. It provides the body of fundamental knowledge essential to the task of undertaking proper cultivation toward higher stages of attainment.

"The BUDDHA FA [meaning law, way, or principles] is most profound," the book begins. "It is the most intricate and extraordinary science of all the theories in the world. In order to explore this domain, people must fundamentally change their conventional human notions. Failing that, the truth of the universe will forever remain a mystery to humankind, and everyday people will forever crawl within the boundaries set by their own ignorance."

Li believes that there were human beings on Earth millions of years ago and that many scientists have already publicly recognized the existence of a prehistoric culture and civilization that was exterminated. The practices of *qigong* were inherited from this remote prehistoric culture.

A nuclear reactor was discovered in Gabon, he says, that was constructed 2 billion years ago and was in operation for 500,000 years. "I made a careful investigation once and found that humankind has undergone complete annihilation eighty-one times," Li writes. "We have found that whenever human societies in prehistoric times experienced periodical destruction, it always took place when humankind was morally corrupt to the extreme."

Li claims that he is the only person genuinely teaching *qigong* "toward higher levels at home and abroad." He states: "The human moral standard is declining tremendously, and human moral values are deteriorating daily. . . . As a practitioner, one must then conduct oneself by following this nature of the universe rather the standards of everyday people."

The book includes discussions of the origins of *qigong*, the roots of illness, and the fundamental *qigong* method of healing. "I do not talk about illness here, nor will we heal illness." Li writes "As a genuine practitioner, however, you cannot practice cultivation with an ill body. I will purify your body. . . . To really dispel such tribulations, karma must be eliminated."

"It is known that what actually causes people to be ill is seventy percent psychological and thirty percent physiological. Once you improve your *xinxing* [mind or heart nature, moral character], your body will undergo a great change."

Li also describes supernormal abilities that he believes "will naturally emerge" through future cultivation practice. Six supernormal abilities are recognized in the world today, he says, including clairvoyance, precognition, and retrocognition. "Yet they are not limited to these alone. I would say that over ten thousand genuine supernormal abilities exist." He cites occasions when Falun Gong practitioners were protected from injury because of their high level of cultivation: One practitioner was struck by a car but was not injured because she had "a very high *xinxing* level" and another was about to be hit by a car when it stopped suddenly. "It was Teacher who protected me," the practitioner said.

Li recommends integrating Falun Dafa practice into ordinary daily life and warns against zealotry. "The fundamental enlightenment that we talk about refers to this: In one's lifetime, from the outset of cultivation practice, one will constantly move up and let go of human attachments and various desires, and one's *gong* will also grow until the final step in cultivation practice. . . . His Third Eye will reach the highest point of its level, and he can see at his level the truth of different dimensions, the forms of existence or different lives and matter in different space-times, and the truth of our universe."

CENSORSHIP HISTORY

Li began to teach the practice of Falun Gong in China in 1992. It was one of many *qigong* groups that sprang up after Cultural Revolution–era restrictions were lifted during the 1980s. Li set up his first study center in Beijing and toured the country between 1992 and 1994 to lecture about his beliefs, often speaking at police and army educational institutions.

In January 1994, *Falun Zhuan* was published in Beijing and assigned an official publishing number. The book became a best seller, reflecting the widespread appeal of Falun Gong. The movement claimed a membership of 70 million in China and 30 million in 40 other countries. But because Falun Gong is a loose network of practitioners with no membership requirements, the number of its adherents is difficult to verify. Clearly Falun Gong's followers numbered in the millions in China and included many Communist Party members and officials. In 1998, the Chinese government estimated that Falun Gong had 40 million adherents; in 2001, after several years of government repression, official Chinese sources cited 2.1 million. The group set up thousands of teaching centers and practice areas in China and abroad and an extensive network of Web sites.

China's officially approved religions are Taoism, Buddhism, Christianity, Confucianism, and Islam. The government condemns any other religious activity as superstition. Falun Gong adherents, however, contend that the movement is not a religion but rather a network for transmitting information and practices.

Li was a member of China's government-approved Qigong Research Society, a body that oversees the various *qigong* groups. After three years of teaching, Li withdrew from the society and became estranged from the official structure. In 1996, the Chinese government's Press and Publications Administration issued a notice banning five Falun Gong publications, including *Falun Zhuan*, for propagating ignorance and superstition. But copies of the book produced in Hong Kong continued to be widely circulated in China. That year, Li announced that he had completed his teachings in China. He traveled in Europe and Asia and then settled in New York.

On April 25, 1999, Chinese officials were stunned when more than 10,000 Falun Gong adherents appeared outside the Chinese government leadership compound in Beijing and stood for 12 hours in a silent protest against government harassment and denigration of their movement. This was the largest mass demonstration since the Tiananmen Square prodemocracy demonstrations in 1989, and it marked a change in the official attitude toward Falun Gong. The government now saw it as a threat to authority and social order.

On July 22, the government declared that Falun Gong, as "an evil cult" that advocated superstition and jeopardized social stability, was now an illegal organization. The government accused the group of causing the deaths of more than 1,600 followers by encouraging them to avoid modern medical care or to commit suicide. It was prohibited "to distribute books, video/audio tapes or any other materials that propagate Falun Dafa (Falun Gong)," "to hold gatherings or demonstrations that uphold or propagate Falun Gong, such as sit-ins or appeals," and "to organize, coordinate or direct any activities that go against the government."

Security forces arrested Falun Gong leaders, ordering that senior members of the movement be "punished severely," and an arrest order was issued for Li. Nearly 30,000 participants nationwide were rounded up, detained, and questioned, many for days in open stadiums with inadequate food, water, and sanitary facilities. Practitioners who refused to renounce the movement were expelled from schools or fired. More than 1,200 government officials who had practiced Falun Gong were compelled to break their ties to the movement.

The police closed Falun Gong instruction centers and exercise areas, raided bookstores and homes of Falun Gong practitioners, and seized and destroyed videotapes and million of books. They arrested booksellers on charges of "illegal business practices" for selling Falun Gong publications. The government shut down or blocked Falun Gong Web sites and filtered Internet search engines such as Google to block access to information on the group.

As Falun Gong demonstrations continued around the country during the summer and fall of 1999, thousands of people were sent to labor camps, psychiatric wards, or prison. International human rights organizations reported abuse, torture, and deaths of practitioners in police custody. Falun Gong claims that more than 900 people have died in custody.

On October 31, 1999, Chinese authorities announced a new anticult law, which specified prison terms of three to seven years for cult members who "disturb public order" or distribute publications. "Banning cult organizations and punishing cult activities goes hand in hand with protecting normal religious activities and people's freedom of religious belief," the law stated. "The public should be exposed to the inhuman and anti-social nature of heretic cults, so that they can knowingly resist influences of the cult organizations, enhance their awareness of the law and abide by it."

In August 2001, the government said that it would summarily close down publications that reported on taboo topics, including press reports that "advocate murder, violence, obscenity, superstition or pseudo-science."

Ten years after the Chinese government began its crackdown on Falun Gong, the repression against the group's adherents continued unabated. In April 2009, the *New York Times* reported that as many as 8,000 practitioners had been detained in the previous year, and at least 100 had died in custody. Scores of practitioners had received long prison terms.

Although the Chinese government has succeeded in suppressing the distribution of Falun Gong publications in China, *Falun Zhuan* has been translated and published in more than 30 languages and is available without cost on the Internet.

FURTHER READING

Beaumont, Peter. "China's Falun Gong Crackdown: 'The Persecution Is Almost Underground.' " *Guardian* (July 18, 2009). Available online. URL: http://www.guardian.co.uk/world/2009/jul/18/china-falun-gong-crackdown. Accessed June 6, 2010.

Country Reports on Human Rights Practices—2003. Washington, D.C.: U.S. Department of State, 2004.

The Crackdown on Falun Gong and Other So-Called Heretical Organizations. London: Amnesty International, 2000.

Dangerous Meditations: China's Campaign Against Falungong. New York: Human Rights Watch, 2002.

Jacobs, Andrew. "China Still Presses Crusade against Falun Gong." *New York Times* (April 28, 2009). Available online. URL: http://www.nytimes.com/2009/04/28/world/asia/28china.html. Accessed June 6, 2010.

Schechter, Danny. *Falun Gong's Challenge to China.* New York: Akashic Books, 2001.

Literature Suppressed on Sexual Grounds

Actual or perceived sexual content continues to drive many people to try to remove books from schools and libraries. Those who would restrict other people's reading often use terms such as *explicit sexuality* or *age-inappropriateness*, but the specific reasons for the challenges can vary widely. Judy Blume's *Forever* has been removed from school libraries because of its discussions of sexual activity. In contrast, Stephenie Meyer's Twilight series, included in this new edition of *120 Banned Books* for the first time, has been removed from school libraries not because of its open depictions of sexuality—the series features a highly attractive male vampire who refuses to have a sexual relationship outside of marriage—but because parents have objected to the perceived erotic undercurrent that exists throughout the series.

Books banned for containing sexual content were the subject of major legal cases in the 20th century. Courts were compelled to determine whether D. H. Lawrence's *Lady Chatterley's Lover*, James Joyce's *Ulysses*, Vladimir Nabokov's *Lolita*, John Cleland's *Fanny Hill: Memoirs of a Woman of Pleasure*, and Voltaire's *Candide*, among many other works, were simply lewd and indecent and could therefore be banned or instead had "redeeming social importance," the test set by the United States Supreme Court in 1957 as the standard for acceptability. Many other books were banned because they alluded to or discussed unwed pregnancy, prostitution, or adultery. Still others were banned because they contained passages that had the clear intention of titillating readers.

By 1970, the barriers were lowered, and the Report of the United States President's Commission on Obscenity seemed to acknowledge that resisting the freedom to read was futile: "Virtually every English language book thought to be obscene when published, and many similar books translated into English, have been reissued by secondary publishers. The entire stockpile of 'classic erotic literature' (e.g., *Kama Sutra*, Frank Harris, de Sade, etc.)

published over centuries has thus come onto the market." Formerly banned books, such as *Candide, Lolita, Lady Chatterley's Lover*, and *Madame Bovary*, became required reading in college and high school classrooms.

In 1986, the findings of the Meese Commission (more properly known as the Attorney General's Commission on Pornography) seemed to add support to the right to read material containing sexually related content. The panel recommended "extraordinary caution" in regard to prosecuting those who distributed materials that contained no photographs, pictures, or drawings: "The written word has had and continues to have a special place in this and any other civilization." In working toward the goal of defining what is pornography and, thus, unacceptable, the Commission designed as among the "least harmful" types of pornography "books consisting of the printed text only." The Commission observed that such text might not always meet its criteria for pornography, which is material that is "sexually explicit and intended primarily for the purpose of sexual arousal."

Nonetheless, books deemed "sexually explicit" are still challenged today. Parents, concerned citizens, religious organizations, and others frequently submit complaints to their local school officials and municipal governments demanding that the books they find to be offensive be removed from classrooms and school and public libraries. This new edition of *120 Banned Books* includes new entries not only on recently published books or series, such as the Twilight and Gossip Girl series, but also on longtime classics, such as Richard Wright's *Native Son*, Zora Neale Hurston's *Their Eyes Were Watching God*, and *The Epic of Gilgamesh*. Other highly acclaimed works that have suffered recent challenges include Rudolfo Anaya's *Bless Me, Ultima*, Julia Alvarez's *How the García Girls Lost Their Accents*, and Toni Morrison's *Song of Solomon*.

The number of challenges reported annually appears to have decreased in recent years, but the reasons for this may lie simply in the practice of preventive banning, in which officials in school and public library systems neglect to purchase a book that has motivated controversy. This is not a victory over censorship. It should instead open our eyes to the increasingly subtle ways in which others continue to attempt to suppress our right to read.

—Dawn B. Sova, Ph.D.

ALWAYS RUNNING—LA VIDA LOCA: GANG DAYS IN L.A.

Author: Luis T. Rodriguez
Original date and place of publication: 1993, Willimantic, Connecticut
Original publisher: Curbstone Press
Literary form: Autobiography

SUMMARY

Always Running is the memoir of a former Los Angeles gang member that takes readers deep into the poverty, crime, and despair of the barrios of Los Angeles and reveals the often frightening and brutal world in which surviving is a daily struggle. With honesty and eloquence, Luis Rodriguez writes of surviving the gang lifestyle, "the crazy life." He reveals in the prologue how he managed to finally break free from gang life and explains what enabled him to begin focusing on being creative and to work for the advancement of the Chicano people. He explains clearly that, however important, these are not his main reasons for writing the book. Instead, he was motivated to tell his story when he realized that his young son, Ramiro, to whom the book is dedicated, was being swept up in the gang culture. His main concern was to save his son from the suffering he experienced and the threats of violence and death associated with the gang lifestyle.

The memoir begins with Rodriguez's parents' move from Mexico when the author was very young and outlines his early years living in the Watts section of Los Angeles; however, it covers primarily the years he was active in gang life in the Las Lomas barrio, from ages 12 through 18. The author states in the preface that this is a nonfiction work, but he admits that he has changed names and stories to protect people from being hurt by revelations about their lives. "I've changed names and synthesized events and circumstances in keeping with the integrity of a literary dramatic work, as an artist does in striving for that rare instance when, as a critic once said, 'something of beauty collides with something of truth.'"

Luis and his sisters and brothers were born in El Paso, Texas, but the family moved back and forth between there and Mexico while he was a baby. His father, a teacher, was sent to jail in Mexico for reasons that were never clearly revealed to the family. After he was released, the family left Mexico and ended up in Watts, one of the poorest sections of Los Angeles. Young Luis soon found himself surrounded by *la vida loca*, or "the crazy life," a world filled with violence, sex, suicide, drugs, prison, and death.

Luis's attempts to stay in school became increasingly difficult, as Latino students attended school where facilities and learning materials were outdated and the schools were surrounded by drug dealing and violence. The predominantly black and Latino schools of the author's experience did not receive the same funding as schools in other areas of the city, and in the late sixties and early seventies racial and gang-related confrontations were daily occurrences. Luis began a cycle of being suspended from school, then being expelled, and then ending up in jail or on drugs. When he was approximately 14, he began "sniffing" anything he could get his hands on: "I stole cans of anything that could give a buzz: carbono, clear plastic, paint or gasoline. Sometimes I'd mix it up in a concoction and pour it on a rag or in a paper bag we sniffed from." He refers to these mixtures as "spray" and describes their effects on his and his friends' brains in graphic language: "The world became like jello, like clay, something which could be molded and shaped. . . . With spray I became water."

Rodriguez's parents became disgusted with the lack of respect he showed toward the family and their house, so they made him move out of the house and live in their small garage. Soon after, he was initiated into the Lomas gang, and with several friends he began wreaking havoc on the lives of rival gang members, participating in beatings and riots, and having sex with multiple partners. With the increasing accessibility of heroin and PCP on the poverty-stricken streets of Los Angeles, the author's drug use became increasingly self-destructive. He describes his lingering depression throughout his high school years and his two attempts at suicide.

> I tried to commit suicide. I had come home in a stupor from pills, liquor and from sniffing aerosol can spray. I had slithered into the house around 3 A.M. and made it to the bathroom. Everyone else slept. Leaning on a washbasin, I looked into the mirror and stared into a face of weariness, of who-cares, of blood-shot eyes, prickly whiskers poking out of the chin, an unruly mustache below a pimpled nose, a face that as much as I tried could not be washed away.
>
> I staggered out of the house and crossed into a backyard with lemon trees and decayed avocados on the ground, and a tiled ramada with hanging vines. I entered my room in the garage, grabbed the pail I used to pee in, and filled it with water from a faucet on a rusted outdoor pipe. I planned to thrust my arm into the water after I cut an artery (I didn't want any blood on the floor—even at this moment I feared Mama cursing about the mess).
>
> I pressed my street-scarred and tattooed body against the wall and held a razor to my wrist. Closed my eyes. Hummed a song—I don't know what song. But I couldn't do it.

He acknowledges that several times he wanted to leave the gang life but it always managed to pull him back in. He also describes the terrifying brutality of the police, who justified their actions by claiming that their treatment of gang members helped protect the law-abiding citizens of Los Angeles. According to Rodriguez, what they did not admit was that anyone whose skin was brown was likely to get stopped, harassed, and probably arrested.

Rodriguez reveals that from the age of 15, he was writing in his mind and in personal notes what became the beginning of *Always Running*. As he grew older, he tried to remove himself from the gang life, but making the change was very difficult for him. He bounced from school to school and eventually became involved in Chicano organizations. This new interest put some stability into his life, but the deaths of several friends and family members left him feeling empty. At the same time, his family was in the process of breaking down. His sister became involved in the gang life and his brother was murdered shortly after. His father continued to experience frustration in attempting to become an American teacher, and his mother struggled for years to learn English.

Rodriguez never glamorizes the gang lifestyle, but he explains why he could not avoid becoming involved in it. The reader begins to understand that his volatile behavior is a reaction against his young life and that of his fellow gang members. Violent passages such as the following one have been highlighted by opponents of the book: "The dude looked at me through glazed eyes, horrified at my presence, at what I held in my hands, at this twisted, swollen face that came at him through the dark. *Do it!* were the last words I recalled before I plunged the screwdriver into flesh and bone, and the sky screamed."

The author eventually found comfort in writing poetry, and through involvement in volunteer organizations he became involved in helping Chicano people advance. He learned that his organizational skills are far more helpful to his people than a gun or a knife in his hand. He successfully struggled to leave the gang, but his life came full circle when his young son joined a gang. After reading a poem written by his son, Ramiro, Luis helped his son leave his gang and realize that his life was more valuable to his family than to his gang.

CENSORSHIP HISTORY

Luis Rodriguez admits that *Always Running* is "a hard-core book" and presents "a lot of graphic material." He denies that any of the graphic material is gratuitous, claiming that "There's no way you can write this kind of book without getting as close to what these young people are going through." The book won the Carl Sandburg Literary Arts Award, and a *Chicago Sun-Times* Book Award, and it was lavishly praised in reviews by the *New York Times*, the *Washington Post*, and the *National Catholic Reporter*. Parents and educators in several school districts have disagreed with that viewpoint and have banned the book.

In 1996, *Always Running* was the first book ever banned in the Rockford, Illinois, school district. Parents complained to school district officials that passages in the book contained "extreme violence, sexually graphic descriptions, and anti-family rhetoric." The story was picked up by Judy Howard, a local columnist who was affiliated with the conservative organization Citizens for Excellence in Education, and the controversy accelerated. On June 11, 1996, the Rockford School District school board voted 4-3 to remove the book from school libraries throughout the district. In the discussion preceding the vote, school board member David Strommer, who voted against keeping the book, spoke of *Always Running* as "irreligious, anti-family, left-wing, anti-American and radical. . . . What's in the book is harmful, ungodly and wrong." Ed Sharp, another board member who voted against the book, stated, "I challenge anyone who knows how the mind works, after reading this book, not to be more likely to assume the lifestyle of a gang person and not to be more likely to have sex in the back of a car."

In October 1998, controversy over the book arose in San Jose, California, when parent Sarah Gama told school officials that her daughter, a student at Lincoln High School, had complained that the book she had chosen from the supplemental reading list "was not clean" and claimed that a male classmate had made "a sexually explicit comment" to her on the school bus. *Always Running* had appeared on the supplemental reading lists for Lincoln High School and Broadway High School in the San Jose Unified School District for several years without controversy. Lincoln High School has a zero-tolerance policy on sexual harassment, but officials could do nothing because Gama and her daughter refused to identify the boy who had made the comment, "saying only that he was inspired to make the comment by *Always Running.*" The school district gave Gama's daughter the opportunity to select another book, which she did, but Gama insisted that the district remove the book from the classrooms and libraries. When school officials refused to comply, she appeared on a local radio talk show and accused the district of "supplying pornography to children." The appearance triggered numerous angry telephone calls to school district officials. The *San Francisco Chronicle* reported on May 16, 1998, that a group called the Justice Institute threatened the school district with legal action, claiming that the district was promoting child pornography by keeping the book on the reading list. School officials yielded to the protestors and removed the book from school classroom and library shelves until a 10-member panel of parents, teachers, and community members could hear public testimony and readings of controversial passages. San Jose resident Adele Hernandez read aloud a long passage "detailing a variety of sexual acts in the back seat of a car" and then told members of the panel, "I'm sure none of you are exactly shocked by this. But I was. I'm sure there's a lot more out there other than this to teach our children." At the hearing, the chair of the English department at Lincoln High School, Kris Morrella, stated, "This book is an easy target. It's easy to take those few passages out of context." The panel recommended that the school district retain *Always Running*, but the book remained on junior and senior reading lists, and students who wished to read alternative books would have that option.

A May 1998 meeting was attended by nearly 100 people and lasted two-and-a-half hours, during which parents, teachers, and community members expressed heated opinions. In the end, the school board agreed with the panel's decision and voted to keep the book on the reading list. After two students spoke and defended the book, parent Rene Moncada stated to those present that teenagers are at "the stupidest time of their life. To me, their opinion doesn't count." He then read aloud an obscenity-filled passage from the book. Another parent, Deborah García, claimed that she was "embarrassed to read the book out loud" and said that she disliked the negative manner in which Hispanics are portrayed in the book: "I'm a proud American, but my history is Mexico, and the people and culture I know is very different from this." On July 23, 1998, a group of San Jose parents called the Parental Rights Organization, formed right after the school board voted to keep the book on the supplemental reading list, officially informed three board members that they would be subjected to a recall campaign.

In Modesto, California, in spring 2003, Patricia LaChapell, the parent of a home-schooled student in the school district, discovered that the supplemental reading lists for three advanced English classes at Beyer High School taught by teacher Melissa Cervantes contained *Always Running*. LaChappell contacted the board of education and requested that the board remove the book from the advanced English classes and from the approved list on which it appeared. The seven-member board declined to do so and, instead, recommended that administrators provide parents with more information about books, including a summary of the text. They also asserted that parents can choose to excuse their child from any assignment they find objectionable. In October 2003, LaChappell approached school administrators to complain a second time about the book. As the American Library Association Office on Intellectual Freedom reported, "After taking a second look at the board-approved book, district administrators told Cervantes that she could no longer use the book in her class." In defending the move, David Cooper, director of secondary education in the district, said the book was "not well-written and does not have the same literary value as other novels."

The swift and unilateral action by school district administrators outraged Barney Hale, executive director of the 1,800-member Modesto Teacher's Association. He said that the administrators had violated their own policy by pulling the book without going through the appropriate channel of taking the matter back to the board that had already approved it. To quell the uproar, the district sent the book for review to a committee of high school English department chairs. Members of the committee disagreed with the complaint and recommended reinstatement of the book, which is on a state-approved book list. In a vote of 4-3, the school board reaffirmed the decision to retain the book.

FURTHER READING

"Censorship Dateline: Schools: Modesto, California." *Newsletter on Intellectual Freedom* 53 (March 2004): 51–52.

Frey, Christine. "Parents Notify 3 SJUSD Trustees of Their Intention to Recall Them." *Willow Glen Resident*, July 29, 1998.

Gaura, Maria Alicia. "Parents in San Jose Criticize School Book—District Reviewing Use of Explicit Novel." *San Francisco Chronicle*, May 16, 1998.

"Modesto School Board Votes to Allow Controversial Book to Stay on List." KXTV News 10 Broadcast, December 16, 2003.

"Success Stories—Libraries: Modesto, California." *Newsletter on Intellectual Freedom* 53 (January 2004).

Sullivan, Patrick. "Luis Rodriguez Casts a Skeptical Eye on Attempts to Ban His Autobiography." *Sonoma County Independent*, February 4–10, 1999.

BLESS ME, ULTIMA

Author: Rudolfo Anaya
Original Date and Place of Publication: 1994, United States
Original Publisher: Warner Books, Inc.
Literary Form: Young Adult Novel

SUMMARY

Bless Me, Ultima is the coming-of-age story of seven-year-old Antonio Marez, who struggles to make sense of the changes happening within his family and in life surrounding him in New Mexico in the years immediately following World War II. The novel resonates with sounds of the Spanish language, which Anaya uses in chapter titles and throughout the work, and with the cultural traditions and the beliefs that define Antonio's world.

In 22 chapters, titled from "Uno"(one) through "Veintidos" (22), Antonio observes the actions and reactions of his parents, his brothers, the people in his small town, and the healer, Ultima. Antonio's parents differ in their goals for his future, and both draw upon their own backgrounds to derive their dreams for the little boy. The daughter of farmers, Maria Marez is a devout Catholic who prays that Antonio will become a priest, while his father, Gabriel, once a vaquero who wandered the New Mexico llano, wants him to become a vaquero and to wander the great plains as he once did. Their argument over his future has already resulted in problems when Ultima reenters their lives. She is a well-respected healer with an extensive knowledge of plant lore and a reputation for using white magic to help the people of the small town of Guadalupe. As a midwife, she has been present at the births of many people in the town, and Antonio's parents believe that only Ultima truly knows their son's future because she helped him to enter the world and only she knows where she buried his afterbirth.

Ultima moves into the Marez home, and Antonio follows her around as she gathers herbs to make her healing concoctions. As they work together, he learns both about the plants and the nature surrounding him, as well as about the spiritual world, of which he has largely remained ignorant. Antonio is forced to begin thinking seriously about sin and death after seeing Lupito shot to death by a crowd in retaliation for Lupito's murder of the sheriff. Lupito suffers from post-traumatic shock disorder—a malady undiagnosed among soldiers of the time—which led to his momentary madness during which he shot and killed the sheriff. Ultima takes the troubled little boy to church with her the next morning and speaks with him about the moral choices all people must make in their effort to confront the world. Her words seem vague to him at the time, but he refers to that conversation later as his brothers return from the war and he senses in them the trauma that led Lupito to such a violent end.

When Antonio begins school, after helping his mother's brothers to harvest their crops, his parents become increasingly anxious about his future. Pressed by Maria to reveal Antonio's future, Ultima tells the family that he will "be a man of learning," a prediction that leaves Gabriel dissatisfied, and he turns his hopes for the success of the family to his older sons, who return from serving in World War II. Gabriel anticipates that their return will enable the entire family to leave New Mexico and move to California, where he feels the opportunities for success will be greater. Rather than fulfill his hopes, Antonio's older brothers are restless and angry and unable to achieve peace with their father and instead leave the small town to pursue independent lives without the family. Their exodus further confuses Antonio, who cannot understand why his father and his brothers were not able to be happy together. His mother is saddened when her older sons leave, and she is unable to explain their behavior to Antonio and can only tell him that he will understand many things when he has his First Holy Communion, an event to which he looks forward eagerly.

The world surrounding Antonio becomes increasingly complicated for him, as he hears stories and learns truths about Ultima that are difficult to reconcile with the Catholic faith his mother has worked hard to instill in him. His friend Samuel tells him about a river god in the form of a golden carp that protects mankind, and he feels guilty for believing the story because it conflicts with his religious upbringing. He learns that the satanic Trementina sisters have cursed his uncle Lucas and finds that the Catholic priest cannot rout the curse, but Ultima can with Antonio's help. He then worries how to reconcile his respect for Ultima's abilities with his Catholic faith.

Antonio faces a major crisis one afternoon in a blizzard when he sees a fight between Narciso, the town alcoholic, and Tenorio, whose daughters had cursed his uncle Lucas. One of the sisters has died, and Tenorio blames Ultima for her death and plans to kill Ultima. Narciso tries to prevent the murder, and Tenorio shoots and kills him while Antonio watches. Afterward, the young boy develops a life-threatening fever and experiences horrifying dreams.

Through all of the traumatic experiences, Antonio holds fast to the belief that he will understand everything that has occurred once he has experienced his First Holy Communion, and he struggles to balance the dissenting voices of his father, his mother, and his friend Florence, who points out to him the weaknesses in Catholic teachings. Antonio expects to experience an epiphany on Easter Sunday, when he takes his First Communion, and he feels seriously let down afterward because he feels no change. As Ultima helps Antonio to build moral independence and reinforces for him the very strong existence of good in the world, she also adds to his confusion. He helps her to exorcise ghosts from a house that Tenorio has put under a spell and learns that Tenorio's remaining daughter has become very ill after the incident. He also loses his friend Florence when she drowns in the river. Antonio is sent to stay on his uncles' farm to recover from losing his friend, but conflict follows him there as well. After a relaxing summer, he encounters Tenorio while walking from his uncles' farm to his grandfather's house, and the crazed man chases him and shoots at him. Antonio remains unharmed, but Tenorio shoots Ultima's owl, her spiritual familiar. When the owl dies, Ultima's death becomes inevitable. Antonio sits with the old woman as she dies, and he carries out her wish that he bury her owl after her death.

The novel does not sanitize Antonio's experiences. At school, he hears another classmate confess to spying through a hole in the wall into the girl's bathroom. "I made a hole in the wall . . . could see into the girls' bathroom. . . . could see everything . . . her ass, hear the pee." A friend brags, "I saw a boy and girl fucking in the grass," to which another classmate replies, "Aw, I see them every night under the railroad bridge . . . naked." Tenorio and other characters curse as they express their anger and intermittent sexual references appear in the text, if only briefly.

CENSORSHIP HISTORY

Bless Me, Ultima, which won the Premio Quinto Sol national literary award in 1972, has been praised by literary critics as "the masterwork" of Rudolfo Anaya, who is widely acclaimed as the founder of modern Chicano literature. President George W. Bush awarded the author a National Medal of the Arts "for exceptional contribution to contemporary American literature for bringing national recognition to the Chicano people," and First Lady Laura Bush placed the novel on her "must-read" list. The novel has also been chosen by the National Endowment for the Humanities for its "Big Read" program. In contrast, parents and administrators in several school districts have condemned the novel as "filthy" and asserted that it contains "excessive vulgarity" and removed it from classrooms.

Norwood, Colorado, superintendent of schools Bob Conder said in February 2005 that he removed two dozen copies of the novel from English classes at the high school after a parent complained that the book contained "filthy" language. He then turned the copies over to the complaining parents John and Rhonda Oliver, who "put them in a trash can and it goes to a landfill. . . . This is just our way of knowing it would be gone." When Luis Torres, a professor of Chicano studies at Metropolitan State College in Denver, offered to pay the school district $1,000 to rescue the books, Conder said that the school district "would not sponsor such garbage" and stated that he had given the books to the parents who complained, claiming he "wasn't certain if the books had been burned or otherwise destroyed." Torres told reporters that he and his colleagues were offering the school district far more than the original cost of $7 each because they were concerned about the misreading of the book. "We are offering such a deal to the Norwood School District because 'Bless Me, Ultima' is one of the most significant cultural treasures of the Chicano community in the United States, and we do not want the book destroyed. Its philosophical basis is the combining, or 'mestizage,' in Spanish, of the Spanish and European and Mexican indigenous cultural traditions, the cultural combination that resulted in today's Mexican and Chicano communities." Public outcry was strong. After 20 students staged an all day sit-in in the school gymnasium and took turns reading aloud from the book, Conder apologized to the students and promised that none of the students who demonstrated would be penalized for their action. He also wrote a letter of apology for removing the book "without enough information on the content of the book" and without reading either the book or the school board policy regarding such issues. He stated that he had formed a committee to review the book, as well as the existing curriculum, and to make recommendations about the book. A year later, an article appearing in the *Denver Post* on May 12, 2006, reported that two teachers who had been outspoken in defending the book during the controversy over *Bless Me, Ultima* were not recommended to be rehired in the Norwood School District. Interim superintendent Larry Raney asserted "The book issue never came up," and refused to comment on the teachers' fate, claiming that he could not talk about the situation because "they are personnel matters" and noting that the two teachers were at the end of their three-year probationary period.

On February 2, 2009, the Newman Crows Landing Unified School District, California, school board voted 4–1 to ban *Bless Me, Ultima* from the sophomore reading list at Orestimba High School after a controversy of several months that began when a parent complained that the novel is "sexually explicit." Superintendent of Schools Rick Fauss concurred with the decision to remove the book and expressed his concern that "There was excessive vulgarity or profanity used throughout the book." The controversy began in the summer of 2008, after Nancy Corgiat, the mother of a sophomore student at the high school, contacted the school superintendent and "initially complained about the vulgar language, the sexually explicit scenes and an anti-Catholic bias." Fauss claimed he "followed district policy, had two committees review the book, and ultimately opted to remove it from the classroom. It went through all the procedures as outlined in the board policy and ended up with me." Teachers were told to find a replacement book for classes, despite the protests of parents who voiced concern about the ban and said the board was spending too much time counting "bad words." Fauss and members of the school board expressed concern about the language and noted, "The context didn't make it acceptable." When parents suggested that lawyers with the American Civil Liberties Union might launch a lawsuit to reinstate the book, the superintendent expressed confidence that his position and that of the board would prevail: "We're not afraid of that; we know what our rights are. We have insurance;

we'll fight it." He denied that the school district had engaged in an act of censorship and asserted, "It's not censorship. It's simply a matter of determining our curriculum, which is left to the school district."

FURTHER READINGS

"Censorship Dateline: Schools." *Newsletter on Intellectual Freedom* 58, no. 2 (March 2009): 39–41.

Draper, Electa. "Norwood Book Ban Brings Offer: Metro Prof Will Pay $1,000 to Retrieve Copies of 'Bless Me, Ultima.'" *Denver Post*, February 4, 2005, p. B–05.

Florio, Gwen. "Award-Winning Book Headed for Landfill." *Rocky Mountain News*, February 4, 2005. Available online. URL: http://www.rockymountainnews.com/drmn/state/article/0,1299, DRMN_21_3522696,00.html. Accessed June 14, 2010.

Lofholm, Nancy. "Town Fights to Retain Teachers: 2 Vocal Advocates: Norwood School District Officials Deny That a Book-Banning Incident Last Year Imperiled the Educators' Jobs." *Denver Post*, May 12, 2006, p. B-05.

Mehta, Seema. "California District Bans Book Lauded by Laura Bush." *Record*, February 2009, p. A07.

THE BLUEST EYE

Author: Toni Morrison
Original date and place of publication: 1970, United States
Original publisher: Holt, Rinehart and Winston
Literary form: Novel

SUMMARY

The Bluest Eye is a sad and tragic novel that recounts the abuse and destruction of Pecola Breedlove, a young African-American girl whose mother knew that her very dark baby would grow into an unattractive young girl. The novel, which takes place in 1940, is narrated by Claudia MacTeer, two years younger than Pecola and her only friend. Black in a white-dominated world, Pecola begins to believe that life would be prettier and better if she were white, and she views blue eyes as symbolic of whiteness. She watches her father, Cholly Breedlove, become increasingly violent as his shattered dreams and constant humiliations as an African American heighten his frustrations, and her mother, Pauline, escapes into the clean and orderly life of working as a maid in a white family's home.

 Pecola is raped by her father one spring afternoon when he returns home drunk and the two are alone. She becomes pregnant after he rapes her a second time. Traumatized by the attacks, she drifts further from reality and visits fraudulent minister Micah Elihue Whitcomb, known commonly as Soaphead Church, to ask him to give her blue eyes. For a fee, Soaphead claims that he can help her, but she must perform a task for him. He has wanted to rid himself of an old, sick dog, so he gives Pecola poisoned meat to feed the dog but tells her only that feeding the dog will result in a sign regarding her wish. Pecola is horrified as she watches the dog stagger around the yard and then die.

The combination of the rapes and this incident drives Pecola mad, leading to her complete loss of touch with reality. Pecola believes that she does have blue eyes and invents an imaginary friend who is always nearby for reassurance that her eyes are the bluest in the world.

CENSORSHIP HISTORY

Several incidents in the book have sparked controversy. The two rapes of Pecola have been criticized for being too graphic in description, and the novel describes the sounds that Pecola hears of her parents having sex in the room next to hers. Another incident that is specifically described is Cholly's first sexual encounter, during which he is surprised by three white hunters who focus a flashlight on the young people and force them to conclude their sexual act.

The Bluest Eye has been challenged in several school districts because of its "vulgar" and "obscene" language as well as for its "graphic sexual description." In 1994, the novel was removed from the 11th-grade curriculum at Lathrop High School in Fairbanks, Alaska, after parents complained that the language was "obscene" and that it contained explicit sexual episodes. School administrators ordered the book removed from the required reading list and stated as their reasons that "it was a very controversial book; it contains lots of very graphic descriptions and lots of disturbing language."

That same year, the novel was challenged in the West Chester, Pennsylvania, school district and at Morrisville (Pennsylvania) Borough High School. Parents in both districts complained to the school board of education about the "sexual content" of the novel and its "objectionable language." After reviewing the complaint and the book, the boards in both districts rejected the parents' request to remove the book from the school libraries and reading lists.

In November 2003, in Bakersfield, California, parents of a student attending East Bakersfield High School in the Kern High School district filed a complaint with the school superintendent requesting to have *The Bluest Eye* removed from the school district curriculum. Sue and Fred Porter initiated the process after their 16-year-old daughter brought the novel home from school and told her mother that the book made her feel uncomfortable, especially the sexual descriptions. Sarah was not bothered by the rape of Pecola by her stepfather; rather, it was "the description of how his genitalia enlarged while he was raping her that I had a problem with." In the formal complaint, Sue Porter asserted that the book "is obscene, according to a dictionary definition. When you say that an illegal act such as pedophilia or incest is not repulsive or offensive to modesty, that's just not true." She acknowledged that the novel "may be great literature—and may not—but it's not appropriate for children. Teachers are not qualified to speak on incest and pedophilia. We're going to put this in our kids' laps and we're not giving them any counseling for it?" Kern

High School district superintendent William Hatcher organized a committee of parents, teachers, counselors, ministers, and librarians to review the book. In their report, they determined that the book is not obscene and stated, "It is neither prurient nor titillating. More importantly, taken as a whole, it has serious literary value." The committee and Hatcher did agree, however, that parents would be notified by letter that their child is reading *The Bluest Eye* and, at the parents' request, students can ask for an alternative assignment. The superintendent approved the use of the novel in the junior and senior honors and advanced placement classes. At the January 12, 2004, meeting of the Kern High School district school board, several school board trustees raised the issue of removing the novel from the classroom. Trustee Sam Thomas expressed "grave reservations about the book's sexually explicit material" and said that he could not support the book with a clear conscience, but he would not pull the book from class reading lists because "What I support is not the book, but the process." Board member Larry Starrh stated that he had read the book and several articles and letters discussing it, and he had decided that it was not appropriate for the classroom. "I would like to recommend that we overrule the superintendent," he stated, and asked to have the item added to the next board meeting agenda, scheduled for February 2, 2004. State law prevented the trustees from voting at the January 12th meeting because the public had not been previously informed that a vote would take place. The controversy attracted the attention of faculty at California State University, Bakersfield, who defended *The Bluest Eye*. In a resolution, the Academic Senate voted to

support the decision made by Kern High School District Superintendent Hatcher and urge the members of the Kern High School District Board of Trustees to vote against banning of *The Bluest Eye* from honors and advanced placement high school reading lists. . . . as a university faculty, we have an obligation to protect freedom and to guard against undue censorship. The complaint in question is an effort to ban *The Bluest Eye* from all high school classrooms, resulting in the censorship of a world-renowned and critically acclaimed literary work by Nobel laureate Toni Morrison.

The district school board trustees voted on February 2, 2004, to support the decision of the superintendent to retain the book in the honors and advanced placement classrooms. The Porter family, who initiated the review, filed a lawsuit against their daughter's English teacher "on the grounds that assigning the novel constituted sexual harassment." The lawsuit was dismissed.

In August 2005, the Littleton (Colorado) Public Schools district school board removed *The Bluest Eye* from the media-center shelves of the Heritage and Arahapoe High Schools after one parent complained of the book's "explicit description of sex in telling the story of an 11-year-old girl who is raped by her father." The book had been approved for students in the 10th grade and up, but the complaint came from the parent of a Heritage High School ninth-grade student who chose the book from a list of optional reading. The district formed a study group made up of parents, teachers, and administrators to review the complaint. The group recommended that the board restrict the book to juniors and seniors, a recommendation the board rejected in a 3-2 vote at the August meeting and, instead, voted to remove the book entirely. District policy required that the book could not be reconsidered until the end of the school year, but students and teachers actively voiced their displeasure and worked for reinstatement of the book. On October 5, 2005, high school students conducted sit-ins in their respective school libraries and read aloud excerpts from the novel. That evening, English teachers and students appeared in front of the school board to defend the book. Amanda Hurley, an English teacher in Heritage High School, acknowledged that the novel is "painful, difficult to read," but she also stated, "We have to discuss it, we have to learn from it." Students spoke in favor of the book and expressed fear that banning it was a dangerous precedent. Camille Okoren, Heritage High School senior, stated, "Once you ban one book, parents and teachers think it's OK to ban another book. Everyone is offended by different things." The board refused to reconsider the August decision and suggested that any member of the community can initiate the process of adding a book to the list of approved volumes, which would bring the issue back to the board before the end of the school year. Judy Vlasin, a Littleton High School English teacher, filed an application for reinstatement of the novel and included materials to support the educational value of the book. The novel has since been returned to the classroom for use by ninth and 10th grade students.

In Howell, Michigan, in 2007, the revision of the high school English curriculum and reading lists to comply with new state graduation requirements led to protests and complaints at a Howell Board of Education meeting that attracted the attention of national groups, including the National Coalition Against Censorship (NCAC), the American Booksellers Foundation for Free Expression (ABFFE), and the Woodhull Freedom Foundation. Members of the Livingston Organization for Values in Education (LOVE) singled out *The Bluest Eye* and *Black Boy* by Richard Wright as "smut," although the books had been read for two years in American literature classes. Anne Blaine, resident and author of a Christian novel, read aloud to school board members several graphic paragraphs and stated, "I've never read such smut like that in my life." On February 6, 2007, Chris Finan, ABFFE president, and the executive directors of NCAC and the Woodhull Freedom Foundation, respectively, Joan Bertin and Ricci Joy Levy, wrote an open letter to the Howell Board of Education and President Susan L. Drazic. The letter defended study of the novels in the classroom and asserted that the insistence upon the sexual references in the novels were distortions.

The sexual content and profanity in *The Bluest Eye* and in *Black Boy* represent small but essential parts of the novels, consistent with the kind of material that high school students frequently read. Indeed, if students were precluded from reading literature with sexual content, they would be deprived of exposure to vast amounts of important material, including Shakespeare, major religious texts such as the Bible, the works of Tolstoy, Flaubert, Joyce, Faulkner, D.H. Lawrence, and Nabokov, and contemporary books such as *I Know Why the Caged Bird Sings*, and many of the texts regularly assigned in high schools throughout the State of Michigan.

The challengers' focus on the sexual content of *The Bluest Eye* and *Black Boy* is misleading. These books are primarily concerned not with sexuality but with the important issues created by differences in social class and race.

At a heavily attended meeting on February 12, 2007, the school board voted 5-2 to return the novels to the Howell High School curriculum. Prior to the meeting, LOVE president Vicki Fyke contacted the county prosecutor David Morse and asked him to investigate the assignment of the books as a criminal violation. Fyke asserted that the assignment of the novels in a classroom was equivalent to the "distribution of sexually explicit materials to minors." Morse complied with the request and decided that no laws were being violated. In a letter to Fyke, Morse wrote that teachers assigning books that have been approved by the school board are exempt from prosecution: "Since the school board has approved use of these books, the teachers and administrators have complied with the school code and are excepted from criminal prosecution under the statute." Morse also asserted that the novels did not meet the criminal standard of being harmful to minors "because the sexually explicit scenes that Fyke and others objected to did not only appeal to readers' prurient interest in sex, and the books as a whole have substantial literary value." After the Howell School Board approved reinstatement of the novels, Fyke contacted the U.S. attorney for the Eastern District of Michigan, who forwarded her case to the Federal Bureau of Investigation (FBI) to investigate her claim that the school district teachers were distributing pornographic material to minors. In an interview on March 1, 2007, with reporter Tony Tagliavia of station WLIX, Fyke stated, "If anybody else gave them this material, it's against the law." On March 10, 2007, ABFFE released the following statement regarding Fyke's efforts: "Late yesterday, U.S. Attorney Stephen J. Murphy III and the Michigan attorney general's office announced that the complaints of obscenity by LOVE are without merit, and there has been no violation of federal law by placing the above-mentioned books on the Howell school approved reading list." Although represented as a local group, LOVE was assisted by the American Family Association, a larger organization that has initiated restrictions and banning in other states. The Michigan chapter assisted in filing the complaint with the state attorney general and the U.S. Department of Justice, claiming that the books violate laws against child pornography and child sexual abuse.

FURTHER READING

"Award Winning Books Challenged in Michigan School." Letter to the Howell School District Board of Education, February 6, 2007. Available online. URL: http://www.

ncac.org/literature/20070206~MI-Howell~Award_Winning_Books_Challenged_ in_Michigan_School.cfm.

Butler-Evans, Elliott. *Race, Gender, and Desire: Narrative Strategies in the Fiction of Toni Cade Bambara and Toni Morrison.* Philadelphia, Pa.: Temple University Press, 1989.

"FBI Investigates Charge That Howell Books Are Porn." WLIX Broadcast Reported by Tony Tagliavia, March 1, 2007. Available online. URL: http://www.wilx.com/ news/headlines/6240036.htm. Accessed January 31, 2011.

Kuenz, Jane. "*The Bluest Eye*: Notes on History, Community, and Black Female Subjectivity." *African American Review* 27 (Fall 1993): 421–431.

National Coalition Against Censorship. "Michigan Board Retains Challenged Books." (Press Release, February 13, 2007). Available online. URL: http://www.ncac.org/ literature/related/howellpr.cfm. Accessed January 31, 2011.

Newsletter on Intellectual Freedom (May 1994): 86; (January 1995): 25; (March 1995): 44–45; (March 2004): 50–51; (May 2004): 118–119; (November 2005): 29; (January 2006): 13–15; (March 2007): 50–54; (May 2007): 117–118.

Staht, Jayne Lyn. "Howell: A Postscript—Atlantic Free Press—Hard Truths for Hard Times." Atlantic Free Press (March 10, 2007). Available online. URL: http://www. atlanticfreepress.com/news/1/1148-howell-a-postscript.html. Accessed January 31, 2011.

Tirrell, Lynne. "Storytelling and Moral Agency." *Journal of Aesthetics & Art Criticism* 48 (Spring 1990): 115–26.

Weinstein, Philip M. *What Else but Love? The Ordeal of Race in Faulkner and Morrison.* New York: Columbia University Press, 1996.

CANDIDE

Author: Voltaire (François-Marie Arouet)
Original date and place of publication: 1759, Switzerland
Publishers: Gabriel and Philibert Cramer
Literary form: Satire

SUMMARY

Candide, originally *Candide, ou l'optimisme,* is a satire of optimism and of the belief that "the world is the best of all possible worlds and everything in it is a necessary evil," a theory attributed to the philosopher Gottfried Leibniz. Voltaire refused to accept the philosopher's assertion that evil and death are part of a universal harmony, and he structured *Candide* to show the ridiculous nature of such thought. Voltaire hid his identity when publishing the book, noting that it was "translated from the German of Doctor Ralph with the additions which were found in the Doctor's pocket when he died at Minden in the Year of Our Lord 1759."

The work recounts the adventures of Candide, a young man educated by the optimist philosopher Pangloss to believe that the world in which he lives is "the best of all possible worlds." He lives at the castle of Baron Thunder-ten-tronckh and falls in love with the baron's beautiful daughter, Cunegonde.

Caught kissing the young woman, Candide is ejected from the castle and begins to roam the world, penniless and hungry. He is witness to natural and social catastrophes, including the great earthquake of Lisbon and the terror of the Inquisition, in which numerous people suffer. On his journey, Candide becomes reacquainted with Cunegonde, who has her own adventures as the favorite of a series of men. Candide becomes, in turn, a captain in the army, a Jesuit priest, a sheepherder in South America, and a philosopher in Paris, where he also enjoys a love affair. When he finally finds Cunegonde once again, she has suffered several instances of rape and abuse, and she is now a servant. They settle on a farm with the string of characters who have joined Candide on his journey, but they soon become bored. To their good fortune, the group meets an old man who advises them to find contentment in cultivating their own garden.

CENSORSHIP HISTORY

In 1821, *Candide* was among the works to which Etienne Antoine, bishop of Troyne, referred when he wrote a pastoral letter to all clergy in France in which he reaffirmed all censorship orders previously issued by the clergy of France and the individual orders issued by the archbishops of Paris,

> in which these works were condemned as godless and sacrilegious, and as tending to undermine morals and the States. We prohibit, under canonical law, the printing or sale of these books within the territory of this diocese, and we charge the vicar-generals to enforce this regulation and to see to the carrying out of the necessary penances for all who make confession of disobedience to these regulations.

The authority of the Catholic Church in France appears to have been considered sufficient for control of the matter, and no application was made to have the work placed on the Roman Index. Nonetheless, as a means of establishing authority, Pope Pius VII had placed *Candide* on the list of prohibited books of the Roman Index of 1806 and later renewed the prohibition.

In 1893, the American Library Association for the first time offered a 5,000-title book guide for small popular libraries and branches, calling it a collection that "one could recommend to any trustee." Geller observes that no works by Voltaire were included on the list because several of his works might prove to be "offensive" to some readers. Unlike Rousseau, whose biography, but not his works, the ALA at least included in the guide, no mention was made of Voltaire.

Candide was being studied in universities worldwide, was available in libraries, and appeared on college reading lists when United States Customs seized a shipment of the imported edition of the novel in 1928 and declared it obscene. The shipment was ordered by a professor of French at Harvard as assigned reading for his students. Relying on a previous ruling, a Customs official in Boston seized the shipment because the edition was unexpurgated. The professor and his Harvard colleagues contacted officials in Washington, demanding an explanation, and were told that Voltaire was on the list of banned works and that the Customs officer had acted correctly in confiscating the shipment. After the intercession of several influential politicians, the shipment was later released for use in the classroom. After a major setback in the 1933 litigation of *Ulysses*, U.S. Customs recognized that a more discriminating appraisal of books was needed. The appointment of Baltimore attorney Huntington Cairns to assess the problems of Customs censorship resulted in new procedures that, by 1937, deprived Customs collectors and their deputies of their decision-making power. This ended the confiscation of accepted literature, such as *Candide*, in most cases, unless the editions contained illustrations that were "too vulgar or erotic," according to Customs bureau standards.

FURTHER READING

Ayer, Alfred Jules. *Voltaire*. New York: Random House, 1986.
Besterman, Theodore. *Voltaire*. New York: Harcourt Brace & World, 1969.
Geller, Evelyn. *Forbidden Books in American Public Libraries, 1876–1939*. Westport, Conn.: Greenwood, 1984.
Paul, James C. N. *Federal Censorship: Obscenity in the Mail*. New York: Free Press, 1961.
Putnam, George Haven. *The Censorship of the Church of Rome and Its Influence upon the Production and Distribution of Literature*. Vol. 2. New York: Putnam, 1906.

THE CLAN OF THE CAVE BEAR

Author: Jean Auel
Original date and place of publication: 1980, United States
Original publisher: Crown Publishing
Literary form: Novel

SUMMARY

The Clan of the Cave Bear is the story of Ayla, a prehistoric girl orphaned by an earthquake and forced to live for a time by herself in the forest. When a human tribe, the Clan of the Cave Bear, finds her and takes her in, Ayla tries hard to conform to their code despite her obvious differences from them. She is one of the "Others"—taller, blond, and blue eyed—and she also has more developed powers of speech than the members of the Clan, who still communicate largely by gesture. Cared for by the Clan medicine woman, Iza, and her brother, Creb, Ayla learns the customs and the language of the Clan, but she frequently violates their expectations because she does not share their racial memories. Ayla becomes adept at the skill of hunting, forbidden to women of the Clan, and her prowess makes an enemy of Broud, the son of the Clan leader. He torments her continuously as they grow up, and then rapes her when they are older. His actions are acceptable according to tradition, because any female must submit to a male at his will. The members of the Clan have not yet made the connection between sexual intercourse and reproduction, so they are amazed when Ayla becomes pregnant, more so because they had assumed that her differences would make her incapable of bearing children. She gives birth to a son, but when an earthquake destroys the Clan's cave, Broud, now the leader, blames Ayla. He curses her and expels her from the Clan, but she must leave her son behind.

CENSORSHIP HISTORY

In 1988, parents of students attending Berrien Springs High School in Michigan challenged the use of the novel in the classroom and asked that it also be removed from the high school library. Their complaints cited the passages of brutish behavior of the male clan members and the physical abuse and rape of Ayla as "vulgar, profane, and sexually explicit."

In 1992, one parent of a student attending Cascade Middle School in Eugene, Oregon, complained that the rape scene in the novel was offensive. The board of education considered the complaint and ordered the book removed from the middle school library and banned from future use.

The novel was challenged in 1993 at Moorpark High School in Sunneyville, California, after parents objected that the novel contained "hard-core graphic sexual content." It was kept on the recommended reading list.

FURTHER READING

Newsletter on Intellectual Freedom (January 1989): 28; (July 1992): 107; (January 1994): 14; (March 1994): 70; (May 1994): 99.
Wilcox, Clyde. "The Not-So-Failed Feminism of Jean Auel." *Journal of Popular Culture* 28 (Winter 1994): 63–70.

THE EPIC OF GILGAMESH

Author: Unknown
Original date and place of publication: 1928, London
Original publisher: Luzac & Company
Literary type: Epic poetry

SUMMARY

The Epic of Gilgamesh is the world's first epic poem, and versions of it have for decades appeared in world literature anthologies read by high school students throughout the United States. Until Stephen Mitchell published *Gilgamesh: A New English Version* (Free Press, 2004), most readers found the work dense and inaccessible although much of the same content was at their disposal, albeit in different form. Earlier translations of the poem were intended for scholars and students, but Mitchell created a new translation of the poem that was intended for the general reader, and it is accessible and understandable and in an easily read form.

The epic poem is older than the *Iliad*, and it remains only a fragment of a much longer work, although the fragments that have been found and translated create a relatively complete, if episodic, account of the journey of Gilgamesh, the young king of Uruk (now Iraq). Originally inscribed in the Akkadian language on stone tablets, the poem was buried during the fall of Nineveh and was not recovered and deciphered until the late 19th century. The existing fragments appear on 11 tablets, and scholars suggest that many more than that number of tablets have been lost.

The Epic of Gilgamesh opens with an arrogant Gilgamesh, possessed of great wealth, power, and physical attractiveness, who oppresses his people as he satisfies his own selfish needs. The gods hear the pleas of his subjects to free them from their oppression and create Enkidu, a ferocious wild man who is said to be the companion of animals, and they offer him as a double or second self for Gilgamesh. Upon first learning of Enkidu, the young king seeks to conquer him, and he sends Shambat, a temple priestess (sometimes translated as "harlot"), to find the wild man and to defuse his power by seducing him. The plan has the expected result, because coupling with Shambat for six days and seven nights awakens the humanity in Enkidu, pushing his animal identity into the background and strengthening his human characteristics. The wild animals no longer consider him one of their own, and they leave him.

Enkidu, seemingly tamed by his sexual experiences, is taken to the city of Uruk, where he meets Gilgamesh and defies the young king by blocking his attempt to enter a bridal chamber and assert his claim of first night with the bride. The two wrestle fiercely and are nearly equal in strength, but Gilgamesh is lauded as the nominal winner. After the fight, the men bond instantly, becoming soul mates, and they are represented in various translations as engaging in what in modern terminology might be labeled a man crush. Without preamble, Gilgamesh asks Enkidu to accompany him in an act of defiance of the gods as he enters the Cedar Forest with the goal of killing the monster Humbaba, who guards the forest. The sun god Shamash sends violent winds to attack Humbaba and to aid Gilgamesh in the fight. Gilgamesh and Enkidu cut off the monster's head and return triumphantly to Uruk.

Gilgamesh returns as a hero and attracts the attention of Ishtar, the goddess of sexual love, who wants him to be her lover. When the young king rejects her with insults and reminders of the many mortal men she has destroyed or turned into animals after tiring of them, she vows revenge. In a rage, she asks her father, the sky god Anu, to give her the Bull of Heaven to destroy Gilgamesh and his kingdom, which he does. Although the bull rampages and kills hundreds of people, Gilgamesh and Enkidu capture and kill it. Enkidu dreams that a council of gods has convened and determined that one of the two men must die as punishment for killing the bull, and that he is the chosen one. Shortly after having the dream, Enkidu becomes ill and dies after suffering for 12 days.

Gilgamesh grieves deeply after his friend's death, ripping off his clothes and tearing out his hair as he laments loudly. He makes elaborate plans to honor his dead friend and orders artisans to create an opulent statue of Enkidu. He offers jewels, gold, ivory, weapons, and other treasures to the gods and considers damming the Euphrates River to place Enkidu's tomb in the riverbed.

Both grief-stricken and now fearful of death, Gilgamesh goes on a quest for immortality. He begins to live as a wild man, killing lions, eating them, and wearing their skins as he searches for Uta-napishti, who found eternal life and whose secret Gilgamesh wants to learn. To find Uta-napisthi, Gilgamesh must travel to the edge of the world. Before reaching his destination, he must cross an ocean, which he does with the assistance of the ferryman Ur-shanabi, who helps him to avoid the Waters of Death. Uta-napishti does not relate the secret of eternal life to Gilgamesh, but he does give him a plant that is supposed to restore youth. On the journey home, however, Gilgamesh carelessly leaves the plant unguarded as he bathes in a pool and a snake steals it. After his many efforts, Gilgamesh returns to Uruk, not immortal in a traditional sense but able to continue his life and to serve as a much wiser and more compassionate ruler.

CENSORSHIP HISTORY

For decades, the standard text of *The Epic of Gilgamesh* used in schools was the Penguin Classics edition of the poem, translated by N. K. Sanders, which clearly conveys the lustful, sensual nature of the hero, beginning with the first tablet that contains the lament of the people: "Gilgamesh sounds the tocsin for his amusement, his arrogance has no bounds by day or night. No son is left with his father, for Gilgamesh takes them all, even the children; yet the king should be a shepherd to his people. His lust leaves no virgin to her lover, neither the warrior's daughter nor the wife of the noble." Shambat, the temple priestess or harlot, depending upon the translation, is instructed before her seduction of Enkidu: "Now, woman, make your breasts bare, have no shame, do not delay but welcome his love. Let him see you naked, let him possess your body. When he comes near uncover yourself and lie with him; teach him, the savage man, your woman's art." No challenges to these earlier versions have been reported.

In 2006, parents of students attending Clearview Regional High School in Harrison Township, New Jersey, challenged the use of the trade paperback *Gilgamesh: A New English Version* and demanded that the school remove the work from the 10th grade classrooms, where it had been an approved text for two years. In a statement to a reporter for the *Gloucester County Times*, Jennifer Low, the mother of a 10th grade student, said that she did not think the book should be in school. "I don't understand how the school can not allow girls to wear spaghetti straps but can allow them to read something so graphic." A new resident in the district who moved to New Jersey from Texas, the month before the article came out, Low claimed that she did not oppose the entire book, only a specific section that she described as "sexually descriptive and unnecessarily explicit." She said that other parents should be made aware of the offensive sections in the book and asserted that she would not have known about the content if her daughter had not told her that reading the passages "made her feel uncomfortable." Jeff Gellenthin, also a parent of a 10th grade student, told the reporter "Bottom line, that material is bizarre." He complained "in a fiery e-mail" to school officials that the translation is "pornography" and "sheer smut." School officials responded to the parent complaints by allowing students whose parents opposed the approved translation to read a different translation of the work.

FURTHER READNG

Ackerman, Susan. *When Heroes Love: The Ambiguity of Eros in the Stories of Gilgamesh and David*. New York: Columbia University Press, 2005.
"Censorship Dateline: Libraries." *Newsletter on Intellectual Freedom* 56, no.1. (January 2007). Accessed April 4, 2010.
Mitchell, Stephen, trans. *Gilgamesh: A New English Version*. New York: Free Press, 2004.

FANNY HILL, OR MEMOIRS OF A WOMAN OF PLEASURE

Author: John Cleland
Original dates and places of publication: 1748, England; 1821, United States
Original publishers: G. Fenton (England); Peter Holmes (United States)
Literary form: Novel

SUMMARY

Fanny Hill, or Memoirs of a Woman of Pleasure was written while John Cleland was incarcerated in a London debtor's prison. The story of an orphaned 15-year-old country girl who moves to London to find employment as a household worker but who instead enters a brothel is primarily composed of descriptions of her sexual experiences and those that she observes. Her first job is with a brothel keeper who trains Fanny for her future profession as a woman of pleasure. Those who have sought to ban the novel over the course of more than two centuries have complained that it contains numerous incidents of heterosexual and lesbian sexual activity, female masturbation, flagellation, and voyeurism. Typical of the criticism leveled at the novel is that of U.S. Supreme Court Justice Thomas C. Clark, who observed in a dissenting opinion in 1966:

> In each of the sexual scenes the exposed bodies of the participants are described in minute and individual detail. The pubic hair is often used for a background to the most vivid and precise descriptions of the response, condition, size, shape, and color of the sexual organs before, during and after orgasms.

Such criticism ignores the many instances in which the language is ornate and metaphorical as Cleland refers to genitalia through such euphemisms as "engine," "champion," and the "machine," as well as "the tender small part framed to receive it," the "pit," and the "wound." Although the novel may be "essentially a guidebook to erotic variations," the author presents them with humor. The author uses none of the "four-letter" words that are usually labeled "obscene," although he does use such candid terms as "maidenhead" and "defloration." The frequent labeling of the novel as priapic is also due to the fascination that Fanny shows with the male anatomy, as in the scene in which she and her first lover, Charles, have sex:

> a column of the whitest ivory, beautifully streak'd with blue veins, and carrying, fully uncapt, a head of the liveliest vermilion: no horn could be harder or stiffer; yet no velvet more smooth or delicious to the touch. . . . a pair of roundish balls, that seem'd to pay within, and elude all pressure but the tenderest, from without.

At the end of the novel, after having experienced every variation of sexual intimacy, Fanny leaves her life of sin and marries Charles, providing the reader with her observation that "looking back on the course of vice I had run, and comparing its infamous blandishments with the infinitely superior joys of innocence, I could not help pitying even in point of taste, those who, immers'd in gross sensuality, are insensible to the so delicate charms of *virtue*."

CENSORSHIP HISTORY

In 1749, less than one year after publication of *Fanny Hill, or Memoirs of a Woman of Pleasure*, John Cleland was imprisoned on the orders of Lord Newcastle, the British secretary of state, on a charge of "corrupting the King's subjects." The action was taken after high-ranking officials of the Church of England had protested the nature of the book and demanded the arrest of Cleland, his publisher, and his printer. The bishop of London had personally contacted Newcastle, asking him to "give proper orders, to stop the progress of this vile Book, which is an open insult upon Religion and good manners, and a reproach to the Honour of the Government, and the Law of the Country."

The trial of *Fanny Hill* in 1821 in Massachusetts was the first obscenity case involving a book to be heard in the United States. The novel had been surreptitiously published in the United States for many years, beginning with several expurgated editions of the novel published by Isaiah Thomas between 1786 and 1814, but not until Peter Holmes published the first edition of the novel in its original form in 1821 did censors take notice. The publisher was convicted for publishing and printing a "lewd and obscene" novel. Holmes appealed to the Massachusetts Supreme Court, claiming that the court had not seen the book and that the jury had only heard the prosecution's description. In delivering a decision on the appeal, Chief Justice Isaac Parker observed that the publisher was "a scandalous and evil disposed person" who had contrived to "debauch and corrupt" the citizens of the commonwealth and "to raise and create in their minds inordinate and lustful desires." Of the novel, he stated that "said printed book is so lewd, wicked and obscene, that the same would be offensive to the court here, and improper to be placed upon the records thereof." In short, Holmes lost his appeal because the judge refused to review the book, to have the jury read the book, and to enter passages from the book into the court record, for to do so "would be to require that the public itself should give permanency and notoriety to indecency, in order to punish it."

In 1930, while the Massachusetts legislature debated a revision of censorship laws, *Fanny Hill* was among 300 books seized in a raid on a Philadelphia bookshop. The city district attorney led the raid and announced at the same time that Philadelphia officials would undertake an extensive campaign to curb sales of "obscene" literature.

In 1963, G. P. Putnam's Sons announced that it would issue an unexpurgated edition of *Fanny Hill*. New York City prosecutors with city attorney Leo A. Larkin decided to take legal action against the publisher. Because Putnam had a reputation as a responsible firm with book sales in many of New York City's largest bookstores, the city decided against arrests and criminal charges. Instead, city officials utilized the state injunctive procedure that allowed them to order the listing of inventories and to freeze stocks to prevent further sales until *Larkin v. G. P. Putnam's Sons*, 40 Misc. 2d 25, 243 N.Y.S2d 145 (Sup. Ct. N.Y. Co. 1963) was decided. A further advantage to the prosecution in proving the book was pornographic was that the injunctive procedure required the lesser proof of a civil case rather than the proof beyond a reasonable doubt of a criminal case. Judge Charles Marks issued an order to restrain sales of the novel. The case then went before the state supreme court and was tried without a jury before Justice Arthur G. Klein in *Larkin v. G. P. Putnam's Sons*, 14 N.Y.2d 399, 200 N.E.2d 760 (1964). Expert witnesses argued that the novel portrayed the economic realities of the times and emphasized its literary merit. The reporting of the British Profumo scandal, a sex-and-spy scandal that threatened to topple the British government, occurred while Justice Klein was deliberating. He dissolved the restraining order and dismissed the city's action, asserting that

> if the standards of the community are to be gauged by what it is permitted to read in its daily newspapers, then Fanny Hill's experiences contain little more than the community has already encountered on the front pages of many of its newspapers in the reporting of the recent "Profumo" and other sensational cases involving sex.

The prosecution appealed the decision in 1964, and in a 3 to 2 split decision in *Larkin v. G. P. Putnam's Sons*, 20 A.D.2d 702, case no. 2, 247 N.Y.S.2d 275 (1st Dep't 1964), the New York State intermediate appeals court reversed Justice Klein's action and ordered Putnam to refrain from selling the novel in the state of New York. Putnam then took the case to the New York Court of Appeals, which in a 4-3 decision reversed the decision of the lower court and granted final judicial amnesty to *Fanny Hill* in New York.

In 1963 the United States Supreme Court considered the validity of a Massachusetts Supreme Judicial Court decision that the novel was "pornographic" in *A Book Named "John Cleland's Memoirs of a Woman of Pleasure" v. Massachusetts*, 383 U.S. 413 (1966). The court cleared *Fanny Hill* of obscenity charges in a conditional decision. Justice William J. Brennan stated in the majority decision that historical importance is a factor, and "the circumstances of production, sale and publicity are relevant in determining whether or not the publication and distribution of the book is constitutionally protected."

In London in 1963, the publication of unexpurgated paperback versions of the novel motivated the director of public prosecutions to secure a seizure order for all copies of the novel that were currently displayed in the window of a small Soho bookstore. The store proudly proclaimed on a sign in the window that the novel was "Banned in America." The trial was held early in 1964; after four days of testimony, the novel was determined to be obscene and the seized copies were ordered to be destroyed.

In 1965, Paul's Book Arcade of Auckland, New Zealand, sought to avoid censorship and applied to the Indecent Publications Tribunal for a determination regarding the expurgated paperback edition of the novel, published by Mayflower Books Limited of London in 1964. In a decision rendered on May 20, 1965, the tribunal ruled:

> The book has no substance other than to relate the experiences of a prostitute and we think that it might arouse interest in the one form of perversion it describes . . . . We accordingly make a ruling which the statute permits classifying it as indecent in the hands of persons under eighteen years of age, though we feel considerable doubt as to how far, if at all, such a classification will have the effect sought.

FURTHER READING

Cooper, Morton. "Fanny Hill vs. the Constitution." *Pageant* 14 (June 1964): 14–20.

Foxon, David F. "John Cleland and the Publication of *Memoirs of a Woman of Pleasure*." *Book Collector* 12 (Winter 1963): 476–487.

Kuh, Richard H. *Foolish Figleaves? Pornography In and Out of Court.* New York: Macmillan, 1967.

Rembar, Charles. *The End of Obscenity: The Trials of "Lady Chatterley's Lover," "Tropic of Cancer" & "Fanny Hill" by the Lawyer Who Defended Them.* New York: Random House, 1968.

Rolph, Cecil Hewitt. *Book in the Dock.* London: Deutsch, 1961.

Sebastian, Raymond F. "Obscenity and the Supreme Court: Nine Years of Confusion." *Stanford Law Review* 19 (November 1966): 167–189.

Stuart, Perry. *The Indecent Publications Tribunal: A Social Experiment.* Christchurch, New Zealand: Whitcombe and Tombs, 1965.

Wald, Emil W. "Obscene Literature Standards Re-examined." *South Carolina Law Review* 18 (Spring 1966): 497–503.

FLOWERS FOR ALGERNON

Author: Daniel Keyes
Original date and place of publication: 1966, United States
Original publisher: Harcourt Brace Jovanovich
Literary form: Novel

SUMMARY

Flowers for Algernon is a novel about a daring human experiment that transforms a mentally retarded man with an IQ of 68 into a genius with an IQ of 185, thus forcing him to cope with the adult world. The experimental surgery that makes Charlie Gordon "normal" is only temporary, and he must suffer the growing realization that he will lose all that he has achieved and, once again, lapse into mental retardation.

Related as a series of progress reports written by Charlie, the novel shows his early inadequacies through the writing in the halting manner of expression, the considerable misspellings, and the lack of grammar skills, in the reports. As his abilities increase, so does the quality of the reports. Thirty-two-year-old Charlie has worked at a bakery for 17 years, after being "rescued" by his boss, Mr. Donner, from the Warren State Home, where his mother had committed him. Charlie attends classes three nights a week at the Beekman College Center for Retarded Adults, where he joins others in practicing speaking and writing skills. He has no memory of his family or other details from his past, only nightmarish flashes of his mother yelling at him and slapping him, and his father saying, "He can't help it if he gets an erection. It's normal."

After the surgery, which had also been performed on a mouse named Algernon who remains under study in the laboratory, Charlie works hard to obtain the needed skills to utilize his new intelligence, and his former teacher, Alice Kinnian, works with him. His rapidly developing mind can process great amounts of information, and he soon begins to trade ideas with experts in various fields, as he also enjoys artistic experiences. Newspaper accounts refer to him as the "moron-genius."

As he develops mentally, Charlie also develops emotionally and falls in love with Alice, who is attracted to him but urges him to become acquainted with other women. Charlie finds that he is haunted by the specter of the younger, retarded boy that he once was. He finally overcomes his fear by drinking a little too much and having sex with his neighbor, the bohemian painter Fay.

Through his scientific studies, Charlie learns that his improvement is only temporary and the deterioration will begin quickly. This fear is confirmed by abrupt changes in Algernon's behavior and the death of the mouse. Before the end, Charlie and Alice spend a long night making love and holding each other, fearing the inevitable. At the end of the novel, Charlie is living in the Warren State Home, his deterioration nearly complete.

CENSORSHIP HISTORY

The novel was banned from the public schools in Plant City, Florida, in 1976 because of its "references to sex" as well as for the sexual encounter between Charlie and his teacher. In 1977, the novel was removed from use in the 11th-grade classrooms in the Cameron County School District after parents protested to the district board of education. They complained that the book was "sexually oriented trash" and that it had no place in a high school classroom. The board agreed and ordered that all copies of the book be removed from the classrooms and that teachers no longer include references to the work in the curriculum.

In 1981, the novel was banned from the Glen Rose (Arkansas) High School library because parents complained about Charlie's first sexual encounter, claiming that it was too detailed and "explicit." In 1983, the novel was challenged, for the same reason, as a suggested reading at the Oberlin (Ohio) High School.

In 1984, parents of students at the Glenrock (Wyoming) High School challenged use of the novel as a required reading, claiming that several "explicit love scenes were distasteful." In 1986, the novel was removed from a 10th-grade supplemental reading list in the Charlotte-Mecklenburg (North Carolina) school district after parents protested its use and charged that the book was "pornographic."

FURTHER READING

Lambert, Robert. "Charley: Metamorphosis by Media." *Media and Methods* 5 (February 1969): 29–31.

Newsletter on Intellectual Freedom (July 1976): 85; (May 1977): 73; (July 1981): 91; (January 1984): 26; (July 1984): 122; (January 1987): 12; (March 1987): 54; (May 1987): 103; (July 1987): 150.

Shugert, Diane P. "Rationales for Commonly 'Challenged' Taught Books." *Connecticut English Journal* 15 (Fall 1983): 145–146.

THE FLOWERS OF EVIL (LES FLEURS DU MAL)

Author: Charles Baudelaire
Original dates and places of publication: 1857, France; 1909, England
Original publishers: August Poulet-Malassis (France); Constable and
   Company (England)
Literary form: Poetry collection

SUMMARY

First published as *Les Fleurs du mal*, the collection contained 100 poems grouped under the following headings: Spleen and Ideal, Parisian Scenes, Wine, Flowers of Evil, Rebellion and Death. The sole collection of Baudelaire's poems to be published in his lifetime, the volume became notorious for its themes of eroticism, lesbianism, morbidity, perversity, and rebellion. His observations of and emphasis upon subjective experiences among prostitutes, drug users, the poor, and other images of Parisian ruin vie with images of unexpected beauty that he discerned beneath the perversity and corruption of modern civilization. To Baudelaire's contemporaries, the modernity of his rendering of the antithesis of good and evil was too great a deviation from contemporary work.

Although critics halfheartedly protested Baudelaire's "religious immorality" in such poems as "Saint Peter's Denial," "Abel and Cain," and "Satan's Litanies," the greater criticism was launched at his glorification of physical pleasures. Particular objections were raised against such lines as "Like a poor profligate who sucks and bites the withered breast of some well-seasoned trull" ("To the Reader") and the adoration of a lover's body in "Jewels," in which the poet glories in "the sleek thighs shifting, shiny as oil, the belly, the breasts—the fruit on my vine." When the book, author, and publisher were placed on trial in 1857 for "immorality," the prosecuting attorney made a point of quoting lines from "Jewels" and "Lethe" ("the reek of you that permeates your skirts . . . those entrancing pointed breasts"). He also declared that "the most intimate habits of lesbian woman" were depicted in "Lesbos," "Damned Women," and "Metamorphoses of the Vampire."

CENSORSHIP HISTORY

The Flowers of Evil was published in an edition of 1,100 copies in 1857 and immediately motivated an uproar among critics for the startling imagery and daring metaphors of the poems. Baudelaire had expected that his poems would offend readers, but he counted on the recent acquittal in the trial of *Madame Bovary* and the preoccupation of the government with elections to protect his work from prosecution. In a letter to his mother dated July 9, 1857, the poet stated, "People have been spreading the rumour that I am going to be prosecuted, but it won't happen. A government with the terrible Paris elections on its hands won't have time to prosecute a lunatic." He was wrong, for attacks on several poems had already begun in the form of articles in the satiric publication *Figaro*, which drew the attention of the courts to Baudelaire's work. On July 5, 1857, his publisher, Poulet-Malassis, received a letter from the Paris distributor stating that the rumor abroad, "especially in high society," was that *Les Fleurs du mal* was going to be seized.

The minister of the interior declared *Les Fleurs du mal* to be "one of those unhealthy and profoundly immoral works destined to have a *succes de scandale*, and he apprised the office of the public prosecutor of his opinion that the book was "an outrage of public morality." Police were sent to seize all copies of the work from the offices of the publisher and the printer. On August 20, 1857, Baudelaire appeared before the Sixth Criminal Court, faced by Deputy Imperial Prosecutor Ernest Pinard, a future minister of the interior. Pinard identified "Saint Peter's Denial," "Abel and Cain," "Litanies of Satan," and "The Murderer's Wine" as breaches of religious morality but did not press the point, so the court dropped the charge of blasphemy. Instead, the emphasis was placed upon the "immoral passages" of other poems, lines from which Pinard eagerly read, including "Jewels," "Lesbos," "Lethe," "Against Her Levity," "Metamorphoses of the Vampire," and two poems entitled "Damned Women." Baudelaire's defense attorney, Chaix d'Est-Ange, pleaded that the poet's work depicted vice in a way that made it odious to the reader, but the court was not convinced and ruled that the book contained "obscene and immoral passages or expressions." The poet was fined 300 francs, and the publisher and printer, were each fined 100 francs. All three were also deprived of their right to vote. Further, the court ordered the first five "immoral" poems named above and the version of "Damned Women" subtitled "Delphine and Hippolyta" to be deleted from future editions of *Les Fleurs du mal*. The ban on the poems in France remained until May 31, 1949, when the French Appeals Court declared that the poems contained no words either obscene or vulgar, "though certain descriptions may, by their originality, have alarmed certain minds at the time."

FURTHER READING

Bergeron, Katherine. "The Echo, the Cry, the Death of Lovers." *Nineteenth Century Music* 18 (Fall 1994): 136–151.

Cohen, Emily Jane. "Mud into Gold: Baudelaire and the Alchemy of Public Hygiene." *Romanic Review* 87 (March 1996): 239–255.

Morgan, Edwin. *Flowers of Evil: A Life of Charles Baudelaire*. Freeport, N.Y.: Books for Libraries Press, 1943.

Pichois, Claude. *Baudelaire*. London: Hamish Hamilton, 1989.

Ramazani, Vaheed K. "Writing in Pain: Baudelaire, Benjamin, Haussmann." *Boundary* 223 (Summer 1996): 199–224.

FOREVER

Author: Judy Blume
Original date and place of publication: 1975, United States
Publisher: Bradbury Press
Literary form: Young adult novel

SUMMARY

Forever is a novel about first love and the chaotic feelings that accompany the romance and the sexual desire of teenagers Katherine and Michael. After meeting at a New Year's Eve party, the two date for several weeks, becoming closer and more sexually aroused each time that they meet. Katherine is a virgin and hesitant to "lose control," but Michael's passionate overtures eventually overcome her doubts. Their first few times having sex are unremarkable for Katherine because Michael reaches orgasm before she is completely aroused. After they finally synchronize their desire, Katherine becomes an enthusiastic aggressor, enjoying their lovemaking and seeking times to be alone with Michael. They pledge to love each other "forever," and for her 18th birthday, Michael gives Katherine a silver necklace on which her name is inscribed on one side of a disk with the words "forever, Michael" inscribed on the other.

Both partners act in a responsible manner, discussing their concerns regarding birth control and the prevention of sexually transmitted diseases and substituting mutual masturbation for sexual intercourse until birth control is available. Their encounters are detailed for the reader, who can trace the growing intensity of their desire from Michael's sensitive exploration of Katherine's breasts to their later frequent and varied lovemaking. Sexual activity is also integral to the subplots involving several friends. Sibyl, who "has a genius I.Q. and has been laid by at least six different guys," has a baby whose father she cannot identify. Erica seeks to help talented high school actor Artie determine if he is gay by having sex with him, but her efforts push him to attempt suicide.

Concerned that Katherine is too young to make a lifetime commitment to Michael, her parents urge her to date others and eventually demand that she work at a summer camp several hundred miles away to test the relationship. When her grandfather dies, Katherine rushes into the arms of fellow counselor Theo, who wisely tells her he wants her but "not with death for an excuse." This makes Katherine realize that she really will not love Michael "forever." When they next meet, she breaks off the relationship, leaving Michael angry and embittered.

CENSORSHIP HISTORY

Forever has been repeatedly challenged and banned in schools and libraries because of the detailed sexual descriptions and the perceived frequency of the sexual activity in the novel. In 1982, the parents of students attending Midvalley Junior-Senior High School in Scranton, Pennsylvania, challenged the book, charging that it contained "four-letter words and talked about masturbation, birth control, and disobedience to parents." The book was also challenged that year in the Orlando, Florida, schools and at the Park Hill (Missouri) South Junior High School library, where librarians were required by the school board to place the book on the "restricted" shelves. In 1983, parents called for the removal of the book from the Akron, Ohio, school district libraries and from the Howard-Suamico (Wisconsin) High School library because "it demoralizes marital sex." In 1984, challenges to the book by parents resulted in its removal from the Holdredge (Nebraska) Public Library young adult section to the adult section because of claims that the "book is pornographic and does not promote the sanctity of family life." That same year, parents challenged inclusion of the book in the Cedar Rapids (Iowa) Public Library because it was "pornography and explores areas God didn't intend to explore outside of marriage."

The Patrick County, Virginia, school board, responding to parent complaints in 1986, ordered the novel placed on a "restricted" shelf in the high school library, and challenges were raised against its inclusion in the Campbell County (Wyoming) school libraries because it was "pornographic" and would encourage young readers "to experiment with sexual encounters." Parents of students in the Moreno Valley (California) Unified School District sought to remove the novel from the school libraries in 1987 and claimed that it "contains profanity, sexual situations, and themes that allegedly encourage disrespectful behavior." In 1987, charging that the "book does not paint a responsible role of parents," that its "cast of sex-minded teenagers is not typical of high schoolers today," and that the "pornographic sexual exploits are unsuitable for junior high school role models," parents of students attending Marshwood Junior High School in Eliot, Maine, demanded its removal from the classroom library. In 1988, the principal of West Hernando (Florida) Middle School yielded to parents' complaints that the novel was "inappropriate" and asked that it be removed from the school library shelves.

The challenges to *Forever* continued in the 1990s. In 1992, the novel was placed on the "reserve" shelf at the Herrin (Illinois) Junior High School library because it was "sexually provocative reading," and students could only check out the book if they had written permission from their parents. In 1993, the novel was removed from the Frost Junior High School library in Schaumberg, Illinois, after parents charged that "it's basically a sexual 'how-to-do' book for junior high students. It glamorizes sex and puts ideas into their heads." Also in 1993, the superintendent of schools in Rib Lake, Wisconsin, filed a "request for reconsideration" of the book after determining that it was "sexually explicit." The novel was placed on the "parental permission shelf," then later confiscated by the high school principal. High school guidance counselor Mike Dishnow, who spoke out against the district book policy and criticized the actions of the principal in restricting student access to the novel, was not rehired for the following academic year. He sued the school district, and a federal jury in Madison, Wisconsin, awarded him $394,560 in damages and lost wages. In summer 1996, the courts reversed their decision and, in agreement with the insurance company of the school district, determined that the board was responsible only for paying the legal fees and not lost wages to Dishnow. The school district took out a nine-year loan to pay off the settlement with interest, an amount of $232,000. In addition, teaching and administrative positions were cut and a bus route dropped to cover costs.

In 1994, school officials in Mediapolis, Iowa, responded to parent complaints about the novel and removed it from the school libraries because it "does not promote abstinence and monogamous relationships and lacks any aesthetic, literary, or social value." The book was returned a month later, but only to the high school library.

In 1995, parents in the Elgin Area School District U-46 in Elgin, Illinois, pressured the school board to remove *Forever* from the middle school library. The parents who lodged the complaint expressed concern about the sexuality in the book. Attempts to reinstate the book failed repeatedly for four years until school librarians in the district were able to convince a special faculty and parent committee to vote unanimously to lift the ban. The committee vote was presented to the Elgin Area School District U-46 Board, which voted 5-2 on January 22, 2002, to lift the ban and return *Forever* to the middle school library's bookshelves.

In 2003, *Forever* was challenged by a parent of a student attending the Spring Hill Elementary School in Hernando County, Florida. In the complaint, the parent charged that the novel is inappropriate for students at the elementary school level because it contains passages that speak openly about masturbation. After reviewing the complaint, the school board decided to retain the title but to make it available only to students who had written parental permission to read the novel.

In 2005, the *Pasadena Citizen* reported that Dr. Rick Schneider, Pasadena Independent School District superintendent, had banned the novel from all of the libraries in the school district after the parent of a student attending the Thompson Intermediate School submitted a formal complaint to the district. Before the district made the decision to remove the book, the district followed a formal policy that included the formation of a campus review committee composed of administrators, instructors, and parents who studied the book and presented their findings to the superintendent. The initial recommendation of the committee was that the district should remove the novel from only the intermediate school libraries and retain the novel in the high school libraries, but school superintendent Schneider made the decision to remove *Forever* from all of the libraries in the school system because he determined that the novel contains "sexually explicit content." A district spokesperson defended the decision. "The superintendent has the responsibility to put materials in the system that are educationally suitable and appropriate. In this particular case, after reading the book, he felt that, though the theme is not unsuitable, certain passages are and decided to remove the book. . . . Certain passages were not appropriate for any students of the school district"

The same year, *Forever* was on a list of 50 books challenged by parents of students attending the Fayetteville middle and junior high school who charged that the books are too sexually explicit and promoted homosexuality.

The novel was not the object of any major challenges for several years until late 2009, when parents of students attending the Sugarloaf School in Summerland Key, Monroe County, Florida, became upset over the description of preteen sex in the book and asked school officials to remove the book from the shelves of the school district libraries. The challenge asserted that the novel contains "a distorted view of sex, promiscuity, [and is] usurping parental control." The school district refused the request until a committee could review the book and decide whether to remove access to the book for all levels of students or to make it accessible only to high school students. Sugarloaf school principal Theresa Axford reassured parents that the committee, which consisted of the principal, the school librarian, a district administrator, a teacher, and a member of community, would read the book and evaluate its literary merit. Tami Fletcher and Heather Fowler, two of the parents who initiated the request for removal of the book, asserted that their 13-year-old children had been subjected to listening to parts of the book being read aloud on the school bus. "This book was discussed with other children who had no choice but to hear it." The National Coalition Against Censorship (NCAC) urged its members to write letters to the school district to urge officials to retain the novel in the school libraries. In the letter, executive director of NCAC Joan Bertin reminded officials that "No book is right for everyone, and the role of the library is to allow students to make choices according to their own interest, experiences and family values. No one has to read something just because it's on the library shelf." NCAC reported in a posting on the organization's Web site dated February 18, 2010, that the school district review committee recommended keeping *Forever* in the school district libraries.

FURTHER READING

Doyle, Robert P. *Books Challenged or Banned in 2005–2006*. Chicago: American Library Association, 2006

"'Forever'—Banned." *Pasadena Citizen*. Available online. URL: http//www.freerepublic.com/focus/f-news/1381149/posts. Accessed September 20, 2010.

Forman, Jack. "Young Adult Books: 'Watch Out for #1.'" *Horn Book* 61 (January/February 1985): 85.

Guerra, John L. "Parents: Books too Racy for Youngsters." Available online. URL: http://ww.keysnews .com/node/20059. Accessed September 20, 2010.

"The Long and the Short of It." *Censorship News* 74 (Summer 1999).

Maynard, Joyce. "Coming of Age with Judy Blume." *New York Times Magazine*, December 3, 1978, pp. 80+.

Newsletter on Intellectual Freedom (July 1982): 124, 142; (May 1982): 84; (May 1983): 85–86; (March 1984): 39; (May 1984): 69; (March 1985): 59; (September 1985): 167; (March 1986): 39; (March 1987): 66–67; (July 1987): 125; (November 1987):

239; (March 1988): 45; (May 1992): 80; (May 1993): 70; (July 1993): 98, 104–05; (September 1993): 146–147; (May 1994): 83, 86; (July 1994): 109; (March 1995): 56; (January 2003): 8–9; (March 2004): 48–49; (May 2004): 95–96; (May 2005): 108; (July 2005):185–186.

"Parents in Florida Object to Judy Blume's 'Forever.'" Blog of the National Coalition Against Censorship. Available online. URL: http://ncacblog.wordpress.com/2010/02/18/parents-in-florida-object-to-judy-blumes-forever. Accessed September 21, 2010.

"Schools Liable for Censorship Damages." *Censorship News*, Iss. 62 (summer 1996). Available online. URL: http://www.ncac.org/projects/bit2.html. Accessed December 22, 2005.

Slivinski, Krystyna. "Schools Can Reinstate Banned Book: District 46 Board Will Let Libraries Stock Racy Novel." *Chicago Tribune*, January 24, 2002, p. 5.

Thompson, Susan. "Images of Adolescence: Part I." *Signal* 34 (1981): 57–59.

GOSSIP GIRL SERIES

Author: Cecily von Ziegesar
Original date and place of publication: 2002–Present, United States
Original publisher: Little, Brown and Company
Literary form: Young adult novel series

SUMMARY

The Gossip Girl series, written by Cecily von Ziegesar, is sophisticated, witty, edgy, and irreverent. It chronicles the alcohol- and sex-filled lives of the privileged children of wealthy parents in contemporary Manhattan. The novels are written from the perspective of an anonymous blogger who posts observations and interacts with e-mail correspondents on the Web site www.gossipgirl.net. She is mean and nasty and reveals awful details about everyone, all the while remaining anonymous. In a disclaimer that appears at the top of the gossipgirl.net Web page, the narrator states "All the names of places, people, and events have been altered or abbreviated to protect the innocent. Namely me."

Gossip Girl, the first book in the series, introduces readers to the world of "the people who are *born to it*—those of us who have everything anyone could possibly wish for and who take it all completely for granted." Manhattan is their playground and attending single-sex private schools is merely a diversion.

Welcome to New York City's Upper East Side, where my friends and I live and go to school and play and sleep—sometimes with each other. We all live in huge apartments with our own bedrooms and bathrooms and phone lines. We have unlimited access to money and booze and whatever else we want, and our parents are rarely home, so we have tons of privacy. We're smart, we've inherited classic good looks, we wear fantastic clothes, and we know how to party. Our shit still stinks, but you can't smell it because the bathroom is sprayed hourly by the maid with a refreshing scent made exclusively for us by French perfumers.

It's a luxe life, but someone's got to live it.

Although Gossip Girl is a member of the crowd she (or he) observes, the narrator freely shares their secrets and reports their adventures to anyone who ventures onto the Web site. "I'll be watching closely. I'll be watching all of us. It's going to be a wild and wicked year. I can smell it." In an interesting bow to the popularity of the Internet, the format of the novel alternates between presenting the Gossip Girl blog page and chapters of text that provide the back story for what the Web site only hints at.

The characters in the novels spend most of their time going to clubs, smoking marijuana, drinking Cosmopolitans in trendy bars, consuming scotch or whatever high-priced liquor is in their parents' liquor cabinets, agonizing over their social lives, and having sex. The continuity of characters in the novels has created a large following among adolescent girls. To many teenage girls, the novels represent "a stirring fantasy of freedom and an equally stirring fantasy of conspicuous consumption." Cindy Egan, an editor at Little, Brown and Company, which publishes the series, credits the popularity of the series to the way in which it speaks to young girls. "In 'Gossip Girl' you've got sophisticated subject matter with the girls having anxiety about dating and getting into college. But they're all doing the same things that high schoolers are doing, partying behind their parents' backs." The novels do not pretend to represent rites of passage or to provide a moral blueprint for readers. "In any event there is no discontent that can't be soothed through a tumble in the luxury marketplace." The novels are also not concerned about dealing with the emotional and psychological problems of their characters. In *All I Want Is Everything*, "As they kissed she couldn't help but think that sex with Dan would be a whole lot more meaningful than sex with Clark." "If sex is presented without much association to psychological tailspins, bulimia is depicted as a habit attached to even less. Bingeing and purging are shown more or less as another lifestyle choice available at relatively unburdensome cost."

One of the objections to the Gossip Girls novels is that the author has no moral tale to tell, and opponents have noted their "alarming lack of moralism about teen sex and drugs." "In von Ziegesar's universe, kids have sex without pregnancy scares; they get high in the Sheep Meadow and still make decent grades. Antiheroine Blair's bulimia is more of an icky weakness than a full-fledged pathology. At worst, von Ziegesar's characters end up embarrassed on the Internet or during an Ivy League interview" (Nussbaun 40).

CENSORSHIP HISTORY

Books in the Gossip Girls series have appeared on the American Library Association's list of the most frequently challenged books since 2006. The complaints have cited homosexuality, sexual content, drugs, material unsuited to its age group, and offensive language as the reasons for the challenges. According to the ALA record of challenges, the series has been challenged 13 times since 2004, in several states, including Florida, Texas, Arizona, and Indiana. The ALA also reports "It is unclear how many times libraries have banned the books."

The language in the novels is admittedly "steamy," and bookstore managers have made attempts to keep the novels out of the children's and junior sections. In Darien, Connecticut, Diane's Books and Barrett's Bookstore moved the novels out of the children's sections and into especially created teenage areas within the adult sections. Dottie Bush, the manager of the Barrett's Bookstore children's section, told a *New York Times* reporter, "We try to keep them separate. The language is bad and there's no value to them."

In August 2008, two mothers of students living in Leesburg, Florida, asked the Leesburg Public Library Advisory Board to remove two books from the Leesburg Public Library: *The Bermudez Triangle* by Maureen Johnson and *Only in Your Dreams: A Gossip Girl Novel* by Cecily von Ziegesar. Dixie Fechtel, who said she "was shocked" when she read parts of the two novels that her 13-year-old daughter brought home after checking them out from the Leesburg Public Library, told a reporter that "a parent or student walking into the youth section should not have to get something off the shelf as shocking as this." Fechtel was joined by another parent, Diane Venetta, in submitting the complaint. The two mothers expressed their outrage through letters to library officials accompanied by a signed petition containing 120 names of "friends and like-minded community members" that asked for the removal of both books and others, a request that Leesburg Public Library Director Barbara Morse denied. Dixie Fechtel claimed that she was horrified by what she read: "sexual innuendo, drug references, and other adult topics." After Morse denied her request, Fechtel engaged the formal book-challenge process of the public library in January 2009, which was designed to formally contest the book and to bring the decision to the five-member library board. Fechtel asserted that she welcomed the opportunity to speak with the board because "It's distasteful for youths. It's so farfetched that we would allow this to happen in the first place." In September 2009, the library board decided that the library should create a special shelf for high school reading and place the novels in the Gossip Girl series and similar teen-oriented books in that area. Librarians were told to place the label "High School" on the books and to place them on a special shelf in the young adult section. After achieving that goal, Fechtel told a reporter for the *Orlando Sentinel* that she would pursue the same goal in the nine municipal and six branch libraries of the Lake County system. She hopes to have all books that contain references to sex or illegal activities provided with a label stating: "Warning: Mature Content."

In 2007, a teen drama series *Gossip Girl* (based on the book's) was created and debated on the CW network. As of 2010, the show is in its fourth season and remains very popular.

FURTHER READINGS

Bellafante, Ginia. "'Gossip Girls' Series Aims Low, Sells High." *Chicago Tribune*, August 30, 2003, p. 7.

Burton, Connie O. "The Most Frequently Challenged Books of 2006." *Teacher Librarian* 35 (December 2007): 67.

Donald, David. "Gossip Girl Book at Center of Library Debate." Available online. URL: Daily Commercial.com/060909book. Accessed July 20, 2010.

Gay, Jason. "Dirty Pretty Things." *Rolling Stone* (April 2, 2009): 40–47.

Nussbaum, Evelyn. "Psst! Serena Is a Slut. Pass It On." *New York* 38 (May 30, 2004): 40–43.

O'Briant, Don. "Books with an Edge Lure Younger Set." *Atlanta Journal-Constitution*, July 6, 2005, p. E1.

Rippel, Amy C. "Leesburg Mom Not Giving Up on Library Book Warning-Label Campaign." *Orlando-Sentinal*. Available online. URL: http://articles.orlandosentinel.com/2010-04-16/news/os-lk-book-policy-leesburg-20100413_1_leesburg-library-six-branch-libraries-bermudez-triangle. Accessed July 18, 2010.

Steele, Margaret Farley. "Books for Teenage Girls Are a Little Too Popular." *New York Times*, August 20, 2006, p. 14NJ6.

THE HANDMAID'S TALE

Author: Margaret Atwood
Original date and place of publication: 1986, United States
Original publisher: Fawcett
Literary form: Novel

SUMMARY

The Handmaid's Tale provides a view of a frightening future in which racism and homophobia run rampant, personal freedom is lost, sexual practices are ritualized, and the earth has become polluted beyond reclamation. The satire depicts a postrevolutionary world run by religious and political conservatives who deport Jews to Israel, execute homosexuals, and resettle African Americans in North Dakota. Critics reviewing the novel have noted that these characteristics reflect real-world abuses, such as Romania's anti-birth-control edicts, the religious fanaticism of Iran's government, and the stringent rules of Puritan society in colonial New England.

Set in a thinly disguised Cambridge, Massachusetts, the novel is framed as a taped interview with narrator Offred, who is a Handmaid and one of the few remaining women who have not been made sterile by nuclear disasters and toxic waste. Her narrative poignantly alternates between her present mechanized life and a past when she was a young working woman with a loving husband and a child. All women have become enslaved, but the fertile Handmaids exist solely to be made pregnant by the Commanders (referred to throughout with the capital *c*), and their babies will be raised by the Commanders' Wives (referred to throughout with a capital *w*).

The novel contains numerous sexual scenes describing the fertilizations, encounters in brothels patronized by the high-ranking Commanders, and the secret sexual liaisons that spring up in this totalitarian state, yet their effect is more apocalyptic than erotic. The brothels are staffed by women who wear such prerevolutionary costumes as Playboy Bunny outfits and other fetish-related items. Working in one such brothel is Moira, a prerevolutionary lesbian friend of Offred's and a strong and rebellious character. Atwood not only depicts the excesses of conservatism but also presents the results of militant feminism gone awry. Pornography of all sorts has been outlawed, women shun all makeup and clothing that hints of sex appeal, and the Handmaids kill any man accused of rape. No one can be trusted, and even after Offred falls in love with Nick, the chauffeur of a Commander, she is uncertain if he will keep his promise to spirit her out of the United States into Canada or England.

CENSORSHIP HISTORY

In 1990, the novel was challenged as a reading assignment in a 12th-grade English class at Rancho Cotati High School in Rohnert Park, California, for being "sexually explicit" and "profane." A local minister asked that the book be withdrawn from the curriculum because the main character of the novel was a woman and young men were unable to relate to her. In a campaign to have the book removed from the schools, one parent circulated a letter to local residents stating, "If you as parents do not rise up and go to your schools over issues such as these, we will continue to educate our kids for the gutter." The school board formed a committee to review the novel, and the work was subsequently retained.

In 1992, parents in Waterloo, Iowa, challenged the use of the book as an optional reading in 12th-grade English classes because of "profanity," "lurid passages about sex," "themes of despair," and statements that they claimed were defamatory to minorities, women, God, and the disabled. The school board rejected the protestors' complaints by a vote of 6 to 1, and one member stated, "The objectors are trying to take away the rights of others to read the books." The protestors appealed to the Iowa Department of Education, which informed them that school districts determined the content of the reading lists.

The novel was removed from the Chicopee (Massachusetts) High School reading list in 1993 because parents complained that it contained "profanity" and "sex."

In 2001, the parents of several students enrolled in an Advanced Placement English class for seniors in Dripping Springs, Texas, challenged the use of the novel as part of the course curriculum, claiming they were offended by the sexual encounters described in the book. The school district board of education considered the parents' request for removal of the book, but the board decided to move the book from the curriculum to an optional reading assignment list.

In March 2006, one parent who felt it was her "duty to ensure no student be able to read *The Handmaid's Tale* in class" succeeded in having the book removed from the Judson Independent School District in San Antonio, Texas. Parent Cindy Pyo complained to Judson school superintendent that the book is "sexually explicit and offensive to Christians" after her son was assigned to read the book as part of the advanced placement English curriculum. Pyo requested an alternative assignment for her son, which the school honored, assigning him Aldous Huxley's *Brave New World* with a few other students. Dissatisfied that other students in the school district were still reading the novel, Pyo submitted a complaint to Judson superintendent Ed Lyman, in the belief that she has "a responsibility to the country and our community to speak up for the values that will strengthen our society." *The Handmaid's Tale* had been in the school district's curriculum for advanced placement English for nearly 10 years, time during which some parents had requested an alternative reading assignment, but no one previously had formally challenged the book. Lyman made the unilateral decision to pull the novel from the AP curriculum despite the recommendations of a committee of teachers, students, and a parent who had approved its use. In an interview reported in the *Houston Chronicle*, the superintendent stated that he believed the book "does not meet community standards" and claimed that some of the descriptions in the book are too sexually explicit for high school students. "The tone of the book does not support, in my opinion, the effort by our state legislature to encourage abstinence outside the bonds of marriage." The recommendation committee appealed the decision to the Judson School District board of trustees, who met on March 23, 2006, to determine whether to uphold the superintendent's ban of the novel or to overrule his decision, which they did in a 5-2 vote. The well-attended meeting contained three hours of public comment and debate before the vote. Near the end of the meeting, board vice president Richard Lafoille stated that he did not see how the trustees could uphold the ban and told the audience of more than 200, "You kids want this book, I'm going to give it to you."

FURTHER READING

Benhuniak-Long, Susan. "Feminism and Reproductive Technology." *Choice* 29 (October 1991): 243.

Cooper, Pamela. "Sexual Surveillance and Medical Authority in Two Versions of *The Handmaid's Tale*." *Journal of Popular Culture* 28 (Spring 1995): 49–66.

Ferns, Chris. "The Values of Dystopia: *The Handmaid's Tale* and the Anti-Utopian Tradition." *Dalhousie Review* 69 (Fall 1989): 373–382.

"Judson Board Set to Write Final Chapter on Sci-Fi Book." *My San Antonio*, March 22, 2006. Available online. URL: http://www.mysanantonio.com/news/MYSA032206_01A_book_ban_86b7db6_html23805.html. Accessed December 12, 2009.

"Judson Makes Right Call, Restoring Book to Class." *My San Antonio*, March 27, 2006. Available online. URL: http://www.mysanantonio.com/opinion/MYSA032706_01O_judson2ed_56c2de7_html.html. Accessed December 12, 2009.

Newsletter on Intellectual Freedom (January 1991): 15; (July 1992): 126; (May 1993): 73; (July 2001): 174; (May 2006): 153–155.

"School's Purchase of Four Books Ignites a Furor in Waterloo." *Des Moines Register*, April 15, 1992, p. M2.

Stein, Karen. "Margaret Atwood's Modest Proposal: *The Handmaid's Tale.*" *Canadian Literature* 23 (Spring 1996): 57–73. .

Tait, Sue, and Christy Tyson. "Paperbacks for Young Adults." *Emergency Librarian* 16 (October 1988): 53–54.

Wilson, Sharon Rose. *Margaret Atwood's Fairy-Tale Sexual Politics.* Jackson: University of Mississippi, 1993.

HOW THE GARCÍA GIRLS LOST THEIR ACCENTS

Author: Julia Alvarez
Original date and place of publication: 1991, United States
Original publisher: Algonquin Books
Literary type: Novel

SUMMARY

How the García Girls Lost Their Accents offers a realistic view of the experiences of young women whose previously secure and protected live have been disrupted. Carla, Sandra, Yolanda, and Sofia have enjoyed lives of privilege in the Dominican Republic, but their lives are reduced when they immigrate to the United States. The immigration is a hurried affair, enabled by the American Central Intelligence Agency to move the family to safety after their father, Carlos García, becomes the target of the Dominican secret police for working underground against the military dictatorship.

As the daughters of wealthy parents, the girls grew up being careless with their possessions and in their treatment of others who did not enjoy the same wealth and luxurious circumstances. While living in the Dominican Republic, they received expensive gifts from FAO Schwarz, which they viewed as located in what appeared at that time in their lives to be an almost mythical United States. Their perceptions change radically after they flee to New York City and confront their new material and cultural realities that do not include chauffeured cars, maids to pick up after them, and cooks to cater to their finicky eating habits. Their mother, Laura, also has a difficult adjustment to make, because she had always lived a life of privilege in the Dominican Republic. She was raised in a wealthy family and her drop in social and financial status is a harsh reality.

The novel opens 29 years after the Garcías moved to the United States, and it is not until the 14th chapter, "The Blood of the Conquistadors," that the novel addresses the political situation in the Dominican Republic and identifies the reasons and the circumstances that made necessary the family's sudden move. The Dominican dictator Trujillo has been overthrown long before, the elder Garcías now have a house on Long Island, and the daughters have been in and out of marriages, relationships, professions, and mental institutions. Yolanda has returned to her homeland and finds that she is a stranger to both the culture and to the language that were once second nature to her. She mistakes farmworkers with machetes for criminals, travels unaccompanied unlike Dominican women who travel in pairs, and falters when speaking in Spanish. She has felt uncomfortable and foreign in the United States, but she is no more comfortable in her homeland and feels that she has no home.

Throughout the chapters that follow, moving between years in the girls' lives in the United States, the reader learns that Laura García sought to distinguish among her daughters when they were young by dressing them in specific colors and repeating symbolic stories for each. She dresses Carla in yellow and relates how she wanted red sneakers badly but the family finances only allowed for common white sneakers, so the young girl used her mother's red nail polish to paint her white sneakers red. Laura dresses Yolanda in pink and speaks of her daughter's abilities as a poet, while ignoring the truth that Yolanda makes her living as a teacher and has a mental breakdown because of the stress of living in two worlds but fitting into neither. Sofia is dressed in white, and Laura proudly supports her defiance of her father's overprotectiveness. Sandra, dressed in blue, is used by a sculptor in forming the face of the Virgin Mary, but her battle with anorexia and mental breakdown leave Laura without a story to tell because she feels that she is a failure as both a Dominican and an American mother.

The novel relates vignettes, some of them containing sexual references, that are integral to the growth and development of the four girls. Sofia has "nonstop boyfriends," and when she is sent as a punishment to the Dominican Republic for a year with her grandmother, she experiences a sexual relationship with her uncle's illegitimate son Manuel. As a young adult she has to go on vacation to Colombia in order to escape her father's prying nature and to evade his condemnation, as well as to have an opportunity to share an intimate relationship with another boyfriend. After having sex with her boyfriend while in Colombia, she leaves him, takes up with a German tourist named Otto, has sex with him four days after they meet, then returns to Germany with him. They later marry and present Carlos with a namesake grandson.

Yolanda was very close to her cousin Mundin, with whom she often played. He has a doll and modeling clay, which their grandmother bought at FAO Schwarz, and which Yolanda wants. When they are alone, he asks her to show him that she "is a girl." She complies and takes off her panties to show him her genitals in exchange for the doll and the clay. Yolanda experiences college life in the late 1960s and despite writing "pornographic poems" with classmate Rudy Elmenhurst, in a chapter titled with his name, she remains a virgin as an undergraduate. She is attracted to Rudy, but the language he uses to describe sexual acts—"balled," "laid," "fucked"—leaves her cold and detached. He accuses her of being "frigid" because she will not sleep with him. When she is in graduate school, the two meet again and he asks her "want to fuck?" She refuses him, then, drinks wine straight out of the bottle "like some decadent wild woman who had just dismissed her unsatisfactory lover."

Carla is at fault for a maid being fired from the family home when they were still living in the Dominican Republic and makes no effort to correct the error that leads to the firing. The girls were given iron banks bought at FAO Schwarz, and Carla's bank was in the form of the Virgin Mary. When Carla placed a coin in the slot, the figure's arms stretched outward, and the figure appeared to ascend to heaven. She left the bank on a shelf in her room and ignored it until one of the family maids asked if she could buy it from Carla with Christmas gift money. Carla simply gave the bank to the maid but did not tell her parents because she did not want to admit that she had not liked the gift and out of fear that they might deny her future gifts. When Laura discovers the bank missing from the shelf in Carla's room, then finds it in the maid's room, she accuses the girl of stealing the bank and dismisses her. Carla does not speak out. When the Garcías have been in the United States for a year, Carla is accosted by a sexual predator who lures her to his car and startles her when she sees he is naked from the waist down. After she runs home and her mother calls the police, both she and Laura feel humiliated because they do not have sufficient command of English to explain the incident completely to the police officers who arrive to take their statements, and no complaint is filed.

Sandra seems to have the most difficult time growing up of the four girls. She wants to be an artist, but she is asked to leave her art class because she wants to sketch and paint kittens and not follow the lessons provided by the teacher. She later encounters an apparently insane sculptor in his studio, where she finds him naked and chained and slashing violently at the face of the sculpture he is creating. He lunges for her, and she falls and breaks her arm, which takes months to heal correctly. In a gallery some time later, she and Laura see a sculpture with a face that is Sandra's. Her encounter with the sculptor had provided him with model for his vision of the Virgin Mary. She has the misfortune of witnessing her father being kissed on the lips by Mrs. Fanning, whose husband, a doctor, worked to help Carlos obtain a medical license in the United States. Rather than tell, Sandra insists that the couple buy her a flamenco doll despite her mother's protests that the girls should not receive any special gifts.

The novel ends with a story that takes place right before the Garcías leave the island. Yolanda has taken a very young kitten from its mother and named it Schwarz. When the mother cat appears, she hides the kitten in her drum that was bought at FAO Schwarz, then beats on the drum with spoons, sticks, and drumsticks in an effort to obscure the plaintive cries of the kitten trapped in the drum. She later pulls the kitten out of the drum and throws it to the ground, injuring its leg, then watches it limp away. That night and for many nights after, Yolanda dreams of the mother cat appearing and feels both fear and sadness for what she did to the kitten.

CENSORSHIP HISTORY

In 2006, *How the García Girls Lost Their Accents* was among nine books on the required reading list that were challenged in the second-largest high school district in Illinois, an act that "triggered debate over whether works praised in literary circles are high art or smut." The controversy began when Leslie Pinney, a Township High School district 214 board member, identified books on the reading list that she considered to "contain vulgar language, brutal imagery or depictions of sexual situations inappropriate for students." The novels Pinney identified as inappropriate reading material, in addition to *How the García Girls Lost Their Accents*, are *Slaughterhouse-Five* by Kurt Vonnegut, *The Things They Carried* by Tim O'Brien, *The Awakening* by Kate Chopin, *Freakonomics* by Steven D. Levitt and Stephen J. Dubner, *The Botany of Desire: A Plant's-Eye View of the World* by Michael Pollan, *The Perks of Being A Wallflower* by Stephen Chbosky, *Fallen Angels* by Walter Dean Myers, and *Beloved* by Toni Morrison. The school board member admitted that she had not read most of the books she targeted and claimed that she did not want to ban the books from the district libraries, but in class she wanted "to replace them with books that address the same themes without explicit material." Her objection to *How the García Girls Lost Their Accents* identified the descriptions of sexual behavior in the novel, which she contended are entirely gratuitous. The challenges were the first in more than 20 years that someone had attempted to remove books from the reading lists in the Arlington Heights–based district, which employed an extensive review process based on established reading lists. In defense of the choices, English and fine arts department head Chuck Venegoni told a reporter for the *Chicago Tribune*, "This is not some serendipitous decision to allow someone to do what they felt like doing because they had something about talking about something kinky in front of kids. It's insulting to hardworking people who really do care about kids." He criticized Pinney's approach of taking a few passages out of context to condemn entire books and observed, "there is nothing in any of those books that even remotely approaches what an objective person would call pornography." Although the school district had an opt-out clause that allowed parents to request that their child read another book if they found the assigned material objectionable, Pinney found the current measures ineffectual "because unless you're digging around the student's backpack, looking at the books and reading them, how exactly will you know what your student is reading?"

Five hundred people attended the school board meeting on Thursday, May 25, 2006, to debate whether to keep *How the García Girls Lost Their Accents* and the other novels on the school reading lists. Supporters of the ban asserted that their efforts were "to protect students from smut" and some people, such as Arlington Heights resident Brude Ticknell, claimed that "teachers promoting the books were motivated by their own progressive social agendas." Students took the debate to the social networking site MySpace.com, and sophomore Scott Leipprandt placed a petition against the ban on the Prospect High page which nearly 500 students and alumni from the six high schools in the district signed. Leipprandt told a *Chicago Tribune* reporter that fighting the banning of books is important. "It's important because it shows us things. All these things happen in real life. By banning it, it doesn't give us the opportunity to talk about it before we encounter it in real life." After a long meeting during which hundreds of people spoke, the school board voted 6-1 in favor of approving the required reading list without change. The following year, the school board voted to provide parents with the reading lists for courses before voting on materials.

In 2007, *How the García Girls Lost Their Accents* was removed from the school libraries in the Johnston County, North Carolina, school district after parents of students attending the West Johnston High School "challenged its sexual content and profane language to the school board." The removal of the novel led to the creation of a districtwide committee that was given the responsibility of reviewing titles in the schools and in the school libraries that might contain material similarly offensive to parents. The associate superintendent for curriculum and instructional services Keith Beamon asserted, "We are simply looking back through the titles to see if there are any red flags out there. It's not that we are looking for any particular title; it's a broad review to see if there is anything out there that jumps out at us. . . . If you've got a leak in one place in your house . . . we're just kind of checking everywhere else to make sure there are no other leaks."

The controversy in Johnston County began when the 15-year-old daughter of Georgia Roberts brought the novel home to read for her English class. Roberts said that her daughter told her multiple times that the book was very hard to read and that the deeper she got into the novel, the more upset she became. "She came to me and she was very upset and crying because the more you got into the book, the worse it got." The school assigned Roberts's daughter *All Quiet on the Western Front* as an alternative reading assignment and scheduled a parent-teacher conference. Roberts said that the teacher, school principal, and adviser defended use of the book by telling her that each of the scenes is a lesson in language barriers. That response angered Roberts, who told reporters,

"I said to the teacher, 'Well, Ma'am, you can learn about language barriers at the DMV . . . you can go anywhere in Johnston County and come up with a language barrier situation. . . . It doesn't have to be done with a man's private parts rising and him taking care of himself." Roberts agreed that learning about diversity and different cultures is important, and said that she was willing to learn about the Latin culture "but not with the foul language and sexually explicit situations in the book." The West Johnston Media and Technology Advisory Committee reviewed the novel and suggested the book should stay on the library shelves and in the classroom curriculum. Ms. Roberts appealed the decision, and the matter was taken up by the district media and technology committee, who reviewed the work and recommended its removal from all county schools.

FURTHER READING

"Censorship Dateline: Libraries." *Newsletter on Intellectual Freedom* 57, no. 2 (March 2008): 59–61.
Francisco, Jamie. "Book-Ban Debate Is Long, Impassioned: More Than 350 Sign Up to Speak to School Board." *Chicago Tribune*, May 26, 2006, p. 2NW.1.
_____. "Explicit Move Is Made to Ban Books from Reading List." *Chicago Tribune*, May 24, 2006, p. 2NS.8.
Megan, Graydon. "Parents to Get Look at School Reading Lists: Controversy Led to Move by District in Arlington Heights." *Chicago Tribune*, May 12, 2007, p. 13.

LADY CHATTERLEY'S LOVER

Author: D. H. Lawrence
Original dates and places of publication: 1928, Italy; 1959, United States
Original publishers: Orioli; Grove Press
Literary form: Novel

SUMMARY

Lady Chatterley's Lover conveys Lawrence's bitter and deep dissatisfaction with the stultifying effects of industrialization and modern sterile society upon the natural life of all English classes. In general, he portrays the manner in which the upper classes have become devitalized and the lower classes debased by the increasing artificiality of their emotional and physical relationships. The novel relates the experiences of a young woman named Connie Chatterley, married to a baronet who is paralyzed from the waist down after severe injuries incurred fighting in World War I. She is sexually frustrated and becomes increasingly dissatisfied with the artificial and sterile nature of the society in which she lives. A brief affair with a man within her husband Clifford's social circle proves to be unsatisfying and leaves her even more restless and unhappy.

Repelled by her husband's suggestion that she become pregnant by another man and produce a child whom he might make his heir, Connie turns further away from him. Instead, she feels attracted to their gamekeeper, Mellors, Lawrence's example of the "natural man," whom society has neither devitalized nor debased. His coarse exterior and verbal expression mask a highly developed spiritual and intellectual independence, and the two become lovers. Their affair is deeply passionate and their lovemaking extremely tender, as Mellors gradually leads Connie to abandon her preconceived views of propriety and her inhibitions. A number of passages contain detailed and candid descriptions of their sexual pleasures and their uncensored utterances and descriptions of both genitals and body functions.

> "Th'art good cunt, though, aren't ter? Best bit o'cunt left on earth. When ter likes! When tha'rt willin'!"
>
> "What is cunt?" she asked.
>
> "An' doesn't ter know? Cunt! It's thee down theer; an' what I get when I'm i'side thee; it's a' as it is, all on't."
>
> "All on't," she teased. "Cunt! It's like fuck then."
>
> "Nay, nay! Fuck's only what you do. Animals fuck. But, cunt's a lot more than that. It's thee, dost see: an' tha'rt a lot besides an animal, aren't ter? even ter fuck! Cunt! Eh, that's the beauty o' thee, lass."

Such passages, although relevant to the plot and to the development of the characters, became the basis for numerous attempts to ban the novel.

At the end of the novel, Connie is pregnant with Mellors's child and plans to marry him after obtaining a divorce from Clifford.

CENSORSHIP HISTORY

Lady Chatterley's Lover was suppressed long before the case of *Grove Press v. Christenberry* went to trial in 1959. The decision was made to publish the novel in Italy in 1928 and then to send copies to subscribers in England to avoid censors. Publishing in this way made it impossible for Lawrence to obtain an international copyright, so the author lost substantial money through the appearance of numerous pirated editions. The United States government had declared the novel obscene in 1929, and the post office ruled the novel barred from the mails. Travelers returning from Europe with copies of the novel faced having the book confiscated by United States Customs. Objections to the novel arose over both the explicit sexual description in the novel and the language used by the characters. As Charles Rembar, the lawyer who defended the novel in the 1959 trial, observed in his account of the case,

> not only did the Lawrence novel devote more of its pages to the act of sex and deal with it in greater detail than anything ever before sold over the counter; it had language that had never been seen in a book openly circulated, except

when used for tangential and occasional purposes, and not often then. . . . *Lady Chatterley's Lover* presented the forbidden acts in forbidden detail, and described them in forbidden language.

In 1929, John Sumner, secretary of the New York Society for the Suppression of Vice, alerted officials at the Boston Watch and Ward Society that bibliophile and former Yale librarian James A. DeLacey, now proprietor of Dunster House Bookshop, had ordered five copies of the novel. An agent went to the bookstore to purchase the book and, after repeated refusals, finally obtained a copy. The society then instituted legal proceedings against DeLacey and his clerk, Joseph Sullivan, who were found guilty on November 25, 1929, by Judge Arthur P. Stone in Cambridge district court. DeLacey was fined $800 and sentenced to four months in jail, and Sullivan was fined $200 and sentenced to two weeks in jail. The convictions were appealed, but despite strong community support for the two men and attestations to their character, on December 20, 1929, Judge Frederick W. Fosdick upheld the lower court conviction. The case was then taken to the state supreme court.

A year later, the novel was the key element of the "Decency Debates" that raged in the U.S. Senate between Senator Bronson Cutting of New Mexico and Senator Reed Smoot of Utah. Cutting worked to modify the censorship laws while Smoot opposed reform ("Senator Smoot Smites Smut," read one newspaper headline). That same year, a Philadelphia prosecutor authorized a raid on a bookshop and the seizure of 300 books, among them *Lady Chatterley's Lover*, *Fanny Hill*, and *The Perfumed Garden*, marking the beginning of an extensive campaign to eliminate the sale of "obscene literature" in that city. Also in 1930, the Massachusetts Supreme Court affirmed DeLacey's conviction, and he was sentenced to four months in jail.

In 1944, John Sumner, acting in the name of the New York Society for the Suppression of Vice, seized copies of *The First Lady Chatterley* (Dial Press, 1944), and the book remained on the blacklist of the National Organization of Decent Literature until 1953.

The novel had appeared in expurgated form over the 30 years since it had first appeared, but the Grove Press edition was the full edition with all of the "four-letter words" and sex scenes created by Lawrence. As soon as the novel was published by Grove, Postmaster General Christenberry issued an order to ban the novel from the mails. The publisher went to court and *Grove Press Inc. v. Christenberry*, 175 F. Supp. 488 (S.D.N.Y. 1959) was heard in federal district court by Judge Frederick van Pelt Bryan, who agreed with the publisher and lifted the ban. He stated in his opinion that the application of a rule of contemporary community standards to the case signals acceptance of the book throughout the country:

> the broadening of freedom of expression and of the frankness with which sex and sex relations are dealt with at the present time require no discussion. In one best selling novel after another frank descriptions of the sex act and "four-letter"

words appear with frequency. These trends appear in all media of public expression, in the kind of language used and the subjects discussed in polite society, in pictures, advertisements and dress, and in other ways familiar to all. Much of what is now accepted would have shocked the community to the core a generation ago. Today such things are generally tolerated whether we approve or not.

I hold that at this stage in the development of our society, this major English novel does not exceed the outer limits of tolerance which the community as a whole gives to writing about sex and sex relations.

In *Grove Press Inc. v. Christenberry*, 276 F.2d 433 (2d Cir. 1960), the circuit court of appeals agreed with Judge Bryan's decision.

In 1959, Postmaster General Summerfield made the decision to continue to suppress copies of *Lady Chatterley's Lover* from the mail, declaring that the book was filled with "filthy," "smutty," "degrading," "offensive," and "disgusting" words, as well as with descriptions of sexual acts. He claimed that such "filthy words and passages" outweighed any literary merit that the book might have.

In England in 1960, the director of public prosecutions brought a criminal action against Penguin Books, Ltd., when the publisher announced its intention to openly publish the first unexpurgated British edition of *Lady Chatterley's Lover*. The prosecutor, Senior Treasury Counsel Mervyn Griffith-Jones, asked jurors to test the obscenity of the book themselves by answering these two questions: "Is it a book that you would have lying around your house? Is it a book that you would even wish your wife *or your servants* to read?" The defense attorneys argued that the novel as a whole was not obscene, despite language and sexual content in various passages. Thirty-five defense experts stressed the literary merit of the work, and the jury deliberated for three days before acquitting Penguin Books of all charges. Kuh relates that when the House of Lords debated the trial that cleared the novel, with its sexual episodes between a lady and her gamekeeper, a peer who agreed with the decision was asked, "Would you want your wife to read it?" He replied, "I would not object to my wife reading it, but I don't know about my gamekeeper."

In 1965, the Indecent Publications Tribunal of New Zealand reviewed the paperback edition of *Lady Chatterley's Lover* to determine if it was indecent, despite an earlier decision that no action would be taken regarding the import or sale of the cloth-bound edition of the novel. At the time, the cloth-bound edition sold in New Zealand for 16 shillings and the paperback edition for 5 shillings. The tribunal acknowledged that the novel "is a seriously written work by an author who has an established place in the field of English literature" and that "the text of the story is in the case of each identical; there is no difference between the two editions save in regard to the preface of the one and the introduction of the other and the form of each respectively."

Nonetheless, tribunal members considered if the novel should be kept out of the hands of persons under 18 years of age, and the issue became the difference in cost between the cloth-bound and the paperback editions, the low price of the paperback making it easily available to minors. This consideration motivated dissent among the members of the tribunal, two of whom asserted that "the sale of the Penguin [paperback] edition should be restricted to persons of seventeen years or over. . . . They think it is a matter for regret that the free circulation of the hardcover edition should have prejudiced the issue, embarrassed the Tribunal and made it virtually impossible in a particularly clear instance to invoke the provisions of the statute." The other three tribunal members felt that, given the unrestricted circulation of the hardcover edition, "it would be futile to classify the paperback edition as indecent in the hands of juveniles." Viewing any restrictive action against the paperback edition as futile, the majority view of the tribunal determined on April 7, 1965, that "the paperback edition of *Lady Chatterley's Lover* published by Penguin Books is not indecent within the meaning of the Indecent Publications Act of 1963."

FURTHER READING

Boyer, Paul S. *Purity in Print: The Vice-Society Movement and Book Censorship in America.* New York: Scribner, 1968.

Grant, Sidney S., and S. E. Angoff. "Censorship in Boston." *Boston University Law Review* 10 (January 1930): 36–60.

———. "Recent Developments in Censorship." *Boston University Law Review* 10 (November 1930): 488–509.

Maddox, Brenda. *D. H. Lawrence: The Story of a Marriage.* New York: Simon & Schuster, 1993.

Paul, James C. N., and Murray L. Schwartz. *Federal Censorship: Obscenity in the Mail.* New York: Free Press, 1961.

Perry, Stuart. *The Indecent Publications Tribunal: A Social Experiment.* London: Whitcombe and Tombs, 1965.

Rembar, Charles. *The End of Obscenity: The Trials of Lady Chatterley's Lover, Tropic of Cancer & Fanny Hill by the Lawyer Who Defended Them.* New York: Random House, 1968.

Roeburt, John. *The Wicked and the Banned.* New York: Macfadden Books, 1963.

U.S. President's Commission on Obscenity and Pornography. *The Report of the Commission on Obscenity and Pornography.* New York: Random House, 1970.

LOLITA

Author: Vladimir Nabokov
Original dates and places of publication: 1955, France; 1958, United States; 1959, England
Original publishers: Olympia Press; Weidenfeld and Nicholson; G. P. Putnam's Sons
Literary form: Novel

SUMMARY

Lolita is structured as a psychiatric case study of the pedophiliac protagonist, Humbert Humbert, the middle-aged lover of 12-year-old Lolita. The book traces Humbert's sexual obsession with young girls; his marriage to Lolita's mother, Charlotte; and the long cross-country trip that he takes with Lolita after her mother's death. Near the end of the novel, the nymphet (as Humbert dubs her), now 16, married, pregnant, and physically worn out, writes and asks for money. Still obsessed with the image of the young Lolita, Humbert hysterically begs her to leave with him but she refuses. In desperation, he offers her a check for $3,600 and $400 in cash if she will reveal the name of the man with whom she ran off. That man is Quilty, a friend of her late mother's and Lolita's old lover from the time when Humbert was still ogling and desiring the 12-year-old.

Humbert seeks revenge, and he is later incarcerated for shooting and killing Quilty.

Humbert's obsession dominates his adult life as he considers every attractive adolescent a seductress. As he intellectualizes his lust, Humbert places the blame for his obsession on the girls, whom he feels lead him on deliberately. Sitting in parks, he "throbs with excitement," "pulses with anticipation," struggles to control the feelings that make him "race with all speed toward [his] lone gratification." Before meeting 12-year-old Dolores ("Lolita") Haze and her mother, Humbert has had three breakdowns and confinements in sanatoriums. He refers to adventures with a succession of girl-like prostitutes and relates that he frequents brothels looking for young girls.

The initial meeting with Lolita is sexually charged, as Humbert notes each sensuous detail of her childlike body and then becomes obsessed with determining how to appease his sexual desire. In one early scene, he teases Lolita by taking her apple as she sits beside him on the couch. Humbert experiences "a glowing tingle" that develops into a "deep hot sweetness" that he can barely control. He feels that "the nerves of pleasure had been laid bare" and "the least pressure would suffice to set all paradise loose." As he sits "suspended on the brink of that voluptuous abyss," he moves his hand up Lolita's leg "as far as the shadow of decency would allow."

After Humbert marries Charlotte, with the aim of having freer access to Lolita, he daydreams of "administering a powerful sleeping potion to both mother and daughter so as to fondle the latter through the night with perfect impunity." Charlotte dies when she runs into traffic after reading Humbert's secret diary that details his fantasies, and Humbert tries out his sleeping pill scheme when he retrieves the orphaned Lolita from camp. The pills don't make her comatose as he had planned, but he seduces her anyway. That begins their two years of travel, posing as father and daughter as they go from motel to motel, encountering the seedy side of the American landscape. After Lolita runs away, Humbert once again has a breakdown and enters a sanatorium, which he later leaves with the intent of finding Lolita and avenging his loss.

CENSORSHIP HISTORY

Lolita was denounced as "filth" and "sheer unrestrained pornography" when it was first published. Author Nabokov claimed that *Lolita* was a comedy and disagreed with those who considered it erotic writing, yet he argued strenuously to have the novel published anonymously in order to protect his career as a professor at Cornell University. American publishers were similarly reticent about an association with the topic, and the novel was promptly refused by many when Nabokov's agent circulated it in 1954. Pascal Covici of Viking Press and Wallace Brockway of Simon & Schuster thought it would strike readers as "pornographic." James Laughlin of New Directions refused the book because "we are worried about possible repercussions both for the publisher and the author" and suggested publication in France. Before giving up, Nabokov sent the manuscript to Roger Straus of Farrar, Straus and Young and to Jason Epstein of Doubleday, who also rejected the manuscript. When the novel failed to find a publisher in the United States, Nabokov's agent took it to Olympia Press in Paris, which published it in two volumes.

After Olympia Press published *Lolita* in English in 1955, France banned the book in December 1956. The publisher, Maurice Girodias, asked Nabokov for help in fighting the ban, but the author replied, "My moral defense of the book is the book itself." He also wrote an essay entitled "On a Book Entitled Lolita" that was a lengthy justification, later attached to the American edition, in which he claimed that readers who thought the work erotic were misreading his intentions. Rather, Nabokov stated, "That my novel does contain various allusions to the physiological urges of a pervert is quite true. But after all we are not children, not illiterate juvenile delinquents, not English public school boys who after a night of homosexual romps have to endure the paradox of reading the Ancients in expurgated versions."

Olympia Press won its case in 1957 in the Administrative Tribunal of Paris, and the novel was back on sale in January 1958. When the Fourth Republic fell in May 1958 and General Charles de Gaulle assumed power, the French minister of the interior appealed to the Conseil d'Etat, the highest court in France. By December of that year, the book was again banned in France after the government successfully appealed the initial judgment. No appeal was possible, but the publication of the novel in French by the prestigious French publisher Gallimard in April 1959 gave Olympia Press foundation for a suit. The publisher sued the French government on the basis that the legal principle of equality among French citizens had been violated by the banning of the Olympia Press edition of *Lolita* and not the Gallimard edition. The English version was placed back on the market in France in September 1959.

British Customs banned the book in 1955, the same year that Graham Greene, in the *Sunday Times*, named *Lolita* one of his three favorite books of the year. Greene's article led John Gordon to remark in the *Sunday Express*: "Without doubt it is the filthiest book I have ever read. Sheer unrestrained pornography." Several British publishers were eager to bid for the rights to the novel, but they waited for the enactment of the Obscene Publications Bill in 1959, which would permit literary merit to be taken into account should the book be placed on trial. They expected prosecution because reviewers were already waging a war against the novel, several stating that the novel should be suppressed in England if it could be proven that "even a single little girl was likely to be seduced as a result of its publication." Conservatives in Parliament urged Nigel Nicholson, a member of Parliament as well as a publisher, not to publish the book, claiming that it would be detrimental to the party image. He lost his next bid for reelection, partly because of *Lolita*.

In contrast, United States Customs determined in February 1957 that the book was not objectionable and could be admitted into the country. Therefore, the book could not be legally exported from France, but people who smuggled the book out could import it legally into the United States. Despite its admissibility by Customs, U.S. publishers refused to publish *Lolita* until G. P. Putnam's Sons took the chance in 1958. A year later, the bans in England and France were lifted and the book was published openly in those countries. In the United States, however, the Cincinnati Public Library banned the book from its shelves after the director observed that "the theme of perversion seems to me obscene."

The novel was also banned in 1959 in Argentina, where government censors claimed that the book reflected moral disintegration. In 1960, the minister of commons in New Zealand banned import of the novel under the Customs Act of 1913 that prohibited importing books deemed "indecent" within the meaning of the Indecent Publications Act of 1910. To fight the ban, the New Zealand Council of Civil Liberties imported six copies of the book and successfully challenged the Supreme Court. Mr. Justice Hutchin delivered the judgment, noting that the book had been written with no pornographic intent and for the educated reader. Basing his decision on the recommendation of a ministry advisory committee that individual orders should be permitted, the justice observed that New Zealand Customs did admit certain books addressed to authorized individuals or intended to be sold to restricted classes. The ban on *Lolita* in South Africa, instituted in 1974 because of the "perversion theme" of the novel, was lifted in 1982, and the South African Directorate of Publications gave permission for its publication in paperback form.

FURTHER READING

Baker, George. "*Lolita:* Literature or Pornography." *Saturday Review*, June 22, 1957, p. 18.

Centerwall, Brandon S. "Hiding in Plain Sight: Nabokov and Pedophilia." *Texas Studies in Literature & Language* 32 (Fall 1990): 468–484.

Dupee, F. W. "*Lolita* in America." *Encounter* 12 (February 1959): 30–35.

Feeney, Ann. "*Lolita* and Censorship: A Case Study. *References Services Review* 21 (Winter 1993): 67–74, 90.

Hicks, Granville. "Lolita and Her Problems." *Saturday Review*, August 16, 1958, pp. 12, 38.

Levin, Bernard. "Why All the Fuss?" *Spectator*, January 9, 1959, pp. 32–33.

"Lolita in the Dock." *New Zealand Libraries* 23 (August 1960): 180–183.

Patnoe, Elizabeth. "Lolita Misrepresented, Lolita Reclaimed: Disclosing the Doubles." *College Literature* 22 (June 1995): 81–104.

Roeburt, John. *The Wicked and the Banned.* New York: Macfadden Books, 1963.

Scott, W. J. "The *Lolita* Case." *Landfall* 58 (June 1961): 134–138.

MADAME BOVARY

Author: Gustave Flaubert
Original dates and places of publication: 1857, France; 1888, England
Original publishers: Michel Levy (France); Henry Vizitelly (England)
Literary form: Novel

SUMMARY

Madame Bovary relates the story of Emma Roualt, a young Frenchwoman married to hardworking doctor Charles Bovary, and the manner in which she allows impossible romantic ideals to destroy her marriage and her life. Despite her husband's infatuation with her, Emma feels little for him and, instead, seeks the passionate love she has read about in romance novels. When the couple attends a fancy dress ball at the estate of a marquis, Emma dances with royalty and mingles with the rich; she leaves believing that this was the life she was born to lead.

She becomes extremely unhappy, and Charles decides that she needs a change of scenery. As they move from Tostes to Yonville, Emma learns that she is pregnant. This knowledge and the attentions of notary clerk Leon, who shares her interests in art and literature, distract her at least until the baby is born. Having hoped for a boy, Emma is disappointed when a daughter is born, and she begins to borrow money from dry goods merchant Lheureux to buy luxury items that she believes she deserves.

As Emma becomes increasingly unhappy, she gravitates toward Leon and the two profess their love but do not begin an affair. Instead, to avoid temptation, Leon moves to Paris. Emma, however, begins an affair with a patient of her husband's, the wealthy Rodolphe Boulanger, who wants only to add her to his list of conquests. Each morning Emma obsessively rushes to Boulanger's estate, where the two make passionate love, and she meets him some evenings after Charles is asleep.

After the novelty wears off and Boulanger ends the affair, Emma sinks into a deep depression, staying in bed for two months. When she recovers, Charles takes her to Rouen to enjoy the opera, but she secretly meets Leon, and they begin an affair. She lies to Charles, telling him that she will take weekly piano lessons in Rouen, but she meets Leon in a hotel room each week to continue their affair.

At the same time, her debt to Lheureux increases, and she begins to borrow money elsewhere to pay him back. She becomes desperate when he confronts her and threatens to confiscate all of her property unless she immediately pays him 8,000 francs. Unable to raise the money, Emma commits suicide by ingesting arsenic after writing a letter of explanation to Charles. Her death weakens Charles, who dies soon after, leaving their daughter, Berthe, to work in a cotton mill to earn her living.

CENSORSHIP HISTORY

Madame Bovary was censored before publication as a novel, when it appeared in installments in *Revue de Paris*, a literary publication run by Flaubert's friend Maxime DuCamp. Before agreeing to publish the work, DuCamp asked to excise a single passage, about a page and a half in length, near the end of the novel. The passage relates Emma's extended tryst with Leon behind the closed curtains of a cab, and DuCamp felt that getting it past the censors would be "impossible." Flaubert agreed, but he was not prepared for the following editorial note inserted by the editors in place of the passage: "Here the editors found it necessary to suppress a passage unsuitable to the policies of the *Revue de Paris;* we hereby acknowledge this to the author." The editors later requested that cuts be made in the sixth and final installment of the novel—a move that Flaubert first fought and then reluctantly accepted, adding his own disclaimer regarding the quality of the now-fragmented work.

The omission of the offensive passages did not prevent government action being taken against *Madame Bovary*, though Flaubert felt the action was aimed more at the overly liberal *Revue* than at his novel. *Madame Bovary* went on trial on January 29, 1857, in highly formal court proceedings in which Imperial Advocate Ernest Pinard admitted that the language of the law of 1819 was "a little vague, a little elastic." He also asserted that the prosecution faced "peculiar difficulty" because reading the entire novel to the jury would be too time consuming, but reading only the "accused passages" would be too restrictive. To solve the problem, Pinard summarized the novel in detail and read verbatim the offending passages. When his version reached the appropriate point in the narrative, Pinard called upon the jury to apply "limits and standards" and noted, "Yes, Mr. Flaubert knows how to embellish his pictures with all the resources of art, but without art's restraints. No gauze for him, no veils—he gives us nature in all her nudity and crudity!"

In defense, Flaubert's lawyer portrayed the novel as a handbook of bourgeois respectability, noting that it taught the consequences of straying from moral behavior. The jury, which waited a week to deliver a verdict, acquitted the author, publisher, and printer without costs on the basis that their guilt had been "insufficiently established." In essence, the jury asserted that Flaubert "committed the wrong of occasionally neglecting the rules which no self-respecting writer should transgress, and of forgetting that literature, like art, must be chaste and pure not only in its form but also in its expression, in order to accomplish the good effects it is called upon to produce." A few months later, the novel was published in its entirety, all cuts restored, and sold 15,000 copies in two months.

In 1888, Flaubert's English publisher, Vizitelly, came under attack by the National Vigilance Association (NVA), a group composed mainly of clergymen who founded it in 1886 to continue the work of the Society for the Suppression of Vice, which had ceased operations a few years before. *Madame Bovary*, translated from French into English by the publisher's son, was specifically cited, as were works by Zola, Goncourt, Maupassant, Daudet, and Bourget. The NVA gained the attention of House of Commons member Samuel Smith, M.P., who spoke in May 1888 against Vizitelly, "the chief culprit in the spread of pernicious literature." The House passed a motion that "the law against obscene publications and indecent pictures and prints should be vigorously enforced and, if necessary, strengthened." The government would leave the initiation of proceedings to private individuals.

Other politicians and the newspapers joined the campaign against pornography, widening the scope of the battle. The Roman Catholic newspaper *Tablet* attacked Vizitelly as a "pornographer." The law firm Collette & Collette, retained by the NVA, obtained a summons on August 10, 1888, against Henry Vizitelly. The defense argued that Vizitelly had carefully expurgated the books while translating them into English, and it pointed out that the unexpurgated French versions were being freely circulated and sold in England at the same time. The prosecution declared the fact irrelevant, and the publisher went to trial at the Old Bailey in October 1888, where a jury charged him with "uttering and publishing certain obscene libels." Vizitelly was fined and ordered to desist publishing the offensive works. When he repeated the offense in 1889, the publisher received a four-month prison sentence, despite impaired health.

In 1893, the American Library Association for the first time offered a 5,000-title book guide for small popular libraries and branches, calling it a collection that "one could recommend to any trustee." No works by Flaubert were included in the list.

FURTHER READING

Elliott, Desmond. "The Book That Shocked Paris: The Strange Story of *Madame Bovary.*" *Books and Bookmen* 5 (June 1960): 11, 46.
Geller, Evelyn. *Forbidden Books in American Public Libraries, 1876–1939.* Westport, Conn.: Greenwood, 1984.
Kendrick, Walter. *The Secret Museum.* New York: Viking, 1987.
Mancuso, Ludwig. *The Obscene: The History of an Indignation.* London: MacGibbon & Key, 1965.
Steegmuller, Francis. *Flaubert and Madame Bovary.* Boston: Houghton Mifflin, 1970.

NATIVE SON

Author: Richard Wright
Original date and place of publication: 1940, New York

Original publisher: Harper and Sons
Literary type: Novel

SUMMARY

Native Son is the story of Bigger Thomas, a character whom Richard Wright revealed was a composite of the many angry oppressed black men he knew growing up, those who "consistently violated the Jim Crow laws of the South and got away with it, at least for a sweet brief spell. Eventually, the whites who restricted their lives made them pay a terrible price. They were shot, hanged, maimed, lynched, and generally hounded until they were either dead or their spirits broken." As Arnold Rampersad writes in his introduction to the HarperPerennial edition of *Native Son*, the novel "is a story that is at one level a seedy melodrama from the police blotter and, at the same time, an illuminating drama of an individual consciousness that challenges traditional definitions of character."

The novel is divided into three parts, rather than chapters, each division named for the experiences and emotions that envelop Bigger Thomas, the eldest of three children living with the impoverished Mrs. Thomas in a seedy, rat-infested apartment on Chicago's South Side. The first third of the story is entitled "Fear," and it opens with a view of the grim little apartment in which four people share one bedroom and struggle to maintain their dignity and modesty while sleeping, dressing, and undressing in the same small cramped room. Of the three children, Bigger is the most rebellious and most aware of the many opportunities that have been denied him, and he is also the least likely to acquiesce to the demands of the white world. As the novel begins, Bigger and his brother, Buddy, attempt to kill a rat that has terrorized their sister, Vera, and their mother. As the women scream in fright, Bigger and Buddy corner the rat behind a trunk and, although the creature defiantly slashes Bigger's trousers with its sharp teeth, they kill it by slamming it with a skillet, after which Bigger crushes the rat's skull by pounding it with his shoe. After the excitement subsides, Mrs. Thomas and Vera repeat their earlier reminders that Bigger has a job interview that day. Mrs. Thomas taunts him with the charge that they could afford to live in better and safer housing if he did have a job and warns him that the way he now lives, hanging out with friends at the pool hall and remaining unemployed, will land him in jail. Vera exhibits her conscientious nature and worries that she will be late for her sewing classes at the YWCA, and Buddy appears to share the same concerns for making a go of life, but Bigger expresses disdain for their concerns.

As the day passes and Bigger waits until his 5:30 P.M. appointment with Mr. Dalton, a very rich white man whose daughter is involved with a communist and whose picture often appears in the society news columns, Bigger considers robbing Blum's Delicatessen with his friends Gus, Jack, and G. H. They have robbed businesses owned by African Americans, but this would be their first robbery of a white-owned business. Gus expresses doubts about the robbery, and Bigger taunts him for being a coward, but Gus responds that Bigger is afraid, afraid that Gus will say "yes." Jack steps between the two when Bigger attempts to attack Gus and distracts Bigger by going with him to the movies. Earlier, Bigger and Gus had played a game they called "white," in which they spoke and acted as they perceived wealthy and snobbish white people did. When a skywriting plane passes overhead, Bigger states that he could fly a plane if he were given the chance, a remark that makes both young men laugh bitterly and conclude that no white people would ever give Bigger or any other Negro the chance.

The films Jack and Bigger see provide a startling dichotomy of the way in which the white and black races are represented. The first movie shows a married rich white woman, who takes a lover, and who is seen golfing, swimming, and going to cocktail parties and to exclusive nightclubs. She returns to her husband after communists try to kill him, which leads Bigger and Jack to try to ascertain what a "Red" is, and they conclude that they must be violent people who live in Russia. The second movie stereotypically depicts naked African tribal women and men dancing wildly to the sound of beating drums. Bored by the second film, Bigger thinks about how he will soon be "getting hold of money" if Dalton hires him as a chauffeur. He begins to express hopefulness about his life and rejects the idea of robbing Blum's because he sees a possibility of having a job that will lead to money and success. Once he arrives at the Dalton residence in the all-white neighborhood, his confidence falters as he agonizes over which door to knock on, the front or the back. When the white housekeeper admits him to the house, he feels uncomfortable in the elegant surroundings, with its fine artwork, smooth white walls, and lovely furniture. Mr. Dalton welcomes him and asks about Bigger's family and past, and the reader learns that the old man's company owns the slum in which Bigger and his family live. As Dalton explains the duties of a chauffeur, his daughter Mary appears and begins a brief inquisition, talking about capitalists and trade unions with a familiarity that aggravates Bigger, although Dalton seems indifferent to what she says. Dalton bluntly reveals that he knows Bigger's reputation as a troublemaker, but as a supporter of the National Association for the Advancement of Colored People, he will give him the job. After the interview, the housekeeper Peggy provides Bigger's supper and explains that he will also be expected to tend to the furnace. In the kitchen, he also meets Mrs. Dalton who, although blind, startles Bigger by her keen perception of where he is and what he is doing.

In his first act of employment, Bigger is expected to drive Mary to the university, but the spoiled young white woman has other plans. She tells him that they will pick up her friend Jan Erlone, and the two make a big show of interacting with Bigger as equals and asking him to use their first names, actions that embarrass Bigger and cause him to feel a "dumb, cold, inarticulate hate" toward them. Mary and Erlone sit in the front seat, and Mary presses against Bigger as he drives. When the two ask him to join them in eating at Ernie's Kitchen Shack, "a place where colored people eat," Bigger is seen by his friend Jack and his sometime girlfriend Bessie, which displeases him.

Mary and Jan direct Bigger to drive them around the park while they drink beer and then rum and talk idealistically about communism, before a very drunk Erlone is taken to the train. Bigger drives a similarly drunk Mary home, where she stumbles noisily, leading him to carry her upstairs and to place the unconscious and suppliant young woman into bed, where he kisses her and begins to go further. "He lifted her and laid her on the bed. Something urged him to leave at once, but he leaned over her, excited, looking at her face in the dim light, not wanting to take his hands from her breasts. She tossed and mumbled sleepily. He tightened his fingers on her breasts, kissing her again, feeling her move toward him. He was aware only of her body now; his lips trembled."

As her body begins to respond to him, the door opens and Mrs. Dalton enters the room and calls out Mary's name. Bigger panics when Mary mumbles a response and, afraid that his presence will be revealed, he briefly presses a pillow against her face to keep her quiet. Mrs. Dalton leaves after accusing Mary of being "dead drunk," and Bigger realizes that he may have escaped discovery but has accidentally suffocated the young woman. Faced with the problem of saving his own life, Bigger thinks of a way to cast suspicion on Erlone and devises a plan for getting rid of Mary's body by placing it in her trunk, which he was supposed to take to the train the next day, then attempts to burn it in the furnace in the basement. The plan is temporarily blocked when he cannot fit the body entirely in the furnace, and he is forced to cut off her head with a hatchet and put both her head and body into the furnace then place a fresh load of coal into the fire. After removing the large amount of cash from Mary's purse, he returns to his home and sleeps.

Book Two, "Flight," opens the next morning, a bright and sunny Sunday. He hides the evidence he has accidentally taken home with him and runs out of the house, feeling that he has created a new life for himself. Convinced that he has murdered and gotten away with the act, he feels invincible. He knows that white people might accuse him of robbing, getting drunk, or raping, but he feels that they would never believe a black man would have the audacity to kill a white woman. The thought makes him brazen, and he spends some of the money he took from Mary's purse buying cigarettes for Gus, Jack, and G. H., then takes a streetcar to the Dalton home. While on the way, Bigger thinks of the murder and begins to feel pride in what he did, considering her murder a justification for the fear that white people have caused him over the years. "Now that the ice was broken, could he not do other things? What was there to stop him?" The action takes on a greater importance in his mind, and he thinks of the relationship between the races, characterizing white people as a "great natural force" against which blacks should join in a group and fight back to "end fear and shame."

Once at the Dalton home, Bigger is momentarily shaken from his newfound confidence when he finds Peggy looking into the furnace, but she expresses no suspicions, so he merely adds more coal and pretends to wait for Mary to come downstairs. After Peggy chastises him for leaving the car out all night, he responds that Mary had told him to do so and mentions that a man had visited her that night. While the family speculates where Mary has gone, Bigger delivers her empty trunk to the train station, then returns to hear Peggy tell Mrs. Dalton that Mary had not packed any clothes. When questioned, Bigger repeats his story about the night before and says Erlone had gone up to Mary's room, in an attempt to shift the guilt onto the young communist. After leaving, he visits Bessie and shows her the roll of money, after which she responds to his kisses and "she drew him to her bed." Afterward, "his body felt free and easy now that he had lain with Bessie." She tells him about a kidnapping case that occurred in the neighborhood where she worked, the real life case of Leopold and Loeb, who sent ransom notes to the family of a young boy they kidnapped and killed. The case gives Bigger a further idea to cover his crime, and he enlists Bessie's help in creating a ransom note to extort $10,000 from the Dalton family.

Britten, a private investigator hired by Dalton, confronts Bigger when he returns to the Dalton home and asks rapid-fire questions intended to trap him into admitting involvement with the Communist Party. In a clever move, Bigger, although frightened by Britten's approach and suspicions, manages to turn suspicion more fully in Erlone's direction and make himself a potential witness against the other man.

After coercing Bessie into helping him write the ransom note, Bigger returns to the Dalton home to surreptitiously deliver it. He is confronted again by Britten and several policemen who question him, asking insistently about Jan's activities with Mary the night before in the car, "Did Jan lay the girl?" "Did he lay her?"

Bigger runs away from the Dalton house after Mary's bones are found in the furnace, and he runs to Bessie and confesses what he did. She cries and tells him that no one will believe the death was accidental and, instead, "They'll say you raped her."

They would say he raped her and there would be no way to prove he had not. That fact had not assumed importance in his eyes until now. He stood up, his jaw hardening. Had he raped her? Yes he had raped her. Every time he felt as he had felt that night, he raped. But rape was not what one did to women. Rape was what one felt when one's back was against the wall and one had to strike out, whether one wanted to or not, to keep the pack from killing one. He committed rape every time he looked into a white face. He was a long, taut piece of rubber which a thousand white hands had stretched to the snapping point, and when he snapped it was rape. But it was rape when he cried out in hate deep in his heart as he felt the strain of living day by day. That, too, was rape.

He and Bessie bundle up some bedding and leave her apartment to hide in an abandoned house, where Bigger plans to kill her. First, however, he wants to have sex. "He kept kissing her until her lips grew warm and soft. A huge warm pole of desire rose in him, insistent and demanding; he let his hand slide from her shoulder to her breasts, feeling one, then the other; he slipped his other arm beneath her head, kissing her again, hard and long." Despite her pleading to stop, and her attempts to push him away, Bigger rapes her. Hours later, because she could identify him and "It was his life against hers," he smashes her head with a brick, killing her. After he throws her body and the bloody bedclothes down an air shaft, he realizes that the money he had stolen from Mary's purse was in her dress pocket, but he decides not to retrieve it.

The police identify Bigger as Mary's killer and a manhunt throughout the city results in thousands of young black men being detained and questioned, while Bigger moves from one hiding place to another. He is finally captured when the police direct the fire department to turn the powerful hose on him in the freezing night, in an attempt to avoid his shooting anyone. As he is dragged away, he hears the shout of the crowd, "Kill that black ape!"

In the final book, Bigger faces trial for killing Mary. Despite Bigger's attempts to frame him, Jan tries to help him and obtains the services of a communist lawyer named Max. As Max would later acknowledge, Jan tells Bigger that knowing him has taught him a lot about the suffering of black people and revealed a plethora of details about the relationship between the races. Bigger also uses the time in jail to analyze his familial relationships and his attitude toward the world. He recognizes that his anger has driven him to commit heinous acts that have destroyed his chance for a future and removed all possibility of a meaningful life. At the end, despite all efforts by Max to defend him, Bigger is found guilty and sentenced to die.

CENSORSHIP HISTORY

Native Son was the object of censorship while still in manuscript form. In the Introduction to *New Essays on Native Son*, Kenneth Kinnamon quotes from letters between Wright and his editor, Edward Aswell. The original manuscript contained a masturbation episode in the scene where Bigger and Jack view several movies on the day that Bigger has his job interview with Mr. Dalton. Kinnamon relates that the episode appeared in several drafts until it was removed from the galley proof.

Bigger and Jack are hardly seated when the graphic description begins: 'I'm polishing my nightstick,' Bigger said. Seen by a passing woman, Bigger and Jack are reported to the manager. The masturbation scene continues for a full page, ending when the two change seats because of the mess they have made.

As the original episode in the Regal Theatre continues, the movie begins with a newsreel showing wealthy young white women on a Florida beach. One of these is Mary Dalton, who is shown in a close-up embracing Jan Erlone as the narrator comments: *"Mary Dalton, daughter of Chicago's Henry Dalton, 4605 Drexel Boulevard, shocks society by spurning the boys of La Salle Street and the Gold Coast and accepting the attentions of a well-known radical while on her recent winter vacation in Florida."* Other sexy scenes with mildly lewd comments by the narrator follow. Recognizing the address as the one at which he will make application for employment that very afternoon, Bigger and Jack discuss the sexual possibilities with Mary.

Referring to the censored galley proof, Kinnamon identifies other passages that Wright removed after reading marginal notes written by Aswell. The scene in which Bigger drives Mary and Erlone around the park was initially more sexually explicit and included a reference to Bigger's response that included "fighting off the stiffening feeling in his loins." A similar excision occurred in the scene in which Bigger carries the drunk Mary up to her room. In the galley passage, "He tightened his arms as his lips pressed tightly against hers and he felt her body moving strongly. The thought and conviction that Jan had had her a lot flashed through his mind. He kissed her again and felt the sharp bones of her hips move in a hard and veritable grind. Her mouth was open and her breath came slow and deep." The daring nature of the instances of interracial sexuality were not only shocking, but they might have prevented the book from being distributed. Kinnamon writes, "As Aswell knew, and as he must have argued to Wright, to retain such highly charged sexual scenes would risk censorship and thus prevent the larger political message from being conveyed, or at best undercut that message by diverting the salacious reader's attention."

Native Son has been challenged many times since its publication. In 1978, parents in Goffstown, New Hampshire, and in Elmwood Park, New Jersey, challenged use of the book in high school classrooms due to "objectionable language." In 1981, parents of Drury High School in North Adams, Massachusetts, petitioned the school to keep the novel out of the classroom. A member of the parental rights committee, Gerald Delisle, told a reporter, "There's enough pornography in movies and television. Why teach the kids something like that?" In response, the principal Roger F. Cirone defended the decision, based on the report compiled by a committee of parents, teachers, and students who "indicated it was proper to use the book, which had been in the school system at least 10 years." The parents took their complaint to school superintendent Robert Maroni, calling it a "garbage book filled with sex and violence." The superintendent turned down the parents' request to ban the book, saying, "I firmly believe that no parent or group of parents has a right to determine what students other than their own children may or may not read." The group then launched an appeal to the school committee, which heard their arguments in September 1981, and denied their request.

In 1988, the novel was challenged for use in both the classrooms and in the library of Berrien Springs, Michigan, high school because parents asserted that the novel is "vulgar, profane, and sexually explicit." The novel was retained for use in the Yakima, Washington, schools in 1994 after a five-month dispute over what advanced high school students should study in class. Two parents complained to school officials about the profanity and "images of violence and sexuality" in the book and asked for it to be removed from the reading list. In 1996, parents of students enrolled in advanced placement

English classes at Northwest High School in High Point, North Carolina, asked the school board to remove the novel because it is "sexually graphic and violent." In 1998, the novel was removed from the high school curriculum in Fort Wayne, Indiana, because of the "graphic language" and "sexual content."

FURTHER READING

Blades, John. "The Uncut Version of Richard Wright's Original 'Native Son,' 'Black Boy' Restores Power of His Themes." *Chicago Tribune*, October 7, 1991, p. 1.

Doyle, Robert. *2007 Banned Books Resource Guide*. Chicago, Ill.: American Library Association, 2007.

Kinnamon, Kenneth, ed. *New Essays on Native Son*. New York: Cambridge University Press, 1990.

"New England News Brief: 'Native Son' Ban Sought." *Boston Globe*, July 15, 1981, p. 1.

"New England News Briefs: School Book Ban Still Sought." *Boston Globe*, July 14, 1981, p. 1.

"New Try in N. Adams Tonight to Ban 'Native Son' at School." *Boston Globe*, September 1, 1981, p. 1.

Rampersad, Arnold. Introduction. *Native Son*. New York: HarperCollins, 1993.

Tolbert, Kathy. "Parents' Bid to Cut Book from Reading List Rejected." *Boston Globe*, July 24, 1981, p. 1.

THE PERKS OF BEING A WALLFLOWER

Author: Stephen Chbosky
Original date and place of publication: 1999, United States
Original publisher: MTV Books
Literary type: Young adult novel

SUMMARY

The Perks of Being a Wallflower is an epistolary novel written by a 15-year-old high school student using the pseudonym "Charlie" to a friend whose name is never revealed. As Charlie tells the recipient of his letters, he is writing the letters because "I just need to know that someone out there listens and understands and doesn't try to sleep with people even if they could have." He does not want the reader to learn his identity and relates that he will call people by different names or by "generic names" because he does not want the reader to find him. For the same reason, he does not include a return address. Although this method of contact is secretive and might appear to be threatening, Charlie reassures the reader, "I mean nothing bad by this." Instead, he plans to relate the events and emotions he encounters as an adolescent making his way through an often confusing and sometimes painful life. "So, this is my life. And I want you to know that I am both happy and sad and I'm still trying to figure out how that could be." Each letter contains a specific date during the

1991–92 school year, and he greets the reader consistently as "Dear friend" and signs the letters, "Love always, Charlie."

The letters begin on August 25, 1991, a few months after his best friend, Michael, commits suicide, although the catalyst for the first letter appears to be his fear of high school. He ends the first letter by telling what he believes to be his reason for writing: "I don't know why I wrote a lot of this down for you to read. The reason I wrote this letter is because I start high school tomorrow and I am really afraid of going." Charlie writes about his reaction to the suicide and of his feelings that Michael could have talked to him if he were having problems. From that beginning, Charlie shares many experiences with the reader. He writes proudly of watching his brother on television playing football for Penn State. He talks about his family and home life, how his parents both cried after the final episode of *M*A*S*H*, and tells the reader about his beautiful mother and his hardworking father. At intervals, he inserts references to his Aunt Helen, and mentions his sister's love life, including an incident when he walked in while she is having sex with her boyfriend. "And I opened the door to the basement, and my sister and this boy were naked. He was on top of her, and her legs were draped over either side of the couch. And she screamed at me in a whisper. 'Get out. You pervert.'"

The novel does not shy away from dealing with controversial topics that are also a part of an adolescent's experience and growing awareness of the world. The letters explore Charlie's feelings and observations about drug use, homosexuality, oral sex, masturbation, teenage sexuality, and suicide. He asks if the reader knows what masturbation is, then answers his own question stating that the reader is older than he and must know, but he decides to tell anyway. "Masturbation is when you rub your genitals until you have an orgasm. Wow!" In the following letter, he informs the reader where he learned about it. "I guess I forgot to mention in my last letter that it was Patrick who told me about masturbation. I guess I forgot to tell you how often I do it now, which is a lot. I don't like to look at pictures. I just close my eyes and dream about a lady I do not know. And I try not to feel ashamed. . . . One night, I felt so guilty that I promised God that I would never do it again. So, I started using blankets, but then the blankets hurt, so I started using pillows, but then the pillows hurt, so I went back to normal."

Charlie also writes about a teenage couple and watching what amounts to an incident of date rape. He is ordered by his older brother and sister to stay in his room when they give a party while his parents are away, but couples repeatedly come into the room, trying to find a private place to make out. All of the couples except one leave when they see him, and he later learns that they are "very popular and in love." They ask if they can use the room even if he must remain present, and he agrees, then watches as they proceed to undress and as the girl protests.

And the boy kept working up the girl's shirt, and as much as she said no, he kept working it. After a few minutes, she stopped protesting, and he pulled her shirt off, and she had a white bra on with lace. I honestly didn't know what to do by this point. Pretty soon, he took off her bra and started to kiss her breasts. And then he put his hand down her pants, and she started moaning. I think they were both very drunk. He reached to take off her pants, but she started crying really hard, so he reached for his own. He pulled his pants and underwear down to his knees.

"Please. Dave. No."

But the boy just talked soft to her about how good she looked and things like that, and she grabbed his penis with her hands and started moving it. I wish I could describe this a little more nicely without using words like penis, but that was the way it was.

After a few minutes, the boy pushed the girl's head down, and she started to kiss his penis. She was still crying. Finally, she stopped crying because he put his penis in her mouth, and I don't think you can cry in that position. I had to stop watching at that point because I started to feel sick, but it kept going on, and they kept doing other things, and she kept saying "no." Even when I covered my ears, I could still hear her say that.

Charlie also reveals a lot about his own life and his experiences navigating through the world of adolescence. He watches as two male friends of his kiss, then sees them having sex with each other in Patrick's room. Other than to tell the reader that "Brad assumed the role of the girl in terms of where you put things" and to reveal that Brad cried and would not allow Patrick to console him, Charlie refrains from providing graphic details. About two-thirds of the way through the novel, Charlie describes his own near-homosexual experience with Patrick which is limited, at first, to a long, slow kiss. "We didn't do anything other than kiss." Later, Charlie hopes that Patrick will want to spend more intimate time with him, as well.

For the most part, although he experiments with drugs and sex to a limited degree, Charlie is a "wallflower," an observer who stands on the sidelines, watching and reporting the activities surrounding him, but his observations about other people reveal much about his life and his fears. As he comments on the activities of his friends, Charlie also learns more about his feelings, and he becomes conscious of long-hidden memories that have had a negative influence in his life. In the final letter, Charlie writes that he has just returned home after spending two months in the hospital, where he was taken after his parents found him sitting in a catatonic state.

CENSORSHIP HISTORY

Stephen Chbosky has told interviewers that he was highly influenced by J. D. Salinger's *The Catcher in the Rye*, and that novel is one among many controversial novels that Charlie mentions reading. The protagonists of both novels experience the angst of adolescence and the feelings of being outsiders. Moreover, both novels portray the thoughts and feelings of teenage boys with realistic candor. As a result of this realism, *The Perks of Being a Wallflower* has shared a similarity with the earlier novel in having become a target of people who wish to ban the novel because of its honest discussion of suicide and references to sexuality.

In 2003, a group named Parents Against Bad Books in Schools challenged the retention of the novel in the Fairfax, Virginia, school libraries because of what the group claimed were "profanity and descriptions of drug abuse, sexually explicit conduct and torture." The following year, the novel was removed from the Massapequa (N.Y.) school district reading assignment list in an elective sociology course due to "offensive content." In 2005, the novel was challenged and retained as optional reading in the Arrowhead High School curriculum in Merton, Wisconsin.

In 2006, the grandmother of a sixth grade student in the Apache Junction, Arizona, school district sent a letter of complaint to the state school superintendent of public instruction Tom Horne, stating that her grandchild had brought home from school *The Perks of Being a Wallflower*, a book that contained numerous sexual references, including a scene where a girl is forced to have oral sex with a boy during a party. In an interview with the *Tucson Citizen*, Horne said that this was the only page of the book he read after receiving the complaint. "The page is not just oral sex. It's nonconsensual oral sex that's described in detail. There's nothing in *Catcher in the Rye* that's remotely comparable to this." He took action and sent a cautionary memorandum on November 22, 2005, to school districts statewide to look at their school policies regarding library books, which led many schools to remove the book from their libraries. He told a reporter, "I'm hoping that if they have this book on the shelves they make sure it is no longer available to minors or any other students for that matter and they will check to see if there are any other books like that on their shelves. I wouldn't dream of trying to stop adults from reading it, but schools should not make this book available to students in their charge." Although he did not ask that schools remove the book, he told school principals and county superintendents that they should "reconsider keeping the book," since he believed that the accelerated reader had inappropriately labeled it as reading for fourth graders. Although he admitted to not have read the book in its entirety, he stated, "There's a page of description of forced oral sex. . . . That's a little much for a 12-year-old."

In February 2009, West Bend, Wisconsin, residents Ginny and Jim Maziarka sent a letter of concern to the West Bend Community Memorial Library asking for the removal and/or relocation of a long list of gay-positive titles and young adult books that contained sexual content. The following month, the Maziarkas sent the library a specific objection to *The Perks of Being a Wallflower* and asked the staff to relocate the novel and several other books to the adult book section. When the library trustees failed to comply, the town common council members asserted that the trustees were not serving the community interests. When trustee Reilly-Kliss approached Alderman Terry Vrana and tried to explain the library reconsideration policy, he told her, "I don't care about your policy. I want those books off the shelves." In April 2009, Reilly-Kliss and three other library trustees who were originally recommended for reappointment were removed from the board "for not satisfying the Maziarkas." After months of "nasty e-mails, phone calls and even accusatory comments at the grocery store," the library board voted on June 2, 2009, to maintain the collection exactly as it was—with young adult materials clearly marked as such and shelved geographically separated from both children's and adult titles. Additionally, the library agreed to add several reparative-therapy titles on becoming heterosexual that the couple had recommended.

Also in 2009, the novel was removed from the Portage High School classrooms in Indiana, after claims that it was inappropriate reading material because it contains such topics as homosexuality, drug use, and sexual behavior.

FURTHER READING

"Apache Junction, AZ." *School Library Journal* 52 (January 2006): 24.
Goldberg, Beverly. "Wisconsin Board, Staffers Cope with Would-Be Book Burners." *American Libraries* 40 (August/September 2009): 23–24.
Newsletter on Intellectual Freedom 55 (January 55): 9–14.

RABBIT, RUN

Author: John Updike
Original date and place of publication: 1960, United States
Original publisher: Alfred A. Knopf
Literary form: Novel

SUMMARY

Rabbit, Run relates the story of onetime high school basketball star Harry "Rabbit" Angstrom, 26, who impulsively deserts his pregnant wife. The novel is set in the small town of Mt. Judge, a "suburb of the city of Brewer, fifth largest city in Pennsylvania," in the spring of 1959. Rabbit feels trapped in his life as a lower-middle-class family man who now demonstrates "a penny's worth of tin called a friggin' MagiPeeler in five-and-dime stores." His wife, Janice, pregnant with their second child, spends her days in an alcoholic stupor, watching television. Despite his contempt for her, Rabbit sometimes finds wisdom in *The Mickey Mouse Club*, especially in the daily advice offered by head Mouseketeer Jimmy.

Little in Rabbit's life is what it appears to be. The fame and success of his high school basketball career have left him with an idealized view of those years that extends to his old coach, Marty Tothero, now unemployed and living in a tenement. As Rabbit tries to recapture some of the order and certainty of his earlier life, he realizes that Tothero is only a broken old man with a penchant for being beaten by his stern lover, Margaret, who refers to him as "an old bloated bastard." The young minister, Jack Eccles, sent to find Rabbit and return with him to Janice and her family, is ineffective. Unable to make Rabbit return, Eccles suggests that they play golf sometime. Rabbit arrives at the Eccles house and finds the minister's young wife in tight orange shorts, and he cannot resist slapping "her sassy ass" and then ruminating on its firmness. When Rabbit eats in a Chinese restaurant, the waiters speak in heavily accented English as they take his order but speak in perfect English once he leaves.

Throughout the novel, Rabbit remains constantly aware of his sexuality. When he first runs off, he thinks of finding "hard-bodied laughers" in West Virginia and remembers the "young whores in Texas," whom he frequented when in the army. Through Tothero, Rabbit meets Ruth, a warmhearted, voluptuous prostitute into whose apartment he moves. He rhapsodizes about her body and their sexual relationship in specific detail at various points in the novel.

When Janice goes into labor, Rabbit returns home, but he moves out again when Janice rejects his sexual advances as signs of "his whore's filthiness." She accidentally drowns their baby while drunk. The day of his baby's funeral, Rabbit sees "two teenage girls in snug shorts" and is unable to resist ogling "their perky butts and expectant sex." After the funeral, Rabbit returns to Ruth, who is pregnant with his child, but she refuses to resume their relationship unless he chooses between his wife and her. The novel ends with the panicked Rabbit running blindly down the street.

CENSORSHIP HISTORY

Rabbit, Run was banned in Ireland on February 20, 1962. A prohibition order was published in the *Iris Oifigiuil*, "the only official source from which booksellers [and readers] might learn of a new prohibition order," in which all articles blacklisted by the Irish Board of Censors were listed. According to the Censorship of Publications Bill of 1928, "the notice in *Iris Oifigiuil* should be sufficient evidence in the courts of summary jurisdiction as to the character of the publication," despite the acknowledgment by justices quoted in Adams's thorough study of Irish censorship laws that "this gazette is not a publication which booksellers are addicted to reading." The Irish Board of Censors found the work "obscene" and "indecent," objecting particularly to the author's handling of the characters' sexuality, the "promiscuity," and the "explicit sex acts." The work was officially banned from sale in Ireland until the introduction of the revised Censorship Publications Bill in 1967.

In 1976, parents of students in six community high schools in Aroostook County, Maine, challenged the inclusion of *Rabbit, Run* in the high school libraries because of its references to sex and to an extramarital affair. Parents cited as one of several objectionable scenes Rabbit's first sexual encounter with Ruth, in which Updike first describes Rabbit caressing her breasts and then provides a detailed description of them having sex:

> He kneels in a kind of sickness between her spread legs. With her help their blind loins fit. . . . [S]he reaches her hand down and touches their mixed fur and her breathing snags on something sharp. Her thighs throw open wide and clamp his sides and throw open again so wide it frightens him. . . . His sea of

seed buckles, and sobs into a still channel. At each shudder her mouth smiles in his and her legs, locked at his back, bear down.

They also raised objections to Rabbit's constant fantasizing about sexual experiences with most of the women he meets and the language in which he expresses such desires. His two-month affair with Ruth, after he leaves Janice for the first time, motivated further objections because the book "seems to make his wife at fault for the affair."

The county school board established a review committee to consider the complaints and recommended that the book be retained. In making the final decision on the book, the school board voted 8 to 6 against banning the book from the libraries but determined that some restriction was required. In a vote of 7 to 6, with one abstention, the board decided that the novel should be placed on the reserved shelf in each of the six county high school libraries and only charged out to students who brought signed permission slips from their parents.

In 1986, the novel was removed from the required reading list for the high school English classes in Medicine Bow, Wyoming, because of the sexual descriptions and profanity in the book. In their complaint to the school board, parents cited Rabbit's cursing, including "shit," "bastard," and "son of a bitch," and Tothero's use of the word "cunt." They also identified the sexually explicit passages between Ruth and Rabbit and his "sexually explicit fantasies."

FURTHER READING

Adams, Michael. *Censorship: The Irish Experience.* Tuscaloosa: University of Alabama Press, 1968.

Galloway, David D. *The Absurd Hero in American Fiction: Updike, Styron, Bellow.* Rev. ed. Austin: University of Texas Press, 1970.

Hunt, George W. *John Updike and the Three Great Secret Things: Sex, Religion, and Art.* Grand Rapids, Mich.: Wm. B. Eerdmans, 1980.

Markle, Joyce. *Fighters and Lovers: Theme in the Novels of John Updike.* New York: New York University Press, 1973.

Newsletter on Intellectual Freedom (March 1977): 36; (March 1987): 55.

Updike, John. "The Plight of the American Writer." *Change* 9 (April 1978): 36–41.

Wright, Derek. "Mapless Motion: Form and Space in Updike's *Rabbit, Run.*" *Modern Fiction Studies* 37 (Spring 1991): 35–44.

THE RAINBOW

Author: D. H. Lawrence

Original dates and places of publication: 1915, England; 1915, United States

Original publishers: Methuen and Company (England); B. W. Huebsch (United States)

Literary form: Novel

SUMMARY

The Rainbow spans three generations of the Brangwen family, moving from the beginning of the English industrial revolution in 1840 through the first decade of the 20th century. Lawrence shows the destruction of the traditional way of life and the ways in which the Brangwen family must accommodate themselves to their changing lives. The early Brangwens farm the land and live in harmony with their surroundings, but the second generation of Brangwens move into the industrial town of Beldover, where the seasonal cycle is replaced by a man-made calendar. Will and Anna no longer participate in the rhythms of nature, and their relationship suffers. They fall into a fixed domestic routine, and Anna begins to live through her children.

Ursula, daughter of Will and Anna, represents the modern woman, becoming the first Brangwen female to support herself and to enter a profession. She also rejects the traditional expectations of her family, such as religion, marriage, and love, becoming involved in unsatisfying relationships with fellow teacher Winifred Inger and shallow aristocrat Anton Skrebensky. She becomes pregnant by Skrebensky but takes ill with pneumonia and miscarries. The novel ends on a hopeful note as Ursula awakens one morning and sees a rainbow, "as if a new day had come on the earth."

CENSORSHIP HISTORY

The Rainbow contains several passages that have aroused challenges. Lawrence believed that the passage in the book that prosecutors found most offensive was likely the one in which the pregnant Anna dances naked in her bedroom:

> She would not have had any one know. She danced in secret, and her soul rose in bliss. She danced in secret before the Creator, she took off her clothes and danced in the pride of her bigness. . . . She stood with the firelight on her ankles and feet, naked in the shadowy, late afternoon, fastening up her hair.

Other passages that generated numerous complaints by editors at Methuen were scenes that were characterized in editorial notes as "lesbian" incidents. In one beach scene, Winifred suggests that she carry Ursula into the water, and in another the two are caught in the rain and "after a while the rain came down on their flushed, hot limbs, startling, delicious." B. W. Huebsch, the publisher of the first American edition of the *The Rainbow*, deleted these two passages and a third that had "generated the most complaints" from reviewers about the Methuen edition:

> Ursula lay still in her mistress's arms, her forehead against the beloved, maddening breast.
> "I shall put you in," said Winifred.
> —But Ursula twined her body about her mistress.

The Rainbow was censored by Lawrence before publication after editors at Methuen and Company sent the manuscript back to the author's agent, J. B. Pinker, "for alteration." Lawrence made cuts, but the altered manuscript was still unacceptable, and the editor again returned the work with portions marked for cutting. Lawrence refused to make further cuts, writing in a letter to Pinker, "I have cut out as I said I would, all the *phrases* objected to. The passages and paragraphs marked I cannot alter." The publisher recognized that the 13 passages the author refused to cut were likely to cause trouble. As soon as the novel was published, book reviewers alerted circulating libraries and legal authorities, calling it "an orgy of sexiness," "windy, tedious, boring and nauseating," and "a monstrous wilderness of phallicism."

The novel was condemned in 1915 after a private citizen complained to the London police. They, in turn, acquired a copy of the novel and took it to Sir John Dickinson, a Bow Street magistrate who issued a warrant under the Obscene Publications Act of 1857. The warrant called for the seizure of the 1,000 copies of the novel found on the publisher's premises. Dickinson also issued a summons that was served on Methuen, requiring that the publisher "show cause why the said books should not be destroyed." The police solicitor charged that the obscenity was so extensively distributed throughout the book that "I am at a loss, Sir, to understand how Messrs. Methuen came to lend their name to its publication."

Methuen claimed that Lawrence had been asked twice to modify the language of the manuscript but had refused, so they published as it stood. A destruction order was granted by the court under Lord Campbell's Act of 1857 to legal authorities without prosecution "or, therefore, any chance of its adequate defence." Thus, the police action against *The Rainbow* was not a criminal proceeding that would result in a jail term. The benefit to such a proceeding for the legitimate publisher was that it carried no risk of stigmatization by the government, nor did the publisher face fines or imprisonment.

The magistrate ordered all 1,000 copies to be destroyed and chided the publisher that he was sorry "that a firm of such high repute should have allowed their reputation to be soiled as it has been by the publication of this work." As publisher Algernon Methuen stated, "The [Scotland Yard] solicitors, in consideration of the reputation of our firm, kindly suggested that we might prefer to hand over the books rather than submit to actual search, and this we did." Aside from the loss of book stock, the publisher paid costs that amounted to 10 guineas, about $30 in contemporary currency. Methuen then requested that Lawrence return the advance it had paid him for the work, but he refused and the firm dropped the request. The novel was not available in an unexpurgated edition again until 1949, when Penguin Books published an edition.

In the United States, B. W. Huebsch published the novel in 1915, using the corrected proofs from Methuen and deleting the 13 "offensive" passages without obtaining permission from the author for the expurgations.

FURTHER READING

Ben-Ephraim, Gavriel. *The Moon's Dominion: Narrative Dichotomy and Female Dominance in Lawrence's Earlier Novels.* Rutherford, N.J.: Fairleigh Dickinson University Press, 1989.

DeGrazia, Edward. *Girls Lean Back Everywhere: The Law of Obscenity and the Assault on Genius.* New York: Random House, 1992.

Doherty, Gerald. "The Art of Appropriation: The Rhetoric of Sexuality in D. H. Lawrence." *Style* 30 (Summer 1996): 289–308.

Geller, Evelyn. *Forbidden Books in American Public Libraries, 1876–1939: A Study in Cultural Change.* Westport, Conn.: Greenwood, 1984.

Lawrence, D. H. *The Quest for Rananim: D. H. Lawrence's Letters to S. S. Koteliansky, 1914–1930.* Ed. and intro. by George J. Zytaruk. Montreal: McGill-Queen's University Press, 1970.

Rolph, Cecil Hewitt. *Books in the Dock.* London: Deutsch, 1961.

SANCTUARY

Author: William Faulkner
Original date and place of publication: 1931, United States
Publisher: Cape & Smith
Literary form: Novel

SUMMARY

In brief, *Sanctuary* tells the story of sexually provocative 17-year-old Temple Drake, a socially prominent judge's daughter and college student, who accidentally witnesses a murder and then falls victim to a sadistic rape. Temple is taken to the isolated house of former convict Lee Goodwin and his common-law wife, Ruby, one evening by her date, Gowan Stevens, after the two have had too much to drink; Stevens wants to buy bootlegged liquor. While there, he remains drunk for three days. When he finally sobers up and realizes that he is outnumbered, he runs off and leaves Temple. Temple is sexually harassed and then raped with a corncob by an impotent bootlegger named Popeye, who also kills Tommy, a mentally retarded gang member who witnessed the act. Afterward, Popeye confines Temple in a Memphis brothel, where she is forced to engage in sexual acts with a stranger named Red while Popeye watches. When Temple begins to enjoy her involvement with Red, Popeye shoots him and then disappears.

Temple is located at the brothel by the lawyer assigned to defend Goodwin on the charge of murdering Tommy, but she falsely identifies him as the killer to protect her reputation. Both she and her prominent father want to hide her sexual involvement with Red and her experiences at the brothel, so they guarantee that her testimony and the trial will be over quickly by implicating Goodwin. Without remorse, Temple is escorted from the courtroom after testifying and leaves for vacation in Luxembourg. The innocent Goodwin is burned to death by a lynch mob.

Despite the persistent sexual undercurrent of much of the novel, none of the sexual acts is described in detail. Even the rape by corncob is referred to obliquely and only Temple's bleeding afterward is described. Throughout, anatomical references are limited to the thighs or the loins. The erotic passages emerge in images of Temple's appearance, with her short dress that permits "fleet revelations of flank and thigh," and the voyeurism in the brothel. Popeye's advances are detailed: "Then it touched me, that nasty little cold hand, fiddling around inside the coat where I was naked. . . . his hand was going inside the top of my knickers." Later in the novel, after becoming eroticized by Red, Temple sits "in a floating swoon of agonized sorrow and erotic longing, thinking of Red's body," and then begs him to have sex with her: "Please. Please. Please. Don't make me wait. I'm burning up." The novel was unusual for its time in its topics of rape and voyeurism as well as for the brothel setting, in which a major part of the action takes place.

CENSORSHIP HISTORY

William Faulkner's sixth novel, *Sanctuary* gained notoriety as much for its erotic passages and inclusion of rape, voyeurism, and prostitution as for the author's claim in his introduction to the 1932 Modern Library edition that he had written about these topics for financial rather than artistic reasons.

In 1948, *Sanctuary* was one of nine novels identified as obscene in criminal proceedings in the Court of Quarter sessions in Philadelphia County, Pennsylvania. Indictments were brought by the state district attorney, John H. Maurer, against five booksellers who were charged with possessing and intending to sell the books. The other allegedly obscene novels were Harold Robbins's *Never Love a Stranger*, James Farrell's *Studs Lonigan* and *A World I Never Made*, Erskine Caldwell's *God's Little Acre*, Calder Willingham's *End as a Man*, and Faulkner's *The Wild Palms*.

In his March 18, 1949, decision in *Commonwealth v. Gordon*, 66 D. & C. 101 (1949) that *Sanctuary* is not obscene, Judge Curtis Bok stated: "There are no vulgar Saxon words in the book, but the situations are stark and unrelieved. It makes one shudder to think of what can happen by misadventure." Bok refused to declare *Sanctuary* "obscene" because the definition in cases that he cited in his decision restricted the meaning of the term "to that of sexual impurity, and with those cases that have made erotic allurement the test of its effect." The work also failed to meet Bok's definition of sexual impurity in literature, which he defined "as any writing whose dominant purpose and effect is erotic allurement—that is to say, a calculated and effective incitement to sexual desire."

Faulkner was awarded the Nobel Prize in literature in 1950. Although *Sanctuary* did not go to court again, by 1954 it was again condemned as obscene by numerous local censorship groups throughout the United States, and the National Organization of Decent Literature placed it on the disapproved list. Also in 1954, Ireland banned *Sanctuary*, along with most of the author's other works, because of the language such as "son of a bitch," "whore," "slut," and "bastard" combined with the brutal violence of the story. Irish and U.S. censors also objected to the character Ruby, who prostitutes herself to obtain money to free her common-law husband from jail, to obtain legal fees, and to pay their expenses. Changes in society have removed most objections to the book, although scattered local censorship continues throughout the United States.

FURTHER READING

Gladstein, Mimi. *The Indestructible Woman in Faulkner, Hemingway, and Steinbeck*. Ann Arbor, Mich.: UMI Research Press, 1986.

Heller, Terry. "Mirrored Worlds and the Gothic in Faulkner's *Sanctuary*." *Mississippi Quarterly* 42 (Summer 1989): 247–259.

Loe, Mary Hong. "Case Studies in Censorship: William Faulkner's *Sanctuary*." *Reference Services Review* 23 (Spring 1995): 71–84.

Page, Sally R. *Faulkner's Women: Characterization and Meaning*. De Land, Fla.: Everett/Edwards, 1972.

Tanner, Laura E. "Reading Rape: *Sanctuary* and *The Women of Brewster Place*." *American Literature* 62 (December 1990): 559–582.

Williams, David. "Faulkner's Women: The Myth and the Muse." Montreal: McGill–Queen's University Press, 1977.

Wilson, Andrew J. "The Corruption in Looking: William Faulkner's *Sanctuary* as a Detective Novel." *Mississippi Quarterly* 47 (Summer 1994): 441–460.

SNOW FALLING ON CEDARS

Author: David Guterson
Original date and place of publication: 1994, United States
Publisher: Harcourt Brace Jovanovich
Literary form: Novel

SUMMARY

Snow Falling on Cedars takes place in 1954 on San Piedro Island, off the coast of Washington in the Pacific Northwest. The story opens on December 6, one day before the 13th anniversary of the bombing of Pearl Harbor, and the tension between Japanese Americans and Anglo citizens in the town remains high. Kabuo Miyamoto, who fought on the American side in World War II, is on trial, charged with killing Carl Heine, also a veteran of World War II and the son of a man who once had an agreement to sell land to the Miyamoto family before they were sent to internment camps. Kabuo and Carl had been childhood friends, despite the simmering anti-Japanese tensions on the island. Watching the trial are Ishmael Chambers, another World War II veteran who has lost an arm in the war and who is now editor of the town newspaper, the *San Piedro Review*, and Hatsue, Kabuo's wife. Many years earlier, Ishmael and Hatsue had had a secret romantic relationship, which Hatsue ended without explanation. Ishmael has information that could clear Kabuo, but he hesitates to bring it up, hoping that he might be able to recapture Hatsue's love if Kabuo is convicted.

Sheriff Art Moran appears on the witness stand and describes pulling Carl Heine's body out of a net on Carl's boat. He explains that he arrested Kabuo after learning from the island's coroner, Horace Whaley, that the autopsy showed that Carl had head injuries consistent with injuries inflicted with gun butts by Japanese soldiers trained in stick fighting, or kendo. Kabuo is an expert in kendo. The sheriff also learns that 14 years earlier, Heine's father, Carl Sr., had made an arrangement to sell seven acres to Kabuo's family and had accepted installment payments. When the family had only two more payments left, the Miyamoto family and other Japanese-American families were moved to internment camps as the other citizens of San Piedro Island stood silent. Carl Sr., promised to hold the land and take the final two payments when the families return, but he died before the war ended, and his wife Etta, who holds a bitter hatred for the Japanese Americans, sold the land to Ole Jurgensen. When Kabuo returned from the war, he was upset by the betrayal but decided to remain patient and wait until Ole decided to sell. His chance came a few days before Carl's death; he learned that Ole decided to sell but found that Carl Heine already had made an offer. Based on the accumulated information, the sheriff decides that Kabuo had substantial reason to want Carl dead.

The novel takes place in a series of flashbacks interspersed with the events of the trial, and readers are made aware of the complicated relationships that exist among the major characters. Detailed descriptions of the heated love affair between Ishmael and Hatsue suggest that the two would have stayed together had prejudice not created obstacles to their love. The efforts of Zenhichi Miyamoto, Kabuo's father, to buy the land and the fair agreement of Carl Heine, Sr., provide a stark contrast to the hatred that Etta Heine holds for Japanese Americans and her disgust that anyone of Japanese background might own her family's land.

Kabuo testifies that he pleaded with Carl, his childhood friend, to sell him the parcel of land that Zenhichi had paid for years earlier and that he felt hopeful that Carl would sell it to him. He also tells the court that he saw Carl the night of the murder. Carl had taken his boat out on the foggy night of September 15, 1954, to think about Kabuo's request, but his boat ran out of power and stranded him in the dense fog in the middle of a shipping lane, leaving him in a dangerous position should a large freighter come through the channel. Kabuo found Carl and the disabled boat and helped him, a kindness that led Carl to decide to sell the land to Kabuo. Later that night, a large freighter passed through the shipping channel, and the force of its huge wake shook Carl's boat violently, knocking him from the mast he had climbed to untangle a lantern and throwing him to the deck. Unconscious, he fell into the water and drowned.

The only person who can save Kabuo's life is Ishmael, who on the evening of the second day of the trial acquires the logbook of a nearby lighthouse. The radioman's assistant is no longer stationed at the lighthouse, but he had recorded that on the night of the murder a large freighter lost its way and the radioman attempted to put it back on course by advising the crew to steer directly through the channel in which Carl was fishing. The logbook reports that the freighter passed through the channel just five minutes before the time on Carl's waterlogged watch. Ishmael struggles between his desire to turn over the logbook to clear an innocent man and his desire for Hatsue. The trial ends, and all but one of the jurors declare Kabuo guilty, leading the judge to adjourn for that day. In the evening, Ishmael reveals the contents of the logbook to Hatsue and then to the sheriff. After a reexamination of Carl's boat, the sheriff finds the rope on the mast where the lantern hung, as well as the blood and hair where Carl hit his head when he fell. The charges against Kabuo are dropped.

CENSORSHIP HISTORY

Snow Falling on Cedars was on the *New York Times* best-seller list for more than a year, and it was cited as best book of the year by the American Booksellers Association and awarded the PEN/Faulkner Award in 1995, but two school districts in Texas and another in the state of Washington found the book "obscene" and "vulgar." In Boerne, Texas, Lake Highlands High School principal Sam Champion officially reprimanded teacher Frances Riley for using "poor judgment" in teaching the book although she had obtained prior permission from the head of the English department to do so. Parents and students complained that the book was "offensive" because it contained racial epithets, and they objected to "sexually graphic passages." Labeling the book "highly offensive," school superintendent John Kelly ordered the book to be removed from the high school curriculum and the library shelves until a study could be made of the contents. The Texas office of the American Civil Liberties Union (ACLU) contacted the school, and the superintendent responded to the query that the book "contained elements that are deemed obscene and graphic and inappropriate by parents and others." In the official school board record of the incident, officials stated that the book was removed from the curriculum because of "obscenity, graphic depiction of sex, mutilation." The *Spokane Spokesman Review* reported on September 11, 1999, that 17-year-old student Jerald Meadows told a reporter that students were annoyed with the length of the book (460 pages) and "complained to their parents about it just to get out of reading it."

Also in 1999, parents of students attending Vidor (Texas) Junior High School in the Vidor Independent School District formally requested the removal of *Snow Falling on Cedars* from the school library. The complaint charged that the novel contains "profanity" and "inappropriate language" for readers in junior high school. According to the 1999–2000 report by the Texas ACLU, the book was banned from the library.

In May 2000, the South Kitsap school board in Port Orchard, Washington, voted 3 to 2 not to place the novel on the district-approved reading list, after critics complained about "sexual content" and "profanity" in the book. The *Newsletter on Intellectual Freedom* reported that a parent, Doug Bean, addressed the board and charged, "This book is extremely vulgar. This book doesn't teach respect; it teaches self-indulgence." The book was withheld until committees at the high school and district levels could review it. Both committees recommended inclusion of the novel in the approved reading list, but students were not required to read it if they or their parents disapproved of it.

In January 2007, school district officials in the Dufferin-Peel Catholic District in Ontario, Canada, removed *Snow Falling on Cedars* from the high school library after one parent complained that the novel contains "objectionable sexual content." The novel was on the reading list for the 11th grade English class at Father Michael Goetz Secondary School in Mississauga, before teachers and librarians were directed by district administrators to remove the book from circulation until a board-appointed committee could review the book. Although the school officials insisted that they were not banning the novel from the district, only making it inaccessible to students until the review committee completed its work, teachers in the district viewed the action differently. One teacher-librarian, who requested to remain anonymous, stated in a news article for the *Star* that "Pulling a book off the shelf and 'banning' it are pretty much the same thing, since they both mean nobody will be able to read the book in the school library." The district "challenged materials" policy required that a committee consisting of library services and religious education coordinators, two trustees, a parent, and the superintendent of schools review the novel and recommend whether to retain the novel in the curriculum or to support its removal. The parent who filed a formal complaint with the school district objected to the detailed description of the young married couple's first sexual encounter and to a description of a sexual relationship between two teenagers.

In January 2008, the school board in the Coeur d'Alene School District voted 3-2 to retain the novel as a reading choice for high school junior English classes after a lengthy review process that was initiated by parents who objected to the "adult material in the novel." Mary Jo Finney, one of several parents who filed a complaint to have the book removed from the curriculum, objected to "depictions of masturbation, genitalia and intercourse" and asserted that the book contains "vulgar language" and that "the 'F-word' appears nine times on one page." The parents told the school board that the book is "too explicit for high school readers, who don't have the life experience or sophistication to read controversial scenes in context." The school district created an 11-member committee that included Finney to review the book. Other members of the committee praised the manner in which the novel deals with racism and prejudice, and the majority agreed that the "adult content" was "tastefully written, not gratuitous, and important to the plot and character development." The majority report issued by the committee stated that mature students need challenging literature that "comes with the realities of life and [is] rich in human experience." The committee voted to reinstate the novel in the curriculum and to allow students who object to the content to request another novel.

FURTHER READING

American Civil Liberties Union. *Free Speech: Banned and Challenged Books in Texas Public Schools 1999–2000.* Austin: Texas ACLU, 2000.
Kalinowski, Tess. "Peel Board Pulls Novel After Parent Complains." Available online. URL: http: //www.thestar.com/News/article/ 17655. Accessed August 13, 2010.
Kramer, Beeky. "'Snow Falling' Survives School Curriculum Challenge." Available online. URL: http:// www.spokesmanreview.com/breaking story.asp?ID=13078. Accessed August 10, 2010.
Newsletter for Intellectual Freedom (November 1999): 163; (July 2000): 106.

SONG OF SOLOMON

Author: Toni Morrison
Original date and place of publication: 1977, United States
Original publisher: Alfred A. Knopf
Literary type: Novel

SUMMARY

Song of Solomon by Toni Morrison examines the ramifications that the actions of past generations have on their descendants and explores the topic largely through the experiences and emotional conflicts of the third Macon Dead.

The novel opens on February 18, 1931, on the sidewalk outside of Mercy Hospital, a charity hospital in Michigan given the name "No Mercy Hospital" by African-American residents of the area because only white patients are admitted for treatment. A crowd has gathered to watch as insurance agent Robert Smith, wearing blue silk wings and positioning himself on the hospital roof, prepares to leap into the air as the promised at three o'clock in the afternoon and to fly to the other side of Lake Superior. Among the onlookers is a very pregnant Ruth Foster Dead, the daughter of a deceased African-American doctor who had never been given hospital privileges by Mercy and whose patients, aside from two who were white, had never been granted admittance. As the crowd watches with excitement, the scene takes on a further surreal cast. Red velvet rose petals fall from the basket Ruth holds and swirl around in the air, and a woman sings loudly, "O Sugarman done fly away" while Smith prepares to soar. Ruth's labor pains begin when the insurance agent hits the ground. The shock of the man's leap appears to overcome the racial prejudices of the hospital attendants, who take Ruth into the hospital where, the next day, her son Macon becomes the first African-American child born in Mercy Hospital.

The third Macon Dead, whose grandfather received the name during the American Civil War from "a drunken Yankee in the Union Army" who completed his paperwork and ignored whatever the true name may have been, is pampered and babied by his mother, Ruth. Born 15 years after his two sisters First Corinthians and Magdalene, he acquires the nickname "Milkman" when a janitor named Freddy looks through a window of the Dead home and sees Ruth nursing the boy who is old enough that his feet nearly touch the floor. She knows that her husband would be horrified to see her sitting with her son at her breast. "She sat in this room holding her son on her lap, staring at his closed eyelids and listening to the sound of his sucking. Staring not so much from maternal joy as from a wish to avoid seeing his legs dangling almost to the floor." Ruth views the nursing as "a pleasure she hated to give up," but discovery by Freddy makes her panic. "Ruth jumped up as quickly as she could and covered her breast, dropping her son on the floor and confirming for him what he had begun to suspect—that these afternoons were strange and wrong." Freddy realizes that his discovery gives him a hold over Ruth. Macon Dead Jr. hears his son's nickname used repeatedly by people in the town, but no dares to reveal its origin because he is a difficult man to approach and most are afraid of him. Still, "he guessed the name was not clean. . . . He knew that wherever the name came from, it had something to do with his wife and was, like the emotion he always felt when thinking of her, coated with disgust." He is also estranged from his sister, Pilate, because he disapproves of the way in which she lives her life.

Milkman has an unhappy childhood in which he is hated at first by his father, who recognizes that his son has replaced him in Ruth's affections. Later, the young man distances himself from Ruth and works with his father, who has become a brutal landlord. He also becomes sexually involved with his cousin Hagar, who is unable to maintain a casual relationship and, instead, pursues him, to the amusement of the people in town. As Milkman grows older, his life appears to lack direction and he feels stifled working with his ruthless father, but he sees no way out. He is also disheartened to learn that his mother had tried repeatedly to abort him because his father had not wanted her to remain pregnant so many years after the birth of his two sisters. He feels as if "everybody was using him for something or as something. Working out some scheme of their own on him, making him the subject of their dreams of wealth, or love, or martyrdom. Everything they did seemed to be about him, yet nothing he wanted was part of it. Once before he had a confidential talk with his father, and it ended up with his being driven further from his mother. Now he had a confidential talk with his mother, only to discover that before he was born, before the first nerve end had formed in his mother's womb, he was the subject of great controversy and strife."

The chance to escape and to start a new life appears when his father tells him that a green tarpaulin suspended from the ceiling of Pilate's dilapidated house may contain millions of dollars in gold, a possibility that leads

Milkman to plot a robbery with his friend Guitar Bains. While Milkman views the promised riches as a means of escaping his present life, Guitar seeks the money to fund his work with a secret society named the Seven Days, which murders randomly selected white people in retaliation for the centuries of injustices African Americans have experienced.

The expected bounty consists of only a few rocks and a human skeleton, which Milkman learns is that of his grandfather, the first Macon Dead. Unable to give up the possibility of finding gold to start a new life, he travels to the old farm in Pennsylvania his father owns and believes that he will find gold hidden in a cave on the farm, after promising Guitar half of any gold he finds. Rather than gold, he discovers his family's history when he meets Circe, the midwife who delivered his father and aunt, and he learns his grandparents' names, Jake and Sing, an Indian woman. The search for his family's history, and his own, intensifies as he travels to Shalimar in Virginia, where his grandfather once lived. Guitar follows Milkman secretly and plans to murder him and take the gold that he believes Milkman has found. The family history Milkman uncovers is tragic. He learns that his great-grandfather Solomon, known as the legendary flying African, escaped slavery by flying to Africa but abandoned his family to do so. He left behind a wife who went insane and 21 children who were scattered when they were taken in by different families. Milkman's grandfather Jake, the first Macon Dead, was raised by an Indian woman named Heddy, whose daughter Sing he married.

The discovery of his family's history and of information regarding his immediate ancestors transforms Milkman into a mature man. He survives Guitar's attempt to murder him and returns home to reveal his discovery to his father and his aunt. When he arrives, he learns that Hagar has died and that the family continues to deal with several tragic events. His aunt Pilate returns with him to Shalimar, where the two bury his grandfather's bones on the mountain that is known as Solomon's Leap because that is the promontory from which his great-grandfather jumped as he began his "flight" to Africa. After the burial, Milkman watches as Pilate is struck and killed by a bullet fired by Guitar. After she dies in Milkman's arms, he shouts to Guitar to take his life if he needs it, then "he leaped. . . . For he knew now what Shalimar knew: If you surrendered to the air, you could *ride* it."

CENSORSHIP HISTORY

The winner of both the National Book Critics Circle Award and the American Academy of Arts and Letters Award, *Song of Solomon* is also the first novel by an African-American woman to become a Book-of-the-Month Club selection. That pedigree did not prevent people from labeling it a "filthy and inappropriate piece of trash" in the 1990s, nor has it prevented efforts to remove it from schools as recently as 2009.

In 1993, parents in Columbus, Ohio, submitted a complaint to the school administration asserting that the novel "contains language degrading to African

Americans" and charged that it is "sexually explicit." Their objections focused on the early scene that describes Ruth Foster Dead breast-feeding Milkman and her admitted shame at being discovered in the act with a child who appears to be nearly the age of an adolescent. Parents in the Richmond City, Georgia, school district voiced a similar complaint in 1994 regarding that passage and others that they labeled "filthy and inappropriate." In this later challenge, those complaining specified additional scenes that they felt were "sexually graphic," including Milkman's sexual affair with his cousin Hagar and one particular scene that takes place after Hagar attempts to kill Milkman with a knife when he tries to end the affair, but he escapes and taunts her: "If you keep your hands just that way and then bring them down straight, straight and fast, you can drive that knife right smack into your cunt."

In 1998, the superintendent of the St. Mary's County, Maryland, public schools removed *Song of Solomon* from the required reading list for the advanced placement English class, despite the recommendations of a faculty committee that advised the school administration to retain the book. Parents who filed the complaints told the superintendent that they were "troubled" by the "sexual matter" in the book and labeled the novel "repulsive filth," and "trash" and demanded its removal from the schools. African-American community leaders asserted that the removal of the book was racially motivated and threatened to file a lawsuit if the superintendent's decision was supported by the school board. In response to the threat, Barbara Thompson, president of the St. Mary's County Board of Commissioners, stated that the superintendent had the right to remove the novel from the required reading list, a decision that the board voted unanimously to support. In defense of her move, Thompson told reporters, "She did not ban the book from the school library. She just said it wasn't required reading. Unfortunately, people keep misinterpreting it and making a much bigger issue of it. If you read the book, you know that it has very sexually explicit things in it." The board president admitted that she did not read the entire book, only the two pages she presented to the board. She claimed that after she read the passage, she ripped up the book.

FURTHER READING

Doyle, Robert P. *2007 Banned Books Resource Guide*. Chicago: American Library Association, 2008.
Zeitchik, Steven M. "Md. Schools Veto Morrison, Angelou Titles." *Publishers Weekly*, January 19, 1998, 236.

SOPHIE'S CHOICE

Author: William Styron
Original date and place of publication: 1979, United States
Original publisher: Random House
Literary form: Novel

SUMMARY

Sophie's Choice is a novel set in 1947 in New York City that describes the intertwined lives of three people renting rooms in the same house: Stingo, a young aspiring writer from the South whose small legacy has allowed him to move north to Brooklyn and write; Sophie Zawistowska, a beautiful Polish emigrant who has survived the Nazi concentration camps at great personal cost; and Nathan Landau, a mentally unstable Jewish man who suffers from paranoid schizophrenia. The story is told by Stingo, who describes his interactions with Nathan and Sophie and who acts as an observer of their individual lives and of their relationship.

Through a series of monologues and flashbacks, Stingo slowly reveals the misery that preceded Sophie's arrival in the United States and her growing unhappiness in her relationship with Nathan. She arrived in America a broken woman, suffering both mentally and physically, after having been widowed twice and losing her two children in the concentration camps. When she meets Nathan in the library, she feels that she has found a man who will help her to forget her painful past and offer her true happiness. At the beginning of their relationship, Nathan, a financially successful biologist, is a commanding presence in Sophie's life. He nurses her back to health and shows her a tender love that makes her feel secure once again. The two become lovers, and Sophie learns that Nathan has a very dark side and is filled with hate. He is a paranoid schizophrenic who drinks excessively and suffers from an addiction to benzedrine sulfate. He frequently flies into rages during which his face becomes contorted and he screams and hits anyone near him, including Sophie. He taunts her: "You're a cheater. You're worse than any little yenta that ever came out of Brooklyn." Despite Sophie's loyalty and fidelity to him, he accuses her of having sex with other men. At one point, he threatens her and hits her, shouting, "Let me out of here before I murder you—you whore! You were born a whore and you'll die a whore!"

Nathan increases his drug use, and on one occasion, the depth of his psychological problems is shown when he takes six amphetamines and snorts two lines of cocaine. He pulls Sophie into a car with him and begins to drive recklessly at high speed, while Sophie screams for him to stop. Stresses continue to build and, after Stingo returns to his family farm in Virginia, Sophie travels there for a break and the two become lovers for a night. Sophie is torn between staying with Stingo, with whom she would be able to relax, and her concern for Nathan, despite his hate for life and his abuse of her. She also reveals the horrible choice that the Nazis had forced her to make: to select which of her two children she will keep and which will be taken by the Nazis. For the rest of her short life, she questions, "Suppose I had chosen Jan to go . . . to go to the left instead of Eva. Would that have changed anything?" Sophie returns to Brooklyn, followed by Stingo a few days later. He arrives at the rooming house to find police, an ambulance and a milling crowd, and he learns that Nathan and Sophie have committed suicide by ingesting sodium cyanide. Although the newspapers glamorize the suicides as the result of love and devotion, Stingo recognizes that the two chose suicide because they could no longer stand the pain they suffered.

CENSORSHIP HISTORY

Sophie's Choice, which won the National Book Award in 1980, was removed from the school library of La Mirada High School in La Mirada, California, on September 17, 2001, after a parent complained that the book contains "profanity" and "extreme sexual content." Students in the district who fought the ban were joined in their efforts by the American Civil Liberties Union (ACLU) of Southern California; the law firm of Greines, Martin, Stein, and Richland; and the American Library Association.

The problem began when Joseph Feres took his 17-year-old daughter to the local public library to obtain a copy of *Sophie's Choice*, which she had selected from the 12th-grade English literature supplemental reading list. As Feres looked through the book, he came across passages that contained sexual activity and found several instances of profanity. He then sent a large number of letters to school administrators, local church leaders, and school board members expressing his outrage. He also confronted principal Andrew Huynh and voiced concerns about the judgment of the teacher who provided the supplemental list. In an interview with the *Los Angeles Times*, Feres stated, "There are ways to teach the lessons without getting into the gutter to teach it. You don't have to use profanity and extreme sexual content." In the same interview, he claimed that he was "saying the book should be banned. . . . It's just not appropriate for high school kids."

Huynh wrote to Feres, saying that he had held a conference with the 12th-grade English teacher, and he had spoken with her about the book and directed her to remove *Sophie's Choice* from the supplemental reading list. Huynh also reassured Feres that the book had been removed from the school library. School board members defended the principal's action and told reporters that instructional materials should be reviewed to determine their appropriateness and that Huynh acted appropriately to review instructional material that a parent found to be objectionable.

Student Kat Kosmala and other students contacted the ACLU, charging that the school district had committed an act of censorship and calling for a return of the novel to the school library. In December 2001, the ACLU, in coordination with the private law firm of Greines, Martin, Stein, and Richland, began to prepare a case against the Norwalk–La Mirada Unified School District, threatening to sue the school district if the book was not restored. The ACLU expressed concern regarding the way the decision to ban the book was made. Attorneys pointed out that the school district had an established policy that allowed for a systematic review of materials that are challenged, but the school principal circumvented the policy and removed the book without review.

Reporters contacted author William Styron, telling him about the ban, and the author expressed outrage at the action. He told a reporter for the *Los Angeles Times* that he found the action "reprehensible" and "shocking," and stated, "It's improper to allow people to be browbeaten about books in this country." When told that the ban was based on charges that the book contained "profanity" and "extreme sexual content," Styron defended the use of language and the sexual activity as being very important in developing the nature of the characters and integral to the story.

On January 11, 2002, the ACLU of Southern California issued a press release stating that the novel had been returned to the La Mirada High School Library and that the school district had agreed to return the novel "after First Amendment issues were cited." The school district had also received letters and calls from a number of organizations dedicated to free expression, including the American Library Association and the National Coalition Against Censorship. The ACLU stated in the press release, "Once the district was informed of the possible First Amendment violations, it was swift in reviewing and remedying the situation and we appreciate the prompt action."

FURTHER READING

"ACLU Announces 'Sophie's Choice' Has Been Returned to La Mirada High School Library." ACLU Press Release. Formerly available online. URL: http://www.aclu-sc.org/print/NewsRelease/100039. Accessed November 30, 2005.

"ACLU Takes Action after Acclaimed Novel *Sophie's Choice* Is Removed from School Library." ACLU News and Publications. Formerly available online. URL: http://www.aclu-sc.org/News/Releases/100030. Accessed November 21, 2005.

"Censorship: Whose 'Standards' Are They?" *Los Angeles Times*, December 28, 2001, p. B16.

Goldberg, Beverly. "Second-Guessing Sophie's Choice." *American Libraries* 33 (March 2002): 25.

Helfand, Duke. "Students Fight for 'Sophie's Choice.'" *Los Angeles Times*, December 22, 2001, p. B1.

"Local High School Backs Off Censoring *Sophie's Choice*: Quick Action Brings Novel Back to School Library." *ACLU Open Forum* (Winter 2002). Formerly available online. URL: http://www.aclu-sc.org/News/OpenForum/1004/100441. Accessed October 10, 2004.

Perera, Andrea. "Controversial Novel Returns to Library." *Los Angeles Times*, January 12, 2002, p. B4.

Stillman, Peggy, and Andrea Kross. "Why Is Everyone Reading *Sophie's Choice*?" *Digital Library and Archives—Virginia Libraries* 46, no. 3 (July/August/September 2000).

TESS OF THE D'URBERVILLES

Author: Thomas Hardy
Original dates and places of publication: 1891, England; 1892, United States

Original publishers: Osgood, McIlvaine (England); Harper (United States)
Literary form: Novel

SUMMARY

Tess of the D'Urbervilles was subtitled "A Pure Woman Faithfully Presented," and Hardy intended to portray a woman whose intentions had been good throughout despite eventually becoming a mistress and a murderess. The novel opens as John Durbeyfield learns that he is the last descendant of one of England's oldest and most powerful families. A poor and powerless working man and a heavy drinker, Durbeyfield sends his eldest daughter, Tess, to the still-wealthy branch of the D'Urbervilles at their estate at Trantridge to claim kinship.

The D'Urbervilles are actually wealthy people named Stokes who have taken the unused ancestral title as their own, and innocent Tess is unaware that Alec D'Urberville is not her cousin. He gives Tess a job caring for his mother's chickens to keep her nearby and rapes her one night in the woods. She stays with him for a few weeks and then returns home pregnant. Their child dies soon after birth.

Grieving for her child and disgraced, Tess takes a job on a distant farm, where she meets Angel Clare, who claims to follow the spirit but not the letter of the Bible. They fall in love, and, on their wedding night, Tess and Angel confess to each other. Angel tells of a brief affair, and Tess forgives him. She then tells him about Alec, and Angel rejects her.

Angel leaves for Brazil, and Tess returns briefly to her family before taking a job at another dairy at Flintcomb-Ash, where she again meets Alec, now a fire-and-brimstone preacher. He wants her back, but she is still married to Angel and does not love Alec. When Tess's father dies the family loses its home, and Alec steps in, promising to educate her brothers and sisters and to protect her mother if only Tess will live with him. She resists Alec and sets up camp with her family at the ancient D'Urberville burial vaults. Alec reappears, and a disheartened Tess relents, because her letters to Angel have gone unanswered.

Angel returns, ready to forgive Tess, and finds her at the luxurious sea resort of Sandbourne, where he begs her forgiveness. She tells him about Alec and orders him to leave. He refuses, and Tess loses control of her senses. She murders Alec, the source of her unhappiness, and then runs away with Angel, whom she believes will now truly forgive her because she has eliminated the root of their problems. They hide in a deserted mansion and then move on to Stonehenge, where Tess falls asleep on a sacrificial altar. The police arrive and arrest her, and Tess is tried for murder. Before she is hanged, Tess asks Angel to care for and to marry her innocent younger sister 'Liza-Lu. The novel ends as Angel and 'Liza-Lu watch the hanging, then walk off together, hand in hand.

CENSORSHIP HISTORY

Hardy consented to the bowdlerization of many of his works before they reached the public just to get them published, and his experience with *Tess of the D'Urbervilles* was no exception. Hardy had great difficulty finding a publisher for the novel, and magazines demanded radical revisions before serializing it. Tillotson and Son, a Lancashire newspaper syndicate, contracted with Hardy in 1889 to serialize the novel, but their suggestions that he make changes in the scene in which Tess is seduced and in the improvised baptism of her dying baby alienated the author. He refused to agree to their suggestions and, instead, asked the publishers to cancel the contract. Hardy then took the still incomplete work to *Murray's Magazine*, whose editor, Edward Arnold, rejected the piece because the magazine "preferred girls to grow up in ignorance of sexual hazards." Mowbray Morris, editor of *Macmillan's Magazine*, rejected the novel because he was "profoundly upset by the book's sexuality."

Before offering the novel to another magazine, Hardy revised the work to produce a version that would not cause offense. In November 1890, Hardy agreed to terms with *Graphic* to begin serialization in July 1891 and for serialization in *Harper's New Monthly* in the United States soon after. Several passages were excised from the novel. Hardy had to remove the seduction scene and the improvised baptism. He was also forced to include a mock marriage staged by Alec to make Tess believe that she was actually his legal wife. The illegitimate baby was also omitted.

In addition to objections to the illicit relationship between Tess and Alec, Hardy was accused of taking a "low" view of women. His sensuous descriptions of Tess were labeled "French" and critics said that it was "degrading" to see women portrayed as in the following example from the novel:

> She had stretched one arm so high above her coiled-up cable of hair that he could see its delicacy above the sunburn; her face was flushed with sleep and her eyelids hung heavy over their pupils. The brimfulness of her nature breathed from her. It was a moment when a woman's soul is more incarnate than at any other time; when the most spiritual beauty inclines to the corporeal; and sex takes the outside place in her presence.

In 1891, the novel was banned by Mudie's and Smith's circulating libraries, leading to a virtual censorship over popular reading in England. The popular circulating libraries had significant influence on book sales during the second half of the 19th century. Novels were expensive and authors made little money in sales unless the circulating libraries accepted their books. The same year, the novel was also the object of banning by the Watch and Ward Society in Boston, which charged that the novel contained illicit sexuality and immorality. The society forced Boston booksellers to agree that they would not advertise or sell *Tess of the D'Urbervilles*, and most adhered to the request.

While attempting to find a publisher for *Tess*, Hardy published in 1890 in *New Review* an essay called "Candour in English Fiction," in which he noted that "the novels which most conduce to moral profit are likely to be among those written without a moral purpose." Hardy, far in advance of the court decisions in such novels as James Joyce's *Ulysses*, D. H. Lawrence's *Lady Chatterley's Lover*, Henry Miller's *Tropic of Cancer*, and others, recognized the need to portray life honestly: "the passions ought to be proportioned as in the world itself." Viewing life as a "physiological fact," he felt that life's "honest portrayal must be largely concerned with, for one thing, the relations of the sexes, and the substitution for catastrophes as favor the false coloring best expressed by the regulation finish that 'they married and were happy ever after,' of catastrophes based upon sexual relationship as it is. To this expansion English society opposes a well-nigh insuperable bar." He concedes that satisfying "the prudery of censorship" is "the fearful price that he has to pay for the privilege of writing in the English language—no less a price than the complete extinction, in the mind of every mature and penetrating reader, of sympathetic belief in his personages."

FURTHER READING

Cowley, Malcolm. *After the Genteel Tradition.* Rev. ed. Carbondale: Southern Illinois University, 1964.

Hardy, Thomas. "Candour in English Fiction." In *Thomas Hardy's Personal Writings: Prefaces, Literary Opinions, Reminiscences*, edited by Harold Orel, 125–133. Lawrence: University of Kansas Press, 1966.

Pinion, F. B. *Thomas Hardy: His Life nd Friends.* New York: St. Martin's, 1992.

Seymour-Smith, Martin. *Hardy: A Biography.* New York: St. Martin's, 1994.

THEIR EYES WERE WATCHING GOD

Author: Zora Neale Hurston
Original date and place of publication: 1937, United States
Original publisher: J. B. Lippincott and Company
Literary type: Novel

SUMMARY

Their Eyes Were Watching God is the story of the past 20 years of Janie Crawford's life as she perceives it to have happened and as she tells it to her best friend, Pheoby Watson. Janie returns to town looking younger than her 40 years and dressed in a man's shirt and coveralls, giving the town women enough to gossip about. Then she increases their resentment by not acknowledging them but simply walking past them to her house. "Seeing the woman as she was made them remember the envy they had stored up from other times. So they chewed up the back parts of their minds and swallowed with relish. They made burning statements with questions, and killing tools out of laughs. It was mass cruelty." Fully aware of their gossip about her and about the way she had left town some time before with a man 10 years younger, Janie decides to tell her story to Pheoby and let her friend decide how much to tell the rest. "You can tell 'em what Ah say if you wants to. Dat's just de same as me 'cause mah tongue is in mah friend's mouf."

Janie recalls her early years being raised by her grandmother Nanny, who grew up under slavery and whose daughter, Leafy, Janie's mother, was the product of a rape by a white man. Leafy suffered a similar fate and gave birth to Janie after being raped by a white schoolteacher. Soon after Janie's birth, Leafy abandoned her daughter to the care of Nanny. Janie recalls growing up and living in the backyard of a white family named the Washburns and the close friendships she shared with their children. "Ah was wid dem white chillum so much till Ah didn't know Ah wuzn't white till Ah was round six years old." After a roving photographer takes photographs of the children and Janie sees her image, she realizes, " 'Aw, aw! Ah'm colored!' "

Nanny has had a difficult life, always feeling repressed and never having enough money to buy what she wanted and only barely able to buy what was needed. She wants more for her granddaughter and, when she sees 16-year-old Janie let Johnny Taylor kiss her at the front gate, the old woman decides that Janie should marry Brother Logan Killicks, an older settled man who she believes will protect the girl. When Janie rejects the idea, Nanny explains the great hopes that she has always held for her granddaughter, and she shares her sorry story with the girl. She recounts the abuse she suffered at the hands of "Mistis," the wife of the plantation owner who knew that her husband had been Nanny's lover and had fathered Leafy, a baby "wid gray eyes and yaller hair." A week after the birth, Nanny had been forced to flee the plantation with her infant, because Mistis planned to have the overseer tie her to the whipping post and have her whipped until the skin peeled off her back. Although she is helped by a good white family in West Florida and raises her daughter with the hope of educating Leafy to become a teacher, she cannot protect her from rape by a white schoolteacher. Sadly, Nanny relates that soon after Janie's birth Leafy began to drink and run around with men, eventually leaving altogether.

Janie does marry Killicks, but she is not able to love him. Two months after the marriage, she tells her grandmother that despite his seeming adoration and the way he does everything for her, she hates the way his head looks, feels that his belly is too big, thinks that his toenails are like those of mules, and "He don't even never mention nothin' pretty." Instead of sympathizing with her, Nanny tells her to feel proud that people tip their hats to her and call her "Mis' Killicks," yet she is distressed by Janie's unhappiness and dies a month later.

After less than a year of marriage, Killicks stops treating her well and orders her to work hard on the farm. When he leaves one day to buy a mule in a nearby town, Joe Starks walks into her life, "a cityfied [sic], stylish dressed man with his hat set at an angle that didn't belong in these parts." He is well-dressed and a glib speaker "from Georgy" who dazzles the young woman with his plans to turn the $300 in his pocket into a fortune by exploiting the new opportunities "down heah in Floridy." They laugh and joke together and promise to meet each day in the scrub oaks across the road until he would move on. Starks tells Janie, "Ah wants to make a wife outa you" and promises to treat her like a lady, swearing that he is a man of principles. That night, she asks Killicks what he would think if she ran away from him, but he dismisses that suggestion and tells her that no other man would want her given her family history. The next morning, after Killicks insists that Janie help him to move the manure pile, she makes up her mind to leave with Starks. The two drive off in a hired rig to Green Cove Springs, where they marry the same day and he buys her new clothes of wool and silk.

Starks and Janie move into a small town named Eatonville, where his money buys them land and a house and where he builds a general store and acquires a post office for the town. As a man of position, he becomes mayor, which forces Janie to play the role of hostess both in his store and for the functions that his new position requires. Rather than enjoy a happy and love-filled marriage as she had expected, Janie is confined to the store six days of the week, and her thoughts and opinions are ignored by Stark. He is jealous of her beautiful hair and forces her to wear a headrag so no other man can see its beauty. After her great hopes, the marriage is a disappointment to her. Seven years later, Starks becomes physically abusive, slapping Janie when dinner is spoiled or when she talks back to him. Soon, after a particularly violent argument in front of customers in the store, Starks begins to deteriorate physically, and suspicions around Eatonville are that Janie has been poisoning him, a rumor fed by a root-doctor who is profiting from the illness. When he is too sick to leave his bed, he refuses to see Janie and depends, instead, on a parade of people from the town to look after his needs. Janie learns from a physician that Starks is suffering from kidney failure and will die soon, and she enters his sickroom shortly before his death to let him know how disappointed she has been with their marriage. "All dis bowin' down, all dis obedience under yo' voice—dat ain't what Ah rushed off down de road tuh find out about you."

After Starks dies, Janie enjoys her freedom for the first time in her life. She refuses the offers of many men to help her with the business, and she rejects their claims that she needs someone to protect her. After six months, she changes from mourning black to her mourning white clothing and with the change appears a suitor more than 10 years younger than she, who was born Vergible Woods but who tells her "Dey calls me Tea Cake for short." Janie becomes enamored of his carefree attitude and with the way he listens to her and makes her laugh. She also enjoys his impetuous behavior. Her store clerk warns her about Tea Cake and tells her "Dat long-legged Tea Cake ain't got doodly squat. He ain't got no business makin' hisself familiar wid nobody lak you." Janie thanks him, but she already knows she is infatuated with Tea Cake. "He looked like the love thoughts of women. He could be a bee to a blossom—a pear tree blossom in the spring. He seemed to be crushing scent out of the world with his footsteps. Crushing aromatic herbs

with every step he took. Spices hung about him. He was a glance from God."
After they spend the first night together, she "awoke the next morning by
feeling Tea Cake kissing her breath away. Holding her and caressing her as if
he feared she might escape his grasp and fly away."

The town watches as Janie and Tea Cake become a couple and "got mad."
Pheoby's husband tells his wife to warn Janie about the gossip that Tea Cake
is after her money and that she is wearing colors too soon after her husband's
death. Eager to shed her past, Janie looks forward to marriage with Tea Cake
and proclaims "Dis ain't no business proposition, and no race after property and
titles. Dis is uh love game." The two marry, and life with the unpredictable Tea
Cake both frightens and fascinates Janie. He persuades her to go with him to
the Everglades to go "on de muck" where the soil is rich and fertile. While they
wait for the season to begin, Tea Cake teaches her to shoot with pistol, shotgun,
and rifle. She is soon so good a shot that she could "shoot a hawk out of a pine
tree and not tear him up." They work side by side picking beans from the rich
soil, and their house becomes the center of social activity for the workers. Other
women try to lure Tea Cake away from her, and, after finding him wrestling in
the cane field with a woman named Nunkie, Janie strides angrily home and later
physically attacks him when he comes in. They struggle from room to room.
"They wrestled on until they were doped with their own fumes and emanations;
till their clothes had been torn away; till he hurled her to the floor and held her
there melting her resistance with the heat of his body, doing things with their
bodies to express the inexpressible; kissed her until she arched her body to meet
him and they fell asleep in sweet exhaustion."

Mrs. Turner, a light-skinned African American, creates trouble for Janie
when she brings her brother to the house, hoping to make Janie like him
enough to leave Tea Cake and to bring her inheritance from Starks with her.
That night, Tea Cake "whipped Janie. Not because her behavior justified his
jealousy, but it relieved that awful fear inside him. Being able to whip her
reassured him in possession." Aware as they are of Mrs. Turner's pretentious-
ness and her disdain for dark skin, the men join Tea Cake in concocting a plan
to run her out of town, and they destroy her restaurant in the effort.

A violent hurricane drives the couple and the other muck workers out
of the Everglades. As Tea Cake and Janie struggle to reach dry ground, he
is bitten by a rabid dog while protecting Janie. Four weeks later, Tea Cake
becomes sick with headaches and is unable to drink water without gagging.
The doctor tells Janie that the dog bite has infected Tea Cake with rabies and
that too much time has passed to cure him. The rabies soon makes him go
mad, and he attempts to shoot her, but Janie grabs a rifle and shoots at nearly
the same time, killing him but not moving quickly enough to avoid "his teeth
in the flesh of her forearm." Janie is arrested but given a speedy trial and
acquitted of murder. Afterward, as she tells Pheoby, she gave away everything
she and Tea Cake owned and returned to Eatonville. As Janie ends her story,

she tells Pheoby that she is home again and she is satisfied to be there because she has truly known love.

CENSORSHIP HISTORY

Their Eyes Were Watching God received a mixed reception when it was first published in 1937. Critics such as Lucille Tompkins, writing in the September 26, 1937, *New York Times Book Review*, praised the novel as being "a well nigh perfect story—a little sententious at the start, but the rest is simple and beautiful and shining with humor" and commended the author for "not being too much preoccupied with the current fetish of the primitive" (Sheila Hibben, *New York Herald Tribune Weekly Book Review*, September 26, 1937). In a review published in *New Republic* on October 13, 1937, Otis Ferguson opened his review with the statement, "It isn't that this novel is bad, but that it deserves to be better." He writes that the inclusion of dialect selectively throughout the novel "is to set up a mood of Eddie Cantor in blackface." Richard Wright is harsher in his criticism. In an article published in *New Masses* on October 5, 1937, he chastises Hurston for seeming "to have no desire whatever to move in the direction of serious fiction." With a dismissive tone, he contends that "Miss Hurston can write; but her prose is cloaked in that facile sensuality that has dogged Negro expression since the days of Phillis Wheatley. Her dialogue manages to catch the psychological movements of the Negro folk-mind in their pure simplicity, but that's as far as it goes." Instead of furthering the cause of literature, Wright asserts that Hurston "voluntarily continues in her novel the tradition which was forced upon the Negro in the theater, that is the minstrel technique that makes the 'white folks' laugh."

More recently, *Their Eyes Were Watching God* was challenged for being sexually explicit by parents of students attending Stonewall Jackson High School in Brentsville, Virginia. In 1997, the parents asked school officials to remove Hurston's novel as well as *The House of the Spirits* by Isabel Allende and *One Hundred Years of Solitude* by Gabriel García Márquez from the international baccalaureate program, a standardized interdisciplinary program for advanced students. The parents contended that students should not have to read the novels, which contain "explicit sexual descriptions, including necrophilia and rape scenes." In a letter to the school board, parent Jeff Smelser described the offensive passages in the books as "graphic descriptions of sexual perversion" and "glorified fornication." A committee consisting of parents, teachers, and administrators approved retaining the work on the advanced reading list, but Smelser appealed the decision. In response, associate superintendent for instruction Pamela K. Gauch appointed a countywide committee consisting of teachers, parents, students, and a librarian to consider the appeal. The new committee did not contain members from Stonewall High School because the original decision to approve retaining the book was made by an all-Stonewall committee. For the appeal, the school officials chose to create a committee having geographic, gender, and ethnic diversity. The original challenge occurred when Amy Smelser selected to read

Their Eyes Were Watching God for the summer reading program prior to her junior year in high school. The family was troubled by the book, but the two alternatives they selected were equally disturbing. After circulating flyers and "numerous meetings with Stonewall teachers and administrators," the Smelsers filed a formal complaint. When the appointed committee responded that the IB program is optional and that the books would remain in the curriculum, Jeff Smelser filed his appeal and the countywide committee was formed. The decision of the earlier committee was upheld by both the countywide committee and the elected school board, and the books have remained in the IB curriculum at Stonewall Jackson High School.

FURTHER READING

Gates, Henry Louis, Jr., and K. A. Appiah. *Zora Neale Hurston: Critical Perspectives Past and Present.* New York: Amistad, 1993.

Hurston, Zora Neale. *Their Eyes Were Watching God.* New York: J. B. Lippincott, 1965.

O'Hanlon, Ann. "Family Appeals Book Decision: County School System Asked to Reconsider Reading List." *Washington Post,* October 12, 1997, p. 1:4.

THIS BOY'S LIFE

Author: Tobias Wolff
Original date and place of publication: 1989, United States
Original publisher: Grove Press
Literary form: Memoir

SUMMARY

This Boy's Life relates incidents of the author life that take place in the United States during the 1950s and the 1960s, in the post–World War II period that is often portrayed as a time of peace, prosperity, and strong family values. The memoir opens as the adolescent Toby Wolff joins his mother, Rosemary, on a journey to Utah, where she hopes to reverse their luck and to provide a financially secure future for herself and for her son by mining uranium. Rosemary has recently left Florida and her second husband, Roy, an abusive and volatile man who follows Toby and his mother as they travel to Utah. The pair feel constantly oppressed by their fugitive status and by their impoverished circumstances. In contrast, Toby's father, who abandoned his wife and youngest son shortly after Toby was born, is living a life of luxury in Connecticut after marrying a wealthy woman. Toby's brother, Geoffrey, attends Princeton University.

Toby romanticizes his nomadic existence and renames himself Jack both to honor his favorite author Jack London and to distance himself from his father and from the shabbiness of life with his mother. Their shared troubles make him emotionally close to his mother, who loves him very much, although she finds herself unable to overcome her abusive childhood and to function as the strong protective parent he needs. Rosemary's emotional scars run deep, and she continuously becomes involved in relationships with men who abuse her and Jack, both physically and emotionally. After Toby/Jack's father leaves her, she marries Roy, whose volatile nature provides a harrowing environment for Jack and his mother, and they attempt to escape their nightmare by leaving Florida and traveling to Utah. When Roy leaves Rosemary, she uproots Toby/Jack and moves to Seattle, where she meets Dwight, the man who will become a major force in her son's life and the source of his most intense discomfort. Dwight is a bully who constantly belittles and berates Jack, assigning him chores for no better reason than to exhibit the control that he exerts over Rosemary and her son. He taunts and criticizes Jack and claims that he wants to make a man out of the boy, but his behavior shows him to be petty and mean-spirited. To obtain spending money, Jack must deliver newspapers, but Dwight takes all of Jack's earnings and uses it for his own needs. Whatever Jack does is never quite good enough for Dwight, who expresses little genuine interest in him aside from making him an object of ridicule and bullying. Dwight tries to turn Jack into the aggressive individual he is and teaches the boy to fight, then expresses one of his few moments of approval when Jack appears ready to engage in a confrontation with Arthur Gayle, a "notorious sissy" with whom Jack had once been friends.

The attempts to cope with his miserable existence lead Jack to escape into his vivid imagination, and he fantasizes a life that is far from the reality of his life in Chinook. In the effort to escape Dwight and Chinook, Jack applies to private boarding schools and forges praise-filled letters of his accomplishments to accompany his applications. Although he is a member of a group of boys that are repeatedly in trouble with the authorities, Jack creates a perfect self for his applications, one in which he is a straight-A student, a star athlete, and a model student. He writes the lies so often that he soon becomes convinced that he is a gifted student and virtuous human being, despite the daily evidence to the contrary.

As Jack grows older, he makes several attempts to run away, but his plans always go awry. He plans to run away with Arthur to Alaska after a Boy Scout meeting, but he is sidetracked by another troop's request for help. In the process of offering help, Jack alienates Arthur and is defrauded of all of his money. He decides to run away to live with his brother, Geoffrey, at Princeton, but he sabotages his own plans when he is caught forging a bank check.

Despite all of his often self-imposed troubles, Jack receives the opportunity to escape Dwight and Chinook when he is accepted into the prestigious Hill School. An alumnus of the school, Mr. Howard, interviews Jack and attempts to serve as his mentor. The attention that both Mr. and Mrs. Howard give Jack in buying him a new wardrobe and preparing him to attend the school enhances Jack's self-esteem, and he thrives on their attention. Shortly before he is supposed to leave home to attend the school, he has an altercation with

Dwight, who pushes Jack in front of Rosemary, an action that motivates her to leave Dwight and to take Jack with her. At Jack's request, Rosemary allows him to live with the family of his friend Chuck Bolger, and Jack promises that he will keep out of trouble while living with the Bolgers. He is unable to keep that promise and is caught stealing gasoline from the nearby farm owned by the Welch family. Despite his remorse for the action, Jack refuses to apologize for his action. At the same time, Jack watches as his friend Chuck Bolger faces arrest on a statutory rape charge. Tina Flood might be pregnant, but the sheriff lets Chuck know that he can avoid arrest if he agrees to marry her, a deal that Chuck refuses. Fortunately for Chuck, a third friend Huff agrees to marry Tina.

Jack's chaotic life continues when he chooses to visit his father and brother the summer before beginning the Hill School. When Jack arrives, his father leaves immediately for Las Vegas with his latest girlfriend. Jack feels alone and detached from his surroundings. Attending Hill does not improve his life because he has lied his way into the school and he cannot keep up with its academics. Midway through his senior year, Jack is expelled from the school. He feels that he has few options left, and the memoir ends as Jack enlists in the army and faces service in Vietnam.

CENSORSHIP HISTORY

This Boy's Life was nominated for the National Book Award in 1994 and praised extensively by critics, but such esteem has failed to insulate the work from challenges. In 2003, parents of high school students in the Blue Valley school district in Overland Park, Kansas, petitioned the school board to remove the memoir and Walter Dean Myers's *Fallen Angels* from district classrooms "due to vulgar language, sexual explicitness, or violent imagery that is gratuitously employed." The school board reviewed *This Boy's Life* and decided in August 2005 to remove the work from the school curriculum but allowed it to remain in the school library. The decision was the result of a long debate. In 2003, Janet Harmon and her husband challenged the use of the memoir in the classroom "because of references to alcohol and sexual explicitness" and cited passages in which the adolescent Jack speaks of watching the Mickey Mouse Club and turns the wholesome activity "disgusting" by noting that "It was understood that we were all holding a giant bone for Annette." They also raised objections to the repeated uses of such "sexually graphic language" as "fuck you" and references to the homosexual kiss between Jack and his friend Arthur, as well as a range of sexual fantasies in which Jack engages. In one passage during which the adolescent boys trade fantastic stories, Jack relates that "they were good friends with a guy who lost his dick in an automobile accident. He crashed his convertible into a tree and his girlfriend was thrown high into the branches. When the police got her down, they found the guy's dong in her mouth." After receiving the initial challenge filed by the Harmons, school officials refused their request and retained the book in the curriculum but created a special review committee to assess the suitability of the work and other books and plays assigned in the Blue Valley communications arts classes. The review of all books being used in the district was conducted by 25 to 30 communication arts teachers who developed new rationales for use of the books and who provided information regarding content of the works and explanations of how each work fits into the school curriculum. After two years, the special review committee recommended removal of *This Boy's Life* because it was "no longer the best fit for the curriculum." On August 8, 2005, the school board voted to remove the work from use in the school district. Vermeda Edwards, director of curriculum and instruction in the school district, asserted that "No titles were removed because of violence, language, or sexual content." The parents who led the challenge to *This Boy's Life* and 13 other books viewed the move as verification of the initial challenge, and one told a reporter for the *Kansas City Star* that she and other "concerned parents" would remain vigilant and "see that the best and the highest quality books are taught and used."

FURTHER READINGS

Newsletter on Intellectual Freedom 54 (November 2005): 282–283.

TWILIGHT SERIES

Author: Stephenie Meyer
Original date and place of publication: United States, 2005–2008
Original publisher: Little, Brown and Company
Literary type: Novel

SUMMARY

The Twilight series, written by Stephenie Meyer, consists of four books: *Twilight, New Moon, Eclipse,* and *Breaking Dawn.* Like *Romeo and Juliet,* the series centers upon teen lovers from widely disparate worlds who must overcome forces and people that seek to separate them. The additions of the paranormal and the macabre suggest the stories of Edgar Allan Poe, whose works contain several instances of love between human beings and vampires. The four novels span several years and take the main character, a human teenager named Isabella (Bella) Swan, from first love in high school through marriage and early motherhood. Throughout the four novels, the forces of good and evil clash, and high levels of melodrama characterize the works.

In the first novel, Bella has moved from Phoenix, Arizona, to Forks, Washington, where she lives with her father because her mother has to travel extensively with her new husband, a minor league baseball player. Bella meets the 100-year-old, still-teen Edward Cullen, a darkly handsome, brooding member of a vampire family who drinks animal rather than human blood.

The two fall in love, but she also attracts the attention of the sadistic James, a member of a rival vampire family. James pursues Bella, and the Cullen family tries to protect her, but she feels compelled to run away to Phoenix, where James follows her and attacks her. Edward's family retaliates and kills James, after which Bella feels she can return safely to Forks.

In the second novel, *New Moon*, Bella sinks into a deep depression after Edward and his vampire family leave Forks because they feel that their continued presence has endangered her life. After the Cullen family leaves, Bella becomes emotionally close to Jacob Black, a member of a werewolf tribe, whose family joins him in protecting Bella when James's mate Victoria tries to avenge his death by killing Bella. A misunderstanding ensues, and, like Romeo, Edward believes that his beloved is dead and travels to Italy, where he plans to commit suicide. Bella finds him and stops him, but they are detained by members of the powerful vampire coven the Volturi, who release them only after the couple promises that she will shortly become a vampire. Having found each other again, Bella and Edward return to Forks.

The conflict increases in *Eclipse*, the third novel, in which Victoria has gathered a large number of vampires in an attempt to destroy Edward's family and to kill Bella as vengeance for the murder of James. At the same time, Bella is forced to choose between Jacob and Edward. She chooses Edward, but Jacob's wolf family joins forces with the Cullen family to combat Victoria's vampire family, over which the vampire-wolf forces triumph. After the victory, Bella agrees to marry Edward.

In the final novel, *Breaking Dawn*, Edward and Bella shorten their honeymoon on an island off South America after they discover she is pregnant. The rapidly progressing pregnancy debilitates Bella, and she nearly dies giving birth. Edward saves her by injecting her with his venom. The member of a rival vampire coven mistakenly believes that Bella and Edward's half-vampire, half-human daughter, Renesmee, is an "immortal child," a being against vampire law. She reports the assumed violation to the Volturi, and the couple struggles to acquire evidence and testimony to prove that Renesmee is no danger to the vampires or to their secrets. The series ends happily, as Jacob makes peace with Bella's love for Edward and the Volturi leave the couple in peace.

The novels are written from the first-person point of view and relate events largely through Bella's perspective, although the epilogue of *Eclipse* and a segment in *Breaking Dawn* are related by Jacob Black. The vampires in the Twilight series differ in several ways from those that appear in other novels featuring vampires, a fact that Stephenie Meyer explains is the result of her not having been "informed about the canon vampires." "*Twilight* vampires have strong piercing teeth rather than fangs; they glitter in sunlight rather than burn; and they can drink both animal as well as human blood." Meyer claims that she was not concerned with creating stories about vampires and that her emphasis was upon creating relationships among her characters without regard to their status as human or vampire.

CENSORSHIP HISTORY

The novels in the Twilight series have been honored by critics. *Twilight* was named one of the Best Children's Books of 2005 by *School Library Journal* and identified as "Best Book of the Year" by *Publishers Weekly*, in addition to being named one of the "Top Books of 2008" by *USA Today*. In 2009, *New Moon* won the "Young Reader's Choice Award," and *Eclipse* and *Breaking Dawn* were both top-selling works. The reception by parents and educators has not always been as enthusiastic because of what reviewers have described as "adolescent erotic tension, but note that the sexual themes are tastefully presented and the star-crossed lovers remain chaste until married."

In October 2008, instructional materials specialist Linda Myers in the Capistrano unified school district ordered the library staff in the 12 middle schools of the district to remove the books in the Twilight series from their shelves and to send them to the school district office, which would place them in the high school libraries. She noted in her e-mail directive the school district coordinator of literacy programs had reviewed the books and "determined them to contain subject matter which is deemed too mature for our middle school–level students." Four days later, the school district reversed the decision and announced that the books would remain in the middle school libraries until a committee could undertake a more thorough review of the books and their content. Julia Hatchel, a spokesperson for the school district, assured a reporter for *School Library Journal* that "no one in the district is interested in banning the books." Instead, she noted, "We had some concern that we might be pushing this too quickly and held off on a decision until we have more time to determine the proper placement. I think of it as a realignment." The district announced that they will follow an existing procedure to make the final decision: "There's a process that we go through to determine the appropriateness of placement of library books, and we will go through that process to determine the best placement for these books." The article notes that Hatchel had been a school principal when she participated in an earlier "realignment" in which she ordered an atlas containing images of ancient Greek and Roman statues removed from the district elementary schools because "It was inappropriate for kindergartners through fifth graders."

In April 2009, Deseret Books, a store owned by the Church of Jesus Christ of the Latter-day Saints, more commonly known as the Mormon Church, of which the author Stephenie Meyer is a member, announced that it had removed the Twilight series from sale in its 38 stores because the books "are met with mixed reviews." The chain did not so much ban the book as make it inconvenient to acquire, because would-be purchasers have to place a special order to buy it from Deseret Books.

Conservative Christian groups have been divided in their reactions to the series. The Christian Coalition of America gave serious thought in July 2009 to launching a campaign against both the books and the movies in the

Twilight series after having attempted to ban the Harry Potter series several years earlier. In an interview with a reporter for *USA Today*, Roberta Combs, president of the Christian Coalition, claimed that despite the pro-abstinence stance of the books the presence of vampires as role models is troubling. "We can let our voices be heard, and anytime you do that you have an effect one way or another. These Twilight books are very disturbing books for family values. Teen marriage is not a standard, but the part that is more troubling is the vampire. It's just not normal for young people to idolize a vampire." In contrast, Gordon Robertson, chief executive officer of the Christian Broadcasting Network, which condemned the Harry Potter books "for fear that the books would inspire young people to try casting spells," has taken a more liberal view of the Twilight series and suggests using the books as a means of opening a dialogue with children. Kathryn Darden, a Christian freelance writer and frequent contributor to faith-based publications, observes that the distinction emerges because of references in the Bible: "One reason for the division is that witches are specifically condemned in the Bible, while vampires are not even mentioned."

In September 2009, school administrators and school librarians at Santa Sabina College in New South Wales determined that *Twilight* is "too racy for schoolchildren to read" and removed copies of the novel from the school library shelves. The school also cautioned parents that they should not allow their children to bring their private copies of the novel to school. The concern about the sexual and supernatural themes in the book motivated teachers in the school to run a seminar for Year 6 students during which they could discuss the themes and deal with what they considered to be issues of concern. Helen Schutz, the head librarian of the school, told a reporter for the *Daily Telegraph* that "We don't have a policy of censorship but the issues in the Twilight series are quite different from the Harry Potter classics. It is not available in our junior library for these reasons. . . . We wanted to make sure they realise [sic] it's fictitious and ensure they don't have a wrong grasp on reality." Not all Catholic schools in New South Wales agreed with the decision. Mark Rix, a spokesperson for the Catholic Education Office, stated that "Individual schools had to decide whether the books were suitable. It comes down to the discretion of the school to keep an eye on what the kids read. Some primary students are not ready to read *Twilight*. That said, some secondary students may not be either." At the Balmoral Queenwood School for Girls, only senior school students were allowed to borrow the novels from the school library, and school officials at St. Anthony's Catholic elementary school in Picton, New South Wales, refused students' requests to bring their copies of the books to school.

FURTHER READING

Barack, Lauren. "CA District Reinstates Twilight Books after Ban." *School Library Journal* (November 2009): 207–208.

Dickson, Lauren. "Schools Ban Racy Twilight Books by Stephenie Meyer." *Daily Telegraph*. Available online. URL: http://www.dailytelegraph.com.au/entertainment/schools-ban-racy-twilight-books-by-stephanie-meyer/story-e6frewyr-1225772090737. Accessed October 13, 2010.

Gaulin, Pam. "Banned Books Week: The Twilight Series." *Yahoo! News*. Available online. URL: http://news.yahoo.com/s/ac/20100924/en_ac/6833034_banned_books_week_the_twilight_series. Accessed September 26, 2010.

Martindale, Scott. "School District Briefly Bans Vampire Book from Middle Schools." *Orange County Register*. Available online. URL: http://www.ocregister.com/common/printer/view.php?db=ocregister&id=194237. Accessed September 27, 2010.

Puente, Maria. "Adults Fret That *Eclipse* Lacks Good Role Models for Teens." *USA Today*. Available online. URL: http://www.usatoday.com/life/movies/news/2010-07-07-eclipse07_CV_N.htm. Accessed September 27, 2010.

Thomas, Ethan. "Twilight Loses Luster with Deseret Books." *Deseret News*. Available online. URL: http: www.deseretnews.com/article/print/705299108/Twilight-loses-luster-with-Deseret -Book.html. Accessed September 26, 2010.

"Twilight Banned at Australian School—Deemed Too Racy." Available online. URL: http://www.lisnews.org/twilight_banned_australian_school_deemed_too_racy. Accessed September 26, 2010.

ULYSSES

Author: James Joyce
Original dates and places of publication: 1918, England; 1933, United States
Original publishers: Sylvia Beach's Shakespeare & Co. (England); Random House (United States)
Literary form: Novel

SUMMARY

Written in the stream-of-consciousness style, *Ulysses* takes places on one day, June 16, 1904, and relates the thoughts, feelings, words, and actions of Leopold Bloom, his wife Molly, and Stephen Dedalus. The novel was severely criticized because it explicitly describes physical and sensual pleasures, makes excretory references, and depicts sexual incidents in frank terms. In addition, complaints were made about the language, which contains numerous uses of "fuck," as well as frequent genital references such as "vagina," "scrotum," "penis," "hymen," and euphemisms for the genitals.

Most of the erotic references emerge through the characters of Bloom and Molly. Wandering through the city of Dublin and stopping at various bars throughout the day, Bloom reflects the journey of the epic hero Ulysses, who wandered 10 years before reaching his home and family. Bloom, who is obsessed with physical and sensual pleasures, recalls his sexual experiences while on his daylong journey, remembering one instance in which "Wildly

I lay on her, kissed her; eyes, her lips, her stretch neck, beating, woman's breasts full . . . fat nipples upright." He is also explicit in excretory references, describing in detail a bowel movement in the outhouse and relating the physical sensations produced. He enjoys eating "grilled mutton kidneys which gave to his palate a fine tang of faintly scented urine."

Molly is equally concerned with excretory matter and sex. When she has run out of a skin cosmetic, she thinks, "I suppose Ill [*sic*] only have to wash in my piss." She thinks of sex with her lover, Blazes Boylan, noting, "I think he made them a bit firmer sucking them like that so long he made me thirsty titties he calls them I had to laugh yes this one anyhow stiff the nipple gets for the least thing Ill [*sic*] get him to keep that up." Molly describes the male sexual organ as a "tremendous big red brute of a thing" and "some kind of a thick crowbar" as she prepares to have sex near the end of the novel. In rhapsodizing about the encounter, she describes taking off her clothes and experiencing "one the size of that to make you feel full up . . . like a stallion driving it up into you. . . . I made him pull it out and do it on me considering how big it is so much the better in case any of it wasnt [*sic*] washed out properly the last time I let him finish it in me." The sexual references are numerous, but the descriptions emerge in a fragmentary manner, most appearing as interior monologues of the characters.

CENSORSHIP HISTORY

In 1922, the U.S. Department of the Post Office burned 500 copies of the novel when an attempt was made to import the book and court decisions ruled against the book. The first court trial of the book, however, actually occurred in 1921, when John Sumner, the secretary for the New York Society for the Suppression of Vice, and his followers seized an issue of the *Little Review*, which contained one chapter of the serialized version of the novel. The trial took place in the court of general sessions with magazine editors Margaret Head and Jane Heap as defendants. Author John Cowper Powys and playwright Philip Moeller, called as witnesses, testified that Joyce's style was too obscure to be understood by most people, but the court ruled against the *Little Review* and the novel.

Bowdlerized and bootlegged copies of the novel appeared, but no further action occurred until 1932, when the collector of Customs seized a copy of the book sent to Random House and declared it obscene under the Tariff Law of 1930. Random House intervened in the case because the publisher was, at that time, producing copies of the book with the intent to distribute it to the American reading public. The publisher demanded the court hearing required by the tariff law and asked for exculpation of the work. In pleas to the Federal Court of New York, Random House asked that the book be read in its entirety and that the passages declared to contain "the dirtiest language" be viewed in the context of the whole. In *United States v. One Book Entitled "Ulysses,"* 5 F. Supp. 182 (S.D.N.Y. 1933), later affirmed in *United States v. One Book Entitled "Ulysses,"* 72 F.2d 705 (2d Cir. 1934), Judge John M. Woolsey rejected the claims of obscenity, stating that despite the "unusual frankness" of the novel, "I do not anywhere detect the leer of the sensualist. I hold, therefore, that it is not pornographic." He further observed that he viewed the language and actions to be entirely consistent with the types of people whom Joyce describes. As to "the recurrent emergence of the theme of sex in the minds of his characters, it must always be remembered that his locale was Celtic and his season Spring." Judge Woolsey ruled that the book was not obscene when judged by its effect on the average man, *l'homme moyen sensuel*. He stated the following:

> In many places it seems to be disgusting, but although it contains, as I have mentioned above, many words usually considered dirty, I have not found anything that I consider to be dirt for dirt's sake. Each word of the book contributes like a bit of mosaic to the detail of the picture which Joyce is seeking to construct for his readers.

The government appealed the decision in the circuit court of appeals where, in *United States v. One Book Called "Ulysses,"* Judge Augustus Hand and Judge Learned Hand upheld the earlier decision. In the majority decision, they noted, "We think that *Ulysses* is a book of originality and sincerity of treatment, and that it has not the effect of promoting lust." The government chose not to appeal to the Supreme Court, and thus ended a decade-long struggle with the United States government and local censorship groups. It also provided a step toward freedom in the struggle between the moralists and publishers. In essence, the court ruled that the harm of an "obscene" book must be judged not from reading select passages but as a result of the whole book. Therefore, if the book as a whole had merit and the allegedly obscene parts were germane to the purpose of the book, then the book could not be viewed as obscene. In summing up the new interpretation of the law, Judge Augustus Hand stated:

> We believe that the proper test of whether a given book is obscene is its dominant effect. (I.e., is promotion of lust the dominant effect of reading the whole book?) In applying this test, relevancy of the objectionable parts to the theme, the established reputation of the work in the estimation of approved critics, if the book is modern, and the verdict of the past, if it is ancient, are persuasive pieces of evidence; for works of art are not likely to sustain a high position with no better warrant for their existence than their obscene content.

A significant result of the verdict was that it led judges and prosecutors to examine a book in its entirety rather than according to isolated passages. The decision also admitted *Ulysses* into the United States.

The controversy over *Ulysses* appeared to have been settled by the court in 1932, and the length of the novel and its difficult language have made it an unpopular choice for students when it has appeared on high school suggested reading lists. As a result, Apple's decision to demand cuts from *Ulysses Seen*, a graphic adaptation of the novel by Rob Berry and Joseph Levitas, before the company would approve the application for use on their iPhone and iPad surprised many people and resulted in such cyber headlines as "Joyce's *Ulysses* Banned Again—by Apple," "A Publishing Tradition: Apple Censors Joyce's *Ulysses*—a Century After the U.S. Did the Same," and "Tiny Cartoon Penis Disqualifies Ulysses Comic from iPad Store." The offending panel contains the sketch of a nude, physically out-of-shape Buck Mulligan diving into the sea. Although the application does not contain offensive language and the cartoon is an abstract rendering, which the authors thought they "might have to pixelate or cover with 'fig leaves,' " Apple's policy forced them "to either scrap the idea of moving the tablet with Apple or re-design our pages." Berry and Levitas chose to crop the images "to remove any offending genitalia." The outcry against Apple's act of censorship was quick and strong. By June 16, 2010, the day that Bloomsday is celebrated worldwide by readings from Joyce's tome, Apple reversed its decision. Berry told an interviewer, "They said they had decided to change their policy in our case and we should resubmit the original unedited versions of all the pages. They told us they'd push it through for Bloomsday." Eight hours after Berry and Levitas resubmitted *Ulysses Unseen*, the application was available from the iTunes Store "for free download but restricted to users aged 17 or older."

FURTHER READING

"Another Repeal: Joyce's *Ulysses* Is Legal at Last." *Nation*, December 20, 1933, p. 693.

Arnold, Bruce. *The Scandal of "Ulysses": The Sensational Life of a Twentieth-Century Masterpiece.* New York: St. Martin's, 1994.

Brown, Damon. "A Publishing Tradition: Apple Censors Joyce's Ulysses—a Century After the the U.S. Did the Same." Available online. URL: http://www.bnet.com/blogmedia/a-publishing-tradition-apple-censors-joyces-ulysses-a-century-after-the-us-did-the-same/8534. Accessed August 21, 2010.

Bryer, J. R. "Joyce, *Ulysses*, and the *Little Review*." *South Atlantic Quarterly* 66 (Spring 1967): 148–64.

Ernst, Morris L., and Alan U. Schwartz. *Censorship: The Search for the Obscene.* New York: Macmillan, 1964.

"In Reversal, Apple Approves 'Ulysses' Comic with Nudity." Available online. URL: http://www.google.com/hostednews/afp/article/ALeqM5i5NWT-KZ7ilmOyU47WzdRw28SmxA. Accessed August 23, 2010.

Kelleher, Kevin. "Joyce's *Ulysses* Banned Again—by Apple." Available online. URL: http://www.thebigmoney.com/blogs/app-economy/2010/06/09/joyce-s-ulysses-banned-again-apple-not-government?page=full. Accessed August 21, 2010.

Marcuse, Ludwig. *The History of an Indignation.* London: MacGibbon & Key, 1965.

Paul, James C. N., and Murray L. Schwartz. *Federal Censorship: Obscenity in the Mail.* New York: Free Press, 1961.

St. John-Stevas, Norman. *Obscenity and the Law.* London: Secker & Warburg, 1956.

Spence, Nick. "Ulysses Seen iPad Webcomic Gets Apple Approval After Cuts." Available online. URL: http://www.macworld.com/article/151821/2010/06/ulysses.webcomic.html. Accessed August 17, 2010.

United States President's Commission on Obscenity and Pornography. *The Report of the Commission on Obscenity and Pornography.* New York: Random House, 1970.

WOMEN IN LOVE

Author: D. H. Lawrence
Original date and place of publication: 1920, United States
Original publisher: Thomas Seltzer
Literary form: Novel

SUMMARY

Women in Love deals with the psychological explorations and the interrelationships of sisters Ursula and Gudrun Brangwen as they deal with love and life in a small English mining town. Alike in many respects, the sisters mirror the goals and desires of other modern young women of the early 20th century in their reservations about getting married and having children, as well as in their hatred of their middle-class origins. Ursula, however, is different from Gudrun in her ability to respond both spiritually and physically to Rupert Birken, although the two struggle mightily before Ursula and Rupert reach an understanding in which "He wanted sex to revert to the level of the other appetites, to be regarded as a functional process, not as a fulfillment." When they do consummate their relationship, Lawrence blends the physical passion with a spiritual bonding.

> They threw off their clothes, and he gathered her to him, and found her, found the pure lambent reality of her forever invisible flesh. Quenched, inhuman, his fingers upon her unrevealed nudity were the fingers of silence upon silence. . . . She had her desire fulfilled. He had his desire fulfilled.

In another segment of the novel, their sexual interaction is more fully revealed: "Kneeling on the hearth-rug before him, she put her arms around his loins, and put her face against his thighs."

Gudrun, on the other hand, and her lover Gerald are too self-absorbed to establish any true communication, and references to their sexual relationship are brief.

Beyond the sensual passages between Ursula and Rupert, critics have objected to Rupert's desire for intimacy with Gerald Crich. Rupert believes that men are capable of establishing an intimate friendship that a man can never attain with a woman. At one point in the novel when the two men wrestle in the nude, Rupert believes that he and Gerald are about to reach a plateau of trust and understanding, but Gerald appears unable to surrender his feelings entirely to anyone.

CENSORSHIP HISTORY

Overall, although *Women in Love* does not contain language that is usually identified as "obscene," nor are passages graphically sexual, the sexual relationship between Ursula and Rupert and the homoerotic relationship of Rupert and Gerald evoked strong objections from critics. The novel first appeared in 1920 in a limited edition of 1,250, marked "for subscribers only." The title page omitted Seltzer's imprint and carried, instead, the phrase "Privately Printed" to protect the company from attacks by censors. That move alone might have signaled to would-be censors that even the publisher thought the book too erotic to be published as part of the company's usual list. Two years later, Seltzer published the novel in a regular trade edition with the company imprint. In 1922, the limited edition of *Women in Love* became one of three titles published by Thomas Seltzer that were involved in a well-publicized censorship case. The other two were Arthur Schnitzler's *Casanova's Homecoming* and the anonymous *A Young Girl's Diary*. The magistrate's court ruled in favor of the publisher.

In 1923, Supreme Court Justice John Ford tried to suppress *Women in Love* after his daughter brought the book home from the circulating library that had recommended it to her. Ford founded the Clean Books League and worked with John Sumner, secretary of the New York Society for the Suppression of Vice, to achieve the passage of a "clean books" bill in the New York legislature. He also favored upholding and strengthening existing obscenity laws. Incensed by the action, Lawrence sent Ford a telegram from Taos, quoted on page 580 of the February 24, 1923, issue of *Publishers Weekly:*

> Let Judge John Ford confine his judgment to courts of law, and not try to perch in seats that are too high for him. Also let him take away the circulating library tickets from Miss Ford, lest worse befall her. She evidently needs an account at a candy shop, because, of course, 'Women in Love' wasn't written for the Ford family. . . . Father and mother and daughter should all leave the tree of knowledge alone. The Judge won't succeed in chopping it down, with his horrified hatchet. Many better men have tried and failed.

FURTHER READING

Boyer, Paul S. *Purity in Print: The Vice-Society Movement and Book Censorship in America.* New York: Scribner, 1968.

"Censorship Beaten in New York Case." *Publishers Weekly*, September 16, 1922, pp. 801–904.

De Grazia, Edward. *Girls Lean Back Everywhere: The Law of Obscenity and the Assault on Genius.* New York: Random House, 1992.

Ford, John. *Criminal Obscenity, a Plea for Its Suppression.* New York: Revell, 1926.

Lawrence, D. H. "On Obscenity." *Publishers Weekly*, February 23, 1923, p. 580.

Loth, David. *The Erotic in Literature.* New York: Dorset, 1961.

LITERATURE SUPPRESSED ON SOCIAL GROUNDS

Most books challenged for social reasons in the past century have suffered because of the "vulgar" language or behavior of their characters or the relationships portrayed within the books. "Socially unacceptable" behavior has, in the past, fallen under the broad label of "obscene." The vague nature of obscenity laws has made possible a wide interpretation of what constitutes an essentially obscene literary work. Often what this has meant in reality is that works containing words or activities deemed vulgar by specific members of a community or depicting nontraditional personal relationships have been considered unacceptable for social reasons, which are quite distinct from the political, religious, or sexual factors discussed elsewhere in this book.

Language, particularly the use of the "n-word," and unflattering portrayals of ethnic groups have motivated challenges to such disparate books as Mark Twain's *Adventures of Huckleberry Finn* and the recent nonfiction work *Freakonomics*. In the last few decades, would-be censors have widened their definition of what is socially unacceptable content to include the discussion or the depiction of same-sex relationships. The mere suggestion that healthy relationships might be forged between partners of the same sex and that families might consist of a combination different from mother-father-child has been enough to motivate numerous challenges to books. Many of these books do not depict overt sexuality, make no appeal for readers to enter the homosexual lifestyle, and contain nothing offensive in language or illustration. For challengers, however, none of that is needed. The nature of what is considered socially unacceptable has been widened.

The books discussed in this section are literary works that have been banned, censored, or challenged because of their language, their depiction of unacceptable activities such as drug use, and the sexual orientation of their characters. This new updated edition of *120 Banned Books* contains entries on recently published controversial works, such as Sherman Alexie's

The Absolutely True Diary of a Part-Time Indian, which won the National Book Award for Young People's Literature in 2007; the international best seller *The Kite Runner*; and the popular children's book *And Tango Makes Three*, about two male penguins that together manage to raise a rejected baby penguin chick. Other books discussed in this new edition for the first time include longtime American classics such as *The Great Gatsby* and recent works of powerful literary fiction such as Toni Morrison's *Beloved*.

The definition of what is socially unacceptable remains fluid, changing with the rise and fall in power of diverse social groups. What must remain constant, however, is a steadfast resistance to all those who would restrict our freedom of expression.

—Dawn B. Sova, Ph.D.

THE ABSOLUTELY TRUE DIARY OF A PART-TIME INDIAN

Author: Sherman Alexie
Original date and place of publication: 2007, United States
Original publisher: Little, Brown and Company
Literary form: Young adult novel

SUMMARY

The Absolutely True Diary of a Part-Time Indian is a semiautobiographical novel that relates the hopes, fears, disappointments, and eventual triumphs experienced by the 14-year-old budding cartoonist Arnold Spirit, Jr. (better known as Junior), who lives on the Spokane (Washington) Indian Reservation ("the rez"). He dreams of becoming a wealthy and respected artist and draws because "I feel like it might be my only real chance to escape the reservation." Despite his talent, displayed in cartoons scattered throughout the novel, Junior's problems appear to be insurmountable, and he views himself as "really just a poor-ass reservation kid living with his poor-ass family on the poor-ass Spokane Indian Reservation." Junior was born with too much cerebral fluid in his skull that leaves him "susceptible to seizure activity" and brain damage that makes him "nearsighted in one eye and farsighted in the other, so my ugly glasses were all lopsided because my eyes were so lopsided," a mouth containing 42 instead of 32 teeth, huge hands and feet paired with a too-skinny body, and a lisp and a stutter. Although "Dad is a drunk and Mom is an ex-drunk," they love their son and want him to escape the cycle of poverty and despair that destroyed their dreams, so they agree to allow him to transfer to Reardon, a small school in "a rich, white farm town" 22 miles away that will provide him with an excellent education. *The Absolutely True Diary of a Part-Time Indian* is the story of Junior's freshman year at Reardon.

The first four chapters—"The Black-Eye-of-the-Month Club," "Why Chicken Means So Much to Me," "Revenge Is My Middle Name," and "Because Geometry Is Not a Country Somewhere Near France"—provide readers with depressing views of Junior's life on the rez. His schoolmates humiliate him, call him names, stuff his head into toilets, and beat him up regularly, "at least once a month." He copes with this abuse by staying at home as much as he can, and he draws "all the time." His lisp and stutter make spoken communication difficult, "words are too unpredictable . . . words are too limited," but "when you draw a picture, everybody can understand it." Junior also suffers because his family is poor, although he acknowledges that most of the Indian families on the reservation are poor. He occasionally misses a meal "and sleep is the only thing we have for dinner," but he reassures readers that "sooner or later, my parents will come bursting through the door with a bucket of Kentucky Fried Chicken. Original Recipe." The lack of money forces Junior to face a heartrending tragedy when he does not have the money for medical attention for his "best friend Oscar," an adopted stray dog who develops seizures, vomiting, and diarrhea and who whimpers in pain while his "red, watery, snotty eyes" plead for help. Junior's parents cannot afford the cost of a veterinarian, and he realizes that there was nothing he could do to save Oscar. "Nothing. Nothing. Nothing." His father offers the only solution he can, to end Oscar's misery by shooting him, a solution that first infuriates Junior, then reinforces his feelings of despair. "So I heard the boom of my father's rifle when he shot my best friend. A bullet only costs about two cents, and anybody can afford that."

Junior turns to his "best human friend" Rowdy, "the meanest kid on the rez," after Oscar dies. Rowdy is "mean as a snake" and fights with others constantly, but he is protective of Junior, whose home is a safe place where he can avoid his father's hard drinking and brutal beatings. Rowdy takes revenge on the 30-year-old Andruss triplets after Junior tells him that they played catch with him "and then kneed me in the balls." He waits until they fall into a drunken stupor and then shaves their eyebrows and cuts off their braids that have taken five years to grow. In a prelude to discussing his first day of high school, Junior reveals that he spends "*hours* in the bathroom with a magazine that has one thousand pictures of naked movie stars. *Naked woman + right hand = happy happy joy joy*." Addressing the reader, Junior becomes expansive:

> Yep, that's right, I admit that I masturbate.
>
> I'm proud of it.
>
> I'm good at it.
>
> I'm ambidextrous.
>
> If there were a Professional Masturbators League, I'd get drafted number one and make millions of dollars.
>
> And maybe you're thinking, 'Well, you really shouldn't be talking about masturbation in public.'
>
> Well, tough, I'm going to talk about it because EVERYBODY does it. And EVERYBODY likes it.
>
> And if God hadn't wanted us to masturbate, then God wouldn't have given us thumbs.
>
> So I thank God for my thumbs.

Despite the poverty, humiliation, and abuse, Junior seems relatively accepting of life until his first day as a high school freshman. He looks forward to geometry class, but his excitement turns to anger when he receives his book and finds his mother's maiden name written inside the cover. He loves his mother, who gave birth to him when she was 30, but her name on the book means that the textbook is at least 30 years old, a fact that hits his heart "with the force of a nuclear bomb" and makes him feel his poverty and sense of hopelessness more keenly. Without thinking, he throws the book at his teacher Mr. P, breaking his nose and earning a suspension from school. The action serves as the turning point in Junior's life.

In "Hope Against Hope," the fifth chapter, Mr. P visits Junior at home, speaks about the incident, and commends him for having retained the spirit and hope for change that most of the reservation residents, including Rowdy and Junior's parents and older sister Mary, have lost. Mr. P reveals that Mary, once his student who now spends most of her day in front of the television in the basement with no ambition to do anything else, "was the smartest kid" he had ever had in class. Much to Junior's surprise, Mr. P says that she had wanted to be a writer, but "she always thought people would make fun of her." Mr. P counsels Junior to leave the reservation and to save himself rather than to give up as everyone else, including the white teachers, have. "You're going to find more and more hope the farther and farther you walk away from this sad, sad reservation." In the following chapter, "Go Means Go," Junior tells his parents that he wants to transfer out of his reservation school and into Reardan, located in a town "filled with farmers and rednecks and racist cops who stop every Indian that drives through." Junior's father had been stopped in Reardan five times in one week for DWI: "Driving While Indian." Despite their fears and the difficulty of transporting him 22 miles each way, and while acknowledging that many residents of the reservation will be angry and resentful, Junior's parents agree that he can transfer schools. Rowdy, however, is not happy, and the two exchange insults in "Rowdy Sings the Blues," one calling the other "dickwad" to the response "kiss my ass." Junior exudes praise for his soon-to-be schoolmates, which Rowdy counters by shouting, "you retarded fag."

Once at Reardan, Junior learns that, aside from the school mascot, he is the only Native American. The girls ignore him, as did girls on the reservation. The boys do not physically attack him, but they call him such names as "Chief," "Tonto," and "Squaw Boy." Addressed by his true name Arnold in class and by Penelope, with whom he becomes infatuated, Junior is intimidated and awed by the tall white farm boys until one, Roger, steps over the line with what he calls a joke: "Did you know that Indians are living proof that niggers fuck buffalo?" Junior lashes out in blind anger, "defending Indians, black people, *and* buffalo," and punches Roger in the face, knocking him to the ground. The farm boy is stunned and surprises Junior in return by refusing to agree to the challenge to meet after school to finish the fight. In a later discussion with his grandmother about the incident, Junior realizes that his rash move has gained him respect.

As the school year progresses toward Thanksgiving, Junior remains physically safe at the high school but also very lonely, a major hazard because "whenever I get lonely, I grow a big zit on the end of my nose." He realizes that he does not feel fully comfortable either at school or at home: "Zitty and lonely, I woke up on the reservation as an Indian, and somewhere on the road to Reardan, I became something less than an Indian. And once I arrived at Reardan, I became something less than less than less than an Indian." His father becomes unreliable in driving Junior to school, so some days he hitchhikes, other days he takes the bus, and on several occasions he walks the 22 miles home. Although everyone and everything seems to turn against Junior, he persists in attending Reardan. He learns that his sister Mary, a persistent runaway, has left for Montana and married a Flathead Indian, and the knowledge buoys him because he feels it means that she has not given up on life. Mary sends letters filled with glowing accounts of her new home and life, which Junior learns later are fiction. The large "gorgeous" home she claims to have is actually a cramped trailer, and her new life is simply a continuation of the old. He also becomes study friends with Gordy, an acknowledged genius at Reardon, but as much of an outsider as Junior. In one silly exchange the two discuss "a metaphorical boner," by which Gordy means joy but which Junior understands "in the sexual sense." Junior also learns that Penelope, with whom he has been in love since his first day at Reardan, is bulimic, and sharing this secret forges a friendship between them, despite threats by her father Earl. At school, Junior, whom Penelope prefers to call Arnold, is suddenly popular, and he enjoys his new celebrity, even though he knows it is fleeting. Gordy brings him down to earth by telling him that adoring the pretty, blonde Penelope "means you're just a racist asshole like everybody else."

Junior's parents try to help him to retain his pride at Reardan by giving him as much spending money as they can, although it is far less than other students have. Fearful of being exposed as poor, he tries to keep up and to impress Penelope, but when the group goes out to eat after the prom to which Junior has worn with great success his father's bell-bottomed leisure suit, Roger reveals that he has known all along that Junior has financial difficulties and he kindly offers $40 to cover dinner. The same night, Roger also drives Junior home to the reservation, and he does so for many nights following. This leads Junior to state, "If you let people into your life a little bit, they can be pretty damn amazing."

Through the remainder of the school year, Junior continues to move between his life on the reservation and his newfound life in Reardan. While in the computer lab with the genius Gordy, Junior opens an e-mail from Rowdy who "was exactly the kind of kid who would e-mail his bare ass (and bare everything else) to the world." When Gordy asks if the image is a "posterior," he responds, "That is a stinky ass. You can smell the thing, even through the computer." Gordy learns that Rowdy is angry with Junior, whom he considers to be an "apple," red on the outside and white on the inside. Gordy explains to Junior that the evolution of both boys in relation to the concept of tribe is completely to be expected.

Major changes occur in rapid succession in Junior's life. He tries out for the high school basketball team—dreaming big as his father advised—and makes the team; he later stars when Reardan plays against the team from his reservation school. His chronically drunk father disappears on Christmas Eve, yet manages to keep $5 aside to give Junior when he returns the day after New Year's Day. Sadly, his beloved grandmother is killed by a drunk driver, and when Junior attends the wake he is fearful of the reaction of the other 2,000 Indians who attend. He is surprised and pleased to hear no harsh words and no criticism because he has left the reservation. His father's friend Eugene is shot in the face and killed by another friend named Bobby in a fight over a bottle of wine. In jail, Bobby hangs himself using a bedsheet. Junior watches as his father reacts by going on "a legendary drinking binge" and his mother goes to church every single day. "It was all booze and God, booze and God, booze and God." A few months later, Junior is taken out of school early and told that his sister has died. Alcohol has been responsible for her death, as well. His father tells him through tears, "They had a big party . . . And your sister and her husband passed out in the back bedroom. And somebody tried to cook soup on a hot plate. And they forgot about it and left. And a curtain drifted in on the wind and caught the hot plate, and the trailer burned down quick." Rowdy lashes out at Junior, blaming him for Mary's death, telling him that Mary would not have run away from the reservation and married so quickly if Junior had not left to attend Reardan. Unable to face a house full of grieving friends and family who "would be drinking booze and getting drunk and stupid and sad and mean," Junior returns to Reardan where the students and teachers greet him and let him know that they care about him and are sorry his sister died.

When the school year ends, Junior reacclimates himself to being home on the rez. He joins his parents in cleaning the family gravesites, and he mourns the "ten or fifteen more Spokanes [who] would die during the next year, and that most of them would die because of booze." He also recognizes that his journey from the reservation toward a better education and future is no different from the journey taken by millions of immigrants "who had left their birthplaces in search of a dream." He also thinks about the many people on the reservation who would not survive, and Rowdy comes to mind. He recalls their friendship and their summers spent swimming, watching television, playing video games, and insulting each other. In one exchange, after Junior looks at the "monster pine tree" and says he loves the tree, Rowdy calls him a "tree fag." When Junior denies this, Rowdy asks, "Then how come you like to stick your dick inside knotholes?" to which Junior replies, "I stick my dick in girl trees." Junior feels that those times together are over, but Rowdy surprises him soon after the school year ends. The two make peace, and Rowdy admits that he is happy for Junior and wishes him a successful future.

CENSORSHIP HISTORY

The Absolutely True Diary of a Part-Time Indian was awarded the National Book Award for Young People's Literature in 2007 and was named one of the *Los Angeles Times*'s Favorite Children's Books of 2007 and one of the *New York Times*'s Notable Children's Books of 2007. Further, the audio version earned the Odyssey Award in 2009, but such honors have not insulated the novel against controversy. Parents of students attending Antioch (Illinois) Community High School, located in a predominantly lower-middle-class Chicago suburb halfway between Chicago and Milwaukee, asked school officials in June 2009 to remove the novel from the summer reading list and claimed to be "appalled by certain passages." Jennifer Andersen, whose son would be a freshman at the high school in September 2009, said that she was "stunned by descriptions of masturbation, racist language, graphic depictions of sex, and references to bestiality." She read the book so that she could help her son with discussion of the content, but "I wasn't prepared for what I read. It was shocking. If there were just swear words, I could deal with that. But sections of this book are just vulgar." In an interview with the *Chicago Tribune*, Andersen said that she understands that children use profanity but protested that if it is part of the curriculum, the students will believe the school condones it. Six other parents joined Andersen to formally petition the school board to remove the book and contacted local news media to air their complaint. The novel had been selected by a committee of English teachers at the high school and approved by John Whitehurst, chairman of the English department, who defended the book and asserted that the passages condemned by parents "need to be read in context." He praised the novel for its "life-affirming values" and reminded parents that even in the controversial paragraphs the words are authentic. "This is honest and realistic language for a boy of this age. Though he has sexual thoughts, he records them but doesn't act on them." Whitehurst also reminded parents that the novel has "a strong anti-drug, anti-alcohol message." The English committee admitted to selecting the novel specifically to appeal to boys who often do not like to read. "We were looking for a book that is engaging for boys. We wanted a main character that they could relate to." The school district offered parents an alternative reading, *Down River*, until the controversy could be settled. The Antioch school superintendent Jay Sabatino told parents that he wanted to complete reading the book before making a decision, and he asked school board members to also read the book before meeting to decide the fate of the novel. Although the superintendent was sensitive to the concerns of parents, he stated, "We don't want to make a knee-jerk reaction." While she awaited the decision of the board, the parent who initiated the controversy sent an e-mail to high school principal Michael Nekritz telling him that, at the very least, she "would have appreciated a warning from school officials about the potentially offensive content." Andersen said that she wanted this protest to begin a national conversation about placing warning labels on books. "We rate movies and put warnings on music and TV. What about books? There is no warning whatsoever if there is vulgar language in a book."

In a closed meeting a week later, the superintendent and the school board of School District 117 "voiced strong support for the book as an educational tool that engages young readers," but they also decided to write a letter to parents of incoming students and invite them to discuss any concerns they may have. They also offered all students the opportunity to read the alternate selection, *Down River* by John Hart. Further, the district will form a committee made up of parents, teachers, and administrators that will meet each March to review books and to select summer reading titles. Jennifer Andersen praised the school board for proposing the committee, but she remained adamant in her disapproval of *The Absolutely True Diary of a Part-Time Indian* and told reporter Lisa Black, "There are so many great stories out there without the vulgarity—Why bother with this book? I don't believe we need swear at our kids to get them engaged."

In an interview with *Publishers Weekly*, the English department chairman John Whitehurst said that there had been opposition in the past to books selected by the faculty for required reading, but "talking to the parents about the selection and offering an alternative has always defused the situation. But it didn't satisfy them this time around." In response to the decision by the school district to retain the novel, the publisher Little, Brown and Company released a statement that it "applauds the school board's decision to have the book remain on the Antioch High School summer reading list for the incoming freshman class. Based on his own experience of growing up, *The Absolutely True Diary of a Part-Time Indian* is ultimately a story about hope, resilience and self-discovery."

FURTHER READING

Black, Lisa. "Antioch School Won't Ban Book: District Calls It a Valuable Read but Offers Alternative." *Chicago Tribune*, June 23, 2009, p. 18.
Fuller, Ruth. "Some Parents Urge Board to Ban Book: School Official Says Book Is Relevant to Incoming Freshmen." *Chicago Tribune*, June 22, 2009, p. 18.
Kirch, Claire. "Chicago School Keeps Alexie Novel on Summer Reading List." *Publishers Weekly* (June 25, 2009). Available online. URL: http://www.publishersweekly.com/article/CA6666906.html?nid=2788&source=title&rid=630002055. Accessed December 15, 2009.
Pierri, Vincent. "Books Stirring Controversy at Antioch High School." *Daily Herald*, June 19, 2009. Available online. URL: www.dailyherald.com/story/?id=302477. Accessed December 16, 2009.
"Recorded Book Wins 2009 Odyssey Award for *The Absolutely True Diary of a Part-Time Indian*." *Young Adult Library Services* 7, no. 3 (Spring 2009): 18–19.
"Sherman Alexie Gets National Book Award." *Seattle Post-Intelligencer*, November 15, 2007, p. C-1.

ADVENTURES OF HUCKLEBERRY FINN

Author: Mark Twain (Samuel Langhorne Clemens)
Original date and place of publication: 1884, London
Original publisher: Self-published
Literary form: Novel

SUMMARY

This novel relates the adventures and struggles of a rambunctious young southern boy in the early 19th century. Told from the first-person point of view, *Adventures of Huckleberry Finn* portrays river life in a developing America and young Huckleberry Finn's adventures while on the journey from boyhood to manhood. The story begins with Huck's escape from his brutal father and follows him up the Mississippi River as he and his slave friend Jim run from authorities and various other scoundrels.

As the novel opens, Huck reminds readers that many of his adventures have already been detailed in Mark Twain's *The Adventures of Tom Sawyer*. He states that the $12,000 that he and Tom had found in the previous novel was invested for them and was earning interest. Huck, who now lives with the Widow Douglas and Miss Watson, expresses annoyance with the amount of concern placed on making him conform to society. Huck sees no point in this lifestyle and yearns to be a rambunctious youth, as is his nature.

As the narrative progresses, Huck's father, the town drunk and a general burden on society, learns of Huck's recent wealth. He kidnaps Huck and holds him hostage in a shack in a remote area outside the town. While Huck waits to be either freed or rescued, his father repeatedly beats him, leaving Huck convinced that escape is the only feasible solution. To accomplish this, he conjures up a plan to make it appear that he has been murdered. Succeeding in his plan, Huck flees to safety on Jackson's Island, where he is reunited with Miss Watson's runaway slave, Jim. Jim is also hiding, fearful that he will be caught and punished for leaving his mistress. Huck agrees not to speak of Jim to anyone, and the two become partners. Aware that men are looking for Jim, the two decide to leave the island in search of adventure and the free states.

They board a raft that they found on the island and begin their journey. By day they hide on land, and by night they travel on the river. All goes well until one night when, during a violent storm, the raft is torn apart by an oncoming steamship. This experience not only almost ends Huck's young life, but it also separates him from Jim.

Huck swims to shore and finds himself in the midst of a feud between two families, the Grangerfords and the Shepherdsons, and he is immediately attacked by members of the Grangerford family. He states his name as George Jackson and explains quickly that he fell off a riverboat and was washed ashore. He stays with the family for a short time, enjoying their lifestyle and making new friends along the way, and he even manages to be reunited with Jim. When the family feud escalates and Huck and Jim watch numerous members of both families die, they decide to resume their adventure on the river, where they meet two men known as the Duke and the King. The unscrupulous men specialize in robbery and deceit, and they do not hesitate to pose as a dead man's next of kin in order to receive a rather large inheritance. The innately moral Huck refuses to cooperate, and he reveals the Duke and the King's deceit. The scoundrels flee, but they first sell Jim to Silas Phelps.

Seeking to obtain Jim's freedom, Huck visits the Phelps farm, where he is mistaken for Tom Sawyer, who is expected to arrive the same day. Huck allows the deception to continue, then meets with the real Tom, who agrees that Huck will continue to pose as Tom, and Tom will pose as his brother Sid. The two also agree to free Jim as soon as possible. After many attempts, Jim finally escapes, but Tom is accidentally shot in the leg during the effort.

Although Jim has been portrayed as ignorant throughout the novel, he is a morally decent man who temporarily puts aside his dreams of freedom to nurse Tom back to health.

The novel closes as Jim and the boys learn that Jim is already a free man, as decreed by the last will and testament of Miss Watson, his former owner. This puts an end to all escape plans and allows Jim to be the one thing that he has always wanted to be, free. Huck also decides to leave and wander on his own, convinced that the civilized world is no place for him.

CENSORSHIP HISTORY

The novel excited controversy from the outset, when Concord (Massachusetts) Public Library banned the book in 1885, charging that the novel was "trash suitable only for the slums." Conventional morality was offended by the street vernacular spoken by Jim and Huck, as well as by their coarse behavior. Denver Public Library banned the novel in 1902, and Brooklyn (New York) Public Library removed it from the children's room on the charge that "Huck not only itched but he scratched, and that he said sweat when he should have said perspiration." In 1930, Soviet border guards confiscated the novel, along with *The Adventures of Tom Sawyer.*

In the United States, the furor quieted down for five decades, as the novel became an American classic and a mainstay of school reading lists. A new challenge emerged in 1957, when the National Association for the Advancement of Colored People protested the racist aspects of the book and demanded that it be removed from high schools in New York City. African-American author Ralph Ellison noted that Huck's friendship with Jim demeaned the stature of black males, because the adolescent Huck is portrayed as equal or superior to the adult Jim in decision-making capability. In 1969, Miami Dade (Florida) Junior College removed the novel from the required reading list, charging that the book inhibited learning in black students by creating an emotional block.

In 1973, the Scott, Foresman publishing company yielded to the demands of school officials in Tennessee and prepared a version of the novel that omitted material to which officials objected. The version omits the passage in Chapter 18 in which the young men of the Grangerford family toast their parents each morning with alcohol. It appears in *The United States in Literature*, a textbook distributed and used nationally.

The most frequent objection to the novel has been its language in reference to African Americans. Yielding to pressures from school districts across the nation, textbook publishers up to 1975 met challenges by substituting euphemisms for the term *nigger*. Scott, Foresman rewrote passages to eliminate the word, Singer replaced the term with *slave*, and McGraw-Hill replaced the term with *servant*. In a 1975 dissertation, Dorothy Weathersby found that Ginn and Company was the only textbook publisher to retain the word, but their textbook included an essay by Lionel Trilling to explain the need to include the word in the novel.

The novel has been frequently banned or challenged by school districts for its language, particularly its racial references and the use of the slur *nigger*. A significant number of such challenges have come from well-educated, middle-class, African-American parents who wish to prevent their children from exposure to such insulting references. The Winnetka (Illinois) school district challenged the novel as being racist in 1976, as did school districts in Warrington, Pennsylvania, in 1981; Davenport, Iowa, in 1981; Fairfax County, Virginia, in 1982; Houston, Texas, in 1982; State College, Pennsylvania, in 1983; Springfield, Illinois, in 1984; and Waukegan, Illinois, in 1984.

In 1988, Rockford (Illinois) public schools removed the book from their required reading list because it contained the word *nigger*. Berrien Springs (Michigan) High School challenged the novel that same year, while Caddo Parish (Louisiana) removed the novel from both its school libraries and required reading lists, charging that it contained racially offensive passages. The following year, the novel was challenged at Sevierville County (Tennessee) High School due to perceived racial slurs and the use of ungrammatical dialect.

The 1990s brought new challenges and continued antagonism to the novel. Citing derogatory references to African Americans, parents challenged its inclusion on the supplemental English reading list in Erie (Pennsylvania) High School in 1990. That same year, the novel was challenged as being racist in Plano (Texas) Independent School District.

In 1991, citing the repeated use of the word *nigger*, parents in Mesa (Arizona) Unified School District challenged inclusion of the novel in the curriculum and claimed that such language damaged the self-esteem of young African Americans. For the same reason, that year the novel was removed from the required reading list in the Terrebone Parish public schools in Houma, Louisiana. Also in 1991, it was temporarily removed from the Portage (Michigan) curriculum after African-American parents charged that the portrayal of Jim and other African Americans made their children "uncomfortable."

In 1992, the school superintendent of Kinston (North Carolina) School District removed the book from the middle school in the belief that the students were too young to read a work containing the word *nigger*. Concern with the same word, as well as additional "offensive and racist language," motivated a 1992 challenge to including the novel on the required reading list in Modesto (California) High School. In 1993, challengers charged in the Carlisle (Pennsylvania) school system that the racial slurs in the novel were offensive to both African-American and Caucasian students. In contrast to other areas, the Lewisville (Texas) school board retained the novel on school reading lists in 1994, despite challenges of its racism. The most comprehensive objection to the novel regarded its use in English classes at Taylor County (Butler, Georgia) High School in 1994, when challengers not only claimed that it contained racial slurs and improper grammar, but it also did not reject slavery.

Also in 1994, in Enid, Oklahoma, a group called the Southern Heights Ministerial Alliance challenged the novel as required reading in American literature classes and brought the issue to the textbook review committee.

The committee recommended that the book be restricted to students taking advanced-placement American Literature classes, a move that the school board soundly rejected in a 7-0 vote. Instead, the board passed a resolution to keep the book in the curriculum and enacted a measure to require teacher training to be led by Harvard professor and African-American Twain scholar Jocelyn Chadwick.

In 2002, an African-American student in Portland, Oregon, challenged the use of the novel as a required reading and claimed that he was offended by the use of ethnic slurs in the novel. The board considered the challenge and voted to retain the novel.

In 2003, parents of students in the Community High School in Normal, Illinois, sophomore literature class challenged use of the novel in the curriculum. They asserted that the novel is degrading to African Americans. The school board considered the challenge and decided to retain the novel in the curriculum and to offer students an alternative. Students who do not feel comfortable reading *Adventures of Huckleberry Finn* are given the option of reading *The Chosen* by Chaim Potok.

In October 2003, an African-American student and her grandmother in Renton, Washington, complained to school officials that the novel degraded all African Americans and their culture. Calista Phair and Beatrice Clark objected to the use of the word *nigger*, and they contended that the book "reinforces institutional racism." The novel was not required reading, but it was on the supplemental reading list for approved assignments to 11th-grade students in the three high schools in the Renton district; thus, students who objected to being assigned the book could be excused from reading it and were permitted to select an alternate work. Phair and Clark demanded the removal of the work throughout the district. In response, school administrators ordered the book removed from the readings lists in the three high schools and asked teachers to stop teaching it until guidelines could be developed. The district formed a committee of language arts teachers, chaired by Ed Sheppard the district curriculum director, to work with the education chairman of the Seattle branch of the National Association for the Advancement of Colored People (NAACP) to develop guidelines for teaching the novel. The resulting one-half-inch thick book of guidelines was distributed to the teachers and posted on the Renton district Web site. The guidebook included information on the history of the objectionable word and explained the place of Huck Finn in the canon of Western literature, information bolstered by articles from educational journals and diverse sources instructing how to teach the novel. Roy Matheson, a Renton school district spokesperson, said that the district did not ever consider banning the book from the curriculum, because doing so would force the school district to consider eliminating such works as *Black Boy* by Richard Wright or *Narrative of the Life of Frederick Douglass, an American Slave*, which also contain the racial epithet. The novel was reinstated on the supplemental reading list.

The controversy over the N-word and the portrayal of African Americans in the novel has continued. In 2007, African-American parents of students attending St. Louis Park High School in Minneapolis challenged the mandatory reading of *Adventures of Huckleberry Finn* in a 10th-grade honors English class and asked the school to remove the novel from the required reading list. Parents Kenneth and Sylvia Gilbert, the main opponents of the requirement, claimed that they did not want the book banned from the school, but they did not want it to be required classroom reading. Mr. Gilbert told school officials that the novel is "a racial issue," and the use of the racial epithet "brings you to a lower level. . . . It makes children feel less equal in the classroom." In response to the parents' protests, a 12-member committee composed of parents, teachers, a community member, and a school administrator reviewed the request and reevaluated the book for classroom use. They determined that the novel should remain. Students at the high school actively opposed removal of the book. Some created posters saying "Save Huck Finn" and others posted a Web site that supported retention of the novel. In a letter to parents, St. Louis Park High School principal Robert Laney wrote that the committee acknowledged that some of the language in the novel is offensive but determined "the literary value of the book outweighed the negative aspect of the language employed." Parents appealed the decision, but the district retained the book as required reading.

The responses to complaints regarding the racial stereotyping and racial epithets in the novel have changed significantly in the last two decades. Rather than remove the book permanently—or for long periods of time—from the classroom or library until the furor has abated, school districts have chosen to place a hold on teaching the novel while assembling committees that are representative of the community to formulate plans to retain the work while making it an effective and acceptable teaching tool. A recent widely publicized challenge provides an example. In 2008, a group of African-American parents in Manchester, Connecticut, challenged the use of the novel as required reading in Manchester High School. The school administrators asked teachers to stop teaching the book until the district could devise a series of seminars that would provide them with the tools to deal with the issues of race before bringing the book back into the classroom. The seminars were presented with the assistance of Reverend John Selders, of the Amistad United Church of Christ, who worked with teachers to handle class discussions about the book. School administrators viewed the seminars as a means of putting the book into perspective and of providing the opportunity to "create a dialogue on race, white privilege, satire and stereotyping." The assistant school superintendent Anne Richardson praised the retention of the book as providing "a very good platform to talk about racial issues," and Manchester High School principal Kevin O'Donnell expressed the belief that the seminars would provide students "with a new opportunity to have those courageous conversations about race and all of the elements that surround race, as difficult as they might be." Reverend Selders was less expansive in his praise of the results of the committee and noted that some teachers "may need to do some more work," although he expressed optimism that the new approach to the novel would be beneficial and justified its retention.

In February 2011, NewSouth Books, a publisher based in Alabama, released a new and more politically correct edition of Twain's classic work in which the word *nigger* was replaced by *slave* and the word *Injun* by *Indian*. Auburn University professor Alan Gribben, who edited both *Adventures of Huckleberry Finn* and *The Adventures of Tom Sawyer* and combined both works into a single volume entitled *Mark Twain's Adventures of Tom Sawyer and Huckleberry Finn: The NewSouth Edition*, claimed in interviews with various news media that his work is not an attempt to censor Mark Twain. He said that he produced the edited version because he had become increasingly worried in recent years that Twain's works were being removed from reading lists in schools because of the 219 uses of the word *nigger* and other racial slurs and felt that his version would revive interest in teaching the work at the high school level.

In an interview with the *New York Times*, Gribben claimed that he had not changed the essential character of Twain's work. "I'm by no means sanitizing Mark Twain," he said. "The sharp social critiques are in there. The humor is intact. I just had the idea to get us away from obsessing about this one word, and just let the stories stand alone."

Reactions to the revised edition have been diverse. Some critics have seen the move as unconscionable censorship or bowdlerization, while others contend that the modifications to the novel will make it more accessible to a wider audience. To date, the planned print run is only 7,500 copies, and Gribben admits that no school districts have expressed plans to reintroduce the book into their curricula because of the revisions. The *New York Times* reported that NewSouth received a large number of negative e-mails after plans for the new edition were announced.

FURTHER READING

Bach, Deborah. "'Huck Finn' Back in Renton; School District Now Provides More Guidance to Teachers." *Seattle Post-Intelligencer*, March 17, 2004, p. B2.

Beam, Alex. "In Other Words . . . , Why Stop with Mark Twain's 'Huckleberry Finn'" *Boston Globe*, January 11, 2011, p. G23.

Bosman, Julie. "Publisher Tinkers with Twain." *New York Times*, January 5, 2011, p. A12.

Bradley, Julia T. "Censoring the School Library: Do Students Have the Right to Read?" *Connecticut Law Review* 10 (Spring 1978): 747–771.

Cloonan, Michele. "The Censorship of the Adventures of Huckleberry Finn." *Top of the News*, Winter 1984, pp. 191–194.

Geller, Evelyn. *Forbidden Books in American Public Libraries, 1876–1939: A Study in Cultural Change*. Westport, Conn.: Greenwood Press, 1984.

Greenlee, Steven. "Sanitized Huck Finn." *Boston Globe*, January 8, 2011, p. G 4.

Leider, Paula. "Does Huck Finn Belong in My Classroom? Reflections of Curricular Choice, Multicultural Education, and Diversity." *Multicultural Education* 13, no. 4 (Summer 2006): 49–50.

Nelson, Randy F. "Banned in Boston and Elsewhere." *The Almanac of American Letters.* Los Altos, Calif.: William Kaufman, 1981.

Newsletter on Intellectual Freedom (May 1969): 52; (July 1976): 87; (September 1976): 116; (November 1981): 162; (January 1982): 11, 18; (May 1982): 101; (July 1982): 126; (September 1982): 171; (January 1984): 11; (May 1984): 72; (July 1984): 121–122; (November 1984): 187; (January 1985): 38; (September 1988): 152–153; (November 1988): 201; (January 1989): 11; (March 1989): 43; (May 1989): 94; (January 1991): 17–18; (March 1991): 43–45, 64; (May 1991): 90–92; (July 1992): 126; (September 1992): 140; (May 1993): 73; (May 1994): 99–100; (March 1995): 42; (July 2000): 125; (January 2003): 11–12; (May 2004): 91; (January 2009): 22–3).

People For the American Way. *Attacks on the Freedom to Learn, 1990–91.* Washington, D.C.: People For the American Way, 1991.

Reichman, Henry. *Censorship and Selection: Issues and Answers for Schools.* Chicago: American Library Association; Arlington, Va.: American Association of School Administrators, 1993. A joint publication.

Teachout, Terry. "Unpleasant Truths." *Wall Street Journal,* January 16, 2011, p. A22.

Tucker, Cynthia. "The Error of Editing History." *The Atlanta Journal-Constitution,* January 16, 2011. p. A22.

Wascoe, Dan, and *Minneapolis Star Tribune.* "'N-word' Fight over Classic: Couple Want 'Huck Finn' Off Reading List." *The Record* (Bergen County, N.J.), March 23, 2007, p. A20.

Weathersby, Dorothy T. *Censorship of Literature Textbooks in Tennessee: A Study of the Commission, Publishers, Teachers, and Textbooks.* Ed.D. dissertation, University of Tennessee, 1975.

THE ADVENTURES OF TOM SAWYER

Author: Mark Twain (Samuel Langhorne Clemens)
Original date and place of publication: 1876, United States
Original publisher: Self-published
Literary form: Novel

SUMMARY

The novel is a first-person account of the life of young Tom Sawyer along the banks of the Mississippi before the Civil War.

When the novel begins, Tom is missing, and his Aunt Polly is worriedly searching for him. She is furious when she learns that he has been swimming all day instead of attending school. As punishment, Tom must whitewash a fence on Saturday, instead of playing as usual, but he tricks his friends into doing the job.

After Tom shows off "his" work on the fence, Aunt Polly agrees to let him play for the remainder of the day. Tom later spots Becky Thatcher and attracts her attention with flamboyant antics, earning a flower from her as his reward.

In catechism class the next morning, Tom receives a Bible for having enough tickets to indicate that he memorized 2,000 passages in the Bible. But

Tom cheated and traded various items with friends in order to amass the correct number of tickets. When the Sunday School teacher asks him to answer a Scripture question, he is unable to do so. Later that morning, Tom creates chaos in church when his pinch bug attacks a wandering dog.

On Monday, Tom once again attempts to avoid school, but Aunt Polly forces him to go. On the way, Tom meets Huckleberry Finn, and the two plan to take the corpse of a cat to the cemetery at midnight in order to cure warts. Once Tom reaches school, he is automatically punished for his tardiness and made to sit in the female section of the schoolroom. Tom sits next to Becky, but she acts repelled by his presence. As soon as they can, Tom and Joe Harper leave and take the rest of the day off.

That night Huck and Tom go to the cemetery with the cat. While there, the two boys see Dr. Robinson, Injun Joe, and Muff Potter unearthing a recently interred body. The three men argue and struggle, leaving Muff Potter unconscious, after which Injun Joe stabs Dr. Robinson to death and leaves. The frightened boys swear never to tell anyone about the murder, even when they hear the next day that Injun Joe has named Muff Potter as Dr. Robinson's slayer.

Tom, Huck, and Joe Harper decide to become pirates for a short while, so they run away to Jackson's Island. Days go by, and the boys continue to enjoy their carefree, adventurous life, while the townspeople frantically search for them. After their efforts prove fruitless, the townspeople legally declare the boys dead and plan a memorial service. On a brief return to his house to leave his Aunt Polly a note, Tom hears that there will be church services the following Sunday for the repose of the three boys' souls. The three guests of honor interrupt the services and casually stroll down the main aisle of the church.

The boys agree to retire from piracy and to return home. Back in school, Tom continues his courtship of Becky, finally winning her admiration by taking the blame and the punishment for something that she does. Tom and the others are able to have their revenge when, on the last day of school, Tom humiliates the schoolmaster by exposing his bald head to the entire school.

When Muff Potter is placed on trial for the murder of Dr. Robinson, Tom is called as a surprise witness. He tells the court that it was not Muff Potter but Injun Joe who ruthlessly murdered Dr. Robinson, and Injun Joe escapes the court and imprisonment by jumping through a window and fleeing.

Days later, Tom and Huck are exploring an abandoned house when two men enter, one of whom is Injun Joe disguised as a Spaniard. The men take gold and silver coins to use at a tavern, and the boys overhear Injun Joe state that he isn't going to leave the area until he can take revenge upon the boys.

At a picnic a few days later, Tom and Becky become lost in McDougal's cave. Later that night, Huck overhears Injun Joe plot to attack the Widow Douglas in retaliation for a whipping that he received from her late husband. After Huck informs Mr. Jones of the plot, Injun Joe and his companion are quickly driven off. Huck then becomes ill, but the Widow Douglas takes care of him.

The townspeople discover that Tom and Becky are missing and search for the two children. In the cave, Tom sees Injun Joe, who is in hiding. The two children finally find a back opening to the cave and return to town. After hearing about Tom and Becky's ordeal, Judge Thatcher orders the cave sealed, unintentionally trapping Injun Joe. When Tom learns that the cave has been sealed, he tells Judge Thatcher that Injun Joe is inside, and Injun Joe's body is later found near the cave entrance.

Tom and Huck return to the cave to recover $12,000 of treasure, which is divided between the boys and invested for them. Tom returns to live with Aunt Polly, and Huck is taken into the Douglas home, to be educated in the moral lifestyle by the Widow Douglas. He agrees to this ordeal and seems placated as long as he can join Tom's newly established robber gang.

CENSORSHIP HISTORY

The novel was censored from its first publication, although it has not provoked as much controversy as Twain's later novel, *Adventures of Huckleberry Finn*. In 1876, Brooklyn (New York) Public Library banned the book from the children's room; that same year, Denver (Colorado) Public Library removed it from the library shelves. Five decades later, in 1930, guards at the USSR border confiscated the novel, along with *Adventures of Huckleberry Finn*.

The novel proceeded to earn a reputation as an American literary classic and remained unchallenged until 1985, when education officials in London removed the novel from all school libraries after determining that the book was "racist" and "sexist." In 1990, the novel was challenged, along with *Adventures of Huckleberry Finn*, as being racist in the Plano (Texas) Independent School District. In the O'Fallon (Illinois) schools in 1992, parents challenged the inclusion of the book on the required reading list and charged that the use of the word *nigger* was degrading and offensive to black students. They won the right to request that an alternative reading choice be offered. In 1994, parents of seventh-grade students in the West Chester (Pennsylvania) schools claimed that the book contained an abundance of racially charged language, and it was removed from the curriculum.

FURTHER READING

Burress, Lee. *Battle of the Books: Literary Censorship in the Public Schools, 1950–1985.* Metuchen, N.J.: Scarecrow Press, 1989.

Geller, Evelyn. *Forbidden Books in American Public Libraries, 1876–1939: A Study in Cultural Change.* Westport, Conn.: Greenwood Press, 1984.

Newsletter on Intellectual Freedom (September 1985): 156; (January 1991): 18; (March 1991): 45–46; (May 1991): 92; (May 1992): 97; (September 1994): 152.

AND TANGO MAKES THREE

Authors: Justin Richardson and Peter Parnell; illustrated by Henry Cole
Original date and place of publication: 2005, United States
Original publisher: Simon & Schuster Children's Books
Literary form: Children's picture book

SUMMARY

And Tango Makes Three is a charming children's picture book based on the true story of two chinstrap penguins living in the Central Park Zoo who adopt a rejected egg, work together to hatch it, and raise the little girl chick together. The book's watercolor illustrations depict the activities of the two adult penguins, whom the zookeepers admit are "a little different." Roy and Silo do everything together. They cuddle, they play together, they bow to each other, and they look lovingly at each other. "They sang to each other. And swam together. Wherever Roy went, Silo went too."

The two male penguins also share a nest that they realize is very different from the nests of other penguin couples, because their nest is empty. They watch as female penguins sit on their nests and hatch fertilized eggs, and they wait futilely for their nest to fill. The illustrations portray the two bewildered penguins craning their necks toward their nest, which was "nice, but a little empty." After a long while, they drag an egg-sized rock to their nest and try to hatch it, but they are unsuccessful.

The zookeeper watches as Roy and Silo try desperately to hatch the rock, caring for it and keeping it warm, and he sees their frustration and sadness when they are unsuccessful. Once he realizes what they have been trying to do, he helps them. He finds a female penguin with two fertilized eggs, one that she is ignoring, and places the egg in Roy and Silo's nest. The two immediately tend to the egg, taking turns to keep it warm and safe, until their penguin girl chick emerges to greet the two loving fathers who "knew just what to do." The zookeeper gives the baby penguin her name, "We'll call her Tango, because it takes two to make a Tango." The illustrations both on the cover and in the book show the happy family of three, the two loving male penguins and their downy chick Tango, "the only penguin in the Central Park Zoo with two daddies."

CENSORSHIP HISTORY

And Tango Makes Three was the most frequently challenged book in the United States in 2006, and its presence in school and public libraries continues to create controversy. Parents demanding its removal have labeled the book "brainwashing" and condemned what one parent in Lodi, California, characterized as its "homosexual story line that has been sugarcoated with cute penguins." The president of the California-based Campaign for Children and Families, Randy Thomasson, told a *Los Angeles Times* reporter that

"The huge majority of parents would avoid this book if they knew it was brainwashing their children to support and experiment with homosexual behavior." Marketed toward children ages 4 through 8, the book has also received extensive praise from educators and parents who endorse its role in opening up a discussion of diverse lifestyles and who view it in a positive light. Christine Jenkins, associate professor at the Graduate School of Library and Information Science at the University of Illinois, asserted in an interview with a reporter for the *St. Louis Post-Dispatch*, "It's different from many other gay-themed children's books because it was published by the mainstream press, and homosexuality isn't a source of conflict." Instead, "The characters are just gay and living their lives. The plot doesn't grapple with being homosexual as do many books for youths of the same nature."

In 2006, parents of students attending Shiloh Elementary School in Shiloh, Illinois, questioned the "appropriateness of the subject matter" and asked school officials to move the book from the regular shelves in the school library to a restricted section "for mature issues." Lilly Del Pinto, the parent who first complained, told school officials that she was surprised by the content. "When it came to the point where the zookeeper saw that the penguins were in love I redirected [my daughter]. That was the end of the story for her." Del Pinto and "a group of like-minded parents" approached the school board and asked to have the book removed to a separate shelf that required parental permission before checkout. School Superintendent Jennifer Filyaw opposed the plan but did concede that "parents could restrict their children from checking out certain titles, and this request would appear when the librarian scans the student's card."

The book did not fare as well that same year in two Rolling Hills Consolidated Library branches in Savannah and St. Joseph, Missouri, after two parents expressed concern about its content. The library director Barbara Read moved the book from the children's fiction to the children's nonfiction section after having read the book and "consulted with zoologists about penguin behavior." The American Library Association's *Newsletter on Intellectual Freedom* reported in its May 2006 issue that, despite Read's claim that she moved the book because it tells a true story, she originally told a local newspaper that she had reshelved *And Tango Makes Three* in juvenile nonfiction because "Given that patrons rarely browse the nonfiction section, there was less of a chance that the book would 'blindside' someone."

In December 2006, Peter Gorman, the superintendent of schools in Charlotte, North Carolina, ordered the district school libraries to remove the book after several parents voiced concerns and after he received an e-mail from Republican county commissioner Bill James. The commissioner, who had read an article online about the book, told a reporter, "I am opposed to any book that promotes a homosexual lifestyle to elementary school students as normal." James contacted the school superintendent and on November 30, 2006, top school officials sent a memo to principals and media specialists in the district explaining the decision to ban the book. "First, it is a picture book that focuses on homosexuality. Second, we did not feel that such information was vital to primary students. Next, we did not believe the book would stimulate growth in ethical standards, and the book is too controversial." Parents who opposed the ban placed pressure on school officials to reconsider their decision and to let a committee review the decision, but the book would remain inaccessible until the committee had reached a decision and their recommendation would be accepted by the school officials.

In 2007, Johanna Habeisen, a school librarian in Southwick, Massachusetts, received an intimidating letter from her principal Kimberley Saso after a substitute teacher took *And Tango Makes Three* to Saso and questioned its appropriateness. In her letter, Principal Saso warned Habeisen against use of the book. "Hopefully you will take this matter seriously and refrain from disseminating information that supports alternative styles of living. Further infractions may result in discipline up to and including suspension and/or termination of employment." *School Library Journal* reported that Saso considered the book "questionable for young readers." She said, "I'm not against alternate lifestyle. I'd love that to be available for counselors that work with families that maybe have this situation. But in this society here, in this town anyways, I don't know if it's our job to expose children." Ms. Habeisen said in the same article that after the challenge to *And Tango Makes Three*, she began "pulling everything that had any reference to families with two moms and dads." She remarked that the irony was not lost on her that such a challenge could occur in Massachusetts, a state in which same-sex marriage has been legal since 2004. In March 2007, the *Newsletter on Intellectual Freedom* reported that the Charlotte-Mecklenburg school district received extensive negative international news coverage after the ban. After the reporters working for the *Charlotte Observer* questioned the ban, Superintendent Gorman returned copies of the book to the school libraries and determined that "the book will be reviewed only if parents ask for its removal."

Parents have had strong negative reactions to the book that are not always shared by school and library officials. In April 2007, Stephanie Bramasco, the parent of a 17-month-old child in Lodi, California, spoke at a public meeting and asked the Lodi Public Library board of directors to remove *And Tango Makes Three* after she admitted that she did not check the book out but "had a stronger urge to present the issue to the board of directors than her friend did." Bramasco charged that the illustration of the two adult penguins and the baby penguin on the book cover was deceptive because it "does not indicate the adult penguins are a same-sex couple." She further admitted that she "struggles with the idea of explaining to her 17-month-old the reasons why two male penguins would be unable to hatch an egg on their own or why two male penguins would have such an intimate relationship together." In a 4-1 vote, the library board of directors refused the request to ban the book.

Parents in Chico, California, in 2009 complained that *And Tango Makes Three* is offensive, and three challenged shelving of the book in the library among picture books and easy-to-read children's literature. After the district received formal complaints from parents at two elementary schools in the Chico Unified School District, officials formed a review committee composed of parents, teachers, librarians, and school administrators, which decided unanimously to retain the books on their current shelves. Also in 2009, in Prince Frederick, Maryland, parents complained to the Calvert County Board of Library Trustees and asked that it be removed. Beth Bubser, a parent who filed a formal complaint, expressed concern that there "is no warning on the book that it is about same-sex parents." The library board reviewed the complaint and the book and decided to keep the book in the children's section, a decision that Bubser and three other mothers appealed. The women expressed dismay that the book would remain in the library and "expressed concerns about their young children being exposed to information contrary to their values, such as homosexuality." Patricia Hoffman, the library director, was supported in her decision by library trustees who concluded that the job of a library is to disseminate information and not "take the role of a parent." As library trustee Laura Holbrook stated about segregating books such as *And Tango Makes Three*, such actions would be the equivalent of passing value judgments of same-sex families and "would censor what readers could easily find in the library."

In Ankeny, Iowa, school board members voted 6-1 to keep the book in circulation at two elementary school libraries. At the same meeting, the board also voted to develop a new process for selecting materials for the school libraries. Controversy began in the school district when a kindergarten child checked out the book from the East Elementary School library, where it was in open circulation. Parents Cindy and James Dacus asked the school board to place the book in "a parents-only section" and argued that it "normalizes homosexuality for children who are too young to understand the risky lifestyle." The challenge attracted the attention of national advocacy groups that sent letters to the district, urging officials to keep the book available to students. Dr. Justin Richardson, a coauthor of the book, expressed skepticism about the suggestion made by Ankeny school superintendent Matthew Wendt and the school board to institute a new process for selecting school library materials. While admitting that he did not know the superintendent's intentions, Richardson told a reporter for the *Des Moines Register*, "It's more troubling to think a school might screen out a book because a parent might complain about it in the future. That could really limit the kinds of books that children have access to."

FURTHER READING

"'And Tango Makes Three' Prompts Serious Challenge in Massachusetts School." *School Library Journal*. Available online. URL: http://www.schoollibraryjournal. com/index.asp?layout=articlePrint&articleID=CA6440187. Accessed January 6, 2010.

Levantis, Angie, and *St. Louis Post Dispatch*. "Children's Book on Gay Penguins Has Parents Concerned." *The Record* (Bergen County, N.J.), December 8, 2006, p. A27.

McClatchy Newspapers. "Schools Chief Bans Book on Penguins." Available online. URL: http://www.boston.com/news/nation/articles/2006/12/20/schools_chief_bans_book_on_penguins?mode=PF. Accessed January 15, 2010.

"Success Stories: Libraries." *Newsletter on Intellectual Freedom* 56, no. 2 (March 2007): 71–72.

"Success Stories: Libraries." *Newsletter on Intellectual Freedom* 56, no. 4 (July 2007): 163–164.

"Success Stories: Libraries." *Newsletter on Intellectual Freedom* 57, no. 3 (May 2008): 115–117.

"Success Stories: Libraries." *Newsletter on Intellectual Freedom* 58, no. 1 (January 2009): 21–22.

"Success Stories: Libraries." *Newsletter on Intellectual Freedom* 58, no. 2 (March 2009): 55–56.

Swanson, Stevenson. "Penguin Papas Lead a List of Literary Controversies." *Los Angeles Times*, October 7, 2007, p. A20.

ANNE FRANK: THE DIARY OF A YOUNG GIRL

Author: Anne Frank
Original date and place of publication: 1947, The Netherlands
Original publisher: Contact
Literary form: Diary

SUMMARY

Anne Frank: The Diary of a Young Girl is a compilation of the notebooks and papers left behind by a 15-year-old Jewish girl, Anne Frank, when she and her family were taken from their hiding place in Amsterdam by German soldiers during the Nazi occupation of the Netherlands in World War II. The hiding place was a "secret annex," a group of rooms at the top and back of a building that served as a warehouse and office for a Dutch-owned business. Those hiding remained quiet by day, while business was conducted in the lower part of the building, but they moved freely at night when the building was deserted. After the Frank family was taken, members of the Dutch family that had sheltered them gathered the papers and hid them in a desk without reading them. When Otto Frank, Anne's father and the only one of the family to survive the war, returned from the death camps, he took the papers and sought to publish them. He would thus fulfill his late daughter's dream for her work and make her live again through her writing.

The final published diary is the combination of Anne's original text with the later edited version that she began, modifying her earlier, more childish phrasing. She also used pseudonyms for the other occupants of the annex, as well as for their protectors, to prevent hurt feelings in instances in which she is critical of them. She writes at several points in the diary that she wants it to live on long after her death and would like it published as *Het Achterhuis* (The house behind), the title under which the work first appeared.

The small, red-checkered diary, which Anne named "Kitty," was a present from her father on her 13th birthday, June 12, 1942, less than a month before they would enter the annex. She began the diary on her birthday, writing in it and in notebooks for the family's 25 months in hiding, from July 5, 1942, through August 1, 1944, three days before Gestapo sergeant Silverbauer and four soldiers broke in and took them away. In the diary, Anne followed the course of the war and recorded her hopes, dreams, fears, and desires, as well as her observations of daily life. The increasingly bad news brought by their protectors, as well as what they heard on the English radio, also prompted Anne's reflections.

Anne's observations about her family as well as the dentist, Mr. Dussel, and the Van Daan family (a father, mother, and 16-year-old son), who share the annex with the Franks, are followed in the diary. She irritably records Mrs. Van Daan's attempts to flirt with Otto Frank, noting that "she strokes his face and hair, pulls her skirt right up, and makes so-called witty remarks," and registers her relief that her father "doesn't play ball." She also records the idiosyncrasies of the other inhabitants, as well as her coldness toward her mother. The reader also learns that the three young people managed to read a lot during their stay and even completed a correspondence shorthand course. Anne also manages to maintain her sense of humor as conditions worsen, remarking at one point when food becomes scarce, "Whoever wants to follow a slimming course should stay in the 'Secret Annexe'!"

CENSORSHIP HISTORY

Censorship of *Anne Frank: The Diary of a Young Girl* began with its initial publication in the Netherlands. Anxious to spare the feelings of their protectors and the memory of the other occupants, Otto Frank excised details of the squabbling among the occupants of the annex and sections in which Anne complained about the selfishness or insensitivity of others. Because she viewed the diary as her private writing, Anne frequently expressed unadorned thoughts and concerns and used the diary as a means of venting her frustrations with the situation. Her father removed such passages without changing significantly the overall representations of the others or their relationships.

Once Otto Frank sought a publisher, additional censorship was required. The Dutch publisher, Contact, required the removal of certain passages that the editors viewed as "tasteless" or "unseemly." These included Anne's references to her and her sister's menstruation. Anne's growing sexual curiosity was also deemed unacceptable, despite the naturalness of such curiosity in an adolescent. Therefore, a passage in which she recalls a friend's developing breasts and muses about wanting to touch them was removed. The publisher also asked that Otto Frank delete all "offensive" remarks made by Anne about her mother.

In 1950, the German publishing firm of Lambert Schneider commissioned a German translation, and additional censorship occurred. The Critical Edition notes that material that would have been especially offensive to German readers was removed. One such passage written by Anne related the rule in the annex that everyone was required "to speak softly at all times, in any civilized language, therefore not in German," which Lambert Schneider changed to "All civilized languages . . . but softly."

The 1952 publication of the diary in England restored most of the excised material. More recent challenges have focused on Anne's growing sexual awareness. In a January 5, 1944, entry Anne recollects sleeping with a girlfriend and having "a strong desire to kiss her," which she did. She states further that she was terribly curious about the other girl's body, "for she had always kept it hidden from me. I asked her whether, as proof of our friendship, we should feel one another's breasts, but she refused. I go into ecstasies every time I see the naked figure of a woman, such as Venus, for example. . . . If only I had a girl friend!" At the same time, she develops a crush on Peter Van Daan, who shows her "the male organs" of a cat, and with whom she experiences her first ardent kiss on the mouth, questioning if she "should have yielded so soon." She also observes increased flirting between the dentist and Mrs. Van Daan and notes that "Dussel is beginning to get longings for women."

In 1982, parents in Wise County, Virginia, challenged the use of the book in school and asserted that Anne's discussion of sexual matters was "inappropriate" and "offensive" and that the criticism of her mother and of the other adults "undermines adult authority." Others have objected to the discussion of "the mistreatment of the Jewish people," and one parent of Arab ancestry objected to the portrayal of a Jewish girl. In 1983, four members of the Alabama Textbook Commission wanted to reject the title for use in the schools because it was "a real downer."

FURTHER READING

Frank, Otto. "Introduction." In *Anne Frank. The Diary of a Young Girl: The Definitive Edition*, edited by Otto Frank and Mirjam Pressler. New York: Doubleday, 1995.
Newsletter on Intellectual Freedom (March 1983): 39.
Wisse, Ruth. "A Romance of the Secret Annex." *New York Times Book Review*, July 2, 1989, p. 2.

THE AUTOBIOGRAPHY OF BENJAMIN FRANKLIN

Author: Benjamin Franklin
Original date and place of publication: 1791, France
Original publisher: Buisson
Literary form: Autobiography

SUMMARY

The Autobiography of Benjamin Franklin is an honest and sometimes lusty chronicle of a man who lived life fully. Franklin originally began to write his memoirs for his son, William Franklin, from whom he later became estranged. The *Autobiography* relates the author's rise from poverty as the youngest of 17 children of a soap and candle maker through his apprenticeship as a printer and to his role as Pennsylvania's agent in England in 1757. Franklin provides details regarding his constant struggle to improve himself in education and in business and explains his passion for improvement, of both self and the public. The *Autobiography* ends when Franklin's activities reach an international scope, and he becomes a truly public figure.

Despite the emphasis upon moral improvement in much of the *Autobiography*, Franklin also admits to human failings. He acknowledges that the "hard-to-be-governed passion of youth had hurried me frequently into intrigues with low women that fell in my way, which were attended with some expense and great inconvenience, besides a continual risk to my health by a distemper." He also admits that he has been the victim of passionate bouts of indulgence and that he has not always stood by his beliefs. Instead, he changed "opinions which I had thought right but found otherwise."

In one episode, Franklin speaks of his hasty departure from Boston in 1723 and writes that he left people to speculate that his exit was because he "got a naughty Girl with Child." In a later episode, Franklin recounts the incident that caused a breach with a friend named James Ralph, who left behind a wife and child when he traveled to England with Franklin to find work. Ralph began an affair with a young Englishwoman, Mrs. T., and they had a child. Unable to find work teaching in London, Ralph left to teach in a country school and asked Franklin to look after Mrs. T. Franklin lent her money and responded to her frequent calls for assistance. On one of those visits, he "attempted familiarities, which she repulsed with proper resentment," and later told Ralph.

The *Autobiography* presents a very human view of a well-known historical figure.

CENSORSHIP HISTORY

Franklin's *Autobiography* is one of the most frequently expurgated books ever published in America, and it was censored from its first publication. In 1789, Franklin sent copies of the manuscript to friends Benjamin Vaughn and Guillaume Le Veillard, the mayor of Passy, France, asking for their advice. After Franklin died in 1790, a pirated edition of the book appeared in France. With the goal of publishing a more "acceptable" version, Franklin's grandson, William Temple Franklin, edited the French version, which he published in 1818 as part of the comprehensive *Works*. This edition made 1,200 changes in the phrasing of the original *Autobiography*, with the expressed aim of modernizing the language for the 19th century. Instead, the changes altered Benjamin

Franklin's sometimes salty tone and word choice, providing a vastly different view.

In 1886, Houghton Mifflin published an edition of the *Autobiography* that included the story of James Ralph's affair with the young woman but removed Franklin's admission of a sexual advance. Instead, the editor inserted this explanation of the strained relationship between the old friends: "In the mean time other circumstances made a breach." In 1888, Ginn & Company removed the entire episode. Houghton Mifflin retained the expurgated account in its 1892 edition, but the editor, Middlebury College professor Julian Abernethy, changed the substituted statement to read, "In the mean time another matter which gave offense made a breach." The publishers justified these and similar changes in nearly a dozen editions on the grounds that they were meant for high school students, who must be protected.

Franklin published more overtly bawdy works that earned the approval of his peers but which are not frequently found among suggested readings. In his "Advice to a Young Man on the Choice of a Mistress," Franklin suggests that more pleasure can be found with an older woman than with a younger because "regarding what is below the Girdle, it is impossible of two Women to tell an old one from a young one" and "They [old women] are so grateful!" In "Polly Baker's Speech," printed in *Gentleman's Magazine* in 1747, he purports to speak as a New England woman who defends herself for being brought to trial, yet again, for having another illegitimate child. Franklin takes flatulence as his subject in "To the Royal Academy at Brussels," in which he parodies scientific reports in the suggestion that chemical additives to food might make "Wind from bowels" less offensive and puns using the slang term *fart*.

As Chief Judge Clarke noted in *Roth v. United States*, 345 U.S. 476 (1957), the discussed works by Franklin "which a jury could reasonably find 'obscene,' according to the judge's instructions in the case at bar" would also have subjected a person to prosecution if sent through the mails in 1957 and "to punishment under the federal obscenity statute." The judge further noted that Thomas Jefferson wrote approvingly of "Polly Baker's Speech" and that James Madison not only praised Franklin's humor but also wrote similarly Rabelaisian anecdotes. That Franklin is popularly known as "the father of the Post Office" (he was designated postmaster general by the First Continental Congress) is ironic, because his own works, with their tongue-in-cheek sexual references, would have been considered too obscene to mail according to federal statutes such as the Comstock Act, which applied to such matters until recent years.

FURTHER READING

Haney, Robert W. *Comstockery in America: Patterns of Censorship and Control.* Boston: Beacon Press, 1960.

Larabee, Leonard W., ed. *The Autobiography of Benjamin Franklin.* New Haven, Conn.: Yale University Press, 1964.

Padover, Saul Kussiel. *The Complete Jefferson.* New York: Duell, Sloan & Pearce, 1943.

————. *The Complete Madison*. New York: Harper & Brothers, 1953.

Perrin, Noel. *Dr. Bowdler's Legacy: A History of Expurgated Books in England and America*. Boston: David R. Godine, 1992.

Van Doren, Carl. *Ben Franklin*. New York: Bramhall House, 1987.

THE AUTOBIOGRAPHY OF MALCOLM X

Author: Malcolm X, with Alex Haley
Original date and place of publication: 1965, United States
Original publisher: Grove Press
Literary form: Autobiography

SUMMARY

The autobiography articulates the anger, the struggle, and the beliefs not only of Malcolm X but also of many African Americans during the 1960s. The work charts the development of the African-American leader from his birth as Malcolm Little in 1925 in Omaha, Nebraska, to his assassination in New York City in 1965. Throughout, he uses fiery rhetoric to preach revolution to African Americans as the only means by which they can achieve full social equality.

As background to his beliefs, he relates the main abuses that occurred in his own life. He recalls his father's adherence to the philosophy of black separatist Marcus Garvey and relates the threats he and his seven siblings endured because of his father's fiery preaching. The work not only chronicles the author's life, but it also presents a sociological examination of the changing roles and growing social and political awareness of African Americans in the United States over four decades.

Particular bitterness is aimed at the welfare system, with its white caseworkers, which strikes a final blow against his family. After their father is murdered, his mother is left a widow with eight children to support, and she works hard at whatever jobs are available to keep the family together. Yet intrusive caseworkers keep a constant watch on the Little home, finally placing the children in foster care and committing Mrs. Little to the state mental hospital at Kalamazoo, Michigan, after she has a mental breakdown when her children are removed. Such images stayed with the author, despite his early efforts to be a "good Negro" and to play the role that white society expected of him.

The autobiography candidly admits that he "tried to be white," like many other lighter-skinned African Americans of his day. From having his hair "conked" (straightened) to buying a "zoot suit," to conducting a five-year affair with a blonde white woman, he allows himself to be "brainwashed." He becomes involved in substantial illegal activity, from running a numbers racket to pimping, selling drugs, and committing robberies. When caught, he claims that he received a much longer jail term than usual because he was involved with a white woman.

At the age of 21, he begins serving seven years in jail, where he learns about the Nation of Islam and becomes a member of the Black Muslim faith. After his conversion and release from prison, the author drops the name Little, his "slave name," and takes "X" to denote an unknown quantity as his last name.

The second half of the autobiography relates the author's efforts to advance the Black Muslim cause, his gradual disillusionment with Black Muslim leader Elijah Muhammad, and his eventual expulsion from the Nation of Islam. He describes his experiences in visiting Africa as well as in the United States, speaking frequently at college campuses and influencing new converts. He also relates the betrayal that he experienced when rumors of an assassination plot surfaced from within the Nation of Islam.

The final three chapters of the work detail the reasons why Malcolm X left the Nation of Islam to form his own organization, Muslim Mosque, Inc. Later called the Organization of Afro-American Unity, its tone was one of militant black nationalism. As threats on his life occurred, the author became certain that the Nation of Islam was the source of the various attacks and threats. In the Epilogue, Alex Haley notes that Malcolm X became convinced that he would be murdered and felt that he would be a martyr "in the cause of brotherhood." His final hope for the autobiography was that it would motivate social action.

CENSORSHIP HISTORY

The Autobiography of Malcolm X was deliberately kept out of classrooms and school libraries when it first appeared because the work openly criticized the role of white society in restricting the achievements and accomplishments of African Americans in the United States. Parents complained that the language was "filthy" and "racist," and the work was viewed for years largely as a radical text that had no place in the high school curriculum, although it enjoyed substantial popularity on college campuses during the 1960s and 1970s. Librarians used "selection" as the criterion for excluding the work from public libraries in predominantly white communities. By the 1980s, the work had come to be viewed as a historical work, and the language and situations, including those in which Malcolm X uses street vernacular and candidly describes the illegal and immoral activities of his early life, seemed commonplace. The 1992 film, *Malcolm X*, directed by Spike Lee, reawakened interest in the book, and high schools added it to their reading lists.

In 1993, parents in the Duval County (Florida) public schools challenged the use of this book in the curriculum, charging that the anti-white racism and the violence espoused by the assassinated Black Muslims leader were disruptive of racial harmony. Citing passages from the book, the parents identified "vulgar" language and "criminal" acts that they felt did not provide decent models for their children to emulate.

The Jacksonville (Florida) school district restricted the availability of the book in the middle school libraries in 1994, after parents complained to the school board that the book was a "how-to" manual for crime and that it represented white people as racist in their views. Only students who had notes from their parents were allowed to take out the book.

FURTHER READING

Carson, Clayborne. *Malcolm X: The FBI File.* New York: Carroll & Graf, 1991.
Dyson, Michael Eric. *Making Malcolm: The Myth and Meaning of Malcolm X.* New York: Oxford University Press, 1994.
Early, Gerald. "Their Malcolm, My Problem." *Harper's* 285 (December 1992): 62–74.
Newsletter for Intellectual Freedom (September 1993): 147; (May 1994): 83.
Vincent, Ted. "The Garveyite Parents of Malcolm X." *Black Scholar* 20 (March 1989): 10–13.

THE BELL JAR

Author: Sylvia Plath
Original date and place of publication: 1963, United Kingdom
Original publisher: William Heinemann Ltd.
Literary form: Novel

SUMMARY

The Bell Jar, first published under the pseudonym of Victoria Lucas, is a thinly veiled autobiographical account of the inner conflict, mental breakdown, and later recovery of a female college student in the 1950s. The novel covers approximately eight months in the life of Esther Greenwood, the 19-year-old narrator, and the plot is divided into three parts. In the first part, Esther embarks on a one-month residence in New York City as a guest editor for the college issue of a fashion magazine. Once in the city, she recalls key incidents from the past, exhibiting her emotional and mental disintegration as the recollections become more real and meaning-filled to her than incidents in her daily life. Her unsatisfactory relationships with men dominate her thoughts, and the reader learns of her disappointing date with Constantin, who makes no attempt to seduce her; the brutal and woman-hating Marco, who beats her up; and her conventional and ordinary college boyfriend Buddy Willard, who wants marriage and a traditional life. At the end of the first part, her last night in New York, Esther throws all her clothes off the hotel roof in a mock ceremony that reveals her disorientation.

In the second part, covering chapters 10 through 13, Esther's psychological deterioration continues as she returns home to see the "white, shining, identical clap-board houses with their interstices of well-groomed green

[that] proceeded past, one bar after another in a large but escape-proof cage." Increasingly depressed, Esther cannot work or sleep, and she refuses to wash her hair or to change her clothes. Shock treatments deepen her depression and increase her obsession with death and suicide. At the end of this part, Esther visits her father's grave, then crawls beneath her house and consumes sleeping pills until she becomes unconscious.

The third section of the novel, chapters 14 through 20, details Esther's slow and painful recovery after the suicide attempt. She resists all efforts to help her when first hospitalized in the psychiatric ward of a public facility, but her move to a private mental hospital produces great progress. During short leaves from the hospital, she goes to Boston and obtains a diaphragm, then experiences her first sexual encounter, a wholly unpleasant experience. Despite this disillusionment, and despite the death of Joan, another mental patient to whom she has become close, Esther looks forward to leaving the mental asylum and returning to college. Yet she remains unsure if she will have another breakdown: "How did I know that someday—at college, in Europe, somewhere, anywhere—the bell jar, with its stifling distortions, wouldn't descend again?"

CENSORSHIP HISTORY

The Bell Jar has been challenged for its characters' discussions of sexuality and because it advocates an "objectionable" lifestyle. In one instance, the main character observes that her boyfriend's genitals are disappointing because they remind her of "turkey neck and turkey gizzards." The young college women yearn for sexual experience, and the main character purchases a diaphragm and seeks an anonymous sexual encounter. Beyond perceived obscenity, the novel aroused challenges because it openly rejects traditional marriage and motherhood. Characterizing marriage as a prison of dull domestic duties, Plath describes mothers as drudges with dirty, demanding children, while wives are subservient and inferior to their husbands.

In 1977, in Warsaw, Indiana, Teresa Burnau, a first-year English teacher at Warsaw Community High School, was assigned to teach an elective course entitled "Women in Literature" using texts that had previously been approved and ordered for the course. Before school began in September, the principal ordered Burnau to remove the literary anthology *Growing up Female in America* and the novel *The Stepford Wives* from the reading list. The books were removed because "someone in the community might be offended by their criticism of traditional roles for women." By mid-October, the principal demanded that *Go Ask Alice* also be removed from the list because it contained "dirty" words. In November, the principal directed that Burnau remove *The Bell Jar* from her list, after reviewing the book and determining that it was "inappropriate" because it spoke of a birth control device (the diaphragm) and used "profanity." Burnau's written protest brought the warning that she would be dismissed for insubordination if she included that book. Although Burnau complied with the demand and dropped the book, the principal later wrote in her evaluation that she exhibited "resentment and a poor attitude" when told not to use *The Bell Jar*. The school board did not rehire Burnau, giving only the reason that she failed to meet her responsibilities and displayed "a poor attitude."

A 17-year-old Warsaw Community High School student and her family challenged the decision of the board. In early 1979, Brooke Zykan, her brother Blair, and her parents became the plaintiffs in a suit that charged the school district with violating the First and Fourteenth Amendment rights of students and called for the court to reverse the school board decision to remove the books, which also included *The Feminine Plural: Stories by Women about Growing Up* and *The New Women: A Motive Anthology of Women's Liberation*. A group called People Who Care was formed to deal with the controversy and to further the aim of removing "filthy" material from the classroom and to press their agenda. One member stated, "School decisions should be based on the absolutes of Christian behavior." In *Zykan v. Warsaw (IN) Community School Corporation and Warsaw School Board of Trustees (1980)*, the plaintiffs claimed that the school board had removed the books from classrooms because "words in the books offended social, political, and moral tastes and not because the books, taken as a whole, were lacking in educational value."

The American Civil Liberties Union attorney associated with the case hoped that the state would recognize academic freedom as a First Amendment right. The suit charged that the school officials had violated students' "right to know" and the constitutional guarantee of academic freedom, but on December 3, 1979, the Indiana District Court rejected these claims and dismissed the suit. The plaintiffs appealed the decision, but the Court of Appeals sided with the school board and proclaimed that the school board had not violated anyone's constitutional rights because the right of "academic freedom" is limited at the secondary school level. On August 22, 1980, Judge Walter J. Cummings of the Seventh Circuit Court determined that "the student's right to and need for such freedom is bounded by the level of his or her intellectual development" and noted that the local school board has many powers to regulate high school classrooms. This case further strengthened the authority of school boards to select and remove books from school libraries and classrooms and provided warning to individuals who sought academic freedom within the school structure.

FURTHER READING

Alexander, Paul. *Rough Magic: A Biography of Sylvia Plath*. New York: Viking Press, 1991.

Butscher, Edward. *Sylvia Plath: Method and Madness*. New York: Seabury Press, 1975.

Hawthorn, Jeremy. *Multiple Personality and the Disintegration of Literary Character: From Oliver Goldsmith to Sylvia Plath*. New York: Ballantine Books, 1983.

MacPherson, Pat. *Reflecting on the Bell Jar*. New York: Routledge, 1991.

Newsletter on Intellectual Freedom (March 1980): 40; (July 1981): 102.

BELOVED

Author: Toni Morrison
Original date and place of publication: 1987, United States
Original publisher: Alfred A. Knopf
Literary form: Novel

SUMMARY

Beloved opens with an ominous message, the declaration that ". . . 124 was spiteful. Full of a baby's venom" and alerts the reader to the sadness and loss that the novel will reveal. Mirrors shatter without reason, and tiny handprints appear in cake icing in a house where no baby lives any longer, while kettles of chickpeas are mysteriously dumped on the floor to join soda crackers that have been crumbled and lined up meticulously along a door sill. The home at 124 Bluestone Road, a seemingly innocuous gray-and-white residence in Cincinnati, Ohio, in 1873, has lost most of its inhabitants to either death or flight due to fear. The sole inhabitants are former slave Sethe and her 18-year-old daughter Denver, whom many believe to be mentally slow, and the constant presence of Sethe's long-dead baby girl Beloved. The often surreal narrative, a complex blend of events past and present told from diverse viewpoints, examines the profound influence of the past on the lives of the characters.

Divided into three parts, the novel relates in flashbacks a story that begins five years before the start of the American Civil War and continues into the decade following the war's end. Part I is nearly twice as long as Parts II and III and provides an account of the years Sethe spent as a slave, recounts the details of her escape and her murder of her infant daughter Beloved and the attempted murder of her sons that led the community to shun her, and provides an account of her reawakening to life through the appearance of Paul D. Part I also relates the appearance of a young woman who seems to be the adult embodiment of her dead daughter Beloved. She is the person to whom Denver turns in an obsessive manner for companionship and attention. In Part II, Sethe's re-entrance to the outside world is reversed, as Paul D leaves and the young stranger Beloved dominates both Denver and Sethe, who believes her to be the reincarnation of her infant daughter. Stamp Paid, who reveals the newspaper clipping that results in Paul D's exit from 124 Bluestone Road, tries to visit Sethe, but the door remains closed to his knocking and he hears voices, "loud, urgent, all speaking at once" that he attributes to ghosts of black people that have suffered at the hands of whites. Paid also attempts to find a home in the community for Paul D, who lives in the church basement after leaving Sethe's home and who finds himself unable to forgive her for her crime nor forgive himself for allowing the young stranger to seduce him repeatedly and, as he claims to himself, against his will. He admits to being afraid of Sethe because of her crime and cries out despondently to Paid, "How much is a nigger supposed to take?" to which Paid responds, "All he can."

In Part III, what began as a happy bonding among the three women—Sethe, Beloved, and Denver—turns bitter as Sethe lavishes love on the woman she believes to be her long-dead daughter and the closeness of the two closes out Denver. Beloved voices recriminations for Sethe's actions, expressing anguish for what she has suffered, thus leading Sethe to plead for forgiveness and to protest that she used a handsaw to try to kill her sons and succeeded in killing her daughter because of her great love for them and the desire to keep them from being taken into slavery when the schoolteacher arrived to recapture her. Sethe's obsession with Beloved leads her to report to work at Sawyer's restaurant later each day, until she is fired. With no income, the household nearly starves, until Denver takes control, searches for a job, and, through her efforts, reignites the concern and respect of the community, which brings the family food. The extent to which Sethe has become mentally unhinged is clear when Denver's new employer, a white man named Bodwin, arrives to drive Denver to work. Sethe attacks him with an ice pick, because she believes him to be one of the men who had walked the same path to the house 18 years earlier as they came to enforce the Fugitive Law and to return her to slavery. While women who had crowded into the yard after hearing the altercation wrest the pick from Sethe's hand, Beloved leaves the porch and disappears. When Paul D later returns to the house to Sethe, he finds her lying in Baby Suggs's bed, looking confused and ready for death. She cries out to him that she has lost her "best thing," Beloved. Paul D holds her hand and responds, "You your best thing." The novel closes with her question, "Me? Me?"

The sometimes harsh details of the characters' experiences reveal the multiple indignities and the suffering the characters endured while slaves and continue to endure in the aftermath of the war when seemingly freed. Aside from setting the historical context of the main character's actions and the brief mention of sons who said they left to fight, Morrison makes no use of the war in developing her characters and in explaining their circumstances. Rather, she castigates the system of slavery for its role in destroying black families, separating children from their "ma'ams," setting a value on black women as breeders and black men as studs, and treating them as nothing more than livestock to be bought, sold, and bartered for the profit of "whitepeople."

Sethe, a "used-to-be-slave woman," and Denver live in isolation at 124 Bluestone Road, a formerly happy house that once served as a way station for slaves running away to freedom in the North and that was often filled with friends of Sethe's mother-in-law, Baby Suggs, a "holy" woman. They have become used to hearing the sounds of the spirit baby crawling up the stairs that were painted white especially for her many years before and of cleaning up the damage and resituating furniture moved by the spirit.

When the novel begins, Baby Suggs has been dead for nearly a decade, Sethe's sons have left out of fear of the seemingly malevolent spirit of their baby sister Beloved, and the other "coloredpeople" in the town refuse to go near the house. The sudden appearance of Paul D, who knew Sethe and

Halle at Sweet Home, and who is one of the few "Sweet Home men" still alive, angers the spirit into a violent rage of thrown objects and furniture. Paul D fights back and succeeds in driving the spirit from the house, leaving Denver feeling deprived of a presence that had lessened her loneliness. Only days later, when the three return from a carnival, they find a young woman wearing a black dress and new shoes sitting on the stump in their yard. She professes to have no memory of her past and claims that her name is Beloved.

Eighteen years before the novel opens, Sethe, in the later stages of her pregnancy carrying Denver, sent her two sons and baby daughter Beloved to the safety of Baby Suggs's house, expecting to follow soon after with her husband Halle, Baby Suggs's son. Sethe was living in Sweet Home, a plantation formerly owned by a benign master whose death brought his sadistic brother-in-law the schoolteacher as overseer, who made the worst abuses of slavery a reality for the plantation inhabitants. While preparing to run, Sethe was caught and abused by the schoolteacher's nephews and learns later from Paul D that Halle had watched the attack, too frightened to intervene, and had later gone mad from the knowledge. The memory of the experience haunts her. "I am full God damn it of two boys with mossy teeth, one sucking on my breast the other holding me down, their book-reading teacher watching and writing it up. I am still full of that, God watching, above me in the loft—hiding close by—the one place he thought no one would look for him, looking on what I couldn't look at all. And not stopping them—looking and letting it happen."

Paul D also reveals a range of indignities that he and other former slaves have suffered. Incarcerated in Alfred, Georgia, as part of a chain gang, he was weakened and exhausted by the heavy chains on his legs and wrists, and "his hands quit taking instruction. They would not hold his penis to urinate or a spoon to scoop lima beans into his mouth." He thinks of the steel bit that he has worn in his mouth, like a restrained horse, and he is bitter when he recalls the sexual abuse perpetrated by white chain gang guards.

> Kneeling in the mist, they waited for the whim of a guard, or two, or three. Or maybe all of them wanted it. Wanted it from one prisoner in particular or none—or all.
>
> "Breakfast: Want some breakfast, nigger"
>
> "Yes, sir."
>
> "Hungry, nigger?"
>
> "Yes, sir."
>
> "Here you go."
>
> Occasionally a kneeling man chose gunshot in his head as the price, maybe, of taking a bit of foreskin with him to Jesus. Paul D did not know that then. He was looking at his palsied hands, smelling the guard, listening to his soft grunts so like the doves', as he stood before the man kneeling in the mist on his right. Convinced he was next, Paul D retched—vomiting up nothing at all. An observing guard smashed his shoulder with the rifle and the engaged one decided to

skip the new man for the time being lest his pants and shoes got soiled by nigger puke.

References are made throughout the novel to the violence that slaves endured at the hands of their white masters and the white authorities on a routine basis and of Baby Suggs for whom slave life had "busted her legs, back, head, eyes, hands, kidneys, womb and tongue." Sethe recalls the whipping she endured and describes the scars that remain on her back, branching out like a tree up her spine and across her shoulder blades.

One of the most graphic descriptions of violence is of Sethe's use of a handsaw to murder her baby daughter Beloved by slicing under her tiny chin, her attempted murder of her sons, and their discovery.

> Inside, two boys bled in the sawdust and dirt at the feet of a nigger woman holding a blood-soaked child to her chest with one hand and an infant by the heels in the other. She did not look at them; she simply swung the baby toward the wall of planks, missed and tried to connect a second time.

Such passages have created consternation in parents who seek to remove the novel from school reading lists.

CENSORSHIP HISTORY

Beloved has been challenged in school districts because of the violence that permeates the novel. In 1995, parents of students attending St. Johns County Schools in St. Augustine, Florida, challenged the use of the book as part of the required reading, but the school board voted to retain the book after receiving recommendations from a review committee composed of parents, teachers, and administrators. In 1996, parents of students attending the Round Rock, Texas, Independent High School submitted a formal complaint to the school board and asked to have the book removed from the required reading list because it is too violent. After reviewing recommendations by a committee composed of students, teachers, and administrators, the school board voted to retain the novel on the district required reading list. In 1997, a member of the Madawska, Maine, School Committee challenged the use of the book as a required reading in the advanced placement English classes. The book had been a required reading for six years and had not previously been the object of complaints. The school district board honored the recommendations of an especially created committee composed of parents, teachers, and school administrators to retain the book. In 1998, a parent of a student attending the Sarasota County, Florida, schools filed a complaint requesting removal of the novel from the reading lists because it contained "inappropriate sexual material." The school board voted to retain the book.

In 1998, the Anaheim Union High School District school board in Illinois banned *Beloved* from the school district curriculum in a 4-1 vote because a member of the community complained that the novel contained material that was "too graphic." The novel, originally approved by an instructional materials review committee, was removed from the proposed reading list for advanced placement English classes. Commenting on her vote to ban the novel, school board trustee Katherine Smith told a reporter for the *Chicago Tribune*, "I think that there are so many other wonderful creative works of literature out there we could use. . . . We need literature that is uplifting and positive."

More recently in 2006, *Beloved* was among nine books on the required reading list that were challenged in the second-largest high school district in Illinois, an act that "triggered debate over whether works praised in literary circles are high art or smut." The controversy began when Leslie Pinney, a Township High School District 214 board member, identified books on the reading list that she considered to "contain vulgar language, brutal imagery or depictions of sexual situations inappropriate for students." The novels Pinney identified as inappropriate reading material, in addition to *Beloved*, are *Slaughterhouse-Five* by Kurt Vonnegut, *The Things They Carried* by Tim O'Brien, *The Awakening* by Kate Chopin, *Freakonomics* by Steven D. Levitt and Stephen J. Dubner, *The Botany of Desire: A Plant's Eye View of the World* by Michael Pollan, *The Perks of Being a Wallflower* by Stephen Chbosky, *Fallen Angels* by Walter Dean Myers, and *How the Garcia Girls Lost Their Accents* by Julia Alvarez. The school board member admitted that she had not read most of the books she targeted and claimed that she did not want to ban the books from the district libraries, but in class she wanted "to replace them with books that address the same themes without explicit material." Her objection to *Beloved* focused on an early scene in the book in which Paul D remembers the way in which the five "Sweet Home" men, deprived of the company of women, left Sethe alone when "the iron-eyed girl" arrived as "a timely present" for their master's wife Mrs. Garner. "They were young and so sick with the absence of women they had taken to calves. . . . And so they were: Paul D Garner, Paul F Garner, Paul A Garner, Halle Suggs, and Sixo, the wild man. All in their twenties, minus women, fucking cows, dreaming of rape, thrashing on pallets, rubbing their thighs and waiting for the new girl. . . . She waited a year. And the Sweet Home men abused cows while they waited for her." The challenges were the first in more than 20 years that someone had attempted to remove books from the reading lists in the Arlington Heights–based district, which employed an extensive review process based on established reading lists. In defense of the choices, English and Fine Arts department head Chuck Venegoni told a reporter for the *Chicago Tribune*, "This is not some serendipitous decision to allow someone to do what they felt like doing because they had something about talking about something kinky in front of kids. It's insulting to hardworking people who really do care about kids." He criticized Pinney's approach of taking a few passages out of context to condemn entire books and observed, "there is nothing in any of those books that even remotely approaches what an objective person would call pornography." Although the school district had an opt-out clause that allowed parents to request that their child read another book if they find the assigned material objectionable, Pinney found the current measures ineffectual "because unless you're digging around the student's backpack, looking at the books and reading them, how exactly will you know what your student is reading?"

Five hundred people attended the school board meeting on Thursday, May 25, 2006, to debate whether to keep *Beloved* and the other novels on the school reading lists. Supporters of the ban asserted that their efforts were "to protect students from smut" and some people, such as Arlington Heights resident Brude Ticknell, claimed that "teachers promoting the books were motivated by their own progressive social agendas." Students took the debate to the social networking site MySpace.com, and sophomore Scott Leipprandt placed a petition against the ban on the Prospect High page, which nearly 500 students and alumni from the six high schools in the district signed. Leipprandt told a *Chicago Tribune* reporter that fighting the banning of books is important. "It's important because it shows us things. All these things happen in real life. By banning it, it doesn't give us the opportunity to talk about it before we encounter it in real life." After a long meeting during which hundreds of people spoke, the school board voted 6-1 in favor of approving the required reading list without change.

FURTHER READING

Doyle, Robert P. *2007 Banned Books Resource Guide*. Chicago: American Library Association, 2007.

Francisco, Jamie. "Book-Ban Debate Is Long, Impassioned: More Than 350 Sign Up to Speak to School Board." *Chicago Tribune*, May 26, 2006.

———. "Explicit Move Is Made to Ban Books from Reading List." *Chicago Tribune*, May 24, 2006.

Keilman, John, and Jamie Francisco. "Book-Ban Fights Are Far from Over: Reading Lists Face Scrutiny across the State." *Chicago Tribune*, May 28, 2006.

"School Board Bans Morrison's 'Beloved.'" *Chicago Tribune*, May 17, 1998.

BRAVE NEW WORLD

Author: Aldous Huxley
Original date and place of publication: 1932, England
Original publisher: Chatto & Windus Collins
Literary form: Novel

SUMMARY

Brave New World is a satire in which science, sex, and drugs have replaced human reason and human emotion in the "perfect" society to which Huxley gives the name "Utopia." The novel depicts an orderly society in which scientifically sophisticated genetics and pharmacology combine to produce a perfectly controlled population whose entire existence is dedicated to maintaining the stability of society. People are genetically engineered to satisfy the regulated needs of the government in regard to specific mental and physical sizes and types. Sexual promiscuity is demanded by the state for the sake of pleasure, not procreation, and women are equipped with contraceptive cartridge belts to avoid pregnancy. The only respectable way to enter the world is through incubation in a bottle—people are decanted rather than born—and learning occurs through preconditioning.

Inhabitants are created and conditioned to fit into specific social slots. Thus, in the Hatchery and Conditioning Center, varying amounts of alcohol are placed into the decanting bottles that contain the embryos to stunt mental growth and create a hierarchy of genetic classes.

Those who will be conditioned to do the monotonous and hard labor of this society receive the highest doses of alcohol to create a low mentality. Labeled in descending order of intelligence as Gammas, Deltas, and Epsilons, they are the most numerous and are produced by subjecting the fertilized egg to the Bokanovsky Process, a budding procedure that enables division of the egg into as many as 96 identical beings from one egg and up to 15,000 brothers and sisters from a single ovary. The Alphas and Betas, who carry out the work of the government, remain individualized, yet they, too, are manipulated through early conditioning. The concept of family is unknown, and the words *mother* and *father* are viewed as smut. In this systematically promiscuous world, men and women are encouraged to experience many sexual partners to avoid the development of intimate emotional relationships that might threaten their obsessive loyalty to the state.

The expected ills of human life have all been eliminated, and inhabitants of this brave new world have been freed of the worries of disease, pain, unhappiness, old age, and death. Disease has been eradicated through sterilization, and pain and unhappiness are easily banished by liberal doses of *soma*, a drug that provides a high without side effects. Smaller dosages are used to counteract depression, while larger dosages are taken to provide a long-term sense of euphoria, described by one character as a two-week vacation. Blind happiness is necessary for social stability, so all emotions are dulled. Even death takes on a new appearance. People are given treatments that keep them youthful-looking until they near the age of 60, at which time their bodies are allowed to experience a brief, soma-controlled period of aging before they disappear into the prominently placed crematoria that turn human bodies into phosphorus to be used in fertilizer.

Huxley exhibits the undesirable aspects of such a world through the characters of the Alpha-class misfit Bernard Marx and the savage John, who lives on the Savage Reservation, a pre-civilized region that has been preserved for study. John is the son of the director of Hatcheries and Conditioning (DHC) and a Beta woman who was left on the reservation by the DHC.

Taken to England by Marx, John is highly uncomfortable in the emotionless and intellectually vacuous Utopia. He wants love and rejects the promiscuity of Lenina Crowne, a Utopian woman to whom he is sexually attracted but whose morals are repugnant to him. Treated as a curiosity by Utopians who clamor to see him and who gawk at him, John finds only misery in this brave new world and decides that suicide is his only solution.

CENSORSHIP HISTORY

Brave New World has evoked a range of responses from those who are made uncomfortable by Huxley's satire of society. The novel has been charged with being sordid, immoral, and obscene, and it has been condemned for vilifying the family, for giving too much attention to sex, and for encouraging illegal drug use. Many cite the sexual promiscuity of the Utopians, as did the Board of Censors of Ireland when it banned the novel in 1932, yet the novel contains no graphic scenes of sexual behavior. For the most part, people who seek to ban the novel believe that *Brave New World* is "depressing, fatalistic, and negative, and that it encourages students to adopt a lifestyle of drugs, sex and conformity, reinforcing helpless feelings that they can do nothing to make an impact on their world."

The novel has been frequently challenged in schools throughout the United States. In 1965, a teacher of English in Maryland claimed that the local school board had violated his First Amendment rights by firing him after he assigned *Brave New World* as a required reading in his class. The district court ruled against the teacher in *Parker v. Board of Education*, 237 F. Supp. 222 (D.Md) and refused his request for reinstatement in the teaching position. When the case was later heard by the circuit court, *Parker v. Board of Education*, 348 F.2d 464 (4th Cir. 1965), the presiding judge affirmed the ruling of the lower court and included in the determination the opinion that the nontenured status of the teacher accounted for the firing and not the assignment of a particular book.

In 1979, a high school principal in Matthews County, Virginia, requested that a history teacher in the high school withdraw an assignment that included *Brave New World*. The teacher assigned it anyway, and the school board terminated the teacher's contract. No further actions were taken by either party.

Use of the novel in the classroom was challenged in 1980 in Miller, Missouri, where it was removed from the curriculum, and in 1988, parents of students at Yukon (Oklahoma) High School demanded the removal of the book as a required reading because of its "language and moral content." In 1993, parents challenged the novel as a required reading in Corona-Norco (California) Unified School District based on charges that it "centered around negative activity." After consideration by the school board, the book was retained on the list, but students who objected to the novel were given alternative choices.

In September 2000, the *Mobile Register* reported that *Brave New World* was removed from the Foley High School Library after parent Kathleen Stone complained. Stone asserted that the novel, which was assigned reading in one 11th-grade English class, showed contempt for marriage and family values. High school officials removed the book from the library pending review and, as the newsletter *Intellectual Freedom* reports, emphasized that the book was not banned, but removed.

In 2003, parents of students attending a summer science academy in the South Texas Independent School District in Mercedes, Texas, challenged the use of this novel and *Stranger in a Strange Land* by Robert Heinlein in the curriculum. They objected specifically to the themes of sexuality, drugs, and suicide in the novels and asserted that such adult themes were inappropriate for students. School officials retained the novels in the summer curriculum. The school board considered the matter further and voted to require school principals to automatically offer an alternative to any challenged books in order to provide parents with greater control over their children's readings.

FURTHER READING

"Another Furor over Books." *Ohio State University Monthly* 55 (December 1963): 8–12.

Bedford, Sybille. *Aldous Huxley: A Biography.* 2 vols. London: Chatto & Windus Collins, 1973–74.

Massie, Dorothy C. "Censorship in the Schools: Something Old and Something New." *Today's Education* 69 (November/December 1980): 56–62.

Matter, William W. "The Utopian Tradition and Aldous Huxley." *Science Fiction Studies* 2 (1975): 146–151.

Nahmod, Sheldon H. "Controversy in the Classroom: The High School Teacher and Freedom of Expression." *George Washington University Law Review* 39 (July 1974): 1,031.

Newsletter on Intellectual Freedom (May 1980): 52; (September 1981): 127; (July 1988): 140; (January 1994): 14; (March 1994): 70; (November 2000): 193; (November 2003): 249–250.

THE CANTERBURY TALES

Author: Geoffrey Chaucer
Original date and place of publication: 1387–1400, England
Original publisher: Unknown
Literary form: Short story collection

SUMMARY

The Canterbury Tales is a group of stories, mostly in verse, written in the closing years of the 14th century. Chaucer establishes the framework for the book in a lengthy prologue, in which he describes the 29 individuals who meet with their host at the Tabard Inn in preparation for a pilgrimage to the popular shrine of Thomas à Becket at the Canterbury Cathedral. They agree that, to pass the time on the journey, each pilgrim will tell four stories, two on the way to the shrine and two on the way home. The host will judge the best tale, and the winner will receive a sumptuous feast at the inn. Chaucer originally planned a book of 120 tales but died in 1400 before completing the work. Only 24 of the tales remain. Of these, 20 are complete, two are deliberately left incomplete because the pilgrims demand that the tellers cease, and two others were left unfinished by Chaucer's death.

The pilgrims extend across all levels of 14th-century English society, from the nobly born Knight, Squire, and Prioress to the low-born Miller, Cook, and Yeoman. None are spared Chaucer's critical examination of the human condition as he uses his characters and their tales to expose the absurdities and inadequacies of all levels of society. The travelers quarrel, interrupt, and criticize each other; become drunk; and provoke commentary. Members of the religious hierarchy are shown to be corrupt, women are lusty, and the dark underbelly of society is exposed. The tales reflect the tellers, from the gentle Knight, "modest as a maid," who describes an abstraction of womanhood in his pure Emily, to the bawdy Miller, who describes his Alison as a highly provocative physical object.

Risqué language and sexual innuendo pervade most of the tales. "The Cook's Tale" describes "a wife [who] whored to get her sustenance." In "Introduction to the Lawyer's Prologue," provocative images of incest emerge in "Canace, who loved her own blood brother sinfully" and "wicked king Antiochus [who] bereft his daughter of her maidenhead." "The Reeve's Tale" tells of a miller named Simpkin whose wife "was a dirty bitch" and whose daughter was "with buttocks broad and round breasts full and high." "The Wife of Bath's Tale," one of the two most commonly anthologized of all the tales, offers an extraordinary view of women and sexuality. Described in the prologue as having had five husbands, "not counting other company in her youth," the Wife of Bath questions the concern over virginity and asks "Tell me also to what purpose or end the genitals have been made?" She lustily promises, "In wifehood I will use my instrument as freely as my Maker has sent it."

The second of the two most popularly anthologized stories is "The Miller's Tale," a story about adultery. Alison, an 18-year-old woman married to a middle-age miller, is courted by Absalom the parish clerk, but she is already having an affair with the boarder, a student named Nicholas. Absalom serenades her outside her window and promises to leave her alone only if she will let him kiss her. She agrees and, when he arrives at her window in the dark, she offers "her naked arse," which he kisses. He soon realizes the trick, for "it seem somehow amiss, for well he knew a woman has no beard; he'd felt a thing all rough and longish-haired." Seeking revenge, Absalom returns to the Miller's house carrying a red-hot poker from the fireplace and calls to Alison for another kiss. This time Nicholas, who "had risen for a piss," decides "to have his arse kissed" to carry on the joke. And, "showing the whole bum," he is shocked when Absalom "was ready with his iron hot and Nicholas right in the arse he got." Later, John, the other student boarder, mistakenly climbs into bed with Alison, who thinks it is Nicholas, and he "pricked her hard and deep, like one gone mad."

CENSORSHIP HISTORY

Canterbury Tales has been expurgated since its first appearance in the United States in 1908 in the Everyman's Library edition. Seventeen of the tales were translated into modern English with extensive expurgation, and seven were left intact but in the original Middle English language. In 1953, the tales were innocent victims of the "Red Scare," when critics approached the Texas State Textbook Commission and demanded that the commission bar the Garden City editions of *Canterbury Tales* and *Moby-Dick* from their schools. The two works were illustrated by Rockwell Kent, charged by critics with being a communist.

For the most part, however, the off-color references of the original text and blunt "Anglo-Saxon" terms related to the anatomy or to bodily functions have raised concerns among parents and those who select textbooks. Thus, they are routinely omitted from most editions, as are curses or oaths uttered by characters in the original tales. Editing has led to such absurdities as "He caught her by the queynte" being transformed into "He slipped his hand intimately between her legs." Challenges to the inclusion of "The Miller's Tale," "The Wife of Bath's Tale," and even the "Prologue" have sought to remove the readings from classrooms because of the "unhealthy characters" and the "nasty words" of the text. Risqué language and characters have made the tales a ready target for textbook evaluators and community and school watchdogs.

In 1986, a lengthy case arose over the use of a textbook that included "The Miller's Tale" and Aristophanes' play *Lysistrata* in an elective humanities course for Columbia County High School students in Lake City, Florida. The tale appeared in *The Humanities: Cultural Roots and Continuities Volume I*, a state-approved textbook that had been used for 10 years without incident. In 1985, the daughter of a fundamentalist minister had enrolled in the course and objected to the two selections, even though they were not assigned readings but portions referred to and read aloud by the teacher. In lodging a formal complaint, the minister identified "sexual explicitness," "vulgar language," and "the promotion of women's lib" as his reasons for demanding that the text be withdrawn from use. His specific objections identified concern over the inclusion of the terms "ass" and "fart" in "The Miller's Tale," as well as the jocular way in which adultery appears to be treated. An advisory textbook committee made up of Columbia County High School teachers read and discussed the two selections, then recommended that the textbooks be retained and that the two selections not be assigned. The school board rejected their suggestions and voted to confiscate all copies of the book and to lock them in the book room. Anxious to avoid the charge of censorship, board members also voted to allow a copy to remain in the high school library, but it was placed on "the mature shelf."

In 1988, the American Civil Liberties Union submitted an initial brief against the school board in *Virgil v. School Board of Columbia County*, 677 F. Supp. 1547, 1551-51 (M.D. Fla. 1988) and argued that the actions of the board in removing the textbook from the classroom suppressed the free thought and free speech of students. The ACLU based its arguments on decisions made in *Board of Education, Island Trees Union Free School District No. 26 v. Pico*, 457 U.S. 853, 102 S.Ct. 2799, 73 L.Ed.2d 435 (1982), in which the court decided that school boards violate the First Amendment rights of students when they arbitrarily remove books. The defense attorney for the school board relied on *Hazelwood School District v. Kuhlmeier*, 484 U.S. 260, 108 S.Ct. 562, 98 L.Ed.2d 592 (1988) in presenting the case, although the case applied to the right of school administrators to censor articles in a school newspaper that was produced as part of a high school journalism class.

The case went to court, and in deciding *Virgil v. School Board of Columbia County*, 862 F.2d 1517, 1525 (11th Cir. 1989), the judge determined that the *Hazelwood* case was the relevant precedent. The limited scope of that case in interpreting the First Amendment rights of students influenced the court to decide in favor of the school board. In the *Virgil* decision, the U.S. Court of Appeals for the 11th Circuit concluded that no constitutional violation had occurred and the school board could decide to remove books from the classroom provided that the removal was "reasonably related" to the "legitimate pedagogical concern" of denying students exposure to "potentially sensitive topics." The written contention of the board that the two selections contained "explicit sexuality" and "excessive vulgarity" was judged to be a sufficient basis for the removal of *The Humanities: Cultural Roots and Continuities* from the classroom. The plaintiffs decided to appeal the case to the United States Supreme Court and directed the ACLU attorney to file a Petition for Writ of Certiorari in 1988. After more than a year passed, the plaintiffs learned that the Supreme Court had never received the petition because a secretary newly hired in April 1989 by the office of the ACLU attorney had never sent it out. The plaintiffs decided not to pursue the matter because the changed character of the higher court did not promise success even if the motion to argue the case were approved.

In September 1995, parents of seniors in the Eureka, Illinois, High School complained to the Eureka School Board that parts of this classic are "too racy." Board members directed the teacher, Nancy Quinn, to stop teaching the work until the board could review the material further. School Board president Eric Franz stated that the parents were particularly concerned with classroom discussions about marriage and adultery that were prompted by the tales. He characterized the action of the board as "about education, not censorship" and said that the board had to determine "whether the community's standards are violated by any particular piece of literature." The board voted to ban the full version of *The Canterbury Tales* and to replace it with an expurgated version, which they described as "annotated."

FURTHER READING

"The Censor's Tale." *St. Louis Post-Dispatch*, September 25, 1995.
"Chaucer's Tales Get Suspension from Illinois High School Class." *St. Louis Post-Dispatch*, September 22, 1995.
Johnson, Claudia. *Stifled Laughter: One Woman's Fight against Censorship.* Golden, Colo.: Fulcrum Publishing, 1994.
Scala, Elizabeth. "Canace and the Chaucer Canon." *Chaucer Review* 30 (1995): 15–39.

CATCH-22

Author: Joseph Heller
Original date and place of publication: 1961, United States
Original publisher: Simon & Schuster
Literary form: Novel

SUMMARY

Catch-22 is a comic novel about World War II that literary critics have described as among the best to have come out of that era. The novel concerns the efforts of Capt. John Yossarian, a bombardier with the 256th U.S. Air Force Squadron, to be removed from combat duty after he witnesses numerous friends being killed in action. He acts insane to achieve his goal, but his efforts are thwarted by military regulation number 22, which states that no sane person would willingly go into combat. Thus, anyone who seeks to avoid combat duty must be considered sane.

Set on the fictional Mediterranean island of Pianosa, from which the squadron makes regular bombing runs to southern France and to Italy, the novel contains graphic descriptions of sex and violence and exhibits strong rebellion against authority. Yossarian lies, sabotages military procedures, and exhibits gross irresponsibility. He also walks around naked for a few days, even when he is being awarded a medal. Given light duty censoring letters written by enlisted men, Yossarian plays games and blacks out words randomly, sometimes adding the chaplain's signature to romantic letters home. The unpleasant experience of his tent mate Orr in a brothel is carefully detailed, as the "whore" beats him with her high-heeled shoe. Readers learn that the two are naked and of "her wondrously full breasts soaring all over the place like billowing pennants in a strong wind and her buttocks and strong thighs shim-sham-shimmying this way and that way." Another character visits a brothel in the Eternal City, then kills the prostitute because she might damage his reputation should she tell others about their encounter. Throughout the novel, the men casually refer to and address each other as "son of a bitch," "prick," or "bastard." At one point, Yossarian loses his temper and rants, "That dirty goddam midget-assed, apple-cheeked, goggle-eyed, undersized, bucktoothed, grinning, crazy sonofabitchinbastard!"

The women in the novel are largely stereotypes to whom other characters refer as "whore." The woman whom "he had longed for and idolized for months" is "perfect for Yossarian, a debauched, coarse, vulgar, amoral, appetizing slattern . . . . She was interested in fornication." However, he also hopes that "Nately's whore" will find him a woman who is just as eager for sex as she. At the end of the novel, as Yossarian leaves the base to run off to Sweden, "Nately's whore was hiding out just outside the door." She attempts to kill him, but he escapes.

CENSORSHIP HISTORY

Catch-22 is part of the school censorship case that set precedent by supporting the student's right to know. In 1972, the Strongsville, Ohio, board of education used its discretionary power over textbook selection to disapprove purchase of *Catch-22* and Kurt Vonnegut's *God Bless You, Mr. Rosewater*, despite faculty recommendation. The board refused to allow teachers to use the books as part of the English curriculum, charging that they were "completely sick" and "garbage." The board then ordered the two books and *Cat's Cradle*, also by Vonnegut, removed from the high school library and "all copies disposed of in accordance with statutory procedure."

Five high school students and their families brought a class-action suit against the school district, the school superintendent, and the board of education, claiming that their rights under the First and Fourteenth Amendments had been violated. The families argued that the board had not followed proper procedure and had not given good reason for rejecting the novels. In 1974, the U.S. District Court for the Northern District of Ohio ruled that the board did not violate First Amendment rights because it had followed the law. Ohio law granted school boards the authority to select textbooks, and the board had held open meetings and consulted enough teachers, administrators, and citizens to make a reasonable decision. The judge dismissed the complaint of the families regarding the removal of the books from the school library.

The case was then heard in 1976 by the U.S. Court of Appeals for the Sixth Circuit, and a different decision emerged. The court upheld the right of the school board to determine the choice of textbooks, but it stood firmly against the right of the school board to remove already purchased books from the school library.

A public school library is also a valuable adjunct to classroom discussions. If one of the English teachers considered Joseph Heller's Catch-22 to be one of the more important modern American novels (as, indeed, at least one did), we assume that no one would dispute that the First Amendment's protection of academic freedom would protect both his right to say so in class and his students' right to hear him and to find and read the book. Obviously, the students' success in this last endeavor would be greatly hindered by the fact that the book sought had been removed from a school library.

The court also chastised the school board for withdrawing books from the school library. Stating in the decision that "a library is a storehouse of knowledge," the presiding judge warned that libraries are created by the state for the benefit of students in the schools. As such, they are "not subject to being withdrawn by succeeding school boards whose members might desire to 'winnow' the library for books the content of which occasioned their displeasure or disapproval." The judge ordered the Strongsville school board to replace the books in the school library. In response, the school district appealed to the U.S. Supreme Court, but the court refused to hear the case.

The use of the word *whore* at several places in the novel to refer to women resulted in challenges in the Dallas (Texas) Independent School District in 1974, where parents demanded that the novel be removed from all of the high school libraries. The same objection motivated a challenge in the Snoqualmie Valley (Washington) School District in 1979. Critics observed that the use of *whore* and Heller's failure to name one woman, calling her only "Nately's whore," represented a stereotyping of women that was harmful to students. In attempts to remove the novel from use in the school system as well as from the Mount Si High School library, critics also cited the "overly descriptive passages of violence" and the increasingly bizarre threats by squadron members against each other. The efforts to remove *Catch-22* were unsuccessful.

FURTHER READING

Green, Daniel. "A World Worth Laughing At: *Catch-22* and the Humor of Black Humor." *Studies in the Novel* 27 (Summer 1995): 186–196.

Moore, Michael. "Pathological Communication Patterns in Heller's *Catch-22*." *Et Cetera* 52 (Winter 1995): 431–459.

Newsletter for Intellectual Freedom (January 1975): 6; (July 1979): 85.

O'Neil, Robert M. *Classrooms in the Crossfire: The Rights and Interests of Students, Parents, Teachers, Administrators, Librarians, and the Community.* Bloomington: Indiana University Press, 1981.

Pinsker, Sanford. *Understanding Joseph Heller.* Columbia: University of South Carolina Press, 1991.

Potts, Stephen. *Catch-22: Antiheroic Antinovel.* Boston: Twayne, 1989.

———. *From Here to Absurdity: The Moral Battlefields of Joseph Heller.* San Bernardino, Calif.: Borgo Press, 1982.

THE CATCHER IN THE RYE

Author: J. D. Salinger
Original date and place of publication: 1951, United States
Original publisher: Little, Brown and Company
Literary form: Novel

SUMMARY

The Catcher in the Rye tells the story of a middle-class, urban, late-adolescent boy in the 1950s who confronts crisis in his own life by escaping into the disordered and chaotic adult world. The story, told from the first-person point of view of Holden Caulfield, details 48 hours in his life and describes how he views and feels about society and the world in which he lives. As Holden experiences his misadventures, he muses about sex, society, and American values. He seeks to remain idealistic, but he is confronted at every turn by the phoniness of society.

Holden narrates his story while in a rest home in California, and the reader becomes aware that he is relating a story from his recent past. He flashes back to his school days, in particular to Pencey Prep, where he was a student until his expulsion. It is just after this expulsion that the action takes place. For most of the novel, Holden appears to search for someone or something in which to believe, but he finds that his generally pessimistic view of human nature and human values is reinforced rather than refuted.

Before Holden makes the decision to leave school, he visits his history teacher for one last time and receives a lecture regarding his lack of motivation and poor scholarship. Mr. Spencer even goes so far as to read Holden the last examination he took. The disappointments accrue, as Holden returns to his room in the dormitory and learns that his roommate, Ward, has a date with a girl whom Holden had wanted to date. To compound the pain, Ward asks Holden to write a composition, which he later criticizes severely. After an ensuing physical fight, Holden packs a bag and leaves the campus.

Holden boards a train bound for New York City and registers at a hotel upon arrival. When loneliness sets in, he makes several telephone calls without success, then visits a crowded nightclub, but he still cannot fill the void he feels inside. When Holden returns to the hotel, he asks the doorman to arrange for a prostitute, but he sends her away unpaid because he is too scared and too depressed to enjoy her. The doorman and prostitute later awaken him and demand the five dollars, and the doorman beats Holden to obtain payment.

After meeting a friend at a bar and indulging in underage drinking, Holden sneaks into his family's apartment to see his younger sister, Phoebe, with whom he discusses his fears that he may "disappear" into himself. He tells her that he has a mission in this world: "I keep picturing all these little kids playing some game in this big field of rye and all . . . . And I'm standing by on the edge of some crazy cliff. What I have to do, I have to catch everybody if they start to go over the cliff." In his further idealism, he becomes upset when he finds "Fuck You" scrawled on the walls of Phoebe's elementary school and on the wall of the museum where Phoebe will meet him.

Holden plans to hitchhike to the West but changes his mind and agrees to return home when Phoebe packs a suitcase and insists on going with him. He later watches Phoebe ride the carousel in Central Park and realizes that he really cannot protect her from all of the world's abuses and that he has to let her take chances without interfering.

By the end of the novel, after fending off the advances of a male former English teacher and reviewing his disappointments with the adult world, Holden appears resigned in the rest home and predicts that he will soon be returning to school.

CENSORSHIP HISTORY

The novel has long ignited disapproval, and it was the most frequently banned book in schools between 1966 and 1975. Even before that time, however, the work was a favorite target of censors. In 1957, Australian Customs seized a shipment of the novels that had been presented as a gift to the government by the U.S. ambassador. The books were later released, but Customs had made its point that the book contained obscene language and actions that were not appropriate behavior for an adolescent. In 1960, a teacher in Tulsa, Oklahoma, was fired for assigning the book to an 11th-grade English class. The teacher appealed and was reinstated by the school board, but the book was removed from use in the school.

The following year in Oklahoma City, the novel became the focus of a legislative hearing in which a locally organized censorship group sought to stop the Mid-Continent News Company, a book wholesaler, from carrying the novel. Members of the group parked a "Smutmobile" outside the capital building during the hearing and displayed the novel with others. As a result of public pressure, the wholesaler dropped the criticized novels from its inventory. In 1963, a delegation of parents of high school students in Columbus, Ohio, asked the school board to ban *Catcher in the Rye*, *Brave New World*, and *To Kill a Mockingbird* for being "anti-white" and "obscene." The superintendent of schools and the school board refused the request and expressed confidence in the ability of their teachers and librarians to choose reading material for the school system.

After a decade of quiet, objections again arose in 1975 in Selinsgrove, Pennsylvania, and the novel was removed from the suggested reading list for an elective course entitled "Searching for Values and Identity Through Literature." Based on parents' objections to the language and content of the book, the school board voted 5-4 to ban the book. The book was later reinstated in the curriculum when the board learned that the vote was illegal because a two-thirds vote was needed for removal of the text.

In 1977, parents in Pittsgrove Township, New Jersey, challenged the assignment of the novel in an American literature class. They charged that the book included considerable profanity and "filthy and profane" language that promoted premarital sex, homosexuality, and perversion, as well as claiming that it was "explicitly pornographic" and "immoral." The board of education had originally approved the novel for study. After months of controversy, the board ruled that the novel could be read in the advanced-placement class for its universal message, but they gave parents the right to decide whether or not their children would read it.

In 1978, parents in Issaquah, Washington, became upset with the rebellious views expressed in the novel by Holden Caulfield and with the profanity he uses. The woman who led the parents' group asserted that she had counted 785 uses of profanity, and she alleged that the philosophy of the book marked it as part of a communist plot that was gaining a foothold in the schools, "in which a lot of people are used and may not even be aware of it." The school board voted to ban the book, but the decision was later reversed when the three members who had voted against the book were recalled due to illegal deal-making. In 1979, the Middleville, Michigan, school district removed the novel from the required reading list after parents objected to the content.

Objections to the novel were numerous throughout the 1980s. In 1980, the Jackson-Milton School libraries in North Jackson, Ohio, removed the book, as did two high school libraries in Anniston, Alabama. In 1982, school officials removed the book from all school libraries because it contained "excess vulgar language, sexual scenes, and things concerning moral issues." In 1983, parents in Libby, Montana, challenged the assignment of the book in the high school due to the "book's contents." Deemed "unacceptable" and "obscene," the novel was banned from use in English classes at Freeport High School in De Funiak Springs, Florida, in 1985, and it was removed from the required reading list in 1986 in Medicine Bow, Wyoming, Senior High School because of sexual references and profanity. In 1987, parents and the local Knights of Columbus chapter in Napoleon, North Dakota, complained about profanity and sexual references in the book, which was then banned from a required sophomore English reading list. Parents of students attending Linton-Stockton (Indiana) High School challenged the book in 1988 because it "undermines morality," and profanity was the reason why the book was banned from classrooms in the Boron, California, high school in 1989.

The challenges to the novel continued well into the 1990s. In 1991, the novel was challenged at Grayslake (Illinois) Community High School for profanity, and parents of students in Jamaica High School in Sidell, Illinois, cited profanities and the depiction of premarital sex, alcohol abuse, and prostitution as the basis for their 1992 challenge. Three other major challenges to the novel occurred in 1992. The novel was challenged and removed from the Waterloo, Iowa, public schools and the Duval County, Florida, public school libraries because of the "lurid passages about sex" and profanity, and a parent in Carlisle, Pennsylvania, objected to the book because it was "immoral" and contained profanity. In 1993, parents in the Corona-Norco (California) School District protested the use of the novel as a required reading because it was "centered around negative activity." The school board voted to retain the novel but instructed teachers to select alternative readings if students objected to it. The novel was challenged but retained for use in select English classes at New Richmond (Wisconsin) High School in 1994, but it was removed as mandatory reading from the Goffstown, New Hampshire, schools the same year because parents charged that it contained "vulgar words" and presented the main character's "sexual exploits."

In May 2000, *American Libraries* magazine reported that the Limestone County School District (Alabama) voted on attempts to ban the book from high school library collections. Elkmont High School parent Mike Taylor had challenged use of the book, complaining that "the Lord's name is taken in vain throughout." The move had the support of Joel Glaze, a board member, who asserted that the book is "teaching debauchery" and stated that a nearby Bible school refused to teach the book. On March 13, 1999, the school board voted 4-3 to retain the book.

In 2001, parents of students in the Dorchester District 2 school in Summerville, South Carolina, complained to the school board that the novel is immoral and asked for the school officials to remove it. The school board reviewed the book and voted to remove it from the school, with one school board member supporting the decision and stating it "is a filthy, filthy book." The same year, a school board member in Glynn County, Georgia, challenged use of the book because of the profanity, but school district officials voted to retain the book.

In 2004, parents of students attending Noble High School in North Berwick, Maine, challenged the use of the novel as an assigned reading. School officials decided to retain the novel, but they planned to create a program in which teachers would provide more information to parents regarding why certain books are studied.

FURTHER READING

Alvino, James. "Is It Book Burning Time Again?" *New York Times*, December 28, 1980, pp. 11, 18.

"Another Furor over Books." *Ohio State University Monthly* 55 (4): 8–12.

Booth, Wayne C. "Censorship and the Values of Fiction." *English Journal* 53 (March 1964): 155–164.

Corbett, Edward P. J. "Raise High the Barriers, Censors." *America* 54 (January 7, 1961): 441–444.

Newsletter on Intellectual Freedom (November 1978): 138; (January 1980): 6–7; (May 1980): 51; (March 1983): 37–38; (July 1983): 122; (July 1985): 113; (March 1987): 55; (July 1987): 123; (January 1988): 10; (September 1988): 177; (November 1989): 218–219; (July 1991): 129–130; (May 1992): 83; (July 1992): 105, 126; (January 1993): 29; (January 1994): 14; (March 1994): 56, 70; (May 1994): 100; (January 1995):

12; (July 2000): 123; (November 2001): 246–247, 277–278; (January 2005): 8–9; (March 2005): 73–74.

Oboler, Eli M. "Idaho School Librarians and Salinger's *Catcher in the Rye:* A Candid Report." *Idaho Librarian* 15 (October 1963): 137–139.

THE COLOR PURPLE

Author: Alice Walker
Original date and place of publication: 1982, United States
Original publisher: Harcourt Brace Jovanovich
Literary form: Novel

SUMMARY

The Color Purple, winner of the 1983 Pulitzer Prize for Fiction and the American Book Award, is composed of personal letters written by the main character, Celie, to God and to her sister Nettie. Written in the vernacular of poor Southern African Americans, the letters allow Celie to tell the story in her own words and permit the author to describe the community of women who support and eventually rescue each other from the restrictions placed on them by society.

The primary setting of the novel is Georgia in the years between World War I and World War II. The novel opens with the first letter written to God by 14-year-old Celie, the victim of continual sexual abuse by her stepfather Alphonso, whom she and her sister call "Pa" and whom they believe to be their natural father. When he first rapes her, he tells her to tell no one but God, and so begin her tragic and painful letters. Poor, uneducated, and unattractive as Celie believes herself to be, she finds no means of preventing the abuse to herself, but she strives to protect her younger sister, Nettie, from becoming a victim. Celie's two children born of the sexual abuse by her stepfather are taken from her and adopted by missionaries bound for Africa, a couple who also befriend Nettie and take her with them. Soon after, Celie is forced into a harsh and poverty-stricken marriage with Albert, a much older widower who mistreats her, leaving her letters to God and to Nettie as her only comfort. She never receives Nettie's responses because Albert hides the letters for years.

Victimized by men and by the failure to resist her ill treatment, Celie can conceive of no other life and views herself as ugly, talentless, and insignificant until the beautiful, sensual, confident, and independent Shug Avery enters her life. Albert's former lover and the mother of three of his children years earlier, Shug is a flamboyant blues singer. She returns as Albert's lover, then becomes Celie's lover, awakening her to experience love for the first time and to truly value her body and her talents. After learning that Albert has hidden her sister's letters for years, Celie leaves Albert to live with Shug and discovers her creative talent as she begins a pants company in Memphis. Years later, having become a confident and valued human being, Celie returns to Georgia to claim her family home. Her sister Nettie returns from Africa with Celie's children, and the family celebrates the survival of the human spirit.

CENSORSHIP HISTORY

The novel has been criticized for including such taboo themes as incest, birth of children outside of marriage, rape, sexual pleasure, and lesbian activity. Aggressive Shug Avery has not only given birth to three children outside of marriage, but she later becomes sexually intimate with both her former lover and his present wife, Celie. Critics of her behavior emphasize that she shows no remorse for her moral transgressions and, instead, exhibits daring boldness in her pleasure seeking. Some members of the African-American community find the novel insulting to African-American males with its emphasis on Celie's sexual abuse by her stepfather and her physical abuse at the hands of her husband. Parents have also objected to the lesbian theme within the novel, claiming that the book would not have been acceptable for use in schools had the lesbian characters been white. In only rare instances have critics challenged the book for its language, but those who have cite the several instances in which such terms as *tits* and *pussy* appear as the cause of their objections.

The novel was first challenged in 1984, when parents of students in the Oakland (California) High School honors English class complained that the book was inappropriate reading because of its "sexual and social explicitness," especially its "troubling ideas about race relations . . . and human sexuality." The book was removed from the classroom, pending review by the Oakland board of education. After nine months of discussion, the board reluctantly gave approval for use of the book in the honors curriculum. The following year, school trustees in Hayward, California, rejected a purchase order for copies of the novel based on their views that it contained "rough language" and "explicit sex scenes." In 1986, school librarians in Newport News, Virginia, removed the novel from the open shelves because of its "profanity and sexual references." The work was made available only to individuals over age 18 or to students who provided written permission from their parents. In 1989, a challenge was raised at the Saginaw (Michigan) Public Library, on the charge that the book was "too sexually graphic for a 12-year-old," but the challenge failed, and the book remained on the open shelves. The novel was also challenged but remained in Chattanooga, Tennessee, in 1989, when it appeared as a summer youth program reading assignment.

Challenges to *The Color Purple* continued into the 1990s. A parent in Ten Sleep, Wyoming, complained in 1990 about the inclusion of the book as an optional reading assignment for a sophomore English class. The superintendent of schools refused to remove the book and, instead, reminded parents that the students had numerous alternative readings from which to choose. That same year, parents in Tyrone, Pennsylvania, objected to the inclusion of the novel on a high school supplementary reading list. They found the language and the sexual activity embarrassing. The school board formed a committee to review guidelines for reading lists and to set standards for material that did not appear on approved curriculum lists. Parents of students in New Bern (North Carolina) High School raised objections to the novel, one of the 10th-grade reading assignments, after they read the passage in which Celie is raped by her stepfather. The high school principal appointed a review committee and allowed parents to select another book for their children. The review committee created restrictions that determined how the novel would be taught to future students. Also in 1992, the novel was banned from the Souderton (Pennsylvania) Area School District 10th-grade reading lists, when parents protested that the language and sexual situations of the novel made it more "smut" than literature.

The *Los Angeles Times* reported that many of the parents were believed to be members of religious organizations. Parents called for the resignation of Marion Dugan, director of curriculum, because she supported retention of the book, although after a long defense she retained her job.

In 2001, the *Atlanta Constitution* reported that *The Color Purple* had been removed from the Accelerated Reader Program in Cobb County in metropolitan Atlanta, Georgia. Until April 2001, the novel was recommended for reading by children as young as 11 in the reading program that encouraged younger students to read material with mature content aimed at teenage readers. Angry parents contacted Cobb County school officials and insisted on removal of the book because of the sexually explicit situations and the incidents of incest that occur. Pam McClure, the parent who led the challenge against the novel, told reporters, "The topic of incest was not appropriate . . . Sexually explicit situations—not appropriate."

FURTHER READING

American Library Association. *Censorship and Selection: Issues and Answers for Schools.* Chicago: American Library Association, 1993.

"Book Ban Includes *The Color Purple.*" *Chicago Tribune,* November 9, 1997, p. 11.

Christian, Barbara. *Black Feminist Criticism.* New York: Pergamon Press, 1985.

Gentry, Tony. *Alice Walker: Author.* New York: Chelsea House Publishers, 1993.

Kramer, Barbara. *Alice Walker: Author of "The Color Purple."* Springfield, N.J.: Enslow Publishers, 1995.

MacDonald, Mary. "Parents Say Preteens in Cobb Get Too Raunchy a Reading List." *Atlanta Constitution,* April 23, 2001, p. A-1.

People For the American Way. *Attacks on the Freedom to Learn: 1991–1992 Report.* Washington, D.C.: People For the American Way, 1992.

Shogren, Elizabeth, and Douglas Frantz. "Political, Religious Right Lead School Book Ban Efforts Censorship: A Survey by a Liberal-Leaning Group Finds 41% of 347 Attempts to Restrict Reading Material Succeeded. *The Color Purple* Is One Target." *Los Angeles Times,* September 2, 1993, p. 14.

Young Adult Services Division, Intellectual Freedom Committee. *Hit List: Frequently Challenged Young Adult Titles: References to Defend Them.* Chicago: YASD, American Library Association, 1989.

FAHRENHEIT 451

Author: Ray Bradbury
Original date and place of publication: 1953, United States
Original publisher: Ballantine Books
Literary form: Novel

SUMMARY

Fahrenheit 451 relates the story of an oppressive society in which books are forbidden objects and firemen are required to burn all books they encounter. The novel, an expanded version of a 1950 story entitled "The Fireman," takes its title from the temperature at which paper ignites: 451°F. One of a number of dystopic novels published after World War II, the work portrays humans as having lost touch with the natural world, with the world of the intellect, and with each other. As the fire captain observes, "the word 'intellectual' became the swear word it deserved to be."

People hurry from their homes to their workplaces and back, never speaking of what they feel or think but only spouting meaningless facts and figures. At home, they surround themselves with interactive picture walls, wall-size television screens on three walls (four walls if one can afford them) containing characters who become accepted as family in an otherwise unconnected life. The streets have become dangerous as *minimum* speed limits of 55 miles per hour must be maintained, and speeds well over 100 miles per hour are more common. Teenagers and daring adults race their cars through the streets without concern for human life. War with an unnamed enemy is imminent.

For one fireman, the realization that there is a better life comes in the form of a 17-year-old girl named Clarisse, whose appreciation of nature, desire to talk about feelings and thoughts, and appreciation for simply being alive mark her as an "odd duck." Guy Montag likes his job as a fireman, but he has clandestinely taken books from several sites where he and his fellow firemen have burned books and the houses in which they were hidden. Clarisse's questions as to why Montag became a fireman and her observations that the job does not seem right for him are disconcerting. A call to burn the books and house of a woman who refuses to leave the premises and, instead, ignites herself with the books increases Montag's discontent. He tries to speak with his wife, Mildred, but she blocks him out with her Seashell ear thimbles, tiny radios worn in the ear that play continuously, and her involvement with her "family" on the picture walls.

Montag learns that the major reason for the abolition of books was to keep everyone happy. His fire captain explains that without books there is no conflicting theory or thought, and no one learns anything more than anyone else. With books, "Who knows who might be the target of the well-read man?"

After his wife reports that Montag has books in the house and their home is destroyed by the firemen, he seeks the help of former English professor Faber, who is part of a broader movement to preserve the knowledge of the past. Following Faber's directions, Montag goes to the railroad yards, where he meets a group of old men, all former university professors who have each memorized specific literary works. They claim to be part of a network of thousands of individuals who will keep literature alive in their heads until the time when the oppression ceases and they can set the literature in type once more. Montag, who has memorized several books of the Old Testament, joins them, and the novel ends on a hopeful note.

CENSORSHIP HISTORY

Fahrenheit 451 is an indictment of censorship and expurgation, so the fact that this book was expurgated and marketed by the publisher that way for 13 years before the author became aware of the abuse is particularly ironic. In 1967, Ballantine Books published a special edition of the novel to be sold in high schools. Over 75 passages were modified to eliminate such words as *hell*, *damn*, and *abortion*, and two incidents were eliminated. The original first incident described a drunk man who was changed to a sick man in the expurgated edition. In the second incident, reference is made to cleaning fluff out of the human navel, but the expurgated edition changed the reference to cleaning ears. No one complained about the expurgation, mainly because few people were aware of the changes and many had not read the original. The copyright page made no mention of the changes, but thousands of people read only this version of *Fahrenheit 451* because the edition ran to 10 printings. At the same time, Ballantine Books continued to publish the "adult" version that was marketed to bookstores. After six years of the simultaneous editions, the publisher ceased publication of the adult version, leaving only the expurgated version for sale from 1973 through 1979, during which neither Bradbury nor anyone else suspected the truth.

In 1979, a friend alerted Bradbury to the expurgation, and he demanded that Ballantine Books withdraw completely the expurgated version and replace it with his original. The publisher agreed, and the complete version has been available since 1980.

This act of censorship had far-reaching effects for authors in regard to the school book clubs. The incident set in motion the American Library Association (ALA) Intellectual Freedom Committee, Young Adult Division. In 1981, the committee looked into expurgation by school book clubs, such as Scholastic, and found that all of them expurgated books to some extent. Using its clout, the ALA reminded the book clubs that it awards the Newbery and Caldecott medals for children's books, and the ALA also noted that buyers are attracted to books designated as "ALA Best Books." The organization warned that it would strip the award announcements from expurgated books. The ALA also alerted teacher groups to demand that an expurgated book in a school book club be clearly identified on the copyright page as an "edited school book edition."

In a coda that now appears in editions of *Fahrenheit 451*, Bradbury states, "I will not go gently onto a shelf, degutted, to become a non-book."

The "adult" version still has its critics. In 1992, students at Venado Middle School in Irvine, California, were issued copies of the novel with numerous words blacked out. School officials had ordered teachers to use black markers to obliterate all of the "hells," "damns," and other words deemed "obscene" in the books before giving them to students as required reading. Parents complained to the school and contacted local newspapers, who sent reporters to write stories about the irony of a book that condemns bookburning and censorship being expurgated. Faced with such an outcry, school officials announced that the censored copies would no longer be used.

FURTHER READING

Johnson, Wayne L. *Ray Bradbury.* New York: Frederick Ungar, 1980.
Moore, Everett T. "A Rationale for Bookburners: A Further Word from Ray Bradbury." *ALA Bulletin* 55 (May 1961): 403–404.
Newsletter on Intellectual Freedom (July 1992): 108–109.
Seed, David. "The Flight from the Good Life: 'Fahrenheit 451' in the Context of Postwar American Dystopias." *Journal of American Studies* 28, pt. 2 (August 1994): 225–240.

A FAREWELL TO ARMS

Author: Ernest Hemingway
Original date and place of publication: 1929, United States
Original publisher: Charles Scribner's Sons
Literary form: Novel

SUMMARY

A Farewell to Arms is both a powerful war novel and a love story. Told from the first-person point of view of American Frederic Henry, who becomes an ambulance driver for the Italian army in 1916, it chronicles fighting against the Austrian army along the Italian-Yugoslavian border. With the other officers, Henry first spends a lot of his time drinking and visiting the officers' brothel. On the battlefield, he is reckless in rescuing wounded soldiers and, after valorous conduct in his 11th battle, he is awarded a decoration. He also becomes involved with an English nurse named Catherine Barkley who serves in an Italian military hospital. He begins the relationship as a way to fill the time, after he learns that Catherine's fiancé was killed in the war and she is vulnerable.

After Henry is wounded and hospitalized, the affair intensifies, and he discovers that he really loves Catherine. He asks Catherine to marry him, but she refuses, knowing that she would then be sent back to England and away from him. However, the war imposes physical separations on them, when Henry is sent to the front just as Catherine learns that she is pregnant. His disillusionment with war escalates as he is involved in the retreat from Caporetto, which begins in an orderly, disciplined manner but eventually turns into a panicking mob as authority breaks down and self-preservation becomes paramount. Henry is captured with other officers and held for execution but manages to escape, thus completing his disillusionment with the war. He locates Catherine, and the two escape together to Switzerland, where they await the birth of their baby. They spend idyllic months, despite Catherine's worry that her narrow hips will make the birth difficult. When they seem about to achieve happiness together, their child is stillborn, and Catherine dies after suffering internal hemorrhaging, leaving Frederick Henry alone.

CENSORSHIP HISTORY

A Farewell to Arms has been censored both for its language and for sexual innuendo, as well as for the sexual relationship between Henry and Catherine and her unmarried pregnancy, although no graphic sexuality occurs in the novel. The soldiers frequent "bawdy houses" or the officers' "brothel." Henry has had "gonorrhea" and a military officer fears having "contracted syphilis from a prostitute." A dead sergeant who had attempted to desert the army is referred to as a "son of a bitch." Early in the novel, a boisterous officer teases a priest that he is often seen with the girls. When the priest protests, the officer jokingly accuses him of masturbating, saying, "Priest every night five against one." At one point, Catherine teases Henry, who says that he is lost without her and states that he at least had something to do at the front. She says, "Othello with his occupation gone." He replies, "Othello was a nigger."

In the few instances in which Hemingway seemed unable to substitute an innocuous word for what might be viewed as a vulgar term, he used dashes. When speaking about their chances against the Austrians, one of two Italian soldiers says, "They'll shell the———out of us." When the soldiers pass through a small Italian town, they pick up two girls and place them in a jeep, while they speculate about having sex. As they speak, the soldiers reassure the girls that there will be no sex, "using the vulgar word," but Hemingway places dashes in the four places where the "vulgar word" should appear. Then the soldiers bluntly ask the girls if they are sexually inexperienced: "Virgin? . . . Virgin too?"

An officer visits the wounded Henry in the hospital, and he tells Henry that the priest is making big preparations to visit. He teases Henry, "Sometimes I think you and he are a little that way. You know." Catherine visits Henry when he is moved to an American hospital in Milan, and they make love in his room, but the reader has to pay careful attention to the dialogue to know this has occurred. Their lines alternate between Catherine asking if Henry *really* loves her, and Henry reassuring her that he does. Afterward, as she sits in a chair by the bed, "the wildness was gone" for Henry, and Catherine asks, "Now do you believe I love you?" As the novel progresses, they discuss marrying, and the point is clearly made that Henry wants "to make an honest woman" out of Catherine. They are concerned about legitimizing her pregnancy.

The censorship of *A Farewell to Arms* began before the novel was published, leading to Hemingway's complaints to editor Maxwell Perkins that too many necessary "unsavory" words had been removed from the manuscript. In letters to Perkins, he stated that "if a word can be printed and is needed in the text it is a weakening to omit it." Perkins had warned Hemingway in 1926 in regard to the earlier novel *The Sun Also Rises* that "papers now attack a book, not only on grounds of eroticism which could not hold here, but upon that of 'decency,' which means *words*." He had suggested that in that novel another word be substituted for the bull's "balls," as well as for other terms.

Two years later, Hemingway was faced with eliminating the natural speech of men at war. Thus, in the original manuscript in the section that detailed the retreat from Caporetto, Hemingway wrote the following: " 'Tomorrow maybe we'll sleep in *shit*,' Piani said. 'I'll sleep with the queen,' Bonello said. 'You'll sleep with *shit*,' Piani said sleepily." The italicized words appear as blanks or dashes in the final novel. Other passages in that same section of the novel have dashes to substitute for "the *fucking* cavalry" and in "So do you, *cocksucker*," as well as in other instances.

In 1929, *Scribner's Magazine* contracted to serialize the book with certain changes. As the editor Robert Bridges explained to the author in a letter:

> we have in several places put in dashes instead of the realistic phrases which the soldiers of course used. This was not done from any particular squeamishness, but we have long been accepted in many schools as what is known, I believe, as "collateral reading," and have quite a clientage among those who teach mixed classics. Things which are perfectly natural and realistic in a book are not viewed with the same mind in a serial reading.

Bridges excised the following words from the manuscript that could not be used in a magazine: *balls, cocksucker, fuck, Jesus Christ, shit, son of a bitch, whore,* and *whorehound*. He also deleted a passage in which Henry fantasizes about his weekend in bed with Catherine, a passage that would later be returned to the novel when it was published. The second installment contained increased deletions of passages, including the sanitization of the seduction scene. Despite all of the changes, the June 1929 issue of *Scribner's Magazine* was banned from the bookstands in Boston, by order of the superintendent of police.

When Max Perkins edited the novel for publication, the following words deleted by Bridges were returned: *Jesus Christ, son of a bitch, whore,* and *whorehound*. However, Perkins suggested that Hemingway remove the following question: "Would you like to use a bedpan?" He also asked Hemingway to change " 'Miss Van Campen,' I said, 'did you ever know a man who tried to disable himself by kicking himself in the balls?' " to substitute the word *scrotum* for *balls*. Hemingway fought to retain use of the word *cocksucker* by the soldiers, and he claimed that eliminating it would completely emasculate the novel. His suggestion to use the term *c—s—r* was considered still too strong, so only dashes appear for that word.

In spite of the modifications to the text, the novel was considered too ris-qué. In a strongly negative review entitled "What Is Dirt?" in *Bookman*, Robert Herrick claimed that he was "adamantly opposed to censorship" but found that *A Farewell to Arms* presented one of those times when it was necessary. Other guardians of morality sent scathing letters to *Scribner's Magazine* threatening to cancel subscriptions because of the "vileness" of the novel, calling it "vulgar beyond express" and condemning the magazine for exploiting "such disgusting situations."

The novel was banned in Italy in 1929 because of its painfully accurate account of the Italian retreat from Caporetto during World War I. In 1930, the Watch and Ward Society in Boston, buoyed by the earlier successful outcry against the serialization in *Scribner's Magazine*, placed pressure on booksellers to remove the book from their store windows. In 1933, the novel was one of numerous books burned by the Nazis in Germany, allegedly for its "prurience." In 1938, the National Organization for Decent Literature (NODL) found the novel to be "objectionable" and placed it on their list of blacklisted books that was then sent to cooperating book dealers who agreed to remove the books from their racks. Such NODL blacklists resulted in elaborate collegial pressure among booksellers, although not legal enforce-ment against a work. The novel was also banned in Ireland in 1939 because of the "fornication" of Henry and Catherine and the pregnancy outside of marriage.

The novel has experienced more recent challenges. In 1974, parents of students in the Dallas (Texas) Independent School District demanded that it be removed from the high school libraries, along with Arthur Miller's *Death of a Salesman*, William Golding's *Lord of the Flies*, and Robert Penn Warren's *All the King's Men*. They complained that the novel contained a depressing view of life and "immoral" situations. After reviewing the work, school offi-cials retained the novel. The book was also challenged in the Vernon-Verona-Sherrill (New York) School District in 1980 for being a "sex novel," along with *A Separate Peace*, *To Kill a Mockingbird*, *The Grapes of Wrath*, *Of Mice and Men*, and *The Red Pony*.

FURTHER READING

Benson, Jackson J. *Hemingway: The Writer's Art of Self-Defense.* Minneapolis: Univer-sity of Minnesota Press, 1969.

Cohen, Peter F. " 'I Won't Kiss You. . . . I'll Send Your English Girl': Homoerotic Desire in 'A Farewell to Arms.' " *Hemingway Review* 15 (Fall 1995): 42–53.

Donaldson, Scott. "Censorship and 'A Farewell to Arms.' " *Studies in American Fiction* 19 (Spring 1991): 85–93.

Hemingway, Ernest. *Selected Letters: 1917–1961,* edited by Carlos Baker. New York: Charles Scribner's Sons, 1981.

Herrick, Robert. "What Is Dirt?" *Bookman* 70 (November 1929): 258–262.

Mandel, Miriam. "Ferguson and Lesbian Love: Unspoken Subplots in 'A Farewell to Arms.' " *Hemingway Review* 14 (Fall 1994): 18–24.

Meriweather, James B. "The Dashes in Hemingway's *A Farewell to Arms.*" *The Papers of the Bibliographical Society of America* 58 (Fourth Quarter 1964): 449–457.

Oldsey, Bernard. *Hemingway's Hidden Craft: The Writing of "A Farewell to Arms."* University Park: Pennsylvania State University Press, 1979.

Reynolds, Michael S. *Hemingway's First War: The Making of "A Farewell to Arms."* Princeton, N.J.: Princeton University Press, 1976.

Solotaroff, Robert. "Sexual Identity in 'A Farewell to Arms.' " *Hemingway Review* 9 (Fall 1989): 2–17.

FREAKONOMICS: A ROGUE ECONOMIST EXPLORES THE HIDDEN SIDE OF EVERYTHING

Authors: Steven D. Levitt and Stephen J. Dubner
Original date and place of publication: 2005, United States
Original publisher: HarperCollins
Literary type: Nonfiction

SUMMARY

Freakonomics: A Rogue Economist Explores the Hidden Side of Everything, written by economist Steven D. Levitt and journalist Stephen J. Dubner, applies the conventional theories of economics in an unconventional manner to challenge modern assumptions about crime, parenting, teaching, drug dealing, and sumo wrestling, among many other topics. Rather than writing a book centered upon a unifying theme, the authors have chosen "a sort of treasure-hunt approach" that "allows us to follow whatever freakish curiosities may occur to us. Thus our invented field of study: Freakonomics." Despite this freewheeling description, the authors do acknowledge that the book "has been written from a very specific worldview, based on a few fundamental ideas: Incentives are the cornerstone of modern life. . . . The conventional wisdom is often wrong. . . . Dramatic effects often have distant, even subtle, causes. . . . 'Experts'—from criminologists to real-estate agents—use their informational advantage to serve their own agenda. . . . Knowing what to measure and how to measure it makes a complicated world much less so."

The authors' theories and discussions are neatly compartmentalized into six chapters: chapter 1—What Do Schoolteachers and Sumo Wrestlers Have in Common?; chapter 2—How Is the Ku Klux Klan Like a Group of Real-Estate Agents?; chapter 3—Why Do Drug Dealers Still Live with Their Moms?; chapter 4—Where Have All the Criminals Gone?; chapter 5—What Makes a Perfect Parent?; and chapter 6—Perfect Parenting, Part II; Or, Would a Roshanda by Any Other Name Smell as Sweet? In the introduction, the authors assert that "if morality represents how people would like the world to work, then economics shows how it actually does work," and they proceed to show in the six chapters that follow why conventional wisdom is often wrong.

In "What Do Schoolteachers and Sumo Wrestlers Have in Common?" the authors explore the important role that incentives play in motivating behavior and examine why they often fail to achieve the desired behavior. The chapter also discusses the reasons why teachers will change children's answers on standardized tests and why sumo wrestlers in Japan may deliberately lose certain high-stakes matches. In the second chapter, the authors identify the ways in which the Ku Klux Klan resembles a group of real estate agents. They examine the role that information asymmetry plays and argue "nothing is more powerful than information, especially when its power is abused." The third chapter questions the validity of experts and asserts that "the conventional wisdom is often found to be a web of fabrication, self-interest, and convenience." The chapter reveals the secret financial operations of a street drug-dealing operation and exhibits the close similarity between the numerous levels of the drug gang hierarchy and the organizational chart of the fast food giant McDonald's.

In "Where Have All the Criminals Gone?" the "facts of crime are sorted out from the fictions." This is the most controversial chapter in the book. Levitt and Dubner postulate a strong link between the legalization of abortion in the United States in 1973 and the dramatic drop in crime in the mid-1990s, the time when, had abortions not occurred, the children born unwanted and into crime-ridden areas would have reached their mid-to-late teens and begun active adult criminal careers. In the discussion of the impact of *Roe v. Wade* on the nation's crime rate, the book states: "Jane Roe, crime stopper: how the legalization of abortion changed everything."

Chapters 5 and 6 focus on the roles of parents and suggest that the parents' socioeconomic status has more to do with children's academic achievement than the advice commonly given by experts that parents should read to their children. The chapter also questions "from a variety of angles, a pressing question: Do parents really matter?" and assesses "the importance of a parent's first official act—naming the baby."

In the epilogue, the authors assert that the net effect of reading *Freakonomics* will probably be subtle: "You might become more skeptical of the conventional wisdom; you may begin looking for hints as to how things aren't quite what they seem; perhaps you will seek out some trove of data and sift through it, balancing your intelligence and your intuition to arrive at a glimmering new idea." At the very least, the authors express a simple hope: "You might find yourself asking a lot of questions."

CENSORSHIP HISTORY

In 2006, *Freakonomics* was among nine books on the required reading list that were challenged in the second-largest high school district in Illinois, an act that "triggered debate over whether works praised in literary circles are high art or smut." The controversy began when Leslie Pinney, a Township High School district 214 board member, identified books on the reading list that she considered to "contain vulgar language, brutal imagery or depictions of sexual situations inappropriate for students." The books Pinney identified as inappropriate reading material, in addition to *Freakonomics*, are *Slaughterhouse-Five* by Kurt Vonnegut, *The Things They Carried* by Tim O'Brien, *The Awakening* by Kate Chopin, *How The Garcia Girls Lost Their Accents* by Julia Alvarez, *The Botany of Desire: A Plant's Eye View of the World* by Michael Pollan, *The Perks of Being a Wallflower* by Stephen Chbosky, *Fallen Angels* by Walter Dean Myers, and *Beloved* by Toni Morrison. The school board member admitted that she had not read most of the books she targeted and claimed that she did not want to ban the books from the district libraries, but in the classrooms she wanted "to replace them with books that address the same themes without explicit material." Her objection to *Freakonomics* was the discussion of abortion appearing in chapter 4 in which Levitt and Dunbar examine the extent to which crime decreased throughout the United States in the mid-1990s, nearly two decades after abortions were legalized in 1973. Pinney expressed dismay that the authors would postulate an abortion-crime link. In the book, the authors anticipate such reactions and assert, "This theory is bound to provoke a variety of reactions, ranging from disbelief to revulsion, and a variety of objections, ranging from the quotidian to the moral. . . . To discover that abortion was one of the greatest crime-lowering factors in American history is, needless to say, jarring." The challenges were the first in more than 20 years that someone had attempted to remove books from the reading lists in the Arlington Heights–based district, which employed an extensive review process based on established reading lists. In defense of the choices, English and fine arts department head Chuck Venegoni told a reporter for the *Chicago Tribune*, "This is not some serendipitous decision to allow someone to do what they felt like doing because they had something about talking about something kinky in front of kids. It's insulting to hardworking people who really do care about kids." He criticized Pinney's approach of taking a few passages out of context to condemn entire books and observed, "There is nothing in any of those books that even remotely approaches what an objective person would call pornography." Although the school district had an opt-out clause that allowed parents to request that their child read another book if they find the assigned material objectionable, Pinney found the current measures ineffectual "because unless you're digging around the student's backpack, looking at the books and reading them, how exactly will you know what your student is reading?"

Five hundred people attended the school board meeting on Thursday, May 25, 2006, to debate whether to keep *Freakonomics* and the other books on the school reading lists. Supporters of the ban asserted that their efforts were "to protect students from smut" and some people, such as Arlington Heights resident Brude Ticknell, claimed that "teachers promoting the books were motivated by their own progressive social agendas." Students took the debate to the social networking site MySpace.com, and sophomore Scott Leipprandt placed a petition against the ban on the Prospect High page, which nearly 500 students and alumni from the six high schools in the district signed. Leipprandt told a *Chicago Tribune* reporter that fighting the banning of books is important. "It's important because it shows us things. All these things happen in real life. By banning it, it doesn't give us the opportunity to talk about it before we encounter it in real life." After a long meeting during which hundreds of people spoke, the school board voted 6-1 in favor of approving the required reading list without change. The following year, the school board voted to provide parents with the reading lists for courses before voting on materials.

More recently, in 2009, the Texas Department of Criminal Justice (TDCJ) prevented an inmate from receiving the copy of *SuperFreakonomics*, the followup to *Freakonomics* that he ordered from Amazon, because it is "racially provocative." When author Steven Levitt heard about the incident, he contacted Texas officials who told him that they had made an error and that *Freakonomics* is the book that violates their censorship policies and the book that they had meant to ban. The incident began when Thomas Glesburg, a prisoner serving a 65-year sentence for murder, ordered a copy of *SuperFreakonomics*. The TDCJ confiscated the book, and Levitt wrote about the incident on his blog, after which Jason Clark, a spokesman for the TDCJ, contacted him and told him that the director's review committee had decided on May 25, 2005, to deny prisoners access to the book because it contained "racial material" on pages 50, 59, 67, and 90. Pages 50, 57, and 69 appear in chapter 2, "How Is the Ku Klux Klan Like a Group of Real-Estate Agents?" Writing in the *Statesman*, Dexheimer reports that page 57 contains a "rather tame and factual history of the Klan, with a single quote containing the use of the n word to describe blacks. Page 59 relates how a young reformer goes undercover and learns exactly how bigoted Klan members really are. It contains two uses of the n word, again both quotes. Page 60 adds details of the man's study, such as the Klan's hilarious secret handshake, which he describes as 'a left-handed, limp-wristed fish wiggle.' It, too, quotes a Klansman using the n word." The objection to page 97 is similar to the others and contains a single blue passage. In it, a drug dealer explains the hard life: "It's a war out here, man. I mean, every day people struggling to survive, so you know, we just do what we can. We ain't got no choice, and if that means getting killed, well shit, it's what niggers do around here to feed their family." Dexheimer observes that page 96 is not cited as part of the reason for the ban, yet it contains several uses of the N-word. He asked TDCJ officials about that omission and learned that the "detailed reason for originally denying the book in 2005 has been purged. All that remains is the ban."

FURTHER READING

Dexheimer, Eric. "Is SuperFreakonomics Inappropriate? No—but Freakonomics Is." *Statesman*. Available online. URL: http://www.statesman.com/blogs/content/shared-gen/blogs/austin/investigative/entries/2010/01/08/is_superfreakonomics_racist_no.html. Accessed July 29, 2010.

Francisco, Jamie. "Explicit Move Is Made to Ban Books from Reading List." *Chicago Tribune*, May 24, 2006.

GORILLAS IN THE MIST

Author: Dian Fossey
Original date and place of publication: 1983, United States
Original publisher: Houghton Mifflin
Literary form: Zoological study

SUMMARY

Gorillas in the Mist, written by the world authority on the endangered mountain gorilla, relates Dian Fossey's experiences over the 14 years in which she conducted field studies among four gorilla families in the Virunga Mountains shared by Zaire, Rwanda, and Uganda. The scientist became well known to villagers, who signaled her approach by shouting, *"Nyiramachabelli!"* meaning, "The old lady who lives in the forest without a man."

To gain the acceptance of the gorillas, Fossey imitated their feeding and contentment sounds, as well as other behavior such as self-grooming and averting her eyes from their glances. After gaining their trust, she tracked the various groups and identified the adult animals with names, then gave names to the offspring that were born during the course of the study. Fossey viewed the gorillas as individuals, and she relates their unique characteristics in the book. She was eventually fully accepted by one gorilla group and made history when a fully mature male gorilla reached out to touch her.

As she studied the gorillas, Fossey meticulously documented male-female interactions, parent-child interactions, mating behavior, parenting skills, and both intragroup and intergroup behavior. Fossey's report of the sexual behavior and mating patterns of the gorillas is equally detailed. In one instance, the scientist reports that a young gorilla named Puck goes off alone and Fossey sees him "actively masturbating."

The author also documents mating behavior in careful detail, as well as other behavior of the young, sexually immature but curious gorillas. The book includes a photograph of a female being mounted by a male in her group. Fossey also tells of three-year-old Pablo, who is so obsessively interested in sexual activities that "he often tried to examine the penises of the older males but was usually shoved away." He also engages frequently in sex play with Poppy, a female gorilla 20 months his junior.

In addition to studying the lives of the gorillas, Fossey informs readers of the devastation that poachers have wreaked in the gorilla population and calls for a stop to their actions. She also relates instances in which she stood up to poachers and reported them, thus placing her life in danger.

CENSORSHIP HISTORY

The work was acclaimed by scientists as a breakthrough study, and Fossey was later thrust into the international spotlight after one of the gorillas was killed by poachers. She spoke to groups to focus attention on the rain forest and the plight of the gorillas, and she was brutally murdered in 1985. The passages regarding masturbation and mating behavior in her book are integral to the study and were accepted as such by scientists, but the same passages raised objections when the books appeared in schools and school libraries.

The book was kept out of many classrooms and not ordered for school libraries to avoid controversy over the details of the gorillas' sexual behavior. Many school administrators viewed the study as suitable for older students but unsuitable for or of less interest to middle school or younger students.

In 1993, teachers in Westlake Middle School in Erie, Pennsylvania, were instructed by school administrators to use felt-tip pens to black out "objectionable" passages in the book. Parents had challenged the use of the book in the classroom, claiming that the passages about gorilla sexual behavior and mating habits were "filthy," "unnecessary," and "inappropriate." The following passage regarding the masturbating gorilla was one of the "objectionable" passages blacked out:

> His head was flexed backward, his eyes were closed, and he wore a semismile expression while using his right forefinger to manipulate his genital area. For about two minutes, Puck appeared to be obtaining great pleasure from his actions. . . . It was the only time I have ever seen a gorilla in the wild actively masturbate.

The teachers were also required to block out lines detailing the sex play of three-year-old Pablo and one-year-old Poppy which "could result in an erection for Pablo, who with a puzzled smile, lay back and twiddled his penis" while Poppy watched with interest "or, occasionally even sucked his penis."

Farley Mowat's *Woman in the Mists* (Warner Books, 1987), which recounted Dian Fossey's dedication to her cause and her brutal death, was also subject to censorship. In 1991, the work was removed from a required reading list in the Omaha, Nebraska, school district. Parents who objected to the book claimed that it contained racial slurs, as well as "profanity" and passages that degraded women. They also objected to Mowat's long discussion of the aftermath of Fossey's abortion.

FURTHER READING

Montgomery, Sy. *Walking with the Great Apes.* Boston: Houghton Mifflin, 1991.

Morrell, Virginia. "Called 'Trimates,' Three Bold Women Shaped Their Field." *Science* 260 (April 16, 1993): 420–425.

Newsletter on Intellectual Freedom (March 1992): 44; (July 1993): 109.

Webb, C. Anne. "The Battle Continues." *English Journal* 48 (September 1995): 123–124.

THE GREAT GATSBY

Author: F. Scott Fitzgerald
Original date and place of publication: 1925, United States
Original publisher: Charles Scribner's Sons
Literary form: Novel

SUMMARY

The story of *The Great Gatsby* is well known, and the name continues to suggest an age of opulence, decadence, and wild abandon. Hidden by the facade of the large, overdecorated mansions, wild parties fueled by illegal liquor, flashy big cars, and mistresses is a world of lonely individuals all unable to find a sort peace in the post–World War I world. Rather than a celebration of such decadence, the novel functions as a cautionary tale in which an unhappy fate is inevitable for the poor and striving individual, and the rich are allowed to continue without penalty their careless treatment of others' lives. Narrated from the perspective of Nick Carraway, a veteran of World War I, Yale graduate, and would-be Wall Street bond seller, the novel relates the downfall of a socially ambitious man who rises from an obscure and impoverished Midwestern childhood to become a wealthy and sought-after center of Long Island society. Nick is a second cousin once removed of Daisy Buchanan, whom Gatsby met nearly a decade earlier when he was a young and poor army officer. His love for her, and his desire to become socially and financially acceptable to her, seems to have driven him to obtain wealth and property through unscrupulous means. Rumors about Gatsby and about the source of his wealth abound, and people who attend his lavish parties speculate where his money was made. Later in the novel, readers learn that Gatsby is a bootlegger who has built his wealth upon the illegal production and sale of liquor and associates with shady characters such as Meyer Wolfsheim.

Nick Carraway stands outside the action of the novel for the most part and relates and comments upon the simultaneous activities of the characters. His cousin Daisy Buchanan is bright, attractive, and flighty, careless in her parenting of her three-year-old daughter Pammy and indifferent to the intense obsession that Jay Gatsby has held for her for nearly a decade. He describes Daisy's husband, the arrogant and extremely wealthy Tom Buchanan, in unflattering terms but has little interaction with him, aside from characterizing him as a former athlete now long past his glory days. For a time Nick becomes romantically involved with Jordan Baker, Daisy's friend and a professional golfer with a tarnished reputation, but the affair begins with the clear knowledge that it will not last long. He expresses his most sympathetic perceptions when relating the character and activities of George Wilson, a mechanic and the owner of the garage located near the homes of the wealthy, and his wife, Myrtle, who is Tom Buchanan's mistress.

The novel portrays the wealthy in an unsympathetic light and exhibits the manner in which they exploit the feelings of others. Tom Buchanan may enjoy Myrtle Wilson physically as his mistress, but his behavior toward her and attitude of superiority show that he views her as only a temporary amusement. Daisy had once before rejected Gatsby when he was a poor army officer and, although she engages in an affair with him while married to Tom, she remains socially aloof and emotionally beyond his reach. Myrtle Wilson exists only to be used by the rich Tom Buchanan, as does her husband. However friendly Tom may appear when he brings his big car into the station for gas or service, he treats George as someone who exists only to serve him. Even James/Jimmy/Jay Gatsby, once a nobody from North Dakota and now in possession of wealth and a huge mansion on Long Island Sound, remains forever inferior to the old wealth represented by the Buchanans. He may have money, but he is not able to elevate his social value nor does he share the elite privileges of the wealthy.

While at the Plaza Hotel in Manhattan, Tom and Daisy quarrel and Daisy leaves, driving Gatsby's car in an effort to relax. The tragedy that occurs is threefold. While racing through the village of West Egg on her way home, Daisy runs down Myrtle with the car, which belongs to Gatsby. The next day, the grief-stricken George Wilson tracks down Gatsby and, believing that he was driving the car that killed Myrtle, he shoots Gatsby and leaves him floating dead in the pool, then commits suicide. Despite all of the people that attended Gatsby's parties, drank his liquor, and ate his food, only three show up at his funeral: Nick, Jay's estranged father, and a man identified only as "Owl eyes," whom Nick once met admiring books in Gatsby's library. After the funeral, disreputable individuals appear at the mansion and take art and other of Gatsby's belongings in payment for debts.

The tragedies do not touch Tom and Daisy Buchanan, and they are left to continue their lives, indifferent to the destruction that they have left behind them. Nick Carroway expresses one of the most revealing sentiments in the book after Tom rationalizes having falsely implicated Gatsby in the death of Myrtle: "They were careless people, Tom and Daisy—they smashed up things and creatures and then retreated back into their money or their vast careless-ness, or whatever is was that kept them together and let other people clean up the mess they had made. . . ." The novel ends as Nick has sold his car and packed his possessions, ready to return to the Midwest, because after Gatsby's death, "the East was haunted for me like that, distorted beyond my eyes' power of correction. So when the blue smoke of brittle leaves was in the air and the wind blew the wet laundry stiff on the line I decided to come back home."

CENSORSHIP HISTORY

The Great Gatsby excited controversy even before the book was published for its daring expose of the wild decadence of the wealthy. In 1923, as Fitzgerald edited and revised the proofs, he explored serialization of the book in various magazines. The 1923 option contract had provided Hearst magazines with the right of first refusal for the serial rights, and the author's expectations of earning from $15,000 to $20,000 were destroyed when editor Ray Long declined the novel. In *Some Sort of Epic Grandeur, The Life of F. Scott Fitzgerald*, Matthew J. Bruccoli relates, "Inoffensive as the material now seems, it was regarded as too strong for magazines whose readership was largely female." Fitzgerald's literary agent Harold Ober attempted to sell the rights to editor John Wheeler for *Liberty* magazine, a weekly magazine. Wheeler also turned down the offer and told Ober, "It is too ripe for us. Running only one serial as we do, we could not publish this story with as many mistresses and as much adultery as there is in it."

In more recent decades, as *The Great Gatsby* has become a perennial selection on high school and college reading lists, challenges have emerged in various areas of the United States, although many receive little publicity because they remain unreported to the American Library Association. Every Web site dedicated to celebrating the freedom to read identifies the novel as having been "challenged at the Baptist College in Charleston, SC (1987) because of 'language and sexual references in the book,'" but the details of the challenge as well as all actual news accounts are not available.

In the same year, however, the Bay County School Board, in Panama City, Florida, and superintendent of schools Leonard Hall created a censorship controversy when they announced a "three-tier book classification system" to evaluate and to eliminate books on the current high school reading list. Superintendent Hall, who claimed that he was "elected to restore Christian values to the schools," developed the categories. The first category consisted of works that contained "no vulgarity or explicit sex," and the second category or tier contains books that the board and superintendent assessed as containing "a sprinkling of vulgarity." The third tier, made of books that were removed from classroom discussion, were those the school officials characterized as having "a lot of vulgarity" and the curse "goddamn." Among the works in this third tier were *The Great Gatsby, Fahrenheit* 451, *The Red Badge of Courage*, and *The Old Man and the Sea*. Students, teachers, and parents brought suit against the school district to challenge the school board policy banning the classroom use of these classics. In May 1987, 44 residents filed a class action lawsuit in federal district court in Pensacola, Florida, in which they contended that their constitutional rights had been violated by the book policy instituted by the Bay County School Board and superintendent Hall. A day after residents filed the lawsuit, the school board and superintendent retracted their earlier actions, a move influenced both by the lawsuit and by the lengthy school board meeting attended by hundreds of area residents, which was also broadcast on local radio and television stations. Students arrived at the school board meeting wearing black armbands and asking to be allowed to speak. A member of the Bay County School Board, Deane Bozeman told reporters that the censorship attempt actually had an effect opposite from what had been intended: "The only thing we succeeded in doing is making sure every child in Bay County reads the books we banned." After meeting for eight hours and listening to hundreds of residents speak, the board moved to change its policy and to approve all books that were currently being used in the county of 110,000 people.

In 2008, the Coeur d'Alene, Idaho, school board developed an approval system to assess and remove books from the school reading lists after some parents complained that teachers had selected and were discussing books that "contained vulgar, profane language and dealt with subjects inappropriate for students." The books were removed from classrooms before the school year began and teachers were instructed to refrain from making reference to the novels until the appropriate approval process had been completed. The school district created a committee of parents, educators, district officials, and community members to review the 26 books that had raised objections. Included on the list were *Brave New World, Alice's Adventures in Wonderland, The Grapes of Wrath, The Scarlet Letter, 1984, The Catcher in the Rye*, and *The Great Gatsby*. Nearly 100 people attended the December 15, 2008, meeting. The board listened to public comments for more than an hour, then voted unanimously to return the books to lists of novels from which teachers can select for required assignments for students in sixth through 12th grades.

FURTHER READING

Bruccoli, Matthew J. *Some Sort of Epic Grandeur: The Life of F. Scott Fitzgerald*. New York: Harcourt Brace Jovanovich, 1981.
"Florida Officials Yield on Book Ban." *New York Times*, May 15, 1987, p. D18.
"Idaho City's School Board Drops Book Ban." Associated Press. Available online. URL: http://www.firstamendmentcenter.org/news.aspx?id21029. Accessed January 12, 2010.
LeVot, Andre. *F. Scott Fitzgerald: A Biography*. New York: Doubleday & Company, 1983.
Rimer, Sara. "Gatsby's Green Light Beckons a New Generation of Strivers." *New York Times*, February 17, 2008, p. A1.
"Suit Challenges School Book Ban." *New York Times*, May 14, 1987, p. A18.
Yardley, Jonathan. "'Gatsby': The Greatest of Them All." *Washington Post*, January 2, 2007, p. C1.

HEATHER HAS TWO MOMMIES

Author: Leslea Newman
Original date and place of publication: 1989, United States
Original publisher: Alyson Publications
Literary form: Children's book

SUMMARY

Heather Has Two Mommies is the story of a three-year-old girl being raised by a lesbian couple. For her, having two mothers feels perfectly normal, until she becomes part of a play group. Heather listens to the other children and realizes for the first time that many of them have one mother and a father, and she becomes upset. The leader of the play group encourages the children to talk about the different types of families that exist. As the children learn more about families, they realize that many children are growing up in nontraditional families. They also realize that the most important part of any type of family is love.

In the first part of the book, the events leading to Heather's conception through artificial insemination and her birth are dealt with in a matter-of-fact manner. The choices being made by the two "mommies" are discussed, as are their reasons for those choices. The second half of the book focuses on the family structure and shows that Heather's family is similar to those of other children, except for the "two mommies."

CENSORSHIP HISTORY

Heather Has Two Mommies has been challenged repeatedly since it was first published. In 1992, this book and *Daddy's Roommate* were removed from the first-grade reading list in the Bay Ridge School District in Brooklyn, New York; challenged but retained in Fayetteville (North Carolina) County Library and Springfield (Oregon) Public Library; and placed in the adult section of the Bladen County Library in Elizabethtown, North Carolina.

In 1993, *Heather Has Two Mommies* and *Daddy's Roommate* were moved from the children's room to the adult section in Mercer County Library System in Lawrence, New Jersey. They were also challenged but retained in the public library in Mesa, Arizona; North Brunswick (New Jersey) Public Library; Cumberland County (North Carolina) Public Library; Wicomico County Free County Library in Salisbury, Maryland; and Dayton and Montgomery County (Ohio) Public Library. In 1994, the two books were taken out of the Lane County Head Start program in Cottage Grove, Oregon, and challenged but retained by Chandler (Arizona) Public Library.

Heather Has Two Mommies was also challenged in 1993 by patrons of Chestatee Regional Library System in Gainesville, Georgia, who believed that the book was "not suitable" to be shelved in the children's section. Librarians moved the book to the young adult section, but three state legislators who became involved in the case wanted it removed. The legislators stated, "We could put together a resolution to amend the Georgia state constitution to say that tax dollars cannot be used to promote homosexuality, pedophilia or sado-masochism." The book remained in the young adult section, and the controversy faded away.

In 1994, parents challenged the inclusion of the book in an Oak Bluffs, Massachusetts, elementary school library. The parent who led the protest spoke out at a public meeting and stated that the subject matter of the book "is obscene and vulgar and the message is that homosexuality is okay." The school board created a review committee to examine the book and voted unanimously to keep the book in the library.

FURTHER READING

Buttenweiser, Susan. "A Child's Garden of . . . Diversity." *Ms.*, January 1993, pp. 61–62.

"Heather's Two Moms, Three Censors." *The Atlanta Journal* and *The Atlanta Constitution*, July 27, 1993, p. H4.

Hildebrand, Joan M. "Books for Children: *Heather Has Two Mommies*." *Childhood Education* 70 (1994), p. 305.

I KNOW WHY THE CAGED BIRD SINGS

Author: Maya Angelou (Marguerite Johnson)
Original date and place of publication: 1969, United States
Original publisher: Random House
Literary form: Autobiography

SUMMARY

I Know Why the Caged Bird Sings is the first of five autobiographical books written by the author. The others are *Gather Together in My Name* (1974), *Singin' and Swingin' and Gettin' Merry Like Christmas* (1976), *The Heart of a Woman* (1981), and *All God's Children Need Traveling Shoes* (1986). The first book chronicles Angelou's life from age three to age 16 and the birth of her only child, Guy, to whom she dedicates this book.

The book describes the divorce of her parents and her own difficulties as she is sent with her brother from Long Beach, California, to live with her grandmother and uncle in Stamps, Arkansas, spends a year in St. Louis with her mother, then returns to Stamps and eventually moves to California to be with her mother. The years in Stamps are largely happy years as her grandmother, "Momma," protects and shields the young girl. There are, however, some social realities from which she cannot be protected. The book recalls the despair often felt by the black cotton pickers as they filed into Momma's general store, returning from the fields on bad days. The rampant racism is evident in incidents such as the one in which her uncle must be hidden after a former sheriff warns the family that "Some of the boys'll be coming over here later" because Willie had "messed with a white lady today." When Maya is in need of a dentist, she overhears her grandmother being told by a white dentist to whom she had lent money during the Depression, "my policy is I'd rather stick my hand in a dog's mouth than in a nigger's."

Maya also suffers personal indignities as a child. When she moves to St. Louis to live with her mother, she is raped by her mother's live-in lover, who is later murdered. When she travels to Los Angeles to spend a summer with her father, the woman with whom he lives stabs Maya with a knife. Maya is nearly six feet tall, flat-chested, and unsure of sexuality at 15 when she decides to have sex with a handsome neighborhood boy. He forgets her name the next day, but she becomes pregnant and later gives birth to her only child, her son.

The autobiography ends with 16-year-old Maya holding her child protectively and going peacefully to sleep.

CENSORSHIP HISTORY

The majority of the challenges to *I Know Why the Caged Bird Sings* have resulted from parents' complaints about the rape scene and Maya's pregnancy out of wedlock. In 1983, the Alabama State Textbook Committee rejected the book because they believed that it "preaches bitterness and hatred against whites." The book was challenged at Mount Abram Regional High School in Strong, Maine, in 1988, because parents objected to the rape scene. In 1990, a parent in Bremerton, Washington, objected to the book as a required reading for the gifted ninth-grade class because of the "graphic" description of the molestation. The parent also complained that the book "raised sexual issues without giving them a moral resolution." Despite the teacher's defense that the molestation passages were only a small part of the book and that the main focus was the fulfillment that Angelou reached in spite of adversity, the school board removed the book from the classroom. The board president justified the action by explaining that his constituents expected him to uphold a higher level of moral standard than is evidenced by the book.

In 1991, several parents in Benning, California, complained about the explicit passages involving child molestation and requested that the book be removed from the eighth-grade curriculum. One parent complained that her son did not want to go back to class to read that "gross" book, and another characterized the work as "morally and religiously offensive smut." The book was removed from the curriculum. In 1992, the work was retained after the parent of a student in Amador Valley High School, in Pleasanton, California, complained of the sexually explicit language.

The work was challenged but retained in several 1993 incidents, all of which objected to the passage in which the rape of the seven-year-old Maya is discussed. The book was temporarily banned from Caledonia Middle School, in Columbus, Mississippi, on the grounds that it was too sexually explicit. In Haines City, Florida, parents objected to the same passage and challenged inclusion of the book in both the English curriculum and the high school library. The same challenge occurred in Hooks (Texas) High School, where the book was assigned in a freshman honors history class.

In 1994, the work was challenged but retained as required reading for Dowling High School sophomores in Des Moines, Iowa, and the book became an issue at Ponderosa High School in Castle Rock, Colorado, when parents charged that it was "a lurid tale of sexual perversion." In their 1994 challenge to the book, parents at Westwood High School in Austin, Texas, claimed that the book was "pornographic, contains profanity, and encourages premarital sex and homosexuality." The challenge motivated a new policy at the school for the reading of potentially controversial literature. The superintendent decreed that children would have to obtain their parents' permission in writing before they would be taught controversial literature.

In 2002, parents of students in freshman English classes in Hamilton, Montana, took issue with the references to rape and premarital sexual intercourse in the book, as well as the author's description of her molestation as an eight-year-old child. The parents also criticized the book for its suggestions of homosexuality. The same year, a group named the Parents Against Bad Books in Schools (PABBIS), represented by parents Richard and Alice Ess, complained to the school officials in Fairfax County, Virginia, that this book, along with 17 others, should be removed from elementary and secondary school libraries. They asserted that the book "contains profanity and descriptions of drug abuse, sexually explicit conduct, and torture."

FURTHER READING

Elliot, Jeffrey, ed. *Conversations with Maya Angelou*. Jackson: University of Mississippi Press, 1989.

Fox-Genovese, Elizabeth. "Myth and History: Discourse of Origins in Zora Neale Hurston and Maya Angelou." *Black American Literature Forum* 42 (Summer 1990): 221–235.

Newsletter on Intellectual Freedom (March 1983): 39; (January 1989): 8; (March 1989): 38; (November 1990): 211; (March 1992): 42; (July 1992): 109; (July 1993): 107; (January 1994): 34; (July 1994): 130; (January 1995): 11; (May 1995): 56; (November 2002): 258; (January 2003): 10.

Pettit, Jayne. *Maya Angelou: Journey of the Heart*. New York: Lodestar Books, 1996.

Shuker, Nancy. *Maya Angelou*. Englewood Cliffs, N.J.: Silver Burdett Press, 1990.

THE KITE RUNNER

Author: Khaled Hosseini
Original date and place of publication: 2003, United States
Original publisher: Riverhead Books (A Penguin Books Imprint)
Literary form: Novel

SUMMARY

The Kite Runner, which derives its name from the Afghan custom of kite fighting, focuses on the relationship between two boys of different social classes and religious backgrounds and the lasting effect that one boy's moment of cowardice has on their lives. A large portion of the novel is told in flashback, opening in December 2001 in San Francisco and moving back to 1975 and relating events through 1981 in Afghanistan and subsequent years in the United States. The story is as much an account of the trials faced by the nation of Afghanistan in those years as it is the story of one man's efforts to achieve redemption and to make peace with his past. The "kite runner" of the title refers to the friend he betrayed when a boy.

Amir and Hassan have grown up in the same household, one the acknowledged son of Baba, a wealthy businessman in Kabul, and the other the putative son of Ali, a servant in the same household. Amir, the narrator, is a Pashtun and a Sunni Muslim, and Hassan, one year younger, is a Hazara and a Shi'a. Their ethnic and religious differences create tensions between the two boys who, nonetheless, become constant companions and share a deep bond from infancy. Both have lost their mothers early in life and are raised by their fathers. Amir's mother died giving birth to him, thus depriving his rigid, successful father of his "beautiful princess," and Hassan's mother left his much-older, impoverished father five days after giving birth, disgusted by both her husband's physical disfigurement and her baby's cleft palate. The boys were also breast-fed by the same woman, whom Baba hired first for Amir, then for Hassan a year later. He

> would remind us that there was a brotherhood between people who had fed from the same breast, a kinship that not even time could break.
>
> Hassan and I fed from the same breasts. We took our first steps on the same lawn in the same yard. And, under the same roof, we spoke our first words.
>
> Mine was *Baba*.
>
> His was *Amir*. My name.
>
> Looking back on it now, I think the foundation for what happened in the winter of 1975—and all that followed—was already laid in those first words.

Baba's father, a judge, had brought an orphaned, five-year-old Ali into his household years earlier, and Baba had grown up with Ali in the same manner as Amir and Hassan. Baba's father had provided for the young Ali's physical wants, but he did not educate the child nor did he move him above his presumed station in life as a Hazara. Ali became a servant, a role he would continue to play in Baba's household, and a role in which his son Hassan would follow, each knowing his place in Afghan society. "When the sun dropped low behind the hills and we were done playing for the day, Hassan and I parted ways. I went past the rosebushes to Baba's mansion, Hassan to the mud shack where he had been born, where he'd lived his entire life." Each morning, Hassan enters the mansion to make Amir's breakfast, to iron his clothes, to gather and to pack his school supplies, and to help him get dressed, before attending to other duties around the house with Ali while Amir goes to school. Hassan is illiterate, but he is an eager learner who asks Amir the meanings of words and who enjoys Amir's reading to him. His illiteracy sometimes tempts Amir to "tease him, expose his ignorance," as when Hassan asks the meaning of "imbecile," a word he hears in a story Amir reads aloud. To Hassan's question, Amir responds in a condescending manner, "But it's such a common word!" At the other boy's persistence, he replies, "Well, everyone in my school knows what it means. Let's see. 'Imbecile.' It means smart, intelligent. I'll use it in a sentence for you. When it comes to words, Hassan is an imbecile."

Baba maintains a social distance from Ali and Hassan, but he is kind and generous toward them. He remembers Hassan's birthday with especially selected gifts, and he arranges for a renowned Indian surgeon to correct the boy's cleft palate. Baba also recognizes that, although a year younger than his son, Hassan is fiercely loyal to Amir and defends him against physical attacks on many occasions. One such instance creates an enemy who later retaliates, changing forever the lives of Amir and Hassan.

Amir has no interest in sports or other physical activity, nor does he exhibit the courage and bluster for which the demanding Baba is known. Instead, he is a dreamer who enjoys reading rather than roughhousing and who acknowledges that he "aspired to be a coward." He is jealous of Baba's approval of and kindness toward Hassan. In a desperate move to win his father's love and approval, Amir becomes involved in the sport of kite fighting and, at age 12, wins the annual tournament in Kabul, a victory he owes largely to Hassan who trains with him and shows an exceptional skill as a kite runner. The kites are made of tissue paper with glass-coated cutting lines that are used to sever the lines of the other kites. The tournament ends when only one winning kite remains in the sky. Kites that have been cut loose are pursued by "kite runners," children who chase the spiraling and drifting kites, shoving each other aside as they grasp for the falling kites.

> For kite runners, the most coveted prize was the last fallen kite of a winter tournament. It was a trophy of honor, something to be displayed on a mantle for guests to admire. When the sky cleared of kites and only the two final remained, every kite runner readied himself for the chance to land his prize. He positioned himself at a spot that he thought would give him a head start. Tense muscles readied themselves to uncoil. Necks craned. Eyes crinkled. Fights broke out. And when the last kite was cut, all hell broke loose.
>
> Over the years, I had seen a lot of guys run kites. But Hassan was by far the greatest kite runner I'd ever seen. It was downright eerie the way he always got to the spot the kite would *before* the kite did, as if he had some sort of inner compass.

After the kite-fighting tournament, Hassan runs through the streets of Kabul and retrieves the final kite Amir cut down to win the tournament. Months earlier, three older boys had trapped Amir and Hassan and threatened to beat them, but the boys were frightened away when Hassan aimed his slingshot at Assef, the most aggressive of the boys, and threatened to knock out his eye. Assef, the son of an Afghan airline pilot father and German mother, has known Amir's family for years, and Baba greatly admires him for his aggression, sports ability, and swagger, but he is not aware of Assef's propensity for violence and his intense admiration for Adolf Hitler. More than a year later, on the night of the kite-fighting tournament, Assef exacts his revenge. As Baba stands on a rooftop and cheers loudly for his son, following Amir's victory at the kite-fighting tournament, Hassan races away to run down the blue kite, the last one cut down and a trophy that Amir will present to his father. Hours pass, and Amir searches for Hassan, eager to obtain the blue kite, and finds him in an alley trapped by the three older boys who had threatened him earlier. Without revealing himself, Amir watches and listens as Assef berates Hassan and tries to wrest the blue kite from him. Loyal to Amir, and knowing how much the blue kite means to him, Hassan steadfastly refuses to hand it over, despite Assef's insults and threats. Amir also watches as Assef decides to let Hassan keep the kite, "I'll let you keep it so it will always remind you of what I am about to do." Amir sees Hassan's corduroy pants thrown carelessly on a pile of rubble and listens as Assef attempts to coerce his friends Wali and Kamal into "teaching a lesson to a disrespectful donkey." When they refuse, he calls them weaklings and orders them to hold Hassan down.

> Assef knelt behind Hassan, put his hands on Hassan's hips and lifted his bare buttocks. He kept one hand on Hassan's back and undid his own belt buckle with his free hand. He unzipped his jeans. Dropped his underwear. He positioned himself behind Hassan. Hassan didn't struggle. Didn't even whimper. He moved his head slightly and I caught a glimpse of his face. Saw the resignation in it. It was a look I had seen before. It was the look of a lamb.

Amir hesitates for a moment and thinks that he had one last chance to make a decision, one "final opportunity to decide who I was going to be. I could step into that alley, stand up for Hassan—the way he'd stood up for me all those times in the past. . . . Or I could run." He ran. As Amir runs away, he tells himself that he does so because he is a coward, "I actually *aspired* to cowardice," but he knows that his real reasons is more sinister. "Maybe Hassan was the price I had to pay, the lamb I had to slay to win Baba. . . . He was just a Hazara, wasn't he?" When the boys finally meet later in the evening, Hassan is carrying the blue kite, fulfilling his promise to Amir, who lies and says that he has been searching for the other boy. Hassan's voice cracks, but all he says is "Agha sahib [Baba] will worry," as he turns and limps away. Amir pretends he does not hear, and he pretends that he does not see "the dark stain in the seat of his pants. Or those tiny drops that fell from between his legs and stained the snow black."

After his moment of cowardice, Amir avoids Hassan, too ashamed to look the younger boy in the eye. A confused and hurt Hassan tries to reestablish their relationship, but Amir rebuffs his attempts and continues to suffer the guilt of his actions, surrounded as he is by the numerous signs of Hassan's presence in the breakfast each morning, the freshly ironed clothes, the warm slippers left outside his door. Hassan's continuing loyalty tortures Amir to the point that he can no longer stand to see Ali and his son and feels compelled to ask Baba about getting new servants. Baba's response is swift and definite as he refuses and warns Amir to never ask that question again. The pain of Amir's shame intensifies at his 13th birthday party, where Assef appears with his friends and gives him a biography of Hitler. Between flashes of fireworks, Amir watches as Hassan serves drinks to Assef and Wali on a silver platter, then sees Assef "grinning, kneading Hassan in the chest with a knuckle."

The discomfort of seeing Hassan continue to carry out his duties without complaining and to remain loyal without question is too much for Amir to bear. He decides to frame Hassan as a thief and hides his birthday watch and some Afghani money under Hassan's mattress, then lies to his father, calling Hassan a thief and hoping the incident will finally drive Hassan out of his life and end his guilt. Baba confronts Ali and Hassan about the presumed theft, and neither fights the accusation, but Amir knows from the way they look at him that Hassan has told Ali about the sexual attack and that they will leave without a fight.

In 1981, after the Russians invade Afghanistan, Amir and his father take a long and dangerous journey through their country and go to the United States. They settle in San Francisco, where the formerly wealthy and powerful Baba finds adjusting difficult. He barely speaks English and responds with disdain when Amir suggests that he take English-as-a-second-language classes. Rather than managing employees, he joins his son in gathering old and discarded objects to sell in the flea market that hosts the booths and tables of many Afghan immigrants. Amir graduates from high school and junior college and continues to write stories, as he had as a boy. And he falls in love with Soraya Taheri, the daughter of a former Afghan general and ministry member. In the United States, Baba and Amir have grown emotionally closer, and Amir turns to his father to ask General Taheri for his daughter's hand in marriage. Once they are married and Baba is stricken by cancer, Soraya nurses the old man in his last months of life. After 15 years, Amir receives a telephone call from his father's close friend Rahim Khan, who is dying, and who asks to see him. Khan has left the chaos and escaped to Pakistan, where Amir meets with him and learns that Hassan is actually his half brother, fathered by Baba months after the death of Amir's mother in childbirth. He learns that Khan had lived in Baba's mansion in Kabul with Hassan and his family, including a son Sohrab, named after Hassan's favorite hero from a book Amir used to read to him. Khan tells him that soon after he left Kabul, the Taliban accused Hassan and his wife of illegally occupying the mansion and executed them in the street, but they took Sohrab away. Khan begs Amir to find the little boy.

Amir protests that he has a wife and a good life in the United States, and he has a novel to finish, but Khan reminds him of the debts he owes to the past and reawakens the guilt he has carried for a quarter of a century. Frightened and with great reluctance, Amir travels to Kabul and searches for Sohrab, whom he finds has been sent to an orphanage. At the orphanage, he learns that a local Taliban commander stops by regularly to give the director money to help the orphanage and routinely leaves with a little girl or a little boy, some of whom are later returned to the orphanage bearing signs of abuse. Amir is horrified to learn that Sohrab is one such child, but he has not been returned. Despite the great difficulty and danger, he approaches a guard after two public executions that take place during halftime of a soccer game and requests an appointment with the Taliban commander who has carried out the stonings and who matches the description provided by the orphanage director. He is granted the appointment, and at the meeting learns that Sohrab has become a sexual victim of the commander who reveals himself to be Assef, the bully who had raped Hassan in the alley years before when Amir failed to act. The little boy has eyes "darkened with mascara, and his cheeks glowed with an unnatural red"; jingling bells encircle his ankles. Enraged by the victimization of his childhood friend's son, Amir demands to be given the boy, but Assef tells him that he must fight to the death for that right. Assef uses brass knuckles and viciously attacks Amir, breaking bones and slashing at his face, stopping only when Sohrab calls for him to stop. The little boy, like his late father, is a great marksman with his slingshot, which he is holding poised to shoot with a brass ball from the table decorations firmly in the pouch. Assef lunges, and Sohrab releases the sling, catapulting the ball firmly into one eye socket and knocking Assef to the ground. The little boy half drags and half carries Amir to the waiting car, and Amir is taken to a hospital where he endures many surgical procedures and begins a lengthy recuperation process.

As soon as Amir is able to move, he removes Sohrab from Afghanistan to the United States, where he and Soraya will adopt the boy. For months after Sohrab reaches the United States, he remains silent and unapproachable, until Amir gives him a kite and shows him how he and Hassan used to fly kites in Kabul. As Sohrab relaxes his guard and flies the kite, Amir tells him that Hassan was the best kite runner he had ever known, and he offers to be Sohrab's kite runner, telling him he would do so, as Hassan had once told him, "For you, a thousand times over."

CENSORSHIP HISTORY

The Kite Runner earned the praise of *Publishers Weekly* upon publication as being "an incisive, perceptive examination of recent Afghan history . . . a complete work of literature that succeeds in exploring the culture of a previously obscure nation that has become a pivot point in the global politics of the new millennium." The novel was on the *New York Times* list of best-selling books, and reviewers of the novel have echoed this praise and lauded the author for creating a sensitive portrayal of the devastating effects that the political turbulence in Afghanistan has had upon its citizens. Parents across the United States have not been as admiring, and their protests against the novel made *The Kite Runner* one of the top books challenged in 2008. Although the book was published in 2003, little attention appears to have been given to formal challenges until after the filmed version of the movie was released in 2007.

In January 2008, Burke County, North Carolina, school board member Tracy Norman criticized the use of the book in the Freedom High School honors class because of the scene of male rape and the use of "profanities" throughout the novel. She charged that the book contains content that is "inappropriate for high schoolers" and recommended removing it from the county public school system curriculum. In an interview with the *Charlotte Observer*, Norman stated, "I don't think it's the public schools' place to be the one exposing them to this." Buddy Armour, another school board member, contradicted Norman's view and defended the novel, "It's not about vulgarity or the rape scene that's depicted. It's a look into the culture, and there's value there. Our kids need to know a little bit about the world, and it's not all pretty and lovely." Other parents defended the book, including Tony Matthews, pastor at the North Morganton United Methodist Church and a parent of a 10th-grade daughter. Matthews observed that "The point of the book was to show the horrors of living under an oppressive regime such as the Taliban. Getting a set of facts on a piece of paper is a way to sterilize the problem. A character in a book becomes someone you're familiar with and you bond with. By telling the story in a piece of fiction . . . it makes the horrors more real."

The novel was taught in the fall semester 2007 to a 10th-grade world literature class at Freedom High School and intended as a text to teach honors students about other parts of the world. The school board refused to act on Norman's attempt to remove the book and, instead, decided to rely on the challenge procedure, begun in 2006 in the school system, which allows parents and community members the right to file formal complaints with the school system for materials they believe are not appropriate for students. The challenge is then reviewed by a media advisory committee made up of teachers, students, and parents who review the complaint and content at issue and decide whether the materials should be removed from the system. School superintendent David Burleson stated that such a decision cannot be made by just one person. "Where do you draw the line? That's a fair and valid question. You draw the line based on your community make-up and what the community expects. That's why we have the advisory committee." Board member Norman asserted that teenagers were being forced into reading content that is too mature for a high school setting and said there must be other ways "to teach students about other cultures without depending on scenes of sexual abuse and books with foul language." She expressed her concern with not only *The Kite Runner* but with "all books that use profane language and include graphic sex scenes and other potentially offensive material." Her comments caused fellow school board member Armour to observe that "what Norman proposes borders on censorship. If *The Kite Runner* is banned from Burke schools, other material will likely also be forced from the curriculum." No media reports have been located to determine the outcome of the committee review.

In May 2008, David McGowan, the parent of a Marianna High School student in Jackson County (Florida) School District, protested to staff and administration at the high school that *The Kite Runner* was disturbing and should not be required reading. In response, the high school principal Randy Ward removed the book from the required reading list but ordered that the book remain in the school library. The action did not go far enough for McGowan who sent a letter in July 2008 to the district director of middle and secondary education and requested that the district form a committee to consider removing the book entirely from the school district. He wrote, "I do not wish to stand in the way of any educational advantage that literature provides. I am simply asking for your help in shielding my children from this particular book." McGowan also appeared before the school board in early August 2008 and read aloud excerpts from the book that contained "profane language and sexual situations" and asked them to remove the book. The school board formed a district review committee of seven consisting of parents, a media specialist, a teacher, members of the community, and a student. The committee voted five to two in favor of keeping the book in the school district. The decision went before the school board members, who had mixed reactions to the report of the committee. In the discussion before the school board's final vote, board president Dr. Terry Nichols, who cast the sole opposing vote, stated, "I think it's a good book. But in looking at this I think it's a book that's good for the adult population. There are vivid scenes that don't promote evil, but are a little bit too vivid for our younger students in high school." Chris Johnson, another board member, voted in favor of keeping the book and said that he would not want his child reading the book but feared that banning *The Kite Runner* "could lead to the issue of banning other books, such as Huck Finn and Macbeth." Johnson expressed concern that the book is available for students in the sixth grade or higher: "When the librarian told me that was a sixth grade book I almost fainted. But what I ban today might be something that hurts me tomorrow." School board member Kenneth Griffin asserted that the passages were offensive and made a motion for the board to consider making the book available only to juniors and seniors, but the school board attorney Frank Bondurant stated that "legal complications might occur in trying to enforce such a rule," so Griffin withdrew the motion.

In November 2008, Laura Stovall, a parent in the Okaloosa County (Florida) School District, expressed concern about the "mature content" of the novel and filed a "Request for Reconsideration of Educational Materials" with the school district after learning that the novel would be taught in the Choctawhatchee High School English classes in the International Baccalaureate (IB) program. The novel was also taught in the Fort Walton Beach High School. Stovall's son was only a ninth-grade student at the time, but she told a reporter for the *Northwest Florida Daily News* that "the book's obscene and profane content should not be a part of the curriculum at any level." The district routinely sent a letter to parents of Choctawhatchee High School students to inform them about the IB program, which noted that students "may encounter literature with mature content." Stovall obtained both of the books mentioned—*To Kill a Mockingbird* and *The Kite Runner*—and read them both. "I thought 'To Kill a Mockingbird' was one of the most pleasant and intriguing books I had read and I hoped to be as pleasantly surprised by 'Kite Runner.' I wasn't." Stovall told school officials she was "mortified" by the book's content and stated that it was "unacceptable to present such R-rated material to high school students who cannot even get into R-rated movies." To support her concerns, Stovall compiled five pages containing passages from the book that she found offensive. In the "Request for Reconsideration," she wrote "The level of profanity and 'R-rated' content of the book is altogether inappropriate in our high schools."

In response to Stovall's challenge, Fort Walton Beach High School and Choctawhatchee High School formed committees to review the novel and to make recommendations to the school district officials based on the novel's instructional and educational merits. Both committees quickly and unanimously recommended that the school district keep *The Kite Runner* as part of the curriculum and on the school district reading list. Their decisions were then reviewed by a district-level committee, which also recommended to the Okaloosa County School Board to retain the book. On January 12, 2009, the school board voted unanimously to keep the novel on the reading lists of both high schools in the Advanced Placement and International Baccalaureate curricula, as well as on the recommended readings lists and in media centers.

FURTHER READING

"BOOKS Library Group Finds *Kite Runner* Problematic." *Houston Chronicle*, April 16, 2009, p. 4.

"Censorship Dateline: Schools." *Newsletter for Intellectual Freedom* 57, no. 3 (May 2008): 97–99.

Hernandez, Kelli. "Choctaw Committee: Keep *Kite Runner*." *Northwest Florida Daily News* (Fort Walton Beach), November 21, 2008. Available online. URL: http://www.nwfdailynews.com/news/school-12902-committee-district.html. Accessed December 26, 2009.

———. "District Committee Recommends 'The Kite Runner' Stay on Reading Lists." *Northwest Florida Daily News* (Fort Walton Beach), December 14, 2008. Available online. URL: http://www.nwfdailynews.com/news/book-13508-district-school. html. Accessed December 27, 2009.

———. "Parents Object to 'Kite Runner.'" *Northwest Florida Daily News* (Fort Walton Beach), November 15, 2008. Available online. URL: http://www.nwfdailynews. com/news/book-12772-school-stovall.html. Accessed December 27, 2009.

———. "School Board Approves 'Kite Runner.'" *Northwest Florida Daily News* (Fort Walton Beach), January 13, 2009. Available online. URL: http://www.nwfdaily-news.com/news/board-14162-school-schools.html. Accessed December 26, 2009.

Kern, Kate McCardell. "'Kite' Still Flies: School Board Rejects Book Ban." Available online. URL: http://www2.jcfloridan.com/jcf/news/local/article/kite_still_flies_ school_board_rejects_book_ban/32549. Accessed October 25, 2010.

"Kite Runner, The." *Publishers Weekly* (May 12, 2003): 43.

"Kite Runner Joins Gay Penguins on Top 10 Books Americans Want Banned." *Europe Intelligence Wire*, April 16, 2009. *General Business File ASAP*. Gale Research. Available online. URL: http://find.galegroup.com/gps/start.do?prodId=IPS&user GroupName=bergen_main. Accessed December 27, 2009.

Young, Marcie. "Book Too Raw for School?" *Charlotte Observer*, February 24, 2008. *General Business File ASAP*. Gale Research. Available online. URL: http://find.gale group.com/gps/infomark.do?&contentSet=IAC-Documents&type=retrieve&tab ID=T004&prodId=IPS&docId=CJ175296057&source=gale&userGroupName= bergen_main&version=1.0>. Accessed on December 28, 2009.

LEAVES OF GRASS

Author: Walt Whitman
Original date and place of publication: 1855, United States
Original publisher: Self-published
Literary form: Poetry collection

SUMMARY

Leaves of Grass appeared in 1855 as a quarto of 95 pages that had been typeset by Whitman in the Brooklyn print shop of Andrew and James Rome. Whitman's name did not appear on the title page, nor did the name of a publisher or printer appear. He did not hide his authorship, however, for the copyright notice was credited to "Walter Whitman" and his portrait faced the title page. The 12 poems in the 1855 edition had no titles, but Whitman created titles for them, with which we are now familiar, in later editions: "Song of Myself," "A Song for Occupations," "To Think of Time," "The Sleepers," "I Sing the Body Electric," "Faces," "Song of the Answerer," "Europe the 72d and 73d Years of These States," "A Boston Ballad," "There Was a Child Went Forth," "Who Learns My Lesson Complete," and "Great Are the Myths." The collection went through five more editions in Whitman's lifetime. The third edition of the collection, published in 1860, contained more than 100 additional poems, many of them with homosexual overtones that brought more notoriety to the work.

The first edition fulfilled Walt Whitman's goal to write a serious work in a clearly sensuous manner. His subject is the common man, unlike other writers of his time who wrote about and for an educated elite. He chose to draw attention to the ordinary people who made up American society. He also had another purpose to his poetry. Whitman stated in the preface to the 1855 edition of *Leaves of Grass* his purpose of uniting the physical aspect of the human with the spiritual, and this purpose appears in the poetry, as in "Song of Myself," which contains the line "I am the poet of the body, / And I am the poet of the soul."

In developing his theme of accepting everything in life equally, excluding nothing, Whitman included blunt anatomical references that offended many of his readers for whom such references remained taboos for many decades into the future. In accepting all of nature, he wrote of "the litter of the grunting sow as they tug at her teats" and "where the bull advances to do his masculine work, and the stud to the mare, and the cock is treading the hen." He similarly accepted people in all stations and situations of life, as he wrote that "the keptwoman [sic] and sponger and thief are hereby invited—the heavy-lipped slave is invited—the veneralee is invited." He offered friendship and brotherhood "to a drudge of the cottonfields or emptier of privies . . . on his right cheek I place the family kiss."

Throughout the poems, Whitman speaks of the physical actions and realities that his contemporaries strained to keep hidden as not being "nice" or "appropriate" to speak of:

Copulation is no more rank to me than death is.
I believe in the flesh and the appetites,
Seeing hearing and feeling are miracles, and
each part and tag of me is a miracle.
. . . .
The scent of these arm-pits is aroma finer than prayer, . . .
. . . .
I turn the bridegroom out of bed and stay
with the bride myself,
And tighten her all night to my thighs and lips.
. . . .
Darkness you are gentler than my lover—
his flesh was sweaty and panting,
I feel the hot moisture yet that he left me.

In numerous lines throughout the collection, Whitman celebrated sensuality and reminded people of their most primitive desires.

CENSORSHIP HISTORY

Leaves of Grass was declared obscene from its first publication. The first bookseller to whom Whitman took his book refused to sell it, claiming that it was "too sensual." Whitman met Lorenzo and Orson Fowler, who agreed to distribute the book, but sales were low and Whitman gave away many copies of the first edition. As cries of "immorality" were raised against the work, the Fowler brothers became frightened and gave existing copies of the second edition of the work to Whitman and resigned the whole edition. Libraries refused to buy the book; the Library Company of Philadelphia is the only one on record in America to have bought a copy when it was first published. Thus, other libraries effectively censored the book by their refusal to buy it.

Critic R. W. Griswold, writing on November 10, 1855, in the *New Criterion*, observed, "Thus, then we leave this gathering of muck to the laws which, certainly, if they fulfill their intent, must have power to suppress such obscenity." A review in the English magazine *Saturday Review* also condemned the collection and stated in March 1856: "After every five or six pages . . . Mr. Whitman suddenly becomes very intelligible, but exceedingly obscene. If the *Leaves of Grass* should come into anybody's possession, our advice is to throw them immediately behind the fire." In 1865, Walt Whitman lost his job with the U.S. Department of the Interior because Chief Secretary James Harlan found an annotated copy of the poetry collection in Whitman's desk drawer and determined that he was "the author of an indecent book." In 1870, Noah Porter, president of Yale University, wrote in *Books and Reading* that "a generation cannot be entirely pure which tolerates writers who, like Walt Whitman, commit, in writing, an offense like that indictable at common law of walking naked through the streets."

Many people, among them Ralph Waldo Emerson, who had praised the book in a letter that Whitman arranged to have published in the *New York Times*, urged Whitman to permit an expurgated version of the collection. He remained staunchly opposed to expurgation, and American copyright law protected him unless he consented to it. From the time that the collection appeared in 1855, his editors suggested that a bowdlerized version for the general public would be good for sales. Whitman violently opposed expurgation, viewing such books as "the dirtiest book in all the world." Not until 1892, not long before his death, did he finally agree to an expurgated version as a gesture of friendship for Arthur Stedman, whose father, Edward Clarence Stedman, had done many favors for Whitman.

Leaves of Grass was not expurgated in the United States until 1892, but it was banned entirely, if informally, in New York and Philadelphia bookstores in the 1870s and legally in Boston in the 1880s. As per their usual practice, the Watch and Ward Society in Boston and the New York Society for the Suppression of Vice placed pressure on booksellers to suppress the sale of the book in their shops. Booksellers agreed not to advertise the book nor to suggest its sale to customers.

In 1881, the Society for the Suppression of Vice sought to obtain a legal ban of a proposed new edition of *Leaves of Grass* in Boston. At the urging of the society, the district attorney threatened criminal action against a publisher who had planned a new edition of the work unless it were expurgated. The edition was withdrawn.

In 1883, author, publisher, and free-love advocate Ezra Heywood was arrested by Anthony Comstock, the head of the New York Society for the Suppression of Vice, on the charge of sending obscene matter through the mail. The material consisted of *Cupid's Yokes*, a pamphlet that contained "unconventional social and sexual views," and an anthology entitled *The Word Extra* that contained two poems from *Leaves of Grass*, "To a Common Prostitute" and "A Woman Waits for Me." When the case went to trial, the grand jury declared the Whitman poems "too grossly obscene and lewd to be placed on the records of the court." This meant that members of the jury would decide Heywood's fate without being permitted to review copies of the poem nor to hear lines from the poem read before making their decision; they were expected to accept the decision of the prosecution that the works were obscene. Judge T. L. Nelson, presiding in the U.S. Circuit Court in Boston, threw out the case, "on the grounds that the allegation in the indictment was untrue."

The English bowdlerized the collection from its first appearance in England in 1868. Pre-Raphaelite ex-bohemian William Michael Rossetti, the editor of the expurgated collection, explained in the preface that he had omitted about half the poems of the 1860s edition because he and Whitman lived in "this peculiarly nervous age." He also proudly proclaimed that he was not bowdlerizing the work, because "I have not in a single instance excised *parts* of poems." Noel Perrin observed, "it is the sort of preface a liberal poet might write if he happened to get involved in bowdlerism." Although Rossetti did not excise parts of any poems, he did make numerous changes in Whitman's preface to the original 1855 edition of the collection, excising even the term *prostitute*. The expurgated version of *Leaves of Grass* became part of the Everyman Library in 1886 and existed well into the twentieth century. Ernest de Selincourt used that version for Oxford's "World Classics" series in 1920, removing several more poems. Late in life, Whitman considered his work and expressed his dissatisfaction with the English editions, noting that "I now feel somehow as if none of the changes should have been made: that I should have assumed that position: that's the only possible, final, logical position."

FURTHER READING

Blodgett, Harold. *Walt Whitman in England.* Ithaca, N.Y.: Cornell University Press, 1934.
Broun, Heywood, and Margaret Leech. *Anthony Comstock.* New York: Albert & Charles Boni, 1927.
Cavitch, David. *My Soul and I: The Inner Life of Walt Whitman.* Boston: Beacon Press, 1985.
Cowley, Malcolm, ed. *Walt Whitman's Leaves of Grass: The First (1855) Edition.* New York: Viking Press, 1959.
Everson, William. *American Bard: The Original Preface to "Leaves of Grass."* New York: Viking Press, 1982.
McCoy, Ralph E. *Banned in Boston: The Development of Literary Censorship in Massachusetts.* Urbana: University of Illinois Press, 1956.
Mordell, Albert. *Notorious Literary Attacks.* New York: Boni & Liveright, 1926.
Perrin, Noel. *Dr. Bowdler's Legacy.* Boston: David R. Godine, 1969.

LORD OF THE FLIES

Author: William Golding
Original dates and places of publication: 1954, England; 1955, United States
Original publishers: Faber and Faber; Coward-McCann
Literary form: Novel

SUMMARY

Lord of the Flies is an allegorical novel that relates the adventures of a group of English schoolboys whose plane crashes on a deserted island, killing all adults aboard. Using their instincts, early social training, and education, the boys attempt to form an organized society. Their efforts result in some of the boys' emerging as leaders or bullies, while others remain destined to follow or to be bullied. Rather than develop a caring and harmonious society free of the corrupting influences of adults, the boys revert to savage behavior and primitive rites.

The novel seems at first to be a simple adventure story of survival, but the growing brutality of the boys toward each other reveals the second level of meaning that questions the nature of civilization and the effect of instinct versus society on behavior. Told from the third-person point of view, the novel opens with a conversation between Ralph and Piggy, who are walking through a tangled jungle on their way back to the beach. The reader learns that they and a large number of other boys, ranging in age from five to 12, were being transported out of a besieged England in the midst of an atomic war when their plane crashed.

The boys emerge in different, seemingly natural roles as the novel progresses. Ralph takes the initiative of calling the boys together, and he emerges as leader of the group, much to the disappointment of Jack, one of the older boys who had hoped to become sole leader. The two boys attract followers. Ralph becomes the builder and organizer who takes a careful and rational look at their needs, while Jack hunts with his followers and becomes increasing brutal and primitive in behavior. The two groups take turns at maintaining a signal fire on the beach in the hope of attracting passing ships, but Jack's group irresponsibly allows the fire to go out while they hunt and kill a pig. Aroused by their success, Jack's followers urge the others to join them in hunting, and the boys seems nearly overcome by a blood lust that almost leads to the death of one of the boys.

The island paradise soon becomes filled with fear. The younger boys cry out that they see beasts in the darkness despite the contention of Simon that it is only the beast inside themselves. As Jack fights more strongly for a leadership role, he gathers around him a majority of the boys, and they form their own "tribe." They kill a mother pig whom they have surprised while she is nursing her young, and the feast draws all of the boys. As if to worship the dead animal, Jack's followers place the pig's head on a stake as their offering to the beast on the mountain. As flies cover the head, Simon realizes that it represents the potent emergence of the boys' wickedness.

The boys soon begin to direct their brutal behavior at each other. One of the younger boys burns to death when the signal fire rages out of control. Then Simon, the poetic, level-headed member of the group, is beaten to death by the boys in a frenzied ritualistic dance. The last to die is Piggy, one of the remaining boys to continue to act with civilized restraint, killed by the sadistic Roger, who crushes him by deliberately rolling a boulder down the mountain. After Piggy's death, Jack hurls a spear at Ralph in a failed attempt to kill him. Forced into hiding, Ralph collapses in exhaustion on the beach and is found by naval officers who have arrived to rescue the boys.

CENSORSHIP HISTORY

The novel has raised objections regarding its use in the classroom because of its pessimistic view of human society as well as for the scenes of brutality. The novel was challenged in Dallas (Texas) Independent School District high school libraries in 1974 and at Sully Buttes (South Dakota) High School in 1981. Critics at Owen (North Carolina) High School challenged the book in 1981 for being "demoralizing" by implying that man is little more than an animal, and the appropriateness of the novel as a reading assignment was challenged at Marana (Arizona) High School in 1983. The school district in Olney, Texas, challenged the use of the book in the classroom for containing "excessive violence and bad language." The Toronto (Ontario, Canada) board of education ruled on June 23, 1988 that the novel is "racist and recommended that it be removed from all schools," after parents and members of the black community complained that it degraded blacks because the boys paint themselves and savagely hunt and kill both wild boars and later several of their group, while they refer to themselves as a "tribe."

The novel was challenged by parents who demanded that it be removed from the junior high school reading list in Rocklin, California, in 1990. The parents claimed that the book did not provide a good model of "the social standards" and "good citizenship" that are expected of students. The school board rejected the complaint and retained the novel on its lists. The same year, the Gloucester County, New Jersey, school district quietly acquiesced to the protests of parents who claimed that the author's notes to the novel were not appropriate reading for the eighth-grade honors English class. With no formal fanfare, the school simply removed the novel from use until new copies of the novel, minus the author's notes, were obtained.

In 1992, the novel was challenged as indecent by protesters in the Waterloo, Iowa, schools. The challenge was based on perceived profanity, lurid passages, and statements viewed as being derogatory to minorities, women, and the disabled. The protesters pointed out that Piggy, who suffers from asthma and cannot see without his glasses, is ridiculed by the others and deprived of his glasses. They also identified as offensive a passage in which the boys trap a sow, who is feeding her piglets, pursue her and stab her repeatedly until she falls; then, one boy proudly proclaims that he has stuck a spear "Right up her ass!" In several instances when the boys act in a manner that is out of step with expected masculine behavior, they are criticized as acting "just like a girl." Despite the opposition, only one of the seven school board members voted against purchasing the book for use in the classroom.

FURTHER READING

Barr, Donald. "Should Holden Caulfield Read These Books?" *New York Times Book Review* 91, May 4, 1986, pp. 1, 50–51.

Egan, John M. "Golding's View of Man." *America* 108 (January 26, 1963): 140–141.

Newsletter on Intellectual Freedom (January 1975): 6; (July 1981): 103; (January 1982): 17; (January 1984): 25–26; (July 1984): 122; (September 1988): 152; (July 1992): 126.

Slayton, Paul. "Teaching Rationale for William Golding's *Lord of the Flies.*" In *Censored Books: Critical Viewpoints*, edited by Nicholas J. Karolides, Lee Burress, and John M. Kean, 351–357. Metuchen, N.J.: Scarecrow Press, 1993.

OF MICE AND MEN

Author: John Steinbeck
Original date and place of publication: 1937, United States
Original publisher: Viking Penguin
Literary form: Novel

SUMMARY

Of Mice and Men is the story of two men, big and simpleminded Lennie and small and cunning George, who drift from one ranchhand job to another as they pursue their dream of owning their own place. Despite their mismatched intellectual capabilities, the two men are good friends who share the same dream, the simple desire to have their own farm where Lennie will be able to raise rabbits. As they travel from job to job, George becomes frustrated with Lennie's limitations and often loses patience, but he does not desert the childlike giant. George knows that Lennie will inadvertently become involved in a situation from which he will be unable to extricate himself, so vigilance is necessary.

Although the two men are thrilled to be given a ranch job, George must, as usual, cover for Lennie and make him appear to be more capable and intelligent that he really is. The boss's son Curley bullies the childlike Lennie, who finds himself drawn to the bully's lovely young wife. Curley's wife, however, does not treat Lennie fairly and she teases him playfully, unaware of how seriously he perceives her actions. He sees her as being similar to the soft and cuddly puppy that he once had, and he wants only to stroke her soft hair as he had stroked the puppy's soft fur. When Lennie approaches Curley's wife to stroke her hair, she becomes frightened and struggles and starts to scream. He places his hand on her mouth to quiet her, but he is not capable of judging his strength and breaks her neck. When George finds them, Lennie apologizes and cries that he has hurt her just like he had hurt the puppy. George is aware that the ranchhands led by Curley will not have pity for Lennie, so he tells Lennie to pack up so that they can leave. A short time later, as the two sit on a riverbank, George shoots Lennie to death to save him from the more terrifying tortures of a mob.

CENSORSHIP HISTORY

Of Mice and Men earned the dubious prestige of being the second most frequently banned book in the public school curriculum of the 1990s, second only to the reading anthology *Impressions*, and challenges were frequent in earlier decades and continue today. Censors claim that the novel contains crude heroes who speak vulgar language and whose experiences exhibit a sadly deficient social system in the United States.

The novel was placed on the banned list in Ireland in 1953 because of "obscenities" and "vulgar" language. It was banned for similar reasons in Syracuse, Indiana, in 1974; Oil City, Pennsylvania, in 1977; Grand Blanc, Michigan, in 1979; and Continental, Ohio, in 1980. In 1977, in Greenville, North Carolina, the Fourth Province of the Knights of the Ku Klux Klan challenged the use of the book in the local school district, for containing "profanities and using God's name in vain." The same reason was given by parents who challenged the book in Vernon-Verona-Sherill (New York) School District in 1980 and in school districts in St. David, Arizona, in 1981 and Tell City, Indiana, in 1982. The school board of Scottsboro, Alabama, banned the novel from Skyline High School in 1983 because of "profanity," and the chair of the Knoxville, Tennessee, school board vowed to remove all "filthy books" from the local school system, beginning with *Of Mice and Men* because of "its vulgar language."

The novel was challenged as "vulgar" and "offensive" by parents in the Christian County, Kentucky, school district in 1987, but it was later reinstated in the school libraries and English classes. "Profanity" was also the reason for the 1988 challenges in Marion County, West Virginia, schools; Wheaton-Warrenville (Illinois) Middle School; and Berrien Springs (Michigan) High School. In 1989, the school board ordered the novel removed from Northside High School in Tuscaloosa, Alabama, because of "profanity," and it was challenged as a reading assignment at a summer youth program in Chattanooga, Tennessee, because "Steinbeck is known to have had an anti-business attitude." That same year, the novel was also removed from all reading lists and all copies were stored away in White Chapel High School in Pine Bluff, Arkansas, because parents objected to the language. "Offensive language" was the reason that parents in the Shelby County, Tennessee, school system challenged the appropriateness of including the novel on the high school reading list.

The 1990s brought an increase in the number of challenges to *Of Mice and Men*. In 1990, a parent in Salinas, Kansas, challenged the use of the book in a 10th-grade English class because it contained "profanity" and "takes the Lord's name in vain." The school board review committee considered the complaint and recommended that the work be retained as a required reading but cautioned that no excerpts from the book should be read aloud in the classroom. That same year, a parent in Riviera, Texas, complained that the novel contained profanities and requested that it be removed from the 11th-grade English classes. At an open school board meeting to consider the request, 50 teachers and administrators and 10 high school students appeared to support continued use of the book. The only person who spoke against the novel was the parent who raised the original challenge. After the parent went through two more levels of appeal, the school board voted to continue assigning the novel.

In 1991, a Fresno, California, parent demanded that the book be removed from the 10th-grade English college preparatory curriculum, citing "profanity" and "racial slurs." The book was retained, and the child of the objecting parent was provided with an alternative reading assignment. In Iowa City, Iowa, a parent complained of the use of *Of Mice and Men* in the seventh-grade literature courses because of the profanity in the book, such as the word "Goddamn." She claimed that her daughter was subjected to "psychological and emotional abuse" when the book was read aloud and expressed the hope that her daughter would "not talk like a migrant worker" when she completed school. The district review committee retained the book. "Profanity," "excessive cursing," and "sexual overtones" were behind challenges to reading of the novel in high schools in Suwanee, Florida; Jacksboro, Tennessee; Buckingham, Virginia; and Branford, Florida.

A large number of challenges arose in 1992. A coalition of community members and clergy in Mobile, Alabama, requested that local school officials form a special textbook screening committee to "weed out objectionable things." Their first target was to be *Of Mice and Men*, which they claimed contained "profanity" and "morbid and depressing themes." No formal complaint was lodged, so school officials rejected the request. Challenges in Waterloo, Iowa, and Duval County, Florida, were made because of "profanity," "lurid passages about sex," and "statements defamatory to minorities." A parent in Modesto, California, challenged the novel on the basis of profanity for the use of the word *nigger*, and the NAACP joined in demanding that the novel be removed from the reading list. "Profanity" prompted the challenge at Oak Hill High School in Alexandria, Louisiana, where it was retained.

One of the more detailed complaints emerged in 1992 in Hamilton, Ohio, where the book was temporarily removed from the high school reading list after a parent complained that it contained "vulgarity" and "racial slurs." The parent, vice president of the Parents' Coalition in Hamilton, stated that the novel contained 108 profanities and 12 racial slurs. The school board suggested the use of alternative reading assignments, which the coalition refused, and the novel was temporarily removed from the optional reading list. At the meeting of the board-appointed review committee, 150 parents, students, and teachers appeared and enthusiastically supported the book. One student submitted a petition bearing 333 signatures of people who favored retaining the book. A local minister who opposed the book told the board, "Anybody that's got a child shouldn't want them to read this book. It should be burned up, put in a fire." The board of education voted unanimously to retain the book.

The novel was challenged in 1993 as an appropriate English curriculum assignment by parents of students at Mingus (Arizona) Union High School who were concerned about the "profane language, moral statement, treatment of the retarded, and the violent ending." In 1994, the school superintendent of Putnam County, Tennessee, removed the novel from the classroom "due to the language in it, we just can't have this kind of book being taught." That same year, parents of students at Loganville (Georgia) High School called for a ban of the book because of "its vulgar language throughout."

In spring 1997, after 13 years of teaching *Of Mice and Men*, eighth-grade teacher Dan Brooks, in Peru, Illinois, was told to stop teaching the book. The school had received three anonymous letters complaining that the language of the book was "inappropriate." Although Peru school superintendent John Jacobson stated that he viewed the novel as a "quality piece of literature," he supported the ban. The National Coalition Against Censorship (NCAC) stepped in to point out the lack of clear policies for responding to challenges, and the Peru, Illinois, school board lifted the ban while the board developed formal curriculum selection policies. In 1998, Brooks told NCAC that since the incident he has been observed more often and reprimanded frequently.

In 2002, the novel was challenged by parents in Grandville, Michigan, who wanted the book removed from high school classes as required reading, because it "is full of racism, profanity, and foul language." School officials considered the complaint but decided to retain the novel as required reading. That same year, after parents in George County, Mississippi, complained to school officials about "profanity" in the novel, the school board voted to ban *Of Mice and Men* from the school system.

In Lucedale, Mississippi, in January 2003, the school board voted to ban the novel. *School Library Journal* reported that a grandparent complained *Of Mice and Men* contains excessive profanity and violence. The book was removed from all classrooms and libraries in the district.

Also in 2003, parents of a student attending Community High School in Normal, Illinois, challenged the use of the novel in the classroom because it contains "racial slurs, profanity, violence, and does not represent traditional values." After a school district review committee considered the challenge and voted to retain the novel, the school district provided the student with the option of reading *The Pearl*, another Steinbeck work, as an alternative, but the family challenging the novel rejected the offer. The committee reconsidered, then recommended two other alternatives, *The House on Mango Street* and *The Way to Rainy Mountain*, which the family accepted.

In 2007, parents of students attending high school in Newton, Iowa, submitted a formal complaint to the local board of education to remove *Of Mice and Men* from the curriculum, charging that it contained "profanity" and expressing concerns about its portrayal of Jesus Christ. The novel had been part of the high school curriculum since the early 1980s, and the nearby city of Des Moines included it in both the required reading list for ninth-grade English students and the 11th-grade special education classes. Despite repeated attempts by several parents to have the board remove the novel, it was retained in the curriculum. That same year, parents in Olathe, Kansas, also sought to remove the novel from the school curriculum and in their complaint characterized the novel as "a worthless, and profanity-ridden book," that is, "derogatory to women, African Americans, and the developmentally disabled." Their request was denied, and the school board voted to retain the book in the curriculum.

In 2008, the parents of a 14-year-old student attending Washington High School in Kansas City, Missouri, filed a complaint with school officials to have the novel removed from the school district reading list. Dana Washington said in a television interview that she did not feel that her request was radical: "I'm not asking for the book to be banned, but for it to be removed from the list of required reading in the USD 500 school list." The parent said that her son had been "uncomfortable" when the teacher asked students to read aloud from the text and the N-word occurred repeatedly throughout the text. School officials responded to Washington and another parent who joined her in the complaint by offering students an alternative reading choice if they were uncomfortable with the language in *Of Mice and Men*. Washington rejected the offer by the school district and told a reporter for the local television station KMBC: "I want them to find another book that doesn't use the word so violently and profusely." She promised to continue her fight to remove the novel from the required reading list.

FURTHER READING

Carrington, Ildiko de Papp. "Talking Dirty: Alice Munro's 'Open Secrets' and John Steinbeck's 'Of Mice and Men.'" *Studies in Short Fiction* 31 (Fall 1994): 595–606.

"Censorship Round Up." *School Library Journal*, February 2003.

Johnson, Claudia. *Stifled Laughter: Woman's Story about Fighting Censorship*. Golden, Colo.: Fulcrum Publishing, 1994.

"The Long and Short of It." *Censorship News* 69 (Spring 1998). Available online. URL: http://www.ncac.org/censorship_news/20030305~cn069~The_Long_And_The_Short_Of_It.cfm. Accessed August 10, 2010.

Newsletter on Intellectual Freedom (March 1975): 41; (November 1977): 155; (January 1978): 7; (March 1979): 27; (May 1980): 62; (July 1980): 77; (May 1982): 84–85; (July 1983): 198; (July 1984): 104; (May 1988): 90; (July 1988): 140; (September 1988): 154, 179; (November 1988): 201; (January 1989): 28; (November 1989): 162; (January 1990): 10–12; (March 1990): 45; (March 1991): 62; (July 1991): 110; (January 1992): 25; (March 1992): 64; (July 1992): 111–112; (September 1992): 140, 163–164; (January 1993): 29; (March 1994): 53; (March 1995): 46, 53; (November 2002): 280; (March 2003): 55; (January 2004): 11; (September 2004): 177–178; (July 2007): 146–147; (January 2008): 27–28.

Noble, Donald R. *The Steinbeck Question*. Troy, N.Y.: Whinston Publishing, 1993.

"*Of Mice and Men* 'Inappropriate in Illinois.'" *Censorship News* 65 (Spring 1997). Available online. URL: http://www.ncac.org/censorship_news/20030305~en065~Of_Mice_and_Men_Inappropriate_in_Illinois.cfm. Accessed August 10, 2010.

"Woman: School Should Drop Steinbeck Book." Available online. URL: http://kmbc.com/education/17530918/detail.html. Accessed August 10, 2010.

ONE FLEW OVER THE CUCKOO'S NEST

Author: Ken Kesey
Original date and place of publication: 1962, United States
Original publisher: Viking Press
Literary form: Novel

SUMMARY

One Flew over the Cuckoo's Nest is told from the point of view of Bromden, a tall and heavyset schizophrenic Native American called the Chief, who is an inmate of a mental hospital ward. He pretends to be mute as a defense against his surroundings, but the arrival of Randle Patrick McMurphy, a fast-talking con artist who has feigned insanity to enter the mental hospital rather than a prison work farm, gives Bromden confidence and helps him to rebel against the sterile, domineering Miss Ratched. Known to the inmates as Big Nurse, she runs a tightly controlled, efficient ward in which the heavily medicated patients mechanically follow her orders without question and even the orderlies stand at attention, "ready to quell even the feeblest insurrection." McMurphy disrupts her efficiency with his irrepressible high spirits and his goal to create havoc on her well-run ward. The chilling authority of Nurse Ratched appalls McMurphy, who provides a direct contrast to the other patients. They "long ago gave up the struggle to assert themselves. Cowed, docile, they have surrendered completely to her unbridled authority."

The boisterous, fun-loving, rebellious McMurphy is a lusty and profane fighter whose brawling and gambling challenge the rigidly structured world over which Nurse Ratched presides. Against all hospital rules, he initiates gambling among the inmates and smuggles women and wine into the ward. As he openly defies Big Nurse, the other men gradually emerge from their fear-induced inactivity and learn to express happiness, anger, and other emotions that have long been repressed. Such behavior becomes dangerous for McMurphy because he has been committed by the state, not voluntarily as have most of the men, and his behavior will determine the length of his stay. The greater his rebellion against the repressive atmosphere created by Big Nurse, the greater the danger that he will be forced to remain in the hospital for a longer period of commitment.

From taking forbidden cigarettes left at the nurses' station to stealing a fishing boat for an inmates' fishing expedition, McMurphy shows a disregard for the rules that have long dominated the lives of the other inmates, as his vitality and enthusiasm radically change them. His escapades have sometimes tragic consequences that result from the clash of authority with the inmates' newfound freedom. One man drowns in the therapeutic swimming pool when his fingers become stuck in the grate at the bottom of the pool, while young Billy Bibbit takes his own life after Nurse Ratched threatens to tell his mother that he has had sex with a prostitute whom McMurphy sneaked onto the ward. Even McMurphy must eventually yield to the misguided technology of the mental hospital after he attacks Big Nurse, blaming her brutal treatment and threats for young Billy's death. A few weeks after the attack, McMurphy disappears from the ward for a week. When he returns, the other inmates refuse to accept the changed man and claim that he is an impostor who looks "like one of those department store dummies . . . a crummy sideshow fake lying there on the Gurney." A lobotomy destroys all that has made McMurphy human and makes him the perfect example of what happens to a man who bucks the system. Unable to bear seeing their friend deprived of his vitality, the remaining inmates decide to provide him with a dignified end. The Chief smothers him with a pillow, then escapes from the hospital to freedom.

CENSORSHIP HISTORY

The novel has been frequently censored and challenged as being racist, obscene, and immoral because of its raw language and for its emphasis upon the defiance of authority. The white inmates repeatedly refer to the black orderlies with such racial slurs as "coons," "boys," and "niggers," while the Japanese nurse from the Disturbed ward is spoken of as the "Jap." Numerous obscenities pepper McMurphy's speech, and he appears to purposely taunt the doctors and nurses, as when he challenges their question regarding his psychopathic tendencies: "'Is it my fightin' tendencies or my fuckin' tendencies? Must be fuckin', mustn't it? All that wham-bam-thank-you-ma'am . . .'" He further describes Nurse Ratched as having "the too big boobs" and as "a bitch and a buzzard and a ballcutter."

Identified as containing "obscene, filthy language," the novel was challenged in 1971 in Greeley, Colorado, where parents in the public school district demanded that it be removed from the nonrequired American Culture reading list along with *I Never Promised You a Rose Garden* and *Love Story*. In 1974, five residents of Strongsville, Ohio, sued the board of education to remove *One Flew over the Cuckoo's Nest* and *Manchild in the Promised Land* from the classroom. Labeling both books "pornographic materials," they charged that the works "glorify criminal activity, have a tendency to corrupt juveniles, and contain descriptions of bestiality, bizarre violence, and torture, dismemberment, death, and human elimination." In 1975, the book was removed from public school libraries in Randolph, New York, and Alton, Oklahoma, and school officials in Westport, Massachusetts, removed the novel from the required reading list in 1977.

In 1978, the novel was banned from St. Anthony Freemont (Idaho) High School classrooms, and the contract of the instructor was not renewed after parents complained about the language in the book. The school superintendent did not read the book, but he collected all copies from students without attempting to determine its literary or scholastic value. The teacher claimed to have sent home a list of books to be read with the condition that alternative titles would be provided for students who chose not to read a specific assigned book, and no one had objected. The teacher worked with the American Civil Liberties Union to file a complaint in the United States District Court for the District of Idaho, claiming that his rights and the rights of his students under the First and Fourteenth Amendments had been violated. *Fogarty v. Atchley* was filed but not decided. The novel was also challenged in 1982 by parents of students in Merrimack (New Hampshire) High School, where it was removed, but in a 1986 challenge to the novel as part of the honors English curriculum at Aberdeen (Washington) High School, the school board voted to retain the novel.

In 2000, parents of students attending Esperanza High School in the Placentia-Yorba Linda Unified School District complained to school officials that *One Flew over the Cuckoo's Nest* provides a "glorification of prostitution, murder and obscenity," and asked the school district to remove the novel from the schools. The California Department of Education had recommended the inclusion of the novel in the curriculum, and educators and other academic experts categorized the novel as "a valuable teaching tool," but the protesting parents described it as "dangerous." Anna Marie Buckner, the parent of three children ages seven, eight, and 17, told a newspaper reporter that the novel "teaches how very easy it is to smother somebody. I don't want to put these kinds of images in children's minds. They're going to think that when they get mad at their parents, they can just ax them out." After learning that her son would be required to read the novel in spring 2001, Buckner filed a two-page complaint in November 2000 with school officials. She was joined by the mother of four children Jenelle Cox in gathering 150 signatures on a petition that requested the removal of the novel from the classroom. Cox told a reporter for the *Los Angeles Times* that the situation was "frustrating. They can choose the best books, but they keep choosing this garbage over and over again." Both parents said that their children would read alternative choices, "books with good morals and heroes with values." School district officials turned the issue over to the district "book challenge review committee," 12 teachers, administrators, and parents who were asked to "establish criteria and resolve the issue." The novel had been used for seven years in the district core 11th-grade reading list before the complaint occurred, and the high school principal David Flynn supported retaining the novel in the curriculum. After months of debate, the board of education voted to keep *One Flew over the Cuckoo's Nest* in the curriculum.

FURTHER READING

Newsletter on Intellectual Freedom (May 1971): 59; (November 1974): 152; (May 1975): 41; (July 1975): 108; (May 1978): 57; (July 1978): 96, 100; (May 1980): 52; (September 1982): 170; (November 1986): 225.

O'Neil, Robert M. *Classrooms in the Crossfire: The Rights and Interests of Students, Parents, Teachers, Administrators, Librarians, and the Community.* Bloomington: Indiana University Press, 1981.

Tebbel, John. *A History of Book Publishing in the United States.* Vol. 4. New York: R. R. Bowker, 1981.

Tran, Mai. "Parents Ask School District to Ban 'Cuckoo's Nest.'" *Los Angles Times*, December 3, 2000. Avilable online. URL: http://articles.latimes.com/2000/dec/03/local/me–60611. Accessed August 10, 2010.

A SEPARATE PEACE

Author: John Knowles
Original date and place of publication: 1960, United States
Original publisher: Macmillan Company
Literary form: Novel

SUMMARY

A Separate Peace takes place at a small New England preparatory school named Devon, where the narrator, Gene Forrester, has returned 15 years after graduation. He visits the tree from which his close friend Finny fell and broke his leg the first time and the First Academy Building, where the second break occurred. These locations stimulate a flashback to the summer of 1942, between his junior and senior years, when the novel really begins.

The main character is Gene's friend Phineas, "Finny," who forms the Super Suicide Society of the Summer Session. Seemingly fearless, his foolhardy behavior, athletic prowess, and quirky sense of humor make him a leader of the boys, whom he repeatedly challenges to jump from a tree on the riverbank into the cold water below. As the summer progresses, all except Finny speak of the threat of enlistment after graduation.

Despite their friendship, a rivalry exists between Gene and Finny. Gene tries to do well academically, but Finny's games interfere with his studies. When Gene fails a math test after Finny convinces him to go to the beach rather than study, he believes that his friend wants him to fail. Finny again distracts Gene on the evening before an important French examination by leading him to a jumping session at the riverbank, and Gene becomes vengeful. As the two boys crawl out onto a tree limb, Gene moves on the branch and causes Finny to fall and break his leg. This incident drastically changes Finny's life because he can no longer participate in sports, so he returns home.

As fall term begins, Gene decides that he might as well enlist in the army, but when Finny returns with his leg in a cast, Gene changes his mind and serves as the injured boy's guide and helper. As the year progresses, the two boys make their peace with each other, and Finny's leg heals imperfectly. Other students who are jealous of Gene's attention to Finny decide to hold a mock trial to determine what really happened. One student testifies that Gene shook the tree limb, a statement that upsets Finny and sends him racing out of the room toward a flight of marble stairs, where his cane slips and he falls, breaking the same leg. Finny dies when the doctor sets the bone a few days later; the official diagnosis is that some of the bone marrow must have escaped into his bloodstream and stopped his heart.

After graduation, Gene and many other Devon graduates enlist, but for Gene the war is of little consequence compared with the enemy he has overcome in trying to achieve a separate peace with Finny's death. He observes at the end of the novel, "my war ended before I ever put on the uniform; I was on active duty all my time at the school; I killed my enemy there."

CENSORSHIP HISTORY

The novel was challenged in 1980 by parents in Vernon-Verona-Sherrill (New York) School District for being a "filthy, trashy sex novel." In their challenge, the parents claimed that the novel contained homosexuality as an underlying theme, which "encourages homosexuality." They also complained of "swear words" to which their children should not be subjected, including "bastard," the barely disguised "f———ing," and "damn." The school board voted to offer students another selection and to remove the book from classroom use. In 1985, parents of students at Fannett-Metal High School in Shippensburg, Pennsylvania, challenged the book because of "offensive language." They claimed that the book was "too adult," for high school students and asked that it be removed from the required reading list. The request was denied, but students whose parents objected to the book were given an alternative assignment. In 1989, the novel was challenged by parents of students in the Shelby County, Tennessee, school system who felt that the "offensive language" in the novel made it inappropriate for the high school reading list. The school board replaced the novel with another book, and the issue ended.

After 22 years of being assigned in the local schools in Champaign, Illinois, without complaints, the novel was challenged by three parents who claimed that "unsuitable language" in the novel made it inappropriate for assignment in high school English classes. The parents specified the use of "damn" and "goddamn" in their complaint. The school board appointed a curriculum review committee to respond to the complaint and agreed with the decision of the committee to retain the novel. In a 1991 challenge to the novel issued by the parent of a high school student in Troy, Illinois, profanity and negative attitudes were cited in the request that the novel be removed from the classroom. The parent identified 34 "profane references" in the book, including "God damn," "Shut up," and "I swear to God." Students were offered alternative assignments while the school board took the matter under advisement, but no further action was taken on the complaint.

A more extensive challenge emerged in 1992, when a parent in Jacksonville, Florida, learned that the high school library contained a copy of *A Separate Peace* and challenged it as being "unsuitable for youth" and "encouraging rebellion against authority." The challenge cited "vulgar language" and characters who skip classes, break school rules, and trespass on school property as offering inappropriate models for students. The "objectionable language" identified includes "for God's sake," "damn," "hell," "Christ," and "Oh God." The district review committee considered the challenge and voted to retain the work that it characterized as "truly a well-written piece of art." In the report of the decision to retain the novel in the high school library, the committee wrote: "To ban or restrict this book reflects the paranoia existing in today's society. Reasons conjured for the banning of the book are unjustifiable."

FURTHER READING

Newsletter on Intellectual Freedom (May 1980): 62; (November 1985): 204; (January 1990): 11–12.

People For the American Way. *Attacks on the Freedom to Learn: 1991–1992 Report.* Washington, D.C.: People For the American Way, 1992.

Rice, Anne M. "Still Good Reading: Adolescent Novels Written before 1967—*A Separate Peace* by John Knowles." *English Journal*, April 1992, p. 88.

THE SUN ALSO RISES

Author: Ernest Hemingway
Original date and place of publication: 1926, United States
Original publisher: Charles Scribner's Sons
Literary form: Novel

SUMMARY

The Sun Also Rises created a sensation when it first appeared because it was the first novel to depict the lives of American expatriates in Paris in the 1920s. It was viewed as a statement of the "lost generation," expressing the disillusionment and the hedonistic attitude brought on by World War I. Young Americans imitated its dialogue, and the novel started a fashion trend, as young women cut their hair and adopted the clothing worn by the female protagonist, Lady Brett Ashley.

The novel is divided into three sections and narrated by Jake Barnes, an American correspondent in Paris. Jake had suffered a severe groin wound in the war that left him sexually impotent, and this makes the love between Jake and Brett torturous because they are unable to consummate it. Thus, Brett seeks physical satisfaction with numerous men, while maintaining her emotional bond to Jake. In reality, all of Jake and Brett's friends are suffering from wounds, most of them psychological. Brett seeks happiness through romantic conquest, Princeton graduate Robert Cohn through romantic novels, and others through frantic and continuous celebrating. Psychological turmoil dominates Jake's days and nights, making him an insomniac as well as emotionally unstable when "his head starts to work."

Brett has her own tragedies: the death of her fiancé from dysentery during the war, a later bad marriage to acquire a title, and present plans to marry the bankrupt Mike Campbell, who drinks heavily, despite her real love for Jake.

In the second section of the novel, the action moves to Spain, where Jake and his friends go for the fiesta and bullfighting. Jake and Bill Gorton spend a few peaceful days fishing and discuss numerous serious subjects before they go to Pamplona for the running of the bulls. During this time, Brett has spent a romantic weekend with Robert Cohn, who becomes possessive of her. When Brett expresses an interest in the young bullfighter Pedro Romero, the competition becomes too much for Cohn, who fights with Jake and Mike and then beats Pedro badly. After heroically fighting the bulls the following day, Pedro runs away with Brett.

With the end of the fiesta, members of the group separate, and Jake goes alone to San Sebastian. He receives a telegram from Brett, who has left Pedro and wants Jake to meet her. Pedro is only 19, and she has left him for his own good. As they drive away in a taxi, Brett tells Jake, "You know it makes one feel rather good deciding not to be a bitch." The novel ends as it began, with Jake and Brett together, locked in a hopeless love for each other.

CENSORSHIP HISTORY

The Sun Also Rises was the only novel that Scribner vice president Max Perkins had ever contracted for completely unseen, and he had only the vaguest idea of its content. He was concerned about the opinion of the 72-year-old head of the publishing firm, Charles Scribner, "who was formidable on certain topics like obscenity." As editor John Wheelock reminded Perkins, "Charles Scribner would no sooner allow profanity in one of his books than he would invite friends to use his parlor as a toilet." When the manuscript was completed, the old-fashioned and gentlemanly Perkins told Scribner that three words might give the firm difficulty, but he could not bring himself to speak the words. Scribner then insisted that Perkins write them, and Perkins hesitantly wrote two of the words, *damn* and *bitch*. He only wrote the third, *balls*, when Scribner insisted that he do so.

In correspondence with Hemingway, Perkins asked the author to modify the language because "it would be a pretty thing if the very significance of so original a book should be disregarded because of the howls of a lot of cheap, prurient moronic yappers." In addition to the words *damn* and *bitch*, Perkins, yet unable to write the offending word, asked the author to consider reworking the statements that referred to the "bulls being without appendages." He also expressed concern about Hemingway's comic passage in which Bill Gorton and Jake speak of a purported accident on a bicycle or tricycle, which left Henry James permanently injured and impotent, as Jake explains his own war wound. Perkins protested because the matter "is peculiarly a personal one" that the publisher would not dare to include had

James been alive and that seemed even more tasteless since James was now dead. In the final version, the story remains but just the name "Henry" is used, to which Bill adds he "was a good writer."

Hemingway claimed to have eliminated as many potentially offensive words as possible, but he retained the phrase, "Tell him the bulls have no balls," that Mike Campbell shouts four times in two pages. Although the publisher did not feel comfortable with the work as it stood, the firm hesitated to turn down the novel because "young writers, who were the future of the firm, would avoid them for their conservative position." After the novel was published, reviewers labeled it "a dirty book." Hemingway's mother wrote him and asked him if he was happy now that he had published "one of the filthiest books of the year" and stated that he must know other words besides *damn* and *bitch*. In 1927, the Watch and Ward Society of Boston added the novel to its list of "obscene" books and requested that booksellers agree not to advertise or to sell the book. In 1953, the novel was banned in Ireland for the "dissipated lives" of its characters, as well as for "profanity."

In 1960, parents of students in the San Jose, California, school district asked the school board to remove the novel from the class curriculum. They expressed concern with the "personal nature of the one character's [Jake's] wound," as well as the "profanity." The school board banned the novel from the schools. That same year, the Riverside, California, school board withdrew all of Hemingway's works from the school libraries after receiving repeated parent complaints regarding the "obscenities" and "sexual situations" in the books.

In a 1977 national survey of high school librarians and English department chairpersons, Lee Burress reported one challenge by a parent in Virginia who requested that the novel be removed from the recommended reading list. The parent claimed that the characters were "too flagrant" in behavior and that their language was "too explicit." After a review committee considered the parent's complaint, the book was removed from the recommended reading list. Burress also reported in a 1982 national survey of librarians that a parent in Indiana challenged the assignment of the book in the classroom because of the "obscene" language. The school board reviewed the book and removed the material from the classroom.

FURTHER READING

Baker, Carlos. *Hemingway: A Life Story.* New York: Charles Scribner's Sons, 1969.

Burress, Lee. *Battle of the Books: Literary Censorship in the Public Schools, 1950–1985.* Metuchen, N.J.: Scarecrow Press, 1989.

Djos, Matt. "Alcoholism in Ernest Hemingway's *The Sun Also Rises:* A Wine and Roses Perspective on the Lost Generation." *Hemingway Review* 14 (Spring 1995): 64–78.

Elliott, Ira. "Performance Art: Jake Barnes and 'Masculine' Signification in *The Sun Also Rises.*" *American Literature* 67 (March 1995): 77–94.

Meyers, Jeffrey. *Hemingway: A Biography.* New York: Harper & Row, 1985.

Pinsker, Sanford. "Individual Authors: A Rotten Way to Be Wounded." *Journal of Modern Literature* 18 (Spring 1993): 277–278.

Reynolds, Michael. *Hemingway: The American Homecoming.* Cambridge, Mass.: Blackwell Publishers, 1992.

Rudat, Wolfgang. "Sexual Dilemma in *The Sun Also Rises:* Hemingway's Count and the Education of Jacob Barnes." *Hemingway Review* 8 (Spring 1989): 2–13.

Strychacz, Thomas. "Dramatizations of Manhood in Hemingway's *In Our Time* and *The Sun Also Rises.*" *American Literature* 61 (May 1989): 245–260.

Wylder, Delbert E. *Hemingway's Heroes.* Albuquerque: University of New Mexico Press, 1969.

TO KILL A MOCKINGBIRD

Author: (Nelle) Harper Lee
Original date and place of publication: 1960, United States
Original publisher: J. B. Lippincott
Literary form: Novel

SUMMARY

Harper Lee's only novel touched a nerve in American society when it was first published, becoming a best seller as well as a critical success that won the Pulitzer Prize in 1961. The author claimed that her story of racial bias in the sleepy fictional Alabama town of Maycomb was pure imagination, but reporters who visited her hometown of Monroeville, Alabama, on the 30th anniversary of the book's publication found remarkable similarities to the novel in both setting and character. In essence, the racial ills chronicled in the novel appear to have been realistically drawn from the author's life.

The novel is told from the point of view of the adult Jean Louise Finch, known as Scout to her friends, who relates the events of three years, beginning with her sixth summer. With her brother Jem, four years her senior, and summer visitor Dill, modeled after a real-life summer playmate who grew up to be the writer Truman Capote, Scout devises a series of projects to make their mysterious next-door neighbor, Arthur "Boo" Radley, emerge from his house. The early chapters of the novel detail the comfortable cocoon of childhood that Scout enjoys, as she enters school, engages in fistfights with boys, and shares confidences with her father, lawyer Atticus Finch.

Scout's comfortable world is shattered when her father agrees to take the unpopular defense of black laborer Tom Robinson, accused of raping white Mayella Ewell. The townspeople want Tom to die, but Atticus believes that Tom is innocent and establishes that Tom's withered left arm could not have made the bruises on the right side of Mayella's face.

As bitterness engulfs the town, Atticus must defend his client not only in court but also from a lynch mob. Atticus manages to prove that Tom is physically incapable of committing the crime, yet the jury brings in a verdict of guilty despite the revelation that Mayella had made sexual advances to

Tom that he had refused out of fear for his life. In addition, townspeople are angered because Tom expresses pity for a white woman.

Atticus plans to appeal the decision, but Tom is fatally shot while trying to escape during a jail exercise period. The final chapters of the novel contain Bob Ewell's attempted revenge against Atticus for having defended Tom and the emergence of Boo Radley from his house to save Jem and Scout from Ewell's knife.

CENSORSHIP HISTORY

Despite its strong annual sales and appearance on required reading lists in numerous high schools throughout the United States, *To Kill a Mockingbird* has frequently been challenged by parents and groups who object to either the language or the way in which race is represented. The Committee on Intellectual Freedom of the American Library Association listed the novel as being among the 10 most frequently challenged books. In 1977, Eden Valley (Minnesota) School District temporarily banned the book because the words *damn* and *whore lady* appeared in the text, and parents in Vernon-Verona-Sherill (New York) School District challenged the book in 1980 as being a "filthy, trashy novel." Black parents in Warren Township (Indiana) schools charged in 1981 that passages in the book that portrayed the submissive behavior of Tom Robinson, Calpurnia, and other blacks and the frequent use of the word *nigger* advocated institutionalized racism and were harmful to the integration process. Despite their vehement efforts, the attempt to censor the book was unsuccessful. As a result, three black parents resigned in protest from the town's human relations advisory council.

The novel was also challenged in 1984 in the Waukegan, Illinois, schools for inclusion of the word *nigger*, and in 1985, Park Hill (Missouri) Junior High School parents challenged the novel because it contained racial slurs and offensive language. In 1985 in Casa Grande (Arizona) Elementary School District, black parents and the National Association for the Advancement of Colored People protested that the book was unfit for use in the junior high school. School officials there changed the status of the book from required reading to retention on a supplemental reading list.

In 2001, a school board member in Glynn County, Georgia, challenged the use of the novel in the classroom because it contains profanity, but no action was taken, and the book was retained.

In August 2002, Terry Saul, the principal of Muskogee High School in Oklahoma, removed the novel from the high school reading list after African-American parents and students complained about racial slurs in the novel. The Muskogee Public Library created a program in response to the action, including showing the movie in two screenings and sponsoring two read-and-discuss programs led by local black educators. The library also adapted the One City–One Book program from the Chicago Public Library and staged a musical and reading program with reminiscences by the child stars of the movie after raising $7,000 in donations. The resulting coalition of participation by community leaders led the school board to vote in October 9, 2002, to reverse the ban.

In 2003, parents of students enrolled in the sophomore literature class in Community High School in Normal, Illinois, challenged the use of the novel and claimed that it is degrading to African Americans. After review by a school district committee, the school board voted in 2004 to retain the novel.

In 2004, Garvey Jackson, an African-American eighth-grade student attending Stanford Middle School in Durham, North Carolina, protested being required to read *To Kill a Mockingbird* because it forced him to repeatedly hear and to read the most offensive word he knew, "nigger." His family joined him in protesting the required reading. Andrew Jackson, his father, stated that the family did not want the book in the school system: "We do want to kill the mockingbird, if it takes until the end of the school year." With the help of his family, the student created a T-shirt that they emblazoned with offensive phrases: "nigger rape," "nigger lover," "nigger snowman," and others. Although the family was aware that the boy might be suspended from school for the action, they thought that making the point during Black History Month was especially important. Jackson's English teacher sent him to the principal's office where, after his parents arrived, Principal David Ebert explained that wearing the shirt was against the school dress code. He also explained to Jackson's parents the formal procedure for challenging a book in the school district. He also told Jackson that he did not have to speak the word "nigger" aloud if it made him uncomfortable. Although Jackson complied with the dress code and removed the shirt, he attempted the following week to protest the screening of the movie version of *To Kill a Mockingbird* and made armbands to pass out to other students. His fellow students refused: "They didn't want to wear them. They said they made them look ugly." Jackson wore his anyway, and his family planned a mock funeral for the book to which they would invite the community. The novel was retained in the curriculum.

In 2007, a resident of Cherry Hill, New Jersey, submitted a request to the school board to remove the novel from the school curriculum because she was concerned that African-American children would become upset by reading about the racism among white members of the community in 1930s Alabama.

In August 2009, the Dufferin-Peel Catholic School Board in Brampton, Ontario, chose not to interfere when the principal of the St. Edmund Campion High School removed *To Kill a Mockingbird* from the 10th-grade English curriculum after one parent complained about the use of the word "nigger" throughout the book. Principal Kevin McGuire stated that he did not ban the book, nor did he remove it from the district, because it was still available in the school library. Rather, he simply made a decision to replace the book at the same time that a parent protested its use in the classroom.

FURTHER READING

"Another Furor over Books." *Ohio State University Monthly* 55 (December 1963): 8–12.

Bruell, Edwin. "Keen Scalpel on Racial Ills." *English Journal* 53 (December 1964): 658–661.

Dave, R. A. "*To Kill a Mockingbird:* Harper Lee's Tragic Vision." In *Indian Studies in American Literature*, edited by M. K. Naik, S. K. Desai, and S. Mokashi, 311–323. Dharwar, India: Karnatak University, 1974.

Doyle, Robert P. *Books Challenged and Banned in 2008–2009.* Chicago: American Library Association, 2009.

May, Jill. "In Defense of *To Kill a Mockingbird.*" In *Censored Books: Critical Viewpoints*, edited by Nicholas J. Karolides, Lee Burress, and John M. Kean, 476–484. Metuchen, N.J.: Scarecrow Press, 1993.

"Mockingbird Returns to Oklahoma High School's Reading List." Associated Press. October 15, 2001. Available online. URL: http://www.freedomforum.org/templates/document.asp?documentID=15150. Accessed August 10, 2010.

Newsletter on Intellectual Freedom (March 1966): 16; (March 1968): 22; (March 1978): 31; (May 1980): 62; (March 1982): 47; (July 1984): 105; (March 1986): 57–58; (November 2001): 277–278; (January 2002): 50; (January 2004): 11; (May 2004): 98–99; (September 2004): 175–176; (November 2009): 202–204.

Skaggs, Merrill. *The Folk of Southern Fiction.* Athens: University of Georgia Press, 1972.

WELCOME TO THE MONKEY HOUSE

Author: Kurt Vonnegut, Jr.
Original date and place of publication: 1968, United States
Original publisher: Delacorte Press
Literary form: Short story collection

SUMMARY

Welcome to the Monkey House consists of 25 short stories, 11 reprinted from Vonnegut's 1961 short story collection *Canary in a Cat House.* All of the stories originally appeared in such diverse publications as the *Atlantic Monthly, Colliers, Cosmopolitan, Ladies' Home Journal,* and *Fantasy and Science Fiction Magazine* from 1950 through 1964, but the title story appeared in *Playboy* magazine the same year that the collection was released.

Many of the 25 stories have as their setting Hyannis Port, Massachusetts, where the Kennedy family has long had its compound, and Vonnegut weaves the Kennedy name throughout many of the stories. The settings vary from the present to hundreds of years into the future, but all offer perceptive criticism of contemporary ills. "Welcome to the Monkey House" is the only story singled out for criticism regarding language and sexual situations, but the entire collection has been removed where such cases have occurred.

The story is set in Cape Cod, Massachusetts, and its environs, in an unspecified future in which antiaging shots make everyone appear no older than 22 and the Earth is overpopulated with 17 billion people. The World Government has launched a two-pronged attack on the problem by encouraging "compulsory ethical birth control" and "ethical suicide." Everyone must take the "ethical birth control pill" three times daily. It is the only legal form of birth control and does not interfere with a person's ability to reproduce, "which would have been unnatural and immoral," but it does "take every bit of pleasure out of the sex act." The pills make people numb from the waist down, and they are so effective that you could "blindfold a man who had taken one, tell him to recite the Gettysburg Address, kick him in the balls while he was doing it, and he wouldn't miss a syllable."

The pills were invented by J. Edgar Nation, a pharmacist from Grand Rapids, Michigan, who created them to "introduce morality into the monkey house at the Grand Rapids Zoo." After he and his 11 children went to the zoo one Easter day and saw a monkey "playing with his privateparts," he rushed home "to make a pill that would make monkeys in the springtime fit things for a Christian to see." The World Government adopted his discovery after the United Nations announced a population crisis and scientists stated that people had to stop reproducing while moralists declared that society would collapse if people used sex for nothing but pleasure. The pill was the solution. "Thus did science and morals go hand in hand."

The Federal Ethical Suicide Parlors are run by Ethical Suicide Service (ESS) hostesses, all of whom are six feet tall or more, seductively made up and dressed, "plump and rosy," skilled in judo and karate, and virgins. They prepare their clients for death by providing pleasant conversation and a last meal before administering the fatal shot with a hypodermic needle.

"Nothingheads," rebels who refuse to take the ethical birth control pills, threaten society. They are "bombed out of their skulls with the sex madness that came from taking nothing." The most notorious nothinghead is Billy the Poet, who specializes in deflowering the hostesses of suicide parlors. He usually sends his potential victims "dirty poems" far in advance, then abducts them, forces them to wait the eight hours until their pills wear off, and "deflowers them with a clinical skill." Afterward, they are "grateful" and join the growing nothingheads movement. After raping Nancy, a 63-year-old virgin ESS hostess, Billy reads a passage from Elizabeth Barrett Browning's *Sonnets from the Portuguese* to her, tells her that lawmakers throughout history "have been absolutely disgusted and terrified by the natural sexuality of common men and women," and gives her a bottle of pills to be taken monthly to prevent pregnancy. The label on the bottle states: "WELCOME TO THE MONKEY HOUSE."

CENSORSHIP HISTORY

In 1970, Marilyn Parducci, a teacher in Montgomery, Alabama, was dismissed for assigning the title story of the collection to her 11th-grade English class.

Three high school juniors of the teacher's 90 students asked to be excused from reading the story, and their parents complained about "vulgarities" and a reference to rape in the story. Objectors stated that the references to the monkey "playing with his private parts" and the phrase "kick him in the balls" were "vulgar." They also objected to lines in two of Billy's poems: "A-goosing statues in the dark," "And when I peed, I peed turquoise" and "Mourn my pecker, purple daughter." The high school principal and the associate school superintendent called the book "literary garbage" and chastised Parducci for teaching a book that promoted "the killing off of elderly people and free sex." Parducci brought suit against the school district in *Parducci v. Rutland*, 316 F. Supp. 352 (M.D. Ala 1970), asking reinstatement and financial remuneration. In rendering his decision, Judge Frank Johnson observed that, despite the "vulgar terms," the story could be considered an appropriate assignment when judged in the larger literary context. He noted that the words objected to were

> less ribald than those found in many of Shakespeare's plays. The reference in the story to an act of sexual intercourse is no more descriptive than the rape scene in Pope's "Rape of the Lock." . . . It appears to the Court, moreover, that the author, rather than advocating the "killing off of old people," satirizes the practice to symbolize the increasing depersonalization of man in society.

The presiding judge stated further, "that teachers are entitled to first amendment freedom is an issue no longer in dispute" and such freedoms of expression should only be restricted if evidence exists that school activities would be disrupted. Because only three students had requested to be excused from the assignment, the judge determined that no disruption of the school schedule had occurred and ruled in favor of the teacher, who was reinstated in her teaching position.

In 1977, a parent in Bloomington, Minnesota, perused the books in the junior high school library and discovered three that contained "sexually explicit language." The parent complained to the school board, indicating that he had been concerned for a while about the materials used in the school "but when this came out, I really became uncoiled." The offending books were *Welcome to the Monkey House* and the two-volume science fiction story collection *Again, Dangerous Vision*, edited by Harlan Ellison. The parent raised objections to use of the words *balls*, *peed*, and *pecker* and noted that the word *fucking* was used in two instances as an adjective. The school superintendent stated his own dissatisfaction over "the fact that the obscene books were purchased and made available to students." He explained that the books were supplementary and had not been ordered through the normal purchase authorization channels, so he had not had the power of veto in advance. Although the superintendent promised that steps would be taken to prevent a reoccurrence, the parent removed his seven children from the Bloomington schools.

FURTHER READING

Allen, William Rodney. *Understanding Kurt Vonnegut.* Columbia: University of South Carolina Press, 1990.

Hipkiss, Robert A. *The American Absurd: Pynchon, Vonnegut, and Barth.* Port Washington, N.Y.: Associated Faculty Press, 1984.

Newsletter on Intellectual Freedom (January 1970): 28; (March 1977): 37.

O'Neil, Robert M. *Classrooms in the Crossfire.* Bloomington: Indiana University Press, 1981.

Vonnegut, Kurt, Jr. *Welcome to the Monkey House.* New York: Delacorte Press, 1968.

INDEX

Note: **Boldface** page numbers indicate major treatment of a topic.